# CHINA'S ECONOMIC DEVELOPMENT

## Also of Interest

† *Economic Reform in the PRC: Assessments by China's Leading Economists,* edited by George C. Wang

† *China Briefing, 1981,* edited by Robert B. Oxnam and Richard C. Bush

*Technology, Politics, and Society in China,* Rudi Volti

† *China: A Political History, 1917–1980* (fully revised and updated), Richard C. Thornton

† *China in World Affairs: The Foreign Policy of the PRC Since 1970,* Golam W. Choudhury

† *The Chinese Agricultural Economy,* edited by Randolph Barker and Radha P. Sinha

† *China, the Soviet Union, and the West: Strategic and Political Dimensions for the 1980s,* edited by Douglas T. Stuart and William T. Tow

† *China Briefing, 1980,* edited by Robert B. Oxnam and Richard C. Bush

*Technology, Defense, and External Relations in China, 1975–1978,* Harry G. Gelber

*Military Power and Policy in Asian States: China, India, Japan,* edited by Onkar Marwah and Jonathan D. Pollack

*Perspectives on a Changing China: Essays in Honor of Professor C. Martin Wilbur,* edited by Joshua A. Fogel and William T. Rowe

*China's Quest for Independence: Policy Evolution in the 1970s,* edited by Thomas Fingar and the Stanford Journal of International Studies

*The People's Republic of China: A Handbook,* edited by Harold C. Hinton

*Urban Development in Modern China,* edited by Laurence J. C. Ma and Edward W. Hanten

† *The Chinese Military System: An Organizational Study of the Chinese People's Liberation Army,* Second Edition, Revised and Updated, Harvey W. Nelsen

† *China's Four Modernizations: The New Technological Revolution,* edited by Richard Baum

† *China's Agriculture: Policies and Performance,* Robert C. Hsu

† Available in hardcover and paperback.

# About the Book and Author

*China's Economic Development: Growth and Structural Change*

Chu-yuan Cheng

How has the government of the PRC transformed traditional economic institutions into a socialist, central-planning system? What has been the impact of this transformation on China's economic growth? What is the essence of the Chinese development model and how successfully has it functioned during the past three decades? What are the prospects for the future? In this first comprehensive and up-to-date analysis of the Chinese economy from 1949 to the present, Dr. Cheng answers these key questions as he discusses China's economic development and the operation of its economic system. Focusing on institutional change as a major determinant of economic growth, he demonstrates how two goals – the substitution of socialist views for deeply embedded traditional values, and the use of China's actual and potential economic surpluses – have together formed the distinctive features of China's economic development.

Based on twenty-five years of intensive research and supported by original Chinese documents, this is an ideal text for upper-division undergraduate and graduate courses on Chinese economic development. It will also be welcomed by China specialists.

Dr. Cheng, a native of Guangdong Province, is professor of economics at Ball State University, Muncie, Indiana. He was for ten years consultant to the National Science Foundation, during which time he served as chief investigator with the Research Project on Scientific and Engineering Manpower in China. Among his many books on China's economy are *Communist China's Economy, 1949–1962; Economic Relations Between Peking and Moscow; China's Allocation of Fixed Capital Investment; The Machine-Building Industry in Communist China;* and *China's Petroleum Industry: Output Growth and Export Potential.*

To Hua

# CHINA'S ECONOMIC DEVELOPMENT

## Growth and Structural Change

Chu-yuan Cheng

Routledge
Taylor & Francis Group
LONDON AND NEW YORK

First published 1982 by Westview Press

Published 2018 by Routledge
52 Vanderbilt Avenue, New York, NY 10017
2 Park Square, Milton Park, Abingdon, Oxon OX14 4RN

*Routledge is an imprint of the Taylor & Francis Group, an informa business*



Library of Congress Cataloging in Publication Data
Cheng, Chu-yuan.
China's economic development.
Bibliography: p.
Includes index.
1. China–Economic conditions–1949-1976. 2. China–Economic conditions–1976– I. Title.
HC427.9.C52178 338.951 81-11671
ISBN 0-89158-788-8 AACR2
ISBN 0-89158-892-2 (pbk.)

ISBN 13: 978-0-367-02211-2 (hbk)
ISBN 13: 978-0-367-17198-8 (pbk)

# Contents

# Tables

# Figures and Maps

*Figures*



*Maps*

# Preface

Much has been written on the Chinese economy during the past two decades, and the existing works fall roughly into three categories. First, there are studies that deal with particular sectors of the Chinese economy – typically, research monographs on various branches of Chinese industry. Second, there are multicontribution symposiums on different aspects of the Chinese economy. Third, there are studies that focus either on the economic system or on economic growth, but not on the two together. The need for a comprehensive and coherent analysis of the Chinese economic development from the inception of the People's Republic of China (P.R.C.) in 1949 to the present day prompted this study.

Previous analyses of the Chinese economy have treated the growth of national product as a function of the factors of production (labor, land, capital, and technology), lumping institutional change under the rubric ceteris paribus. A similar approach has been used in short-run analyses of Western economies, in which institutional change is relatively slow and therefore can be treated as an exogenous variable. In China's case, economic development involves a seminal institutional transformation designed to achieve two goals: (1) the creation of a national outlook in which new socialist views are substituted for deeply embedded traditional values; (2) the orientation of the institutional changes toward mobilizing and using China's actual and potential economic surplus. The pursuit of these two goals has resulted in some distinct features that characterize China's economic development – for instance, the relatively rapid transition to collectivized agriculture, the rationing of staple consumer goods, the nationalization of industry and commerce, and the mobilization of labor for large-scale projects in rural areas. Ample evidence indicates that the ebbs and flows of the Chinese economy have been closely related to periods of major change in the country's economic institutions. These institutional elements warrant a systematic examination in any comprehensive analysis of Chinese economic development.

Although the aim of this study is to provide an analysis of Chinese economic development, institutional transformation as a determinant of Chinese economic growth is also treated and three sets of problems are addressed.

1. How did the Communist government transform the traditional Chinese economic institutions into a socialist, central-planning system? What significant impact did this institutional transformation have on the Chinese economic growth?

2. What is the essence of China's development strategies and how have those strategies affected the Chinese economy? Are the institutional changes and development strategies conducive or detrimental to Chinese economic growth?

3. Given the existing institutional constraints, can the Chinese leadership achieve its ambitious goal of modernizing the national economy? If not, what sort of institutional changes are the Chinese likely to pursue in the years to come?

To answer these questions, a wide range of topics is covered. The first two chapters examine two crucial factors shaping Chinese economic development: natural resources and ideology. Until the death of Mao Zedong in September 1976, his economic concepts dominated policymaking. Arguments for and against Mao's ideas underlay a continuing struggle between two lines within the Chinese Communist Party and culminated in the Cultural Revolution, which affected Chinese economic development for more than a decade. A survey of economic development in China under Communist control therefore requires a brief review of the ideological background of the Chinese leaders and especially of the thought of Mao.

Chapters 3, 4, and 5 analyze the process of agricultural collectivization, the evolution of the commune system, and the transformation of the private enterprises into state enterprises. The main purpose of these chapters is to assess the social and economic consequences of those transformations. As official Chinese records reveal, the decision to collectivize the agricultural sector by organizing the entire rural population into some 50,000 communes had detrimental effects on Chinese agricultural growth. Since the establishment of the commune system in 1958, labor productivity in the agricultural sector has stagnated, despite a substantial increase in agricultural inputs.

In Chapters 6, 7, and 8, the discussion focuses on the establishment and implementation of central planning, the organization and operation of market controls, and the functioning of price and wage systems. Most of the new institutions involved in those processes are modeled on their Soviet counterparts. The institutional changes have enabled the Chinese central planners to achieve a high rate of capital formation and to suppress inflationary forces, but they have also resulted in an entrenched bureaucracy and a decline in efficiency.

Chapter 9 examines the evolution of China's development strategies from the adoption of the Stalin model in the First Five-Year Plan of 1953–1957 to the strategies of the Great Leap Forward in 1958–1960, the new economic policy of 1961–1965, the Cultural Revolution and its aftermath (1966–1976), the New Great Leap in 1977–1978, and the further adjustments in 1979–1985. Chapter 10 examines the quantitative trends of the Chinese economy between 1949 and 1979, analyzes the underlying causes and implications of the economic fluctuations, and discusses the probable pattern of Chinese economic growth in the 1980s.

Chapters 11 and 12 deal, respectively, with the modernization of two major sectors of the Chinese economy: industry and agriculture. The programs and problems of the current modernization drive and its prospects are analyzed in detail. Chapter 13 assesses the changes in the structure of the Chinese economy in terms of sectoral contribution to GNP, relationships between investment and consumption, industrial structure, and spatial distribution of production facilities.

The final chapter focuses on China's economic relations with the rest of the world. It surveys the evolution of China's foreign economic policies, the long-term trends of its foreign trade, the impact of China's modernization on the world economy, and the prospects for increased trade relations during the 1980s with the Western world in general and with the United States in particular.

This study was undertaken at a turning point in the history of the People's Republic. From 1949 to 1976, China was under Mao's shadow. Most of the major socioeconomic measures, such as the establishment of rural communes, the Great Leap Forward, and the Cultural Revolution, were initiated under Mao's leadership. The nationwide campaign of "In agriculture learn from Dazhai, in industry learn from Daqing" and the guideline of "Agriculture taking food grain as the key link; industry taking steel as the key link" were Mao's highly personalized responses to complex socioeconomic problems. Those narrowly conceived policies posed a formidable obstacle to modernization. In only four years after Mao's death, the new leadership in China realized that the old commitments to uninterrupted revolution and the egalitarian distribution of income were detrimental to modernization and economic growth. The success of the modernization program hinges on China's ability to strengthen management, raise labor productivity, and improve the effectiveness of investment. Although still rendering lip service to some tenets of Mao's doctrine, the new leadership has proclaimed economic policies that undercut the principles and institutions held sacrosanct by the Maoists only a few years ago.

The pace of change accelerated in the 1978–1979 period. The ten-year development plan unfurled by the then Party Chairman Hua Guofeng in February 1978 was scrapped in December 1978 and replaced by a seven-year (1979–1985) readjustment plan. That plan is also undergoing constant revision, and it is risky to forecast policy trends over the next decade. Nevertheless, the groundwork for current economic reform and readjustment was laid down by the Third Session of the Fifth National People's Congress in August 1980, and further radical changes seem unlikely over the short term.

This study has drawn heavily on many articles and monographs by students of the Chinese economy and also on my own publications of the past three decades. In the quantitative study of the growth and fluctuations of the Chinese economy, the analysis has benefited immensely from the estimates of the U.S. Central Intelligence Agency.

When the second draft of this study was completed, the Beijing authorities announced the formal adoption of the Chinese phonetic alphabet (*pinyin*) to standardize the romanization of P.R.C. names and places in official documents and publications. Since January 1, 1979, the Chinese have used the *pinyin* system for all personal names, place names, and titles of publications–abandoning the widely used Wade-Giles system. In many cases, the change has caused confusion and created inconsistencies, but since both the U.S. government and major journals in the West have adopted the new system, I have no alternative but to follow the practice.

In any work on China, the author and the reader encounter the problem of style in handling Chinese proper names. In this book, I follow the official Chinese practice of giving surname first and the given name following for the names of those Chinese who live in China, Taiwan, and Hong Kong. For the Chinese living in the Western world, the Western custom is adopted, with the given name preceding the family name. Although most Chinese place names have been converted into the new *pinyin* system, some conventional English names–such as Loess Plateau, Pamir, Tarim, and Tonkin Gulf–are still used in official Chinese publications and also in this book.

The book contains massive statistical data, many of which are gathered from a wide variety of sources published in various periods. Although strenuous efforts have been made to iron out contradictions, some minor discrepancies may still exist. A few percentages in the statistical tables do not add up to 100 due to rounding, but in most cases, the discrepancies are inherited from the original data, and corrections are difficult to make.

I am grateful to the Bureau of Business Research and the Department of Economics at Ball State University for supporting this research venture with travel grants and a reduction in my teaching load. In the long process of preparing the manuscript, I have benefited from the assistance of many colleagues, students, and friends. Professors Liang-lin Hsiao, Katherin H. Hsiao, and Joan Maloney were kind enough to review the manuscript and offered valuable comments. J. B. Black and John Hannaford gave me their deep concern and constant support. Robert Jost and Betty Harris edited the first draft of the first several chapters, and Abera Zegeye reviewed a part of Chapter 10. Barbara Benson typed the entire manuscript; Brenda Turner typed most of the statistical tables; and Charles Martin drew the maps and figures. I should like to express my deep appreciation for all these contributions.

The book would never have been completed without the assistance of Mervyn Adams Seldon, consulting editor of Westview Press, who not only initiated the writing of this book but also edited the manuscript. Her knowledge of contemporary China, skill, and patience in editing the various drafts have significantly improved the presentation and readability of the work. Megan L. Schoeck of Westview Press made a careful review of the final draft. Her critical acumen saved the author from many errors. I am deeply indebted to both of them for their assistance. Needless to say, I alone am responsible for any flaws that remain.

To my wife Hua and my children Anita and Andy, my sincere thanks for their encouragement and understanding during the three years I spent writing the book.

*Chu-yuan Cheng*

# Conversion Equivalents and Terms

I CONVERSION FACTORS

| *Metric* | *Chinese* | *English* |
|---|---|---|
| Meter | *Shichi* (Chinese foot) | Foot |
| 1 | 3 | 3.2808 |
| 0.3333 | 1 | 1.0936 |
| 0.3048 | 0.9144 | 1 |
| Kilometer | *Shili* (Chinese mile) | Mile |
| 1 | 2 | 0.6214 |
| 0.5000 | 1 | 0.3107 |
| 1.6093 | 3.2187 | 1 |
| Hectare | *Shimu* | Acre |
| 1 | 15 | 2.470 |
| 0.0667 | 1 | 0.1647 |
| 0.4047 | 6.0703 | 1 |
| Kilogram | *Shijin* (Catty) | Pound |
| 1 | 2 | 2.2046 |
| 0.5000 | 1 | 1.1023 |
| 0.4536 | 0.9072 | 1 |
| Gram | *Shiliang* (Tael) | Ounce |
| 1 | 0.0320 | 0.0353 |
| 31.2500 | 1 | 1.1023 |
| 28.3495 | 0.9072 | 1 |
| Metric Ton | *Shidan* (Picul) | Long Ton |
| 1 | 20 (2,000 catties) | 0.9842 |
| 0.0500 | 1 | 0.0492 |
| 1.0160 | 20.3209 | 1 |

## II CROPS

| | *Pounds/Bushel* | *1.0 Bushel Equals* | *1.0 Ton Equals* |
|---|---|---|---|
| wheat, potatoes, soybeans...... | 60 | 0.02722 tons | 36.743 bushels |
| rye and corn... | 56 | 0.02540 tons | 39.368 bushels |
| barley........ | 48 | 0.02177 tons | 45.929 bushels |
| oats.......... | 32 | 0.01452 tons | 68.894 bushels |

cotton: 1.0 metric ton: 4.593 bales of 480 pounds each.
4.409 bales of 500 pounds each.

## III TERMS

Metric tons are used throughout.
Dollars refer to U.S. dollars.
Yuan refers to Renminbi (RMB).
The dollar-yuan exchange rates:

| | |
|---|---|
| 1952 | one dollar = 2.24 yuan |
| 1953-1964 | one dollar = 2.62 yuan |
| 1978 | one dollar = 1.677 yuan |
| 1979 | one dollar = 1.549 yuan |
| 1980 | one dollar = 1.494 yuan |

---

Sources: (1) *Handbook on People's China* (Beijing: Foreign Languages Press, 1957), pp. 187–188.
(2) Chu-yuan Cheng, *The Machine-Building Industry in Communist China* (Chicago: Aldine, 1971), pp. 64–65.
(3) U.S. Central Intelligence Agency, *China: International Trade, Third Quarter, 1980* (Washington, D.C.: 1981), p. 2.

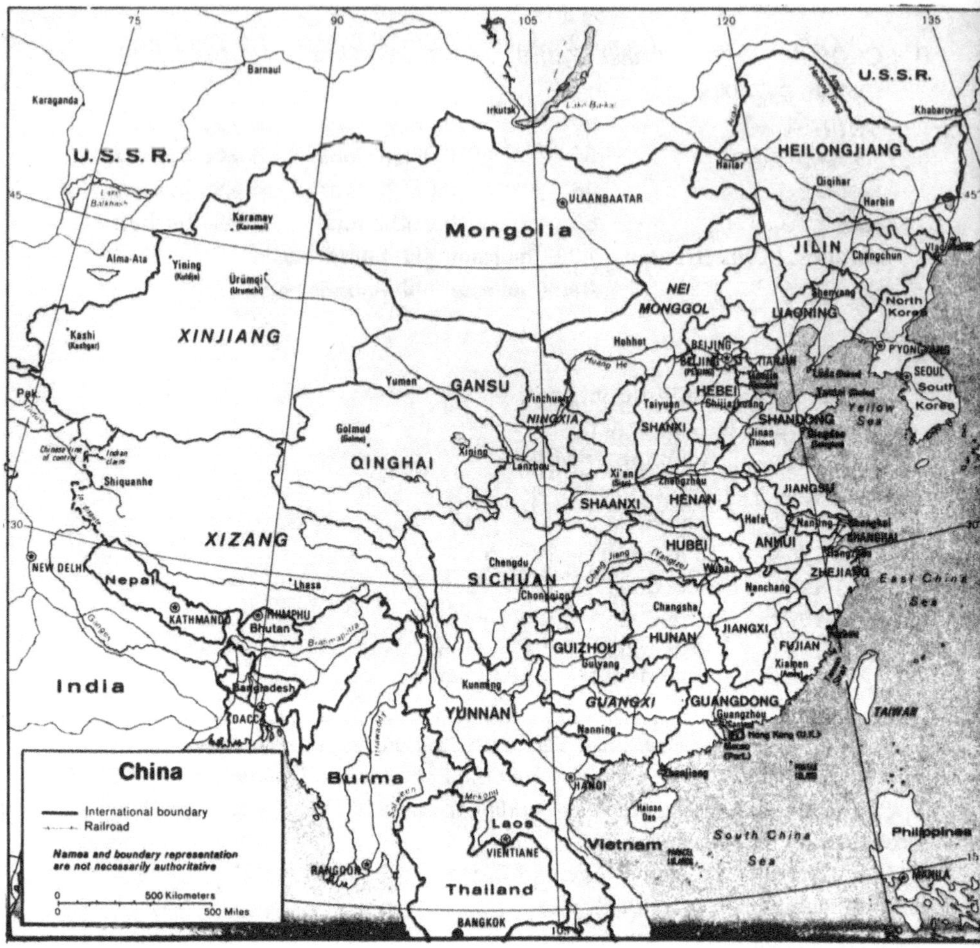


**Province-level Names**

| Conventional | Characters | Pinyin | Pronunciation | Conventional | Characters | Pinyin | Pronunciation |
|---|---|---|---|---|---|---|---|
| Anhwei | 安徽 | Anhui | ahn - way | Kweichow | 贵州 | Guizhou | g_way - joe |
| Chekiang | 浙江 | Zhejiang | juh - jee_ong | Liaoning | 辽宁 | Liaoning | lee_ow - ning |
| Fukien | 福建 | Fujian | foo - jee_en | Ningsia | 宁夏 | Ningxia | ning - she_ah |
| Heilungkiang | 黑龙江 | Heilongjiang | hay - loong - jee_ong | Peking | 北京 | Beijing | bay - jing |
| Honan | 河南 | Henan | huh - non | Shanghai | 上海 | Shanghai | shong - hi |
| Hopeh | 河北 | Hebei | huh - bay | Shansi | 山西 | Shanxi | shahn - she |
| Hunan | 湖南 | Hunan | hoo - nan | Shantung | 山东 | Shandong | shahn - doong |
| Hupeh | 湖北 | Hubei | hoo - bay | Shensi | 陕西 | Shaanxi | shun - she |
| Inner Mongolia | 内蒙古 | Nei Monggol | nay - mung - goo | Sinkiang | 新疆 | Xinjiang | shin - jee_ong |
| Kansu | 甘肃 | Gansu | gahn - soo | Szechwan | 四川 | Sichuan | ssu - ch_wan |
| Kiangsi | 江西 | Jiangxi | jee_ong - she | Tibet | 西藏 | Xizang | she - dzong |
| Kiangsu | 江苏 | Jiangsu | jee_ong - su | Tientsin | 天津 | Tianjin | te_en - jin |
| Kirin | 吉林 | Jilin | jee - lynn | Tsinghai | 青海 | Qinghai | ching - hi |
| Kwangsi | 广西 | Guangxi | g_wong - she | Yunnan | 云南 | Yunnan | yu_oon - nan |
| Kwangtung | 广东 | Guangdong | g_wong - doong | | | | |

Source: *Map*—United States Department of Agriculture, *People's Republic of China Agricultural Situation, Review of 1978 and Outlook for 1979* (June 1979), p. ii. *Province-level Names*—Foreign Broadcast Information Service, September 1979.

# 1

# Geographical Setting and Natural Endowment

The process of economic development involves the eradication of mass poverty, improvements in the material welfare of the population, the introduction of new technology, and changes in socioeconomic institutions. Given the technical know-how and institutional arrangements, the pace of a country's economic development is highly dependent on its human and natural resources. Specifically, in a country like China, where agriculture still constitutes the main sector of the national economy, the relationship between land and population is critical to economic advancement. This chapter will focus on four topics: China's physical geography, its natural resources, the land-population ratio, and the impact of these factors on Chinese economic development.

## PHYSICAL GEOGRAPHY

China is the world's third largest country, with an area of 9.6 million square kilometers. Its latitudinal position corresponds closely to that of the United States, and both countries have the same east-west spread. From east to west, China's territory measures more than 5,000 kilometers, covering 62 degrees in longitude from the meeting point of the Heilong Jiang and the Wusuli Jiang (Amur and Ussuri rivers) to the Pamir. In the easternmost region, the sun rises more than four hours earlier than in the westernmost region. The distance from north to south is more than 5,500 kilometers, extending over 49 degrees in latitude. If the map of China were superimposed on a map of North America, China would reach from Puerto Rico to the Hudson Bay and from the Atlantic to the Pacific. Superimposed on Europe, China would cover the whole of the Mediterranean from end to end.

Heilongjiang Province would coincide with the heart of European Russia, and Hainan Island would lie in the vicinity of Khartoum.[1]

China borders on twelve nations: North Korea on the east; the Soviet Union on the northeast and northwest; Outer Mongolia on the north; Afghanistan, Pakistan, India, Nepal, Sikkim, and Bhutan on part of the west and the southwest; and Burma, Laos, and Vietnam on the south. The coastline stretches 18,000 kilometers, and the land frontier extends for 14,966 kilometers, of which 4,908 kilometers face the Soviet Union, and 3,862 kilometers border Outer Mongolia.[2]

### *Topography*

The relief map of China shows that its land mass is like a three-step staircase, descending from west to east. The highest section is located in the southwest, where the Qinghai-Xizang Plateau rises for the most part to more than 4,000 meters above sea level, thus constituting the highest land mass in the world. The headwaters of most of China's major rivers, which flow east or southeast, are here.

The second section slopes north and east of the Qinghai-Xizang Plateau to plateaus and basins at altitudes of 1,000–2,000 meters. This area includes the Tarim Basin in the northwest, the Nei Monggol Plateau, the Loess Plateau, the Sichuan Basin, and the Yunnan-Guizhou Plateau.

The lowest section, mostly below 500 meters, is made up of the Northeast Plain in Manchuria, the North China Plain, the middle and lower Chang Jiang Plain, and the Southeastern Hills.

Most of China's rivers follow this sloping contour from west to east to empty into the sea. As they rush down from a higher to a lower section, deep and treacherous gorges are formed, such as the Chang Jiang gorges and the Sanmen Gorge on the Huang He (Yellow River). The west-east inclines allow the moist air current from the eastern seas to penetrate to inland areas and bestow abundant rain on vast regions of the Southeast.

### *Landscape*

The Chinese landscape is characterized by diverse physical features. Imposing plateaus, broad plains, vast mountain ranges, rolling hills, and deep basins present an endless variety of scenery. There are great deserts and wilderness areas in the northwest, and rivers, streams, and lakes stud the plains along the middle and lower reaches of the Chang Jiang (Yangtze River). With respect to slope and relief, almost 14 percent of the land consists of plains, 15 percent is basin, 9 percent is hill, 32 percent is plateau, and 30 percent is highland. The distribution of elevation is shown in Table 1.1.

Table 1.1
Distribution of Elevation in China, by percent

| Elevation | Percent |
|---|---|
| More than 5,000 meters (16,404 feet) | 16 |
| 2,000 - 5,000 meters (6,561 - 16,404 feet) | 17 |
| 1,000 - 2,000 meters (3,280 - 6,561 feet) | 35 |
| 500 - 1,000 meters (1,640 - 3,280 feet) | 18 |
| Under 500 meters (1,640 feet) | 14 |
| Total | 100 |

Source: Chiao-min Hsieh, "Physical Geography," in Yuan-li Wu, ed., China: A Handbook (New York: Praeger, 1973), p. 31.

*Plains.* The plains measure more than 1 million square kilometers. The three most significant plains–the Northeast (Manchuria), the North China, and the middle and lower reaches of the Chang Jiang–are each roughly about 300,000 square kilometers. Extending in a north-south band, they form a broad, flat, low region in the eastern part of the country. These three plains are endowed with rich soil and a warm, humid climate. Because irrigation systems have been established on them since ancient times, they have long been China's principal agricultural centers.

*Basins.* Basins occupy about one-sixth of the total land area of China. The four largest are the Sichuan, the Tarim, the Junggar, and the Qaidam. Fringed by great mountains, the Sichuan Basin is a typical stratum containing hills, low mountains, and alluvial plains. It has a humid climate, rich soil, and numerous streams and has long been known as the "land of abundance." The three other basins are located in the hinterland, where a dry climate and poor transportation conditions make them less conducive to cultivation.

*Hills.* Hill regions constitute about 9 percent of the country's total area, and they are found mostly in the eastern coastal provinces. The most important ones are the Southeastern, the Shandong, and the Liaodong hills. Their gentle slopes, interspersed with fluvial plains and small basins, make them ideal for terracing and for the cultivation of a wide variety of crops and trees.

*Plateaus.* Plateaus claim about a third of China's total land area. Situated in the western and central regions, the principal plateaus are the Qinghai-Xizang, Yunnan-Guizhou, Nei Monggol, and Loess. Each of these plateaus has its own special features.

*Highlands.* Highlands make up about another third of the country's territory. There is a striking contrast between the western and eastern sides of an imaginary line drawn directly from Lanzhou in Gansu Province to Kunming in Yunnan Province. On the west are high and steep ranges, and on the east the land is generally lower with gentle slopes.

The Qinling and Nanling (mountain ranges) farther east run from east to west, the former dividing the drainage basins of the Huang He and Chang Jiang, and the latter dividing those of the Chang Jiang and the Zhu Jiang (Pearl River).

### *Climate and Vegetation*

With its vast territory and wide range of altitudes, China has a diversified climate that encompasses six temperature zones: equatorial, tropical, subtropical, warm temperate, temperate, and frigid. The most significant control factors of China's climate are monsoons, mountain barriers, and cyclones.

Because China's land mass stretches more than 5,000 kilometers from east to west, the moisture-laden summer monsoons from the Pacific Ocean cannot penetrate deep into the northwestern hinterland. Also, because the Himalayas and the Xizang Plateau stand in the way, monsoons from the Indian Ocean cannot get into the northwestern region either. As a result, Northwest China has the least rainfall in the country, and in the desert there is no rain the year round. Farmland in that region is irrigated mainly by melted snow from the adjacent high mountains and by underground water.

The annual rainfall increases gradually as one moves from the northwest toward the east, the south, and the southeast. The northeastern region has an annual precipitation ranging from 400 to 1,000 millimeters. In many places along the southeastern coast, the annual rainfall exceeds 2,000 millimeters.[3] The west-east disposition of the mountain ranges also affects the climate by presenting barriers to the rain-bearing winds from the south in the summer and to the cold winds from the north in the winter.

Extratropical cyclones are the usual cause of weather changes in China, especially in the spring season. About 70 percent of those cyclones originate in China, 27 percent in Siberia, and 2 percent in India. Typhoons are an important climatic factor, especially on the southeastern coast during August and September.

With respect to precipitation and evaporation, the country can be divided into four zones: humid, semihumid, semiarid, and arid. The humid zone is the most extensive, and it lies chiefly in Southeast China, where the average annual precipitation is about 750 millimeters. In the semihumid zone, which takes in the Northeast and North China plains and the southeastern part of the Qinghai-Xizang Plateau, the average is 500 millimeters. In the semiarid zone, embracing most of the Nei Monggol, Loess, and Qinghai-Xizang plateaus, it is 300 millimeters. In the arid zone, comprising Xinjiang, the western part of the Nei Monggol Plateau, and the northwestern part of the Qinghai-Xizang Plateau, the annual precipitation is less than 250 millimeters.

Not only is China's rainfall distributed unevenly throughout the country, but it also varies widely from season to season and from year to year. Its unpredictability has a great bearing on Chinese harvests. More than 80 percent of the annual precipitation in China occurs between May and October during the summer monsoon season. In the semiarid and arid regions, the heaviest rainfall is concentrated in July and August. The coincidence of the time of the greatest precipitation with that of the highest temperature is beneficial to agriculture, especially rice cultivation.

The wide range of temperature and humidity from one part of the country to another results in a great variety of plant life. The 9.6 million square kilometers of China consist of about half woodland and half grassland and desert. The woodland is concentrated in the eastern section; the grassland and desert, in the western part. China boasts more than 30,000 varieties of seed-bearing plants; of those varieties, more than 5,000 are woody, and nearly 1,000 are timber trees of excellent quality and high value. Most of the crops grown in other parts of the world can be grown in China. Among the food crops, both paddy rice (which needs a great deal of light, heat, and water) and wheat (which prefers a dry climate) are produced in great quantities. There are also more than twenty lesser staples, including maize, kaoliang, and sweet potatoes. Cash crops are grown in great variety and quantity and include the raw materials used in textile, oil-pressing, sugar-refining, tobacco, and other industries.

## NATURAL RESOURCES

China posses adequate mineral and other natural resources necessary for industrialization. In comparative terms, its known resources are superior to those of Japan or India, but they are probably inferior to those of the Soviet Union or the United States.

### *Mineral Resources*

Early and partially incomplete assessments of China's resources concluded that China was rich in some special varieties of metals but poor in iron and petroleum, two materials considered vital for modern industry. Subsequent intensive geological prospecting has substantially changed those initial assessments. During the past three decades, more than eighty additional minerals and thousands of deposits were located. Chinese officials now claim that China has significant deposits of iron ore, coal, petroleum, molybdenum, asbestos, and pyrites, in addition to many minerals and metals for which China has long been a major supplier, such as tin, tungsten, antimony, mercury, bismuth, fluorspar, magnesite, and talc.[4]

The most vital discovery in the post-1949 period, however, was widespread oil deposits, found first in the northwestern highlands and later in the northeastern Songliao Basin and in the North China Plain. More recently, oil deposits have been found in the offshore shallow seas, from the Bohai Wan (Pohai Gulf) in the north through the Huang Hai (Yellow Sea) and the Dong Hai (East China Sea) all the way down to the Nan Hai (South China Sea). The discovery and exploitation of oil resources in the coastal areas may transform China into one of the world's major oil producers.

Of the myriad mineral resources that will affect China's economic future, the most crucial ones appear to be petroleum, coal, natural gas, iron ore, and nonferrous metals, most of which are abundant in China.

### *Petroleum and Natural Gas*

In the pre–World War II era, Western geologists had long maintained that both the type of rocks and the age of the rocks precluded the existence of any petroleum deposits worthy of exploitation throughout most of China.[5] In 1949, China's probable oil resources were estimated officially at only 200 million metric tons (hereafter, "metric tons" will be referred to as "tons"). In 1956, after extensive prospecting, government sources estimated the possible reserves (or potential reserves) at 1.7 billion tons. The geological prospecting and exploration that accompanied the Great Leap Forward development effort in 1958–1959 significantly enlarged the reserve figures, and in 1960 the total potential reserves were officially cited to be 2.9 billion tons.[6] The most important discoveries in the late 1950s were the Daqing oilfield in the Songliao Basin in Manchuria, the Shengli oilfield in Shandong Province, and the Dagang oilfield in the northern portion of the Bohai Wan. In 1980, those three oilfields produced three-quarters of China's crude oil.

Official Chinese reports indicate that since 1966, large-scale oil prospecting has been going on in many parts of China. The most promising discovery, however, lies offshore on the continental shelf stretching from the Huang Hai between Korea and the Shandong Peninsula to as far as the Xisha and Nansha islands in the South China Sea. Since large-scale exploration has just begun, we do not yet have an accurate picture of China's reserves, and there is a very wide disparity between high and low estimates. In mid-1970, one U.S. government source estimated there were 80 billion barrels of recoverable oil, but in 1977 other researchers tended to agree on a figure of about 40 billion barrels (5.5 billion tons) of ultimately recoverable reserves.[7] In comparison, as of mid-1970, remaining proved-plus-probable reserves were estimated to be 166 billion barrels for Saudi Arabia, 20–26 billion barrels for Nigeria, and 9.5 billion barrels for Indonesia.[8]

Information on China's natural gas has been fragmentary, but the major reserves are believed to be concentrated in southern Sichuan Province. A large supply of natural gas was found in 1960 in the suburbs of Shanghai and, in 1971, in twenty-seven counties and municipalities in Zhejiang Province on the east coast.[9] In 1975, Western experts estimated the total natural gas reserves in China to be 850 billion cubic meters, of which 500 billion cubic meters are located in Sichuan Province.[10]

### *Coal*

In 1980, coal was officially reported to constitute 71 percent of China's primary energy supply, and geologists have long regarded China as a country with vast coal reserves. *The General Statement on the Mining Industry,* issued by the Geological Survey of China in 1935, estimated China's total coal resources in 1934 at 243,669 million tons. In 1947, the figure was revised upward to 444,067 million tons.[11]

After the establishment of the new government in 1949, extensive geological surveys were conducted, and there were numerous upward revisions of coal reserve estimates. The 1955 estimate of 1,500 billion tons escalated to 9,000 billion tons in 1958. There is little evidence to support the reported rapid rise in coal reserve estimates, however. After the euphoria that accompanied the Great Leap Forward had subsided, the State Statistical Bureau published its *Ten Great Years* in 1960, and in that work the volume of proved coal reserves was reduced to something "over 80 billion tons" as of 1958.[12]

In 1980, however, Chinese officials announced that the total coal reserves in China were estimated at 1,500 billion tons, roughly comparable to the reserves of the United States or the Soviet Union.[13] At China's current level of consumption, and assuming a 50 percent rate of recovery, these reserves are equivalent to more than 1,700 years of supply. Proved reserves were officially given in 1980 as 600 billion tons.[14]

Geographically, the richest coal deposits are in northern China. According to a Chinese study, nearly three-fourths of the country's total reserves (71 percent) are in mountainous Shanxi Province and the adjoining provinces of Hebei, Henan, and Nei Monggol. Other large deposits are in northwestern China (Shaanxi, Gansu, Qinghai, and Xinjiang), which accounts for 19 percent of the total, and in northeastern China (Liaoning, Jilin, and Heilongjiang), which accounts for 2.7 percent.[15] Table 1.2 shows a more recent Western estimate of China's regional distribution of coal.

Most of China's coal—an estimated 77 percent—is bituminous, about 19 percent is anthracite, and the remaining 4 percent is lignite. Reserves of coking coal, a vital raw material in the production of steel and in other metallurgical processes, appear adequate to meet China's near-term requirements. Much of the coking coal is of poor quality and requires additional processing for conversion to coke. Major deposits of coking coal are in northeastern China and the eastern provinces of Hebei, Henan, and Anhui (see Figure 1.1). Some reserves are also scattered throughout the western provinces, stretching from the Nei Monggol and Ningxia regions in the north to Sichuan and Yunnan provinces in the south. Only small amounts are in the coal-rich provinces of Shanxi and Shaanxi.

### *Iron Ore*

Estimates of China's iron ore reserves parallel the erratic pattern that characterizes the coal industry. In 1948, according to Chinese officials, the country's total iron ore reserves were estimated to be 5.4 billion tons. After 1949, estimates of potential iron ore reserves in China skyrocketed from 10 billion tons in 1954 to 100 billion tons dur-

Table 1.2
China: Regional Distribution of Coal Production and Reserves
( in percent)

| | Production | Reserves |
|---|---|---|
| Northeast | 22 | 2.7 |
| North | 28 | 70.1 |
| Central | 22 | 4.0 |
| South | 10 | 1.2 |
| Northwest | 9 | 18.7 |
| Southwest | 9 | 3.3 |

Source: U.S. Central Intelligence Agency, Chinese Coal Industry: Prospects over the Next Decade (Washington, D.C., February 1979) p. 1.

ing the years of the Great Leap Forward.[16] There is no evidence that would lend credence to the latter figure, and in later 1980, official sources put the known deposits of iron reserves at 44 billion tons,[17] less than half the Great Leap figure.

Although quantitatively China possesses sufficient iron ore for continuous exploitation well into the twenty-first century, most of the ore is siliceous and of very low quality. The available evidence suggests that Chinese iron ore contains only 25 percent to 35 percent iron, compared with an iron ore content of more than 50 percent in Australia and Japan.

Nearly all the major iron mining areas are located north of the Chang Jiang, with the biggest deposits centering around the Anshan, Daye, Baotou, and Longyun mines. Numerous additional iron ore deposits are dispersed over other parts of the country. The potential output from ore bodies located in Gansu, Guizhou, southern Sichuan, and northern Guangdong provinces appears especially promising.

Besides iron ore, China has rich manganese deposits, much of which is formed from sedimentary ores found along the sea coast, lake floors, or swamps of ancient times. Large manganese deposits are also found in Liaoning, Hunan, and Guangxi provinces. The manganese re-

Figure 1.1
China's Iron and Coal Mining Centers

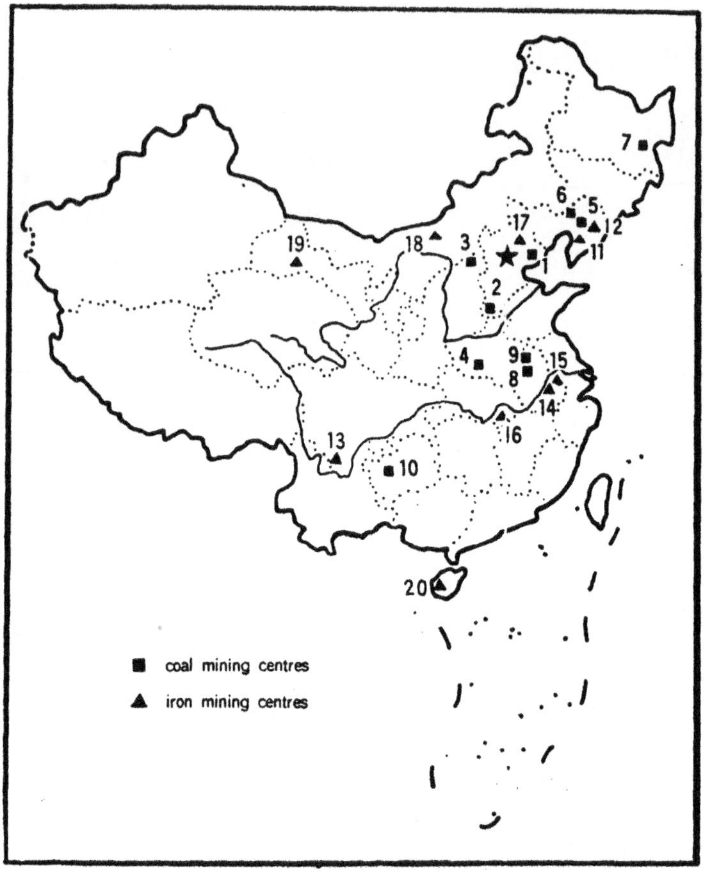


1. Kailuan
2. Fengfeng
3. Datong
4. Pingdingshan
5. Fushun
6. Fuxin
7. Jixi
8. Huainan
9. Huaibei
10. Liupanshui
11. Anshan
12. Benxi
13. Panzhihua
14. Maanshan
15. Meishan
16. Daye
17. Shuichang
18. Bayan Obo
19. Jingtieshan
20. Shilu

Source: *Beijing Review* 23:42 (October 20, 1980), p. 24.

serve has been estimated at 50 to 100 million tons, which makes China's reserve the world's third largest.

*Ferrous and Nonferrous Metals*

In ferrous and nonferrous metals, China is rich in tungsten, antimony, tin, mercury, and uranium but poor in copper, lead, zinc, chrome, and nickel. Many of the reserves have not been fully surveyed, and information generally is lacking.

*Tungsten.* China has the largest tungsten deposits in the world. Estimates of the reserve have varied considerably from 5.2 million tons to 100 million tons (of 1.5–2.5 percent $WO_3$ ore).[18] Most of the tungsten ore in China is high-grade wolframite and is concentrated in Jiangxi Province in South China. It has been China's most important metal export for more than half a century.

*Molybdenum.* Most of China's molybdenum deposits are located at Jinxi in Liaoning Province in Manchuria, but there are also deposits in Xinjiang and Jiangxi provinces and in the Qinling of Shanxi.

*Mercury.* China has long been one of the world's major producers of mercury. Most of the metal has come from the Tongren District of Guizhou Province in Southwest China, but new mines have also been found in Hunan. In 1980, five big mercury mines in Guizhou accounted for 90 percent of the nation's total.[19]

*Tin.* China has both lode and alluvial tin, with total reserves on the order of 1.5 to 2 million tons of contained tin. The most significant deposit is located in Gejiu, Yunnan Province. In early 1979, a large tin mine was opened in the Guangxi-Zhuang Autonomous Region. According to offical Chinese sources, in the first phase alone, the mine will produce 1 million tons of tin ore annually, from which 4,000 tons of tin, 20,000 tons of zinc, 5,000 tons of lead, and 3,000 tons of antimony will be extracted.[20]

*Copper.* Pre–World War II estimates set China's copper reserve at 3 million to 6 million tons. New discoveries of disseminated and porphyry copper ores are located in the Qilian Shan of Gansu Province and in the Zhongtiao Shan of Shanxi Province. Copper has also been found at Hongshan on the Yunnan-Guizhou Plateau and at Tongguanshan in Anhui Province. But for years, China has been a net importer of copper.

*Lead-Zinc.* Estimates for lead and zinc reserves are very tentative for lack of data, but pre–World War II estimates were 3 million to 6 million tons for each. The largest Chinese lead-zinc mines are located in Guangdong and Hunan provinces, and there are also a few small lead and zinc mines in Liaoning and Fujian provinces. In recent years, the country has relied on foreign supplies.

*Uranium.* Rich uranium deposits were found in granite strata in South China in 1956. The deposit was officially identified as the biggest in China, covering an area of 100 square kilometers with nearly 100 rich veins. Part of that reserve has since been tapped. In late 1979, a medium-sized uranium deposit was found in North China.[21]

In summary, of the nonmetallic minerals, China abounds in coal, oil, and oil-shale. In ferrous metals, China has an iron ore deposit that surpasses the combined totals of the United States and Great Britain. In nonferrous minerals, China is rich in some but deficient in others. It is safe to say that China's mineral resources are adequate to support a highly developed industry. The world significance of selected Chinese minerals in 1975 is shown in Table 1.3.

### *Forestry and Water Resources*

Among the other natural resources, forests and water also are significant for industrialization. China has large forest areas, covering nearly 579,350 square kilometers. The most important forest reserve is in the Northeast. A 1947 official estimate put standing timber at 3,730 million cubic meters in Manchuria, chiefly along the Tumen Jiang and Sungari Jiang, the northern part of the eastern Manchurian uplands, and in the Great and Little Hingan Ling (Khingan Mountains). The thick needle-leaf forests distributed over the Great Hingan Ling in northernmost China give those mountains the name, "sea of trees." In addition to larch, the region also has spruce and pine. These are excellent materials for construction of boats, carts, musical instruments, and paper.[22]

The Northwest has only one-twentieth (197 million cubic meters) as much standing timber as the Northeast, most of it in Gansu Province. The Southwest Forestry District reports a total of 1,572 million cubic meters, chiefly in the mountains of western Sichuan and western Yunnan. Southeastern China is credited with only 269 million cubic meters.[23]

Forest types are varied, and there is a wide variety of trees. There are 2,800 kinds of tall trees alone. Timber trees of fine quality and high economic value number close to 1,000 kinds, including such special and rare varieties as Taiwania, which grows to a height of sixty-six meters; red cypress, which has a trunk more than twenty meters in circumference; metasequoia; China cypress; and golden larch. Rich timber reserves supply abundant materials for the construction, paper, textile, furniture, utensil, and tool industries. Oils and essences are extracted from the roots, bark, leaves, and blossoms.

With respect to water resources, four major rivers and five minor ones flow eastward across China. They provide irrigation, support navigation, and offer a great potential for hydroelectric power. From north to south, the major arteries of China's river system consist of the Heilong Jiang, the Huang He, the Chang Jiang, and the Zhu Jiang. There are also the Liao, Hai, Huai, Qiantang, and Min rivers. The only north-south waterway in China is the Grand Canal.

The Chang Jiang, China's premier river, is 6,380 kilometers long.[24] Rising in the Koko Shili Mountains in western Qinghai Province, it traverses Qinghai, Xizang, Yunnan, Sichuan, Hubei, Hunan, Jiangxi, Anhui, Jiangsu, and the Shanghai area to empty into the Dong Hai. It drains a basin of 1.8 million square kilometers – about 19 percent of the country's total area – inhabited by 250 million people, and near it are several of China's greatest cities and industrial centers. Ocean-going vessels reach Hankou 1,014 kilometers upstream. Several large tributaries join the Chang Jiang and greatly increase its commercial value. The Han Jiang enters Boyang Hu (Poyang Lake) and reaches the Chang Jiang from the south. At Hankou, the 1,609-kilometer-long Han Jiang enters from the north, giving its name to the junction city of Hankou. Dongting Hu (Tungting Lake) receives two major tributaries from the south, the Xiang Jiang and the Yuan Jiang, and passes them on to the Chang Jiang. The Jialing joins at Chongqing, and the Min flows past Chengdu and enters the Chang Jiang in western Sichuan. Because the greater part of its length is navigable, the Chang Jiang is China's most important transport artery.

The Huang He is China's second largest river. Originating in the northern foothills of the Bayankara Mountains in Qinghai Province, it flows 4,800 kilometers through Qinghai, Sichuan, Gansu, Ningxia, Nei Monggol, Shaanxi, Shanxi, Henan, and Shandong to empty into the Bohai Wan. The Huang He valley, 740,000 square kilometers in area, is the cradle of Chinese culture.

The Huang He has less commercial value than the Chang Jiang. The Loess Highlands, through which its middle section flows, have sparse vegetation, so the soil is easily washed away. The silt that is carried into the Huang He is deposited in the riverbed as the current slows down while crossing the North China Plain. Throughout history, the

Table 1.3
Mineral Supply Position of the P.R.C., 1975

| Commodity | Share of World output (percent) | Adequacy in production | Reserve potential |
|---|---|---|---|
| Ferrous materials: | | | |
| Chromite | (a) | Little produced | Nothing of consequence |
| Iron ore | 6 | High grade ore short | 1st rank, low grade |
| Iron, pig | 7 | Adequate | Not applicable |
| Iron, scrap | 2-3 | Can use more | Building up |
| Iron, steel ingot | 4-5 | Imports special products | Not applicable |
| Manganese ore | 5 | Slight surplus | Considerable |
| Molybdenum | 1 | Adequate | Promising |
| Nickel | (a) | Greatly deficient | Very poor at present |
| Tungsten, mine | 20-25 | Large surplus | World's largest |
| Nonferrous metals: | | | |
| Aluminum | 1-2 | Considerably short | Sizable, off-grade |
| Antimony | 15-20 | Large surplus | Probably world's largest |
| Copper | 2 | Greatly deficient | Moderate |
| Gold | (b) | Can use more | Moderate |
| Lead | 3-4 | Growing shortage | So far not plentiful |
| Mercury | 7-10 | Large surplus | 1st rank, low grade |
| Silver | 1 | Adequate | Poor, but some stocks |
| Tin | 10 | Large surplus | 1st rank |
| Zinc | 2 | Growing shortage | So far not plentiful |
| Chemical fertilizer materials: | | | |
| Phosphate rock | 3 | Some imports | Sizable, low grade |
| Potassium ore | (a) | Substantially short | Unknown, perhaps moderate |

| | | | |
|---|---|---|---|
| Pyrite | 8 | Generally adequate | Moderate |
| Salt | 15 | Light surplus | 1st rank |
| Sulphur | 1 | Becoming short | Moderate |
| Nonmetallics: | | | |
| Asbestos | 4 | Surplus, demand growing | Considerable |
| Barite | 5 | Surplus, demand growing | Considerable |
| Borates | 1 | Adequate | Could prove moderate |
| Cement | 5 | Meets demand | Extensive raw materials |
| Diamonds | 1 | Adequate | Moderate |
| Fluorspar | 8 | Large surplus | 1st rank |
| Graphite | 10 | Adequate | Moderate |
| Gypsum | 1–2 | Adequate | Considerable |
| Limestone | 5 | Meets demand | 1st rank |
| Magnesite | 10 | Surplus | 1st rank |
| Mica | 1–2 | Adequate | Moderate |
| Quartz (piezo electric) | (c) | Adequate | Moderate |
| Silica (glass quality) | (c) | Adequate | Moderate |
| Talc | 3 | Slight surplus | Moderate, top grade |
| Mineral fuels: | | | |
| Anthracite | 10 | More than adequate | 1st rank |
| Bituminous coal | 15 | Adequate | 1st rank |
| Coke | 7 | Adequate | Coking coal moderate |
| Petroleum, crude | 3 | Growing surplus | Promising 1st rank |
| Petroleum, refined | 2–3 | Building up quickly | Not applicable |
| Natural gas | 3–4 | Potential surplus | Promising 1st rank |

(a) Insignificant
(b) Small
(c) Unknown

Note: Percentages represent order of magnitude. Source: K. P. Wang, "China's Mineral Economy," in U.S. Congress, Joint Economic Committee, Chinese Economy Post-Mao (Washington, D.C.: Government Printing Office, 1978), p. 378.

river has repeatedly overflowed its banks and changed its course, bringing misery to the people living in the river's floodplain. Historically, the Huang He was called "China's sorrow," and it became a liability rather than an asset to the nation's economy. In the past thirty years, vast efforts have been made to control the river by building reservoirs on the upper and middle reaches to serve the purposes of power generation, irrigation, flood control, and silt retardation. In the Loess Highlands, intensive conservation projects have sought to halt soil erosion and water loss. It is hoped that ultimately the river will be under permanent control.

China's river systems carry 2,784 billion cubic kilometers of water a year, which is about 9 percent of the world's fresh water and is surpassed in quantity only by the waters of the Soviet Union and Brazil. The Chang Jiang alone has an annual flow of nearly 1,000 billion cubic kilometers. The river systems are essential to agricultural and industrial development and are among the country's most valuable natural resources. More than 95,000 kilometers of the streams are considered navigable, and the hydropower potential has been estimated at 580 million kilowatts.[25]

Underground water resources in China are as abundant as surface water. In the eastern plains and hilly regions, where precipitation is high, subterranean waters are plentiful and close to the surface, which makes their exploitation easy. On the margins of the North China Plain, which adjoins mountainous terrain, water gushes out of the ground to form springs. Jinan, the provincial capital of Shandong Province, is known as the "city of springs."

Situated at the foot of such great mountains as the Tian Shan and the Qilian Shan, the arid regions of Xinjiang, Gansu, and Qinghai are watered by melting glaciers and snow, and rich water resources are buried underground. Underground water in an arid region is of paramount importance for agriculture.

Because water resources in China are unevenly distributed, marked by an abundance in the South and a scarcity in the North, the Chinese government has recently envisaged a grand scheme to divert Chang Jiang water to northern China. The plan would draw water from the lower reaches of the Chang Jiang near Yangzhou in Jiangsu Province and channel it north to Tianjin. Roughly, the diverted water would flow through the Grand Canal, pass through Hongze, Louma, Nanzi, and Dongping lakes, cross the Huang He and run through the four provinces of Jiangsu, Anhui, Shangdong, and Hebei. The project, which is still in the early planning stages, would eventually bring irrigation to more than 9.7 million acres of farmland and ensure an unfailing water supply to the industrial bases along the route.[26]

China's coastline of 18,000 kilometers touches on three seas of the Pacific Ocean: the Huang Hai, the Dong Hai, and the Nan Hai. Like its land surface, China's sea floors slant from west to east, forming a northwest-southeast descent. For the most part, this slope is gentle, and the seas are less than 200 meters deep and provide good fishing. The seas off the Chinese coast contain more than 1,500 varieties of fish. The Zhoushan Archipelago of Zhejiang Province, visited by both cold and warm currents, is rich in fish of cold and warm water origin. It is now China's biggest fishing ground.

The shallow seas off the coast, especially those less affected by tidal movements, are most suitable for marine products culture. With 11,000 kilometers of such ideal shore waters, China has, in the past three decades, registered rapid increases in the output of marine products. In 1974, the total area of fishery bases amounted to 1,470,000 square kilometers spreading over 5,000 islands.[27]

Of the abundance of salt produced in China, sea salt accounts for some four-fifths of the total output. All the seaboard provinces have salt fields. The major ones are found at Lüshun-Dalian in Liaoning Province, Changlu in Hebei Province, Qingdao in Shandong Province, Huaibei in Jiangsu Province, and Yingge in Guangdong Province. Salt production in 1979 was officially reported at 14.77 million tons, less than half that of the United States, the world's leader.[28] The availability of abundant and widespread resources of various kinds of salt is important for developing a strong chemical industry and for feeding a very large population.

## LAND AND POPULATION

Land and labor are two vital factors of production in China. During the early stage of development, when capital is scarce and technology rudimentary, a country's level of income and growth are largely dependent on land and labor. Although a lot of land is a blessing, a huge population can be an asset as well as a liability, depending on the land-labor ratio. A poor country with a high ratio of people to land has a severe handicap. It lacks the technical capacity and capital that can be substituted for land, and with development, a further expansion of population and a further decline in the ratio of land to people can be expected. Changes in the relationship between land and population have been viewed by some historians as a major factor underlying the fall of the Qing Dynasty in 1911.[29]

Although China has an immense territory of 9.6 million square kilometers, only 15 percent of its total land area, roughly 1.4 million square kilometers (350 million acres), is arable. In 1949, 232.6 million acres were cultivated, roughly 10 percent of the area of the country.[30] This percentage of cultivated land can be compared with the figures of 6 percent in the Soviet Union, 15 percent in Japan, 18 percent in the United States, 30 percent in the United Kingdom, and 35 percent in India and Pakistan at about the same time. Data on cultivated land become more meaningful in per capita terms, for China's average of 0.5 acre per person can be compared with 0.3 in Japan, 0.7 in India and Pakistan, 1.8 in the Soviet Union, and 2.5 acres in the United States.[31] In terms of cultivated acreage per male farm laborer in the middle of the present century, there were approximately 10 acres in China, compared with 8 acres in India and Pakistan, 11 acres in Japan, 81 acres in the Soviet Union, and 208 acres in the United States.[32]

The growth of China's population during the pre-World War II period, which resulted in a shrinkage of per capita land holding, was accompanied by two other problems: an unequal distribution of ownership and a fragmentation of landholding due to the traditional inheritance system.

Prior to the Communist government, most farms were privately owned. J. L. Buck's study shows that around 1930 (1929–1933) the government owned only 7 percent of the farmland; the balance was privately owned.[33] Of the private land, landlord families, which accounted for about 3 percent of the farming households, owned approximately 26 percent of the total cultivated acreage, while poor peasants, who represented 68 percent of the farm families, possessed only 22 percent of the cultivated land. The remaining 52 percent of the land was owned by rich and middle peasant households. Moreover, the land owned by the landlords and rich peasants was largely of good quality, while that owned by the middle and poor peasants was usually marginal.[34]

The average farm in the pre-1949 era was small. Through successive inheritance, family holdings had been divided and subdivided into tiny plots. The plots were often scattered over the radius of 1.6 kilometers from the farmhouse, so that much time was wasted in going from one plot to another. Government data indicate that in the pre-World War II period 33 percent of the farms covered less than 1.6 acres, 25 percent had 1.6 to 3.3 acres, and only 8 percent were larger than 8.4 acres. Most farms were too small for efficient operation. On the average, there were only 3.7 crop acres per farm household, compared with 40 acres in Denmark and 155 acres in the United States.[35]

The scarcity of land became a critical problem when China's population increased considerably. China has had few detailed demographic counts, and the traditional official population records of pre-1949 times were kept primarily for such purposes as taxation collection, labor levies, and military conscription, which makes them unreliable as a source of population data. Even these data are incomplete, and most figures on population are at best guesstimates. Following the general pattern of demographic evolution, from the time of Christ through the sixteenth century, the Chinese demographic pattern was characterized by a high rate of birth and a high rate of death, resulting in a low rate of natural growth. The population appears to have been constant from the Han Dynasty (A.D. 2) to the Ming Dynasty (A.D. 1578). But during the last two centuries, China entered a high demographic growth period, and with high birth rates and declining death rates, the population more than tripled. The totals in Table 1.4 are not precise measurements, but they may show the general trends.

In 1953, in preparation for the election of the National People's Congress and the First Five-Year Plan (FFYP), the new government conducted a census as of June 30, 1953. Of those counted by direct census, 51.82 percent were said to be males. People eighteen years old and more accounted for 58.92 percent of the population. On the basis of a study of 30 million people covered in the 1953 census, the birth rate was put at 37 per 1,000 and the death rate at 17 per 1,000, meaning a natural increase rate of 2.28 percent per year. Population on the Chinese mainland in mid-1953 totaled 582,603,417.

Table 1.4
China's Population in Various Periods

| Period | Year A.D. | Population |
|---|---|---|
| Han Dynasty | 2 | 59,595,000[a] |
| Ming Dynasty | 1578 | 60,700,000[b] |
| Qing | 1740 | 140,000,000[b] |
| Qing | 1812 | 362,000,000[b] |
| Republic (Nationalist) | 1946 | 448,668,546[b] |
| People's Republic (Communist) | 1953 | 587,960,000[c] |

Sources: (a) Hwang Nai-lung, Chung-kuo nung-yeh-fa-chan-shih (A history of agricultural development in China) (Taipei: Chen-chung Book Company, 1963), p. 333. (b) George B. Cressey, Land of the 500 Million (New York: McGraw-Hill, 1955), p. 5. (c) Tongji gongzuo (Statistical work) No. 1 (January 14, 1957), pp. 24-25.

Since the 1953 census, no new census has been conducted, and the size and growth rate of the Chinese population has been a subject of great controversy among Western demographers. Estimates of the Chinese population in 1978 ranged between 800 million and 1 billion. In May 1979, Chinese authorities, for the first time in twenty years, disclosed population figures showing that the 1977 population, including the independent island of Taiwan, had reached 960 million. Subtracting Taiwan's then 16 million people would make mainland China's population 944 million—nearly one-quarter of the world's population of about 4 billion, 3.7 times the Soviet Union's population, and more than four times the U.S. population.[36]

Some foreign analysts accept these figures; others are skeptical. Using the official Chinese figures for 1953 and 1977, the annual growth rate for that period would be 2.1 percent. Judging from the official Chinese growth rate, the Chinese population would have been 966 million in 1979, not counting the 17 million people on Taiwan, and would pass the 1 billion mark in 1982. In fact, U.S. government analysts have estimated that China's population had already passed the 1 billion mark in 1978.[37] The size and rate of increase of population on mainland China between 1949 and 1956, based on the official Chinese figures and on U.S. government estimates for 1957–1980, are reported in Table 1.5.

The increase of population from approximately 450 million prior to World War I to 1 billion in 1978 resulted in a steep rise in population density, which exerted great pressure on Chinese agriculture. First, the dense population required maximum production for each acre of land, and agriculture in China is very intensified in its use of manpower and land. The index of multiple-cropping for China has been very high. In the 1930s, the index stood at 163.20 in the rice region and 131 in the wheat region, with an overall index of 139.70, and the multiple-cropping indexes continued to rise in the post-1949 period. The index was 141 in 1957 and reached 150 in 1978.[38] In some southern provinces, the multiple-crop index in 1980 reached as high as over 200 percent in Zhejiang, Guangdong, Hubei, Hunan, Jiangxi, and Guangxi. Through centuries of intensive use, the Chinese soils have lost much of their initial fertility. The replacement of adequate phosphorus and potash requires high quantities of fertilizers. Consequently, for further development, Chinese agriculture will need more capital investment than many other countries.

Second, although China still possessed 120 million acres of arable land that had not yet been cultivated in 1980, most of the uncultivated lands were located in the border regions, where weather conditions

Table 1.5
Size and Rate of Increase of Population
in P.R.C.: 1949–1980
(in millions as of mid-year)

| Year | Number | Percent Increase | Year | Number | Percent Increase |
|---|---|---|---|---|---|
| 1949 | 538 | 1.20 | 1965 | 753 | 2.31 |
| 1950 | 547 | 1.67 | 1966 | 770 | 2.26 |
| 1951 | 558 | 2.01 | 1967 | 788 | 2.34 |
| 1952 | 570 | 2.15 | 1968 | 808 | 2.54 |
| 1953 | 583 | 2.28 | 1969 | 828 | 2.48 |
| 1954 | 596 | 2.23 | 1970 | 849 | 2.54 |
| 1955 | 610 | 2.35 | 1971 | 870 | 2.47 |
| 1956 | 625 | 2.46 | 1972 | 891 | 2.41 |
| 1957 | 642 | 2.72 | 1973 | 912 | 2.36 |
| 1958 | 657 | 2.34 | 1974 | 933 | 2.30 |
| 1959 | 672 | 2.28 | 1975 | 952 | 2.04 |
| 1960 | 685 | 1.93 | 1976 | 971 | 2.00 |
| 1961 | 696 | 1.61 | 1977 | 987 | 1.65 |
| 1962 | 706 | 1.44 | 1978 | 1,002 | 1.52 |
| 1963 | 720 | 1.98 | 1979 | 1,017 | 1.50 |
| 1964 | 736 | 2.22 | 1980 | 1,032 | 1.47 |

Sources: 1949–1956: Tongji gongzuo, Data Section, "Data on China's Population from 1949 to 1956," Tongji gongzuo (Statistical work) No. 1 (January 14, 1957), pp. 24–25.

1959–1977: Arthur G. Ashbrook, Jr., "China: Shift to Economic Gears in Mid-1970s," in U.S. Congress, Joint Economic Committee, Chinese Economy Post-Mao (Washington, D.C.: Government Printing Office, 1978), p. 208.

1978–1979: U.S. Central Intelligence Agency, China: Major Economic Indicators (Washington, D.C., 1980), p. 1.

1980: Projected figures.

are unfavorable and transport facilities and housing are lacking. Reclamation of land requires substantial amounts of overhead capital investment. During the past two decades, cultivated acreage has decreased by as much as 12 percent, since land reclamation has been outweighed by the encroachment of irrigation systems and other forms of construction.[39] As a result, per capita land acreage in 1980 is much smaller than in the 1950s.

Third, because population increases at a pace of more than 15 million people per year, the demand for food and other necessities continuously increases. Prior to World War II, China had to import nearly 2 million tons of food grains a year, half of which was rice. China was a net food exporter between 1951 and 1960, but between 1961 and 1970, China imported an average of 5 million tons of wheat per annum. In more recent years, the purchase of foreign food grains was stepped up. It reached 9.4 million tons in 1978 and 10.5 million tons in 1979.[40] In October 1980, China signed a four-year grain-trading agreement with the United States, committing itself to buy 6 million to 9 million tons of U.S. grain annually, starting in January 1981. At prevailing prices, the grain would cost $1.4 billion annually.[41] At the same time, China also stepped up imports of cotton. Those two items have absorbed a sizable part of China's foreign exchange and, hence, reduced its capital investment in industry.

Fourth, the rapid growth of population since 1949 has made the Chinese population a young one. In 1980, the number of children under sixteen totaled 380 million, almost equal to the combined population of the United States, Japan, and France. The bulk of the population in China in 1980 was either of working age (fifteen to sixty-four) or waiting to enter the labor market (see Figure 1.2). The task of providing education, housing, and employment to the enormous and growing numbers is prodigious. The size of the population and the limited availability of cultivated land constitute the most crucial hindrances to Chinese economic development.

## EFFECTS ON ECONOMIC DEVELOPMENT

The geographical environment, natural resources, and the land-population ratio have all had a great impact on Chinese economic development. First, China's geographical location and vast territory have made it basically a continental country rather than a sea power. Despite 18,000 kilometers of coastline touching on three seas of the Pacific Ocean, historically China's economic activities have seldom extended beyond its borders. China proper possesses extensive fertile valleys. These display a marked diversity and a rich supply of plants, many of them essential for food, clothing, and shelter. The country is so large that its people have chiefly spent their energy in occupying, developing, and defending it. Not until the seventeenth and eighteenth centuries did the Chinese go beyond the ocean border to Taiwan and Southeast Asia in large numbers. The traditional Chinese economy was primarily a self-sufficient one, in which foreign trade played an insignificant role. During the past three decades, foreign trade accounted for only 3 to 4 percent of the total national product,

## Figure 1.2
## China: Comparison of Age-Sex Distributions, 1958 and 1988

This comparison of 1958 with 1988 shows changes in the age-sex distribution of the Chinese population. some of which are now only beginning to be apparent. but will be much more evident ten years hence.

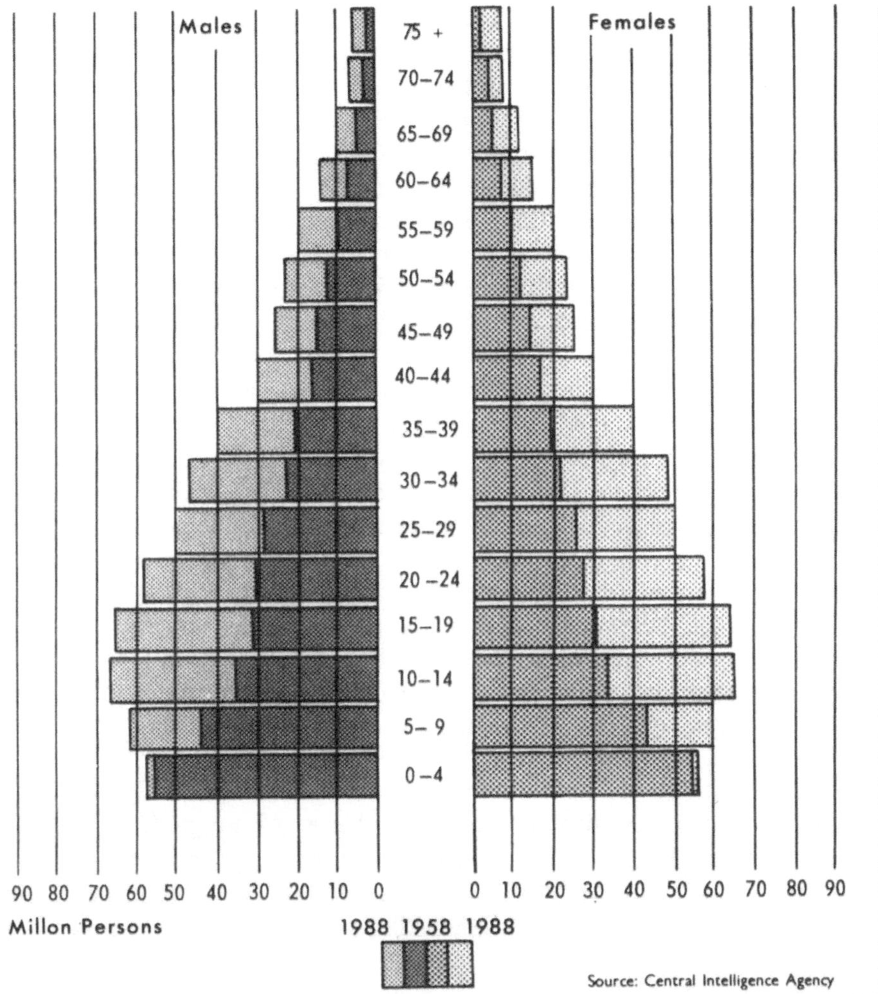


Source: Central Intelligence Agency
China: Economic Indicators, 1978

which is comparable to the situation in the United States and the Soviet Union but is much lower than that in Great Britain, Japan, and West European countries. The principle of self-sufficiency that was strongly advocated by Chinese Communist leaders after 1949 was more dictated by geography than by ideology.

Second, China's mineral resources, although not so rich as those of the United States and the Soviet Union, are considered by both Chinese and Western experts to be sufficient for a modern industrial economy. China has large deposits of iron ore, coal, petroleum, natural gas, aluminum, manganese, and several other major nonferrous metals, and many of those deposits are outstanding by world standards. According to a study by K. P. Wang, of the twenty-three major mineral commodities produced in different countries in 1974, China ranked as one of the first three world producers of eight: hard coal, anthracite, tungsten, antimony, mercury, salt, pyrite, and asbestos. If all minerals were added together in terms of output value, China would rank as one of the world's top five producers of crude minerals.[42] In the world energy crisis of the 1970s, China was one of the few major countries to escape virtually unscathed. Moreover, the long-term outlook for China's supply of energy looks even brighter. Chinese coal reserves are nearly on a par with those of the United States and the Soviet Union, and its petroleum industry has suddenly come into prominence. Its role as a major oil producer also has been enhanced in recent decades. The raw materials prospects for China's nuclear industry are considered reasonably good. While the mineral resources of other industrial nations are rapidly being depleted, China's are still underdeveloped and have great potential. Compared with Japan, which relies on foreign countries to supply most of its iron ore, oil, and coal, China has greater potential as a major industrial power.

Third, China's huge population and its limited amount of arable land impose a constant pressure on agriculture. Although China is the world's third largest country in terms of territory, much of its land cannot be cultivated. Mountains, steep hills, and cold plateaus greatly restrict the amount of usable land. Plains and rolling basins cover less than half of the country, and two-thirds of them are arid. Barely 15 percent is potentially usable for agriculture. Because most of the cultivated land has been tilled intensively for more than twenty centuries, Chinese soils have lost much of their initial fertility. Agricultural development in China, therefore, is much more difficult than in the United States and the Soviet Union, where vast tracts of virgin land are still available and the land under cultivation is more fertile.

Because China's population has continued to grow during the past three decades and now approaches 1 billion, the pressure on the food supply is mounting. In the view of many economists in Chinese studies, the most serious and intractable problem facing Chinese agriculture is not distribution of the product but technological backwardness and the resultant low labor productivity. There is no doubt that the Chinese peasant has used the factors of production at his disposal most intensively at the existing level of technology. Yet, the Chinese Communist Party Vice-Chairman Deng Xiaoping revealed that the output of grain per farm laborer in 1977 amounted to only 1,000 kilograms as compared with more than 50,000 kilograms in the United States.[43] Improvement in agricultural technology and an increase in current input may enable China to raise the crop yield per acre, but the progress is likely to be very slow. How to keep the food supply and population growth in equilibrium, thereby escaping the Malthusian trap, is one of the major tasks for the Chinese.

Finally, the differences in temperature, rainfall, and transport facilities between the coastal and hinterland areas also have great consequences for the economic development of those two areas. The country's population and productive capacity are unevenly distributed. In the crowded eastern part, China's average density is more than 100 persons to a square kilometer, and in a number of places more than 400. The western part is still thinly populated, with an average for most of the area of fewer than 10 persons to a square kilometer. Because the eastern and coastal areas embarked on the path of modernization and industrialization in the 1930s, almost all major economic centers are located there. This "space friction" is also a critical long-term problem for the Chinese economy.

Although China is endowed with a large territory that is rich in mineral resources, as befits a modern industrial power, the high ratio of population to land has become the foremost handicap for China's development in the coming decades.

## NOTES

1. T. R. Tregear, *An Economic Geography of China* (London: Butterworth, 1970), p. 28.
2. *China—A Geographical Sketch* (Beijing: Foreign Languages Press, 1974), p. 1; and Chiao-min Hsieh, "Physical Geography," in Yuan-li Wu, ed, *China: A Handbook* (New York: Praeger, 1973), p. 34. The length of coastline is from *Renmin ribao* [People's daily], November 19, 1980, p. 3.
3. *China—A Geographical Sketch,* p. 54.

4. K. P. Wang, "Natural Resources and Their Utilization," in Yuan-li Wu, *China: A Handbook*, p. 71.

5. Chu-yuan Cheng, *China's Petroleum Industry: Output Growth and Export Potential* (New York: Praeger, 1976), p. 3.

6. A. A. Meyerhoff, "Development in Mainland China, 1949–1968," *American Association of Petroleum Geologists Bulletin* 54:8 (1970), pp. 1567–1580.

7. U.S. Central Intelligence Agency, *China: Oil Production Prospects* (Washington, D.C., 1977), pp. 5–7.

8. U.S., Department of State, "Oil Supply–Prospects and Policy," *Current Policy*, (Washington D.C.) No. 202 (July 1980), pp. 2–3.

9. New China News Agency (hereafter referred to as NCNA)–Chengdu, May 7, 1958; NCNA-Shanghai, January 18, 1960; and *Renmin ribao*, July 30, 1971.

10. K. P. Wang, *Mineral Resources and Basic Industries in the People's Republic of China* (Boulder, Colo.: Westview, 1977), p. 109.

11. Chu-yuan Cheng, "China's Energy Resources," *Current History* 74:435 (March 1978), p. 121.

12. P.R.C., State Statistical Bureau, *Ten Great Years* (Beijing: Foreign Languages Press, 1960), p. 14.

13. According to Xiao Han, minister of the coal industry, China has an estimated 1.5 trillion tons of coal reserves (Foreign Broadcast Information Service [hereafter referred to as FBIS], *People's Republic of China*, September 13, 1978, p. A-9).

14. Editorial Department, "China's Economy in the 80's," *China's Foreign Trade* No. 5 (September-October 1980), p. 3.

15. *Renmin dianye* [People's electric power] No. 20 (October 1958), p. 32.

16. Yuan-li Wu, *The Steel Industry in Communist China* (New York: Praeger, 1965), pp. 48–49.

17. *Beijing Review* 22:42 (October 19, 1979), p. 32, and 23:42 (October 20, 1980), p. 24.

18. K. P. Wang, *Mineral Resources and Basic Industries*, pp. 149–150.

19. *Beijing Review* 23:42 (October 20, 1980), p. 24.

20. *Wall Streeet Journal*, February 1, 1979.

21. *Beijing Review* 22:51 (December 21, 1979), p. 5.

22. *China–A Geographical Sketch*, pp. 88–89.

23. George B. Cressey, *Land of the 500 Million* (New York: McGraw-Hill, 1955), p. 128.

24. In the past, the length of the Chang Jiang was put at 5,520 kilometers or 3,430 miles. The length was raised to 6,380 kilometers (3,965 miles) in 1976, after an expedition team found the new origin of the Chang Jiang. The new discovery made the Chang Jiang the third longest river in the world (*Shih-tai pao* [San Francisco journal], May 20, 1979).

25. In comparison, the United States has 44.5 million kilowatts of developed hydroelectric power and 124 million kilowatts of undeveloped potential

(see Chiao-min Hsieh, "Physical Geography," in Yuan-li Wu, *China: A Handbook,* p. 38).

26. *Peking Review* 21:38 (September 22, 1978), pp. 6–8.

27. *Zhongguo jingji de xianzhuang yu zhanwang* [China's economy: current situation and prospect] (Hong Kong: Chi-shih Nien-tai, 1977), p. 32.

28. P.R.C., State Statistical Bureau, "Communiqué on Fulfillment of China's 1979 National Economic Plan," *Beijing Review* 23:19 (May 12, 1980), p. 13.

29. Ho Ping-ti's interview in *Chi-shih nien-tai* [The Seventies] (May 1979), p. 85.

30. T. H. Shen, *Agricultural Resources of China* (Ithaca: Cornell University Press, 1951), p. 6.

31. George B. Cressey, *Land of the 500 Million,* p. 104.

32. Colin Clark, *The Conditions of Economic Progress,* 3d ed. (London: Macmillan, 1960), p. 308.

33. John Lossing Buck, *Land Utilization in China,* vol. 1 (New York: Council on Economic and Cultural Affairs, 1956), p. 193.

34. Nai-Ruenn Chen and Walter Galenson, *The Chinese Economy Under Communism* (Chicago: Aldine, 1969), p. 4.

35. George B. Cressey, *Land of the 500 Million,* p. 106.

36. *Washington Post,* May 14, 1979, p. A-15.

37. John S. Aird, "Population Growth in the People's Republic of China," in U.S., Congress, Joint Economic Committee, *Chinese Economy Post-Mao,* (Washington, D.C.: Government Printing Office, 1978), p. 465.

38. P.R.C., Ministry of Agriculture and Forestry, Bureau of Foreign Affairs, "Briefing on China's Agriculture" (Paper prepared for Mid-Atlantic International Agribusiness Trade Council, September 8, 1978).

39. Thomas B. Wiens, "Agriculture in the Four Modernizations" (Paper presented at the thirty-first annual meeting of the Association for Asian Studies, Los Angeles, March 30, 1979), p. 5.

40. U.S., Department of Agriculture, *People's Republic of China: Agricultural Situation, Review of 1979 and Outlook for 1980* (Washington, D.C., June 1980), p. 2.

41. *Wall Street Journal,* October 20, 1980, p. 28.

42. K. P. Wang, *Mineral Resources and Basic Industries,* pp. 3–7.

43. Deng's speech to the National Science Conference on March 18, 1978 (*Hongqi* [Red flag] No. 4 [April 1978], p. 12).

# 2

# Ideological Background

Like Communists in other countries, the Chinese Communists consider themselves devoted Marxist-Leninists. In theory, all policies on social, economic, and political affairs are to be formulated in accordance with Marxist-Leninist doctrine. In practice, Mao Zedong's thought dominated policymaking until his death in September 1976 and was promoted almost like some sort of state religion. As early as 1945, Mao's thought had been incorporated into the Party constitution as its guiding doctrine. Although Mao intended to have his concept of socialism define the economic system, not all of China's Communist leaders shared his views. Arguments for and against Mao's doctrine underlay a continuing struggle between two lines within the Chinese Communist Party and culminated in the Cultural Revolution, which affected Chinese economic development for more than a decade. A survey of economic development in China under Communist control therefore requires a brief review of the ideological background of the Chinese leaders and especially of the thought of Mao Zedong.

Any attempt to delineate and assess Mao's economic thought confronts almost insurmountable problems. First, Mao, unlike Karl Marx, was not an economist by training and never wrote systematically on economic problems. On several occasions, Mao frankly acknowledged that he was a layman in economics.[1] Although he did study Marxist theory in Chinese translations during the Yanan period (1937–1945), it was not until 1960 that he read and made detailed notes and commentaries on the Soviet *Textbook on Political Economy,*[2] an official interpretation of Marxian theories. In the absence of any systematic treatment of economic subjects in Mao's *Selected Works,* analysis can only focus upon the economic policies of the People's Republic of China. This presents the researcher with a second serious problem, however – how to discern and distill Mao's ideas from the myriad forces affecting the formation of economic policies pursued by the Communist government. In this chapter, Mao's economic doctrine is interpreted in a broad political-economic context, and the assessment will concentrate primarily on Mao's expressed goals for the Chinese economy, the methods he advocated for achieving those goals, and the discernible impact of his policies on the economic development of the People's Republic of China.

## ORIGINS OF MAO'S ECONOMIC THOUGHT

The evolution of economic doctrine in the Western world has been indelibly influenced by the times in which various economic theorists lived. Similarly, Mao's thought reflects the intellectual currents of his time, as they interacted with his personality and career experiences.

During Mao's lifetime, China was undergoing transformation from a traditional to a modern society. In his youth, the nation was frequently humiliated by foreign invasions and was often on the brink of being dismembered by the major powers. The May Fourth Movement in 1919 was the climax of a period of mounting nationalism. Like most thoughtful young Chinese of his generation, Mao was exposed to a wide variety of modernization and Westernization schemes that were oriented toward saving the country from foreign partition. During the 1920s, when the young republic failed to secure needed moral and material aid from the West, the intellectual class began to turn to communism as an alternative vehicle for modernizing China. Mao was deeply influenced by two intellectual enthusiasts of the Russian Revolution, Li Dazhao (1889–1927) and Chen Duxiu (1880–1942), who saw Marxism as the panacea for the country's plight. According to Mao's account, the influence of Li Dazhao in 1918–1919 converted Mao to Marxism.[3]

Although Mao considered himself a Marxist thereafter, his concepts of revolution, class relations, social transformation, and economic reconstruction were primarily derived from Lenin's writings rather than from those of Marx. According to Marx, the forces or conditions of production are the fundamental determinant of social structures, which in turn breed attitudes, actions, and civilization. The forces of production have a logic of their own, changing according to necessities inherent in them so as to produce their successors. These economic forces inevitably shape society, creating the proletariat that ultimately generates the socialist revolution. Thus, according to Marxist theory, capitalist (bourgeois) social institutions are necessary prerequisites that sharpen the conflict between proletariat and bourgeoisie that must inevitably lead to socialism.[4] Although Marx and Engels laid down the foundation of Marxism, neither of them had the opportunity to lead the revolution. That task was undertaken by Lenin (1870–1924), and Lenin's primary contribution to communism was in organization rather than in ideology.

Lenin amended Marxist theory by contending that in countries where Communists became predominant, the peasant masses could be led to socialism without passing through a capitalist stage of development. Mao appears to have subscribed to Lenin's modification and carried it one step further.[5] According to Mao, the peasantry not only constituted the important revolutionary force but was itself capable of independent revolutionary action.[6] Thus, Mao contended that when revolution flared in Russia during 1917, that country's industrial base was already quite strong and the revolution first succeeded in the cities, with the proletariat playing an important role. In sharp contrast, the peasantry constituted the spearhead of Mao's 1930 revolution. Indeed, when Mao launched the revolution in China, modern industrial workers represented less than 1 percent of the population.[7] The revolution, which started with abortive uprisings in the cities, later became a protracted struggle in the remote and rural areas between Mao's forces and the Nationalist Army and only gradually engulfed the cities in 1947–1948 in what was essentially a peasant-based guerrilla war. During the initial period of revolution in the 1930s, industrial workers played no meaningful role. In this sense, the Chinese revolution was essentially a peasant revolt rather than the proletarian revolution that Marx had envisioned as leading to the socialist state.

Both the peculiar nature of the Chinese revolution as well as the backwardness of the Chinese economy had a profound impact on Mao's economic thought. Marx and Lenin considered the technical-economic foundation as the ultimate force shaping history. Lenin's commitment to technical progress was fully manifest in his famous formula, "Communism equals the soviets plus electrification." Recognizing the "poor and blank" condition of China, and deeply affected by his guerrilla warfare experience, Mao advanced his own theory that men, not weapons, are the decisive factor in revolutionary war. In a similiar vein, he argued that men, not machines, are the most powerful force shaping economic development. Mao's obsession with human willpower rather than with technological development further separated him from orthodox Marxism.

Another manifestation of Mao's economic thought is contained in his proposition that politics always commands economics. The proposition had been advocated by Lenin, but it was reinforced by Mao and became the overriding policy guideline for China with the founding of the People's Republic in 1949. The purge of Vice-Premier Deng Xiaoping in 1976 provides a recent example as the purge was the consequence of Deng's attempt to rank economics above politics. Events after the launching of the Cultural Revolution in 1966 consistently exemplified Mao's desire to subordinate economics to political decisions. These deviations from classical Marxism add substance to the conclusion that although Mao considered himself a Marxist his economic thought represented a heretical version of traditional Marxism. This distorted version was officially justified as the "Sinification of Marxism." In 1938, after Mao had established himself as the Communist Party leader, he asserted in a report to the Sixth Plenum of the Sixth Central Committee:

> A Communist is a Marxist internationalist, but Marxism must take on a national form before it can be applied. There is no such thing as abstract Marxism, but only concrete Marxism. What we call concrete Marxism is Marxism that has taken on a national form, that is, Marxism applied to the concrete struggle in the concrete conditions prevailing in China and not Marxism abstractly used.[8]

The Sinification of Marxism was later hailed by other Chinese Communist leaders as the "great accomplishment" of Mao, who "has created a Chinese or Asiatic form of Marxism."[9] Yet, from the point of view of orthodox Marxists, Mao's thought represents "petty bourgeois fanaticism" and "has betrayed socialism."[10]

## ESSENCE OF MAO'S ECONOMIC THOUGHT

The essence of Mao's economic thought is embodied in his vision of "Communist man" in contrast to the "economic man" concept of classical economic theory. Classical economics, since the time of Adam Smith, has held that man is by nature a creature of self-interest whose behavior is always guided by economic forces. The whole structure of Western economics is based on the assumption that man is a rational being who will deliberately subordinate means to the attainment of definite ends. Men, if allowed to pursue their own rational self-interest, with government confined to protecting private property, will select the most efficient means of allocating resources. This, in essence, is the doctrine of laissez faire, a fundamental bulwark of capitalism.[11]

In contrast, Mao saw the key to an ideal society in the transformation of men's souls into selfless parts of an organic whole. Donald Munro has suggested that in Mao's thought, selflessness is both a means and an end.[12] According to Marx and other socialists, unselfishness is the state of mind of people under communism. In Mao's thought, unselfishness is also the touchstone for achieving a metamorphosis of the state. Thus, Mao envisaged the Communist man as an ideal type. This Communist man, once properly imbued with, indoctrinated into, and committed to the course, would possess both tremendous energy and a consciousness that would enable him to conquer nature and overcome virtually all obstacles. The Communist man would fear no hardship, not even death, and would eagerly perform any task the Party assigned.[13]

Compared with Smith's concept of economic man, Mao's politicized Communist man possessed some unique characteristics. First, he possessed the capacity for total self-denial as well as a wholehearted willingness to overcome natural limitations. Second, unlike Smith's economic man, whose rational self-interest was oriented toward maximizing personal gain, Mao's ideal Communist was a moral creature solely concerned with benefiting the commonwealth. Third, in Smith's model, the harmony between individual self-interest and the good of the commonwealth was achieved through competition, which placed constraints on selfishness. Self-interest was the engine of social progress, and competition provided a brake on its excesses. In sharp contrast, Mao's ideal type became a reality only when the Communist man was willing to subordinate fully his individual self-interest to the goals of the community at large.

Having developed the concept of the ideal Communist man, Mao formulated a corollary proposition that singled out man as the most significant factor in production. In contrast, classical economists ascribe a dominant role to capital in the early stages of economic development. Economic development, according to Adam Smith, was the direct result of three factors: division of labor, expansion of market, and the accumulation of capital. Division of labor was limited by the extent of the market and the extent of the market mirrored the degree of capital accumulation. Thus, in classical economics, the rate of output expansion goes hand in hand with capital accumulation, which is the primary determinant of economic growth.

In Mao's view, man, not the machine, was the most powerful factor shaping economic development. "Of all the things in the world, people are the most precious. As long as there are people, every kind of miracle can be performed under the leadership of the Communist Party."[14] Mao's overwhelming stress on man may have stemmed partly from the fact that China was an underdeveloped country endowed with tremendous manpower but shackled by an extremely low rate of capital accumulation. At the time of the establishment of the People's Republic of China in 1949, the rate of capital formation was approximately 6 percent, compared with 15 to 20 percent in most advanced countries. In 1958, during the Great Leap Forward, Mao said: "China's 600 million people have two remarkable peculiarities: they are, first of all, poor, and secondly, blank. That may seem like a bad thing, but it is really a good thing. Poor people want change, want to do things, want revolution. A clean sheet of paper has no blotches, and so the newest and most beautiful words can be written on it, the newest and most beautiful pictures can be painted on it."[15]

The belief that revolution can change everything, coupled with the will to take advantage of China's poverty and "blankness" in order to build a new society that ultimately would enable the Chinese people to live better than the imperialist countries, has permeated most major economic policy decisions in China since 1949. In 1958, Mao proclaimed policies that mobilized 100 million people to develop an irrigation system and another 60 million to build primitive blast furnaces in order to increase the country's iron production. He apparently assumed that labor and capital were interchangeable and that ideological indoctrination and mass mobilization could take the place of capital equipment and technological expertise.

Associated with Mao's belief in the efficacy of ideological indoctrination and mass mobilization was a power preference for the egalitarian distribution of income. Indeed, a reasonably egalitarian income distribution was apparently almost as important to Mao as economic growth. Realizing that poverty was an almost universal condition in China and that there was no magic way to lift the living standards of the masses overnight, Mao concluded that mass support could best be enlisted by pursuing egalitarian policies. A series of campaigns during the first decade of the People's Republic aimed at eradicating private enterprises (1956) and at the communization of farm households (1958) so as to eliminate private wealth. To ensure a minimum subsistence level for every citizen, a strict scheme of rationing food grains, cotton fabrics, and edible oils was introduced in 1955. These policies resulted in an equal allotment of basic staples to the entire population.

The egalitarian spirit also influenced, if it did not permeate, the wage system. Since 1956, the country as a whole has had a unified wage scale, with industrial workers being classified in terms of seven or eight grades based on levels of tenure and skill. Starting in 1956, the wage spread between the lowest workers and the highest-paid specialists or executives has never exceeded a ratio of 1 to 10. Although Mao never made a theoretical commitment to equal payment regardless of work, the spirit of egalitarianism was undoubtedly part of his social ethic.

This egalitarian spirit extended to women. During the early 1930s in the Jiangxi Soviet Republic, Mao favored freedom for the individual to decide matters of love and backed equal rights for women. In 1955, he said: "China's women are a vast reserve of labor power. This reserve should be tapped and used in the struggle to build a mighty socialist country. To encourage women to join in productive labor, we must put into effect the principle of equal pay for equal work, men and women alike."[16] Following the 1949 revolution, women's liberation in China was symbolized by uniformity in dress and job assignment without regard to sex. Women were allowed to wear work clothing similar to that of working men and to enter occupations formerly monopolized by men. Today, the two sexes participate equally not only in agriculture, industry, and transportation, but in military activities as well.[17] Leadership roles, however, are largely held by men.

Although the ideas of the Communist man and the egalitarian spirit have been shared by many of the leaders associated with Mao, there are fundamental differences between Mao and other Communist leaders in several major aspects of ideology. The most crucial one concerns the concept of class struggle. The notion of class struggle, borrowed from Marx, was a pillar of Mao's economic thought. According to Marx, every society, except the final classless society under communism, consists chiefly of a ruling class and an oppressed class. Marx saw human history as a history of class struggle. Mao, following Marx's analysis, thought that even after the bourgeois class had been removed from power, it would retain some of its traditional influence on society for there is a spontaneous tendency toward capitalism among the peasants and small producers. Thus, a continuing class struggle would inevitably find expression within the Party and would be reinforced by lingering bourgeois, revisionist influences as well as by pressure from foreign imperialist powers.[18] In 1957, Mao warned that the class struggle was by no means over. In September 1962, at the Tenth Plenum of the Chinese Communist Party's (CCP) Eighth Central Committee, he called for the whole Party never to forget class struggle. Under his initiative, a nationwide Socialist Education Campaign was launched to halt the spread of economic and ideological views akin to Khrushchev's "revisionism," which Mao regarded as renascent capitalism. During the Cultural Revolution, Mao formulated "a basic line for the whole socialist historical stage."

> Socialist society is a fairly long historical period. In the socialist historical stage, there still exist classes, class contradictions, class struggle between the socialist and the capitalist lines, and the danger of capitalist restoration. We must be fully aware of the protracted and complex nature of these struggles. We must be on the alert . . . otherwise, our socialist country will go the wrong way and deteriorate and restoration of capitalism will appear.[19]

In later years, Mao emphasized that class struggle was the key link and everything hinged on it. His stress on class struggle, to the neglect of economic reconstruction, led to an open split between Mao and many Party leaders. In the opinion of former Chairman Liu Shaoqi, Deng Xiaoping, and many others, class struggle was a means, not an end. These opposition leaders contended that after the elimination of capitalists in the urban areas and of landlords and rich peasants in the rural districts, the class struggle should be regarded as basically concluded. In his 1956 political report to the Eighth Party Congress, Liu stated that

> with the exception of a few localities, the feudal landlords have been eliminated as a class. The rich peasant class is also being eliminated. Landlords and rich peasants who used to exploit the peasants are being reformed. They are making a fresh start in life and becoming people who live by their own work. The national bourgeois elements are in the process of being transformed from exploiters into working people.[20]

According to Liu, the task confronting the Party was to build China into a great socialist country as quickly as possible. Such diametrically opposed appraisals of the class struggle were important ingredients in shaping the Cultural Revolution.

The concept of class struggle underlay Mao's theory of "permanent" or "uninterrupted" revolution. Aware of the selfishness of human nature and the spontaneous inclination of peasants and small producers toward capitalism, Mao feared that without an uninterrupted revolution, there was no certainty that the Communist regime would be free from the growing web of bureaucracy and the reemergence of revisionism. In the absence of uninterrupted revolution, Mao direly predicted in 1963 that "it would not take too long, perhaps only several years of a decade or several decades at most, before a counter-revolutionary restoration on a national scale inevitably occurred. The

Marxist-Leninist Party would undoubtedly become a revisionist party or a fascist party, and the whole of China would change its colour."[21]

Another controversial issue between Mao and his opponents was the incentive system. In the Maoist view, self-interest and material gain are the driving forces of the capitalist system, and a socialist system requires a collective ethos and collective institutions. Capitalist and socialist motivations and institutions cannot long coexist; if capitalist motivations persist, there will be a reversion to a form of capitalism.[22] Thus, Mao sought to promote moral incentives by emphasizing the role of people's consciousness and the repudiation of private material gain.

According to Liu Shaoqi and Deng Xiaoping, however, material rewards are indispensable for increasing labor productivity, regardless of differences in social systems. During the post-Great Leap Forward period (1961-1965), when Liu and Deng were in power, a whole set of material incentives was instituted–piecework payment systems, bonuses for workers, the return of private agricultural plots, and the reopening of free markets for some farm produce.

Mao's obsession with class struggle and the need for continuous revolution led him to use mass mobilization and continuous indoctrination as instruments for achieving economic progress. Since 80 percent of the Chinese people were peasants, mobilization of the peasantry provided the key to production and revolution. Perhaps because of his experiences during the 1930s and 1940s, Mao was inclined to apply the basic features of guerrilla warfare to economic affairs–specifically, a greater reliance on human will and mass mobilization than on professional expertise, machinery, and equipment. In 1964, he proclaimed the slogans, "In agriculture learn from Dazhai" and "In industry learn from Daqing," to illustrate his model for China's economic development. The first slogan eulogized the peasants of the Dazhai Production Brigade in northern Shanxi, who according to an earlier official report had successfully terraced the hillsides of Dazhai, replacing the barren soil and enabling the area to become highly productive. The second slogan praised the Herculean efforts of workers to build the Daqing oilfields without promise of financial reward. Both models expressed Mao's reliance upon revolutionary fervor to achieve industrialization.

But according to Liu Shaoqi, Chen Yun, and many other top Party leaders in charge of economic affairs, industrialization involving complicated modern technology, and managerial skill requires rational economic methods and the talents of experts–including factory directors, engineers, and technicians. Under Liu's initiation, a whole set of regulations for running agriculture, industry, and commerce was proclaimed in 1961–1962. The emphasis was placed on expertness rather than "redness." Maoists charged that Liu's Seventy-Point Charter for Industry denied the workers control and put profits instead of politics in command. Deng Xiaoping was quoted as having said, "It doesn't matter whether cats are white or black; so long as they can catch mice, they are good cats."[23] Deng's assertion clearly indicated his desire to free the economy from ideological interference.

## STRUGGLE BETWEEN TWO LINES

The divergent views of Maoists and their opponents on class struggle, incentives, and the path to modernization underlie the serious internal tensions and struggles that have characterized the Chinese Communist Party since 1949. The first bitter contest between the two schools of thought centered on rural policy in the mid-1950s. The issue at stake was whether China should collectivize agriculture before or after industrialization. According to Marxism, economic relations change after the productive forces of society have fully developed. Following this doctrine, Liu Shaoqi and other Russian-trained Chinese leaders believed that China's advance to socialism would be painfully slow, extending years into the future, and would come about only after the country had achieved large-scale industrialization. In 1951, at an All-China Propaganda Work Conference, Liu condemned as "utopian agricultural socialism" the views of those people in the Party who thought that socialization of agriculture could be achieved simply through the establishment of cooperatives. He emphasized that "if there is no adequate development of modern industry, no agricultural collectivization can be achieved."[24]

In contrast, Mao foresaw a spontaneous tendency among the peasantry to develop capitalism in the countryside. "If the position is not held by socialism" he said, "capitalism will definitely occupy it."[25] To forestall this possibility and to release peasant energies for development, Mao believed it essential to change the production system through collectivization. Postponing collectivization would, he thought, reconcentrate land ownership and farm machinery in the hands of new landlords and rich peasants.

In early 1955, when collectivization caused widespread peasant resistance, the majority of leaders on the CCP Central Committee recommended a slowdown in the program, and, with the approval of Liu Shaoqi, 200,000 agricultural cooperatives were dissolved. Moving against the tide, Mao called a meeting of the secretaries of the provincial, municipal, and district Party committees on July 31, 1955. He severely attacked those Party leaders who suggested a deceleration for "tottering along like a woman with bound feet, always complaining that others are going too fast."[26] Overriding the decision of the CCP Central Committee, he demanded a 30 percent increase in the number of agricultural cooperatives to be set up that year. Mao's triumph over Liu on this issue culminated in 1958 in the hasty establishment of people's communes and in the Great Leap Forward.

The second major contest between Mao and his opponents occurred in 1959–1964, in the wake of the disastrous failure of the Great Leap. During the summer of 1959, there was a bitter debate within the CCP hierarchy regarding the validity of the Party's general line, the commune system, and the Great Leap, all credited to Mao's authorship. A group of powerful military leaders led by Marshal Peng Dehuai, the former minister of national defense and one of the founders of the Red Army, openly opposed the communes and the Great Leap. In August 1959, after the Eighth Plenum of the Eighth Party Congress, Peng and his follower Huang Kecheng, former chief of the general staff of the army, were both dismissed. Peng's viewpoints, however, found wide support in the army and among top Party leaders and leading economists.[27] As Premier Zhou Enlai admitted in his December 1964 report to the National People's Congress: "From 1959 to 1962, the class enemies at home launched renewed attacks on socialism. In the countryside, quite a number of people advocated the so-called three-selfs and one-assignment in favor of more private plots with larger free markets and the reintroduction of small enterprises with private responsibility for profit and loss."[28] Zhou's admission bespoke widespread disapproval of Mao's radical economic program and a general preference for a more moderate and liberal policy, which was to some extent similar to the policy then prevailing in the Soviet Union.

In 1961, as the economy reacted to the failures of the Great Leap and the commune movement, the CCP Central Committee suspended the Great Leap and adopted the Sixty-Point Charter for Agriculture, a dramatic revision of the commune system. During this period, the Party Central Committee was under the influence of Liu Shaoqi, chairman of the People's Republic, and Deng Xiaoping, secretary-general of the Party. According to red guard publications during the Cultural Revolution, Liu and Deng had jointly approved such measures as allowing commune directors to assign production work to individual peasant households and even returning farmlands to peasants in some localities.[29] These steps, according to the Maoists, signified the revival of an individual economy and the de facto dissolution of the commune system, which Mao had once hailed as "the ladder to the Communist paradise."

In the industrial sector, the Seventy-Point Charter for Industry initiated by Liu Shaoqi directed that profit play the central role in industrial management and that full responsibility be given to the factory director. Those workers who could increase output or reduce costs and produce profit would get rewards. Political consciousness was no longer emphasized. A complicated bonus system was put into effect, with prizes for good quality, high productivity, and savings on raw materials consumption. Penalties were levied if machines broke down, quality was poor, or quotas were not met. The key words were efficiency and profit instead of revolution and class struggle.

The new economic policy ensured a steady recovery of the national economy and received strong support from many academics and intellectuals. On the role of profits, the importance of rational relative prices, and the orientation of Chinese economic development, a consensus among professional economists in China favored a pragmatic approach that emphasized careful planning, good management, and technical competence. A leading Party economist, Sun Yefang, former director of the Economic Research Institute in the Chinese Academy of Sciences, openly challenged Mao's policies, especially those concerning the communes and the Great Leap. In Sun's view, such grandiose schemes were impractical and subjective for they did not have the support of needed production capacity and modern techniques, they disregarded the economic law of value and the principle of gaining maximum profits at minimum costs, and they totally ignored cost accounting. Sun's suggestion, like the Liberman proposal in the Soviet Union, was to let profit serve as a criterion in socialist economic administration. He also urged the use of material incentives to stimulate individual efforts in production by citing the Soviet experience under Khrushchev, in which materialistic incentives had yielded good results in Soviet agriculture.[30] Some economists even suggested that productive funds be channeled to those enterprises that had proved capable of achieving a higher-than-average profit rate and not to those that had performed inadequately. In addition to measuring performance, they proposed that the profit rate become part of the ethos of a firm.[31]

Opposition to Mao's ideology and policies was not confined to economic affairs and found even stronger expression in the fields of philosophy, history, literature, and the arts—the sphere that Marxists called "superstructure." To most intellectuals within and outside the Party in 1962–1965, Mao's emphasis on class struggle and the primacy of politics had excluded too many other considerations. Consequently, Mao's policy had become impractical, irrelevant, or unnecessary, placing obstacles in the path of the intelligent development of the socalist order. According to Zhou Yang, former deputy director of the Party's Department of Propaganda and in charge of literature and publications for more than three decades, "Politics will lose its meaning if we keep talking about politics at every breath." Hence, he deliberately limited the publication of manuscripts dealing with class struggle and other political subjects.[32] Yang Xianzhen, a top Party ideologist and former president of the Advanced Party Academy, proposed the theory that "two combine into one." This theory, an approach to class reconciliation, echoed Liu Shaoqi's view that China was free of class conflict and directly opposed Mao's dictum that class struggle must be carried through to the end. During the same period (1961–1965), many well-known writers published books and articles on historical subjects related to current events. Many of them rejected Mao's subjectivism as unrealistic and ridiculed his Great Leap as a fiasco.[33] Leaders in the field of culture proposed a reaffirmation of the traditional "moral heritage" as support for the social order. A great deal of traditional literature in the fields of the classics, philosophy, history, prose, poetry, and drama was reissued while the reprinting of Mao's *Selected Works* was substantially curtailed. The major intention in reviving traditional culture, as C. K. Yang has pointed out, was to unify the people by appealing to common historical sentiments and nationalistic pride, thereby mitigating class conflict and enhancing internal peace. It was an intellectual attempt to negate the justification for class struggle.[34]

Aware of the economic crisis and of popular resentment, Mao endured considerable criticism during this period. Starting late in 1962, as the national economy showed signs of recovery, Mao launched his counterattack with the nationwide Socialist Education Campaign in an attempt to reaffirm his policies. In May 1963, Mao claimed that many Party cadres "shut their eyes to the activities of bad elements and ogres of all kinds and in many cases failed to differentiate the enemy from their own, and went so far as to collaborate with the enemy and become corrupted and demoralized." He warned that if the situation continued, "The whole of China would change its color before long."[35] On at least three occasions–in September 1962, the summer of 1964, and September 1965–Mao strove unsuccessfully to reverse the tide through the customary rectification campaign. To recover his absolute authority, Mao sought the collaboration of Lin Biao, who had succeeded Peng Dehuai as defense minister and seemed loyal to Mao. Lin seized the opportunity to consolidate his own position. Thus began a titanic power struggle during the era of the Great Proletarian Cultural Revolution.

The first stage of the Cultural Revolution, the campaign was wrapped in the cloak of ideology. The officially proclaimed goal was the elimination of revisionism, which it was feared would change the course of development and the final goal of the Communist revolution. The campaign began with a purge in cultural circles that involved such famous figures as Yang Xianzhen, the leading Party ideologist, and Wu Han, a scholar specializing in Ming history and a former vice-mayor of Beijing who had published an historical play entitled *The Dismissal of Hai Rui.* (In the play, Hai Rui, a benevolent mandarin of the sixteenth century, served as a symbol for Marshal Peng Dehuai, who had openly criticized Mao's radical line and had been dismissed in August 1959.) However, the convulsive campaign soon swept on to involve the highest leaders in the Party. In the summer of 1966, Peng Zhen, one of Liu Shaoqi's close associates and the powerful mayor of Beijing, and Lu Dingyi and Zhou Yang, two prominent leaders who had controlled the CCP propaganda machine and cultural affairs for more than three decades, were victimized. Hundreds of editors of local Party newspapers, writers, and several dozen presidents and vice-presidents of the nation's top universities and colleges also were ousted. After the Eleventh Plenum of the Eighth Party Congress in August 1966, the spearhead was pointed directly at Liu Shaoqi, who was openly accused of being China's Khrushchev. He lost not only his position as first vice-chairman of the CCP and Mao's heir apparent,[36] but his rank on the Standing Committee of the Politburo descended from number two to number eight. Thereafter, the immediate aims of the campaign shifted from purging reactionary intellectuals to seizing power through the organization of millions of red guards and the destruction of the entrenched, anti-Mao Party machine. A power struggle ensued. As Chen Boda, the man entrusted by Mao to lead the Cultural Revolution in the 1966–1969 period, frankly admitted in a January 18, 1967, speech: "From the very beginning, the Great Cultural Revolution has been a struggle with Peng Zhen, Lu Dingyi, Luo Ruiqing [former chief of staff of the People's Liberation Army] and Yang Shangkun [a member of the CCP Central Secretariat]. This is a struggle for power."[37]

As events unfolded, the Cultural Revolution involved three dimensions: a conflict between Maoists and pragmatists over goals and concomitant policies, Mao's egoistic drive to have his personality and views dominate politics and government, and the struggle over Mao's succession. Between July 1966 and the Ninth Party Congress in April 1969, a political purge unprecedented in scale in CCP history took place. Of the 169 living members of the Eighth Central Committee, 115, or 68 percent of the total, were purged, including such powerful figures as Liu Shaoqi, Deng Xiaoping, Peng Zhen, and Luo Ruiqing. Of the 26 members of the Politburo of the Eighth Central Committee, 19 persons, or 73 percent, were purged or attacked (including 10 persons who were criticized and humiliated but retained their positions). Of the 29 first secretaries of provincial Party committees, 25 persons, or 86 percent of the total, were purged. The Party machine on the central and local levels was smashed. Never in modern history had a Party chairman dismantled his own Party machine as Mao did.

The Cultural Revolution expanded Mao's personality cult and expressed the paternalistic style of his leadership. The thought of Mao Zedong was praised as the acme of Marxism-Leninism in the current era. Nothing is more revealing than an editorial in the army's newspaper, *Jiefang junbao* [Liberation Army daily], which was published immediately after the purge of Peng Zhen.

> The attitude towards Mao Zedong's thought, whether to accept it or resist it, to support it or oppose it, to love it warmly or be hostile to it, this is the touchstone to test and the watershed between true revolution and counter-revolution, between Marxism-Leninism and revisionism. He who wants to make revolution must accept Mao Zedong's thought and act in accordance with it. A counter-revolutionary will inevitably disparage, distort, resist, attack, and oppose Mao Zedong's thought.[38]

During the course of the Cultural Revolution, millions of copies of the Chinese classics were burned, and the publication of most periodicals was suspended in order to devote all available facilities and supplies to the printing of Mao's works. According to an official report, 10 million sets of the *Selected Works of Mao Zedong* had been published between 1949 and 1965. Under the new campaign, the regime printed 15 million sets before the end of 1966 and another 86 million sets in 1967.[39] Such extensive circulation of a single publication was unprecedented in Chinese history. In the high tide of the Cultural Revolution, the nation's broadcasting network spent more than two-thirds of its air time reading from the book *Quotations from Chairman Mao.* Red guards were required to take as their highest obligation the study, dissemination, application, and defense of the thought of Mao Zedong. Propaganda teams were dispatched to factories, government agencies, schools, and army units to turn all major forms of organization into schools of the thought of Mao Zedong. By mid-1967, the craze for Mao had swept the entire country. Giant portraits of Mao gazed down on the throngs at every street intersection, and songs praising him swelled above the hubbub at every public gathering. The innumerable symbols of a personality cult made the entire Cultural Revolution appear as if it were Mao's grand design to resume complete personal dominance, to take revenge upon those who had opposed him after the Great Leap, to establish himself as an unchallengeable leader in the CCP, and to transform his doctrine into sacrosanct dogma. Chinese communism was so identified with the personality of Mao that any expression or action against Mao's thought automatically became an object of struggle.[40]

Although Mao dislodged his opponents and promoted his personality cult through the Cultural Revolution, he failed to solve the problem of his succession. In 1966, Mao chose Defense Minister Lin Biao as his successor to replace the purged Liu Shaoqi. At the Party's Ninth Congress in April 1969, Lin's position as Mao's "most intimate comrade-in-arms and successor" was incorporated into the Party's new constitution. Lin was praised for "having consistently held high the Great Red Banner of the thought of Mao Zedong and defended comrade Mao Zedong's proletarian revolutionary line."[41] Yet, less than thirty months after his designation, Lin was allegedly staging a coup d'etat to assassinate Mao. When the plot was discovered, Lin purportedly attempted to fly to the Soviet Union and was killed–along with his wife, his son, and several aides–when his plane crashed in Mongolia on September 12, 1971.[42]

The death of Lin Biao, no matter what the real cause, dealt a severe blow to Mao's prestige.[43] In a short span of five years (1966–1971), Mao had purged two of his closest comrades-in-arms, his chosen heirs apparent, and had condemned them as traitors, reactionaries, and special agents of the Kuomintang. Even the most naive people began to question the wisdom of the chairman and the correctness of his thought.

After the fall of Lin Biao, the nation was in disarray. Both domestic policy and foreign policy were recharted under Premier Zhou Enlai, who had allied with Mao during the struggle with Liu Shaoqi but was considered flexible and pragmatic. In restructuring the local and regional administrations, Zhou had played a decisive role in arranging compromises, picking candidates, and protecting some military leaders against red guard attacks. He also rehabilitated a number of former Party leaders purged during the tumult. Among them were such influential figures as Deng Xiaoping and Luo Ruiqing. Deng had been the number two target of the Cultural Revolution, next to Liu Shaoqi. Before his disgrace, Deng had served as secretary-general of the Party and first vice-premier of the State Council. He had also been a political commissar of the former Second Field Army.

To allow Deng's rehabilitation must have been a bitter decision for Mao, who was fully aware that Deng, once he had consolidated his power base, might seek to revive his revisionist policies. Yet, in 1973, when Zhou had developed terminal cancer and the threat of the Soviet Union was growing, the only man who could help Zhou reconstruct the Party and revive the national economy was Deng, one of the few experienced administrators available. Simultaneously with Deng's rehabilitation, Mao lent support to a powerful group led by Mao's wife, Jiang Qing. This group, later known as the Gang of Four, also included Wang Hongwen, a young labor union organizer in Shanghai, Zhang Chunqiao, who controlled the Shanghai Party Committee, and Yao Wenyuan, a young writer whose attacks on the playwright Wu Han had led to the outbreak of the Cultural Revolution. By supporting this radical group, Mao had hoped to institutionalize his "uninterrupted revolution" so that it would survive his death.

To ensure the continuation of Mao's revolutionary line, the Tenth Party Congress was convened in August 1973 in utter secrecy. The new Party constitution adopted by the congress and the makeup of the new Politburo showed that the radical left had gained the upper hand. Wang Hongwen, Jiang Qing, Zhang Chunqiao, and Yao Wenyuan all became members of the Politburo, and Wang at thirty-nine was elected to the third-ranking position in the Politburo after Mao and Zhou. Elected as members of the new Central Committee, however, were many rehabilitated leaders who supported the moderate line of Zhou and Deng. As a result, the Party's leadership was again split between the radical leftists, who controlled the Party center, and the pragmatists, who controlled the government administration and many local Party committees.

Between 1973 and 1975, the struggle between the two lines was expressed in the Anti-Confucius campaign. Initiated by the Maoist left, the campaign used Confucius as a symbol for attacks on Zhou Enlai and his followers. Confucius, China's ancient philosopher and moralist, was portrayed as a reactionary and a revisionist. The campaign was ostensibly aimed at Confucius and Lin Biao, but the real target was Zhou Enlai and his economic, political, and educational policies and particularly his rehabilitation of old cadres. Two contradictory lines can be discerned behind the ideological screen. One called for unity and stability and the other for struggle and violence. Zhou was behind the call for unity and emphasized seeking common ground and reserving minor differences, while the leftists stressed the need for continuing struggle and revolutionary violence to bring about the new order of communism. Mao's stand was clear. In 1967, he had foreseen the need for many future cultural revolutions. In December 1973, he further forecast that great disorder would occur every seven or eight years.[44]

During the waning days of Mao and Zhou, the struggle between the two lines intensified. The Anti-Confucius campaign failed to weaken Zhou's and Deng's positions, but it triggered widespread unrest among the workers and split them into fighting factions. This led to large-scale strikes of coal miners and railway workers in twelve provinces. According to a July 1, 1974, document of the CCP Central Committee, factional fighting, labor indiscipline, and an abdication of responsibility by managers had caused the outputs of coal, steel, iron, nonferrous metals, chemical fertilizers, cement, and armaments to all drop sharply.[45] The Maoist leadership had to scale down the campaign. In January 1975, the Second Plenum of the Tenth Party Congress met again in secrecy. It preceded the First Session of the Fourth People's Congress, the first meeting held since the Cultural Revolution. The CCP Plenum made Deng Xiaoping a vice-chairman of the Party, and the People's Congress appointed him the first of the twelve vice-premiers and chief of the staff of the army, thus making him the third-ranking man in China.

From January 1975 to April 1976, Deng was in charge of the government, and the radicals still dominated the Party. Firmly determined to trim off the ultraradical fringes of the system, Deng put forward a General Program of Work in the Party and the Country, together with two documents concerning scientific and industrial development. According to partial disclosures of these documents, Deng s program can be summarized as follows:[46]

1. He advanced a new interpretation of the relationship between politics and economy and construction, emphasizing the urgent need for a general adjustment in all fields in industry, agriculture, transport, finance, public health, literature, and the arts, as well as in the army and the Party.

2. In science and technology, Deng opposed proletarian leadership in science and held that not every scientist need be a convinced Communist. "A white scientist can be useful to the Chinese people. It is better to let him work than to have him sitting in a privy, producing nothing."

3. In industry, Deng reasoned, "If the development of the economy is to be speeded up, it will be necessary to learn all advanced valuable things from abroad and then introduce them at home in a planned manner." He suggested that China import modern equipment and machinery, to be paid for with exports of Chinese coal and petroleum.

4. In industrial management, Deng favored an independent working system of production management under the unified guidance of the enterprise Party committee. "If there is no system of strict responsibility in an enterprise, production will be haphazard."

5. As for incentive systems, Deng stressed that "from each according to his ability and to each according to his work" was a socialist principle. Disregard of rewards for work accomplished would damage the workers' incentive to produce. "It is wrong to practice egalitarianism, denying existing differences and the principle of remuneration according to work." He also suggested that "the wages of a certain number of workers should be raised annually."

Thus, Deng's program ran counter to the radical line advocated by Maoists during the Cultural Revolution and constituted a challenge to the ultraleftists supported by Mao. A counterattack was soon launched by the radicals. The leftist leader Zhang Chunqiao called for the abolition of differential wage systems and for restrictions on bourgeois access to all kinds of legal rights. Deng was described as the unrepentant man on the capitalist road. The death of Zhou Enlai on January 8, 1976, further endangered Deng's position. He was denounced for having distorted Mao's instructions by deliberately ignoring class struggle as the key link in his program and for attempting to revive the revisionist line. The nation's sentiments were on Deng's side, however. On April 5, 1976, a large-scale riot involving some 100,000 residents, workers, and students occurred in Beijing's Tian An Men Square. For the first time since 1949, anti-Mao sentiments were openly aired. When the riot was quashed, Deng was made the scapegoat for the incident. On April 7, 1976, on Mao's recommendation, the CCP Politburo deprived Deng of all his Party and government posts and appointed Hua Guofeng, a member of the Maoist group who was in charge of the police force, as the first vice-chairman of the Central Committee and the new prime minister.[47]

After Mao died on September 9, 1976, the Maoists soon split. The ultraleft wing was led by Mao's widow, Jiang Qing, and consisted of Zhang Chunqiao, Wang Hongwen, Yao Wenyuan, and Mao's nephew Mao Yuanxin, a military leader in Manchuria. A moderate left wing was led by Hua Guofeng and included Mayor Wu De of Beijing, Wang Dongxing (the head of the secret police), Chen Xilian (commander of the armed forces in the Beijing Military Region), and Ji Dengkui (a member of the Politburo). Moving swiftly, Hua Guofeng arrested his ultraleftist rivals on October 7, 1976 (less than one month after Mao's death), and became Mao's successor.

The fall of the radicals paved the way for Deng's second comeback. At the Third Plenum of the Tenth Party Congress in July 1977, Deng regained the posts he had lost in 1976, and he wasted no time in resuming the programs he had put forward in 1975. When the Eleventh Congress of the CCP convened in August 1977, it strengthened Deng's position by expelling the ultraleft wing from the Party center and rehabilitating more veteran cadres, many of whom had been allies of Deng's in the past. In February and March of 1978, the Fifth National People's Congress convened in Beijing to adopt the "four modernizations" program stressed by Zhou Enlai in January 1975 as the overriding program to guide China to the end of the century. The proposal was notable because it marked a shift in the Party's perspective from class struggle and revolution to stability and economic development. The leadership expressed its determination to lessen the emphasis on politics, to foster stability and unity, and to embark on the four modernizations (in agriculture, industry, science and technology, and national defense).

## DEMOLITION OF MAO'S IDEOLOGY

The fall of the radicals in October 1976 marked a new era of ideology in China. In a quiet and subtle way, the new leadership adopted a whole set of measures designed to reevaluate the thought of Mao and to demythologize him as an unchallengable leader – a process similar to Khrushchev's de-Stalinization campaign in 1956, but one that would proceed in a step-by-step manner.

The first step was the reiteration of Mao's early policies so as to bury his later radical programs, such as the Great Leap and the Cultural Revolution. On December 15, 1976, the Party organ, *Renmin ribao* [People's daily], printed an unpublished speech known as the Ten Great Relations, that Mao had delivered to the Party's Politburo on April 25, 1956.[48] Five of the ten relations dealt with the nation's economy. The speech did not outline an economic program, but it presented the moderate and more balanced approach that Mao had espoused at the time. In the speech, Mao had stressed the importance of speeding up production. His method was to balance economic development by shifting investment from heavy industry to light industry and agriculture, by raising workers' wages and peasant income, and by shifting resources from defense to economic development. He had also favored borrowing from other countries in science and technology. The publication of the Ten Great Relations was apparently designed by the new leaders to sanction the revival of material incentives, the increased production of consumer goods, and loans from and trade with the West–all of which the Maoists had strongly opposed during the Cultural Revolution.

Another step in downgrading Mao's personality cult was the official new attitude toward Mao's sayings, which had been treated as gospel in the past. In September 1977, on the first anniversary of Mao's death, Marshal Nie Rongzhen, a veteran Party and military leader, wrote an important article published in *Renmin ribao* and *Hongqi* [Red flag] entitled "Restore and Foster the Good Spirit of the Party." In this article, Marshal Nie appealed to the whole Party to return to the old tradition of honesty and democracy. "It is highly dangerous and does great harm to the leading offices of the Party, if what is said is not the truth but falsehood, and especially if this is justified or legalized." More important, Nie condemned the mechanical application of phrases from the works of Mao and contended that "when we study and apply Marxism-Leninism and Mao Zedong's thought we must grasp its spirit and study its stance, viewpoint and method. . . . We should be firmly opposed to turning phrases of Marxism-Leninism or Mao Zedong thought into dogmas, disregarding the time, the place and the conditions."[49]

Nie Rongzhen's article made it clear that the new Chinese leadership had decided to dispel the magic of Mao's sayings by indicating that many of his writings were time bound or space bound and not relevant under different circumstances. Starting in April 1978, the Party's newspapers stopped carrying a daily quotation from Mao in a special box next to the masthead, a practice that had originated during the Cultural Revolution.[50]

A more direct move to dissipate the cult of Mao was the publication on the Party's fifty-seventh anniversary of a talk that Mao had delivered on January 30, 1962, to an Enlarged Working Conference of the CCP Central Committee. In the speech, which had never been published, Mao had confessed that he had made mistakes during the Great Leap. This was the first public Chinese disclosure of Mao's confession of his own "shortcomings and mistakes." In the speech, Mao had admitted his ignorance concerning economic problems. "Of all the mistakes made by the Central Committee, I am responsible for those directly related to me and I have a share of the responsibility for those not directly related to me because I am its Chairman."[51]

The 1978 release of Mao's 1962 speech conveyed the Party leaders' new message to the people that Mao was not ominiscient. He had made many mistakes in the 1950s and more mistakes in later years. He had lent his authority to many radical measures – such as the purge of large numbers of veteran leaders during the Cultural Revolution, the appointment of Lin Biao as his successor and the stipulation of that decision in the Party's constitution, the promotion of radicals to top Party posts, the launching of the Anti-Confucius campaign (with which the radicals meant to discredit Zhou Enlai), and the dismissal of Deng – and therefore he should bear full responsibility for them.

On July 6, 1978, following the publication of Mao's confession, the army's organ, *Jiefang junbao,* published a substantial article entitled "A Fundamental Principle of Marxism." Its main theme was that theory must derive from practice. "Ideology cannot speak for and prove itself." It must be tested by practice. "Generally speaking, how far a line is accepted by the masses and transferred into a material force shows how correct this line is." The article condemned those who had treated Mao's thought as "something absolute" and "something like religion." It suggested that

> Marxism-Leninism and Mao Zedong's thought themselves need to be tested in practice and their correctness needs to be proved in practice. . . . The result of practice will show whether this line is conducive to the development of the social productive force, whether it has brought real gains to socialism and the masses – this is the only arbiter of the correctness or incorrectness of this line.[52]

The article was the prelude to a general reassessment of Mao's ideology and the political-economic lines he had advocated during the preceding three decades. Since the Great Leap and the Cultural Revolution had severely damaged the national economy, based on the new criterion, both represented incorrect lines that must be rejected and condemned.[53]

By the summer of 1978, a systematic campaign to demolish Mao's influence, particularly his ideology, was in progress. Compared with the de-Stalinization campaign, the new Chinese leaders were more subtle and operated in a slow and covert way. Because the myth of Mao had been constructed over more than four decades and because the veneration of Mao had intensified in the previous fifteen years, it was extremely difficult for the new leadership to discard Mao's thought once and for all. Yet the message was clear: If China was to modernize and industrialize, Mao's ideology must be downgraded and

Mao's fanaticism should be set aside. New practical guidelines to lead the country into a period of economic reconstruction must replace Mao's fantasy of continuous revolution.

## GENERAL EVALUATION

Of all the factors affecting the Chinese economy, the primacy of ideology probably has had the most profound impact. Since the beginning of the People's Republic, the Chinese Communist leadership under Mao Zedong had stressed the key role played by ideological commitment in the course of revolution and reconstruction. In accordance with his version of Communist man, Mao viewed ideological indoctrination, mass mobilization, and organization as effective substitutes for expertise, professionalism, and the availability of capital equipment.

The emphasis on the primacy of ideology had several positive effects. To a certain degree, Mao's ideology rallied the selfless support of the people. Without their ideological commitment, the fierce class struggle underlying land reform and the campaigns against the bourgeoisie in 1949–1952 would have been difficult to carry out so effectively. As Mao's thought assumed the status of a state religion, an intensive mind-remolding process was undertaken that involved the entire population. In response, Chinese society achieved great uniformity in conduct and habit, in expressions of thought, in obedience to a higher authority, and in the subordination of personality to a higher scheme. The rulers in Beijing could mobilize millions of people with a single directive. During the Great Leap Forward, for instance, the regime was able to put 100 million people into irrigation projects and another 60 million people into the backyard blast furnace campaign. Moreover, emphasis on ideological purity helped the government to repress the people's expectations for improvements in their standard of living, thus enabling the government to freeze workers' wages for almost two decades and thereby maintain price stability and a high rate of capital formation.

Mao's ideology differed from Western capitalism in many aspects. As John Gurley put it:

> In many ways, Maoist ideology rejects the capitalist principle of building on the best. . . . While capitalism, in [the Maoist] view, strives one-sidedly for efficiency in producing goods, Maoism . . . in numerous ways builds on "the worst": experts are pushed aside in favor of decision-making by "the masses"; new industries are established in rural areas;

> the educational system favors the disadvantaged; expertise (and hence work proficiency in a narrow sense) is discouraged; new products are domestically produced rather than being imported "more efficiently"; the growth of cities as centers of industrial and cultural life is discouraged; steel, for a time, is made by "everyone" instead of only the much more efficient steel industry.[54]

According to Gurley, the most important aspect of Maoist ideology was its determination "to bring everyone into the socialist development process," or what the Maoists called the "mass line." In many areas, however, Mao's obsession with ideology and his neglect of practical conditions damaged the Chinese economy, and on two occasions—the Great Leap Forward and the Cultural Revolution—it pushed the national economy toward the brink of collapse.

For thirty years, Mao's concentration on class struggle and his concept of continuous revolution underlay numerous social and political campaigns. During the land reform movement of 1949–1952, the landlords were singled out as class enemies and subjected to brutal purges and humiliations. In 1960–1961, there was a new campaign to reclassify some peasants in the villages as landlords in order to continue the class struggle. Under Mao's "one divides into two" theory, the population was divided into "people" and "nonpeople." The former category included workers, peasants, soldiers, and those regarded by the government as "good citizens." The latter included those on the black list—exlandlords, rightists, reactionaries, capitalists, revisionists, and so on. The list of "bad elements" expanded after each social or political campaign. This periodic class struggle created an atmosphere of fear.

The concept of class struggle not only caused instability for the national economy, but it formed many artificial social barriers.[55] An individual's social class determined the entire family's social origin, or *cheng-fen*. During some periods, youths from landlord, bourgeois, or rightist families were automatically deprived of the right to higher education, even if they showed superior talent. During 1969–1976, only children of peasants, workers, and soldiers could enter universities and colleges. The country failed to educate millions of brilliant and gifted youths who had the highest potential to become scientists and engineers.

Continuous class struggle also made China a society without a legal foundation. There was virtually no stable framework of law. Between 1949 and 1978, the country was ruled by the arbitrary will of a few top leaders and by inner-departmental regulations and instructions, which were not made public. At the beginning of the Cultural Revolution, Mao proclaimed, "It is justified to rebel and attack the strongest foes." With his personal blessing, red guards arrested high Party officials and smashed government organizations. Chaos and upheaval became the norm, and China experienced a prolonged period as a society practically without law.[56] When social norms are undermined, men or women in power can do whatever they wish.

The basic weakness of Maoism stemmed from its dogmatic reliance on the outmoded experience of the guerrilla days of the Yanan era for answers to the problems that faced the postrevolutionary state. Moreover, under the concepts of continuous revolution and class struggle, there was no security for any member of the society. The ordinary individual in China–the worker, peasant, student, or cadre member–could not visualize his future with any certainty or plot a rational course toward it. Within a period of ten years (1966–1976), three powerful factions of the Chinese Communist Party were purged in turn: the Liu Shaoqi–Deng Xiaoping group, the Lin Biao faction, and the Gang of Four. Each time, millions of cadres lost their jobs or were sent to prison. These unpredictable shifts created a psychology that meant that Party workers were afraid to act without calling endless meetings. Consequently, many officials became afraid to express an explicit and unambiguous view when a problem arises. As a result, lower-level cadres lacked direction and did not know what to do. The permanent revolution Mao promised to carry on thus became self-defeating and ended with the creation of an immense new bureaucracy.

Nor was the Maoist egalitarian distribution system conducive to economic development. Many experienced Western observers who have traveled in China in recent years have found an unchanged social current underneath an ostensibly puritan society. As one veteran American journalist noted, "The tendency toward embourgeoisement was more plainly visible in the Chinese countryside than the image of a new Chinese man."[57] Mao had tended toward that view in 1955 when he observed that the Chinese peasants have a "spontaneous tendency toward capitalism."[58] Once the government loosens control, the winds of individualism and capitalism are likely to prevail.

The death of Mao and the purge of the radical group ended the era of the primacy of ideology. The new leadership in China, under the strong influence of Deng Xiaoping, swiftly shifted gears toward a relatively pragmatic, nonideological approach to economic development. Material incentives were reaffirmed, and in 1977, workers received their first pay raise in fifteen years. In industry, great attention has been placed on regulation, efficiency, and profit. In education, the traditional examination system was restored in 1977, and educational departments throughout China are now seeking to enroll only those who are academically outstanding. China's intellectuals, whom Mao despised, are recognized as part of the working class. Most of the 400,000 rightists purged during 1957–1976 have been rehabilitated. On many occasions, Deng and other top leaders have stressed the need to abandon the utopian ideological approach favored by Mao in order to follow a pragmatic style concentrating on realistic measures.

In March 1980, the Fifth Plenary Session of the Eleventh Party Central Committee decided to rehabilitate Liu Shaoqi, the chief target of the Cultural Revolution, who had died in disgrace in 1969. In ceremonies throughout China in May 1980, Liu was praised as a great Marxist and proletarian revolutionary, who dedicated the whole of his militant life to the cause of communism. Liu's analysis of the class structure of the society and his policies on economic reconstructions are now upheld by the Party.

The rehabilitation of Liu's reputation marked a new stage of de-Maoization. In July 1980, the giant portrait of Mao that had long adorned Tian An Men Square was removed. In an interview with Yugoslavian journalists, Party Secretary-General Hu Yaobang indicated that Mao's errors were the cause of great misfortunes for the Party and the Chinese people.[59] Even Mao's handpicked successor Hua Guofeng admitted in August that "the Chinese Communist Party made grievous and serious mistakes during the ten years of Cultural Revolution" and that "as Chairman of the Party, Comrade Mao Zedong bore responsibility for those mistakes."[60]

When the National People's Congress convened in August 1980, Zhao Ziyang, a pragmatist supported by Deng Xiaoping, replaced Hua as China's new prime minister. Mao's two favorite models, Dazhai and Daqing, were under open attack. The Dazhai Brigade was officially accused of having systematically falsified grain output figures from 1973 to 1977 to inflate achievements for political purposes. The Daqing oilfield, long considered a brilliant model of industry, has been criticized for being unscientific and inefficient. Reports from China reveal that in an official revision of the Party's history, Mao's role has been reassessed. Some Party leaders have even insisted that no selected works of Mao be published in the future.[61]

The campaign to defame Mao's cult and his thought gained momentum toward the end of 1980 when the Gang of Four and six other important figures of the Cultural Revolution were put in an open trial.

There has been increasing explicit and implicit criticisms of almost every major policy Mao initiated – the agricultural collectivization, the antirightist campaign, the commune system, the Great Leap Forward, the purge of Peng Dehuai, and the Cultural Revolution. Many people in China, particularly the young generation, hold the view that Mao's thought had no merit at all. As the faith for which the Chinese people had fought and made sacrifice for several decades was negated, the country fell into a "crisis of faith."[62] There was a lack of respect for authority and a rapid erosion of the Party's standing.

The Chinese leadership soon realized that a further demotion of Mao's thought and the tarnishment of Mao's image could do more harm than good to the Communist Party. It was against this background that a new consensus of the conflicting leaders emerged. In an important article, "On Appraisal of Chairman Mao and Attitude Toward Mao Zedong's Thought, which appeared in the Army's organ, *Jiefang junbao,* on April 10, 1981, the former chief of staff of the army and the secretary of the Party's Central Discipline Inspection Commission, Huang Kecheng, warned Party members that total negation of Mao and his thought would raise a fundamental question, What should we replace it with? Confucious's thought? or capitalism? Huang asserted that "as long as China remains a socialist country, Mao Zedong's thought will be the spiritual weapon of the CCP members and the Chinese revolutionary people."[63]

Thus, the Chinese leadership has been caught in a dilemma: To steer Chinese society toward modernization, it is imperative for the leadership to discard many of the radical visions of "the great helmsman"; yet by admitting Mao's mistakes, rehabilitating Mao's political rivals, and reversing the Mao cult, the leaders have created an ideological vacuum. In the years ahead, the Chinese leadership may have to continue its pragmatic programs but, at the same time, also stress Mao's doctrinaire ideology to counteract the growing disenchantment of the Chinese youth.

## NOTES

1. On December 8, 1956, in a talk to the delegation of the China Federation of Commerce and Industry, Mao admitted that he was a layman in economics (see *Mao Zedong sixiang wansui* [Long live the thought of Mao Zedong] [Beijing, 1969], p. 61). On January 30, 1962, in a speech to the Enlarged Working Conference of the CCP Central Committee, Mao again admitted that he did not have a grasp of many problems relating to economic reconstruction, particularly in industry and commerce (see *Hongqi* No. 7 [July 1978], p. 5).

2. Mao Zedong, "Comments on Soviet Textbooks," in *Mao Zedong sixiang wansui,* pp. 319–399.
3. Edgar Snow, *Red Star over China* (New York: Random House, 1939), p. 140.
4. Joseph A. Schumpeter, *Ten Great Economists from Marx to Keynes* (New York: Oxford University Press, 1951), p. 13.
5. Stuart R. Schram, *The Political Thought of Mao Tse-tung* (New York: Praeger, 1970), p. 39.
6. Ibid., p. 53.
7. Mao Zedong, "Analysis of All the Classes in Chinese Society," in *Selected Works of Mao Tse-tung,* 5 vols. (Beijing: Foreign Languages Press, 1965–1977), vol. 1, p. 18.
8. Mao Zedong, "On the New Stage," in *Selected Works,* vol. 2, pp. 195–211.
9. See Liu Shaoqi's speech in 1946, quoted in Anna Louise Strong, "The Thought of Mao Tse-tung," *Amerasia* 11:6 (June 1947), p. 161.
10. Stuart R. Schram, *Political Thought of Mao Tse-tung,* p. 118.
11. Adam Smith, *An Inquiry into the Nature and Causes of the Wealth of Nations,* ed. Edwin Cannan (New York: Modern Library, 1959), bk. 4, chap. 2.
12. Donald J. Munro's comments on Benjamin I. Schwartz, "China and the West in the Thought of Mao Tse-tung," in Ping-ti Ho and Tang Tsou, eds., *China in Crisis,* Vol. 1, *China's Heritage and the Communist Political System* (Chicago: University of Chicago Press, 1968), bk. 1, p. 394.
13. Mao Zedong, "Preface to *Socialist Upsurge in China's Countryside,*" in *Selected Works,* vol. 5, pp. 218–224.
14. Mao Zedong, *Selected Works,* vol. 4, p. 454.
15. *Hongqi* No. 1 (June 1, 1958), pp. 3–4.
16. Mao Zedong, "Commentary Notes to *Socialist Upsurge in China's Countryside,*" in *Selected Works,* vol. 5, pp. 246–247.
17. For conditions of women in China, see Delia Davin, *Woman-Work: Women and Party in Revolutionary China* (Oxford: Clarendon Press, 1976), chaps. 4 and 5.
18. Mao Zedong, "On the Correct Handling of Contradictions Among the People," in *Selected Works,* vol. 5, pp. 363–402.
19. Quoted from *Hongqi* No. 10 (October 1967).
20. Liu Shaoqi, *Political Report of the Central Committee of the Chinese Communist Party to the Eighth National Congress* (Beijing: Foreign Languages Press, 1956), pp. 15–16.
21. *Peking Review* 7:29 (July 20, 1964), p. 26.
22. E. L. Wheelwright and Bruce McFarlane, *The Chinese Road to Socialism* (New York: Monthly Review Press, 1970), p. 149.
23. Editorial departments of *Renmin ribao, Hongqi,* and *Jiefang junbao* [Liberation Army daily], "Struggle Between the Two Roads in China's Countryside," *Hongqi* No. 16 (November 23, 1967), pp. 18–29.
24. From Red Guards of Qinghua University in Beijing, *Jing gang shan* [Chingkang Mountains], February 1, 1967, p. 6.
25. Mao Zedong, "On the Question of Agricultural Cooperativization," in *Selected Works,* vol. 5, pp. 168–191.

26. Ibid.

27. Support for Peng's view is expressed in an article by Lu Dingyi, then head of the Propaganda Department of the CCP Central Committee, in *Renmin ribao,* March 8, 1979. Lu stated: "It is now very clear that Comrade Peng Dehuai's proposals at the Lushan meeting in 1959 were correct. It was not Comrade Peng Dehuai but the opposition to him that was wrong."

28. *Renmin ribao,* December 31, 1964. The original Chinese version of this policy is called *"San zi yi bao,"* and it proposed to (1) increase the size of private plots (*zi-liu-di*); (2) increase the number of free markets (*zi-you-shi-chang*); (3) allow small enterprises sole responsibility for their own profits and losses (*zi-fu-ying-kui*); and (4) fix output quotas at the household level (*yi bao*).

29. Red Guards of Qinghua University in Beijing, *Jing gang shan,* February 1, 1967, p. 7.

30, Kung Wen-sheng, "Sun Yefang's Theories Are Revisionist Nonsense," *Renmin ribao,* August 9, 1966.

31. For details, see G. W. Lee, "Current Debate on Profits and Value in Mainland China," in *Australian Economic Papers* (June–December 1965), pp. 72-77; also Nai-Ruenn Chen, "The Theory of Price Formation in Communist China," *China Quarterly* No. 27 (July–September 1966), pp. 33–53.

32. *Renmin ribao,* July 15, 1966.

33. For details, see Chu-yuan Cheng, "Power Struggle in Communist China," *Asian Survey* 6:9 (September 1966), pp. 469–483.

34. C. K. Yang, "Cultural Revolution and Revisionism, in Ping-ti Ho and Tang Tsou, *China in Crisis,* vol. 1, bk. 2, pp. 520–521.

35. Editorial, *Jiefang junbao,* June 6, 1966.

36. According to Marshal Viscount Bernard Montgomery, Mao personally told him in 1961 that Liu would be his successor (see the interview in the *Sunday Times* [London], October 22, 1961).

37. Chen Boda's speech, "Problems of Seizing Power," *Dong fang hong* [The East is red], a red guard newspaper published by the coordination office of red guards in the Beijing area, February 18, 1967, p. 1.

38. Editorial, *Jiefang junbao,* June 7, 1966.

39. *Peking Review* 11:1 (January 3, 1968), p. 14.

40. C. K. Yang, "Cultural Revolution and Revisionism," p. 509.

41. *Hongqi* No. 5 (May 1969), p. 36.

42. Although the real story of Lin's death may never be disclosed, the official explanation was included in a document called "Zhongfa No. 4" (*Zhonggong zhongyang fabu* [CCP Central Committee document, Zhongfa No. 4] dated January 13, 1972) accompanied by the alleged draft outline for a coup d'etat by the son of Lin Biao, Lin Liquo, and the alleged confession of Director of the Political Department, Fourth Air Force, Li Weixin. An English version of this secret document was published in *Issues and Studies* (Taipei) 8:8 (May 1972), pp. 79–82.

43. Some Western experts suspect that an anti-Lin coalition finally obtained, with the support of the secret police and the Beijing Guard Division, Mao's consent to stage a successful coup against Lin, which made Lin or some of his supporters turn to the desperate last resort of a flight to the Soviet Union

(see Jurgen Domes, "The Doom of an Heir or the Failure of an Experiment?" in *Proceedings of the Third Sino-American Conference on Mainland China* [Taipei: Institute of International Relations, 1974], pp. 85–87.

44. C. L. Sulzberger, "China Squares the Circle," *New York Times,* December 8, 1973.

45. *New York Times,* November 15, 1974.

46. The contents of these documents have not been published. Their key points were revealed in several articles in the April 1976 issue of *Xuexi yu pipan* [Study and criticism], a monthly journal published by the radicals in Shanghai. Unofficial versions of the documents have been published in *Issues and Studies* 13:7 (July 1977), pp. 90–113; 13:8 (August 1977), pp. 77–99; and 13:9 (September 1977), pp. 63–70.

47. On November 16, 1978, the Beijing Party Committee, with the approval of the Party Central Committee, reversed the earlier verdicts. The new resolution praised the Tian An Men Incident as a "revolutionary mass action" (see "The Tien An Men Incident in 1976 – A People's Revolutionary Movement," *China Reconstructs* 28:2 [February 1979], pp. 6–17). Zhou Yang, vice-president of the Chinese Academy of Social Sciences, hailed the incident as "another great movement to emancipate people's mind in the history of Chinese revolution" (*Beijing Review* 22:21 [May 25, 1979], p. 11).

48. The English version of Mao's speech appeared in *Peking Review* 20:1 (January 1, 1977), pp. 10–25.

49. *Renmin ribao,* September 5, 1977, p. 1.

50. *New York Times,* April 26, 1978.

51. The English version of the speech was published in *Peking Review* 21:27 (July 7, 1978), pp. 6–22.

52. The English version of parts 1 and 2 of this long article appeared in *Peking Review* 21:28 (July 14, 1978), pp. 5–12, and part 3 followed in 21:29 (July 21, 1978), pp. 9–15.

53. According to Hua Guofeng's report to the Fifth National People's Congress on February 26, 1978, between 1974 and 1976, the influence of the radicals had caused losses worth 100 billion yuan ($53 billion) in industrial output, 40 billion yuan ($21 billion) in state revenue, and 28 million tons of steel production. As a result, the national economy was "on the brink of collapse" (see Hua Guofeng, "Unite and Strive to Build a Modern, Powerful Socialist Country!" *Peking Review* 21:10 [March 10, 1978], p. 12).

54. John G. Gurley, *China's Economy and the Maoist Strategy* (New York: Monthly Review Press, 1976), p. 9.

55. The doctrines of class struggle and uninterrupted revolution were openly challenged in Beijing in early 1979. For instance, on March 9, 1979, the *Renmin ribao* published Zhang Decheng, "Stop Saying 'Grasp Revolution, Promote Production,'" in which the author contended that "for a long time after 1957, class struggle seemed to grow more acute and political movements came one after another. As a result, the whole society was always unstable. . . . This was a major factor in the slow development of China's social productive forces."

56. Some official reports confirmed large-scale strife in various localities. For instance, two Party leaders in Sichuan Province triggered an armed struggle in 1967 in which there were more than 2,000 killed and 8,000 injured (*Renmin ribao*, July 15, 1978).

57. C. L. Sulzberger, "China Squares the Circle."

58. Mao Zedong, "On the Question of Agricultural Cooperativization," in *Selected Works*, vol. 5, pp. 168–191.

59. *New York Times*, August 11, 1980.

60. *Beijing Review* 23:33 (August 18, 1980), p. 14.

61. *New York Times*, July 29, 1980, p. A2.

62. *Wen wei pao* (Hong Kong), April 14, 1981, p. 3.

63. *Jiefang junbao*, April 10, 1981. An English version of Huang's article appeared in Foreign Broadcast Information Service, *Daily Report, People's Republic of China* (hereafter referred to as FBIS), April 13, 1981, pp. K6–K11.

# 3

# Collectivization of Agriculture

The crux of China's economic problems is its growing agrarian population coupled with a scarcity of arable land. Of China's 9.6 million square kilometers of territory, only 15 percent is arable. Since 80 percent of the population is engaged in agriculture for a living, per capita landholding is extremely meager.

Aware of the unfavorable man-land ratio and the poverty of modern farm inputs, the Chinese Communist leadership saw organizational and attitudinal changes as possible substitutes for capital investment as a stimulus for agricultural development. Moreover, the Chinese revolution was essentially an agrarian revolution. For more than twenty-two years, prior to their victory in 1949, the Chinese Communists had penetrated deeply into the villages and transformed many backward rural areas into Communist military bases. To gain peasant support during the civil war, the Communists had called for land redistribution. As far back as 1927, Mao had emphasized that the distribution of land to the peasants was the basic starting point for all other components of the Chinese revolution. He regarded the peasant question as the central revolutionary problem[1] and adhered to Lenin's dictum that the peasantry constitutes the last bourgeois class. Thus, it was not surprising that once the Communists had won nationwide control, they initiated a series of policies to transform the peasants into an agrarian proletariat. In three successive steps spanning a nine-year period, Mao engineered the land reform of 1949–1952, the collectivization of 1951–1957, and the commune movement, which began in April 1958. Through these steps, unprecedented changes were wrought in China's countryside.

This chapter will discuss four problems related to China's agricultural policies during the first decade of the People's Republic: (1) the functions and procedures of land reform, (2) the evolution of agricultural collectivization policies, (3) the organizational features of various farm institutions, and (4) the social and economic consequences of those early initiatives. Chapter 4 will examine agricultural institutions since the establishment of the communes in 1958.

## LAND REFORM, 1949–1952

The first step in the socialist transformation of the Chinese countryside was land reform. In his speech of June 23, 1950, before the Second Session of the National Committee of the Chinese People's Political Consultative Conference, Mao declared that the evolution of Communism in China must pass through three critical stages, each of which is the prerequisite of the succeeding stages of development. The three stages are marked by civil war, land reform, and the realization of socialism. In other words, the advent of socialism would depend on the successful conclusion of the land reform program.

In pre–World War II China, the Nationalist government advocated land redistribution as national policy. Sun Yat-sen, founder of the Nationalist Party of China, the Kuomintang, cited the principle of "land to the tillers" as one of his key economic policies; but, unfortunately, little was accomplished in this area in the decade before World War II, and the issue was taken over by the Communists. In Mao's overall revolutionary strategy, however, land reform meant more than just land redistribution. It was an effective weapon for waging class struggle among the rural population. Thus, the policy had a twofold political function: to win over the masses of landless peasants so as to overthrow the ruling class in the countryside, and thereby to consolidate the Party's control over the peasants.

Since the end of World War II, land reform has been a popular program in most developing countries. It is said to stimulate peasant incentive, release peasant energy, and promote education and community development in general and to have other desirable social effects. Land reform in mainland China has displayed two unique features. First, its purpose was not merely to distribute "land to the tillers," as most countries intended, but to serve as a stepping-stone toward collectivization. As early as 1948, Xu Dixin, a noted economist in the P.R.C., pointed out that equal land distribution would facilitate the voluntary pooling of land in cooperatives.[2] The Chinese Communists did not regard land reform as an end in itself but saw it as part of a long-term strategy for institutional reform.[3] Second, because land reform was primarily a means for overthrowing the former ruling class in the rural areas, the Chinese Communists prohibited any peaceful redistribution of land. Emphasis was placed on class struggle. In his September 1956 report to the Eighth CCP Congress, Liu Shaoqi pointed out:

> In carrying out land reform, our Party did not take the simple and easy way of merely relying on administrative decrees and bestowing land on the peasants. . . . We accomplished the task of land reform through the struggle of the peasants themselves. . . . Thus land reform succeeded not only in eliminating the landlords as a class and weakening the rich peasants in the economic realm, but, also, politically, in overthrowing the landlord class and isolating the rich peasants.[4]

Political considerations lay behind the regime's strong opposition to peaceful land reform measures like those employed in Taiwan and other non-Communist countries. As Mao Zedong explained:

> The giving of land as a grace from the government without mobilizing the activism of the masses, but coming forth purely as a result of the so-called peaceful land reform from above, is not correct and the result, when obtained, cannot be consolidated, for in that case, the land given to the peasants today might be taken back by hook or by crook by the landlord class tomorrow.[5]

Under Chinese Communist land reform, not only were the landlords unable to get any compensation for their land, but even those who donated their land voluntarily were struggled against. Since land reform was considered a key link in the class struggle, CCP policy during land reform was based on four principles: relying on the poor peasants, uniting with the middle peasants, neutralizing the rich peasants, and eliminating the landlord class. To effect these principles, the Party employed three important strategies.

First, in order to satisfy the desire for landownership on the part of the broad masses of poor peasants and rural laborers, the Chinese Communists proclaimed that the purpose of land reform was not to nationalize the land but to transfer the land of the landlords to peasant ownership. The basic law governing land reform adopted on June 30, 1950, stipulated in Article 1 that "the system of peasant landownership shall be carried into effect." The rights of peasant proprietorship were restated and formally guaranteed in Article 20: "Once land reform has been achieved, the People's Government shall issue title-deeds and shall recognize the rights of all landowners to manage, purchase, sell or rent out land freely."[6] The Chinese Communists also averred that the policy of peasant ownership would be maintained until conditions were conducive to the wider use of machinery in farming and to the organization of collective farms, thereby implying that private ownership of land would be a long-term policy of the new government. This recognition of peasant proprietorship differed significantly from Soviet practice during the years just after the 1917 revolution. China's policy was apparently intended to win the support of the farmers in order to ease the overthrow of the anti-Communist forces in the rural areas.

Second, in concentrating on efforts to eliminate the landlord class, the Chinese Communists accepted the middle peasants as allies, despite the latter's strong petty-bourgeois inclinations. As Mao instructed his cadres in 1948, "In the land reform it is necessary to unite with the middle peasants who account for about 20 percent of the rural population. Otherwise, the poor peasants and farm laborers will find themselves isolated and the land reform will fail."[7] Not only did the Chinese Communists generally allow the middle peasants to retain more land than the poor peasants, they also ordered that the Peasants' Associations, which were the executive organizations of land reform, enlist the middle peasants as members.

Third, the Party adopted a new policy toward the rich peasants, who accounted for only 5 percent of the rural population but still constituted the main force in agricultural production. The government abandoned its former policy of requisitioning their land and sought to neutralize that class. The Land Reform Law stipulated that only that part of the land rented out by the rich peasants should be requisitioned; the rest of their land and property should remain untouched.

All of these policies were designed to isolate the landlord class, to reduce peasant resistance, and to destroy the social foundation of the Nationalist government in the countryside. As Mao made clear in his 1948 speech, "The system of feudal exploitation should be abolished step by step, that is, in a tactical way . . . the total scope of attack in the land reform should generally not exceed about 8 percent of the rural households or about 10 percent of the rural population."[8] The implementation of that program was an extremely complicated process involving three basic stages.

In the first, or preparatory, stage, the chief task was to "awaken" the poor peasants by inciting their hatred of landlords. In order to obtain the poor peasants' support, the Party gave priority to rent and interest reduction. The relevant regulation issued by the CCP called for the following measures.

1. a 25 percent reduction of existing rent
2. a rent ceiling equal to 37.5 percent of the normal yield of the principal crop
3. prohibition of advance rent payment, extra obligations to landlords, and secondary renting
4. refunding of rental deposits
5. cancellation of unpaid rent

Having enacted those measures, the Communists began to organize the "positive elements" among the poor peasants. This group was to be the main force in the struggle with the landlords. Peasants' Associations and Assemblies of the Peasants' Representatives were established throughout the rural areas. The Peasants' Associations—which derived their memberships from poor and middle peasants, farm laborers, and artisans—also included "revolutionary intelligentsia" sent by the Party as organizers. This last element constituted the "charter membership" of the associations and, in fact, was their guiding spirit. The assemblies were composed of delegations from Peasants' Associations and other nonassociation members whose representative status had been approved by the associations. Since the assemblies were not always in session, the executive power of the land reform was exercised by the associations and was controlled by the local Party cadres.

The second stage stressed "class differentiation" among the rural population. By the terms of the Land Reform Law of June 1950 and the Decisions Concerning the Differentiation of Class Status in the Countryside issued by the State Administrative Council on August 4, 1950, the rural population was grouped into six classes: landlords, semilandlords, rich peasants, well-to-do middle peasants, poor peasants, and farm laborers. Each of the categories was again subdivided into many strata. Although the government attempted to dictate the criteria for determining class status, the borderlines between classes were extremely hazy, and most classifications were made arbitrarily by the rural cadres. Thus, different localities might classify individuals owning the same amount of land into quite different categories.

Following the designation of class status, properties still retained by landlords were expropriated. Their houses, furniture, and personal possessions were all confiscated in a movement that was characterized by mass trials and executions. Individuals were encouraged at public meetings to relate all past real and imaginary wrongs that they had suffered at the hands of the marked victims or their forebearers. Agents planted in the mob kept the meetings at a high emotional pitch. As a result of frequently hysterical accusations, open violence and bodily harm almost inevitably occurred. Yet Mao Zedong was able to justify this violence in these terms:

> Revolution is violence. It is a violent action in which one class attempts to overthrow the power of another. The agrarian revolution by the peasantry aims at the overthrow of the power of the feudalistic landlord class. . . . Great revolutionary enthusiasm must be generated in the villages in order to arouse the tens of thousands of peasants to forge a tremendous power. All excessive acts possess their revolutionary significance. . . . Every village must go through a short period of terror, without which counterrevolutionary activities cannot be suppressed.[9]

Based on the 8 percent household quota set by Mao for requisition during the land reform, it was estimated that the properties of some 10 million households assigned to the categories of landlords and reactionaries were confiscated.

The final stage, land redistribution, followed immediately. Generally, redistribution was undertaken within the individual rural administrative units known as *xiang,* or townships, each consisting of several villages. The expropriated land within a particular *xiang* was divided among its eligible residents. Consequently, the amount of land an eligible person received basically depended upon the size of the confiscated land and the number of eligible peasants in the *xiang.* Naturally, residents of densely populated areas received much less than those in sparsely populated areas. The beneficiaries of this redistribution were principally determined by class status, however.

Although the two chief categories were poor peasants and farm laborers, Party workers, members of the armed forces, and their families were also to share land and other means of production equally with eligible peasants. According to the official report, in the course of land reform, some 700 million mu (115.5 million acres) of land were redistributed to 300 million peasants. Based on these figures, each person received, on the average, only 2.3 mu, or a third of an acre of land.[10] In many areas where the population was extremely dense, the amount was less.

The immediate effect of land reform was the consolidation of political control in the countryside. The Chinese Communist leaders had foreseen that their strongest opposition would come from the landlord class in the villages. The redistribution of land and the confiscation of the landlords' property eliminated their economic power. The humiliating treatment and physical violence associated with the public accusation meetings, the antidespot campaign, and the public trials had the combined effect of destroying the landlords' social standing and prestige. More important, having waged a brutal struggle with the wealthy class, the poor peasants were forced to cooperate more readily with the new regime.

The land reform resulted in very limited gains for the rural economy, however, for it neither increased per capita landholding nor raised the rate of capital formation in agriculture. Instead, it brought about three new problems.

First, by granting equal shares of land to the family members of Party workers, the armed forces, and the mass organizations, such as the peasants' and women's associations, the new government increased the number of landholders by more than 50 million. That action reduced the size of the average farm and the ability of peasant households to accumulate capital.[11]

Second, land reform caused new frictions among the peasants, and it did not end class stratification in the countryside. Draft animals were one source of friction. Prior to the land reform, the landlord had usually rented draft animals and implements to his tenants or other farmers. This arrangement was equivalent to the pooling of animals and implements for better use. After the redistribution of the landlords' property, some peasants had draft animals but no implements, whereas others had implements but no draft animals. In many cases, draft animals were redistributed to groups of peasants, causing friction among the new owners over their respective obligations to supply fodder and their right to use the animals. Consequently, many animals were overworked and underfed. They died in large numbers.

Indebtedness among the peasants also increased, partly because of the need to buy farm implements for cultivating the land and partly because of rising peasants' propensity to consume after they became landowners. About 60 to 70 percent of the peasants in Heilongjiang and Jiangsu were reported to be involved in borrowing and lending relationships.[12] To settle their debts, peasants sold land and draft animals, thus increasing the concentration of resource ownership.

The impoverishment of the poor peasants and hired workers in the wake of land reform was revealed by a 1954 survey by the Communist government. According to the survey, class composition in the countryside after land reform was roughly as follows: poor peasants and farm laborers constituted 29 percent of the total number of households; the middle peasants, 62.2 percent; the rich peasants, 2.1 percent; the former landlords, 2.5 percent. The remaining 4.2 percent of the peasant households had already been incorporated into agricultural cooperatives. This survey did not distinguish between the upper and lower strata of the middle peasants. Of the total number of peasant households, however, the poor and lower-middle peasants probably constituted about 70 percent, and the well-to-do middle peasants, about 30 percent. On the average, each poor peasant household had only 11.7 mu (1.9 acres) of arable land; there was one draft animal for every two households, one plow for every three households, and one waterwheel for every seventeen households. Therefore, with few tools, the peasants found it extremely difficult to develop production. Their income was sometimes even insufficient to ward off hunger and cold. The well-to-do middle peasants had more and better land, but only the few rich peasants were really better off. According to the same survey, each rich peasant household had, on the average, 34.6 mu (5.7 acres) of arable land, two draft animals, and one plow, and every three households had a waterwheel.[13]

The differing economic conditions of the peasants again separated the rural economy into two extremes. Many poor and lower-middle peasants, having sold or rented their land, were forced to become hired laborers. For example, in Baoying Xian in northern Jiangsu Province, 500 households sold a total of 1,735 mu of land in 1951. In 1952, the number of households selling land increased to 1,705, and the sales involved 6,853.5 mu. In the first ten months of 1953, the number of households selling land jumped to 2,264, and the sales involved 7,472 mu, or four and a half times the 1951 totals. At the same time, the newly rich peasants were gaining strength daily. They hired permanent workers to cultivate their lands and drew much of their income from exploitation, loans, and usury. In fact, the usury rate was reported to be as high as 5–10 percent per month.[14]

It is significant to note that among the rising newly rich peasant class, the majority were rural Party cadres. A 1952 investigation of economic conditions in five villages made by the Heilongjiang Party Committee revealed that 83.27 percent of the Party members in three of the villages had become well-to-do or rich peasants. In the remaining two villages, 80 percent of the Communist Youth League membership had achieved the same status.[15] The degradation of the poor peasants into hired workers and the rise of the newly rich peasants created a new class differentiation in the rural areas. The social structure in the rural areas tended to revert to the structure that had existed prior to the Communist land reform movement.

Third, the redistribution of land increased the peasants' propensity to consume and resulted in a curtailment of grain supplies to the urban areas. Before land reform, under the tenancy system, the grain that the landlords extracted from tenants as rent payment was sold in the urban market. Land reform destroyed that extraction mechanism. Moreover, as Kang Chao rightly pointed out,[16] in non-Communist countries land reform usually includes the obligation that those people who obtain land must make compensation payments, over a number of years, either to the original landowners or to the government, which had advanced money to buy the land. Under such an arrangement, peasants must sell enough grain to make those compensation payments. Thus, the compensation payments serve to secure supplies of grain from the countryside for the urban market. Since no compensation payments were involved in China's land reform, the peasants felt less need to sell grain and tended to increase their home consumption. The result was a severe food crisis in the cities. To solve all these problems and to curb the further growth of capitalism in the rural economy, the cooperatives were introduced in 1952.

## FROM MUTUAL AID TEAMS TO COOPERATIVES, 1951–1957

Although most Communist leaders accepted land reform as a necessary step toward collectivization, the time schedule for collectivization was never settled, and that fact caused a split within the Party leadership. Before the 1949 victory, Mao's concept of collectivization had involved three principles: a stage-by-stage progression, voluntary membership, and mutual benefit. In his 1948 speech to the cadres in the Shanxi-Suiyuan area, Mao had emphasized that "in order to develop agricultural production, we must advise the peasants to organize, voluntarily and step by step, the various types of producers' and consumers' co-operatives based on private ownership."[17] In May 1949, in a report to the Second Plenum of the Party's Seventh Central Committee, Mao again pointed out that "the economy of individual peasants and individual handicraftsmen who produce 90 percent of the total gross value of the national economy can and must be guided, prudently, step-by-step, and yet positively, . . . in the direction of modernization and collectivization.[18] These statements illustrate that although Mao conceived of collectivization as the goal of agricultural transformation, he believed that the process should be pursued voluntarily and gradually.

On December 15, 1951, the CCP Central Committee issued to the local Party organizations its first draft decision on mutual aid and cooperation in agricultural production. The detailed and comprehensive provisions of the decision were put into practice experimentally in some localities. The document was kept secret, however, until February 1953. In accordance with this decision, the process involved three major steps: the establishment of mutual aid teams, the organization of elementary cooperatives, and the formation of advanced cooperatives or collective farms. Each stage marked an economic and political advance, and each provided the basis for higher development. No decision was made as to how much time should elapse between land reform and the inception of socialization of agriculture nor as to how long a period would be needed to complete the whole process.

According to Liu Shaoqi and Bo Yipo, a leading official in economic affairs during the 1950s and 1960s, the new government should encourage peasant initiative under the private farming system after the land reform and not rush into collectivization. Liu and his associates regarded the rising capitalistic attitude of the peasants after the land reform as a healthy development, and Liu is reported to have criticized the activities of those Communist cadres who tried to stop the tendency by forming mutual aid teams and cooperatives as the "action of erroneous, dangerous, and utopian rural socialism."[19] In July 1951, Bo Yipo criticized the cadres for not encouraging peasants to "get rich" instead of entertaining utopian thoughts about the imminence of socialism in the countryside.[20]

Although Liu Shaoqi and Bo Yipo never opposed the long-term goal of collectivization, they postulated that the optimal time to introduce collectivization would be (1) when 70 to 80 percent of the peasant households had attained the income level of rich farmers and (2) after industry had become so well developed that it would be able to supply an adequate number of tractors and other modern farm machines to the agricultural sector. In other words, agricultural mechanization should precede collectivization.[21]

Liu Shaoqi's approach apparently was the antithesis of Mao's continuous revolution approach, which advocated moving on without interruption from the stage of bourgeois democratic revolution to the stage of proletarian socialist revolution. Mao wanted to launch the mutual aid and cooperative movements immediately. He believed that if the CCP were to favor a rich peasant economy, capitalism rather than socialism would win out in the rural areas. Moreover, Mao thought that the majority of the poor and lower-middle peasants would have a potentially inexhaustible enthusiasm for socialism and an intense hatred for the old system. Although China's industry could not provide agricultural machinery in large quantities, it was possible and necessary to arouse the socialist enthusiasm of the poor and lower-middle peasants and first accomplish collectivization.[22]

With Mao's blessing, mutual aid teams mushroomed in the northern and northwestern provinces. Some agricultural cooperatives were also set up in different localities on an experimental basis. From the autumn of 1951 to the autumn of 1952, the number of mutual aid teams rose from 4.7 million to 8 million and membership in them increased from 19.2 percent to 39.9 percent of all peasant households. The number of cooperatives increased from 130 to 3,644, representing 0.1 percent of peasant households.[23] The sudden emergence of cooperatives brought great uncertainty regarding the future of private ownership. In many areas, pigs were slaughtered and trees felled, while all kinds of subsidiary occupations stagnated and peasants stopped collecting fertilizer.[24] Throughout the country, draft animals died from overwork and neglect. Discrimination against individual, independent farmers during the campaign violated the middle peasants' interests and reduced their incentive to produce.

Against this background, a new resolution was adopted by the party's Central Committee on December 16, 1953. A compromise between Mao and his opponents, it hastened the pace of collectivization but reiterated the policy of gradualism. Stressing voluntary participation and denouncing "blind impetuous adventurism," it recommended persuasion as the main method of implementing cooperativization, proposing that one or more model cooperatives be set up in each locality to demonstrate the superiority of cooperative farming. The resolution set a national target of 35,000 cooperatives by autumn 1954, as compared with the 14,000 units existing in December 1953.[25]

The policy of gradualism was not observed uniformly throughout China. In many places, cadres "blindly chased figures" by forcing peasants to join cooperatives. In January 1954, the target was raised to 45,000 to boost cooperativization. By the spring of 1954, almost 100,000 cooperatives were in existence, and in the autumn of that year, the number jumped to 230,000. By the end of 1954, there were 497,000 cooperatives comprising 10.9 percent of peasant households, and in March 1955, the number reached 633,000 with 14.2 percent of the peasant households participating.[26]

Rapid cooperativization proved costly. When the policy of voluntary participation and gradualism was violated, some local authorities withheld loans from independent farmers and members of teams, restricting such funds to cooperatives. Political pressure was exerted to boost membership, and reluctant peasants were crowned with rightist, capitalist hats and further punished by being forced to sell a high quota of grain to the state.[27]

The process of cooperativization was much more complicated and posed many more difficulties than the establishment of mutual aid teams had done. Although private ownership was retained intact, the management of several peasant households was a new experience for the cadres. Lacking appropriate leadership skills, many cooperatives were unable to work out a comprehensive plan. Consequently, most of the elementary cooperatives set up in 1953 and 1954 were shaky and inefficient. According to an official survey in August 1954, of the 95,000 elementary cooperatives established early in that year, only 30 percent could be rated as well organized. About 50 to 60 percent had improper foundations, and the poor formation in the remaining 10 to 20 percent tended to confuse the members and encourage withdrawal.[28]

Fearing the arrival of a second land reform, the rich and middle peasants slaughtered livestock on a large scale and refrained from improving their land. Many other peasants showed no interest in purchasing farm implements or accumulating fertilizer, and in some areas, forests were destroyed. During springtime, official reports revealed that "in numerous areas there is nobody to take charge of spring ploughing and production."[29] As the rural economy deteriorated, opposition to the rapid growth of the cooperatives arose within the Party. This opposition was fully reflected in the Decision on Spring Cultivation adopted by the State Council on March 3, 1955. As the council indicated, "Because the cooperatives were developed rather quickly, and we are without sufficient experience and preparation, we did not provide a concrete policy and unified decision to the cooperative movement."[30] The State Council therefore proposed that the movement be slowed down and that the formation of new cooperatives be suspended until after the spring planting.

That decision occasioned a serious national setback for the cooperative program. Many leading local Party members openly expressed their doubts as to the likelihood of the movement's successful conclusion. They indicated that it was easy to establish cooperatives but difficult to consolidate them. The peasants were too poor to contribute share funds and too illiterate to supply the cooperatives with qualified accountants. The same Party members also declared that the cooperatives would result in considerable surplus labor for which there would be no outlet. Many provincial Party units even adopted a policy of "drastic compression" by dissolving large numbers of local cooperatives. According to Mao's July 1955 report, of the 53,000 cooperatives in Zhejiang Province alone, 15,000 units comprising 400,000 households had been dissolved in one move.[31]

Apart from the Zhejiang case, reports from many provincial Party committees indicated that a majority of their leading cadres also openly advocated a slowdown in the cooperative movement. A statement at the fourth meeting of the Hebei Party Committee in September 1955 revealed that "many cadres realized that the cooperative movement went too fast last winter and this spring and firmly advocated the suspension of further development."[32] Another report noted that "in Shandong Province, many cadres indicated that the development of cooperatives was too fast to be consolidated; therefore, a part of them should be dissolved and return to the level of the mutual aid team."[33] More important, Deng Zihui, director of the Department of Rural Works of the CCP Central Committee and the person responsible for supervising the cooperative movement, also argued against the acceleration of cooperativization.[34]

The policy of gradualism and consolidation was incorporated into the final draft of the First Five-Year Plan (1953–1957), which was adopted in July 1955. According to that plan, collectivization would take fifteen years, and one-third of all farm households were to be brought into elementary cooperatives by 1957. However, Mao opposed this gradualist approach, claiming that it overlooked "the new upsurge in the socialist mass movment" and was "guiding the movement by grumbling unnecessarily, worrying continuously, and putting up countless taboos." On July 31, 1955, he convened a meeting of municipal and provincial Party secretaries and delivered an epochal speech, "On the Question of Agricultural Cooperativization." Putting his prestige and leadership position on the line, he denounced the so-called intra-Party conservatism, castigated those Party members who had suggested a deceleration of the cooperative movement, and demanded that the elementary cooperatives absorb half of all peasant households by 1958, with the remainder to be organized by 1960.

Mao put forth three basic arguments for the acceleration of collectivization. First, industrialization could not be carried out in isolation, separate from agricultural collectivization. Within a period of roughly three five-year plans, China would have to solve the problem of agricultural collectivization by jumping from small-scale farming with animal-drawn farm implements to large-scale farming with machines. If it failed to do so, the contradiction between a rising demand for marketable grain (and industrial raw materials) and a slower rate of growth in agricultural production would make it impossible for the country to achieve its industrialization goals.

Second, Mao argued that much of the capital needed for industrialization would have to come from agriculture (some of it from the agricultural tax) and from light industry. But no large-scale expansion of light industry was feasible within a small peasant economy. The growth of light industry would require large-scale farming, which in turn would require collective agriculture.

Third, Mao went on, the situation in China's countryside was characterized by a spontaneous tendency toward capitalism. Newly rich peasants were springing up everywhere, and many well-to-do peasants were striving to become rich. Many poor peasants, lacking sufficient means of production, were still very poor. If the tendency went unchecked, the separation into two extremes would worsen daily. As a result, "If the position in the countryside is not held by socialism, capitalism will assuredly occupy it."[35]

Mao's intervention was effective. The Sixth Plenum of the Seventh Central Committee, meeting October 4–11, 1955, decided to accelerate the formation of agricultural cooperatives. The immediate targets for collectivization were raised, but only moderately. Elementary cooperatives were to be established in a majority of localities by the spring of 1958, and 70 to 80 percent of the peasantry was to be placed in cooperatives by 1960. However, local and regional authorities were anxious to escape the accusation of "rightist deviation" and tended to carry out the collectivization program with more speed than the new decision had envisaged. In the months following the meeting, various provincial committees revised their schedules for cooperativization. Mao and his supporters interpreted the revisions as a sign of the peasants' spontaneous momentum toward socialization and demanded a further acceleration of the pace. In December 1955, Mao personally edited and prefaced a book, *The Socialist Upsurge in China's Countryside,* in which he estimated that the formation of elementary cooperatives could be basically accomplished in a single year – 1956 – instead of in the estimated three or four years, with total completion in 1960. On January 25, 1956, Mao called a Supreme State Council meeting at which he demanded the adoption of a National Program for Agricultural Development, 1956–1967. The program stipulated (1) that in some areas with favorable conditions, all peasants should be brought into the advanced type of cooperatives (collectives) by 1957, and (2) that the conversion of the whole countryside into advanced cooperatives should be accomplished by 1958.[36] The new program thus telescoped a fifteen-year schedule into only two years. By the end of June 1956, more than 110 million peasant households, or 91.9 percent of the total, had been recruited into cooperatives and collectives. Membership in the collectives rose from 4 percent of the peasant households at the end of 1955 to 63.2 percent by June 1956. The progress of cooperativization is summarized in Table 3.1.

From Mao's viewpoint, the movement from cooperatives to collectives was natural and desirable. It helped to solve the contradiction

Table 3.1
The Progress of Agricultural Cooperativization
in China, June 1955–June 1956
(in percent)

| Year | Cooperatives and Collectives | Cooperatives | Collectives | Others[a] |
|---|---|---|---|---|
| 1955 | | | | |
| June | 14.2 | 14.2 | --- | 85.8 |
| December | 63.3 | 59.3 | 4.0 | 36.7 |
| 1956 | | | | |
| January | 80.3 | 49.6 | 30.7 | 19.7 |
| February | 87.0 | 36.0 | 51.0 | 13.0 |
| March | 88.9 | 34.0 | 54.9 | 11.1 |
| April | 90.3 | 32.1 | 58.2 | 9.7 |
| May | 91.2 | 29.3 | 61.9 | 8.8 |
| June | 91.9 | 28.7 | 63.2 | 8.1 |

[a]Refers to mutual aid teams and independent peasant households.
Source: P.R.C. State Statistical Bureau, Statistical Materials on Agricultural Cooperativization and the Distribution of the Product in Cooperatives During 1955 (Beijing: Tongji Chubanshe, 1957).

between the private ownership of resources and unified management, and it also helped to avoid the revival of rural capitalism. Under the cooperatives, the land was still privately owned. As long as this continued, land consolidation and rationalization were impossible. It was further claimed that the payment of rent impeded growth in two ways. It reduced the incentive to work because those who received rent did not have to work full time to earn their living, and it impeded the accumulation of public property because the cadres regarded rent as a sum that could be diverted to investment.[37]

The hasty formation of collectives created tremendous difficulties in management and incentives. In a speech on the "Current Situation in Agricultural Cooperativization" on May 7, 1956, Deng Zihui listed the defects of the cooperatives as waste and faulty planning, neglect of industrial crops and subsidiary occupations, and defective organization due to the rapid advance of the movement.

In the wake of these difficulties, peasants in many areas again agitated for withdrawal from the cooperatives. In Guangdong Province, it was reported that during the winter of 1956, some 160,000 peasant households had applied for withdrawal – 80,000 of them successfully.[38] During the early months of 1957, peasant resistance became even more apparent, and Party policies were openly and liberally criticized. Former landlords and rich peasants launched counterattacks against the rural Party organizations, and not a few local Party members and cadres were killed. Consequently, pessimism and defeatism again engulfed the Party.

Confronted with this critical situation the Chinese Communist leadership began a nationwide rectification campaign in the autumn of 1957 to strengthen the confidence of both masses and cadres in the cooperatives and to check the disruptive activities of former landlords and rich peasants. At the same time, on September 14, 1957, the CCP Central Committee Directive on Carrying Out Well the Work of Production Management in the Agricultural Producers' Cooperatives introduced a series of reforms. These included:

1. giving more authority to the production brigades and subsidiary occupation brigades so as to facilitate a more flexible use of land and manpower in accordance with local conditions
2. advocating the "three-responsibility" system, which assigned specific quotas to the production or sideline occupation brigades for labor, production, and costs; granting bonuses when a brigade met or surpassed planned goals; and punishing failures to fulfill quotas
3. assigning specific targets within a brigade to field teams, or even households, thereby giving each peasant a sense of individual responsibility
4. limiting the size of cooperatives to no more than 100 households and production teams to no more than 20 households
5. conciliating well-to-do peasants by allowing them to retain fish ponds, pastures, and orchards as private property and refunding their excessive investment into the cooperatives as required by local cadres
6. allowing each member to raise a certain number of domestic animals and poultry, as well as draft animals, and paying the owner a fee when the cooperatives used the draft animals[39]

All of these reforms were designed to offer incentives to the well-to-do peasants, and they signaled a retreat from Mao's radical policy. Efforts made by the conservative elements in the Party to slow the pace of collectivization apparently had gained the upper hand in late 1956 and early 1957. It was officially claimed that a fierce debate concerning the choice between the "two roads"—capitalism and socialism—took place in the whole countryside in the fall of 1957. Mao fought back by launching a Socialist Education Campaign in the countryside in 1957 and by introducing rural communes in 1958 (see Chapter 4).

## ORGANIZATIONAL FEATURES OF VARIOUS FARM INSTITUTIONS

Before narrating the story of Chinese agricultural developments since 1958, it may be useful to describe the features of the institutions established during the first decade of the P.R.C.

### *Mutual Aid Teams*

The mutual aid teams introduced in 1951 were not an innovation of the new government. They were quite similar to the *toz* that prevailed during the Soviet War Communism period (1918–1920) and were already abundant in North and Northwest China before 1949. The teams were formed primarily to exchange draft animals, implements, and manpower during the busy seasons. Compensation for labor, implements, and draft animals borrowed from other member households were settled by members on mutually agreeable terms. The Communists seized upon this traditional practice as the first step in their long-range collectivization program. Thus, beginning in 1951, two types of mutual aid teams were organized in the rural areas.

The elementary type, called a seasonal or temporary mutual aid team, was composed of three to five households. It operated only during the harvesting or sowing seasons and was limited to certain important farm work. Upon meeting that need, the team dissolved. The advanced type was a year-round permanent team that usually consisted of six to ten or more households. Its members, working together throughout the year, might gradually accumulate a small amount of common property, such as farm tools and draft animals.

In both types of team, each peasant household continued its own production. Although the members might use one another's labor power and certain means of production on their own farms, animals and tools were still privately owned. Any disparity in reciprocal use had to be made good in cash or kind.[40] Since the land, farm implements, and animals were still privately owned, these teams were regarded as a type of embryonic socialism.

The teams had two functions. First, they made it possible for the poor peasants to exchange their labor for the use of tools and animals belonging to the middle peasants. Second, the teams forged an alliance between the poor and middle peasants and isolated the capitalistic rich peasants, without destroying the latter's incentive to produce.

The teams, however, failed to stem the tendency toward class differentiation and polarization. Member households with greater economic resources could still use a part of the labor of other member households to obtain greater returns. For instance, a peasant who owned an ox and loaned it to the team always received twice the return of those who lacked a draft animal. Also, speculation in grain and other agricultural products increased after 1952 as a new group of rich peasants emerged. To prevent the development of a rich peasant economy, the government decided to push forward and emphasize the elementary cooperatives.

### *Elementary Cooperatives*

Institutionally, the shift from mutual aid teams to elementary agricultural cooperatives involved a profound change in the size of the organization, its ownership and income distribution system, and the techniques used in managing it. The cooperatives were several times larger than the teams, for each cooperative, on the average, embraced thirty-five households. The new system was marked by a pooling of land as shares under a unified management. Each member household retained title to its land, which was converted into a share of capital contribution to the cooperative. A certain amount of land, not exceeding 5 percent of the average individual landholding, was left for members' private use and was referred to as the "retained plot" or "private plot." Other capital assets, such as farm implements, farm transport, and draft animals, were treated on the same principle: They remained privately owned but under unified control.

With such changes, income distribution assumed a distinctive form. The aggregate amount of agricultural and sideline production, after a part had been deducted to meet the depreciation of the means of production, formed the cooperative's total income for the current year. Of this, part went to the state for taxes, and part went for the reserve and welfare funds of the cooperative; the remainder was distributed among the members in such basic forms as payment for work, dividends on land, and payment for other means of production.[41]

Payment for work was calculated on the basis of workdays, or work points. Members were paid in cash and kind according to the quantity and quality of their work. In some cooperatives, members were rewarded for overfulfillment of output norms, which had been calculated on the basis of seasonal or yearly quotas. The dividends on land were distributed according to the amount of land a member had pooled as shares in the cooperative upon joining it. A ratio was fixed between dividends on land and payment for work. In principle, the former was lower than the latter. Because the members retained private ownership of their land and other means of production, by which they earned a limited income, the elementary cooperatives preserved private ownership to a certain extent. They were therefore regarded as semisocialist in nature and as an important step toward the establishment of collective farms.

In theory, the elementary cooperative was to be superior to the team in two major respects. First, the pooling of land was designed to eradicate the main structural weakness of Chinese agriculture – small, dispersed, and uneconomic holdings. The consolidation of fragmentary plots under a single management would make it possible to remove many boundary lines between private holdings, thereby freeing extra acreage for cultivation. Second, the reduction in the number of producing units and improved planning would enable the government to increase its control over consumption and investment. From the spring of 1953 to the summer of 1955, China experienced two grain crises. Increased consumption in the rural areas led to food shortages in 1953 and resulted in the establishment of a planned purchase system. In 1954, the government made excessive grain purchases, which, according to its own directives, should have been retained by the farmers for food, seed, and animal fodder.[42] A new system of assessing the peasants' grain obligations, the "three-fix" policy (fixed quotas for production, consumption, and procurement), was implemented in August 1955 to reduce the peasants' uncertainty regarding the extent of their burden. The cooperative system was considered conducive to the control of consumption and to the marketing of food grains.

Although those positive arguments were quite true, the new institution also had many negative effects. The foremost problem was management. The pooling of thirty to forty households required a great deal of planning, administration, and bookkeeping. Since farming operations are highly diversified and nonstandardized, the required effort may vary substantially according to such factors as the quality of soil, the distances involved, weather conditions, and so on. It is extremely difficult for the manager of a large farm organization to make perfect job assignments and to evaluate performance properly. The managerial problems were acute in China after cooperativization because the great majority of the Chinese peasants were illiterate and incapable of handling even the simplest bookkeeping.[43]

Equally disturbing was the problem of relating performance and reward–the problem of incentives. The shift from private to cooperative responsibility weakened this relationship. The most complicated job in income distribution was the assessment of land rent, which involved two distinct problems: fixing the relative shares of rent and wages in the distributed product and setting the rents for each piece of land. Too low a rent might discourage middle and rich peasants from joining the cooperatives, and too high a rent might cause resentment among the poor peasants. Government directives stipulated that total land-rent payments should be less than the total wage bill and should not rise as output increased, but the setting of the proportions was left to the cooperatives. The relative shares fixed for rent and wages depended largely on the degree of control exercised by different peasant classes. Cooperatives in which middle and rich peasants had gained control tended to fix higher rents than those over which poor peasants had won control. Rent disputes always caused great antagonism between poor and middle peasants.[44] In order to solve this contradiction, some Party leaders urged the elimination of private ownership through converting the cooperatives into collectives.

### *Advanced Cooperatives (Collectives)*

The advanced cooperatives, or collectives, represented a higher type of collectivization similar to the Soviet *kolkhoz.* When a peasant became a member, his land and other principal means of production were transferred from private to collective ownership, and payments for land shares and other means of production were abolished. The Model Regulation for Advanced Agricultural Producers' Cooperatives, adopted by the Third Session of the First National People's Congress on June 30, 1956, set organizational rules.

*Membership.* All working peasants over sixteen years of age could apply for membership. Former landlords and rich peasants could be admitted as members only after many years of labor reform and the approval of the members' meeting.

*Ownership.* Land and important means of production possessed by members had to be turned over to the cooperative for use under centralized management. Members were permitted, however, to retain small private plots on which to grow vegetables and other produce. These private plots were not to exceed 5 percent of a village's average landholding.

*Share Funds.* The cooperative collected two share funds from its members. One, termed the productive expenditure share fund, was used to cover production costs, such as the purchase of seed, fertilizer, fodder, and the like. The other was used to buy the means of production and was called the common property share fund. Share funds were usually made up of contributions from members based on the amount of land pooled.

*Income Distribution.* After deducting funds for production expenditures for the coming year, for reserve and welfare purposes, and for the payment of state agricultural taxes, the remainder of the income was distributed among the members according to the number of workdays each individual had invested in agricultural production.

*Payment for Work.* Payment for work performed by the members was based on the piecework system in accordance with the principle, "to each according to his work." Norms and rates of payment for the various jobs were reckoned in units of workdays. One workday was usually equal to ten work points, and the value of each work point depended on the total amount of income to be distributed to the members.

*Production Organization.* The cooperative organized its members into production brigades. Serving as the basic unit of the labor organization, each brigade arranged its daily and seasonal schedules of work in accordance with the general production plan of the cooperative. When necessary, a production brigade could be subdivided into temporary production groups.

*Management.* The highest management body of the cooperative was the general meeting of its members. This meeting elected a management committee to conduct the affairs of the cooperative, a supervisory committee to check on the cooperative's affairs, and a chairman to direct all daily activities.[45]

After the adoption of the Model Regulation, most of the elementary cooperatives were transformed into the advanced type. By the end of 1956, 96.3 percent of all agricultural households had joined cooperatives, and 87.8 percent of them were of the advanced type. By the end of 1957, China's 120 million peasant households had been organized into 752,113 cooperatives, of which 668,081 were collectives. The main task for the socialist transformation of agriculture had therefore been fulfilled ten years in advance of the original schedule.[46]

Four features distinguished the collectives from the elementary cooperatives.

1. On the average, a collective consisted of 158 peasant households, about four to five times the size of elementary cooperatives.
2. There were no rent payments to members.
3. There was collective ownership of draft animals.
4. Income distribution was based solely on the work contribution of each member.

The principle "from each according to his ability and to each according to his work" was put into effect. The collectives thus were socialist organizations.

Those who supported collectivization cited three major advantages of the new institutions. First, collectives solved the contradiction between private ownership of resources and unified management, and the abolition of private ownership facilitated land consolidation and rationalization. Second, since land rent constituted a significant part of the rich peasants' income, the abolition of rent payments would increase both the wages of the poor peasants and the level of investment. Third, collectivization was essential in order to carry out a large-scale water conservation campaign in the winter of 1957 and the spring of 1958.

However, the transformation of 120 million independent peasant households into more than 750,000 cooperatives, each with a single management and common ownership, failed to produce the necessary growth of China's agricultural economy. Indeed, it gave rise to several new problems. First, the establishment of common ownership forced the peasants to abandon their dream of becoming landowners, which diminished their incentive to produce and resulted in some indifference to common property. For example, there was a nationwide upsurge in the mortality rate of draft animals. According to a survey conducted in Jiangsu Province, some 60,000 animals died during the winter of 1956 and the spring of 1957. In Shandong Province, 30 percent of the draft animals were declared to be weak or incapacitated. Shanxi Province, which had usually enjoyed an abundance of draft animals, suffered serious shortages in the wake of collectivization.[47] Since draft animals still constituted the basic source of power for farming in China, their decline dealt a severe blow to agricultural production, and agricultural growth slowed in 1957. The alleged superiority of collectivization, at least during that period, cannot be supported by production figures.

Second, the single management system of the collective farms demanded a great number of qualified directors and accountants. Because land fertility and peasant productivity varied widely, centralized management required a sufficient number of experienced personnel. Yet, with the rapid growth of the collectives, there was a universal shortage of accountants. Many units, even after their first year of operation, could not establish regular accounting systems. In turn, it was extremely difficult to distribute income correctly, and irregularities only quenched the enthusiasm of the capable members, thereby exerting a further adverse effect on agricultural production.

Third, when the peasants farmed independently, they had always made effective use of all of their arable land. Slack farming seasons were devoted to sideline production, and the income derived from that production generally represented 30 to 40 percent of their total income. But when the farms were incorporated into collectives, those subsidiary occupations were largely suspended. According to a survey of Liaoning, sideline production registered a 40 to 50 percent decline during the first quarter of 1956, as compared with the corresponding period in 1955. The same situation prevailed in Hebei and other provinces.[48] The drastic decline of pig raising was most striking. In 1954, there were about 100 million pigs in China; by the end of June 1956, their number had fallen to 84 million.[49] This decline not only lowered peasant income, but it also brought about serious shortages of meat in the urban districts.

Finally, numerous difficulties arose over the system of income distribution. The adoption of an egalitarian policy, ignoring the differences of productivity of various teams (villages) within the collectives, led to rising dissatisfaction among hitherto rich and productive villages. The situation became worse when collective managers attempted to increase the size of the collectives, further separating productivity and reward. With rents abolished, private plots squeezed, and pig populations in decline, there was a growing crisis of confidence among the peasants as to the collectives' ability to raise their incomes and improve their living conditions.

The time was again approaching for China's leaders to reach a new decision – to retreat from consolidation or to push a step further. They made the dramatic decision to go forward, and the result was the emergence of the rural communes (see Chapter 4).

## SOCIAL AND ECONOMIC CONSEQUENCES OF AGRICULTURAL POLICY, 1949–1957

Within the short span of eight years, the Chinese countryside had undergone a fundamental change from a traditional farm economy, based on individual ownership and labor, to a collective system. The collectivization movement proceeded with extraordinary and unexpected speed. Its merits and demerits can be evaluated through an examination of its social and economic consequences.

Compared with the collectivization drive in the Soviet Union, the Chinese movement seems to have been more successful. It encountered no organized peasant rebellion and had fewer adverse effects on agricultural production. Soviet land reform had been carried out immediately after the 1917 revolution, and for more than a decade afterward, small, private, peasant farming had prevailed. In late 1929, however, the ruthless drive for forced collectivization began, and by 1936, about 90 percent of Soviet peasant households had been collectivized. An immediate consequence of that forced collectivization was the loss of millions of lives, a severe disruption of agricultural output, and a precipitate decline in livestock. By 1932, the number of cattle in the Soviet Union had declined by 40 percent, pigs by 55 percent, and sheep by 64 percent. It was not until the mid-1950s that herds were restored to their 1928 level.[50] Learning from the Soviet lesson, the Chinese leaders pursued a step-by-step approach, from land reform through mutual aid teams to elementary cooperatives and then collectives. The step-by-step transition in China helped to avoid a feeling of suddenness and shock among the peasants.

The most significant social consequence of the Chinese collectivization was the elimination of the landlord and rich peasant classes and the equalization of living standards in the countryside. At the time of land reform, all peasants were registered as belonging to four broad social classes: landlord, rich, middle (upper and lower), and poor. After land reform, it was claimed that many former poor peasants had risen into the middle peasant class. With the completion of collectivization in 1957, most of the distinguishing features of class, based on private ownership of land and other agricultural capital, ceased to exist. All classes received the same size of private plot per person. Although middle and upper-middle peasants were often better farm managers than the poor peasants–and therefore continued to receive a larger percentage of their income from their private plot and sideline occupations–socioeconomic differences between the poor and the rich diminished rapidly.

Two kinds of evidence concerning class and income document the changes. The first is a 1956 survey of 860 peasant households in two collectives of Yunnan Province, which shows the income differentiation per capita among the different classes of household. Table 3.2, drawn from that survey, shows that there was little difference in per capita income among poor peasants, middle peasants, and former landlords. The income of those lowest on the scale fell only 20 percent below that of the highest.

The second set of data shows the income and living standards of 600 farm households in five collectives in Hebei and Shandong provinces and displays a much wider income gap between poor and upper-middle peasants (see Table 3.3). In terms of food and cloth consumption, however, the difference was usually rather small. In general, a polarization of the peasants into very poor and very rich, which has characterized some developing countries, was effectively prevented.

In an economic sense, collectivization failed to improve the land-population ratio; nor did it improve labor productivity. Because the population continued to grow at a rate of 2.2 percent during the 1952–1957 period while cultivated land increased at a rate of less than 1 percent a year, there was a continuing decline in land per capita.

Table 3.2
Income of 860 Peasant Households
in Two Collectives in Yunnan Province, 1956

| Class of Household | Income per capita (yuan) | Income per capita from collective (yuan) | Income per capita from private sector (yuan) | % of income from private sector (yuan) |
|---|---|---|---|---|
| Poor peasant | 81.3 | 73.6 | 7.7 | 9.5 |
| Middle peasant | 91.6 | 78.9 | 12.7 | 13.9 |
| Former rich peasant | 101.9 | 84.9 | 17.0 | 16.7 |
| Former landlords | 97.8 | 86.8 | 11.0 | 11.3 |
| Former small renters | 90.7 | 75.9 | 14.8 | 16.3 |

Source: Wang Ming, "Several Questions Viewed from Income Distribution in Two Collectives," Xinhua banyuekan (New China semimonthly) No. 24 (1956), pp. 59–60.

Table 3.3
Income and Living Standards of Five Collectives in Hebei and Shandong Provinces, Year-end 1956

| Village | Beidaliu Village | | | Chengzi Village | | | |
|---|---|---|---|---|---|---|---|
| Class of Household | Poor & Lower | Middle | Upper | Poor | Lower | Middle | Upper |
| Income per head (yuan) | 50 | 76 | 84 | 58 | 63 | 75 | 111 |
| Food consumption per head (catties) | 349.1 | 368.9 | 361.6 | 360 | 365 | 361 | 362 |
| Meat consumption per head (catties) | 4.1 | 7.2 | 7.9 | 7 | 8 | 10 | 14 |
| Cotton Cloth consumption per head (feet) | 19.4 | 25.8 | 22.2 | 15 | 14 | 19 | 24.5 |

| Class of Household | Xihe Village | | | | Dafuhuai Village | | | |
|---|---|---|---|---|---|---|---|---|
| | Poor | Lower | Middle | Upper | Poor | Lower | Middle | Upper |
| Income per head (yuan) | 64 | 73 | 90 | 131 | 47 | 60 | 73 | 97 |
| Food consumption per head (catties) | 362 | 369 | 422 | 502 | 319 | 359 | 364 | 386 |
| Meat consumption per head (catties) | 0.28 | 0.32 | 0.55 | 0.95 | 1.1 | 1.5 | 3.5 | 6.0 |
| Cotton cloth consumption per head (feet) | 15 | 15.7 | 20.2 | 33.3 | 13 | 16.7 | 20.4 | 21.3 |

| Class of Household | Kongjia Village | | | |
|---|---|---|---|---|
| | Poor | Lower | Middle | Upper |
| Income per head (yuan) | 47.6 | 64.5 | 79.3 | 121.2 |
| Food consumption per head (catties) | 348.6 | 395.2 | 430 | 511 |
| Meat consumption per head (catties) | 1.6 | 2.6 | 2.9 | 5.5 |
| Cotton cloth consumption per head (feet) | 12.9 | 15.7 | 18.4 | 26.8 |

Source: Yang Yingjie, Survey of Five Agricultural Collectives and 600 Farm Households (Beijing: Caizheng Jingji Chubanshe, 1958), pp. 54–55.

The total amount of cultivated area as reported by the Chinese government and as estimated by Kang Chao is summarized in Table 3.4.

Chao accepted the 1957 official figure as basically reliable but made adjustments for the earlier years on four grounds. First, Communist figures for cultivated areas for 1949–1955 were much smaller than J. L. Buck's estimates for the prewar period, indicating that official cultivated-land figures for the early 1950s may be considerably understated. Second, during collectivization, official sources disclosed that farmland concealment had been consistently uncovered – some 30 million mu of unregistered farmland was discovered from 1953 to 1957. This amount, which was treated as newly cultivated land in the official statistics, should have been added to the original cultivated land in 1949. Third, in the Chinese official statistics, the total cultivated area increased steadily throughout 1949–1956, ceased to rise in 1957, and declined for the first time in 1958. Apparently, part of the increase before 1957 was only statistical and resulted from uncovering concealed holdings. That factor had virtually disappeared by 1957, and the reduction in cultivated land in 1958 was real, reflecting the large quantity of farmland occupied by extensive construction activities in that year. Fourth, of the 77.56 million mu of reclaimed land

Table 3.4
Comparison of Two Estimates of Cultivated Area in Mainland China, 1949–1957
(in million mu)

| Year | Chinese Official Data[a] | Kang Chao's Estimates[b] |
|---|---|---|
| 1949 | 1,468.22 | 1,667.15 |
| 1950 | 1,505.34 | 1,666.74 |
| 1951 | 1,555.07 | 1,665.23 |
| 1952 | 1,618.78 | 1,663.64 |
| 1953 | 1,627.93 | 1,662.95 |
| 1954 | 1,640.32 | 1,662.20 |
| 1955 | 1,652.35 | 1,672.74 |
| 1956 | 1,677.37 | 1,686.55 |
| 1957 | 1,677.45 | 1,677.45 |

Sources: (a) P.R.C. State Statistical Bureau, <u>Ten Great Years</u> (Beijing: Foreign Languages Press, 1960), p. 128. (b) Kang Chao, <u>Agricultural Production in Communist China</u> (Madison: University of Wisconsin Press, 1970), p. 207. One mu = 0.165 acre, or 0.067 ha.

in the period 1953–1957, only 19.80 million mu were reclaimed by the agricultural cooperatives. The increase mainly resulted from the removal of boundary lines, graves, and so on, so the increase represented only a 1.21 percent gain in cultivated land.[51]

Following Chao's estimates, the contribution of collectivization to the increase of cultivated land was very small. One positive effect of collectivization was the increase of double-cropping in food grain, which, according to official statistics, added 128 million mu to the area sown for grain in 1952–1957.[52] Again, much of the claimed increase is only statistical, however, as it came from the recovery of unregistered grain land. Using Chao's estimates, Table 3.5 shows the general deterioration in the ratio between land and rural population in terms of cultivated areas and sown areas between 1952 (the year that land reform was completed) and 1957 (the conclusion of collectivization).

One strong argument for collectivization was that it helped the accumulation of public property, which would promote agricultural growth. Government statistics showed that state investment in agriculture was rather meager during the 1953–1957 period. Of the state's planned capital construction investment, only 7.6 percent was devoted to the agricultural sector.[53] In an attempt to present a more complete picture of total fixed investment in the agricultural sector, I have made a detailed study of both state investment and private investment. Private investment in agriculture includes projects financed by agricultural cooperatives and by peasant households. Part of the private investment can be derived from official data on producer goods sold to the rural areas. This is the portion that went through market channels and was expressed in monetary terms. The other part of private investment is the imputed value of peasants' labor in water conservation projects, land reclamation, soil improvement, afforestation, and housing repair and construction. This part of the investment did not go through market channels and therefore was not counted as investment in official statistics. Since the effect of these labor investments is exactly the same as capital investment, the omission of this portion might result in a sizable understatement of rural investment. I have therefore decided to include my estimates of private investment in the agricultural sector (see Table 3.6).

Total state and private investment in agriculture during the five-year period amounted to 18,986 million yuan, averaging 3.8 billion yuan a year. According to an estimate made by Ta-chung Liu, the total stock of fixed reproducible capital in the agricultural sector in 1957 was 94.57 billion yuan.[54] If an average life span of twenty-five years is assumed for those capital goods,[55] the annual depreciation would

Table 3.5

Land Per Capita of Rural Population, 1952-1957

| Year | Total Cultivated Area (in million mu)[a] | Total Sown Area (in million mu)[b] | Rural Population (1,000 persons)[c] | Landholding Per Capita: Cultivated Area (in mu) | Landholding Per Capita: Sown Area (in mu) |
|---|---|---|---|---|---|
| 1952 | 1,663.64 | 2,233.95 | 503,190 | 3.31 | 4.44 |
| 1953 | 1,662.95 | 2,254.65 | 510,290 | 3.26 | 4.42 |
| 1954 | 1,662.20 | 2,305.66 | 520,170 | 3.20 | 4.43 |
| 1955 | 1,672.74 | 2,301.01 | 531,800 | 3.15 | 4.33 |
| 1956 | 1,686.55 | 2,404.58 | 538,650 | 3.13 | 4.46 |
| 1957 | 1,677.45 | 2,342.72 | 545,650 | 3.07 | 4.29 |

Sources: (a) Table 3.4. (b) Kang Chao, Agricultural Production in Communist China (Madison: University of Wisconsin Press, 1970), p. 213. (c) Chu-yuan Cheng, China's Allocation of Fixed Capital Investment, 1952-1957 (Ann Arbor: Center for Chinese Studies, University of Michigan, 1974), p. 78.

Table 3.6
Public and Private Fixed Investment in Agricultural Sector, 1953-1957
(in million yuan)

| Items | State Investment | Private Investment[a] | Total Amount | Total % |
|---|---|---|---|---|
| Water Conservation | 4,202 | 1,100 | 5,302 | 27.9 |
| Reclamation of new land | 1,431 | 1,000 | 2,431 | 12.8 |
| Purchases of agricultural machinery & implements | 709 | 3,322 | 4,031 | 21.2 |
| Purchases of livestock & carts | 708 | 3,532 | 4,240 | 22.3 |
| Afforestation | 146 | 2,450 | 2,596 | 13.7 |
| Meteorology services | 25 | 0 | 25 | 0.1 |
| Other[b] | — | 361 | 361 | 2.0 |
| Total | 7,221 | 11,765 | 18,986 | 100.0 |

Notes: (a) Includes projects financed by agricultural cooperatives and by peasant households. (b) Mainly repairing of roads and bridges.

Source: Chu-yuan Cheng, China's Allocation of Fixed Capital Investment, 1952-1957 (Ann Arbor: Center for Chinese Studies, University of Michigan, 1974), p. 81.

amount to about 4 billion yuan. The fixed investment during the 1953–1957 period thus was close to the amount needed to replace worn-out assets, such as houses and farming tools, and therefore fulfilled the minimal requirement to prevent farm output from falling.

Because man-land ratio and capital investment failed to improve, the crop yield per unit of sown area increased only moderately between 1952 and 1957, and the averages in the 1952–1957 period fell short by varying degrees of the corresponding estimates for the prewar period (see Table 3.7).

In 1957, the year collectivization was completed, the gross value of agricultural production increased by 3.5 percent, but the volume of food grain output rose by only 1 percent, below the population growth rate of 2 percent. The sown area of food grains also fell by 55 million mu, accounting for a decrease of 6 million tons of grains.[56] In the col-

Table 3.7
Major Grain Yields Per Unit of Sown Areas
in Prewar and 1952-1957 Periods
(unit: catties)

| Crop | Prewar Period | | Communist Period | | |
|---|---|---|---|---|---|
| | 1929-1933[a] average | 1931-1937[b] average | 1952[c] | 1957[c] | 1952-1957[c] average |
| Rice | 447<br>433<br>(glutinous rice) | 338 | 321 | 359 | 336 |
| Wheat | 141<br>(winter) | 144 | 98 | 114 | 106 |
| Potatoes | 264<br>(sweet)<br>213<br>(Irish) | 263<br>(sweet) | 251 | 278 | 246 |
| Coarse grains | 151 | 158 | 136 | 139 | 134 |

Sources: (a) J. L. Buck, Land Utilization in China (Shanghai: Commercial Press, 1937), vol. 3, p. 209. (b) T. H. Shen, Agricultural Resources of China (Ithaca: Cornell University Press, 1951), pp. 347-377. (c) P.R.C. State Statistical Bureau, Ten Great Years (Beijing: Foreign Languages Press, 1960), p. 121. One catty = 0.5 kilograms or 1.1023 pounds.

lectives, peasants demanded reductions in grain taxes and procurement, and many collectives cut their investment by distributing more grain for consumption. General conditions in the autumn of 1957 indicated that the collectives were by no means securely established in the countryside and were doomed to further transformation.

In summary, agricultural collectivization during the 1949–1957 period succeeded more in equalizing the distribution of peasant income than in promoting agricultural output. Land reform eradicated the landlord class and the rich peasants. The collectives equalized living standards and facilitated planned procurement and the rationing of food grains. The drive failed to halt the deterioration of the man-land ratio, however, for the growth of the rural population outpaced the increase in the amount of cultivated land. The increase of fixed capital investment during the period was only able to compensate for the depreciation of capital stock, with very little progress in labor productivity. Numerous difficulties arose in the collectives over the problems of distribution, management, and incentives. The lack of experienced managers and accountants, together with the growing scale of operations, created further disincentive effects among the membership. In view of the low growth rate of agricultural output during the 1952–1957 period, the faults of collectivization probably far outweighed the merits.

## NOTES

1. Mao Zedong, "Report on an Investigation of the Peasant Movement in Hunan," in *Selected Works,* vol. 1, p. 23.
2. Xu Dixin, *New Democracy and the Chinese Economy* (Hong Kong: New Tide Publishing House, 1948), chap. 2.
3. Kenneth R. Walker, "Collectivization in Retrospect: The Socialist High Tide of Autumn 1955–Spring 1956," *China Quarterly* No. 26 (April–June 1966), pp. 4–5.
4. Liu Shaoqi, *Political Report of the Central Committee of the Chinese Communist Party to the Eighth National Congress,* pp. 23–24.
5. Cited in Lin Yizhou, "The Peasant Problem in Democratic Revolution," *Hongqi* No. 5 (March 1961), p. 27.
6. P.R.C., "Land Reform Law," in *Renmin shouce, 1951* [People's handbook, 1951] (Shanghai: Da Gong Bao, 1951), sec. 5, p. 26.
7. Mao Zedong, "Speech at a Conference of Cadres in the Shanxi-Suiyuan (Shansi-Suiyuan) Liberated Area," in *Selected Works,* vol. 4, p. 235.
8. Ibid., p. 236.
9. Mao Zedong, "Report on an Investigation of the Peasant Movement in Hunan," p. 22.
10. Liao Luyan, "The Great Victory in Land Reform During the Past Three Years," in *New China's Economic Achievements (1949–1952),* comp. China Committee for the Promotion of International Trade (Beijing: Foreign Languages Press, 1952), p. 171.
11. For instance, in Guangdong Province, where only 0.82 mu per head was allocated to the beneficiaries of the land reform, the decrease in the average size of farms was conspicuous. An official report stated that in thirteen *xian* (counties) where land reform had been completed by the spring of 1952, there was only one draft animal per 88 mu of land and one farm implement per household. The normal requirement for draft animals was one per 12–35 mu of land (*Nanfang ribao* [Southern daily], March 1, 1952).
12. Gao Gang, "Overcome the Erosion of the Party by Bourgeois Thoughts, Oppose Rightist Thinking Within the Party," *Xuexi* [Study] No. 1 (1952), pp. 9–12.

13. Xue Muqiao, Su Xing, and Lin Zeli, *The Socialist Transformation of the National Economy in China* (Beijing: Foreign Languages Press, 1960), pp. 98–101.

14. Zuo Mu, "The Problems of the Separation of Peasants into Classes During the Historical Period After the Land Reform," *Guangming ribao* [Enlightenment daily], May 29, 1961.

15. *Renmin ribao,* January 8, 1952.

16. Kang Chao, *Agricultural Production in Communist China* (Madison: University of Wisconsin Press, 1970), pp. 43–44.

17. Mao Zedong, *Selected Works,* vol. 4, p. 238.

18. Mao's report was republished during the Cultural Revolution in *Renmin ribao,* November 25, 1968.

19. Liu Shaoqi, "On the Problem of Land Reform," published in an internal document on June 14, 1950, and quoted in *Hongqi* No. 16 (November 23, 1967), p. 22.

20. Bo Yipo, "Strengthen the Party's Political Work in the Villages," *Xuexi* Nos. 6–7 (1951), pp. 30–32.

21. Editorial departments of *Renmin ribao, Hongqi,* and *Jiefang junbao,* "Struggle Between the Two Roads in China's Countryside," *Hongqi* No. 16 (November 23, 1967), pp. 18–29.

22. Ibid.

23. Kenneth R. Walker, "Collectivization in Retrospect," p. 13.

24. CCP, Central Committee, "Directive to Party Committees at All Levels on the Spring Agricultural Production," March 16, 1953, *Xinhua yuebao* [New China monthly] No. 4 (April 1953), pp. 121–122.

25. CCP, Central Committee, "Resolution on Developing Agricultural Cooperatives," December 16, 1953, in CCP, Central Committee, *Cooperative Farming in China* (Beijing: Foreign Languages Press, 1954), Appendix.

26. P.R.C., State Statistical Bureau, *Statistical Materials on Agricultural Cooperativization and the Distribution of the Product in Cooperatives During 1955* (Beijing: Tongji Chubanshe, 1957), pp. 10–12.

27. Kenneth R. Walker, "Collectivization in Retrospect," p. 19.

28. *Renmin ribao,* August 3, 1954.

29. Editorial, *Renmin ribao,* March 5, 1955.

30. *Renmin shouce, 1956* [People's handbook, 1956] (Tianjin: Da Gong Bao, 1956), p. 472.

31. Mao Zedong, "On the Question of Agricultural Cooperativization," *People's China* No. 22 (November 1, 1955), pp. 3–17; Chinese version in *Selected Works,* vol. 5, pp. 168–191.

32. *Renmin ribao,* September 8, 1955.

33. Ibid., August 23, 1955.

34. Deng Zihui's speech, CCP Eighth Party Congress, September 22, 1956.

35. Mao Zedong, "On the Question of Agricultural Cooperativization."

36. *Xinhua banyuekan* [New China semimonthly] No. 4 (1956), p. 1.

37. Kenneth R. Walker, "Collectivization in Retrospect," pp. 38–39.

38. *Renmin ribao,* March 22, 1957.

39. *Renmin shouce, 1958* [People's handbook, 1958] (Beijing: Da Gong Bao, 1958), pp. 518–519.

40. Xue Muqiao, Su Xing, Lin Zeli, *Socialist Transformation,* pp. 112–113.

41. Ibid.

42. Li Xiannian, "Financial Work and Agricultural Cooperativization," *Da gong bao* [Impartial Daily] (Beijing), November 8, 1955.

43. Kang Chao, *Agricultural Production,* pp. 48–49.

44. Kenneth R. Walker, "Collectivization in Retrospect," pp. 37–38.

45. The English version of the Model Regulation appeared in Tong Dalin, *Agricultural Cooperatives in China* (Beijing: Foreign Languages Press, 1958), Appendix 2.

46. *Jingji yanjiu* [Economic research] (Beijing) No. 10 (October 1959), p. 3.

47. *Renmin ribao,* April 19, 1957.

48. *Da gong bao* (Beijing), May 2, 1956.

49. *Xinhua banyuekan* No. 1 (1957), pp. 88–90.

50. Janet Chapman and Shun-hsin Chou, "The Agricultural Sector in the Chinese and Soviet Economies" (Paper presented to the Midwest Seminar on Chinese Economic Studies, Ann Arbor, Michigan, May 1976).

51. Kang Chao, *Agricultural Production,* pp. 204–207.

52. P.R.C., State Statistical Bureau, *Ten Great Years,* p. 129.

53. Ibid., p. 59.

54. Alexander Eckstein, Walter Galenson, and Ta-chung Liu, eds., *Economic Trends in Communist China* (Chicago: Aldine, 1968), pp. 170–171. The amount includes the value of rural residential housing.

55. According to Sun Yefang, then director of the Institute of Economic Research of the Chinese Academy of Sciences, the period of amortization in China amounts to twenty-five years (see FBIS, August 23, 1978, p. A27).

56. Liao Luyan, "Strive to Achieve the Plan for Agricultural Development," in *Xinhua banyuekan* No. 5 (March 1958), pp. 127–132.

# 4

# Evolution of the Commune System

The people's communes, which first appeared in China's countryside in April 1958, have been the most dramatic institutional change undertaken by the Communist government. Praised by the Chinese leaders as the "ladder to Communist paradise," the commune is not a purely agricultural establishment but is intended to serve as a basic unit of the country's social-economic-political system. Since there was little experience in other countries that could provide a guide, it was indeed a novel experiment on a grand scale, involving the well-being of more than 700 million Chinese peasants. Since its inception, the organization and function of the commune have undergone incessant changes, and its main features have altered in striking ways from period to period. The commune system in 1980 differed greatly from the 1958 version. This chapter will analyze the communes of 1958, trace their evolution and identify the factors that caused change, depict the structure and functions of the commune today, evaluate the impact of the communes on agricultural production, and assess the strengths and weaknesses of the system.

## GENERAL BACKGROUND

The emergence of the rural commune was the result of two significant developments in late 1957 and early 1958. The first was the cluster of unsolved problems arising from the agricultural collectives. The second was the widening gap between industry and agriculture created by the First Five-Year Plan.

During their first year of existence, the collectives revealed a series of internal and external contradictions. The three most important contradictions were between the collective economy and the private sector, between the better-off collectives and the poor ones, and between collectives and the state.[1]

The first of those conflicts appeared when the management of a collective, intent on fulfilling state quotas, demanded that the members give priority to assigned work but the members were more interested in cultivating their small private plots and tending their domestic animals and poultry. In the income distribution of 1957, many collective agricultural incomes fell below private agricultural incomes.[2] The competition between the private and collective economies for labor, manure, and water led many cadres to conclude that the abolition of private plots was a prerequisite for consolidating the collectives.

The second contradiction occurred because some collectives had been organized by well-to-do peasants, who owned considerable land and capital, and those collectives had a sound economic foundation. Directors and members of the prosperous units were often more interested in profitable rural business activities than in engaging in agricultural production. When speculative activities reached new heights in 1957, this group was largely responsible. On the other hand, collectives composed predominantly of poor peasants found themselves incapable of expanding their capital stock. Their levels of income were low, and their organizations hovered on the brink of disaster. Rural economic society continued to show a sharp cleavage, despite collectivization.

The third and most serious contradiction was reflected in agricultural tax collection and state procurement. In order to encourage the peasants to join the collectives, the government announced during the 1956 summer tax collection that 70 percent of the total agricultural output should be distributed among the peasants. It also decreed that each collective should first distribute rations to its members and only thereafter pay its agricultural tax to the state. The result was a decline of 1.5 million tons of grain in the tax collection from that of the previous year. Consequently, during the autumn collection of 1956, the government ordered the collectives to fulfill their state collection quotas first and then distribute the remainder of the output among their members. Even so, fifteen provinces, representing 65 percent of the total, failed to fulfill their tax obligations. During the summer collection of 1957, the situation became even more critical. Most of the agricultural collectives concealed their agricultural output in order to lessen their obligations to the state. An August 9, 1957, report of the Party organ, *Renmin ribao,* revealed that many collectives, with the consent of their directors, maintained two sets of accounts. One set recorded the true output for internal purposes, and the other listed faulty figures for submission to the government. Tax collection and unified state procurements declined for all important crops.

The root of the contradictions, according to the Communist leadership, lay in the traditional individualistic Chinese concepts of the family system and private property. To destroy this tradition necessitated a thorough reform of the socioeconomic structure. This situation provided the background for the emergence of the people's communes.

The immediate cause for the establishment of communes, however, was the need to solve the labor shortage created by the Great Leap Forward movement. China's First Five-Year Plan had been completed in 1957. According to official statistics, industrial production grew during those five years (1953–1957) at an annual rate of 18 percent while agricultural production rose 4.5 percent a year and the output of food grains by 3.7 percent, barely surpassing the population's growth rate. Bottlenecks in the production of raw materials forced the planners to reconsider the development plan.

In November 1957, Mao Zedong went to Moscow to seek Soviet economic aid, and the Moscow meeting was followed by a decision of the Communist bloc to launch a comprehensive economic competition with the West. Upon his return to Beijing, Mao promoted the slogan of "surpassing Great Britain in principal industrial output within fifteen years." To achieve this ambitious goal, the government began to construct water conservancy projects on an unprecedented scale as the first major step to stimulate agriculture. Incomplete government statistics for the winter of 1957 to mid-April 1958 show that about 100 million peasants were called to participate in the water conservancy projects for three consecutive months.[3] Hundreds of thousands of peasants were mobilized to build roads and dredge canals, placing a great strain on the rural labor force. The manpower shortage was further aggravated by the Great Leap Forward, which began in March 1958, when some 60 million peasants were assigned to build and operate millions of native-type factories and backyard furnaces. Thus, Mao concluded that the manpower shortage demanded a change in the organization of rural labor and in the traditional peasant mode of living so that women could be drafted into agricultural production. This reasoning gave birth to the rural communes.[4]

The first model commune, popularly referred to as Sputnik, was

Table 4.1
The Establishment of Rural Communes
up to September 1958

| Location | Number of Communes Established | Number of Participating Households | Percentage of Total Peasant Households | Average No. of Households per Commune |
|---|---|---|---|---|
| Beijing | 56 | 663,124 | 100.0 | 11,842 |
| Shanghai | 23 | 256,000 | 100.0 | 11,130 |
| Hebei | 951 | 8,402,639 | 100.0 | 8,836 |
| Shanxi | 975 | 3,483,564 | 100.0 | 3,573 |
| Nei Monggol (Inner Mongolia) | 812 | 1,561,023 | 98.6 | 1,922 |
| Liaoning | 428 | 3,264,579 | 100.0 | 7,628 |
| Jilin | 481 | 1,914,547 | 100.0 | 3,980 |
| Heilong-jiang | 718 | 1,946,478 | 100.0 | 2,711 |
| Shaanxi | 1,673 | 3,232,904 | 100.0 | 1,932 |
| Gansu | 794 | 2,006,389 | 100.0 | 2,527 |
| Qinghai | 144 | 245,624 | 100.0 | 1,706 |
| Ningxia | 53 | 201,815 | 67.3 | 3,808 |
| Xinjiang | 389 | 625,151 | 59.3 | 1,607 |
| Shandong | 1,580 | 11,347,989 | 100.0 | 7,182 |
| Jiangsu | 1,490 | 9,127,234 | 99.4 | 6,126 |
| Anhui | 1,054 | 7,219,244 | 100.0 | 6,849 |
| Zhejiang | 761 | 5,697,412 | 100.0 | 7,487 |
| Fujian | 622 | 2,672,839 | 95.1 | 4,297 |
| Henan | 1,285 | 10,272,517 | 100.0 | 7,994 |
| Hubei | 729 | 6,040,000 | 96.1 | 8,285 |
| Hunan | 1,284 | 8,172,440 | 100.0 | 6,365 |
| Jiangxi | 1,240 | 3,720,000 | 92.0 | 3,000 |
| Guangdong | 803 | 7,905,553 | 100.0 | 9,845 |
| Guangxi | 784 | 4,041,944 | 100.0 | 5,156 |
| Sichuan | 4,827 | 13,676,988 | 99.1 | 2,833 |
| Guizhou | 2,194 | 3,101,205 | 94.5 | 1,413 |
| Yunnan | 275 | 1,137,148 | 31.0 | 4,135 |
| Total | 26,425 | 121,936,350 | 98.2 | 4,614 |

Source: Tongji gongzuo /Statistical work/ (Beijing) No. 20 (1958), p. 23.

organized in the Xinyang District, Henan Province, in April 1958. By the end of August, the 38,497 agricultural cooperatives in Henan Province had been incorporated into 1,280 communes, representing 99.98 percent of that province's rural peasant households. On August 29, the enlarged meeting of the CCP Central Committee's Politburo adopted a Resolution on the Establishment of the People's Communes in the Rural Areas. This directive provided the general guidelines for the entire system. Following its provisions, cooperatives everywhere were merged immediately into communes. By the end of September 1958, there were 26,425 communes in the rural districts, representing 98.2 percent of the total number of peasant households.[5] The number and size of the communes, as of September of that year, are shown in Table 4.1.

## ORIGINAL FEATURES OF THE RURAL COMMUNES

By official definition, "The People's commune is the basic unit of the social structure of our country, combining industry, agriculture, trade, education and the military. At the same time, it is the basic organization of social power."[6] The commune is a much larger and more advanced form of collectivization than the collectives (advanced cooperatives).

When agricultural cooperativization was completed in 1957, China's 120 million peasant households had been organized into 752,113 units, of which 668,081 were of the advanced type. The average number of households per unit (both elementary and advanced) was 158. In the commune system, households per unit averaged 5,000 in 1958, or a membership thirty-two times larger than that of the average cooperative. Thus, the commune could dispose of vastly more manpower and land than the cooperatives could.

In addition to this difference in scale, the original blueprint for the communes differed from that of the agricultural cooperatives in several respects.

*Function.* Whereas the original agricultural cooperatives had been organized purely for agricultural production, the communes merged peasants, workers, tradesmen, students, and militia members into a single unit to engage in afforestation, animal husbandry, and subsidiary occupations, as well as in agriculture. The communes also run factories, banks, and commercial enterprises; handle credit and commodity distribution; undertake cultural and educational work; and control their own militia and political organizations.

*Ownership.* Although the collective membership of the agricultural cooperatives owned the major means of production, individual members retained small plots of land, houses, and orchards and engaged in spare-time occupations. Initially, all means of production and properties, including small garden plots, houses, large farm implements, draft animals, and livestock, were owned solely by the communes. Private ownership of land was basically abolished.

*Income Distribution.* Under the former agricultural cooperatives, each household counted as a unit in distribution, and payment was issued only to the head of the family. Income, in both cash and kind, was distributed among the peasants according to the number of days they had worked, and how they spent the income was up to them. The initial commune structure, however, established a half-wage, half-supply system: The Commune retained the entire food supply, and members received ration tickets redeemable at public mess halls, where food had to be eaten on the premises. Moreover, the commune issued wages on a monthly basis and determined amounts according to the individual's attitude toward labor, technical skill, and physical strength. Gradually, peasants were placed on an equal footing with workers.

*Manner of Life.* Since the agricultural cooperative enforced collectivization only for production, the traditional family life of the peasants was virtually unchanged. In the initial stage of communalization, however, the peasants were required to eat together in public mess halls, to place their children in communal nurseries, to send sewing and mending work to the centralized tailoring teams, and, in some cases, to live in central lodgings. The family, as a unit, was scheduled for elimination.

*Labor Organization.* In the original agricultural cooperatives, labor organization took the production brigade as the basic unit. Under the commune system, the original units of the cooperatives were reorganized into production brigades, and the original brigades became production teams. In September 1959, there were a half million production brigades and some 3 million production teams in the 24,000 rural communes.[7]

*Administration.* In the past, there had been two separate structures in the rural areas: One of government administration had the *xiang* (township) as its basic unit, and the other, a production organization, was the agricultural cooperative. With the establishment of the communes, these two structures merged. Each commune had an administrative committee, which exercised control over a general office, a supervisor's office, and departments of agriculture, water conservancy, forestry, animal husbandry, industry, communications, political affairs, labor, security, finance, food, supplies, marketing, credit, commerce, culture, education, and public health. Each commune also had such special units as planning commissions and scientific research institutes. The organization resembled a county government and was much larger in scale than an agricultural cooperative.[8] The communes were also dissimilar to the Soviet *kolkhoz* and *sovkhoz* in their more comprehensive economic, political, and social organization.

The introduction of the rural commune helped to alleviate the shortages of labor and capital that had been created by the Great Leap Forward. Large numbers of women were drafted into agricultural production. According to official estimates, one woman in each peasant family had done nothing in the past but attend to household chores, but after the formation of communes, one woman was able to manage the domestic affairs of an average of four households.[9] In this way, an estimated 90 million women were released from the 120 million peasant households to take part in production activities. In the seven provinces of Henan, Hunan, Shandong, Shanxi, Jiangxi, Liaoning, and Heilongjiang, more than 20 million women were relieved of domestic duties. In Shandong Province alone, the number of women thus released reached 6.7 million – an increase of one-third of that province's labor force.[10]

The establishment of communes also contributed to capital accumulation in rural areas because income that had previously gone to the private sector was now transferred to the communes. In 1956, 70 percent of the total agricultural income in the collectives was distributed among the members; in 1957, that share was reduced to 53.2 percent.[11] After the establishment of communes, income received by the peasants as compensation for labor dropped to only 30 percent of the total revenue. The remaining part was allocated for welfare and investment.[12] The transformation of private property into commune property also increased public funds for investment. The amount of the transfer income taken over by the government in 1958 was reflected in the sharp increase in extrabudgetary investment, or investment that was not included in the state's original capital construction plan. Official statistics showed an unprecedentedly rapid rise in extrabudgetary investment, which amounted to 5.3 billion yuan, or approximately $2 billion at the 1958 exchange rate, a sum almost equal to the extrabudgetary investment during the entire period of the First Five-Year Plan.[13]

Apart from economic considerations, the regime also attempted to tighten its political control over the rural areas via the regimentation of the communes. Beginning in 1957, peasants in various rural areas had waged a campaign to "get even" with local Communist cadres by resisting government requisition and purchase of grain, thereby making it impossible for the regime to fulfill its collection targets. With the establishment of the communes, however, all grain came under the control of the commune, and the peasants had to obtain all their food from it. As life became intensely collectivized, each and every individual's thinking and behavior came under the direct supervision of Communist cadres.

For long-term purposes, the communes were intended first to destroy the family system and then to lay the cornerstone of collectivized life, or the creation of the so-called Communist man. The Communists believed that individualism could be eradicated only by destroying the traditional peasant concept of the family as the basic social unit. In the initial stage of the communes, official ideology no longer recognized moral obligations between father and son, between husband and wife, or between relatives and friends; the only relationship sanctioned was between "fellow workers." Such drastic policies threatened the family as the fundamental social unit, since they tended to isolate the individual from any sense of personal ties or obligations.

The second long-term goal was the elimination of the peasantry as a class. Accepting Lenin's dictum that "peasants constitute the last bourgeois class," the Chinese Communists argued that the realization of communism would require the abolition of all classes save the proletariat. Under the wage system initially employed in the communes, the distinction between peasants and workers was to diminish daily. When the peasants were eventually transformed into agricultural workers, they would cease to exist as a class. The overall goal of the communes was to mitigate disparities between urban and rural areas, workers and peasants, and mental and manual labor, a goal that Stalin had singled out in 1952 as a prerequisite for the realization of communism.

Affected by the zeal of the Great Leap Forward, the rural communes were organized with unprecedented speed in accordance with the popular belief that they would bring about ownership by the whole people very soon, or would even permit China to enter communism immediately. Under this impetus, the local cadres frequently adopted a variety of radical measures. First, the commune administration confiscated all private property, including the small private plots, existing private consumer stores, houses, bank deposits, domestic animals, poultry, and other items. Second, the system of distribution combined wages with supplies of goods, or, as the Communists proclaimed to the Chinese peasants, from thenceforth everyone could eat without payment. Third, the leadership advocated that the communes follow three working principles, namely, that they organize along military lines, work as if fighting a battle, and live in a collective way. Commune members were organized as a worker-army to engage in shock-tactic methods of production. In many places, peasants and workers "fought" round the clock, eating and sleeping beside the fields. Fourth, the family was regarded as an obstacle to be eradicated as soon as possible. Many local cadres seized and melted down all private cooking equipment and forced the peasants to eat their meals in the public mess halls. Children were placed in communal schools, and women were ordered to enter the labor force. Fifth, immediately after the establishment of rural communes, federations of communes that included whole counties were established in several provinces. Each unit contained about a half million members. At the end of September 1958, statistics covering thirteen provinces indicated that there were already ninety-four such large communes.[14]

These radical policies received official approbation. On August 29, 1958, an enlarged Politburo meeting passed a resolution stating that the people's communes were the "logical result of the march of events" and were based on the "ever-rising political consciousness of a half billion peasants." The resolution approved the formation of the county confederations of communes and the seizure of private plots. It stipulated that each commune would first embrace a *xiang*, comprising about 2,000 peasant households or more; then, as the number of units grew, 2,000 county federations would be formed. It also indicated that private plots of land should be turned over to collective management during the merger of coperatives. Although the Central Committee admitted that the communes were still socialist in nature, it confidently pointed out in the resolution that the communes already contained "some elements of ownership by the people as a whole" and predicted a steady growth of such elements. The Politburo foresaw completion of the transition to complete ownership by the whole people in three or four years in some places and in five or six years or more in other places.[15]

In seeking to implement the August 29 Politburo resolution on people's communes, the local cadres continued and even intensified their radical policies. The official organ of the State Planning Commission, *Jihua jingji* [Planned economy], published a series of articles revealing that several communes were preparing to enter communism by 1963.[16]

The immediate result was turmoil and even sabotage in the rural districts. Zhou Enlai disclosed in a report of August 1959 that the work of reaping, threshing, gathering, and storing the 1958 autumn harvest had been so poorly done that a great part of the crops had perished.[17] Although Zhou's report blamed the shortage of agricultural labor for the waste of crops, it could not be denied that peasant sabotage was the underlying factor.

Recognizing the prevailing rural discontent, the CCP Politburo convened in Zhengzhou, November 2–10, 1958, but that meeting and a subsequent enlarged meeting of CCP provincial first secretaries failed to remedy the situation. Nor was any positive policy adjustment forthcoming until the Resolution on Some Questions Concerning the People's Communes was adopted by the CCP Eighth Central Committee at its Sixth Plenum on December 10, 1958, in Wuhan.

That plenum made four major decisions. First, the Chinese Communists reaffirmed their belief that the commune was the best form for realizing the transition from collective ownership to ownership by the whole people, as well as for the subsequent transition from socialism to communism. But the CCP Central Committee admitted that fifteen to twenty or more years would be needed for the first stage of transition. Even then, the communes would remain socialist in nature, and the principle "from each according to his ability and to each according to his work" would prevail.

Second, commune members would be allowed to retain their means of livelihood as private property and to engage in small domestic sideline occupations, on the condition that these did not harm collective production. Similarly, although the free supply-wage system for income distribution was retained, the portion of wages paid according to work performed was given first place in order to promote individual incentive. The peasants were also promised reasonable freedom of choice within the framework of the free supply system and were guaranteed twelve hours daily for meals, sleep, and recreation.

Third, the system of unified leadership and management on separate levels was enforced. Thus, the communal administrative machinery generally consisted of the commune management committee, the production brigade, and the production team. The commune management committee, somewhat similar to the *xiang* government, was to exercise control over the whole commune and to be responsible for its profits and losses. The production brigades, based on the former advanced cooperatives, were to be the basic accounting units. The production teams, under the jurisdiction of the production brigades, were the basic-level organizations in the rural communes.

Fourth, the CCP Central Committee reiterated its policy of merging the communes in a county. The committee was forced to declare, however, that the complicated situation in the cities prohibited any rapid establishment of urban communes. To compensate for that fact, rural communes were urged to engage in industry "in a big way."

Although popular resistance to radical policies had forced the government to grant concessions, the government expected that discontent would persist. Thus, the Wuhan resolution also called for a large-scale checkup campaign between December 1958 and April 1959 in every province, municipality, and autonomous region. Party secretaries were charged with organizing thousands of cadres to conduct the inspections.

Despite these measures of the winter of 1958, peasant resentment remained almost universal. Rebellious activities–work slowdowns, the slaughter of livestock, attacks on cadres, and damage to public property–became conspicuous.[18] In February 1959, the CCP Central Committee again met in Zhengzhou to formulate further revisions of the commune system. The resultant policy, approved by the CCP Eighth Central Committee's Seventh Plenum in April 1959 in Shanghai, marked the beginning of a new stage for the rural communes.

## THE EVOLUTIONARY PROCESS

After the April 1959 meeting, the Party implemented a series of major concessions to the peasants. The first provided for the return of small plots to commune members. As before, each member was allowed a plot on which to raise vegetables or pigs, but the total was not to exceed 5 percent of the commune's lands. At the same time, Deng Zihui, director of the Department of Rural Work of the CCP Central Committee, publicly acknowledged such defects in the public mess halls as inadequate facilities, waste of grain, and time lost by the peasants in having to walk long distances for meals.[19] Beginning with the 1959 summer harvest, grain rations were distributed to individual households instead of to the public dining halls.

Meanwhile, the CCP Central Committee abandoned the practice of seeking the federation of all communes within a county and the policy of encouraging the development of communal industry. Due to critical manpower shortages, the government ordered that 80 percent of all rural labor power be assigned to agricultural production. The labor power used for commune-run industry was not to exceed 2 percent.[20] Since those two measures had originally been regarded as a means of promoting the transition to ownership by the whole people, their abandonment indicated that the Chinese Communists had lost confidence in their ability to accomplish that transition within the foreseeable future.

The most basic revision formulated at the February Zhengzhou meeting was the introduction of the new system called "the three-level ownership system with the production brigade as the basis." This system was not publicized until the Eighth Plenum of the Eighth CCP Central Committee in August 1959, in Lushan, Jiangxi Province. The new resolution declared that "the right of ownership at the level of the production brigade is basic and the right of ownership at the communal level is only partial. The production teams, too, should have a small portion of ownership."[21] Consequently, the function of the commune level was curtailed drastically. Instead of being merely a subordinate unit, the production brigade was given authority to operate independently, both for administration and production management. The production brigade became independent in its accounting system and exercised control over its production teams. Crop arrangements, production targets, and technical measures were decided upon only after consultation among the production brigades and teams. The commune management committee was limited to making recommendations and to any necessary balancing or adjusting but it could not make direct arrangements or interfere with the production brigades' general plan.

The system of distribution was also revised. The commune was no longer allowed to seize any percentage of the public welfare fund retained by the brigade and was allowed to take over only a small part of the general reserve fund. Similarly, whereas peasants had received about 50–80 percent of their income in the form of food and some other necessities, and only a small portion in wages, under the new system, 70 percent of the disposable income would be distributed in the form of wages, with higher payments going to those performing the most work.[22] The great appeal of free meals for all commune members had become untenable. Since the brigade had become an independent unit, economic relations between brigades and their commune assumed the form of a commodity exchange. Therefore, the rural fairs, which had been banned with the establishment of the commune system, were reopened in 1959.

When the Central Committee adopted the new ownership system in August 1959, allowing the brigade to retain basic ownership for five years was seen as a temporary concession. Nevertheless, according to the Canton *Nanfang ribao* [Southern daily] of September 16, 1960, the Central Committee decided to maintain the system until 1965. But continuing peasant recalcitrance and declining agricultural production forced the government to make further concessions. An official report in the summer of 1960 revealed that peasants had destroyed the crops on about 10 percent of the arable land during the spring sowing that year. In Shandong Province, one-third of the paddy fields were overrun with weeds.[23] Another official report testified that the death rate for newborn pigs in the same period was as high as 50 percent. Peasant subversion was the main source of the disaster.

The drop in agricultural production and rising peasant resentment led to the first open split within the top Communist leadership. At the Lushan meeting, Defense Minister Peng Dehuai had attacked Mao's policy on the communes and the Great Leap in a 10,000-word letter addressed to the chairman but distributed to all participants. Peng characterized the commune as "petty bourgeois fanaticism" and endorsed many peasants' complaints that the introduction of communes was "too early, too fast, and too rude." Besides, he estimated that the waste in the backyard furnace campaign for the steel industry in 1958–1959 had reached 2 billion yuan (or approximately $800 million at the official rate of exchange).[24] Although Mao ousted Marshal Peng from his position as defense minister, the Lushan meeting marked the beginning of the precipitous decline in Mao's prestige and influence. In 1960–1961, a rival camp rallied under Liu Shaoqi and proposed a series of measures to reform the commune system.

China's agricultural crisis worsened in 1960. As a consequence, the government banned the principle of egalitarianism in income distribution and sanctioned the contract between the brigade and the teams under the "four fixes and three guarantees" system. This arrangement allowed the brigade to own land, draft animals, and farm implements and to assign them and manpower to the teams for use. The brigade was to entrust output quotas, cost, and manpower questions to the teams, thus virtually making the team the decision-making unit for determining labor and distribution. In March 1961, the Party Central Committee formulated the Draft Regulations Concerning the Rural Communes. This directive again banned coercive measures, discouraged industrial undertakings, and allowed suspension of the mess halls. It was then revised and finally put into effect in September 1962.[25] Commonly referred to as the Sixty-Point Charter for Agriculture, the directive made further changes in the rural communes.

First, the size of the communes was drastically curtailed. In September 1958, China's 120 million rural households were organized into 26,000 communes with an average size of 4,615 households. The number of the communes was reduced to 24,000 in September 1959, and the average size rose to 5,000 households. By October 1963, the number had risen sharply to 74,000, with a corresponding reduction in size to only one-third of that in 1959. The new communes averaged 1,622 households, which was approximately the size of the traditional marketing community as estimated by G. William Skinner.[26] Each commune, on the average, comprised about ten brigades and sixty to seventy teams. The size of the average brigade was equivalent to that of the former advanced cooperatives, and the size of the team was equivalent to that of the former elementary cooperative.

With the adjustment of the scale of operation, a three-level system of commune ownership was implemented, with the team as the basic accounting unit. The commune management committee became essentially the political-administrative unit linking the state and the locality; the brigade became the coordinating unit linking the commune management committee and the team; and the team became the basic unit for accounting and production. The commune owned only small enterprises, motor vehicles, mills, and farm-tool repair shops. The brigade owned some farm implements and facilities, but the team owned virtually all the important means of production, including land, draft animals, and tools. Without approval of the *xian* government, neither the commune nor the brigade could freely appropriate a team's property.

With these changes, the team became the autonomous unit for distribution and accounting. After computing the gross output, the team set aside grain for the agricultural tax and the unified procurement grain to be delivered to the state. From the balance, the team then deducted production expenses, reserve grain, reserve funds (public accumulation), and welfare funds. After setting aside the share for the state and the collective, the team then distributed the remaining grain and cash among its members.

As the commune and the brigade lost their importance, the government reaffirmed the role of private plots and sideline occupations as component parts of the economy of rural communes.[27] The government encouraged peasants to use their spare time to develop private plots and subsidiary production and allowed them to retain the income derived from those pursuits.

The timetable for the achievement of communism was again extended from a remote target to an indefinite goal. The Hunan Party Committee declared that the transition from brigade to commune ownership would take a fairly long time. Even then, prevailing conditions would determine when the system of ownership by the whole people could be established.[28]

To stimulate peasant initiative, the system of "three guarantees and one reward" was tried on an experimental basis during this period. The team allocated a strip of land or a piece of work either to small groups or to individuals, holding them responsible for production results. The recipients guaranteed output, time, and costs ("three guarantees"); they were to receive a bonus from the team if their output exceeded the assigned quota ("one reward"). During 1960–1961, many teams even gave output quotas to individual households. In the second half of 1961, as the national economy approached collapse, a set of more liberal guidelines, called *san zi yi bao* ("three selfs and one guarantee"), reiterated the gist of the directives, but also ordered that all communal land be distributed among individual households as "responsibility land," on which each household would guarantee to produce a given amount, or quota.

The proposal caused bitter debates within the Party. In a September 1962 Party Central Committee meeting, Mao warned his colleagues never to forget the class struggle. In March 1963, he drafted a Resolution on Some Problems in Current Rural Work to launch a new Socialist Education Campaign in the rural sector, but his proposals were apparently not fully implemented. In the following two years, while the two contending power groups prepared for a showdown, there was an unstable equilibrium in the rural areas, with one group of leaders favoring a continuation of the liberal policy and another group trying to restore ideological commitment. The conflict culminated in the outbreak of the Cultural Revolution.

During the early stage of the Cultural Revolution (1966–1969), as the ideologists gained control of the Party center, the commune system underwent another series of changes. First of all, the size of the communes increased. Between 1968 and 1970, mergers reduced the number of communes from about 75,000 in 1968 to 51,000 in 1970.[29] The average commune in 1970 had about 2,900 households, 13,000 persons, and a labor force of 5,400, as compared with 1,600 households in 1963.

Second, revolutionary committees were established on the commune and brigade levels, with an equivalent group on the team level that replaced the original management committees. The commune revolutionary committee consisted of cadres, poor and lower-middle peasants, and demobilized soldiers or militia. It consolidated power by combining the roles of the Party committee, the management committee, and the military units.

Third, the poor and lower-middle peasants became the main force in the commune. They not only dominated the revolutionary committees, but were also entrusted to supervise the rural schools. In rural finance and trade, the poor and lower-middle peasants gained controlling power in the supply and marketing cooperatives as well as in the credit cooperatives. The radicals condemned many former directors of communes and brigades as followers of Liu Shaoqi and subjected them to brutal struggles.

Fourth, in many areas, private plots were confiscated, sideline occupations were banned, and farm markets were closed. Some communes changed from three-level to two-level ownership by making production brigades the accounting unit instead of teams. In income distribution, many communes abandoned the "labor base–point" system and adopted a system initiated by the Dazhai Brigade in 1963 called "model work point with self-report and public evaluation." Under this system, the brigade's work-point recorder registered each member's performance and the number of days he or she had worked. At the end of the month, the brigade selected a model peasant, who had had the best work performance and political attitude, and decided how many points the model worker deserved for a day. Using this pacesetter as a measuring rod, members evaluated their own work and politics and reported how many points they thought they deserved. All the members discussed each member's claim and finally decided awards case by case. This system, designed to overcome the peasants' obsession with work points, had detrimental effects on motivation, since political activism always counted more than productivity.[30]

The changes resulted in rural unrest and agricultural stagnation. In order to contain extremism and avoid the errors of 1958–1959, the draft state constitution of 1970 reaffirmed the three-level system of ownership, with the team as the basic unit. In February 1971, Mao issued a directive prohibiting any alteration of team management.[31] In December 1971, the CCP Central Committee issued a Directive on Problems of Distribution in the People's Commune. The new document supplemented the Sixty-Point Charter of 1962 and reemphasized the need to avoid "absolute egalitarianism." It set forth several principles for commune management:

1. correct handling of the relationship between collective accumulation and individual payment
2. effective measures for grain distribution
3. allocation of work and income on the basis of "from each according to his ability, to each according to his work"
4. self-reliance
5. implementation of the policy directive to "take grain as the key link and ensure an all-round development"[32]

Since 1972, the rural commune system has gradually returned to the pattern that prevailed in the 1962–1965 period. The basic configuration of the commune has been continued, but its size has been enlarged.

Since the autumn harvest of 1978, a new system called "five items fixed and one reward" has been in effect in Guangdong, Sichuan, and several other provinces. Although the production team still serves as the basic unit of operation and distribution, it is divided into many work groups of several to a dozen households. The team assigns labor, land, output, workpoints, and production costs (the "five items fixed") to the work groups, together with bonuses for exceeding the planned output ("one reward"). Within the work groups, fixed quotas are further laid down for each member who will receive remuneration according to the fixed quotas or—after assessment—according to the hours he or she has worked. This system was intended to establish a responsibility system linking reward to output so as to correct chaotic commune management. During the winter of 1978, some 39.5 percent of the production teams in Guangdong set up this new system. When the CCP Eleventh Central Committee convened its Third Plenum in December 1978, it adopted the new Sixty Articles on Rural Communes and affirmed that work contracts could be assigned to work groups, with remuneration linked to output.[33]

The system was hailed by the Guangdong Party Committee as representing a step forward in the standardization of commune management. However, it caused some new problems. First, after the new system was put into effect, work groups within a team competed with each other for draft animals, manure, and manpower. Peasants began to demand that the teams be divided into permanent work groups so that each group would control its own land and draft animals. Moreover, during the summer distribution of 1979, many work groups distributed the harvest among themselves, thus violating the principle of having the team handle products, income, and distribution in a unified way. In Guangdong and Sichuan, some teams broke down into work groups.[34] The situation warranted an editor's warning in the *Renmin ribao:*

> In fixing work quotas on a group basis and computing remuneration on the basis of output, it is imperative . . . that the production team should conduct the economic accounting, carry out distribution and allocate the labor force in a unified way. A change of ownership or disintegration of a production team could never be permitted since it would result in a situation where groups scramble for land, labor force, draft animals, farm tools, water and fertilizers. Also, the collective economy will be undermined.[35]

Despite these new warnings, the form of management in the rural communes continued moving toward a more personal responsibility system. Official statistics indicate that by the end of 1980, 20 percent of China's peasant households were under the new system of fixing output quotas directly to each household. Although the team still served as the accounting unit, the plots of land were put under the management of individual households on a long-term basis. After harvesting, the peasants had to hand over to the team a fixed amount of their output for unified distribution but were allowed to retain any surplus over the quota assigned.[36] Table 4.2 summarizes the evolution of the rural commune system after 1958 in terms of size, organization, ownership, and distribution.

## ANATOMY OF A RURAL COMMUNE

The preceding survey of rural communes reveals a continuing oscillation between regimentation of the peasants and a more liberal policy. Of course, there is great variation across China in commune management and distribution patterns. Nevertheless, it may be useful to attempt to portray a typical commune today – its organization, management, incentive structure, distribution system, and private sector. The information in this section has been derived from various official documents published in recent years and from Frederick Crook's detailed study of communes, which is based on scattered reports of 1,400 communes in the 1963–1974 period.[37]

### *Organizational Structure*

A typical commune in 1980 consisted of three levels of organization: the commune, the production brigades under it, and the production

Table 4.2
Evolution of the Rural Commune, 1958–1980

| Period | Organization | Planning Unit | Number of Communes | Ownership | Income Distribution |
|---|---|---|---|---|---|
| April 1958 through April 1959 | Three Levels<br>a. Commune management committee<br>b. Administrative division (or large production brigade)<br>c. Production brigade | Commune as the functional organ | 26,000 (Sept. 1958) including: 500,000 brigades and 3 million teams | a. All property owned by commune<br>b. Large brigade as accounting unit<br>c. No private plots allowed | a. Income distributed to each laborer<br>b. Half supply and half wages<br>c. Year-end settlement |
| April 1959 through December 1960 | Three levels<br>a. Commune management committee<br>b. Production brigade (equal to advanced cooperatives)<br>c. Production team (equal to elementary cooperatives) | Production brigade as the functional unit | 24,000 (Sept.1959) | a. Property owned by brigade<br>b. Brigade as accounting unit<br>c. Private plots allowed | a. Food distributed to households<br>b. 70% of income as wages<br>c. Year-end settlement |
| January 1961 through December 1966 | Three levels<br>a. Commune management committee<br>b. Production brigade<br>c. Production team | Production team as the functional unit | 74,000(Oct. 1963) | a. Property owned by team<br>b. Team as accounting unit<br>c. Private plots allowed | a. Food distributed to households<br>b. 70% of income distributed as wages<br>c. Year-end settlement |

Table 4.2 (continued)

| Period | Organization | Planning Unit | Number of Communes | Ownership | Income Distribution |
|---|---|---|---|---|---|
| January 1967 through December 1970 | Three Levels<br>a. Commune revolutionary committee<br>b. Production brigade<br>c. Production team | Production team as the functional unit<br><br>In some communes brigade as functional unit | 51,000 (1970) | a. Property owned by production team<br>b. Team as accounting unit; in some areas property owned by brigade with brigade as accounting unit<br>c. In some areas, private plots were abolished | a. Food distributed to households<br>b. Reappearance of mess halls in some areas<br>c. Year-end settlement |
| January 1971 through June 1978 | Three levels<br>a. Commune revolutionary committee<br>b. Production brigade<br>c. Production team | Production team as functional unit | 50,000 (1978) | a. Property owned by a team is managed by it. Brigade and commune also own some means of production<br>b. Team is basic accounting unit<br>c. Private plots allowed | a. Food distributed to households<br>b. "To each according to his work"<br>c. Year-end settlement |

| | | | | | |
|---|---|---|---|---|---|
| July 1978 through June 1980 | Three levels<br>a. Commune management committee<br>b. Production brigade<br>c. Production team | Production team as functional unit<br>But in many provinces land and labor are assigned to work groups under the team | 50,000 communes<br>680,000 brigades<br>4,800,000 teams<br>(Feb. 1979) | a. Team is basic accounting unit<br>b. Private plots allowed | a. Food distributed to households<br>b. Year-end settlement<br>c. Advance distribution of summer grains allowed |

Sources: Chu-yuan Cheng, Communist China's Economy, 1949-1962: Structural Changes and Crisis (South Orange, N.J.: Seton Hall University Press, 1963), pp. 52-53; "Some Basic Facts About China," China Reconstructs, January 1974, pp. 2-9; Frederick W. Crook, "The Commune System in the People's Republic of China 1963-74," in U.S. Congress, Joint Economic Committee, China: A Reassessment of the Economy (Washington, D.C.: Government Printing Office, 1975), pp. 366-409; China News Analysis (Hong Kong) No. 1124 (June 23, 1978); Foreign Broadcast Information Service, Daily Report, People's Republic of China, May 25, 1979, pp. P1-P2.

teams under each brigade. There were about 50,000 communes, 680,000 production brigades, and 4.8 million production teams in February 1979. As the number of peasant households increased from 120 million in the 1950s to 170 million in 1979, the average commune in 1979 had 14 production brigades and 96 production teams, with 3,400 households and 16,000 people.[38]

The number of brigades and teams varies widely from one commune to another. Some communes have only production brigades without production teams as subdivisions. In the great majority of the communes, however, the number of teams ranges from 55 to 275. In general, suburban communes are larger than rural communes. Crook's study indicates that rural communes have one-half to two-thirds fewer people than communes near the large urban centers. Although Crook's study found no set pattern concerning the relationship between communes and natural villages in China, many natural villages are associated either with brigades or with teams.[39] There are also cases where a single brigade contains a large number of villages. Such cases include a brigade in Fujian (75 villages), one in Guangxi (55 villages), Shanxi (44 villages), Henan (32 villages), and Jiangxi (20 villages).[40]

Each commune has a people's congress and an administrative committee, which serves as the administrative organ under the people's congress. According to the state constitution adopted by the Fifth National People's Congress in March 1978, the "People's congress and [the] revolutionary committees [changed to administrative committees in 1979] of the people's communes are organizations of political power at the grass-roots level, and are also leading organs of [the] collective economy."[41]

The people's congress is the highest organ of power in the commune. Its deputies are nominated through "democratic consultation" among the commune members and are elected by secret ballot for a term of two years. The function of the congress, apart from maintaining law and order, is to examine and approve the commune's economic plans, budget, and accounts.

A typical administrative committee is composed of a chairman, eight vice-chairmen, and twenty-four members, all elected by the commune people's congress. Many functions of government are performed by units in the commune that correspond to units on the national level. Thus, for national defense, the commune has a military affairs office under the *xian* (county) military affairs department, which takes charge of militia training and conscription for the national armed forces. For public security, an officer from the county public security bureau is stationed in the commune to help maintain public order, protect the lives and property of the people, and investigate criminal cases. The commune mediation committee functions as a grass-roots judicial and civil affairs unit, handling disputes between members, complaints expressed in personal visits or letters, and also population and marriage registration.

The commune maintains scientific farming and veterinary stations, and the county bureau of agriculture and forestry sends people to disseminate knowledge on scientific farming, forestry and animal husbandry, and all kinds of agricultural extension services. In the field of finance and trade, the commune credit cooperative handles the work of the state bank in the countryside. It takes deposits and issues loans to the commune or its subdivisions. The commune supply and marketing cooperative, linked with the All-China Federation of Supply and Marketing Cooperatives, sells farm tools and articles of daily use, purchases for the state the products of agriculture and sideline occupations from commune members, and provides instructions for the use of new farm tools. In education and cultural activities, the commune's education office supervises senior middle schools within the commune and maintains a hospital, partly with its own funds and partly with funds from the county health bureau. A commune cultural center organizes mass cultural activities and provides some professional guidance to amateurs.[42]

Although the Party committee is not a part of the commune administration, it is the most powerful institution in the countryside. Party committees interpret policy decisions made in Beijing, adapt policies to local conditions when necessary and ensure that policies and production plans are implemented. As a rule, responsible persons on the Party committees also serve on commune administrative committees.

The brigade operates small industries and other undertakings that are beyond a team's scope. Among these are small water conservation works, tractor stations, farm machinery repair shops, orchards, and workshops for processing agricultural and sideline products. The brigade also runs primary and junior middle schools. The average brigade has approximately seven production teams, about 240 households, and roughly 1,100 persons. It cultivates, on the average, 336 acres of land.[43] Each brigade also has a congress, an administrative committee, and a chairman elected by the congress. The Party branch secretary in the brigade usually is the most powerful leader on the brigade level and concurrently serves in the brigade administration.

The team is the grass-roots organization of the commune and the basic accounting unit. Agricultural production in China is managed by and its proceeds distributed mainly through the team. Land, draft animals, and farm machinery are owned mainly by the teams. As an independent accounting unit, the team manages its own income and distribution and bears its own profit or loss. The number of production teams was estimated at 5 million in 1980, as in 1958. On the average, a team has about thirty-three households, encompassing approximately 160 persons, and cultivates roughly forty-nine acres of land.[44]

Each team has a congress and an administrative committee. It has a team leader and a deputy leader, an accountant or a work-point recorder, a militia platoon leader, a spare-time wire-broadcast repairman, and a custodian to care for the team's tools, animals, and granary.[45] No other institution in China so deeply affects the well-being of the rural population as the production team within each commune.

*Management System*

By 1962, the team had replaced the commune as the basic unit for organizing production. Unlike the commune in early periods, which purported to manage production through mass mobilization, the post-1961 team, following the Sixty-Point Charter for Agriculture, gradually displayed a more stable and autonomous management. There are three types of management arrangements in the fields of production, labor, and finance.

With respect to production, each team receives the annual production targets from the *xian* (these are conveyed through the commune and the brigade), and then draws up its annual plan in accordance with local conditions. The team decides how to use land, manpower, draft animals, and farm tools; it determines when to plow and plant; and it selects seeds and fertilizer. The overall plan must be presented to the team congress for final approval. The team then sends the plan to the brigade and the commune for additional suggestions.[46]

In labor management, all peasants, including women and youngsters, are included in the team's labor plan. Every year, members in the production team must determine by "democratic deliberation" the basic labor day of each person, including the work to be done, its quality, the time needed for each task, and the work points allocated to each job. This is called "fixed-quota management."[47] A 1978 report stated that a man should work 330 days a year and a woman 300 and any worker should ask for leave before being absent for illness or business reasons.[48]

Teams have adopted two principal methods for allotting the collective work among their members: assigning work and fixing work. In grain production and other major farm tasks, the work is assigned to work groups on a rotating basis. Each group is assigned a total allotment of work points for the day, and at the end of the day, each member gets a share of the points according to the quantity and quality of work done. For minor tasks, the work is given to a small group of three or four persons, who often retain permanent responsibility for the job.

In addition to collective work, the team sets aside one or two days every three months for "basic construction," which should not require more than 3 percent of a member's annual workdays. If such work extends beyond that limit, the team's wages are paid from the team's reserve funds. For small-scale construction, such as repairing roads and dikes, the peasants receive work points as they do for other farm work.

In financial management, in principle, all expenditures must be scrupulously regulated. Any purchase should be discussed by the team congress. The accountant and cashier can theoretically veto any expenditure that the regulations prohibit. The team's grain, tools, and other materials are under the control of the custodian. The team chief supervises the financial and custodial operation but, by regulation, does not directly control cash or goods. Neither the commune nor the brigade can meddle in a team's finances, except for auditing purposes. To prevent embezzlement, the team's accountant and cashier keep two identical sets of books for cash and goods. Only when the figures in both books are identical is an outlay made. But in practice, many team chiefs have collaborated with the financial officers and taken public funds for personal spending.[49]

Team members are motivated to work through a combination of material and nonmaterial incentives. According to Party ideology, nonmaterial incentives will become preponderant in the long run, but in the short run, material incentives have received the most attention. Nonmaterial incentives include labor discipline codes, selecting and honoring "model farmers" for outstanding work, and inducing teams to engage in competition with, or emulation of, each other for medals, red flags, or other symbols of achievement. Extensively used during the initial commune period, this sort of incentive has come to be regarded as rhetoric and has lost its stimulation effect. The effects of material incentives on workers' motivations have been influenced by several important factors. Among these are the relative shares of income distributed among the state, the team, and the household; the absolute amount of income allocated to individual households; the correspondence between rewards and work performance; and the availability and price of consumer goods. Those factors, in turn, are affected by the Party's rural policy and by general economic conditions.

Although patterns have varied from period to period and from place to place, scattered reports indicate that the share of the total collective income distributed to the peasants has ranged between 44 and 57 percent. In 1966, the official organ, *Peking Review,* published figures on the income distribution of a team near Beijing (see Table 4.3). In 1972, another official publication revealed how the Chiaoli Production Team of the Teching Commune in Zhejiang Province had distributed its income for the year 1971 (see Table 4.4). It is difficult to say how representative the figures shown in Table 4.3 and Table 4.4 are for China as a whole. Their citation in official publications suggests, however, that they are typical cases. If so, team members receive roughly half the team's total income.

Table 4.3
Distribution of 33,950 Yuan Income in 1966
by the Second Team of Baqing Brigade, Yangtan Commune

| Expenditure | Amount in Yuan | Percentage |
|---|---|---|
| Production expense | 13,124 | 38.6 |
| Agricultural tax | 2,207 | 6.5 |
| Reserve fund | 1,697 | 5.0 |
| Welfare fund | 330 | 1.0 |
| Reserve grain | 1,488 | 4.4 |
| Distribution to members | 15,104 | 44.5 |
| Total | 33,950 | 100.0 |

Source: Peking Review 9:13 (March 25, 1966), p. 16.

Most teams distribute income on the basis of a member's labor contribution to production. The prevailing system is called the "labor-day work-payment" system. It measures the amount and quality of work done in terms of labor days (or work points; one labor day usually equals ten work points). At the end of the agricultural year, the sum of the labor days credited to all farmers and team staff is divided into the income available for distribution to team members in order to obtain the value of one labor day or one work point. The income of each member can then be determined simply by multiplying the figure for one labor day or work point by the number of labor days or work points the individual has accumulated. Under this system, how to measure each farmer's work became the central issue. Crook's study lists seven methods of measurement:

*Equality.* All those who showed up in the field received the same number of labor days. Those who did not appear earned no labor days.

Table 4.4
Distribution of 87,978 Yuan Income in 1971
by the Chiaoli Production Team

| Expenditure | Amount in Yuan | Percentage |
|---|---|---|
| Production & management costs | 21,427 | 24.4 |
| Agricultural tax | 3,386 | 3.8 |
| Public accumulation | 13,068 | 14.9 |
| Distribution to members | 50,097 | 56.9 |
| Total | 87,978 | 100.0 |

Source: "How Chiaoli Production Team Distributes Its Income," China Reconstructs 21:9 (September 1972), pp. 26-29.

*Assessment.* Members periodically assessed each other's work for some period of time and determined the number of labor days each deserved.

*Fixed rate, fixed assessment.* Members were classified into different grades according to their technical skills and capacity for work, and basic work points were attached to each grade. At the end of each workday, those who had worked received their prescribed number of basic work points.

*Fixed rate, flexible assessment.* All workers were assigned to a single grade, and an assessment meeting evaluated the work done by members and determined how many work points each person should receive.

*Piece rate.* Labor days due each person were calculated on the basis of labor norms set up by the team. The work completed by each member was then rated by comparison.

*Labor contracts to individuals and households.* Households were assigned responsibility for cultivating a fixed area of land or husbanding a fixed number of animals. The team guaranteed the households a certain number of labor days for completing production targets and awarded a fixed percentage of output in excess of the targets. This method prevailed in the 1962–1964 period but was condemned as a return to individualism and banned in 1965.

*Labor production contracts to households.* Teams made contracts with individuals or households to complete tasks within a given time period, at a stated quality, in return for a predetermined number of labor days.[50]

In recent years, remuneration for agricultural labor has basically fallen into two categories: the piecework work-point system and the time-rate work-point system. There are two variants in the piecework system: (1) an individual piecework work-point system under which remuneration is based on individual quotas and (2) a collective piecework work-point system under which the team is given a quota to meet, but its work is evaluated on an individual basis.[51]

No matter which system is adopted, there are always contradictions between egalitarianism and incentives, between emphasis on labor productivity and emphasis on collective spirit. None of the methods can simultaneously satisfy both values. Until recently, the allocation of work points in many communes was determined on the basis of the following criteria.

1. the degree of love for the collective
2. alertness to the common good
3. readiness to carry out assignments
4. observance of labor discipline
5. level of exertion
6. attention to the quality of the product
7. precautions against wasting time and materials[52]

When the work-point assessment involved political criteria, there was always a tendency toward an egalitarian distribution of income. The result was peasants' indifference to collective work and attention to their small private plots.

*The Private Sector*

At present, the private sector is considered to be an integral part of the commune system. Article 7 of the 1978 state constitution stipulated, "Provided that the absolute predominance of the collective economy of the people's commune is ensured, commune members may farm small plots of land for personal needs, engage in limited household sideline production, and, in pastoral areas, they may also keep a limited number of livestock for personal needs."

Since earnings from the collective remain rather meager,[53] private plots and subisidary production have provided about 30 percent of peasants' income. In most teams, 5 percent of the arable land is allocated for private plots. According to Crook's study, each household is allowed to cultivate, on the average, about 300 square meters of land, which is a plot about 17.37 meters square.[54] Farmers generally use their plots to raise high-value products such as chicken, pigs, fruits, and vegetables and cash crops such as tobacco and castor bean seed. Therefore, the private 5 percent of the land generates about 10 percent of household income.[55]

Apart from cultivating a small private plot, each household also engages in some sideline occupation such as weaving, knitting, gathering medicinal herbs, and handicrafts. In 1978, one-quarter of the agricultural side products bought by the state commercial networks came from the private sector. An even higher proportion of state purchases of pigs, poultry, and eggs came from private households, which also provided almost all medicinal herbs.[56]

The private plots and subsidiary production have made the farm markets an indispensable institution for the private sector. The farm market is not a free market because it is subject to strict government regulation. Transactions are conducted mainly between commune members. A small number of city residents and city production team members are also permitted to attend, but public agencies and enterprises are not allowed to enter the farm market. Buyers may not resell their purchases, and speculation is strictly forbidden. Commodities for sale in the farm market are confined to sundries and nonstaple products. Teams may sell surplus produce of some important crops in the farm markets only after they have fulfilled their state procurement quotas. Peasants sell in the farm market in order to obtain cash for their own purchases. No exploitation is involved.[57]

Although the private sector (including production from private plots and sideline occupations) provides only 30 percent of farmers' income, the farmers fully control this part of their effort and its output and can count on it to supplement their collective income. For years, the private sector has been the touchstone of official rural policy. When radicals were in control of the Party, as in 1958–1959 and 1966–1969, the private sector was either completely prohibited or under deliberate restrictions. In many communes, private plots were confiscated and restored three or four times between 1958 and 1968. Since the fall of the Gang of Four in 1976, private plots have been justified as being "in accordance with the present objective economic conditions and as the common request of the vast mass of [commune] members."[58] The Chinese peasants are now being told that household sideline occupations "not only can increase social products, improve the commune members' livelihood but also be of benefit to the state, the individual, and the collective."[59] The new policies suggest that the private sector may last for quite a long period.

## APPRAISAL OF THE COMMUNE SYSTEM

In its first twenty or so years of existence, the Chinese rural commune system has had some successes and some failures and has confronted several unsolvable contradictions. The main merit of the system stems from its ability to mobilize rural resources, especially labor, for large-scale construction projects such as water conservation and hill terracing. The system has demonstrated its capacity to weather floods, droughts, and earthquakes, which would have been calamities for independent farmers. With an average of 15,000 people and a labor force of 6,000 at its disposal, a commune can make concerted efforts to cope with the unexpected.

The commune system can also take credit for the mushrooming of rural industry, which has become the main source of rural capital accumulation. An official survey reported in 1977 that some 90 percent of the communes and 70 percent of the brigades ran industrial enterprises of some sort. By October 1977, communes and brigades had set up 1,090,000 enterprises employing a total of 17 million peasants. The value of their output in 1976 amounted to 23.1 percent of the combined output value of communes, brigades, and teams. In some areas, the percentage was as high as 30 to 40 percent.[60] In 1976, according to statistics from fourteen provinces, capital accumulation from the enterprises totaled 3.6 billion yuan, of which 1.3 billion yuan were allocated for rural development. In Hebei Province, for instance, the capital accumulation from commune and brigade enterprises for agricultural development in 1976 was eleven times the state allocation.[61] Official statements have held out the hope that commune accumulation could finance the grand plan for agricultural mechanization.[62]

The commune system can also be credited with a more than 60 percent increase in irrigated farmland, over the past two decades.[63] Nearly one-half of China's cultivated land is now irrigated, compared to less than 10 percent in the United States, the Soviet Union, or most European countries.[64]

Despite these achievements, China's agricultural production under the commune system has not responded to the increase in large-scale farmland capital investment. On January 24, 1979, the Party organ, *Renmin ribao,* assessed the situation as follows:

> China's present agricultural status indicates that its rural productive forces still lag behind; manual operation predominates; labor productivity remains very low; only a small number of marketable products is offered. . . . The rural economy is dull and inefficient and the capabilities for expanding reproduction are small. In some places, agricultural production has been stalled for a long time; the peasants' rations have been tightened and their incomes are still meagre. This serious damage is the result of interference and sabotage of Lin Biao and the "gang of four." But the drawbacks and mistakes in our past work should also be held responsible, namely, the trend toward effecting the transition to Communism prematurely, a work style characterized by exaggeration, improper procurement of products and arbitrary orders.[65]

The U.S. government has estimated that during the twenty years after the establishment of communes, Chinese agricultural production grew at only 2 percent per year. Total grain output increased from 191 million tons in 1957, the year before the establishment of the communes, to 305 million tons in 1978, representing an average annual growth rate of 2.1 percent, which barely kept pace with the population growth. Under the policy of "taking grain as the key link," however, the growth of grains was at the expense of other subsidiary foods, including fish, meat, and edible oils. Consequently, peasants in China probably got fewer calories and less protein per day after communization than before it. Even per capita food grain production registered a decline between 1958 and 1970 and showed only a moderate increase after 1978 (see Table 4.5).

The inadequate growth in agricultural production cannot be attributed to any single factor (see Chapter 12), but the commune system has been a contributing factor because of its violation of the autonomy of the production teams by higher-level organizations. Production teams have been officially recognized as the basic units responsible for production and distribution, yet their right to self-

Table 4.5
China's Agricultural Indicators, 1957-1979

| | 1957 | 1958 | 1965 | 1970 | 1975 | 1978 | 1979 |
|---|---|---|---|---|---|---|---|
| Agricultural production index (1957=100)[a] | 100 | 107 | 101 | 126 | 148 | 156 | 160 |
| Total foodgrain output (million metric tons)[a] | 191 | 206 | 194 | 243 | 284 | 305 | 332 |
| Cotton production (million metric tons)[b] | 1.6 | 1.7 | 1.6 | 2.0 | 2.4 | 2.2 | 2.2 |
| Hogs (million head)[c] | 146 | n.a. | 160 | 196 | n.a. | 301 | 320 |
| Per capita food grain (kilograms)[a] | 294 | 310 | 255 | 283 | 295 | 302 | 307 |

Note: n.a. - data not available

Sources: (a) U.S. Central Intelligence Agency, China: Major Economic Indicators (Washington, D.C., 1980), p. 1. These figures are not identical with those in Table 12.2, which are Chinese official statistics. (b) From Table 12.3. (c) Henry J. Groen and James A. Kilpatrick, "China's Agricultural Production," in U.S. Congress, Joint Economic Committee, Chinese Economy Post-Mao (Washington, D.C.: Government Printing Office, 1978), p. 649.

determination has never been respected by communes or local governments. Many government officers have considered the teams as purely administrative units appended to their higher organs, "like the beads on the abacus that can only move by manipulation from above."[66] Communes and local governments have often formulated production plans that were divorced from reality; they have embarked on big construction projects by requisitioning manpower, materials, and products from the teams; they have also procured excessive grains and made compulsory purchases of farm and sideline products. The violations were so rampant that in July 1978, the CCP Central Committee issued two directives aimed at reducing the needless burdens thrust on the peasants by rural cadre leadership and placed constraints on cadre behavior. These directives reflected conditions in Xiangxiang County in Hunan and Xunyi County in Shaanxi and were intended to dramatize the concern of the central government for the peasants' welfare.[67]

In short, the commune system continues to suffer from the three basic contradictions of the collectives mentioned at the outset of this chapter—between the communal economy and the private sector, between rich and poor communes, and between the communes and the state. Like other collective agricultural organizations in the Soviet Union and Eastern Europe, the commune system has two fundamental defects: insufficient incentives to spur the peasants to produce and inadequacies in management.

The contradiction between the collective economy and the private sector involves the question of incentives to motivate the peasants, and problems with motivation arise from several sources. First, the peasants' rewards do not always correspond to their work performances; second, the peasants are uncertain as to what share of the collective income they will receive; and third, even if the peasants increase their output, their income may decline if the communal cadres are wasteful and extravagant.

A number of factors affect the motivation to work hard. First, under the current distribution system, most staples—food grains, cotton cloth, and edible oil—are strictly rationed, and additional quantities cannot be earned by extra effort. Available supplies are generally evenly divided, and the differences in income among team members are rather small. Second, a notable lack of objective criteria in work-point assessment can also hurt motivation. During the late 1960s and early 1970s, the principle of politics taking command was in effect, and work points were often given on the basis of political posture instead of productivity. Third, since the peasants have the last claim on the team's income, any change in the government's tax and procurement requirements, or any increase in production costs and capital investment, can affect the peasants' share. Fourth, the autonomy of the production team has not been respected by communes and brigades, and many financial burdens have been gradually shifted to the teams. The situation is aggravated when commune and team leaders are corrupt or extravagant. As a result, a considerable number of communes have increased their agricultural output year after year, yet the income of the commune members has either remained stagnant or declined. For instance, in Jiangsu Province, where agricultural output achieved the highest annual growth rate in China (4.4 percent in the 1960s and 5.4 percent during 1970–1978), per capita income for Jiangsu peasants in 1966–1976 rose by less than 1 yuan ($0.6) per annum.[68] In many provinces, the peasants' income actually declined, as was the case in Yunnan, Sichuan, Anhui, and Nei Monggol.[69]

When compared with other farm systems, the Chinese peasants on the rural communes are in a very unfavorable position. They do not have the guaranteed wages and fringe benefits of state farm employees and factory workers, but they do have to assume responsibility for their production and investment. By the same token, they do not have the freedom of the individual proprietors, who can fully dispose of the fruits of their endeavors. Small wonder that many Chinese peasants have lost interest in collective work and devote more time and energy to their private plots and sideline occupations. Moreover, the existence of the private sector constitutes a constant threat to the collective economy. When peasants derive an increasing proportion of their income from the private sector, their desire to work for the collective sector diminishes. The contradiction between individual interest and collective interest that permeated the agricultural cooperatives has not been solved in the communes.

Nor has the commune system succeeded in bridging the gap between rich and poor teams. The original idea in organizing the communes was to incorporate poor and rich collectives into a larger unit, thereby eliminating income differences. Under the current three-level ownership system, with production teams as the basic accounting unit, the 5 million small teams, are really responsible for the country's agricultural production and distribution instead of the 50,000 communes or 700,000 brigades. Because natural endowment and managerial capability differ considerably from one team to another, the gap between rich and poor teams has widened rather than narrowed. Rich teams can afford to purchase farm machinery and chemical fertilizer, which results in high output and income. According to official statistics, under the same water and soil conditions, a team employing machinery can raise output by 15 percent.[70] Poor teams, which lack the capability for investment, are subject to the law of diminishing returns. Their agricultural output has remained stagnant, peasant income has failed to increase, and a great number of households have had to rely on the state to supply a portion of their food grains. Official reports disclose that some 20 percent of the production teams, embracing 1 million units with 140 million people, were classified as "poor teams" in 1972.[71]

According to some Communist leaders, unless the commune changes the basic unit of accounting from the current three-level ownership system to one of two-level ownership, with the brigade as the accounting unit, farmland capital construction for the poor teams cannot be promoted. For this reason, Mao praised the Dazhai Brigade in Shanxi Province as a model for the nation. It abolished the teams in 1961 and returned private plots to the collective in 1963. Any attempt, however, to move the accounting unit from the team up to the large brigade or the commune level immediately encounters numerous difficulties in management and incentives. Such difficulties helped abort the ill-fated attempt during the 1958–1960 Great Leap to make the commune the basic accounting unit. The same sorts of difficulties helped abort a selective attempt to make the brigade the accounting unit in certain places during the Cultural Revolution. But so long as the team remains the basic accounting unit, the contradiction between poor and rich teams will remain unresolved.

Finally, the contradiction between the team and the state also persists. The state's goal is to maximize agricultural output and procurement while the team's goal is to maximize its income and retain as much of its food grain as possible. High output and procurement targets mean high taxes and delivery obligations, and less for team members. In a sense, the team leader is torn between the two obligations. The leader is an integral member of the team, not an outsider. His decisions affect his own income and that of his close friends and relatives. He is an intermediary between the state, on the one hand, and neighboring households, on the other. During periods of strong Party control, the team leader has tended to cater more to the state plan. During periods of lax Party control, the team leader has tended to cater to the interests of his members. The divided loyalities of the team leaders make the system unstable.[72]

In view of these problems, the pragmatic leadership in Beijing has renewed its efforts to improve commune management and to promote peasant motivation. As a symbol of shifting the focus from revolution to production, the commune revolutionary committee was abolished in 1979 and replaced by the commune administrative committee, resembling the management committee prior to the Cultural Revolution. There is a growing demand from agricultural experts and Party officials to separate the commune from local government administration and make the commune a purely economic unit. The separation is deemed necessary to reduce government interference in commune planning and operation.[73] Although the production teams remain the basic accounting units of the commune, farming operations are mostly contracted out to small groups, households, or even individuals.[74] The "three selfs and one guarantee" (*san zi yi bao*) system of private plots, village fairs, and personal responsibility for profit and loss along with a guarantee of production down to the household level – a system that prevailed in 1961–1962 and was banned in 1966–1976 – is again a common practice.[75]

Moreover, on March 30, 1981, the State Council issued a circular instructing that for those areas in which the system of fixing output quotas for each household was not in practice, peasants' private plots might be extended from 5 percent to a maximum limit of 15 percent of the total farmland of each production team.[76] The tripling of the size of private plots signified another marked change in the commune system.

After two decades of experimentation, the commune system has not led China into communism, but rather has represented a retreat to a level of collectivization quite similar to that of the advanced cooperative of the 1950s. For the foreseeable future, it is probable that the Chinese commune system will become a federation of brigades and teams and that the Chinese peasants will learn to live with all the contradictions arising from collectivization without resolving them.

## NOTES

1. *People's China* (Beijing) No. 17 (September 1957), pp. 4–9.
2. Editorial, *Renmin ribao*, February 13, 1958.
3. *Renmin ribao*, May 3, 1958.
4. For details, see Chu-yuan Cheng, *The People's Communes* (Hong Kong: Union Research Institute, 1959), pp. 1–8.
5. Ibid., pp. 8–9.
6. CCP, Eighth Central Committee, "Resolution on Some Questions Concerning the People's Communes," *Xinhua banyuekan* No. 24 (December 1958), p. 7.
7. *Renmin ribao*, August 28, 1959.
8. *Questionnaire on People's Communes* (Guangdong: People's Press, 1958), p. 3.

9. *Xin jianshe* [New Construction] (Beijing) No. 10 (October 1958), p. 20.
10. *Hongqi* No. 9 (October 1958), p. 22.
11. *Tongji yanjiu* [Statistical research] (Beijing) No. 8 (August 1958).
12. *Renmin ribao,* September 19, 1958.
13. Chu-yuan Cheng, *Communist China's Economy, 1949–1962* (South Orange, N.J.: Seton Hall University Press, 1963), pp. 163–164.
14. Chu-yuan Cheng, *People's Communes,* pp. 31–33.
15. CCP, Central Committee, "Resolution on the Establishment of People's Communes in the Rural Areas," NCNA-Beijing, September 9, 1958.
16. CCP, Xushui Xian Committee, "Draft for Accelerating Socialist Construction to Enter Communism," in *Jihua jingji* [Planned economy] No. 10 (1958), p. 15.
17. Zhou Enlai, "Report on Revision of the Major Targets in the 1959 Plan and on Stepping Up the Movement for Increasing Output and Economizing," *Renmin ribao,* August 29, 1959.
18. *Da gong bao* (Beijing), October 25 and December 7, 1958. For details of peasant resistance, see Chu-yuan Cheng, *Communist China—Its Situation and Prospects* (Hong Kong: Freedom Press, 1959), Appendix 2, pp. 16–18.
19. Deng Zihui, "Actively Improve the Mess Halls, Thoroughly Carrying Out the Voluntary Principle," in *Nongcun gongzuo tongxun* [Rural work correspondence] (Beijing), May 1, 1959.
20. *Guizhou ribao* [Kweichow daily] (Guiyang), September 2, 1960.
21. *Xinhua banyuekan* (Beijing) No. 17 (1959), p. 3.
22. Luo Gengmu, "The Three-Level Ownership System in Rural People's Communes," *Zhongguo qingnian* [China's youth] No. 1 (January 1, 1961), pp. 4–9.
23. *Renmin ribao,* August 14, 1960.
24. Peng Dehuai, "Letter to Chairman Mao," reprinted in *Newsletters of Mass Criticism and Repudiation* (Tianjin: Red Guards, 1968).
25. The document was reproduced by the Nationalist Chinese government in Taipei in 1965. Its existence was confirmed by Liu Shaoqi in his confession to the Working Conference of the CCP Central Committee, October 23, 1966 (*1970 Yearbook on Chinese Communism* [Taipei: Institute for the Study of Chinese Communist Problems, 1970], vol. 2, sec. 7, pp. 29–30).
26. According to Skinner, there were about 60,000 market towns in China in 1949. Each town was surrounded by about twenty villages and served as the center of the peasants' economic activities (see G. William Skinner, "Marketing and Social Structure in Rural China: Part I," *Journal of Asian Studies* 24:1 [November 1964], p. 33).
27. *Da gong bao,* July 5, 1961.
28. *Xin Hunan bao* [New Hunan daily] (Changsha), November 13, 1960.
29. The 1968 figure is from Ian Davies, "The Chinese Commune—An Australian Student's View," in *Eastern Horizon* 8:1 (1969), pp. 34–44; the 1970 figure from *Shehui fazhanshi* [History of social development] (Shanghai: Shanghai Renmin Chubanshe, December 1974), p. 340.
30. *Yearbook on Chinese Communism 1973* (Taipei: Chung-kung Yen-chiu

she, 1974), sec. 5, pp. 5–11. Also, Byung-joon Ahn, "The Political Economy of the People's Commune in China: Changes and Continuities," *Journal of Asian Studies* 34:3 (May 1975), p. 647.

31. *Renmin ribao,* February 18, 1971.

32. *1977 Yearbook on Chinese Communism* (Taipei: Institute for the Study of Chinese Communism, 1977), sec. 5, p. 9.

33. The official title of this document is Regulations on the Work in the Rural People's Communes (Draft for Trial Use) (Editorial, *Renmin ribao,* February 23, 1979). This document has not yet been published, but some key points have been revealed in government statements.

34. FBIS, April 17, 1979, p. Q1, and May 25, 1979, p. P1.

35. *Renmin ribao,* March 2, 1979, p. 4.

36. *Beijing Review* 24:11 (March 16, 1981), pp. 3–4.

37. Frederick W. Crook, "The Commune System in the People's Republic of China 1963–74," in U.S., Congress, Joint Economic Committee, *China: A Reassessment of the Economy* (Washington, D.C.: Government Printing Office, 1975), pp. 366–410.

38. According to Crook's study, the average commune in 1974 possessed 15 production brigades and 100 production teams (ibid.). The number of China's peasant households increased from 120 million units in the 1950s to 170 million in 1979 (*Hua-chiao jih-pao* [China daily news] [New York], March 23, 1981).

39. For instance, a commune in Liaoning had 72 natural villages and 72 teams; a commune in Jilin had 211 villages and 200 teams (Frederick W. Crook, "The Commune System").

40. Ibid.

41. *Peking Review* 21:11 (March 17, 1978), p. 11.

42. Most of the information in this section is derived from "How China's People's Communes Are Organized," *China Reconstructs* 27:9 (September 1978), p. 15.

43. Robert J. Birrell, "The Centralized Control of the Communes in the Post 'Great Leap' Period," in A. Doak Barnett, ed., *Chinese Communist Politics in Action* (Seattle: Washington University Press, 1969), pp. 400–443.

44. Frederick W. Crook, "The Commune System," p. 395.

45. "In the Communes–Ownership on Three Levels," *China Reconstructs* 22:1 (January 1974), pp. 35–38.

46. Byung-joon Ahn, "Political Economy of the People's Commune in China," p. 645.

47. *China News Analysis* No. 1,124 (June 23, 1978), p. 4.

48. "Life in a Rural People's Commune," *China Reconstructs* 27:9 (September 1978), p. 6.

49. Byung-joon Ahn, "Political Economy of the People's Commune in China," p. 650; and Chu Ko, "Several Problems Confronting the People's Communes," *Mainland China Monthly* (Taipei) No. 129 (May 15, 1978), pp. 36–38.

50. Frederick W. Crook, "The Commune System," pp. 400–401.

51. China People's University, Department of Agricultural Economy, "A

Discussion on the Forms of Remuneration for Agricultural Labor," *Guangming ribao,* June 19, 1978, p. 4.

52. *China News Analysis* No. 1,124 (June 23, 1978), p. 5.

53. For instance, the average per capita annual income of commune members in Liaoning in 1978 was only 81 yuan or $49 (FBIS, May 29, 1979, p. S4). In Jiangsu, the average income was 85 yuan or $52 per person in 1978 (FBIS, May 25, 1979, p. O3).

54. Frederick W. Crook, "The Commune System," p. 403.

55. Liu Hong, "Supplies Can Be Ensured Only When the Economy Is Developed," *Renmin ribao,* January 24, 1973.

56. "It Is Necessary to Develop Sideline Occupations on a Large Scale in Rural Areas," *Renmin ribao,* March 29, 1978, p. 5. Agricultural sideline products include medicinal herbs, knitting, small handicrafts, and the like.

57. Dong Dai, "Is the Rural Trade Fair the Capitalist Free Market?" *Renmin ribao,* January 31, 1978, p. 3; and Shang Zheng, "It Is Imperative to Bring into Full Play the Positive Role of Rural Trade Fairs," *Guangming ribao,* January 30, 1978, p. 3.

58. *Renmin ribao,* March 29, 1978.

59. NCNA Contributing Reporter, "How to View Legitimate Domestic Sideline Production," NCNA-Beijing, April 20, 1978.

60. *Zhongguo xinwen* [China news service] (Beijing), October 10, 1977.

61. Ibid., December 9, 1977.

62. Editorial, *Renmin ribao,* April 4, 1978.

63. Editorial, *Renmin ribao,* January 24, 1979.

64. Henry J. Groen and James A Kilpatrick, "China's Agricultural Production," in U.S., Congress, Joint Economic Committee, *Chinese Economy Post-Mao,* p. 630.

65. Editorial, *Renmin ribao,* January 24, 1979.

66. Lo Chen-mao, "The Production Team Is also an Enterprise," *Guangming ribao,* November 18, 1978, p. 3.

67. Editorial, *Renmin ribao,* August 3, 1978, and Li Xiannian's speech at the National Conference on Capital Construction in Agriculture in Beijing, August 15, 1978.

68. NCNA-Beijing, February 26, 1979.

69. See *Yunnan ribao* [Yunnan daily] (Kunming), March 12, 1979, and NCNA-Beijing, September 27, 1978 (FBIS, September 28, 1978, p. J1).

70. Shandong Province, Planning Committee, "The Future of Agriculture Depends on Mechanization," *Jingji yanjiu* No. 21 (1978), p. 54.

71. *Renmin ribao,* January 13, 1973.

72. Frederick W. Crook, "The Commune System," pp. 405–406.

73. *Hua-chiao jih-pao* (New York), June 3, 1980, p. 3.

74. Commentator, "Choose a System of Productive Forces," *Banyuetan* [Dialogue semimonthly] (Beijing) No. 12 (October 26, 1980).

75. Jin Guang and Xiong Yan, "A Correct Analysis Should Be Made of 'San-Zi-Yi-Bao,'" *Renmin ribao,* May 12, 1980, p. 5.

76. Xinhua-Beijing, April 5, 1981.

# 5

# Socialist Transformation of the Urban Economy

While agricultural collectivization was under way in the countryside, the Communist government began the complicated task of bringing the private sector in the urban area under state control. In contrast to the ebb and flow of the collectivization process, the urban socialist transformation achieved a remarkable success. Within seven years (1950–1957), the entire private sector of several millions of private firms and tens of millions of independent handicraftsmen and peddlers had been absorbed into the state-controlled economy without severe violence or disruption of production.

The triumph was decisive. Since 1957, the Chinese bourgeoisie has ceased to exist as a class. The historical victory can be partly attributed to the character of the Chinese bourgeoisie, who were always more prone to compromise than to resist. But a more important factor in the achievement was the astuteness of the Communist leaders who sought to avoid the devastation created by War Communism in the wake of the October Revolution in the Soviet Union by following a step-by-step process to induce Chinese capitalists to take the road of socialization. The Chinese Communists hailed the peaceful transformation as "a pioneer effort in the history of proletarian revolution" and proudly proclaimed that "Lenin's idea of state capitalism was not brought into realization in the Soviet Union, but . . . in China."[1]

This chapter will analyze the general guidelines pursued by the Chinese Communist leaders to carry out the socialist transformation, the process of the transformation, and its impact on general economic development.

## POLICIES FOR TRANSFORMATION

At the time of the Communist takeover, the Chinese urban economy consisted of a relatively small modern sector in the major industrial centers, mostly along the eastern coast, and a vast traditional or handicraft sector, which used little or no mechanical power. Although modern factories dominated the machinery, chemical, metal-processing, electrical, and public utilities industries, handicrafts predominated in the production of simple tools and artistic goods and services, as well as goods and services ancillary to modern industry.

The modern or capitalist sector was primarily owned by foreign capitalists, by the Chinese government, and by Chinese capitalists. The traditional sector was owned by small businessmen and handicraftsmen. In mapping the strategy of transformation, the Chinese Communist government classified the national economy into five sectors: the socialist state sector, the sector of individual peasant and artisan ownership, the capitalist sector, the state capitalist sector, and the semisocialist cooperative sector. The first three were the basic sectors, the last two were only transitional. Of the five, the socialist state sector was the leading sector, and the others were destined to be transformed into the socialist sector.

When the new government was formed in 1949, the state sector controlled only 34.7 percent of industrial output and a smaller proportion of commerce, and in 1950, state enterprises handled only 23.9 percent of wholesale trade and 14.9 percent of retail trade.[2] The Chinese urban economy was basically under private control. Large-scale confiscation of private enterprises was bound to cause sabotage and disruption. During this period, rural land reform had barely started, and a landlord-capitalist alliance could have mounted an effective resistance to the Communist regime. In order to isolate the landlord class, Mao instructed the cadres on June 6, 1950, "Do not hit in all directions."[3] For the time being, the new government should not confiscate capitalist enterprises but should adopt a policy of simultaneously uniting and struggling with the bourgeoisie. With this strategy in mind, the new government refrained from mentioning the final goal of socialist transformation and emphasized the principle of coexistence between the capitalist sector and the state socialist sector. This principle was first stipulated in the Common Program (a temporary constitution for the new government), which was adopted by the Chinese People's Political Consultative Conference in September 1949. Government statements in the early years also stressed the principle of giving consideration to both public and private interests for the benefit of both labor and capital. These policy statements tended to nourish the hope of the Chinese bourgeoisie for long-term coexistence.

Nevertheless, in early 1952, as the Korean War was winding down and land reform approached completion, the regime suddenly launched a fierce attack—the "five-anti" campaign—on the capitalists. The regime mobilized the workers and employees of private enterprises to struggle against the capitalists, whom it accused of five evils: tax evasion, bribery of government workers, theft of state property, cheating on government contracts, and stealing economic information from the government for private speculation. People who were found guilty had to pay retroactive taxes or large fines. Communist actions had revealed the real attitude toward the bourgeoisie, and the Communists soon clarified their intentions.

In 1953, the CCP Central Committee's General Line for the Transitional Period delineated the fundamental task for that period as the social transformation of agriculture, handicrafts, and capitalist industry and commerce. On September 7, 1953, Mao talked to the representatives of minor political parties and businessmen and outlined what he called "the only road for the transformation of capitalist industry and commerce." That road was state capitalism.[4] In another statement, Mao defined state capitalism as "the use of various forms of capitalist economy linked with the state-operated socialist economy and supervised by the workers under the control of the people's government."[5]

Mao's strategy of socialist transformation, like his policy of agricultural collectivization, caused controversy within the Party. Some official documents have identified Liu Shaoqi and Bo Yipo as two top leaders who wanted to "consolidate the new democratic order" and "further develop the capitalist economy for a few more decades." Liu was quoted as having commented that "there is merit in [bourgeois] exploitation." In 1953, during a taxation reform, Bo Yipo called for "complete equality between the public and private tax burden." He was criticized for having proposed a sales tax that would harm state commerce and enhance the ability of the capitalists to compete with state enterprises.[6]

## PROCESS OF TRANSFORMATION

Under the influence of Liu Shaoqi, the CCP Central Committee adopted a moderate program that envisaged the completion of socialist transformation within three five-year plans.[7] In 1955, however, Mao criticized right deviations in the agricultural cooperation movement and led the socialist upsurge for agricultural cooperation. At the end of 1955, he urged that China "strive to bring to fruition a bit earlier the socialist transformation of her handicraft industry and capitalist industry and commerce."[8] On March 5, 1956, Mao further instructed the State Council to accelerate the socialist transformation in handicrafts. Consequently, a high tide of socialist transformation appeared in the big and medium-sized cities throughout the country. By the end of 1956, the process of transformation was largely completed, ten years ahead of the original schedule. The program included five major aspects: (1) confiscation of "bureaucrat capital" and foreign enterprises; (2) nationalization of private financial institutions; (3) transformation of private business and industry; (4) cooperativization of handicrafts and peddlers; and (5) the establishment of urban communes.

*Confiscation of Bureaucrat Capital and Foreign Enterprises*

The large-scale development of the state sector of the Chinese economy began in 1949–1950 with the confiscation of all "bureaucrat capitalist enterprises." In Communist terminology, this meant the confiscation of those state-monopoly enterprises that had been controlled by the Nationalist government. According to Mao Zedong, the "bureaucrat capital" amounted to between $10 billion and $20 billion.[9]

The accumulation of such a huge amount of bureaucrat capital was the result of investments made by the Japanese government and private capitalists in Manchuria and North China during the latter stages of the Sino-Japanese War. After the war, those Japanese enterprises were surrendered to the Nationalist government and reorganized into state corporations. In 1948, state-owned enterprises accounted for about two-thirds of the total industrial capital. On the eve of the Communist victory, the National Resources Commission of the Nationalist government controlled 90 percent of the country's iron and steel output, 33 percent of its coal, 67 percent of its electric power, 45 percent of its cement, and all petroleum and nonferrous metals. In addition, state capital also controlled the big banks; all the railways, highways, and airlines; 44 percent of the shipping tonnage; and a dozen or so monopolistic trading corporations.[10]

Following the 1949 victory, the Chinese Communists took over those state corporations which it identified as bureaucrat capital. In a short span of time, the Communists confiscated 2,858 industrial enterprises employing more than 750,000 industrial workers. This laid the foundation for the state sector. In 1949, the new regime's state industrial enterprises accounted for 41.3 percent of the gross output value of China's large, modern industries and 34.7 percent of all industrial output. The state sector owned 58 percent of the country's electric power resources, 68 percent of the coal output, 92 percent of the pig iron production, 97 percent of the steel, 68 percent of the cement, and 53 percent of cotton yarn. It also controlled all railways, most modern communications and transport, and the major share of the banking business and foreign trade.[11]

In the course of confiscation, the Communists adopted a policy of retaining all technical and managerial personnel, as well as the existing production system. This policy prevented any suspension of production or sabotage of equipment and installations during the takeover process. As soon as the regime had consolidated its control over the enterprises, however, the Communists launched a democratic reform campaign. The reform was intended to oust former Nationalist officials from supervisory positions, in which they might retain some influence over the workers. Several hundred thousand "hidden counterrevolutionaries and remnants of the feudal forces" were officially reported to have been removed in the course of the campaign.

During 1949 and early 1950, enterprises belonging to American, British, French, or other Western interests remained intact. They were allowed to continue operations on the condition that they abide by the laws and regulations of the new government. But the government soon increased its restrictions and punitive taxes. More seriously, the government ordered the foreign companies to cut the scope of their operations and to retain all Chinese employees at their usual wages. Thus, the foreign capitalists found themselves pouring money into China in order to keep their firms afloat, and they were unable to reap profits. It was estimated that about 375,000 pounds sterling were being sent monthly from Britain and Hong Kong to finance British firms in Shanghai. Losses were so heavy that the share values of the foreign companies' stocks declined to almost nothing.[12] Some foreign banks and other firms found it impossible to continue and applied for permission to close. Others voluntarily transferred their property to the Communist government without compensation.

The outbreak of the Korean War aggravated the difficulties of foreign enterprises in the area. In December 1950, the U.S. government seized control of China's property in areas under U.S. jurisdiction, and the Beijing government immediately issued a decree to control American property and freeze American bank deposits on the mainland. In April 1951, similar measures were extended to the property of British-owned companies. In the summer of 1952, British merchants elected to leave the mainland. Consequently, the Beijing government obtained British assets valued at 200 million pounds.[13] After almost three centuries, Western investments on the Chinese mainland were totally terminated in 1952.

*Nationalization of Private Financial Institutions*

In the pre-Communist period, private banking corporations had existed side by side with the state banks and had played an important role in the national economy. Most private enterprises relied on the private banks for short-term and long-term investments. According to an official report, there were 446 private banks in six major Chinese cities at the end of 1949. These included both modern and native banks. Between June 1949 and the end of 1952, the Chinese Communists moved to eliminate the private banking establishments so as to strengthen the state sector.

The first step was to gain control of government funds. In March 1950, the CCP Central Committee and the State Administrative Council jointly announced measures in three areas to centralize control of all financial and economic activities. The state treasury assumed authority over state fiscal revenues and expenditures, central control was established over national resources and their allocation, and all government financial resources were placed under the centralized authority of the state bank. Thus, government funds in the private banking system were transferred to the People's Bank (Central Bank of the People's Republic of China). This caused a drastic contraction in public credit and forced many private banks to cease operation. By June 1950, 233 banks, 52 percent of the total, had closed, leaving only 213 private banking establishments.[14]

Following this initial step, the government demanded that the remaining commercial banks increase their capitalization, in conformity with the decision of a national financial conference held in August 1950. Many private banks were thereby forced to close. Special measures were then adopted to deal with any private banks still having adequate financial foundations.

In August 1950 the government also called a joint conference of monetary enterprises and encouraged the private, commercial, and native banks to merge in a series of gradual steps by a process of joint operation. By the end of 1951, the sixty-four remaining private banking establishments had merged into five major groups. In order to consolidate overall control, the Communist government then advised each group to establish a joint administration to exert direct control over member banks and their branches. The highest executive organ of each joint administrative unit was a joint board of directors. Most directors were government appointed, and the joint administrations actually were directly subservient to the state. In November 1952, the five joint administrations and joint boards of directors were merged into a single joint administration, and all privately owned banking establishments were redesignated as its branch offices. By the end of 1952, China's private banking system had disappeared.[15]

Apart from the nationalization of private banks, the Communist government also took stern measures to control exchange transactions and the activities of goldsmiths, pawnshops, and firms dealing with overseas Chinese remittances. All of these had served as agents for special monetary transactions in China and had long occupied an important role in Chinese economic life.

During the hyperinflation that preceded the Communist victory, speculative activities in gold bars, silver dollars, and U.S. currency flourished in every city. In the early days of Communist control, large-scale transactions were still carried out in gold bars, and ordinary buying and selling used silver dollars and U.S. notes. To halt these activities, the new government banned the circulation of gold bars, silver dollars, and foreign currency as exchange media in 1949.

Simultaneously, the government moved to halt the activities of goldsmiths and silversmiths, whose main business had become clandestine gold transactions. The government first limited the scope of their business to the sale of manufactured products and prohibited them from engaging in gold bar transactions and from buying and selling gold jewelry. They were required to report their gold holdings and daily transactions to the local authorities. Second, the government decreed that people wishing to sell gold could do so only at the local offices of the People's Bank or at its authorized agencies at pegged prices, which were much lower than the market quotations. These regulations squeezed the goldsmiths out of business and paved the way for government control of private gold holdings during the land reform and the "five-anti" campaign.

Pawnshops were singled out for government control because of their intimate relationship with the broad masses of people. In the old days, pawnshops had been the only place where the poor could get cash in an emergency. They had also served as the main outlet for stolen goods, however. In September 1950, the government promulgated strict restrictions on pawnshop operations and capital requirements. The basic purpose was the eventual elimination of pawnshops and the establishment of credit cooperatives.[16] The government also moved to gain control over the firms that dealt with overseas Chinese remittances, both to prevent foreign exchange from getting into the free market and to obtain economic information about the recipients, most of whom were landlords and rich peasants.

These controls effectively curbed speculative activities and helped stabilize the new currency. In addition, a raid on the Shanghai stock exchange by Communist troops in June 1949 had practically demolished the center of monetary speculation in the country. In South China, the historical Shi-san Hang (thirteen trades) of Canton, the long-established hub of speculation in the city, folded following persistent Communist raids. All of these moves strengthened the position of the new government and its control over the private sector.

*Transformation of Private Business and Industry*

The socialist transformation of private ownership in the urban areas involved 3 million private firms and factories and directly affected an urban population of 70 million. To avoid disrupting the national economy, the process was conducted circuitously in three stages: utilization, restriction, and transformation.

Although the Communists had developed a blueprint for the process, they did not reveal their whole plan clearly until 1953. In the meantime, the prevailing illusion among the Chinese bourgeoisie was that the private and state sectors of the economy might coexist. In fact, as soon as the regime controlled the money and the commodity markets, it announced its three-step policy and incorporated it into the 1954 constitution of the People's Republic of China. Article 10 of the constitution stipulated:

> The policy of the state towards capitalist industry and commerce is to utilize, restrict, and transform them. The state makes use of the positive sides of capitalist industry and commerce which are beneficial to national welfare and the people's livelihood; restricts their negative sides which are not beneficial to national welfare and the people's livelihood; encourages and guides their transformation into various forms of state-capitalist economy. It gradually replaces capitalist ownership with ownership by the whole people, and this it does by means of control exercised by administrative organs of the state, the leadership given by the state sector of the economy, and supervision by the workers.[17]

Implementation of that policy involved highly skillful political manipulation, and the outcome was far more successful than that of the cooperativization drive in the countryside.

*The Utilization Stage—1949–1952.* Before the Communists came to power, Mao Zedong had defined the Chinese revolution as a "bouregois democratic revolution." He had repeatedly promised Chinese businessmen that the Communists would protect private property and develop capitalism.[18] Misled by these pledges, the Chinese bourgeoisie lent their support to the Communists in the last stage of the civil war. In fact, the promises were temporarily honored. In 1949, private enterprises accounted for 55.8 percent of the gross output value of industry and for 85 percent of retail sales.[19] Without the cooperation of the private sector, the rehabilitation of the national economy would have been impossible. Communist policy during this stage was to fight against speculative activity while aiding the development of normal private business. The first blows struck at the private sector were the sudden closing of the stock exchange in Shanghai and the concentration of all government funds in state banks. Following these moves, more than half of the private banks in Shanghai closed, as did one out of every ten commercial establishments.

Between January and May 1950, on a national basis, private industry's production of cotton cloth dropped by 38 percent, silk and satin by 47 percent, woolen yarn by 20 percent, and paper by 31 percent.[20] In June 1950, with the private sector on the brink of collapse, Mao presented measures for the "adjustment of industry and business" as one of three conditions necessary to improve finance and the economy.[21] He advocated readjusting the relationships between the state and private ownership, between labor and capital, and between production and marketing. Actually, the focal point was the readjustment of the relationship between the state and private sectors. The state began to stimulate private industries and businesses by placing orders with them and purchasing their products. In this way, private firms obtained raw materials, markets, and a certain amount of profit. The state trading organization allowed private commercial enterprises to benefit from the difference between wholesale and retail prices so that they could promote the flow of goods between town and country and between China and foreign countries.

After the People's Republic entered the Korean War in October 1950, orders for military supplies increased tremendously, and the state's dependence on private enterprises also increased substantially. Consequently, the private sector developed considerably during this period. According to statistics for eight major cities, including Shanghai and Tianjin, the number of private industrial and commercial enterprises rose 27 percent in the two years ending December 1951. The total value of private industrial products increased by approximately 70 percent in the three years between October 1949 and

September 1952.[22] In retrospect, the year 1951 was the golden year for the private economy under communism.

The policy of utilization adopted in this period brought a twofold advantage to the new government. It enabled the state to greatly increase its tax revenue from the private sector, and those taxes totaled 35 percent of the 1950 and 1951 state fiscal revenues. The policy also enabled the state to procure industrial products, which were exchanged with the peasants for grain, raw materials, and other agricultural products. Control over these products helped to stabilize the commodity market. Moreover, many leading industrialists who had previously withdrawn their capital from China and taken refuge in Hong Kong now returned. Mao's tactics of exploiting the Chinese capitalists proved very successful.[23]

*The Restriction Stage–1952–1953.* Efforts to restrict the private sector began during the utilization stage and were carried out simultaneously with the policy of utilization. Early in 1950, private firms were called on to make regular reports on their activities. The Provisional Regulations for Private Enterprise of December 31, 1950, detailed the conditions under which the private sector could operate. Private enterprises were required to submit their complete plans of production and records of sales for the approval of the government and to distribute their earnings among dividends, welfare funds, taxes, and reserve funds in specified proportions.

By 1952, the state sector had been greatly strengthened as a result of the completion of land reform and the nationalization of the banking system. In January 1952, in order to check further development of the private sector, the regime launched the ruthless "five-anti" campaign. The targets were those capitalists who committed the crimes of bribery of government workers, tax evasion, theft of state property, cheating on government contracts, and stealing economic information from the government.[24] Although the campaign's stated purpose was "to sever the capitalists' relations with their imperialist, feudal, bureaucratic compradors," its real purpose was to curb the growth of the private sector and to confiscate profits made by that sector during the Korean War.

The January–April campaign was waged with great intensity. Mass meetings in cities throughout the country mobilized millions of workers and employees to denounce their employers. One result was a great increase in suicides by businessmen. According to a report by Bo Yipo, former minister of finance of the State Administrative Council, an investigation of 450,000 private industrial and business undertakings in nine major cities found that 340,000 of those enterprises, or 76 percent, had committed "various illegal transactions."[25] The accused enterprises were ordered to pay large fines, the sum to be determined by the local governments. Bo Yipo also reported a huge surplus in China's state budget in 1952. State revenue figures listed a sum equivalent to $1.7 billion under "other revenues" without any specification as to source.[26] The fines collected because of the "five-anti" campaign undoubtedly constituted a major share of that item.

The fines also drained most private enterprises of their working capital. A 1953 survey of the Bureau of Industry and Commerce of the Tianjin municipal government revealed that in that second largest economic center of China, the amount of working capital private factories and firms had possessed (taking 1949 as 100) was 232 in 1950 and 319 in 1951. In 1952, as a result of the "five-anti" campaign, the working capital dropped to only 182, a 43 percent decline. The share of capital owned by industrialists and businessmen decreased proportionally. Using 1948 as the base year (= 100), their share dropped to 71 in 1949, to 57 in 1950, to 52 in 1951, and in 1952, after the "five-anti" campaign, to 32. Most factories and firms in Tianjin relied heavily on bank loans and commercial credit to tide them over the critical period.[27]

Having largely reduced private enterprise to an empty shell and with the market again in stagnation, the government expanded its purchases of processed and manufactured goods from private factories and permitted private commercial enterprises to act as retail distributors or commission agents for the state. All of these measures were intended to keep the private sector continuously in operation, while diverting it into the orbit of the state sector.

To replace the private sector, the number of state corporations and stores was expanded greatly during this period. By the end of 1952, there were over 30,000 state stores throughout the country, or 4.7 times the number in 1950. Together with the supply and marketing cooperatives in the countryside and the consumers' cooperatives in the cities, the state sector and cooperative sector formed a socialist commercial network. In 1952, total retail sales controlled by state commerce increased by 306 percent, and those of the cooperatives increased by 529 percent, as compared with 1950. Thus, the proportion of state and cooperative commerce in the total value of commodity exchange increased immensely. In 1952, the share of state commerce in the total wholesale trade rose to 63.8 percent, as against 23.9 percent in 1950. The share of state and cooperative commerce in total retail sales rose to 42.6 percent, as against 14.9 percent in 1950. The state sector handled about 93 percent of all foreign trade in 1952. The purpose of restriction was also basically achieved.[28]

*The Transformation Stage–1954-1957.* In the original plan of the Chinese Communists, the policies of utilization and restriction were intended to engineer the socialist transformation of capitalist industry and commerce. This transformation entailed two principal steps: first to transform capitalism into state capitalism; second to transform state capitalism into socialism.

In the Communist concept, state capitalism is not an independent economic form. Its nature and function vary with the political and economic conditions of the whole society. According to Lenin, "state capitalism is capitalism which we shall be able to restrict, the limits of which we shall be able to fix. State capitalism is connected with the state, and the state is the worker's."[29]

In China, when the private sector was diverted into state capitalism, fairly permanent connections were established between it and the state sector through various more or less socialist forms. Based on the extent of these connections and the growth of socialist elements, state capitalism in China was divided into two forms–elementary and advanced. The elementary state-capitalist enterprises were still privately managed by capitalists. Connections of one kind or another were established only by contracts, and the state sector remained outside the enterprises. In the advanced form, by changing capitalist enterprises into joint state-private enterprises, the state sector took over the management function, determination of the operation plan, and personnel policies. Private investors and owners were to be reimbursed by the joint enterprises out of net revenue, with a fixed interest on their original investment. Having accomplished this form, the enterprises became state owned.[30]

State capitalism of industry was introduced in its elementary form during the first stage of industrial and commercial adjustment in 1950. After 1953, it was promoted on a wider scale. Almost every industrial trade operated to fulfill government orders. Official statistics show that the share of state orders in private industrial output rose from 12 percent in 1949 to 29 percent in 1950, 43 percent in 1951, 56 percent in 1952, 63 percent in 1953, 79 percent in 1954, and 82 percent in 1955.[31]

State capitalism of commerce, in its elementary form, makes private firms retail distributing agents for the state. The state supplies the goods and imposes the terms of operation. The income of the private firms, derived from commissions or handling charges, is determined by the state company. In this way, private firms become increasingly dependent on the state economy.

State capitalism in commerce was in its embryonic stage in the period of national economic rehabilitation and was widely developed only after 1954. When the government enforced the planned purchase and marketing of grain at the end of 1953, private grain stores were turned into retail distributors, or commission agents, for the state enterprises. The planned purchase and marketing of cotton cloth and other goods, which began in 1954, further expanded the activities of private enterprises as retail distributors and commission agents and excluded private firms from serving as a wholesale link. After 1953, the government began to replace the private wholesale trade with state commerce in a planned way, transferring private wholesale merchants and their employees to state commercial enterprises. The small wholesalers, who dealt in commodities of secondary importance, were retained and allowed to engage in wholesale activities for the state. Private retailers were forced to rely solely on state commerce for stock supplies. In 1954, the function of the private wholesalers was taken over almost entirely by state commerce. As a result, state capitalism in the commercial field was greatly expanded. According to official statistics, the volume of retail sales handled by the state-capitalist commercial enterprises and cooperative stores was only 1 percent of the total retail sales in 1953, but it rose to 17 percent in 1954 and 45 percent in 1955.[32]

The elementary forms of state capitalism were fundamentally more private in nature, since the assets of those enterprises were still the private property of businessmen, who used them directly in production and exchange. To ensure voluntary acceptance of elementary state capitalism by private industrial and commercial enterprises, the government guaranteed a reasonable amount of profit. In late 1952, the government declared that according to respective conditions and under normal and proper operations, private factories were to receive an annual profit amount to about 10 to 30 percent of their capital. But in 1953, a method of dividing the profits into four parts was introduced to further restrict capitalist "surplus value." The four parts consisted of income taxes, reserve funds for the enterprises, workers' welfare funds, and profit for the capitalists (including dividends and bonuses). As a result of the new division, the capitalists retained only a quarter of the total net earnings of their private enterprises.

The elementary forms of state capitalism also greatly affected the allocation of manpower and resources in the private sector. By assigning tasks of production and operation through contracts and by regulating the price of goods, processing charges, and the difference between wholesale and retail prices, the state could encourage some trades and restrict others.

With the disappearance of the freely competitive market, businessmen became less eager to improve or expand their enterprises. Many lost interest in increasing production and were reluctant to improve management. This, in turn, caused great waste, poor-quality products, unnecessary inventories, the stockpiling of raw materials, and other serious irregularities. Moreover, since the profit for businessmen, which was included in processing charges and the price of the goods, was calculated in terms of cost, businessmen were reluctant to reduce their costs and sometimes even raised them by deliberately wasting raw materials and paying unwarranted higher wages. The Communists soon found it necessary to reorganize all private factories and firms into joint state-private enterprises to facilitate more direct control. Thus, the advanced form of state capitalism came to be adopted.

There were two steps in the development of the advanced form: the joint state-private operation of individual enterprises and joint operation by a whole trade. During the first step, after taking an inventory and making a reappraisal, the assets of the capitalists were turned into private shares, and the investment made by the government became state shares. In this way, the means of production came to be jointly owned by the capitalists and the state. The government also assigned its representatives to participate in and control management. The capitalists and their agents, who previously had held the responsible positions, now received their appointments from the government. Although they continued to participate in management, they no longer played a dominant role. The profit of a joint enterprise was still distributed according to the principle of "dividing profit into four shares"; nevertheless, the amount paid for dividends and bonuses was divided proportionately between the state and private shares. The capitalists' share of the profits diminished even more than it had during the previous stage. The enterprises were therefore semisocialist in nature, or as Lenin called it – "three-fourths of socialism."

In 1949, there were only 193 such joint state-private enterprises, employing 100,000 or more workers and other employees. By 1953, the number of units had increased to a little more than 1,000, with 270,000 workers and other employees and an annual output value of 2 billion yuan. In September 1954, the State Council promulgated its Provisional Regulations for Joint State-Private Industrial Enterprises, marking a new stage in the development of joint enterprises. By the end of 1954, more than 1,700 joint state-private industrial enterprises had more than 530,000 workers and other employees and an annual output value of more than 5 billion yuan. This constituted 12.3 percent of the total industrial output value of the country.

In the latter half of 1955, following the nationwide upsurge of agricultural cooperation, the socialist transformation of capitalist industry and commerce also reached a new stage. In the first quarter of 1956, the high tide of joint operation by whole trades swept over the country. Businessmen, seeing the general trend of events, expressed a readiness to accept their lot, and at the end of the year, joint state-private industrial enterprises constituted 99 percent of private industrial establishments and 99.6 percent of the private industrial output value. In 1956, 112,000 private industrial establishments, with 1.2 million workers and other employees, changed over to joint state-private operation. Simultaneously, 400,000 private commercial establishments became jointly operated, and another 1.44 million units were converted into cooperatives.[33]

After joint operation by a whole trade was established, the means of production that had belonged to the capitalists were placed at the disposal of the state to be utilized under a unified plan. The government then assessed the total value of private capital. According to official statistics, at the end of 1956, the total of the private shares in the joint state-private enterprises was assessed at 2.4 billion yuan ($1 billion). Of this amount, industrial shares totaled 1.7 billion yuan. The shares in the fields of commerce, restaurants, and personal services totaled 600 million yuan, and the shares in communication and transport, another 100 million yuan.[34]

Following this assessment of private shares, the government announced that it would pay a fixed interest to the capitalists. Under the new arrangement, the state would pay capitalists a fixed rate of interest on their shares of their enterprises, regardless of profit or loss during the entire period of joint operation. This rate was generally set at 5 percent per annum. The new policy of "buying off" the capitalists was regarded as the price paid to gain the capitalists' acceptance of a peaceful transformation. Payment of this fixed interest was to start on January 1, 1956, and to continue only until December 1962. Because of the economic crisis in the wake of the Great Leap, however, the regime needed the cooperation of the businessmen, and in March 1962, at the Third Session of the Second National People's Congress, the government extended the payment of fixed interest to the capitalists to 1965.[35]

Annual payments between 1956 and 1965 were set at 120 million yuan a year, or an equivalent of $50 million. The recipients numbered

1,140,000, each receiving an average of $44 per year.[36] Many capitalists elected to forfeit their payment, because they thought it did not pay to be labeled a capitalist in return for a few dollars. After the Cultural Revolution broke out in 1966, the payment of fixed interest ended.

When the amount of the private shares was determined, the legal proprietary rights retained by the capitalists were limited to a fixed sum of interest for a ten-year period. The right of the capitalists to own their property was therefore severed from their right to use it. Except for the fixed interest they drew, they no longer had any authority over the disposition of their property. Thus, they no longer functioned as capitalists but as government-appointed employees working in state enterprises. The result of the socialist transformation of capitalist industry and commerce is illustrated by the statistics in Table 5.1 and Table 5.2.

Table 5.1
Socialist Transformation of Private Industry in China (1949-1956)*
(in percent)

| | | State-Capitalist Industry | | | |
|---|---|---|---|---|---|
| Year | Socialist Industry | Total Percentage | Joint state-private enterprises | Private enterprises executing orders and processing goods for the state | Private Industry[a] |
| 1949 | 34.7 | 9.5 | 2.0 | 7.5 | 55.8 |
| 1950 | 45.3 | 17.8 | 2.9 | 14.9 | 36.9 |
| 1951 | 45.9 | 25.4 | 4.0 | 21.4 | 28.7 |
| 1952 | 56.0 | 26.9 | 5.0 | 21.9 | 17.1 |
| 1953 | 57.5 | 28.5 | 5.7 | 22.8 | 14.0 |
| 1954 | 62.8 | 31.9 | 12.3 | 19.6 | 5.3 |
| 1955 | 67.7 | 29.3 | 16.1 | 13.2 | 3.0 |
| 1956 | 67.5 | 32.5 | 32.5 | --- | --- |

* Percentage distribution of gross output value of industry, excluding handicrafts.

[a]This indicates those produced and marketed privately.

Source: P.R.C. State Statistical Bureau, Ten Great Years (Beijing: Foreign Languages Press, 1960), p. 38.

### *Cooperativization of Handicrafts and Peddlers*

Handicraftsmen and peddlers were two significant components of the traditional economy, and they were scattered throughout the entire country. In 1954, handicrafts accounted for about 17.4 percent of the country's gross output value.[37] According to a nationwide 1954 survey, about 20 million people were engaged in handicrafts in China. Of those, about 9 million were full-time handicraftsmen, and 11 million were peasants who produced handicrafts in their free time. To lead these people along the path of socialization was another difficult task for the Communist government.

In view of the importance of handicrafts in the national economy and their diffusion and small-scale production, the first step was to organize the supply of raw materials and the marketing of the products. In this way, a close relationship was established with the state sector, and the relationship with private commerce was gradually severed. The next step was to organize production and to move from individual ownership to collective ownership. The Communists developed three different models in succession: the small supply and marketing groups, the supply and marketing cooperatives, and the producers' cooperatives. The procedure was quite similar to that of

Table 5.2
Socialist Transformation of Private Commerce in China (1950–1957)*
(in percent)

| Year | Socialist Commerce | State-Capitalist and Cooperative Commerce | Private Commerce |
|---|---|---|---|
| 1950 | 14.9 | 0.1 | 85.0 |
| 1951 | 24.4 | 0.1 | 75.5 |
| 1952 | 42.6 | 0.2 | 57.2 |
| 1953 | 49.7 | 0.4 | 49.9 |
| 1954 | 69.0 | 5.4 | 25.6 |
| 1955 | 67.6 | 14.6 | 17.8 |
| 1956 | 68.3 | 27.5 | 4.2 |
| 1957 | 65.7 | 31.6 | 2.7 |

* Percentage distribution of retail sales.

Source: P.R.C. State Statistical Bureau, Ten Great Years (Beijing: Foreign Languages Press, 1960), p. 40.

the collectivization of agriculture.

The supply and marketing group was an elementary form of handicraft cooperation. It was organized for the purchase of raw materials from and the sale of products to state commercial establishments, or for the receipt of orders for processing goods. The members were generally independent handicraftsmen or small proprietors. Apprentices and hired hands were ineligible for membership, although they took part in production. Members of the supply and marketing groups retained their former means of production and continued to engage in independent production, accounting for their own profits or losses. The function of these groups was to place their members in close contact with the state sector and to accumulate some collectively owned property. This paved the way for the formation of supply and marketing cooperatives.

The more-advanced supply and marketing cooperatives were organized by a number of individual handicraftsmen, both those engaged in small production and those belonging to supply and marketing groups. During the initial stage, and as a general rule, these cooperatives were responsible only for obtaining raw materials and for marketing; production was left to the individual members as before. The members contributed shares but retained ownership of their tools and equipment. Later on, they gradually merged into one unit for production. A portion of the profit was used to purchase collective means of production, and a part of the means of production was turned into common property after the members had agreed to turn over their major means of production to the cooperative. Thereafter, each hired hand, apprentice, or member of the handicraftsmen's families who was participating in production became a member of the cooperative. As soon as the handicrafts producers' cooperatives were established, their management was unified, and profits and losses were shared by all members. The income of the cooperative, after deducting taxes and reserve and welfare funds, was distributed to the members in the forms of wages and bonuses according to the principle of "to each according to his work."

From 1949 to 1952, the membership of the handicrafts cooperatives and groups only increased from 89,000 to 228,000, but the groups and cooperatives developed rapidly in 1955. By the end of that year, membership had expanded to 2.2 million, or 27 percent of the total number of handicraftsmen in the country. At the beginning of 1956, spurred by the upsurge in agricultural cooperation and the socialist transformation of private industry and commerce, a vigorous nationwide campaign commenced for the socialist transformation of handicrafts. The handicraftsmen in entire regions and trades immediately organized into producers' cooperatives based on collective ownership, bypassing the stage of supply and marketing cooperatives. By the end of that year, the number of handicrafts cooperatives exceeded 100,000. They embraced over 6 million handicraftsmen, or 92 percent of the total number.[38] The progress can be seen from the figures in Table 5.3.

In 1958, the year of the Great Leap Forward, the government ordered the reorganization and expansion of some of the handicrafts cooperatives to constitute the basis of local industries. Many handicrafts cooperatives were then transformed into state-local factories owned by the whole people. In that year, according to their membership, 37 percent of the handicrafts cooperatives were transferred from collective ownership into ownership by the whole people; 28 percent retained their collective ownership as cooperative factories or handicrafts cooperatives in cities; and the remaining 35 percent of the handicrafts cooperatives were incorporated into the new rural communes.[39]

Cooperativization, however, was not fully consolidated. In

Table 5.3
Progress of Handicraft Cooperation
in China, 1952-1956

| Year | Number of Persons Engaged in: (thousands) | | | Percentage Distribution | |
|---|---|---|---|---|---|
| | Total | Cooperative Handicrafts | Individual Handicrafts | Cooperative Handicrafts | Individual Handicrafts |
| 1952 | 7,364 | 228 | 7,136 | 3.1 | 96.9 |
| 1953 | 7,789 | 301 | 7,488 | 3.9 | 96.1 |
| 1954 | 8,910 | 1,213 | 7,697 | 13.6 | 86.4 |
| 1955[a] | 8,202 | 2,206 | 5,996 | 26.9 | 73.1 |
| 1956[b] | 6,583 | 6,039 | 544 | 91.7 | 8.3 |

Source: P.R.C. State Statistical Bureau, Ten Great Years (Beijing: Foreign Languages Press, 1960), p. 36.

(a) In 1955 and 1956 the number of handicraftsmen decreased because in the course of forming cooperatives some of the handicraftsmen in the cities were absorbed by the industrial enterprises, while in the countryside some of the handicraftsmen joined the agricultural producers' cooperatives. (b) The figure for handicraftsmen in the cooperatives in 1956 covers more than 1 million handicraftsmen belonging to fishing and salt cooperatives.

December 1961, a secret instruction issued by the Party Central Committee to local cadres ordered that except in special cases, the state-local industrial workshops formed in 1958 by the amalgamation of cooperatives should gradually be divided up again and should resume their identity as separate cooperatives. Eventual transition to all-people ownership was declared inevitable but was ruled out for a long time ahead, and permission was explicitly given for the continuation of individual handicraft enterprises. The new emphasis was on the need to respect the diversity of the industry by allowing a multiplicity of organizational forms.[40]

Under the new policy, the cooperatives were merely to provide capital and to serve as the channel for the distribution of materials. Despite this modification, reports in recent years indicate that handicrafts cooperatives in general have acted as a link between the individual handicraftsman or small group and the local department of commerce. Handicrafts have basically been absorbed into the orbit of the state economy.

Similar procedures characterized the socialist transformation of peddlers. According to official statistics, there were about 2.8 million small units of peddlers employing some 3.3 million people in 1955. These constituted 96 percent of the total number of private commercial establishments. The volume of commodity transactions of the small traders and peddlers in 1955 accounted for 65 percent of the total volume handled by private commerce.

Peddlers differed basically from peasants and handicraftsmen in that they were engaged in commercial operations instead of in production. They were not capitalists but individuals engaged in commercial transactions. As a rule, they possessed little capital and often operated a small shop, stand, or stall or traveled about to peddle their wares. The Chinese Communist policy for their transformation was to draw them into the supply and marketing cooperatives. Hence, the major transitional form was the establishment of cooperation groups or cooperation stores.

The cooperation groups served their members by acting as distributors, commission agents, or purchasing agents for the state commercial establishments. Selling remained the business of the individual member, who alone was responsible for his or her profits and losses. Although the cooperation groups did not change the individual operations of their members, they gradually became an organic part of state commerce. Members had to purchase their merchandise from the state corporations and sell at prices regulated by the state. The members' income came from the difference between wholesale and retail prices or from commissions. Therefore, the position of a member was substantially closer to that of a salaried salesman in a state store. The advanced form of transition, the cooperation store, changed individual operation into collective management. The cooperation store differed from the cooperation groups in that it sold its stock directly to consumers and shared its profits and losses with its members.

The task of transformation among the small traders was begun in 1953 but was not expanded greatly until the latter half of 1955. At that time, large numbers of cooperation groups and cooperation stores were established as part of the nationwide upsurge of socialist transformation. By the end of 1956, 1.15 million small units in the retail and catering trades had organized themselves into cooperation groups. Another 800,000 units, or 32 percent of the total, had become cooperation stores. Other small traders and peddlers had been taken into joint state-private enterprises. Most of the remaining 540,000 units were widely scattered, which made their organization almost impossible.[41]

After 1958 and the nationwide establishment of rural communes, many small traders and peddlers were drawn into the communes. Thus, this sector of individual economy on the Chinese mainland has been almost entirely transformed into the collective economy.

### *The Rise and Fall of Urban Communes*

When the Communist leaders adopted the commune system, they sought the elimination of three basic differences: between workers and peasants, between city and village, and between mental and manual labor.[42] During the high tide of commune formation in 1958, urban communes were also set up in several cities. In view of the complicated situation in the urban areas, the Sixth Plenum of the Eighth CCP Central Committee in December 1958 decided that urban communes should be established cautiously and solely on an experimental basis. Until March 1960, only 20 million of the 90 million urban people were reported to have been organized into the urban communes.[43]

When the Second Session of the Second National People's Congress convened in late March 1960, a high tide of urban commune formation was launched. By the end of that June, some 1,027 units, comprising 52 million people, had been absorbed into communes. This represented a 160 percent increase within that three-month period.[44]

The principal reason for this sudden acceleration was the failure of the agricultural harvest during the summer and autumn of 1959. The government therefore decided to adopt a new policy with agriculture as the foundation and with first priority given to the increase of grain production. Early in 1960, the government called for a nationwide movement to support agriculture. After the spring of that year, some 20 million laborers were shifted from urban districts to the rural areas to reinforce the agricultural front,[45] causing manpower shortages in urban industries. To solve this problem, the CCP followed its rural pattern by mobilizing housewives and idle manpower in the urban districts to participate in production. This required the establishment of welfare facilities to socialize housework so that large numbers of women could be freed for other employment.

Apart from meeting the urgent demands for manpower, the more profound reason behind the acceleration was that the urban commune was regarded as the only means of solving the contradiction between collective production and individual independent livelihood. The Communist leaders believed that a collective mode of production demands a collective mode of life. Despite the socialist transformation of private firms and factories into public and private joint operation in 1957, the mode of living remained individual. The organization of the economic life of the people and the release of great numbers of women for production represented a socioeconomic revolution in the urban areas. Thus, the function of the urban communes, as indicated by the CCP Central Committee, was "to serve as a tool for the reform of old cities and the establishment of the new socialist cities; as an over-all organizer of the production, exchange, distribution and welfare of the people; and as a social organization where workers, peasants, merchants, students and soldiers are coordinated with each other, and where government and commune authorities are integrated into one unit."[46]

Because urban inhabitants followed many different occupations, they were organized into one of three broad categories of urban communes centering on (1) large, state-owned industrial and mining enterprises; (2) government organizations or schools; or (3) a number of streets and their residents.[47] For instance, in Shenyang, the 3.1 million people of the municipality and the suburban areas were organized into twenty-seven communes centered on such big factories and mines as the Northeast Machine-Building Plant and the Shenbei coalfield, three communes were based on neighborhood residency, ten communes involved government organizations and schools, and eight communes were located in suburban agricultural areas.[48]

The urban communes varied in size in response to local conditions. In Shenyang, each commune had 50,000 to 80,000 members. In Harbin, eight urban communes contained more than 1.27 million people, averaging some 158,000 members per unit. In Wuhan in Central China, nine urban communes contained most of the population, and each had more than 300,000 members. In Southwest China, Chongqing's 2 million people were organized into thirty-nine urban communes with 50,000 members each. Beijing had thirty-seven urban communes in July 1960.[49]

The system of ownership in the urban commune differed from that in its rural counterpart. Urban communes had several economic sectors, representing socialist all-people ownership, ownership by the commune as a collective body, and ownership by the collective bodies under the commune. Generally speaking, the socialist pattern of all-people ownership predominated in communes centered on a state-owned factory or mine but was less characteristic of communes composed of the residents of a neighborhood. Usually, however, the urban communes possessed more elements of socialist all-people ownership than did the rural communes.[50]

Members of urban communes universally enjoyed more freedom than did the peasants in the rural communes. For example, many urban public mess halls did not require members to take all their meals in the public dining rooms and could serve staple or nonstaple food, which could be eaten there or taken out. They could even deliver food to the homes of sick or aged persons.[51] A normal pattern of family life was still permitted.

At first, the urban communes exerted a great effort to provide numerous collective welfare and service agencies in order to emancipate women from their household tasks. Statistics compiled in March 1960 showed that in various large and medium-sized cities, 53,000 dining rooms were set up to serve meals to some 5.2 million people. Approximately 50,000 nurseries provided accommodations for some 1.46 million children. In addition, there were centers that provided laundry, tailoring, repairing, hairdressing, bathing, housecleaning and health-protecting services and facilities for the care of the sick and aged. In the beginning of March 1960, there were 55,000 service centers rendering assistance to approximately 450,000 people.[52] Although these public welfare facilities were very poor in terms of equipment and management, they nevertheless showed a constant increase over figures for the previous year. For instance, in Chongqing, there were 1,297 commune-operated mess halls at the end of March 1961, and over 85 percent of the population of that city was reported to be using those facilities. Some 398 children's nursing teams were formed, and over 35 percent of the total number of children there were accommodated in neighborhood communal nurseries and kindergartens. Relieved of many chores by these services, great numbers of housewives joined the labor force. It was reported that by March 1960, the urban communes had provided the state-operated enterprises with more than 3.4 million workers, of whom 80 percent were women.[53]

By the spring of 1960, the urban communes had become an important supplementary production force of the state economy. In the beginning of 1961, commune workshops assumed the task of producing from 30 to 70 percent of all small commodities and of providing a large proportion of all repair services required in the urban districts. The Communist government adopted a new division of work policy, ordering the state factories to concentrate on the development of high-grade, precision, large-sized, or new products and assigning factories in the communes the task of producing small commodities. This decision made it possible to channel scattered productive manpower and resources in the urban communes into the state economy. In early 1961, a new system of "five fixes"–fixed factories (workshops), personnel, production, supplies of raw materials, and cooperative relations with state enterprises–regulated the production teams of the urban communes engaged in special tasks and also made a clear division of work between state and commune factories. By receiving production assignments from the state sector, the commune factories became a part of socialist industry and were included in the state plan.[54]

According to the official Chinese plan, when the urban areas were completely communized, collective ownership in the cities would gradually give way to monolithic, socialist, all-people's ownership. But after the second half of 1961, under the new guideline of consolidation and adjustment adopted by the CCP Ninth Plenum of the Eighth Central Committee in January 1961, the Great Leap Forward in industrialization was abandoned, and millions of small workshops were closed. The shortage of raw materials, due to agricultural disasters and transport deficiencies, hit urban commune industry with special severity. Priority for the allocation of raw materials was given to large-scale concerns, and the decline in industrial activity reduced the demand for ancillary services from the urban communes. This factor, combined with waning enthusiasm and lessened ideological pressure, brought the urban communes to a halt. In many cities, the urban communes were replaced by neighborhood women's committees or by street associations.[55] After 1962, urban communes were scarcely mentioned in Chinese newspapers and official documents. The system seems to have quietly faded away.

## IMPACT OF THE SOCIALIST TRANSFORMATION

The completion of socialist transformation in the urban sector had several profound effects on the planning and growth of the national economy. The foremost long-term impact probably lay in the emergence of an independent economy free of foreign domination. Since the end of the Opium War, the Chinese market had been controlled by competing foreign powers. In 1933–1937, foreign capital accounted for approximately one-third of Chinese modern manufacturing capital and two-thirds of the capital invested in transportation and public utilities. The prohibitive measures adopted by the Communist government toward foreign enterprises after 1949 forced foreign capital to withdraw. Except for some Soviet influence during the 1949–1959 period, China has been free of foreign interference, and its economy has been insulated against any major international disturbances, such as the energy crisis in 1974–1975 and the more recent dollar crisis.

The nationalization of the private banking system unified the monetary system, which in turn helped to suppress speculation in urban areas and to stabilize prices between 1950 and 1978. Nationalization of the private banks made the People's Bank the sole source of short-term credit and thus drained speculative capital. A centralized and unified currency provided a national market in which the supply of money could be planned and its value stabilized. The state banking system has been an all-important instrument of supervision and control over the entire economy. It became a centripetal force that made possible a greater degree of unification by the central government than had ever existed before.

Transformation of private industrial and commercial firms produced mixed results. On the positive side, the transformation laid down the foundation for the centrally planned system. Without the transformation, the planned purchases and planned sales of major products and the rationing in food grains, cotton cloth, and other staples might have been less effective than they are today. The transformation also helped to increase government revenue and accumulation. By buying out the capitalist sector and paying 5 percent fixed interest at a cost of 100 million yuan per year, or a total of 1 billion yuan in ten years, the government was able to channel 95 percent of the after-tax earnings of private firms into the state treasury, a part of which became investment funds. For this small price, the Communist government merged all of capitalist industry and commerce into the socialist sector and averted large-scale unemployment and disruption of production. The program was a remarkable success.

The transformation incurred considerable costs, however. One severe detrimental effect was the loss of entrepreneurship, the human input into innovation in production and management. Although many capitalists were hired by the government as employees in their former enterprises, they had lost their zeal for innovation and initiation. Others were replaced by cadres sent by the state to fulfill management roles. As Joseph Schumpeter has noted, the motive of the entrepreneurial man is "to found a private kingdom. . . . Then there is the will to conquer, the impulse to fight. . . . Finally, there is the joy of creating, of getting things done, of more fully exercising one's energy and ingenuity."[56] The socialist transformation destroyed such motivations among Chinese capitalists. One reason why China has lagged behind Hong Kong, Taiwan, and South Korea in the past three decades in the development of new industrial products is the diminution of private entrepreneurial activities.

The transformation of handicrafts also became detrimental to the national economy and people's lives. For 2,000 years, handicrafts had provided the bulk of essential consumer goods. In contrast to the situation in many developing countries, they had survived the competition from modern industrial plants thanks to China's ability to produce at extremely low costs, the vastness of the country's territory, and the backwardness of the country's transportation. Craftsmen can make many traditional items that cannot be mass produced. The hasty transformation of scattered handicraftsmen into cooperatives made it more difficult for many rural people to obtain needed items and hampered the further development of handicrafts.

In the wake of the collapse of the Great Leap, the government ordered some cooperatives to divide up into individual workshops. Official publications lauded the traditional organization and business methods of the handicraftsmen. In the 1960s, the traditional small handicraft shops and itinerant repairmen were recognized as a precious national heritage and were encouraged to continue.[57] In reviving individual handicrafts, the government recognized that small producers and service businesses play an important role in rural China. In June 1961, the CCP Central Committee adopted the Regulations on Some Questions Concerning Urban and Rural Handicraft Industries, and many handicraft units that had been transferred into state-owned enterprises reverted to their original status of cooperatives.[58]

During the Cultural Revolution, individual handicraftsmen and small peddlers were labeled by the radicals as "tails of capitalism" and banned. The policy was reversed in 1977. The new constitution adopted by the NPC in 1978 stipulated that "the state allows non-agricultural individual laborers to engage in individual labor involving no exploitation of others." During 1979 and 1980, as the urban unemployment problem surfaced, the Chinese authorities regarded individual handicraftsmen and peddlers as an outlet for urban unemployment. In Beijing, Shenyang, and other major cities where millions of youths waited for job placement, licenses were issued to hundreds of thousands of individual laborers, allowing them to engage in repairing, sewing, barbering, and other petty businesses.[59] Some handicrafts in which skills have been handed down from generation to generation have also been restored. Statistics show that as of the end of 1980, there were more than 1.3 million collectively run commercial enterprises throughout the country. Businesses run by individuals had been expanded to nearly 1 million units, a twenty-time increase over that in 1976.[60] As one official document noted: "The individual laborers provide convenience for the people and meet their needs. For a fairly long time to come, they will exist side by side with the state enterprises and enterprises of collective ownership."[61]

## NOTES

1. Xue Muqiao, "Struggle Between the Two Roads in the Economic Sphere During the Transition Period," *Guangming ribao*, August 8, 1977.
2. Ibid.
3. Mao Zedong, *Selected Works*, vol. 5, p. 24.
4. Mao Zedong, "The Only Road for the Transformation of Capitalist Industry and Commerce," in *Selected Works*, vol. 5, pp. 98–99.
5. Mao Zedong, "On State Capitalism," in *Selected Works*, vol. 5, p. 88.
6. Xue Muqiao, "Severing the Ties Between the Bourgeoisie and the Market and Carry Out Planned Management of the Market Economy," *Guangming ribao*, July 18, 1977; also in Mao Zedong, *Selected Works*, vol. 5, pp. 81–82.
7. Liu Shaoqi, *Political Report of the Central Committee of the Chinese Communist Party to the Eighth National Congress.*
8. Mao Zedong, "Preface to *Socialist Upsurge in China's Countryside*," in *Selected Works*, vol. 5, p. 223.
9. Mao Zedong, "The Present Situation and Our Tasks," in *Selected Works*, vol. 4, p. 167.
10. Xue Muqiao, Su Xing, and Lin Zeli, *The Socialist Transformation of the National Economy in China*, pp. 27–28.
11. Ibid., p. 29.

12. *Financial Times* (London), May 31, 1950.

13. T. J. Hughes and D.E.T. Luard, *The Economic Development of Communist China 1949–1958* (London: Oxford University Press, 1959), p. 88.

14. Chu-yuan Cheng, *Monetary Affairs of Communist China* (Hong Kong: Union Research Institute, 1954), p. 46.

15. Ibid., pp. 50–55.

16. Ibid., pp. 44–45.

17. *The Constitution of the People's Republic of China* (Beijing: Foreign Languages Press, 1954), p. 76.

18. Mao Zedong, "On Coalition Government," in *Selected Works,* vol. 4, p. 273.

19. P.R.C., State Statistical Bureau, *Ten Great Years,* pp. 38–40.

20. Xue Muqiao, Su Xing, and Lin Zeli, *Socialist Transformation,* p. 47.

21. Mao Zedong, "Fight for a Fundamental Turn for the Better in the Financial and Economic Situation in China," in *New China's Economic Achievements (1949–1952),* comp. China Committee for the Promotion of International Trade (Beijing: Foreign Languages Press, 1952), pp. 1–11.

22. NCNA-Beijing, September 18, 1952.

23. In his concluding remarks delivered to the Sixth Plenum of the CCP Seventh Central Committee, Mao expressed his high satisfaction in capturing the Chinese capitalists (see his *Selected Works,* vol. 5, pp. 198–199).

24. Liu Shaoqi, *Political Report,* p. 23.

25. Bo Yipo, "The Three Years of Achievements of the People's Republic of China," in *New China's Economic Achievements,* pp. 152–153.

26. Bo Yipo, "A Report on the 1953 Budget of China," *People's China* (Beijing) Supplement (June 19, 1953).

27. *Da gong bao* (Tianjin), June 19, 1953.

28. Zhongguo shehui kexueyuan [Chinese Academy of Social Sciences] *Zhongguo ziben zhuyi gongshangye de shehui zhuyi gaizao* [Socialist transformation of capitalist industry and commerce in China] (Beijing: Renmin Chubanshe, 1978), p. 89.

29. V. I. Lenin, *Selected Works,* vol. 11 (New York: International Publishers, 1952), pt. 2, p. 644.

30. Wu Jiang, "The Development of State Capitalism in the Initial Stage of the Transition Period," *Jingji yanjiu* No. 1 (February 1956), pp. 84–116. Also Wu Jiang, "Transition from Capitalist Economy to State-Capitalist Economy," *Jingji yanjiu* No. 2 (April 1956), pp. 54–99.

31. "The Development of State Capitalism in China's Industry," *Tongji gongzuo tongxun* [Bulletin of statistical works] (Beijing) No. 22 (October 1956), pp. 3-7.

32. Xue Muqiao, Su Xing, and Lin Zeli, *Socialist Transformation,* pp. 194–195.

33. P.R.C., State Statistical Bureau, *Ten Great Years,* pp. 30-31.

34. The assessment of private capital was greatly undervalued. Thus, the state could pay only a token amount of fixed interest to the owners.

35. *Renmin ribao,* March 20, 1962.
36. Xue Muqiao, Su Xing, and Lin Zeli, *Socialist Transformation,* pp. 209–210.
37. P.R.C., State Statistical Bureau, *On the Fulfillment of the 1954 State Economic Plan* (Beijing: Tongji Chubanshe, 1955), p. 21.
38. P.R.C., State Statistical Bureau, *Ten Great Years,* pp. 28–29.
39. Xue Muqiao, Su Xing, and Lin Zeli, *Socialist Transformation,* p. 157.
40. Audrey Donnithorne, *China's Economic System* (New York: Praeger, 1967), pp. 231–232.
41. Ibid., p. 164.
42. CCP, Central Committee, "Resolution on the Establishment of People's Communes in the Rural Areas," NCNA-Beijing, September 9, 1958.
43. Li Jibo, "Speech to the Second Session of the Second National People's Congress," *Renmin ribao,* April 9, 1960.
44. Li Fuchun, "Raising High the Red Banner of the General Line and Marching On," *Hongqi* No. 16 (August 16, 1960), p. 3.
45. Hu Ning-hui, "China's Economy in the Process of Adjustment," *Chi-shih nien-tai* (Hong Kong) No. 113 (June 1979), pp. 13–14.
46. CCP, Eighth Central Committee, "Resolution on Some Questions Concerning the People's Communes," *Xinhua banyuekan* No. 24 (December 1958), p. 7.
47. *Peking Review* 3:10 (April 19, 1960), p. 23.
48. *Liaoning ribao* [Liaoning daily] (Shenyang), April 28, 1960.
49. *Gongren ribao* [Workers' daily] (Beijing), March 29, 1961.
50. Guan Datong, "Characteristics and Superiorities of Urban People's Communes," *Xin jianshe* [New construction] (Beijing) No. 5 (May 7, 1960).
51. Yao Yilin, "Speech to the Second Session of the Second NPC," *Renmin ribao,* April 9, 1960.
52. Ibid.
53. *Gongren ribao,* March 29, 1961, and *Renmin ribao,* April 19, 1960.
54. *Da gong bao* (Beijing), January 25, 1961.
55. Audrey Donnithorne, *China's Economic System,* pp. 230–231.
56. Joseph A. Schumpeter, *The Theory of Economic Development* (Cambridge, Mass.: Harvard University Press, 1934), pp. 93–94.
57. He Yifu, "Encourage Traditional Business Methods," *Gongren ribao,* November 21, 1961, p. 2.
58. Editorial, *Renmin ribao,* June 19, 1980, p. 1.
59. In Liaoning Province, 13,000 individual businesses received licenses in 1979 (*Renmin ribao,* April 1, 1980).
60. Xinhua-Beijing, March 29, 1981.
61. *Beijing Review* 22:49 (December 7, 1979), pp. 5–6.

# 6

# Formulation and Implementation of the Central Plans

The absorption of private enterprises into the state sector and the collectivization of agriculture provided an institutional framework for a central planning system. Since 1949, the Chinese leadership has been firmly committed to the Soviet practice of using centralized plans, rather than the operation of a free market, to coordinate the economy. The commitment stemmed partly from the Communist leaders' adherence to the Marxist-Leninist concept of planned development of the national economy and partly from their perception that a high rate of growth could only be achieved through centralized planning. Official statements argue that the basic difference between socialism and capitalism lies in the fact that a socialist society can develop the national economy according to objective proportions in a conscious and planned way and thus facilitate maximum economy and effective use of the material, human, and financial resources of the country.[1]

Although national economic planning had been introduced in the 1930s by the Chinese Nationalist government, the organization of the entire economy into a colossal plan represents a brand new experience. As a result, there have been erratic twists and turns in the development of the central planning system since 1949, reflecting the prevailing political climate at the pinnacle of the Party. This chapter will survey the development of this system, analyze the pattern and procedure of plan formulation, inquire into the mechanism of plan implementation, and examine the problems confronting the central planning system and the proposals for its reform.

## THE CENTRAL PLANNING APPARATUS

Essentially, central planning in a Soviet-type economy is a hierarchical system of organization, a pyramid-type structure with a planning elite at the top issuing orders concerning output and production technique and a multitude of production units at the bottom carrying out those orders. In a central planning economy, virtually all government organs are in some degree concerned with plan construction and implementation.[2]

The Chinese administrative system consists of three levels. At the top of the hierarchy is the central government, with the National People's Congress (NPC) serving as the highest organ of the state authority and the State Council serving as its executive organ. Under the State Council are thirty to eighty ministries, commissions, general bureaus, and special agencies–the number depends on the emphasis on centralization or decentralization[3] (see Figure 6.1).

The second level of administration includes twenty-one provinces, five autonomous regions and three centrally administered cities (Bei-

Figure 6.1
Administrative Structure of China, 1981

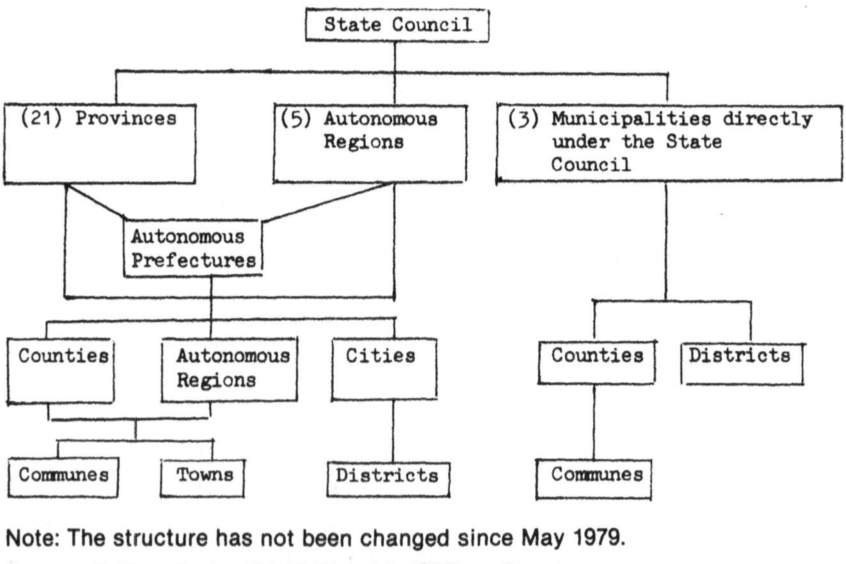


Note: The structure has not been changed since May 1979.

Source: *Beijing Review* 22:20 (May 18, 1979), p. 21.

jing, Shanghai, and Tianjin). Under the provinces and autonomous regions are several hundred prefectures (special districts) or autonomous prefectures, each of which controls several *xian* (counties) or autonomous counties (banners) and cities (see Table 6.1). The third level of administration encompasses 2,138 *xian*, which are further broken down into people's communes and towns.[4]

Of the central and local government organs, three sets of agencies are directly involved in economic planning. They are, respectively, responsible for information collection and evaluation, plan formulation and coordination, and plan implementation and supervision.

### *The Information Collection Agencies*

Since planning implies both knowledge and action, the central planners need to obtain three types of information in order to formulate commands. First, the planners must have knowledge of the physical capacity of the economy to produce. Second, they must have knowledge of the production functions of each commodity (i.e., the number and kinds of inputs necessary for the production of each output). Finally, they must understand the possible trade-offs, in which one output may substitute for another in order to maximize satisfaction. In all existing central planning economies, an extensive information collecting network is a prerequisite for plan construction.

When the Chinese Communists assumed power in 1949, no nationwide statistical network was available. The highest organ in charge of information gathering at that time was the statistical department of the Bureau of Planning, which was a part of the Financial and Economic Committee of the State Administrative Council (the predecessor of the State Council). Later, corresponding departments were set up in the six great administrative regions (each region controlled several provinces). But until the end of 1952 and the eve of the First Five-Year Plan, the overwhelming majority of local governments had no statistical agencies.

The State Statistical Bureau came into existence in October 1952. The bureau, patterned after its Soviet counterpart, consisted of fourteen departments for industry, agriculture, basic construction, trade, distribution of materials, transportation and communications, labor and wages, culture, education and health, comprehensive studies, research, editing and translation, machine calculation, and general offices.[5]

By May 1953, the bureau had opened offices in all provincial-level units, except Xizang, and in provincially controlled municipalities. In 1954, statistical units were set up on the levels of special districts and

Table 6.1
Administrative Divisions of China, 1979

| Provinces | Prefectures | Counties | Cities |
|---|---|---|---|
| Hebei | 10 | 139 | 9 |
| Shanxi | 7 | 101 | 7 |
| Liaoning | 3 | 53 | 11 |
| Jilin | 5 | 48 | 10 |
| Heilongjiang | 9 | 76 | 13 |
| Shandong | 9 | 106 | 9 |
| Jiangsu | 7 | 64 | 11 |
| Zhejiang | 8 | 65 | 3 |
| Anhui | 9 | 70 | 11 |
| Jiangxi | 6 | 82 | 8 |
| Fujian | 7 | 62 | 6 |
| Henan | 10 | 111 | 14 |
| Hunan | 11 | 90 | 10 |
| Hubei | 8 | 73 | 6 |
| Guangdong | 9 | 97 | 11 |
| Shaanxi | 7 | 92 | 5 |
| Gansu | 10 | 74 | 4 |
| Qinghai | 7 | 38 | 1 |
| Sichuan | 14 | 181 | 11 |
| Guizhou | 7 | 79 | 5 |
| Yunnan | 15 | 122 | 4 |
| Autonomous Regions | | | |
| Guangxi Zhuang | 8 | 80 | 6 |
| Xinjiang Uygur | 13 | 80 | 7 |
| Nei Monggol | 4 | 43 | 5 |
| Xizang | 5 | 71 | 1 |
| Ningxia Hui | 2 | 17 | 2 |
| Municipalities | | | |
| Beijing | | 9 | |
| Shanghai | | 10 | |
| Tianjin | | 5 | |
| Total | 210 | 2,138 | 190 |

Source: Beijing Review 22:20 (May 18, 1979), p. 23.

*xian*. In the following two years, an attempt was made to get statistical work under way on the *xiang* (township) and *zhen* (small town) levels. During the 1953–1956 period, a total of 160 offices and a quarter million statistical reporting units were established on the special district and *xian* levels, respectively.[6] A nationwide data collection system had gradually taken shape.

The state statistical network operated under a double-tracked reporting system. Enterprises controlled by the central government ministries were required to report first to the specialized business bureau and subsequently to the State Statistical Bureau. Second, they were also required to report to the provincial bureau and thence to the State Statistical Bureau in the central government. The double-tracked reporting system was designed to attain uniformity and served as a cross-check for all statistical reports.

The efforts to build up a national statistical network were shattered in 1958 by the Great Leap Forward. During that period, the normal functions of data collection and analysis were replaced by the urgent political task of engineering interregional or interplant emulation drives. Many statistical units were abolished and their personnel transferred to other tasks.[7] The result was the statistical fiasco of 1958 and 1959, when there were highly inflated claims that eventually had to be retracted.[8]

In the wake of the Great Leap, the statistical system gradually resumed its functions, and by 1962, a vertical control system over statistical departments on all levels had been reinstituted. The system suffered another disruption, however, when the radicals smashed all bureaucratic agencies during the Cultural Revolution. For almost a decade, the statistical system was paralyzed, and there was widespread falsification of statistics.[9] Official statements in late 1977 indicated that it would take at least three years to clean up the mess so the statistical system could resume its normal functions.[10]

Starting in July 1979, the government resumed publication of the annual communiqué on fulfillment of the national economic plan for the preceding year as well as on the economic plan and fiscal budget for the current year. For the first time in more than two decades, the Chinese authorities revealed statistics on population, foreign trade, and national income. This would indicate that the statistical system had gradually been restored to normal operation.

### *The Plan Formulation Agencies*

In the autumn of 1952, in preparation for the First Five-Year Plan, the State Planning Committee was established as a parallel organization to the then-existing State Administrative Council. Corresponding planning organs were also set up in the economic ministries and in all other government agencies. In 1954, the State Planning Committee was reorganized as the State Planning Commission (SPC) and placed under the jurisdiction of the newly constituted State Council. In May 1956, it was decided that the State Planning Commission would specialize in long-term planning and a State Economic Commission (SEC) would be responsible for the annual and quarterly plan.[11]

In addition to these two planning bodies, a State Construction Commission was created in 1954 to assume responsibility for all capital construction work. In February 1958, it was abolished, and its functions were divided between the other two commissions and the Ministry of Construction Engineering. In October 1958, however, a State Capital Construction Commission (SCCC) was established, only to be abolished in early 1961 and revived in 1965 as the government prepared for the Third Five-Year Plan. During the Cultural Revolution, plans and enterprise regulations were condemned by the Maoists as constraints on worker initiative and dampers on progress. In light of this reasoning, the number and size of the central planning and economic administrative organs were severely curtailed. The State Economic Commission was abolished, and the State Planning Commission was reduced to a shadow of its former self.[12]

As the dust of the Cultural Revolution began to settle, planning organizations came to life again. By 1979, the State Planning Commission had become China's highest planning authority. It establishes broad budget parameters for each component of the economy and engages in both long-range and annual planning. The SPC sets the guidelines, and other planning bodies draw up plans in conformity with them. In 1962, the SPC had twenty-three bureaus for production, foreign trade, communications, agriculture, and construction, as well as other bureaus corresponding to each industrial ministry. The State Economic Commission, which reemerged in 1978, is charged with implementing the production plans of the SPC. Specifically, the SEC coordinates the details of annual and quarterly production plans for the industrial and communications sectors and coordinates the supply and demand of industrial raw materials, energy, and other inputs. As a result, supply shortages in any given sector normally come to the SEC's attention first. If domestic sources are unavailable, the commission may order the necessary items from abroad through the Ministry of Foreign Trade. According to one senior official of the SEC, the commission has a small headquarters staff of about 300 people. Generally, the implementation of plans rests on the ministries, and the SEC becomes involved only when a ministry does not pay enough attention to a particular problem or when there is a conflict of interest between two ministries. Each month, the SEC holds meetings with ministry heads to discuss such problems.[13]

The State Capital Construction Commission is responsible for all investment projects above a certain size. It plans logistics for and oversees major capital construction work nationwide. Once the SCCC's budget receives SPC approval, the SCCC coordinates the investment plans of ministries and, in turn, approves their investment budgets. As with the SPC, the SCCC has liaison bureaus for each ministry–except for agriculture, which is the sole responsibility of the State Agricultural Commission.[14]

Often the appearance or disappearance of the planning apparatus appears to have been the result of changing attitudes in the Party's leadership toward planning and control. During periods when Maoist ideology was the paramount concern, as in the Great Leap Forward and the Cultural Revolution, careful planning and control were generally eschewed, the power of the planning commissions was circumscribed, and their organizations were abolished or cut to the bone. During periods when the pragmatists were in the saddle, planning and control became prime concerns, and the power and organization of the planning machinery were usually greatly expanded. In the First Five-Year Plan period and in the adjustment years after the Great Leap, the influence of the planning commissions was notable. In November 1962, for instance, when more moderate policies were in favor, the State Planning Commission had twenty-two vice-chairmen, which indicates the immensity of its organization.

*The Plan Executive Organs*

The largest group of government agencies is concerned with the implementation of the national economic plan. One set of agencies supervises the financial transactions involved in the physical production plans. Thus, the Ministry of Finance and the People's Bank of China, together with its various subordinate specialized agencies, such as the Construction Bank and the Agricultural Bank, act as the controllers of state enterprises. The banking system is responsible for financing the transactions of enterprises according to their individual plans. The banks, in fact, act as auditors of the plan implementations by making sure that disbursements correspond to plan provisions.

Other agencies are responsible for the supply of factors of production to enterprises. The Bureau of Material Supply (first an agency under the direct jurisdiction of the State Council in 1956, then absorbed into the State Economic Commission in 1958, and again an independent agency in 1963) has been responsible for the allocation of producer goods to all individual enterprises. Supply of imported equipment and raw materials has been provided by the Ministry of Foreign Trade. The allocation of labor force has been the responsibility of the Ministry of Labor, and the training of scientific and technical manpower has been entrusted to the Ministry of Education and the Bureau of Technical Personnel.

Most of the government agencies in economic affairs are directly responsible for industrial and agricultural production. The number of ministries in charge of a single industry has fluctuated almost constantly through mergers, regroupings, and divisions over the years. In 1965, before the Cultural Revolution, there were four ministries in charge of agriculture, forestry, aquatic products, and land reclamation; nineteen ministries dealt with various branches of industry and construction; and three ministries were responsible for domestic commerce and foreign trade. During the Cultural Revolution, the number of ministries in charge of agriculture, industry, and communication decreased by almost half through amalgamations. Thus, the four ministries related to agriculture were merged into the Ministry of Agriculture and Forestry; the three ministries in charge of coal, petroleum, and chemical industry became the Ministry of Fuel and Chemical Industries; the three ministries in charge of railways, communications, and posts and telecommunications were merged into the Ministry of Communications; and the three ministries in charge of textiles and light industry became the Ministry of Light Industry.[15] According to Zhou Enlai, the number of cadres in the organs of the central government numbered only 10,000 in 1971, compared with 60,000 before the Cultural Revolution.[16]

The purge of the radicals in October 1976 presaged the resurrection of many central ministries. Under the subsequent drive for modernization, many ministries, commissions, and other offices under the State Council regained their separate identities. In March 1978, with the reorganization of the State Council, the number of ministries and commissions increased from twenty-nine to thirty-seven. By July 1980, there were forty-nine ministries and commissions, of which forty-two were responsible for economic planning and production (see Figure 6.2 for those extant in 1979).

Most of the central ministries listed in Figure 6.2 are at the apex of a vertical system and have corresponding departments or bureaus in the provincial and city governments. These vertical functional systems have a great influence on plan formulation and implementa-

## Figure 6.2
## Central Economic Administration of China

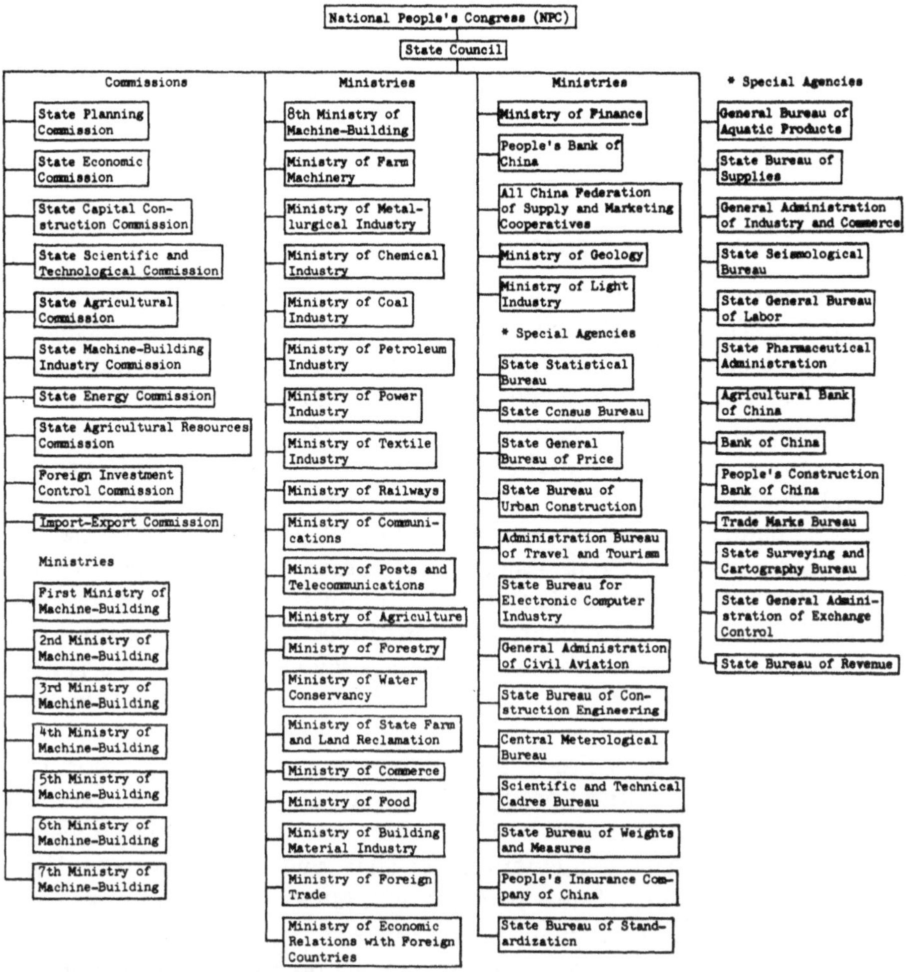


Note: Asterisk* indicates that these agencies are directly under the jurisdiction of the State Council, but do not hold the rank of Ministry. Agencies that are not directly related to economic affairs are not listed in this chart.

Sources: *Beijing Review* No. 20 (May 19, 1979), p. 21; NCNA, March 28, 1979, and June 13, 1979; *The China Business Review* (September-October 1980), p. 9; *China Directory*, Tokyo: Tokyo Radio Press, 1980, pp. 49-55.

tion. In a sense, the ministries resemble holding companies or large, multidivisional, multiplant corporations in the West. Although the corporation is the principal financial, juridical, and accounting unit in the West, in China, the individual enterprises, rather than a ministry, perform those functions.[17] Frequent changes have resulted in a fairly high degree of administrative instability on the national level, but, because bureaus and other subministry bodies have often remained essentially intact – still performing many of their basic tasks despite mergers or splits on the ministry level – there has been more continuity in functions and institutions than one might expect.[18]

## FORMULATION OF THE ECONOMIC PLAN

The primary goal of central planning is balanced and proportionate growth. The methodology employed in central planning is called comprehensive balance – between state revenue and expenditures, between the supply of and demand for commodities, and between the inflow and outflow of cash. The process involves a two-way vertical movement from the central planning organs down to the enterprises and vice versa.

The national plan is formulated in three stages. In the initial stage, the State Planning Commission issues control figures, based on the long-term plan, to the State Economic Commission. The SEC then formulates yearly control figures and directives and passes them on to the central economic ministries and the provincial economic organs, which in turn issue control figures and directives to their subordinate units. The control figures include (1) the rate of growth for national income, industry, agriculture, transportation, and so on; (2) major industrial and agricultural production quotas; (3) investment in capital construction; (4) distribution of important materials; (5) purchase and allocation of major commodities; (6) state budget and currency issuance; (7) number of new workers; and (8) wages for and prices of major industrial and agricultural products.[19]

To translate these targets into concrete action, the central economic plan includes various subordinate plans: (1) a financial plan dealing with the national budget, accumulation and allocation of capital funds, banking, and credit-monetary flow; (2) a material plan dealing with the allocation and supply of materials, the flow of commodities among various geographic areas and trade organizations, and imports and exports; and (3) a production plan dealing with the temporal allocation of users and the maximization of the rate of growth, including a labor plan and a technological plan.[20]

A major portion of the control figures used initially in plan construction and subsequently as instructions to the operating agencies consists of commodity output targets. How are the particular goods and output targets selected? There is no uniform criterion. In the case of some intermediate goods, such as pig iron, the physical output targets can be deduced from the corresponding targets for end products (e.g., finished steel) under the assumption of fairly stable technical input coefficients. In the case of some final products, such as most essential consumer goods, minimum requirements can be estimated on the basis of the physical needs of the population, modified by export requirements. In the case of a number of final and intermediate goods in chronic short supply, the production targets are set at the level of full capacity production by existing plants. The domestic production targets of some products that use import components as input are set by the availability of those components.[21]

Based on these tentative plans, each business bureau will send compulsory targets to the enterprises under its jurisdiction. Prior to November 1957, the Chinese planning system, following the Soviet model, was highly centralized. There were twelve mandatory targets; total quantitative output of major products, total value of output, total number of employees, new varieties to be trial manufactured, total wage bill, important technical and economic norms, amount of cost reduction, rate of cost reduction, number of manual workers at the end of the year, average wage, labor productivity, and profit.[22]

In November 1957, under the decentralization program, the number of targets classified as "mandatory" was reduced to only four: output of major products, total number of employees and workers, total wage bill, and profit. The purposes of reform were to give plant directors more leeway and to remedy many unrealistic decisions made by the central planners.

The number of mandatory targets, like the entire planning system, has varied over time. During the Cultural Revolution, considerable flexibility characterized the planning system, and it is unclear whether the central planners still provided compulsory targets. In 1972, a visitor to the Anshan Iron and Steel Company found that there were six major targets: the output of major products (in physical terms), the value of sales, specified product quality, supply of raw materials and fuels, cost reduction, and profit.[23]

In April 1978, as the central planners resumed tight control over the economy, the CCP Central Committee issued the (Draft) Resolution on Some Problems of Accelerating Industrial Development. The number of control targets was raised to eight: output of major products, variety of product, quality, cost, profit to the state, rate of raw material consumption, labor productivity, and liquid capital.[24] These control targets remained in effect as of the end of 1980.

In the formal planning process, workers and the technical and managerial staffs of the enterprises receive the targets; evaluate the output quotas against production capacity, input requirements, and technological conditions; and map out a concrete plan. Plans submitted by the various enterprises are then aggregated by the business bureaus and transmitted upward to the ministries and the State Economic Commission. The central planners reconcile the enterprises' input requests, using certain goods with output assignments of firms producing those goods to ensure a balance between supply and demand. The method used is the Soviet "material balance" approach. A balance sheet must be drawn up for each of the approximately 200 key materials under unified distribution by the state. The two sides of a material balance are supposed to be estimated separately. The supply side represents the planner's best estimate of what each plant may be capable of producing, and the demand side is based on the material input norms (technical coefficients) the central planners regard as feasible for the enterprises. If the demand and supply sides balance, the consistency problem has been solved for that particular commodity or industry; if the two sides are unbalanced, adjustments must be made. The balancing task is often tedious and time-consuming. The whole process of drafting the annual plan therefore entails some tough bargaining concerning input norms between planning organs and enterprises. Because this bargaining takes time, annual plans have often been promulgated in final form only after the start of the planning year.[25]

After the balance between the input and output of various industries has been worked out, a final plan will be approved by the State Council, the Central Committee of the Communist Party, and, in a purely formal sense, by the National People's Congress or its Standing Committee before the plan becomes the law of the land. Each enterprise and department has the obligation to implement the plan and to fulfill the quotas assigned.

In the planning process, there is an inherent conflict between planning organs and enterprises. Planners have a strong interest in economizing on raw materials and in guaranteeing that output will be maximized per unit of raw materials used. Often planners tend to set "tight" norms in the preliminary plans that are sent down to the enterprises. Enterprises, on the other hand, want to protect themselves against the risk of not fulfilling the output plan and thus have a strong tendency to demand low output quotas and high input requests. Moreover, plan formulation involves a process of aggregation and disaggregation. The commands of the central planners must be disaggregated so as to become meaningful to the individual producers. Yet the production plans of each individual producer are beyond the limited comprehension of the central planners until they are aggregated and presented to the central planners by the ministry. This process inevitably results in distortions. Final plans may be out of balance in that the aggregate may balance, but its components may not.

This problem is particularly keen in China, where the territory is vast and economic conditions vary widely. Many technical norms set by the central planners are unrealistic and inoperative. By 1956, it appeared that the command system had caused severe damage to the economy. Careless plan formulation, followed by repeated revisions, had resulted in a disregard for priorities, the waste of both capital and raw materials, and unbalanced plan fulfillment.[26] It is against this background that the reform of the planning system was promulgated in September 1958.

The reform adopted a double-track system by combining vertical, functional control with horizontal, territorial control. Many control functions of the central ministries were delegated to local authorities, and the territorial principle was to have priority over the functional control of the production branch. Except for the defense industries and some other key industries, textile plants, light industries, and agricultural machinery factories were put under local control. Although the central industrial ministries continued to exist and to draw up plans for all enterprises within their industries, the planning process underwent sharp changes. The plan was to be constructed from the bottom up, primarily on the basis of horizontal, territorial balances. The whole country was divided into seven economic coordinating regions. After provincial plans had been balanced by the economic coordinating regions, they were to form part of the unified national plan. These successive horizontal balances were to compose the primary plans, and the vertical, functional plans compiled by the ministries were to take second place. The final national plan would be constructed on the foundation of both types of plans.[27]

Relaxation of central control in 1958 led to a breakdown in the planning system, first because of the frenzy of the Great Leap Forward of 1958 and then because of the economic crisis of 1959–1961. During that period, the five-year plan was discarded, and the national economy operated on the basis of annual or even quarterly plans. In 1961, efforts were made to return to the functional principle. The nation's economy was described as a chessboard, i.e., action in one sector affected what happened in other sectors, and, hence, moves had to be carefully planned and coordinated. The organs of central planning were expanded and reinforced. In November 1962, the State Planning Commission had twenty-two vice-chairmen, and the number of central ministries had also increased.

These efforts, however, were soon disrupted by the Cultural Revolution of 1966–1969, which severely shook and weakened the organizational structure of the Chinese economy. Not only were large numbers of bureaucrats and technocrats purged, but the planning process also underwent drastic changes. Authority over most of the enterprises formerly under central control devolved to the provinces in which they were situated. Even the huge Anshan Iron and Steel Company appeared to be controlled by its province.[28] The output and requirements of the plants were now included in the local and provincial plans. The planning procedure once again started from the bottom up, although an enterprise still received some control figures from the appropriate ministry and provincial planners. An annual plan, however, was worked out in each workshop, and a draft of the plan was then sent forward to the province. The province carried the proposals of all its enterprises to the State Planning Commission. All major products were given in physical quantities, and the rest were expressed in monetary terms. The province, after reaching agreement with the central planners, disaggregated the plan and divided it among the various enterprises. When the output targets and input requirements of an enterprise had been settled on at the area level, individual industrywide meetings would then be called. Representatives of enterprises in one industry would come to a meeting from all over the country and work out how to dovetail their plans. They would then enter into contracts stipulating quantities, quality, and delivery dates of each product.[29]

Under this loose-jointed style of planning, material balance on a macro level was generally eschewed. The result was economic disarray. As Yu Qiuli, then chairman of the State Planning Commission, summarized the situation in his report to the Fourth Session of the Standing Committee of the National People's Congress on October 23, 1977:

> Some of the proportional relations in the national economy and the normal order of the socialist economy are deranged. . . . Firstly, the growth of agriculture and light industry falls short of demand for the country's

construction and the people's life; secondly, the development of the fuel and power industries and the primary good industry is not keeping pace with the need of the whole national economy.[30]

Determined to correct these problems, the leadership reemphasized the importance of overall planning and all-round consideration. In his report on the work of the government to the National People's Congress in February 1978, Hua Guofeng stated:

Planned economy is a basic feature of the socialist economy. We must resolutely put an end to the anarchy resulting from the interference and sabotage of the Gang of Four and bring all economic undertaking into the orbit of planned, proportionate development. In formulating plans, we must follow the mass line, and both the central departments and the localities should do more investigation and study [and] endeavor to strike an overall balance.[31]

Several months later, Hu Qiaomu, president of the Chinese Academy of Social Sciences, reaffirmed the importance of careful planning and overall balancing in his famous proposal to reform the economic system:

State plans should be formulated by taking into consideration the needs of various sides and all possibilities and, after repeated calculations and comprehensive balancing, they should not leave any loopholes. Additions should not be made to local plans by each level. Production or capital construction projects outside state plans should be included in local plans at the various levels. There should be direct and indirect plans. State plans are a combination of these two types of plans. Production targets issued by the state must be integrated into the enterprise's production contracts to solve current contradictions between supply and demand and between production and needs.[32]

Hua Guofeng's and Hu Qiaomu's statements show that although the leadership had no intention of reviving the highly centralized planning method of the First Five-Year Plan period, it had decided to carry out the double-track planning system adopted during the 1962–1965 period. In doing so, the leadership hoped to effect an integration of balancing by production branches and balancing by various localities, with the legal role ascribed to national balancing.

## IMPLEMENTATION OF THE PLAN

Although plan formulation was entrusted to the central planners, implementation of the plans was the responsibility of the enterprises. The basic pattern of enterprise management in China is the economic accounting system, which resembles the *khozraschet* system of the Soviet Union. Under this system, each enterprise becomes an independent production unit responsible for its own profits or losses. State plans drawn up by the central authorities are broken down into specific targets for each enterprise, but the enterprise is responsible for translating those targets into orders and directives for its subordinate units. The central government judges each enterprise's success or failure in meeting its targets.[33]

To ensure compliance with the state plan, a formal control structure, patterned after that of the Soviet Union, was introduced in the 1950s. The set of control mechanisms included: (1) the one-man management system, with the plant director bearing the responsibility for fulfilling the plan; (2) direct control over major inputs – labor, capital, and raw materials; (3) a complex system of financial controls; (4) an incentive system to induce workers and managers to fulfill the plan; and (5) political pressures and emulation campaigns to obtain plan fulfillment.

The one-man management system was a key part of the vertical command structure. It not only made possible an unbroken chain of command but also enabled the regime to hold individuals responsible for success or failure. Under this system, each firm was headed by a director, who served as chief executive. He shared his responsibility with two deputies, the chief engineer, and the chief accountant. Each enterprise operated on the basis of certain assigned targets, the fulfillment of which was the personal duty of the director. Until September 1956, many economists regarded one-man management as a good system because it provided clear-cut responsibility.

The one-man system, however, often came into conflict with the Party committee of each enterprise and was therefore abolished in 1956. The locus of power then shifted from the director to the enterprise's Party committee, which in a sense began to play a role somewhat equivalent to the board of directors of a Western corporation. All major questions were to be decided by the Party committee; the functions of the managers were confined to routine administration and technical tasks.[34]

In 1961, because of the pressure of economic crisis, the authority of the enterprise managers was once again affirmed, and a strict responsibility system was instituted. Although the Party committee still made decisions on policy matters, the director was charged with the disposition of labor, materials, and financial resources in accordance with state plans. Great importance was attached to the clear-cut allocation of duties through a series of responsibility systems from the factory manager downward, which specified the responsibilities of cadres on every level and of each organization so that "every person may have a specific job to do and everything may have a specific person to take care of it."[35]

During the Cultural Revolution, radicals charged that this management system suppressed the workers' initiative, and one of the Cultural Revolution's essential features was the struggle against managerial authority. Major decisions were made by the factory revolutionary committees, which consisted of army representatives, workers, and cadres. Most of the regulations of the responsibility system were totally neglected, which resulted in lax labor discipline and widespread anarchy.

The ouster of the Gang of Four presaged a gradual return to the responsibility system. In the speech cited above, Hua Guofeng stressed that "a strict system of personal responsibility must be set up at all levels, from the departments under the State Council to the provinces, municipalities and autonomous regions right down to the grass-roots units, so that each leading cadre has his clear-cut responsibilities and nothing is neglected. Fulfillment of the state plan will thus be effectively ensured."[36] Hua's statement in effect called for a return to the strict responsibility system advocated by Liu Shaoqi and Deng Xiaoping prior to the Cultural Revolution.

At the heart of central control is the direct distribution of key intermediate inputs and important capital goods to individual enterprises in accordance with the plant targets. The number of items subject to unified distribution rose quite rapidly during the First Five-Year Plan – there were 28 in 1952, 96 in 1953, 235 in 1956, and 417 in 1958. In 1959, one Communist economist indicated that the state planning system should minimally include 500 products.[37] Materials under unified distribution could not be purchased on the market. Through the allocation of inputs, the central authorities hoped to guide production activities. This method, however, created contradictions between output targets and input requirements, and in many cases, the input allocated by the center was inadequate. Under the impact of decentralization in industrial management, the number of items subject to centralized allocation was reduced to 132 in 1959. Although there is no information on the precise number after 1959, visitors to China in 1972 estimated that there were probably 100 to 200 items under central control.[38] In March 1980, an official source mentioned 100 major industrial products in the state plan.[39] Adding agricultural products to that number, the total number of items subject to centralized allocation must have been around 120 in mid-1980.

Although central planners regard the central allocation of key materials as an effective way to force individual plants to comply with state plans, the central government has often been unable to maintain a firm grip on the distribution of even the most important raw materials. The barter system has prevailed between cities and between enterprises. The situation was particularly severe during the Great Leap Forward and the Cultural Revolution, when central control was loose. In recent years, exchanges of major materials among individual plants have become a common practice, which, according to official reports, has severely "affected the fulfillment of the state production plan, undermined the Party's economic policy, and impeded socialist marketing."[40]

To back up administrative and physical controls, an elaborate system of financial controls was also initiated during the 1950s. Starting in 1950, all state enterprises had to conduct their business with other similar units through the People's Bank of China. All transactions were to be cleared through the bank, and only minor operations could be financed by currency. Copies of all contracts involving any unit within the system had to be deposited with the bank, so that it could act as the government's watchdog in making payments and could play a role corresponding to that of the controller of a giant Western corporation.

In addition, elaborate rules governed how enterprises could obtain funds for their own use and how they could use them once obtained. Working capital had to be kept separate from investment funds. Although the bank supplied part of the former, the state budget alone financed the latter. Between September 1954 and February 1958, between September 1958 and January 1961, and after March 1965, overall control of investment programs was the task of the State Capital Construction Commission. It was responsible for deciding the priority of investment projects, for cooperation between central organs and local authorities, and for general supervision of technical designs and the like. Budgetary grants for investment were paid out through a special bank—the Construction Bank. That bank had to refuse appropriations for all construction projects not included in the state plan.

All capital projects (new, rebuilt, or restored) were classified as either "above-norm" or "below-norm" according to the amount of investment for different industries. In 1957, the norm for iron and steel, motor vehicle, tractor, and rolling-stock manufacturing industries and for shipbuilding was 10 million yuan, but for light industries, it was only 3 million yuan. The norm in 1960 was raised to 20 million yuan for steel plants and 5 million yuan for textile, paper, and sugar industries.[41] All above-norm projects were to be included in the central plan. Even new investment financed out of profits that an enterprise had been allowed to retain had to be made according to the central plan and under the supervision of the Construction Bank.[42]

In industrial enterprises, 70 percent of the working capital was appropriated from the state budget and 30 percent was financed by the People's Bank. In commercial establishments, 70 percent of the working capital came from the bank, and 30 percent came from the state budget.[43] According to regulations, working capital was not to be used for fixed capital investment, nor was it to be used to increase wages beyond the target figure. Moreover, each enterprise had to draw up detailed income and outlay plans for approval by higher-level authorities. Each plan then formed the basis upon which bank loans were given and budget allocations were made. Even the enterprise's own deposits were not to be used for other than approved purposes.

The financial control system, like the other control mechanisms, was not as effective as expected, and after the 1958 decentralization, there was a considerable volume of investment financed out of extrabudgetary funds. In 1958, local authorities were encouraged to use their initiative to provide funds for above-plan investment by diversion of funds from other uses.[44] Investment from extrabudgetary funds had amounted to only 4 percent of the investment from budget in 1957, but it rose sharply to 23 percent in 1958 and 19 percent in 1959.[45] Many enterprises also diverted working capital from bank loans for various unauthorized purposes, such as covering the losses of the enterprise, paying wages for extra workers, and so on.[46] During the Cultural Revolution, the control function of the People's Bank was further curtailed. In more recent years, the People's Bank has been concerned only with wage funds and a part of the capital construction investment, and it has played only an insignificant role in enterprise operations.[47]

In addition to physical and financial controls, economic incentives also played a vital role in plan fulfillment up to the Cultural Revolution. For years, quantitative targets tended to occupy the attention of plant directors and were used as determinants of enterprise bonuses. In the post–Great Leap period, profit also became an important success indicator. In 1961, all industrial economic accounting units recording losses were ordered to shut down. In 1963, Sun Yefang, former director of the Economic Research Institute of the Chinese

Academy of Sciences, openly demanded the use of profits on capital as the chief success indicator for enterprises.[48] Although Sun's idea did not receive official sanction, profit did play an increasing role in enterprise management up to the eve of the Cultural Revolution.

The increasing importance of profit was due to its connection with bonuses for workers and staffs in the enterprises. The November 1957 reform of the industrial management system allowed each industrial ministry to fix different percentages of retainable profits for the enterprises under its control. Retained profits were calculated as a fixed proportion of total profits. In 1957, enterprises' bonuses amounted to 7.3 percent of total industrial profit, and in 1958 they rose to 20 percent.[49]

Of the bonuses to the enterprises, part went to individual workers and employees to provide direct stimulus for plan fulfillment. From November 1957 up to the Cultural Revoilution, enterprises were permitted to derive from the retained profit a sum equivalent to not more than 5 percent of the total wage bill as "socialist emulation prizes" or other bonuses. In 1964, workers at Anshan reportedly received bonuses of up to 14 percent of their basic wages.[50] Bonuses given to the administrators, technicians, and political staffs of enterprises during the 1956–1957 period appear to have been on a notably more generous scale than those of the ordinary workers. At one time, it was reported that senior staffs received bonuses equal to 8–15 percent of their basic wages if the state plan was fulfilled, 25–40 percent for overfulfillment, but that ordinary production workers were given bonuses equivalent to only 2.5–3.5 percent of their wages.[51]

During the Cultural Revolution, the radicals reviled the bonus system as the thin end of the capitalist wedge, and the system was abolished. Since the start of the second quarter of 1978, bonuses have been officially rationalized as ways of "making up for the deficiencies of the time-rate system."[52] According to a 1979 State Council directive, the highest bonuses for workers cannot exceed 12 percent of their monthly wages. In Sichuan Province, however, where the first 100 major enterprises were put under an experimental management reform, bonuses for workers in 1979 were awarded at an average rate of 17 percent of their basic monthly wages, thereby substantially exceeding the ceiling set by the State Council.[53]

In Communist ideology, however, nonmaterial incentives are superior to material ones. In the early years of the new government, nonpecuniary incentives were assiduously developed. These included emulation drives (in which groups of workers competed in raising output or in achieving other targets), mass participation in special campaigns (e.g., "learn from Daqing"), and the awarding of various titles such as model worker or "five-good worker" (good at political thought, completion of assignments, observance of regulations, regular study, and mutual help). The awards could mean mention by name on the plant's honor roll, a certificate of appreciation, or a medal. This kind of incentive appeals to a worker's professional pride, sense of responsibility, empathy, and cooperative spirit. During the Cultural Revolution, the nonmaterial incentives were put in the forefront. Radicals saw moral incentives as an essentially practical way of getting people to take a more active part in production, while avoiding capitalist tendencies. Backing up the nonmaterial incentive is the recruitment of outstanding workers to join the Communist Party, thus smoothing their entry into the managerial elite and leading to their promotion either in industrial administration or as cadres in Party and government agencies.

In short, implementation of the central economic plan in China relies partly on a formal control system based on physical and financial controls of the factors of production and partly on incentives for the administration and workers. During periods when bureaucrats and technocrats have been in command, formal control and material incentives were put into action. In contrast, when ideologists have been in command, formal controls were generally eschewed, and nonmaterial incentives were emphasized.

## PROBLEMS AND PROSPECTS

Despite the fact that China has had a central planning system since 1953, a highly centralized command system has never been fully put into effect, and the performance of the planning system during the past twenty-eight years has proved to be mixed. The central planning system has achieved two significant goals: a high rate of capital formation and a more balanced spatial allocation of investment resources. In the pre–World War II years, China's rate of investment (i.e., gross domestic capital formation as a percentage of gross domestic product) averaged only 5 percent in terms of 1933 prices and 7.5 percent in terms of 1952 prices. As a result of the central allocation of financial and physical resources, the rate of investment in the 1952–1957 period rose to 18.2 percent in 1933 prices and 24 percent in 1952 prices. The central planning system enabled the government to allocate larger portions of current output for accumulation, and from 1959 to 1960, the accumulation rate reached 40 percent of national income. The average accumulation rate from 1970 to 1978 was more than 31 percent, and in 1978, it reached 36.6 percent.[54] In view of the extremely low per capita income, these accumulation rates are exceedingly high.

The guiding principle concerning consumption and investment as expounded by Bo Yipo, former chairman of the State Economic Committee, was that the rate of increase in people's consumption should be less than that of social output and should also be lower than the rate of increase in accumulation. The proportion of capital investment in national income should be set at not less than or a little higher than 20 percent. The normal ratio of state budget receipts to national income should be set at about 30 percent, and the ratio of capital construction to total budget expenditures should be set at approximately 40 percent.[55] Official statistics show that capital construction investment accounted for 41 percent of the state budget in 1959–1977, 40.7 percent in 1978, and 34.8 percent in 1979.[56] Without a central planning system, such a high rate of capital formation would have been impossible.

Moreover, the centralized economic planning and budgetary processes enabled the central authorities to constantly transfer income and wealth from the well-developed provinces to the backward areas, thus reducing the degree of interprovincial inequality. Under the centrally controlled financial system, the maximum level of expenditures permitted in each province is determined by the central government. After estimating the total revenues available to each province, the central government then calculates a revenue remission rate for each province. This rate is set so that each province will have just enough revenue to finance the initially determined level of expenditure. Because of the central government's commitment to reducing regional inequality, backward provinces typically have low remission rates, or may even retain all of their revenues and receive additional subsidies, while the more prosperous provinces are allowed to spend only a small portion of their revenues, the rest being remitted to the central government. In 1956, the five developed provinces (Sichuan, Jiangsu, Zhejiang, Shandong, and Guangdong) were required to remit some 60 percent of their revenues, and the five less developed provinces (Qinghai, Xizang, Gansu, Xinjiang, and Nei Monggol) retained all of their revenues and received additional subsidies from the central government.[57] This system has generated a far-reaching redistributive effect in interregional economic development.

The system also became the source of increasing economic inefficiency, however. This was due both to the difficulties inherent in all central planning and management systems and to the size, diversity, and backwardness of the Chinese economy. When China began its central planning in 1953, each of its twenty-one provinces had more people than all but a handful of the other developing nations. In the 1950s, China had more than 100,000 individual industrial firms. In 1979, the number of state-owned and collective-owned enterprises had increased to 350,000,[58] but the enterprises differed widely in technology, scale of operation, and efficiency. Consequently, the central ministries could not manage their geographically far-flung empires with any single set of technical coefficients as the foundation of the material balance. The rudimentary level on which accounts were kept and the lack of vital statistics prevented the formulation of realistic and comprehensive plans.

The leadership of the Chinese Communist Party was in no better shape. Most of those in charge of planning and economic administration had become leaders during the period of guerrilla warfare in the 1930s and lacked any training in planning and management. In 1955, for example, less than 6 percent of the leadership personnel (plant managers and the like) had a university or an equivalent level of technical education.[59] A more recent official investigation revealed that in some provinces in 1980, none of the leaders on the prefectural and county levels were university or college graduates, and few of the leaders were capable of handling scientific, technical, or managerial matters. In many enterprises, only one or two leaders had a good command of production and planning techniques.[60]

As of 1980, implementation of the central plan was still impeded by several factors: the inability of the central planners to formulate economic plans ahead of the planned period, the absence of horizontal coordination of the plans, and the promotion of self-reliance and self-sufficiency. To serve as an effective guide for the national economy, an economic plan must be formulated ahead of the planned period and must demonstrate a high degree of consistency. The Chinese experience in the past three decades has breached those requirements. The First Five-Year Plan (1953–1957) was first drafted in 1952 but was not put in final form until mid-1955. Preliminary targets for the Second Five-Year Plan (1958–1962) were announced by Zhou Enlai and approved by the Eighth Party Congress in September 1956. The plan was scrapped in the initial year, however, and superseded by the Great Leap Forward. The Third Five-Year Plan did not materialize until 1966, and it was immediately thrown into disarray by the Cultural Revolution. During the tumultuous years of 1967–1969, most of the bureaucrats in charge of planning and economic administration were purged, and it was not possible to implement any long-term planning. There were occasional references in the Chinese press to a Fourth Five-Year Plan (1971–1975), but no details were revealed. It was not until February 1978 that a Ten-Year Plan covering the period 1976–1985 was formally announced. Again, the Ten-Year Plan was published two whole years after its starting date, and one year later, the entire plan was discarded. Official statements in 1980 referred to the years 1979–1985 as a period of recovery and adjustment, indicating that the Ten-Year Plan (1976–1985) was scrapped again. This background indicates that long- and medium-term plans have played a rather limited role in shaping the Chinese economy. In most years, the Chinese planning system has concentrated on annual plans, but even the annual plans have not been ready at the beginning of the year.[61] This delay suggests that for most of a period, individual enterprises have operated without a nationally integrated economic plan.

The absence of horizontal coordination of economic plans on a regional basis has been a frequent source of inefficiency and waste. It was quite common for both a central government ministry and a local government to construct factories in the same area to use local raw materials. Since there was no effective means of coordinating these projects, they competed for the same materials. As a result, both factories operated below capacity. A similar lack of horizontal coordination has also existed in national supply planning. During the First Five-Year Plan period, central ministries established a network of vertically administered supply agencies, but partially overlapping local supply networks were also established at the same time. Consequently, commodity distribution within a single region was fragmented.[62]

The promotion of regional self-sufficiency during the Great Leap Forward and the Cultural Revolution also conflicted with overall planning. Under the principle of self-sufficiency, local authorities tended to ignore the central plan and to pursue local interests. One typical example was the reduction of acreage for cotton and cash plants in order to concentrate on food grain production for local consumption, regardless of the local natural endowment. This kind of problem made it very difficult to achieve material balance on a national scale. At the same time, self-reliance implies the ability to improvise out of one's own resources rather than rely on planned coordination and state investment grants. In recent decades, enterprise expansion has no longer relied on budget appropriations of capital but has mostly resulted from the plowing back of profits or from the diversion of working capital. The economy was leading toward what Audrey Donnithorne has called a "cellular economy"—one consisting of numerous small, self-sufficient units without a unified national plan.[63]

The entire command structure was severely weakened when most members of the experienced economic elite in the fields of planning and administration were purged during the Cultural Revolution. One detailed study indicates that in January 1966, there were 316 known leaders holding 337 top positions (of assistant minister rank or higher) in central government economic agencies in Beijing. By 1969, only one-fourth were presumed to have remained in office. Of the higher-ranking 75 leaders in the economic field (men with Central Committee status), about 70 percent had apparently been ousted.[64] The loss of the services of those experienced experts had a devastating effect on the central planning system. As of October 1978, according to Hu Qiaomu, the national economic base remained in a "semiplanned status."[65]

The post-Mao leaders have deemed it necessary to transform the semiplanned, semianarchist state into a fully planned state, and strenuous efforts have been made to restore the planning structure and control mechanisms since Deng Xiaoping regained power in July 1977. In July 1978, the CCP Central Committee issued a thirty-point document, Decisions Concerning Some Problems in Speeding Up the Development of Industry (Draft), which was to be the basic guide for socialist enterprises in the following years. Although the full text of the document has not been published, official statements have observed that the new guideline was basically adopted from "several previous documents of a similar nature," notably the Seventy-Point Charter for Industry initiated by Liu Shaoqi in 1961 and the Twenty-Point Program drafted under the aegis of Deng Xiaoping in 1975.[66]

In essence, the new guideline made three recommendations. First, it demanded the restoration of direct plant-director responsibility in place of that of the revolutionary committee, and all revolutionary committees in enterprises were abolished in the second quarter of 1978. Second, the guideline established eight economic norms to measure the performance of each enterprise with respect to output, variety, quality, cost, profit to the state, consumption of raw materials, the amount of the circulating fund, and labor productivity. Third, it decreed the restoration of the "five fixed quotas" (or five fixes) and a "five-guarantees" system, which had prevailed during the post–Great Leap era. The state would designate fixed quotas for each enterprise with respect to output, personnel and organizations, raw materials, fixed assets and liquid capital, and the relations of co-operation. In return, each enterprise would submit five guarantees to the state with regard to variety, quality, and quantity of product; total wage bill; costs; expected state profit; and the life span of the major equipment. Enterprises overfulfilling their five guarantees would be entitled to retain a portion of the planned profit in a bonus fund to improve the well-being of the work force. Moreover, under the new management system, an enterprise could reduce the number of its personnel and use part of the saving that resulted for worker and staff bonuses, provided production quotas were fulfilled.[67] Thus, the new guideline points to the return of the planning and management system that existed prior to the Cultural Revolution.

Apart from the reform in management, a fundamental change for the entire planning system was outlined in late 1978 by Hu Qiaomu, president of the Chinese Academy of Social Sciences and a leading Party theoretician. Because Hu's article was published in *Renmin ribao,* it can be regarded as the economic doctrine of the leadership. One notable feature of Hu's proposal was the explicit repudiation of Mao's doctrine of "politics in command." Instead, Hu emphasized the importance of economic laws. In the new planning system, both price and profit would serve as major instruments for economic planning. Four concrete proposals emerged from Hu's article.[68]

First, Hu recommended the substitution of a contract system for direct command. He argued that the current planning system involved coercion and "commandism," because any minor changes in output target required central approval through command channels. He proposed that this system be replaced by a contract system, in which contracts would be reached by mutual agreement between the signatories and equally binding on both parties. The contract system would set up links between grass-roots enterprises; among producers, suppliers, and sellers; between big and specialized companies; among local companies; and between various types of companies and grass-roots enterprises. It would also establish ties between the state and enterprises and even between central and local authorities and between enterprises and their staffs and workers. In other words, under the proposed system, there would be a shift in management from vertical command to bilateral relations. This system was intended to nail down responsibility, to improve efficiency, and to lighten the burdens of administrative organs on all levels.

Second, Hu suggested the reorganization of all industrial enterprises into specialized companies. Industrial establishments in China are organized along vertical lines, and the tasks each plant performs range from basic production processes to auxiliary production processes, with little specialization or coordination. In the machine-building and metal-processing industries, for example, each plant has to produce its own components and parts. As a result, it is impossible for plants to exchange components, and each plant must maintain a great variety of equipment that has an extremely low rate of utilization. Moreover, the addition of a new product requires adjustments in numerous production processes and causes complicated problems of craftsmanship.[69] In the 1960s, a campaign called for the organization of specialized companies patterned after the industrial corporation in the West. Thirteen companies producing tractors, machinery, silk, aluminum, tobacco, and so on were set up on a trial basis. Although the system proved conducive to production and technological progress, the Maoists condemned it as a capitalistic practice during the Cultural Revolution, and it was suspended after 1966. Hu's economic proposal called for the restoration of the specialization companies. Under this guideline, the Ministry of the First Machine-Building Industry began to reorganize its affiliated units and enterprises to ensure specialization and coordination. The reorganization involved three steps: first, the organization of specialized companies or general factories to end overlapping leadership and diffuse management; second, the regrouping of factories according to the type of products they produce; and third, technical reformation to raise the technical level of products needed in large quantities. The reorganization began with the farm machine and motor vehicle industries. In Beijing, 147 machinery plants under the administration of the city's Machinery Industry Department are now under the control of twenty specialized companies. The Ministry of the First Machine-Building Industry anticipated that nationwide reorganization would be completed between 1981 and 1983.[70]

Third, Hu noted that the People's Bank had played a significant part in supervising the activities of enterprises before the Cultural Revolution, regretted its minor position in plan implementation, and stressed the need to strengthen the bank's role. In the March 1978 government reorganization, the bank was elevated to ministry status, signifying its new role.

Fourth, Hu proposed the strengthening of economic legislation and economic judicial work. The change in plan implementation from a command to a contract system could result in complicated disputes. To solve these disputes rapidly, fairly, and correctly, the country needed strict laws and regulations to give the judicial departments clearly defined powers. It also needed economic judicial organs to enforce contracts.

Hu's proposals were not totally new; many had been tried during the 1961–1965 period. What was new was the substitution of bilateral contracts for vertical command and the official sanction of the use of price and profit as planning instruments. Developments in 1979–1980 appeared to follow the corrective measures Hu had outlined. In late 1979, official statistics revealed that 970 specialized companies and general plants of various types had been established throughout the country. The "large and comprehensive" and "small and comprehensive" factories that had produced everything in one plant were dissolved and transformed into specialized companies according to products, spare parts, accessories, and industrial technology. There were also industrywide national companies, such as the China Electronic Supply Industrial General Company, the China Chemical Company, and the China General Company for Textile Machine-Building.

An industrywide company is an independent business unit that assumes sole responsibility for its profits or losses. Each company is also a management unit that supervises supply, production, marketing, personnel, and finance, as well as research and development in the enterprises under its control.[71] The industrywide companies are designed to focus industrial management on a middle level between the supervisory ministry and the individual plant. The system is quite similar to the system of production associations, introduced by the Soviet Union in 1973, which was patterned on the Western corporation system.[72]

The second major reform was the enlargement of the decision-making power of individual enterprises. For three decades, the central departments had imposed rigid norms and regulations on regions and individual enterprises for output, funds, machinery and equipment, marketing, and salaries and wages. The state had not only drawn up production plans, supplied materials, and marketed the products, but it had also taken most of the enterprises' profits and had made up their losses. Consequently, an enterprise's success or failure had had no direct bearing on the economic welfare of the enterprise or its staff and workers. In 1978, more than a quarter of the state enterprises had suffered a loss. To promote management efficiency, experimental reforms were first introduced in 100 industrial enterprises in Sichuan Province and soon extended to 6,600 different types of enterprises in all parts of the country, which contributed 45 percent of the nation's total industrial output value in 1979.

In mid-1979, the State Council issued five directives that formally granted selected state-owned enterprises the right to (1) draw up their own production plans and sell above-quota output directly to other units; (2) retain 5 percent of their assigned profits and 20 percent of their extra profits after state quotas had been fulfilled; (3) promote workers according to the principle of "more pay for more work" and control their own welfare and bonus funds; (4) receive bank loans for investment; and (5) negotiate directly with foreign companies and retain a share of their foreign exchange earnings.[73]

Another new thrust in the same direction was the issuance of bank loans to replace state budget appropriations for capital investment. In the past, all capital construction projects, once approved by the state, had been automatically financed by state budget. That system had caused a great waste of capital and an undue prolongation of the construction period. Between July 1979 and early 1980, 150 capital construction projects were undertaken solely with bank loans. In 1980, textile, power, tourism, metallurgical, building materials, machine-building, and light industries in Shanghai and in eleven provinces were experimenting with the new system. Funds derived from bank loans accounted for 30 percent of the investment in capital construction in Hubei Province and 28 percent of such investment in Fujian Province. Eventually, all capital investment will shift to bank loans.[74]

All these experimental plans seem to have one goal in common: to abolish the highly centralized planning and management system, which seriously shackles the initiative of managers and workers, and to build a system that combines central planning with a market mechanism similar to the market socialism of Yugoslavia and some Eastern European Communist states.[75]

## NOTES

1. Zhong Qifu, "Methods in Formulating National Economic Plans," *Jihua jingji* No. 3 (1955), pp. 28–30.
2. Abram Bergson, *The Economics of Soviet Planning* (New Haven: Yale University Press, 1964), p. 27.
3. In the Soviet Union, the term decentralization refers to the reduction of central control and a greater reliance on the use of the market as a means of resource allocation. In China, the term refers to the transfer of administrative authority to the provincial government.
4. The constitution of the People's Republic of China was adopted on March 5, 1978, by the Fifth NPC (*Peking Review* 21:11 [March 17, 1978], pp. 10–11, and 22:20 [May 18, 1979], pp. 21–23).
5. India, Ministry of Food and Agriculture, *Report of India Delegation to China on Agriculture Planning and Techniques* (New Delhi, 1956), pp. 82–83.
6. Yuan-li Wu, *The Economy of Communist China* (New York: Praeger, 1965), p. 28.
7. Choh-ming Li, *The Statistical System of Communist China* (Berkeley and Los Angeles: University of California Press, 1962), chap. 7.
8. Chu-yuan Cheng, *Communist China's Economy, 1949–1962,* pp. 186–189.

9. For instance, the Party secretary of the Anshan Iron Plant was criticized for having inflated the production figure for the first quarter of 1978 (NCNA-Beijing, August 4, 1978).

10. Harrison E. Salisbury, "China's Leaders View Last 10 Years as Lost," *New York Times,* November 5, 1977, p. C-3.

11. *Zhonghua Renmin Gongheguo fagui huibian* [Compendium of laws and regulations of the People's Republic of China], vol. 4 (Beijing: Renmin Chubanshe, January–June 1956), p. 82.

12. Audrey Donnithorne, "China's Cellular Economy: Some Economic Trends Since the Cultural Revolution," *China Quarterly* No. 52 (October–December 1972), pp. 605–606.

13. *Economist* (London) 268:7045 (September 9, 1978), p. 60.

14. NCNA-Beijing, October 10, 1978; FBIS, October 13, 1978, pp. E5 and E6.

15. Japan, Cabinet Research Office, *The Organization and Personnel of the People's Republic of China* (Tokyo, 1971), pp. 71–72.

16. See Edgar Snow's interview with Zhou in *Epoca* (February 1971), p. 23.

17. Alexander Eckstein, *China's Economic Revolution* (London: Cambridge University Press, 1977), p. 130.

18. A. Doak Barnett, *Cadres, Bureaucracy, and Political Power in Communist China* (New York: Columbia University Press, 1967), p. 9.

19. NCNA-Beijing, September 11, 1977.

20. For details, see "The Contents of the Component Sectors of the National Economic Plan," *Renmin shouce* [People's handbook] (Tianjin: Da gong bao, 1953), pp. 70–72.

21. For more detailed discussion, see Yuan-li Wu, *Economy of Communist China,* pp. 54–55.

22. *Zhonghua Renmin Gongheguo fagui huibian,* vol. 6 (July–December 1957), p. 395.

23. Alexander Eckstein, *China's Economic Revolution,* pp. 96–97.

24. Hu Qiaomu, "Act in Accordance with Economic Laws, Step Up the Four Modernizations," *Renmin ribao,* October 6, 1978.

25. For material balance, see Sun Huiqing, "Charts of Supply Plans of Raw Materials and Technical Equipment," *Jihua jingji* No. 1 (January 1958), pp. 38–41.

26. Yang Yingjie, "On Unified Planning and Decentralized Control," *Jihua jingji* No. 11 (November 1958), pp. 3–4.

27. Audrey Donnithorne, *China's Economic System,* p. 465.

28. *Peking Review* 15:4 (January 28, 1972), p. 22, and *Renmin ribao,* January 15, 1972, p. 1.

29. Information in this section is derived from Joan Robinson, *Economic Management in China* (London: Anglo-Chinese Educational Institute, 1975), pp. 22–23. This description refers to conditions prevailing in spring of 1972 when the author visited Beijing, Shenyang, Wuhan, Nanjing, Shanghai, and Guangzhou.

30. *Far Eastern Economic Review* 98:44 (November 4, 1977).

31. *Peking Review* 21:10 (March 10, 1978), p. 25.
32. *Renmin ribao,* October 6, 1978.
33. Dwight H. Perkins, "Industrial Planning and Management," in Alexander Eckstein, Walter Galenson, and Ta-chung Liu, eds., *Economic Trends in Communist China,* p. 617.
34. CCP, *The Eighth National Congress of the Communist Party of China* (Beijing: Foreign Languages Press, 1957), vol. 11, pp. 304-306.
35. Audrey Donnithorne, *China's Economic System,* p. 198.
36. *Peking Review* 21:10 (March 10, 1978), p. 25.
37. Yang Yingjie, "Several Problems in Current Planning Work," *Jihua yu tongji* [Planning and statistics] (Beijing) No. 14 (November 23, 1959), pp. 10-14.
38. Alexander Eckstein, *China's Economic Revolution,* p. 135.
39. *Beijing Review* 23:12 (March 24, 1980), p. 5.
40. NCNA-Beijing, April 18, 1978; FBIS, April 21, 1978, pp. M2-M3.
41. Audrey Donnithorne, *China's Economic System,* p. 474.
42. Dwight H. Perkins, "Industrial Planning," p. 620.
43. Li Zhengrui and Zuo Zhongtai, *Banking Works Under Socialism* (Beijing: Zhongguo Zaizheng Jingji Chubanshe, 1963), p. 104.
44. Lin Yun, "The 1958 Reform of Our Country's Financial Management System," *Jingji yanjiu* No. 10 (October 1958), p. 47, and No. 11 (November 1958), p. 45.
45. Audrey Donnithorne, *China's Economic System,* p. 476.
46. Li Zhengrui and Zuo Zhongtai, *Banking Works Under Socialism,* p. 60.
47. Hu Qiaomu, "Act in Accordance with Economic Laws."
48. Meng Kuei and Xiao Lin, "On Sun Yeh-fang's Reactionary Political Stand and Economic Programme," *Peking Review* 9:43 (October 21, 1966), pp. 21-25.
49. Audrey Donnithorne, *China's Economic System,* p. 166.
50. Ibid., p. 209.
51. Ibid., p. 211.
52. "Implementing the Socialist Principle 'To Each According to Work,'" *Peking Review* 21:31 (August 4, 1978), pp. 6-15.
53. *Jingji guanli* [Economic management] (Beijing) No. 1 (January 15, 1980), pp. 15-18.
54. Wu Zhenkun and Tan Huazhe, "Do Things According to the Basic Socialist Economic Law," *Renmin ribao,* June 17, 1980, p. 5.
55. Bo Yipo, "On the Correct Handling of the Relationship Between Accumulation and Consumption," *Renmin shouce* (1957), p. 73.
56. The 1959-1977 figure was derived from a statement in *Renmin ribao,* June 3, 1979. According to that source, the profits and revenue provided by light and textile industries from 1950 to 1977 accounted for 29 percent of the state's revenue, or 70 percent of the state's total investment in capital construction. From these two figures, the ratio of 41 percent is derived. The 1978 and 1979 figures are from *Xinhua yuebao* No. 6 (1979), pp. 30-37.
57. Nicholas R. Lardy, "Economic Planning in the People's Republic of China: Central-Provincial Fiscal Relations," in U.S., Congress, Joint Economic

Committee, *China: A Reassessment of the Economy*, pp. 101–102.

58. Hu Ninghui, "China's Economy in the Process of Adjustment," *Chi-shih nien-tai* (June 1979), p. 15.

59. Dwight H. Perkins, "Plans and Their Implementation in the People's Republic of China," *American Economic Review* 63:2 (May 1973), p. 225.

60. Contributing Commentator, "Be Promoter in Reforming the Structure of Cadre Ranks," *Hongqi* No. 11 (June 1, 1980), pp. 2–5.

61. For instance, the state plan was formally approved in February 1953 and 1959, only around mid-year in 1954 and 1957, and in April in 1956 and 1960. In 1966, most of the enterprises did not have their plans approved as of May and June (Alexander Eckstein, *China's Economic Revolution*, p. 93).

62. Nicholas R. Lardy, "Economic Planning in the People's Republic of China," p. 99.

63. Audrey Donnithorne, "China's Cellular Economy; Some Economic Trends Since the Cultural Revolution," *China Quarterly* No. 52 (October–December 1972), p. 611.

64. A. Doak Barnett, *Uncertain Passage: China's Transition to the Post-Mao Era* (Washington, D.C.: Brookings Institution, 1974), p. 240.

65. Hu Qiaomu, "Act in Accordance with Economic Laws."

66. The full text of the Twenty-Point Program, appeared in *Issues and Studies* (Taipei) No. 8 (August 1977), pp. 77–99.

67. This information is based on the following sources: (1) Chi Ti, "Industrial Modernization," *Peking Review* 21:26 (June 30, 1978), pp. 7–9; (2) Wu Qinglian, Zhou Shulian, and Wang Huibao, "Establish and Improve the System of Retaining Earnings for Enterprise Funds," *Renmin ribao*, September 2, 1978, p. 3. Details of the "five fixed quotas" and "five guarantees" are from Hu Qiaomu, "Observe Economic Laws, Speed Up the Four Modernizations," *Peking Review* 21:46 (November 17, 1978), p. 23.

68. Hu Qiaomu, "Act in Accordance with Economic Laws."

69. Chu-yuan Cheng, *The Machine-Buildling Industry in Communist China* (Chicago: Aldine, 1971), pp. 148–150.

70. NCNA-Beijing, August 28, 1978; FBIS, August 28, 1978, p. E9.

71. *Renmin ribao*, April 21, 1980, and NCNA-Beijing, June 13, 1980.

72. For the Soviet system, see Theodore Shabad, "Soviet Ordering Industry Reform for Three Years," *New York Times*, April 13, 1973, p. 1.

73. Zhongguo xinwen, July 29, 1979.

74. FBIS, February 20, 1980, p. L11.

75. Liu Chengrui, Hu Naiwu, and Yu Guanghua, "Link Planning with the Market: A Basic Approach to Reforming China's Economic Management," *Jingji yanjiu* No. 7 (July 20, 1979), pp. 37–46.

# 7

# Material Distribution and Market Control

Since 1949, the Communist government has confronted a fundamental conflict between the backwardness of agriculture and the desire to achieve rapid industrialization. Industrialization requires an enormous capital investment, which in the case of China has to derive from agricultural surplus. The low level of per capita farm output has necessitated the control of consumption and the channeling of agricultural surplus into capital investment. The most effective ways to attain the goal have been a strict rationing system for key consumer goods for the entire population and the direct allocation of raw materials and capital goods to producing enterprises. Although the system has distorted resources allocation, impeded peasant incentives, and in many ways created waste and inefficiency, it has nevertheless ensured the planners' preferences, stabilized consumer goods prices, and become the cornerstone of the Chinese economic system.

This chapter will review the control apparatus; survey the control mechanisms for agricultural products, daily necessities, raw materials, and capital goods; study the consequences of those control devices; and examine recent reforms in the field of material distribution.

## THE APPARATUS OF MARKET CONTROL

In a market economy, the distribution of consumer goods and capital goods is a function of the myriad independent wholesale and retail networks that constitute the mainstay of the market. Under a vertically centralized control economy, a huge bureaucratic hierarchy must be created to perform the coordination and distribution functions.

Prior to the March 1978 reorganization, the top-level government organ directly concerned with China's material distribution was the Office of Finance and Trade under the State Council, and there were four ministries under that office: commerce, foreign trade, finance, and food. With the reorganization of the central government, the Ministry of Food was abolished, and its function was presumably taken over by the Ministry of Commerce. In June 1979, however, the Ministry of Food was restored. As of mid-1980, the Ministry of Commerce was the central organ in charge of material distribution on a national scale. It is concerned with general supply, sales, and inventory planning, and it supervises the inflow and outflow of major consumer goods among different provinces and major cities. It tries to assure proper financial and critical-commodity balancing among local departments and bureaus of commerce.[1]

Under the Ministry of Commerce there are many specialized national trading corporations, the number of which has varied over time. Most of those corporations are organized along product lines. Early in March 1950, twelve special corporations were created to conduct wholesale trade in foodstuffs, raw cotton, cotton yarn and cloth, coal, building materials, tin, mineral products, oil, and various other major products. The six most important corporations were the China Grain Corporation, the China Cotton and Textile Corporation, the China Salt Corporation, the China General Merchandise Corporation, the China Native Products Corporation, and the China Coal and Building Materials Corporation. These corporations, with main offices in Beijing, set up a nationwide network from the great administrative districts down to the provinces, special districts, and *xian*. By the end of 1955, there were thirty-seven specialized corporations, seventeen of which dealt with domestic trade, and the remainder engaged in foreign commerce.[2]

The bulk of the consumer goods distributed from factories to retail outlets has to pass through commercial wholesaling organizations. In general, China's domestic trade sector is characterized by complex networks and overlapping leadership. Municipal-level commerce bureaus typically are subordinate both to the leadership of the municipal people's council for matters of personnel, welfare, and the pricing of various products and to the provincial commerce department and even the Ministry of Commerce for matters involving planning and control, the allocation of various commodities, and the prices of major products. Similarly, the regional corporations are under the joint leadership of their respective national corporations and the regional and provincial departments of commerce.[3]

The organization of wholesaling in the state commercial system has been based on the political administrative region, with wholesale depots set up in provinces, special districts, and *xian*. In most cases, the alignment of the state commercial apparatus has not coincided with natural economic areas. As the scope of market control expanded, so did the organization of wholesale and retail networks. In 1963, there were 900 second-level (special district) wholesale stations throughout the country; by 1978, their number had increased to more than 1,500.[4]

Subsidiary to the state corporations are two types of domestic trade cooperatives–the consumers' cooperatives and the supply and marketing cooperatives. The first serves as a retail outlet to supplement the state retail stores, and the second is under the direct supervision of the All-China Federation of Supply and Marketing Cooperatives. Each individual unit supplies its members with farm implements, fertilizer, and daily necessities and also markets the members' agricultural products. In 1956, there were 178,000 such supply and marketing cooperatives; official reports indicate that in 1965, there were 200,000 supply and marketing cooperatives and departments distributed over China's countryside.[5]

In principle, there is supposed to be a division of labor between the state commercial organs and the supply and marketing cooperatives. Although the former primarily control the higher echelons of the commercial world as well as urban trade, the latter operate mainly in the countryside and concentrate on third-category farm commodities as well as certain "outside the plan" second-category products (see explanation of categories below). In 1963, for example, the All-China Federation took over commercial control of eighty-two third-category agricultural products.[6] In practice, chronic friction appears to exist between the two parts of the system.[7] In the 1978 government reorganization, the role of the supply and marketing cooperatives received new recognition, and the All-China Federation of Supply and Marketing Cooperatives was made a ministry-level organ under the State Council. With the encouragement of rural private sideline occupations and the reopening of rural markets, the supply and marketing cooperatives have assumed a more active role than ever before. The entire domestic distribution system in China in 1979 is shown in Figure 7.1.

Figure 7.1
Domestic Commercial Systems in China

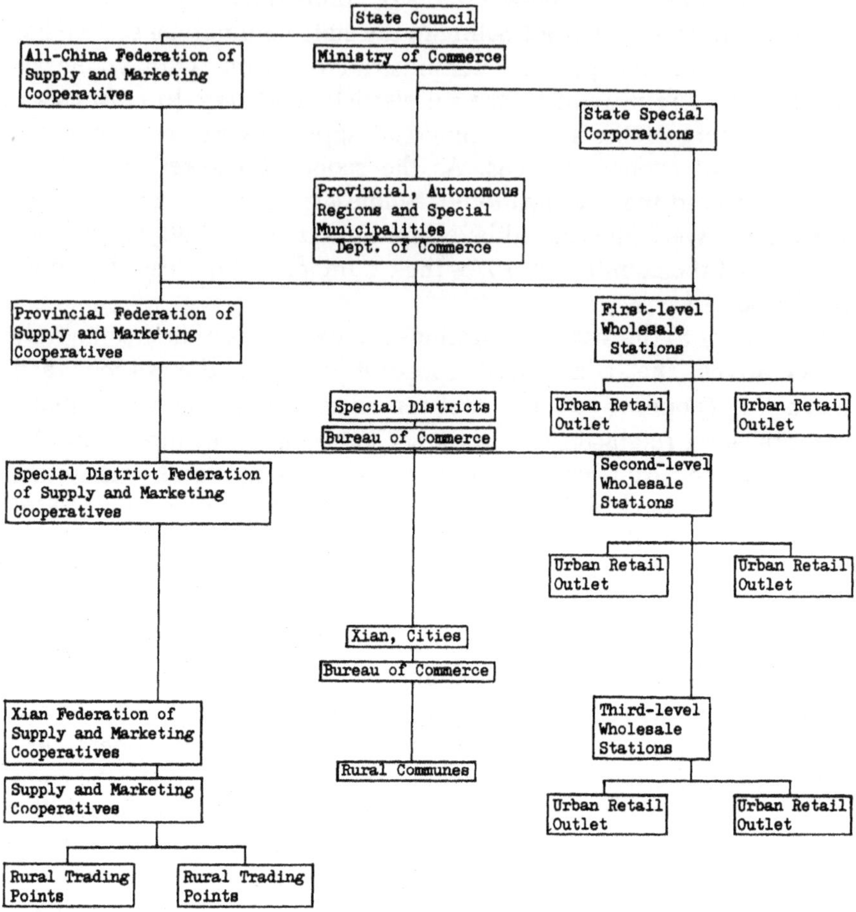


Source: Xue Muqiao, *Zhongguo shehuizhuyi jingji wenti yanjiu* [Study of China's socialist economic problems] (Beijing: Renmin Chubanshe, 1979), pp. 110–113.

## PLANNED PURCHASE AND PLANNED SUPPLY SYSTEM

The core of market control in China lies in the planned purchase and planned supply of major agricultural products and key consumer goods. In an underdeveloped, agrarian economy such as China's, agriculture provides the bulk of the staple foods and raw materials.

The control of agricultural products is therefore the key to control of material allocation.

*The Control of Agricultural Products*

Before the introduction of compulsory purchases and the rationing of grains and other major products in 1953, the wholesale and retail trade in agricultural products and other consumer goods was controlled by both state and private enterprises. In 1952, private commerce still accounted for 36.2 percent of wholesale sales and 57.8 percent of retail sales.[8] In the early years of the Communist government, the central planners used prices to influence the marketing of agricultural products and to affect the allocation of land and other resources between different crops. For instance, when planning authorities were anxious to expand the production of cotton for the cotton textile industry, they would raise the price at which state trading companies purchased raw cotton in relation to the prices of rice and wheat. Thus, the peasants were induced to expand the area sown to cotton. The price mechanism, although proving to be quite effective in resource allocation, was found to conflict with two basic goals: a high rate of capital formation and price stability. The increase in procurement prices of cotton raised the monetary income of the farmers and also their propensity to consume. When the supply of industrial consumer goods failed to meet the demand, farmers tended to consume more agricultural products and to reduce the marketing rate of food grains.[9] The market prices of grains in rural areas in October 1953, just prior to the compulsory purchases, were 20 to 30 percent above the official prices.[10]

The central planner had several options at that juncture. One was to slow down the rate of investment and industrial growth and thus ease the pressure of demand on farm products. The second was to use price as a device to accelerate the growth of farm output, but that step would inevitably increase purchase prices and trigger inflation. Neither option would dovetail with the regime's guiding principles. The only remaining option was to impose direct control over the supply of and demand for staple foods and other key industrial raw materials. Thus, the "planned purchase and planned supply" system was instituted in November 1953, the initial year of the First Five-Year Plan.

The planned purchase and planned supply system virtually monopolized the trade of food grains and edible oils, and in 1954, raw cotton, cotton yarn, and cotton cloth were also placed under central control. All together, those items accounted for 70 percent of the purchasing power of the population. All private wholesale trade in those items was taken over by state corporations, and all private retail stores were converted into state agents. The system became more inclusive in 1954, when a government directive classified all major agricultural products and scrap metals into two categories. The first group covered items most essential to the national economy, including food grains, edible oils, oil seeds, raw cotton, cotton yarn, and cotton cloth. The second group was composed of such diverse products as cured tobacco, hemp, jute, sugarcane and sugar, silkworm cocoons, tea, live hogs, wool, cowhides, handicraft-produced paper, medical herbs, apples, oranges, and marine products.

Products in the first category were subject to planned purchase by the government at prices fixed by the state corporations, after making allowance for tax payments in kind and retention of limited amounts for personal use by the producers. The distribution of commodities in this category was directly controlled by the State Planning Commission. Goods in the second category were assigned purchasing quotas by the government, which the peasants were expected to fulfill on a contractual basis. If quotas in the second category were met, the peasants were permitted to sell any remaining stock in the farm market.[11]

In the summer of 1956, another group of commodities was listed as "minor native products." These could be sold freely, presumably at uncontrolled prices. No purchasing requirements were assigned by the state, but state corporations were urged to draw up contracts with the producers based upon mutual consent.

The classification of commodities into different categories was refined and expanded in April 1959, when the State Council listed 38 items in the first category (under strict central control), 293 items in the second category (less rigid control), and the remainder in the third category (no central control).[12]

Of the products under state control, food grains, edible oils, and cotton are the most vital. The chief control mechanism is the compulsory procurement from peasants of the products at government-set prices. Before the system of planned purchase and planned supply of grains was introduced in November 1953, the government grain supply to the urban population had far exceeded the purchase from the peasants, resulting in a depletion of food reserves for the urban areas. To alleviate the grain crisis, purchase agents apparently procured everything they could get their hands on. Consequently, purchases in November 1953 were 85.52 percent above those for October, and purchases in December 1953 were 72.22 percent above those for

November. Between December 1952 and December 1953, grain procurement increased by 137.34 percent.[13] The rise between July 1954 and June 1955 was even sharper. Overprocurement caused great hardship for and widespread resentment among the peasants. To place a ceiling on the peasants' liability for compulsory sales, the government issued the Provisional Methods of Unified Purchase and Unified Sales of Grains in August 1955, known as the "three-fix" policy–fixed quotas for production, consumption, and procurement.

The new system assigned a standard production quota, based on normal yield, to each piece of land used for growing grain. The normal yields were assessed around the time of the 1955 spring plowing according to area and quality of land, natural conditions, and past yields. Based on the production quota, the state then assigned each peasant household a compulsory sales quota, which was set after assessing the needs of each household or cooperative. The needs for grain were determined on scales set by the provincial governments and equivalent authorities for seed grain and grains for fodder and human consumption. The total, together with the amount of grain for agricultural taxes, was deducted from the figure for fixed production.

As a result of the calculations, the households or cooperatives were divided into three groups: those having a surplus, those that were self-sufficient, and those that were grain deficient. The grain-surplus households or cooperatives would have to sell some 80 to 90 percent of their surplus to the state, while a grain-deficient unit could obtain a fixed supply of grain from the state. Grain-deficient peasants were further divided into two categories: those engaged primarily in grain production yet not growing enough for their own needs, and those short of grain because they had devoted most of their land to the cultivation of cotton and or some other economic crop. For the first category, consumption standards were set slightly below those of the grain-surplus peasants in the same district; peasants in the second category usually received enough rations so they had the same amount as the local grain-surplus households.

Once production quotas had been set, they remained unchanged for three years, beginning with 1955. Under normal conditions, fixed purchase quotas were also to remain unchanged for three years. The purpose of the three-fix policy apparently was to motivate peasants to increase their production.

Compulsory quotas for cotton growers were introduced in September 1954. The content of the directive was much like that for grain, but its purpose was different. Where the purchase of grain could increase supply by raising the marketing rate, cotton purchases could only be increased materially by an increase in output. By 1953, the marketing rate of grain was estimated at only 15 to 20 percent of total output, but the marketing rate of cotton had already reached 80 percent of output.[14] The main purpose of compulsory quotas for cotton, therefore, was to ensure that cotton acreage would not be reduced because of the increasing demand for grains.

Despite the fact that the cotton marketing rate had already reached a plateau, the compulsory quotas enabled the government to procure a larger proportion of the product. The new measure increased the amount of cotton purchased by 53 percent during the good year of 1955 and reduced it only slightly during the natural calamities of 1956.[15] This would indicate that the compulsory procurement in both grains and cotton had proved to be very effective.

### *The Rationing of Grains and Consumer Goods*

Although compulsory procurements helped the government control the supply of food grains and cotton, the procurements still could not ensure an equilibrium between aggregate demand and aggregate supply. To control the demand for food grains and key consumer goods, a nationwide rationing system was established in 1955 and has been kept in effect since that time.

The first item to be strictly rationed was grain, which made up nearly 30 percent of food expenditures and over 15 percent of total consumption expenditures for a typical urban worker's budget in the mid-1950s. Moreover, the income elasticity of the demand for grain for Chinese urban dwellers was estimated by a Japanese expert at less than 0.2.[16] This fact would suggest that control of monetary income alone has little effect on the consumption of food grains. The most effective way to reduce consumption is through rationing.

Local rationing of grains and edible oils for urban residents began in 1953 and was made nationwide by a decree of August 25, 1955.[17] At that time, the Ministry of Food was in charge of the rationing of grains and vegetable oils, and the Ministry of Commerce administered the rationing of subsidiary foodstuffs, cotton cloth, and other commodities.

Food rationing for people in the urban areas varied according to age, type of work, and regional grain-eating habits. In areas where wheat flour was the staple food, rations were 10 percent higher than in areas where rice was the staple food. Rationing took the family as a unit, and each family received a certificate that listed its total ration of grains and allowed it to purchase grain at designated grain stores. There were two kinds of rationing coupons: One could be used in the whole country; the other could be used only within a region. When urban residents visited friends or relatives in other localities, they could, after much red tape, exchange their rations for interregional coupons. Frequently, only people who were authorized to travel were eligible for those coupons. With these coupons, they could take meals at restaurants or purchase cooked food or grain products in the market.[18]

For purposes of rationing, city dwellers were classified into nine categories–heavy, medium, and light workers, higher and other intellectuals, office employees, students, children, and nonproducers (including housewives)–and each category received different rations. Scattered evidence suggests that the amount stipulated was not always supplied. For instance, a comparison of the actual 1956 rationed supply in Guangzhou in South China with the official schedule shows a shortfall ranging from 5 percent for college and high school students to almost 30 percent for people engaged in unusually heavy labor. In the case of Anshan in Northeast China, however, the shortfall was much smaller and some categories even received more than the average (see Table 7.1).

Although food rationing had persisted in the twenty-five years since 1955, rations fluctuated from year to year depending on supply. Official statistics reveal that the average actual monthly per capita ration in 1956 was 25.72 catties and rose to 27.6 catties in 1957 (one catty = 1.1 pounds).[19] In the autumn of 1964, urban grain rations in North China ranged between 26 and 30 catties a month according to category of consumer.[20] In 1973, rice rations reportedly averaged more than 30 catties according to age.[21]

In December 1977, Ross H. Munro, Beijing correspondent for the *Toronto Globe and Mail,* reported that in South China cities teenagers and adults got an actual monthly ration of 25.5 to 60 catties, depending on how heavy their work was.[22] Comparing Munro's report to the figures in Table 7.1 would indicate that monthly rations per capita have risen only slightly, if at all, since the introduction of rationing in 1955. This observation has been verified by Hu Qiaomu, who stated in October 1978 that "the average per-capita grain distribution in 1977 only matched that of 1955."[23]

Subsidiary foodstuffs under strict rationing are edible oils, pork, and sugar. The rationing of edible oils in urban areas, instituted in November 1953, and the rationing of pork and sugar, started in late 1956, remain in effect. The prices of rationed food have remained stable, but other rationed commodities have undergone a substantial rise in price. The purpose of the increase in prices was not primarily to suppress demand but to stimulate production. The shortage of these

Table 7.1
Rationed Supply of Food Grains in Guangzhou in 1956 and in Anshan in 1958
(unit: catties per person)

| Category of people | Amount of rationed grain for areas in which rice is the staple food[a] | | The actual rationed supply of grain in Guangzhou 1956[b] | Amount of rationed grain in areas in which miscellaneous grain crops are the staple food[a] | | The actual rationed supply of grain in Anshan in 1958[c] |
|---|---|---|---|---|---|---|
| | Monthly ration | Average | | Monthly ration | Average | |
| Unusually hard laborers | 45–55 | 50 | 35.89 | 50–60 | 55 | 48.59 |
| Hard laborers | 35–44 | 40 | 31.63 | 40–49 | 44 | 40.40 |
| Light laborers | 26–34 | 32 | 27.52 | 29–39 | 35 | 32.42 |
| White collar employees | 24–29 | 28 | 25.37 | 27–32 | 31 | 29.66 |
| College and high school students | 26–33 | 32 | 30.32 | 29–36 | 35 | 33.98 |
| General public & children over 10 | 22–36 | 25 | 23.35 | 24–28.5 | 27.5 | 28.36 |
| Children between 6 and 10 | 16–21 | 20 | 15.04 | 18–23 | 22 | 21.55 |
| Children between 3 and 6 | 11–15 | 13 | 11.66 | 12–17 | 14 | 14.79 |
| Children under 3 | 5–10 | 7 | 7.09 | 6–11 | 8 | 7.61 |

Note: A catty is equal to 500 grams

Sources: (a) Renmin ribao (People's daily), August 25, 1955. (b) Liangshi (Food grain) No. 6 (June 1957), pp. 7–8. (c) Zhongguo xinwen (China news service), October 3, 1959.

items has been chronic, and no relief is in sight. More than 90 percent of China's edible oils comes from rapeseed, peanuts, soybeans, sesame seeds, and cotton seeds, but the acreage alloted to those oil-bearing plants is extremely limited. In 1978, only 5.8 percent of China's total farmland was allocated to oil-bearing crops, with an average per capita production of 4 catties, or 2 kilograms, a year.[24]

Rations of edible oils are not uniform throughout the country but depend on local supply conditions. They have ranged between 2.4 and 4.8 catties a year in the urban areas and between 1.2 and 2.4 catties in the rural areas. Much higher rations have been granted to government officers, scientists, and families of overseas Chinese in the pre- and post-Cultural Revolution periods. In Manchuria, where soybeans grow in abundance, the official monthly ration of edible oils was half a catty (5 taels) a month for each worker and urban inhabitant when the actual government ration was only 3 taels per person, or 3.6 catties, a year.[25] In December 1977, cooking oil was rationed in Beijing at 1 catty per month for an individual, but the ration was only half that amount for other cities.[26]

Pork rationing was rigidly maintained almost everywhere from 1956 to 1978, and city dwellers could purchase only several ounces a month with their meat tickets. Ross. H. Munro reported in 1977 that in Kunming in the Southwest and in Harbin in the Northeast, the meat ration in the winter of 1976 was 8.8 ounces per person per month. In 1979 and 1980, as a result of new rural policies, the supply of pork increased considerably, and in most provinces, pork rationing has been abolished.

In the rural areas, no ration of meat is available. Peasants are required to raise their own hogs, and when the hogs reach marketable weight, officers from local state-commerce corporations purchase them at fixed prices. The hog owner is allowed either to retain 30–40 percent of a hog for family consumption or to sell that portion at a premier price in the farm market.[27]

In nonfood consumer goods, cotton cloth has ranked as the most sought-after commodity in both urban and rural areas. As early as January 1951, the Financial and Economic Committee ordered the unified purchase of cotton yarn. In September 1954, planned purchase and rationing of cotton cloth were formally instituted.

Under the rationing system, the fiscal year for the planned marketing of cotton cloth runs for September 1 through the following August. Prior to the fiscal year, the Ministry of Commerce issues ration quotas for cotton cloth to various provinces, municipalities, and autonomous regions, which divide the coupons (or tickets) among low-echelon units for distribution to the people. The cloth ration, like that of other consumer goods, has fluctuated over the years. A report by Zeng Shan, former minister of commerce, disclosed that the average consumption of cotton cloth per person was 11.99 *shichi* (Chinese feet; 1 Chinese foot = 0.333 meters), or about 4 meters, in 1950. It rose to 23.08 *shichi* (7.7 meters) in 1953, slipped to 23 *shichi* in 1954, and dropped to 18 *shichi* (6 meters) in 1956.[28] Information gathered from various provinces in 1971–1972 shows that the average annual ration for each person was still around 6 meters (see Table 7.2). Jan Prybyla, who visited China in 1974, was told that the average ration of cotton fabric per person per year remained at 6 linear meters.[29] Travelers' reports in the summer of 1980 indicated that there has been no change in the ration of cotton cloth but the supplies of nonrationed synthetic fabrics have increased rapidly.

In addition to regular rationing, cloth coupons are also issued as subsidies for births, deaths, and marriages. Each newborn baby is entitled to 75 percent of the regular annual ration of cotton cloth. For funerals, 5 to 10 meters are allowed, and for marriages, 4.7 meters, for the couple.[30] Cloth coupons are required not only for purchases of cotton fabric but also for knitwear, garments, shoes, socks, towels, sheets, and other cloth products (see Table 7.3).

Because food and cotton cloth are strictly rationed, excess purchasing power sought an outlet in industrial consumer goods. For years, wristwatches, radios, sewing machines, and bicycles have been the four most sought-after items in China.[31] Since 1979, television sets (particularly color) and cassettes have become the hottest items. All of these goods are also subject to rationing. The scope of rationing extends to most daily necessities, including soap, light bulbs, and toothpaste as well as pans and rice bowls. Rationing of these consumer goods is conducted through the issue of industrial coupons. When the industrial coupons were introduced in Shanghai and Nanjing, they were issued in accordance with the salary or wage scale of workers and employees. In 1962, when Beijing adopted the system, one coupon was awarded for every 20 yuan earned, and city dwellers received one coupon every two months.[32] Later on, when other provinces instituted the system, the family became the basic unit, and each member of a family was entitled to two coupons per month. Table 7.4, which is based on scattered information from South China, shows the number of industrial coupons or tickets needed to purchase daily necessities in early 1978.

Because coupons are required for most necessities, they have become a sort of quasi money, for money alone cannot buy even a tube of toothpaste or a handkerchief. Observers report that "coupons

Table 7.2
Per Capita Cotton Cloth and Raw Cotton Rationing in China, 1971-1972

| Provinces | Annual cotton cloth rationed (meters per person) 1971 | 1972 | Amount of raw cotton rationed (taels per person) in 1971 |
|---|---|---|---|
| Guangdong | 4.5 | 4.5 | 3 |
| Guangxi | 4.5 | 4.5 | 3 |
| Fujian | 4.7 | 4.7 | 4 |
| Shanghai | 4.8 | 5.3 | 5 |
| Jiangsu | 4.8 | 5.3 | 5 |
| Zhejiang | 4.8 | 5.3 | 5 |
| Anhui | 4.8 | 5.3 | 5 |
| Jiangxi | 4.8 | 5.3 | 5 |
| Hunan | 4.8 | 5.3 | 5 |
| Hubei | 4.8 | 5.3 | 5 |
| Sichuan | 4.8 | 5.3 | 5 |
| Yunnan | 5.4 | 5.4 | 5 |
| Guizhou | 5.2 | n.a. | 5 |
| Beijing | 5.76 | 6 | 7 |
| Tianjin | 5.76 | 5.7 | 7 |
| Hebei | 5.76 | 7 | 7 |
| Shanxi | 5.9 | n.a. | 7 |
| Shandong | 5.06 | n.a. | 7 |
| Henan | 5.03 | 5.3 | 7 |
| Shaanxi | 5.7 | n.a. | 7 |
| Gansu | 6.7 | n.a. | 9 |
| Ningxia | 7.3 | n.a. | 9 |
| Nei Monggol | 7.8 | n.a. | 10 |
| Liaoning | 7.17 | 7.17 | 9 |
| Jilin | 7.5 | 7.5 | 10 |
| Heilongjiang | 8.07 | 8.07 | 10 |
| Qinghai | 8 | 8 | 10 |
| Xinjiang | 8.2 | n.a. | n.a. |
| Xizang | 13.4 | 13.3 | 10 |

n.a.- data not available

Sources: Chen Ting-chung, "Planned Marketing by the State: Economic Fetters in Mainland China," Issues and Studies 14:1 (January 1978), p. 34.

are so precious that they draw premium rates when sold in the black market."[33] China seems to have the world's most elaborate rationing system.

### *Distribution of Raw Materials and Producer Goods*

Like food grains and consumer goods, key raw materials and major producer goods are also under unified distribution by the central

Table 7.3
Cloth Coupons Required to Purchase
Various Cotton and Textile Goods
in 1977

| Items of Goods | Cloth Coupon Required |
|---|---|
| A pair of socks | 0.2 meter |
| A pair of stockings | 0.7 meter |
| A towel | 0.5 meter |
| A T-shirt | 0.7 meter |
| An undershirt | 0.83 meter |
| Undershorts | 0.27 meter |
| A shirt | 2.5 meters |
| A light cotton suit | 5 meters |
| A bedsheet | 4 meters |
| A pillowcase | 0.83 meter |
| A pair of cloth shoes | 0.4 meter |
| A cap with visor | 0.43 meter |
| A roll of cotton thread | 0.1 tael of cotton thread ticket |

Source: Chen Ting-chung, "Planned Marketing by the State," Issues and Studies 14:1 (January 1978), p. 37.

authorities. Under the material balance method, a certain number of raw materials and producers' goods are centrally controlled, and others are allocated by provincial or local authorities. In 1952, the number of commodities so distributed was only 28, but it rose to 96 in 1953 and 235 by 1956.[34] The goods are distributed to the departments concerned on the basis of requirements embodied in their production plans. A rationed distribution of these commodities not only backs up plan targets, but also makes it possible to enforce various priorities implicit in the central plans.

Prior to 1959, enterprises under the direct control of central ministries had to apply for their requirements of materials through their own ministries, and local concerns applied to their local authorities. In 1958, the State Planning Commission was made responsible for effecting a nationwide balance of raw materials. In May 1963, a State General Bureau of Raw Materials was established directly under the State Council. In 1964, the bureau was transferred to the Ministry of Allocation of Materials and became the central organ in charge of material allocation for the whole country.

When the main allocation decisions have been made by the national or local organs concerned, their implementation is arranged by con-

Table 7.4
Number of Coupons Required for
Purchasing Daily Necessities
in South China, 1978

| Items | Number of industrial tickets required |
|---|---|
| A small tube of toothpaste | 0.5 ticket together with a used toothpaste tube |
| A toothbrush | 0.5 ticket together with a used toothbrush |
| A cake of soap | 1 ticket |
| A thermos flask (with a capacity of 5 pounds of water) | 10 tickets |
| An aluminum pan (for serving two persons) | 4 tickets |
| A rice bowl | 2 tickets |
| A cup | 2 tickets |
| A pair of socks | 1 ticket |
| A plastic basin | 3 tickets |
| A plastic bedsheet | 4 tickets |
| A pair of leather shoes | 15 tickets |
| A tael of tea leaves | 1 ticket |
| A wristwatch | 75 tickets |
| A bicycle | 120 tickets |

Source: Chen Ting-chung, "Planned Marketing by the State," Issues and Studies 14:1 (January 1978), p. 38.

tracts on the lower levels. There are general contracts between the central organs of the supplying or producing ministry and the ministry requiring some commodity. Within the framework of general contracts, the enterprises producing and consuming the materials would conclude detailed particular contracts. In some cases, direct contracts are made between the two enterprises without any general contracts being made between their superiors. Enterprises consuming large quantities of any product often sign contracts for a long-term, direct supply with the factories or mines that produce it.[35]

In order to facilitate the unified distribution of raw materials and capital goods, the most important institution has been the supply and sales order conference, known as the "material allocation conference." These conferences are organized along commodity or branch-of-industry lines. For centrally allocated commodities of major and strategic importance, the conferences are typically jointly sponsored by the state planning organs, the material allocation agencies, and the ministry in charge of the particular industrial branch. The state planning organ deals chiefly with general coordination, ironing out major conflicts, formalizing contracts, and issuing special allocation certificates, which give industrial organizations the legal right to receive stipulated types and quantities of centrally allocated materials. The material allocation agencies negotiate the various contractual details and supervise the implementation of the contracts.[36]

The major purpose of the national conferences is to bring related industrial buyers and sellers together to negotiate and sign detailed contracts covering supply and sales relationships, specifications, and delivery dates. The conferences are usually held after the parties involved have received their aggregate output targets and resource allocation limits for a given year. Apparently all of the industrial ministries manufacturing important producer goods sponsor and participate in national conferences at least once a year. The participants also typically include representatives of the ministries that are the principal purchasers of the commodity to be produced and the principal suppliers of its material inputs. The conferences thus serve as centrally controlled clearinghouses for material and capital goods.

During the early 1960s, a relatively continuous type of commodity exhibition was set up, at which enterprises or commercial organizations could get cash, credits, or other commodities in exchange for their own surplus materials. These transactions did not come under the central plan.[37]

All of these institutions clearly perform quasi-market and coordinating functions in the area of material and equipment allocation. One notable feature of the material distribution system is its flexibility as it allows some leeway for individual enterprises to acquire needed input. Such flexibility creates numerous loopholes, however, and makes the unified distribution system less effective than it might otherwise be.

Unlike the compulsory procurement of agricultural products and the rationing of food and consumer goods, the allocation of raw materials and capital goods has lacked a stable coordinating mechanism. There have been frequent shifts in the central organ responsible for allocation. The Ministry of Allocation of Materials, which was established in 1964, was abolished during the Cultural Revolution, and it is uncertain which central organ has been in charge of the allocation since then. According to Xue Muqiao, a leading Chinese economist, the situation was still chaotic in the second half of 1979, and no solution was in sight.[38] The lack of central control is illustrated by the prevalence of bartering between enterprises. Many production units exchange their products with other units without the approval of their superiors, and many enterprises that cannot obtain needed materials and equipment through the dilatory mechanism of the planning, allocating, and commercial systems dispatch staffs or agents to scour the country for such supplies. As a result, each enterprise or department of local governments employs purchasing agents similar to the *talkachi* in the Soviet system. For years, some teahouses in Shanghai have been acknowledged places to buy metals and machinery, serving patrons from all parts of China.[39] In recent years, such practices have become even more popular. As one official report testified: "Due to the interference and sabotage by the 'Gang of Four,' unhealthy practices have been fostered among leading cadres. One of these practices is exchanging products with other units. . . . This unhealthy practice has affected the fulfillment of the state production plan, undermined the Party's economic policy and socialist marketing."[40]

The poor coordination of material supplies has been responsible for the large number of unfinished construction projects throughout the country and the extremely high rate of inventory. A recent official report revealed, "In the past, when each unit was responsible for its own supplies, there was often no guarantee of materials."[41] A general survey of the allotment of funds and materials already approved for 1,793 projects in Nanjing disclosed that many projects were three to five years overdue because of the poor coordination in material supplies. For instance, in the first half of 1978, Jiangsu Province could only supply 12 percent of the building materials needed for Nanjing municipal construction projects. When those materials were distributed equally among the various projects, work on many projects could be carried out only intermittently.[42] The fact that materials are supplied everywhere but shortages are also felt everywhere clearly signifies that although the Chinese government has been quite effective in providing subsistence for the population, it has not yet established an effective system of allocation of materials and equipment essential for production and construction.

## EFFECTS OF MARKET CONTROL

The control mechanisms for agricultural products and consumer goods have had both positive and negative effects on the Chinese economy. The system keeps the aggregate demand and supply of basic consumer goods under government control, thus making it feasible to guarantee minimum subsistence levels to most people and to achieve price stability at the same time. For twelve years (1966–1978), the procurement prices of food grains remained unchanged.[43] The prolonged rationing of consumer goods and fixed procurement prices for agricultural products, however, have severely impeded worker and peasant incentives and underlie the economic stagnation of recent decades.

The Chinese Communists, recalling that the Nationalist government succumbed to hyperinflation, have shown an extreme commitment to price stability. With a rapid population growth and a sluggish agriculture, the government faced renewed inflation when it launched large-scale industrialization in 1953. Compulsory procurement and the rationing of foods and cotton enabled the government to suppress the inflationary forces. Since both procurement prices and rationing prices remained basically stable between 1955 and 1978, the government could adjust per capita rationing in accordance with the harvest and the availability of cotton cloth each year. For instance, when China suffered a poor harvest of cotton in 1956, the cotton cloth ration in 1957 was half the ration of preceding years. By tailoring demand to supply, price stability could easily be maintained. Official retail price indexes record an average annual increase of merely 1 percent from 1951 to 1959, with the largest rise being only 3 percent and 2 percent in 1953 and 1957, respectively.[44] There were no indications of prolonged serious inflation between 1953 and 1977. The official indexes undoubtedly reflect a downward bias since they are based chiefly on controlled prices, which were often far below the real equilibrium level. Because the government was able to control the bulk of the consumer goods, however, that bias probably does not negate the basic contention that price increases in China between 1953 and 1978 were quite moderate.

The stability of consumer prices rendered the low wage policy less intolerable for the worker than it would have been with price inflation. Except for some minor adjustments, the wages for most workers were virtually frozen between 1963 and 1977. The system seems to have worked because the regime was able to supply minimum subsistence to the population, but the efficiency and the adequacy of the rationing system have been a subject of controversy. Most visitors' reports have praised the guaranteed minimum level of living for the population.[45] Some people have argued that during the years of scarcity from 1959 to 1961, the available supplies were equitably spread out over the country so that no one actually starved. However that observation has been disproved by a secret military paper of 1961, which disclosed numerous deaths among soldiers' families in the disaster areas.[46] Reports by refugees from Guangdong Province also told of extreme malnutrition and high death rates in those years.[47] In 1979, Li Xiannian, a vice-chairman of the CCP, revealed that 100 million people, representing about 10 percent of China's population, did not have enough food.[48] But compared with other underdeveloped countries, China's rationing system does ensure minimum subsistence to most, if not all, of that country's citizens.

The rationing system also checks unauthorized migration to the towns, enforces labor assignments, and makes possible the rustication of millions of urban youths in the countryside. Under the Provisional Measures for Rationed Supply of Grain for City and Township People, people who wish to transfer their domicile or to add a member to their family have to present their household registration book and credentials to the authorities concerned to obtain grain and oil purchasing rights or permission for additional supply. When people change jobs, they have to present a certificate from the labor department in order to transfer their household registration. When high school or college graduates are ordered to settle in the villages, their household registration and grain coupons are automatically transferred to the place they are assigned to. The young graduates have to obey, or they will lose their rations.

Stability of consumer prices and control over labor assignments have been achieved at a high cost. Since prices are artificially maintained, the system tends to create black markets. References in the official press and reports of those coming out of China indicate that a black market flourishes both in coupons and in commodities. The prices of consumer goods on the black market are always double or triple the official prices. Table 7.5, based on reports of refugees in Hong Kong, compares the March 1961 black-market prices in Nanchang, capital of Jiangxi Province, with the official prices. Reports from Guangzhou, Shanghai, and several local markets in Guangdong, Fujian, Jiangsu, and Zhejiang provinces show that wide discrepancies between black-market prices and official prices also persisted in 1978 (see Table 7.6).

The expansion of black markets has inspired speculative activities in rural areas. Seeking a profitable undertaking, many communes have organized their members to purchase commodities from rural fairs for shipment to urban black markets. Government offices, People's Liberation Army (PLA) units, and state enterprises have also engaged in the illicit purchase of agricultural and subsidiary products. Some state enterprises even exchange machinery, raw materials, and other goods for agricultural and sideline products.[49]

Such unauthorized purchases have cut the supply of foodstuffs to

Table 7.5
Market Prices and Official Prices for Some Subsidiary Foodstuffs in 1961

| Item | Unit | Official Price (yuan) | Market Price (yuan) | Market Price: Official Price (off. price=1) |
|---|---|---|---|---|
| Pork | Catty | 0.70 | 4.00 | 5.7 times |
| Chicken | Catty | 0.80 | 2.00 | 2.5 times |
| Eggs | Unit | 0.08 | 0.40 | 5.0 times |
| Sweet Potatoes | Catty | 0.06 | 0.25 | 4.1 times |
| Fish | Catty | 0.50 | 2.00 | 4.0 times |

Note: 1 catty= 0.5 kilograms or 1.1023 pounds; 1 dollar= 2.6 yuan.

Source: China News Analysis (Hong Kong) No. 364 (March 14, 1961), p. 2.

urban areas. The coastal city of Guangzhou, where fish were formerly abundant, has suffered a critical shortage of marine products in recent years, and in 1978, Beijing also faced a shortage of fruits and vegetables.[50] The main cause of the short supplies was that peasants refused to sell products to the government at the official prices. The 1979 increase in the procurement prices immediately boosted the supply of pork, poultry, and eggs and resulted in a decline of the market prices.[51]

The central distribution system, by taking administrative zones as its basis, has become the underlying cause of inefficiency and waste. According to G. William Skinner, traditional China had standard markets that suited local economic conditions. There were some 42,900 rural standard markets in 1948. The relationships between lower-level and higher-level marketing systems were characterized by interlocking networks, which are difficult to contain within the bounds of discrete administrative units.[52] By organizing the flow of commodities along administrative-zone lines, the government ignored transportation conditions and the relationship between supply and demand. Under the current system, the procurement of agricultural products, which starts at procurement points in rural areas, involves five or six links – from the procurement center in the township and the procurement bureau or department on the *xian* level, commodities are transferred to the city and distributed by the state corporations to their wholesale and retail outlets. The problems include overlapping

Table 7.6
Market Prices and Official Prices for Major Consumer Goods in 1977-1978

| Item | Unit | Official Price (yuan) | Market Price (yuan) | Locality |
|---|---|---|---|---|
| Rice | Catty | 0.142 | 0.55 | Guangzhou |
| Flour | Catty | 0.20 | 0.32 | Guangzhou |
| Peanut Oil | Catty | 1.50 | 3.80 | Puning, Guangdong |
| Pork | Catty | 1.20 | 2.20 | Puning, Guangdong |
| Poultry | Catty | 0.60 | 2.80 | Guangzhou |
| Egg | Unit | 0.08 | 0.20 | Guangzhou |
| Brown Sugar | Catty | 0.36 | 0.58 | Shunde, Guangdong |
| Refined Sugar | Catty | 0.96 | 1.20 | Shunde, Guangdong |
| Soap | Unit | 0.19 | 1.40 | Zhengjiang, Fujian |
| Matches | Packet | 0.02 | 0.04 | Zhengjiang, Fujian |
| Rice (Grade 2) | Catty | 0.18 | 0.50 | Shanghai |
| Rice (Grade 1) | Catty | 0.19 | 0.55 | Shanghai |
| Flour | Catty | 0.20 | 0.60 | Shanghai |
| Pork | Catty | 0.75 | 1.20 | Shanghai |
| Lamb | Catty | 0.78 | 1.30 | Shanghai |
| Chicken | Catty | 1.10 | 1.80 | Shanghai |
| Sugar | Catty | 0.72 | 1.50 | Shanghai |

Source: Kuan Shan-yuan, "The Black Market on the Mainland," Chinese Communist Affairs Monthly (Taipei) 20:10 (April 5, 1978), pp. 58-59.

management and roundabout, redundant transport. Consequently, the commercial departments in China have to keep 3 billion yuan in commodities in the delivery process from procurement points to retail outlets.[53]

The complicated procurement and distribution system also requires a huge bureaucracy. In 1958, there were 7.9 million people employed in the trade and financial system;[54] by July 1978, the number had increased to 12 million.[55] This represents a 50 percent increase in twenty years, while China's food grain output rose less than 40 percent.

The most detrimental effect is caused by the separation of production and consumer demand. Under the state's planned purchase and planned supply system, factories are out of touch with the end-users of their products. They have no knowledge about the market demand but blindly produce according to plan. As a result, useless goods pile up in warehouses at government expense. The waste is astonishing. Official statistics show that at the end of June 1978, unsold products stockpiled in warehouses amounted to 200 billion yuan, equal to half of the annual industrial output value of the country.[56]

## RECENT REFORMS IN MATERIAL DISTRIBUTION

As a part of the drive since the second half of 1978 to streamline economic management, several new distribution measures have been implemented. The first major effort has been to change the commodity flow from administrative to economic zones, and some second-level wholesale stations in Heilongjiang, Sichuan, Hunan, and Hubei provinces have already done so, which has resulted in increased efficiency and lower costs. There are also plans to abolish the existing economic cooperative districts (the whole country is currently divided into six economic cooperative districts) by restoring the historical economic centers. Thus, Shanghai will become the economic center for the Southeast region, Tianjin the economic center for North China and Northeast China, Guangzhou the center for South China, Chongqing for the Southwest, and Hankou and Xian for Central and Northwest China. There will be no boundaries for the economic centers. They will be able to exchange freely and organize according to economic conditions. Economic centers are mainly trading centers but can also organize production. Advanced industrial districts can establish transprovincial corporations to engage in joint ventures with industrially backward areas, thus overcoming obstacles caused by arbitrary administrative districts.[57]

The second major reform has been to eliminate intermediate links by establishing direct contact between producers and consumers. Several state corporations in the machine-building industry have signed contracts with users, thereby bypassing the distribution networks. In Shanghai, the Bureau of Textile Industry set up twenty-six factories and a silk corporation to produce for export. Those factories and the corporation can deal directly with foreign businessmen without hierarchical approval. Decisions that would formerly have taken two to three weeks to reach can now be made on the spot.[58]

The third reform involves a change in the capital goods distribution system. In the past, all capital goods and intermediate goods were classified into three categories according to the level of administration: those distributed by the state, those controlled by the ministries, and those controlled by local governments. The system created unnecessary red tape and proved to be inflexible and inefficient. The new system reclassifies all capital goods and intermediate goods into those distributed under state plans, those to be sold by supply enterprises, and those to be disposed of by production enterprises. Vital materials and equipment, such as fuel and major machinery, are still subject to the state's planned distribution, but the producing enterprises can now sell a part of their products directly to consumers. After the producers of secondary capital goods and materials–such as bearings, tools, chemical products, metallic materials, and construction materials–have fulfilled their contracts, they may sell any surplus in the market. All materials not in the first two groups are available for production and sale.[59] The new reform marks a major step toward the establishment of a capital goods market.

Another reform under consideration is a gradual breach in unified purchase and marketing and the introduction of competition among enterprises, making state enterprises more competitive both at home and in the international market. Although state-owned commerce will continue to be the principal part of the socialist market, collective-owned commerce and free markets for farm and sideline products are also recognized as indispensable. Under the new system, the state will allow a number of small commodity industries to operate independently in terms of production and marketing and to sell directly to retail stores. Rural communes will also be allowed to sell and ship their farm and sideline products directly to the cities as well as to supply and marketing cooperatives.[60]

All these reforms are intended to correct the shortcomings of the existing system. The new guideline is to combine planning with aspects of a market economy, along the lines of the Yugoslav and French models. As Xue Muqiao, a leading Chinese economist has pointed out, "To develop our socialist economy, we should use certain economic forms developed in capitalist countries to organize the circulation of commodities."[61] Since the market control system has operated for three decades, a thorough reform is bound to be slow and complicated, and the outcome is difficult to assess at present.

## NOTES

1. For early commerce organization structure, see Barry M. Richman, *Industrial Society in Communist China* (New York: Random House, 1969), pp. 877–880.
2. Chu-yuan Cheng, *China's Market Under Communist Control* (Hong Kong: Union Research Institute, 1956), pp. 20–21.
3. *Xinhua yuebao* No. 6 (April 1950), pp. 1408.
4. NCNA Reporter's Commentary, "Organize the Flow of Commodities According to Economic Zones," NCNA-Beijing, August 12, 1978.
5. *Xin jianshe* Nos. 1-2 (February 1966), p. 58.
6. *Da gong bao* (Beijing), September 11, 1963, p. 1.
7. *Da gong bao,* editorial, January 15, 1964, p. 5.

8. *Xinhua banyuekan* No. 91 (September 6, 1956), p. 46.

9. According to Xue Muqiao, then director of the State Statistical Bureau, the output of grain increased in 1953, but the peasants sold less. Many well-to-do peasants hoarded grain and waited for higher prices (see Xue Muqiao, Su Xing, and Lin Zeli, *The Socialist Transformation of the National Economy in China,* p. 60).

10. Yang Po, "Planned Purchase and Planned Supply," *Jingji yanjiu* No. 1 (February 17, 1956), p. 37.

11. Sun Huiqing, "Charts of Supply Plans of Raw Materials and Technical Equipment," *Jihua jingji* No. 1 (January 1958), p. 38.

12. *Da gong bao* (Beijing), April 4, 1959.

13. Kojima Reiitsu, "Grain Acquisition and Supply," in E. S. Kirby, ed., *Contemporary China* (Hong Kong) No. 5 (1963), p. 74.

14. Zeng Ling, "The Rural Market in the Surging Tide of Agricultural Collectivization," *Jingji yanjiu* No. 2 (March 1, 1956), p. 13.

15. Dwight H. Perkins, *Market Control and Planning in Communist China* (Cambridge, Mass.: Harvard University Press, 1966), p. 53.

16. Ishikawa Shigeru, *Chugoku ni okeru shikon chikuseki kiko* [Capital formation in China] (Tokyo: Iwanami Bookstore, 1960), pp. 139–185.

17. P.R.C., State Council, "Provisional Measures for Handling Urban Fixed Grain Supply," *Xinhua yuebao* no. 9 (September 28, 1955), pp. 163-164.

18. Chen Ting-chung, "Planned Marketing by the State: Economic Fetters in Mainland China," *Issues and Studies* 14:1 (January 1978), pp. 28-39.

19. Zhu Jingzhi, "A Review of Urban Food Rationing and Some Suggestions for Improvement of the System," *Liangshi* [Food], August 25, 1957. One catty = 0.5 kilograms.

20. Audrey Donnithorne, *China's Economic System,* p. 311.

21. Chi Wen-shun, "Highlights of Economic Conditions in China," *Chinese Economic Studies* 9:1 (Spring 1975), p. 66.

22. Ross H. Munro, "China's Bureaucratic Nightmare: Rationing for 900 Million People," *U.S. News and World Report,* December 12, 1977, pp. 35–36.

23. Hu Qiaomu, "Act in Accordance with Economic Laws, Step Up the Four Modernizations."

24. NCNA-Beijing, August 26, 1978.

25. *Cheng Ming Monthly* (Hong Kong) No. 11 (November 1, 1978), pp. 51–52.

26. Ross H. Munro, "China's Bureaucratic Nightmare."

27. Chen Ting-chung, "Planned Marketing by the State."

28. *Da gong bao* (Tianjin), September 28, 1956.

29. Jan S. Prybyla, *The Chinese Economy* (Columbia: University of South Carolina Press, 1978), p. 66.

30. Chen Ting-chung, "Planned Marketing by the State," p. 35.

31. Ross Terrill, "Peking: Waiting to be Westernized," *Atlantic Monthly* 245:8 (August 1980), p. 10.

32. Audrey Donnithorne, *China's Economic System,* p. 311.

33. Ross H. Munro, "China's Bureaucratic Nightmare," p. 35.

34. "A General Survey of the Distribution of Centrally Allocated Com-

modities During Past Years," *Tongji gongzuo* [Statistical work] No. 13 (July 14, 1957), pp. 29-31.

35. Audrey Donnithorne, *China's Economic System*, p. 174.
36. Barry M. Richman, *Industrial Society*, pp. 712-713.
37. Ibid., p. 714.
38. Xue Muqiao, *Zhongguo shehuizhuyi jingji wenti yanjiu* [Study of China's socialist economic problems] (Beijing: Renmin Chubanshe, 1979), pp. 108-109.
39. NCNA-Beijing, April 18, 1978; FBIS, April 21, 1978, p. M2.
40. Yan Shikuai, "Strive to Complete 'Unfinished Construction Projects,'" *Renmin ribao*, September 25, 1978, p. 3.
41. Ibid.
42. Xue Muqiao, *Zhongguo shehuizhuyi jingji wenti yanjiu*, p. 130.
43. Ibid.
44. P.R.C., State Statistical Bureau, *Ten Great Years*, p. 172.
45. For example, Lloyd G. Reynolds, "China's Economy: A View from the Grass Roots," *Challenge* 17:1 (March/April 1974).
46. *Gongzuo tongxun* [Work bulletin] No. 6 (January 27, 1961), pp. 15-17.
47. Audrey Donnithorne, *China's Economic System*, p. 312.
48. Fox Butterfield, "China's Modernization Said to Cause 1978 Deficit," *New York Times*, June 15, 1979, p. D1.
49. Liaoning, Provincial Revolutionary Committee, "Circular Forbids Unauthorized Purchase of Goods," FBIS, October 18, 1978, pp. L6 and L7.
50. *Renmin ribao*, September 16, 1978.
51. *Zhongguo xinwen* (Guangzhou), September 22, 1979.
52. G. William Skinner, "Marketing and Social Structure in Rural China: Part III," *Journal of Asian Studies* 24:3 (May 1965), p. 374.
53. NCNA Reporter's Commentary, "Organize the Flow of Commodities According to Economic Zones," NCNA-Beijing, August 12, 1978; and Nanchang, Jiangxi Provincial Series, October 31, 1978, FBIS, November 6, 1978, p. G3.
54. John Phillip Emerson, *Nonagricultural Employment in Mainland China, 1949-1958* (Washington, D.C.: Bureau of Census, 1965), p. 159.
55. NCNA-Beijing, July 4, 1978.
56. He Jianzhang, "Problems in the Management of a Planned Economy Under the System of Ownership by the Whole People and the Orientation of Reform," *Jingji yanjiu* No. 5 (May 1979), p. 36.
57. Xue Muqiao, "Some Opinions on Reforming the Economic System," *Renmin ribao*, June 10, 1980, p. 5.
58. NCNA-Shanghai, November 3, 1978.
59. NCNA-Beijing, May 4, 1980.
60. Xue Muqiao, "Some Opinions on Reforming the Economic System," p. 5.
61. Ibid.

# 8

# Price-Wage Structure and Policies

Since 1949, Chinese price and wage policies have tried to achieve two conflicting goals. On the one hand, the government has hoped to suppress inflationary forces by keeping prices and wages as stable as possible. On the other hand, it has sought to use prices and wages to attain certain allocative and distributive ends. As a result, prices have needed continuous adjustment to cope with the changing economic conditions.

The intricacy of the problem of price formation is also reflected in the continuous debates among Chinese economists on whether profits should be calculated as a return on total costs or as a return on invested capital. During the Cultural Revolution, the law of value and the system of differential wages were discarded. Despite a reverse trend in recent years, the role of the price mechanism is still largely undefined.

This chapter will focus on several major aspects of prices and wages in China. It will review various functions performed by prices in the Chinese planning system and examine the structure of prices and the process of their formulation. It will discuss Chinese price policies of differentiation and stability, analyzing in particular the role of profit in price formation and wage structure and policies. A final section will explore the economic consequences of the existing price system and outline recent reforms as well as problems arising from those reforms.

## ROLE OF PRICES IN THE CHINESE ECONOMY

Although physical allocation by administrative order predominates in the Chinese economy, prices still perform certain control, allocative, and distributive functions.

*The Evaluation-Control Function*

As in the Soviet Union, prices in China are mainly used by the central planners to secure the compliance of enterprise managers with the plan and to evaluate the performance of the managers.[1] Prices also constitute a kind of vocabulary that enables the central planners to express complex input and output targets for enterprises in value terms in order to have a common denominator for physically dissimilar units of raw materials, labor, and capital goods.

Until November 1957, five of the twelve control targets issued by the central planners to plant managers were expressed in value terms: total value of output, total wage bill, amount of cost reduction, average wage, and profit. After the decentralization in November 1957, the number of mandatory targets was reduced to four, two of which – total wages and profit – were expressed in value terms. Since April 1978, there have been eight control targets, and three of them – cost, profit, and liquid capital – are expressed in value terms. It is thus easier to evaluate plan performance in terms of price than in physical terms alone.

As an additional measure of administrative and physical control, all state enterprises in China have to conduct their business and clear their transactions with other similar units through the People's Bank of China. The existence of prices enables the financial authorities to control plan execution closely.

*The Allocative Function*

The allocative function of prices is mainly subsidiary and subordinate to allocation by administrative order. Yet in many cases, prices still serve as a useful device of allocation. In agricultural products, price planning has been quite effective in influencing the allocation of land and other resources among different crops. For instance, between 1950 and 1956, planning authorities were anxious to expand the production of cotton to provide an assured source of supply to the cotton textile industry. Therefore, between 1950 and 1952, the raw cotton prices paid by the state trading companies were raised 15 to 30 percent in relation to the prices for rice and wheat. The area sown to cotton consequently increased rapidly between 1950 and 1956.[2] The same practice has been repeated in more recent years. For instance, in 1965 a picul (50 kilograms) of ginned cotton sold for 99.5 yuan, 11.8 times the price of a picul of unhulled rice. In order to promote cotton production, the price of ginned cotton was raised in 1978 to 12.3 times that of unhulled rice.[3]

Prices have also been used to allocate producer goods among the socialized enterprises. In 1956, the state directly controlled 235 industrial producer goods, but its control was not complete. Many producer goods that central planners could not yet handle systematically were sold on the market,[4] and enterprises were free to purchase them or not as they wished. In making their decision, enterprises were guided by several criteria, one of which was the relative prices of substitutes.

Consumer goods classified as essential – such as food grains, cotton cloth, and edible oils – are subject to rationing, and prices play no allocative role. The high prices of consumer goods not in the essential category – such as watches, cameras, bicycles, radios, sewing machines, and television sets – are intended to curtail demand and thereby divert resources to capital goods.

*The Distributive Function*

The distribution of monetary income among workers and peasants is affected by the planners' decisions on wages, agricultural procurement prices, savings, and labor allocation – most of which have an effect on prices. As a matter of principle, the Chinese leaders want to narrow the gap between the incomes of farmers and workers, mental and manual laborers, and urban and rural inhabitants.

During the 1950s, the Chinese Communists followed the Stalin model by squeezing agriculture to support industrialization. The prices that the state paid farmers for agricultural products were set at extremely low levels in relation to the prices that farmers paid the state for industrial products, thus giving rise to the "scissor-gap" phenomenon. Official statistics indicate that the terms of trade between agriculture and industry returned to pre-World War II parity after 1960; since then, they have turned in favor of the farmers.[5] Taking 1950–1952 prices as 100, the government purchasing price for grains rose to 160.0 in 1971 and 165 in 1974; in the same period, the rural retail prices of industrial products fell to 104.6 in 1971 and 97.8 in 1974.[6]

Those figures signal the redistribution of real income between the rural and urban populations. According to an estimate made by Peter Schran, based on official national income (i.e., net domestic material product) data, the ratio between the total consumption levels of worker and employee households and farmer households in 1952 was 2.3 to 1. During the First Five-Year Plan period, as wages for nonagricultural workers and other employees grew much more rapidly in real terms than those of peasants, the income differential between the two segments increased notably. Yet, as the result of a continuous upward adjustment of agricultural product prices, the worker-farmer differential has gradually diminished. In 1977, Peter Schran calculated that the income ratio in 1970–1971 once again approached that of 1952, and the difference declined further in 1979, when the government raised the procurement prices of agricultural products.[7]

Despite these functions, prices do not play an autonomous guiding role in the Chinese economy. To the individual manager, prices do not convey neutral information on the basis of which he can reach a decision but merely convey the planners' orders to the manager.[8] As one official statement pointed out, "Prices in our country are managed by the state according to the principle of unified centralized leadership and local management at different levels. Production and sales units have no power to set prices."[9]

Since prices are determined by the state authorities, not through the interaction of suppliers and users in the market, they are basically administrated prices and do not reflect the relative scarcity of various commodities, services, or factors of production.

## PRICE STRUCTURE AND FORMULATION

Prior to the completion of socialization in the private sector in 1957, a dual pricing system was in effect – one for state-operated factories and the other for the free market (private industry and handicrafts). After 1957 and the elimination of the free market, a unified pricing system prevailed. The entire price structure in China comprises the following five categories:

*Factory Prices.* These prices are the sum of planned factory cost plus planned profit. They are used exclusively for internal accounting purposes.

*Exfactory Prices* (chuchan jiage) or *Transfer Prices* (diaobo jiage). These are the prices at which an industrial enterprise disposes of its products to other enterprises or to wholesalers. They are composed of costs, profits, and taxes. Costs include wages and salaries, basic and supplementary materials, depreciation charges, and various administrative expenses, excluding rent and capital charges. Profits are calculated on the basis of the total current costs. Taxes include the industrial tax and the commercial tax.[10]

*Agricultural Procurement Prices.* The state trading companies pay these prices to the peasants for delivering obligatory quotas. Theoretically, the procurement price of an agricultural product should cover not only production costs but also profit for accumulation by the communes.[11] In practice, however, agricultural procurement prices are determined by the planned profits assigned to the state trading companies and by the government's policy toward the peasantry in various periods.

*Wholesale Prices.* These are the commodity prices that wholesalers charge state retailers, marketing cooperatives, and commercial agencies of the communes. Wholesale prices include, in addition to exfactory prices, the selling expenses of the wholesalers and a profit margin. No taxes are levied on the wholesale level.

*Retail Prices.* The retail price paid by the final consumers includes the wholesale price, taxes, selling expenses on the retail level, and a profit margin for the retailers. The differences between retail and wholesale prices were 10–12 percent in 1952 and 12–16 percent in 1953. In 1958, some agricultural producer cooperatives had profit margins of 16.3 percent, which was said to be "almost as much as that of a state-run store."[12] That last information suggests that the profit margin was probably in the 12–16 percent range.

Of the five sets of prices, the prime constituents are the exfactory prices for industrial products and the procurement prices for agricultural products. In planning and statistics, they are usually expressed in "constant prices," and four sets of constant prices have been enforced in China in various periods. The first set consisted of the 1943 constant prices for products in Manchuria and the 1950 (June) constant prices for China proper, both of which were valid in the 1950–1952 recovery period. The second set comprised the 1952 constant prices for the First Five-Year Plan period (1953–1957), and the third set has been the 1957 constant prices for the period since 1957. Official publications have mentioned a set of 1970 constant prices but have provided no details. In the calculation of 1978 national income, Chinese statisticians used current prices instead of constant prices, indicating that a set of new constant prices may be in the process of formulation.[13]

The contents of the first set of constant prices have not been revealed, but, according to official documents, they were fixed prices for the products of industrial enterprises, presumably state-owned enterprises. The 1952 constant prices were fixed for only two sectors: industry and agriculture. They were officially reported as the average exfactory prices of industrial products all over the country during the third quarter of 1952. In fact, they were merely the outcome of the weighted average of the actual prices enforced among the major enterprises under the control of the central government. Neither regional price differences nor price differences among local industries were taken into account. The prices for some 16,000 commodities were reportedly fixed by the State Statistical Bureau in 1952.[14]

Under the 1952 constant prices, according to a Chinese official statement, producer goods were overpriced in relation to consumer goods and agricultural products. A comparison of 1936 and 1952 price levels shows an increase of 150 percent in the prices of industrial products in general. Among industrial products, the prices of producer goods were triple those of 1936, and consumer goods prices were double those of 1936. Yet prices of agricultural products rose 100 percent in the same period.[15]

The overpricing of producer goods heavily weighted producer goods in the output index, because producer goods usually have had a higher rate of growth than that of consumer goods. In order to correct the upward bias, a new set of constant prices was introduced in 1957. The 1957 constant prices deflated the prices of all industrial products by 10.2 percent. Compared with the 1952 constant prices, prices of producer goods dropped by 13.1 percent, and those of consumer goods dropped by 7.6 percent. This system provided separate procedures for setting constant prices for each of three groups of industrial products.

First, the State Statistical Bureau set constant prices on industrial products with a relatively large output and national economic significance (more than 70 percent of the total industrial output of the country). It calculated the uniform average prices weighted by output quantity all over the nation. Second, the statistical organization attached to each respective ministry, province, autonomous region, or municipality fixed its constant prices on lesser industrial products for use in its area alone. Third, enterprises producing various other products in small quantities or with negligible local price differences used their exfactory prices of January 1, 1957, as constant prices.

These procedures were more practical and flexible than those of 1952 for pricing new products. During the First Five-Year Plan period, the prices of new Chinese products had been based on test manufacturing costs incurred during the final stages of developing a product, with some allowance for a prospective decline in costs upon regular production. Those costs were converted to 1952 prices by a factor based on the current prices of similar products on the constant price list. If no similar domestic product was available, prices of imported products were the basis for price determination. Because it was difficult at the trial manufacture stage to forecast prices of products under mass production, the constant prices of new products tended to be very high. Economists inside and outside of China noted that this practice distorted the price system.[16] In 1958, the State Statistical Bureau decided to base the price of new products on actual costs during the first month or quarter of production. Since actual costs remain very high at this stage and decline only as the volume of output increases, the new method still imparted a substantial upward bias to new product prices, and thereby to the official production index for industrial output.

Although there is no official statement concerning the formulation of the 1970 constant prices, two sets of official statistics on the 1952 agricultural and industrial output values, expressed in both 1970 and 1957 prices, can be used to derive the relationship among the 1952, 1957, and 1970 constant prices as follows:[17]

1. To convert output value from 1952 constant prices to 1957 constant prices, a factor of 0.8898 is used to multiply the 1952 value of agricultural output and a factor of 0.898 is used to multiply the 1952 value of industrial output.
2. To convert output value in 1957 constant prices to 1970 constant prices, a factor of 1.468 is used to multiply the 1957 value of agricultural output and a factor of 0.887 is used to multiply the 1957 value of industrial output.

The 1970 constant prices thus involved an upward adjustment from the 1957 constant prices of 46.8 percent for agricultural prices and a downward adjustment of 11.3 percent for industrial prices.

Under the existing system, price setting follows "average cost-plus" methods for most industrial products. The exfactory price of a product is composed of the average cost of production of all enterprises producing the product in question, a profit margin calculated on the basis of cost, and a specific amount of tax proportionate to sales. On the wholesale and retail levels, selling costs have to be added, including the costs of screening, storing, packing, and transportation. On the retail level, a 3 percent industrial and commercial tax is added to the price.[18] Production cost includes all expenses involved in producing a given product, including raw materials, supplies, fuel, electricity, depreciation of fixed assets, interest on borrowed working capital, wages for workers and employees, social insurance premiums, and administrative and managerial expenses.

Profit is the difference beween price and costs. Since costs cannot be changed at will, the profit rate has played an important role in price formation. According to official statistics, the rates of profit for the eight industrial ministries of the central government, calculated on the basis of production costs, were 32.03 percent for 1953 and 33.05 percent for 1954.[19] As a result of neglect of efficiency, the profit rate has been declining steadily. The average profit rate of industry was 24.3 percent in 1966, but it dropped sharply to only 16.4 percent in 1978, when one quarter of the nation's industrial enterprises suffered a loss.[20]

Profits, calculated on costs, have varied significantly in different industries. In 1955, the profit in the whole of heavy industry was stated to have been 40 percent, far exceeding the average profit for all industry. In 1957, the Anshan Steel Works was reportedly operating at a 120 percent profit,[21] and a 1978 report on the pricing of chemical fertilizer produced by the Wulitun Chemical Fertilizer Plant at the Daqing oilfield revealed a 133 percent profit on the basis of production costs. According to that report, production costs per ton at the plant were 150 yuan while industrial profit was set at 200 yuan, resulting in an exfactory price of 350 yuan (no tax was mentioned in this case). Selling costs added another 100 yuan (including 46 yuan for transportation, loss, and capital interest; 18 yuan for management; with the balance as profit for the wholesaler and retailer). The retail price per ton was set at 450 yuan.[22]

The method of determining the exfactory prices outlined above represents the theoretical norm. According to Nai-Ruenn Chen, several variants are frequently encountered.

> *The model cost method.* Instead of calculating the production costs of all firms making a given product in a particular branch of industry, a group of representative firms is selected. Their average costs then form the basis for prices throughout the industrial branch.
>
> *The backward derivation method.* The exfactory price is obtained by deducting distribution costs and trade profits, which can be historically obtained, from the retail price.
>
> *Historical price data.* This method uses price relationships prevailing in 1930–1936, a period regarded as relatively normal, as the basis for setting the current price.[23]

The prices paid to the rural producers of agricultural products consist largely of prices paid on the urban markets minus shipping costs. The price of grain had originally been fixed on the basis of 1953 prices before the free market for grains was abolished. In 1950, the procurement prices for cotton were fixed at about 30 percent above the 1931-1936 level in terms of grain. The relative price of cotton in terms of grain, however, has fluctuated over time. Official statements have revealed that the changes in price and ratio between two commodities partly reflect changes in material costs of production and partly reflect supply and demand. As production costs continued to rise during the 1970s, the peasants suffered great losses in producing cotton and food grains and had to rely on sideline products to make up those losses. For instance, the cost of production for 100 catties of cotton in Hebei Province rose from 64 yuan in 1965 to 112 yuan in 1976, resulting in a loss of 7 yuan per mu. The cost of wheat per 100 catties rose from 13 to 15 yuan, causing a loss of 4.22 yuan per mu.[24] Many agricultural procurement prices, even with constant upward adjustment, still barely cover production costs.

## PRICE DIFFERENTIATION AND STABILITY

From a macroeconomic point of view, Chinese policy is to maintain price stability, but from a microeconomic point of view, it is to maintain price differentiation. Differentiation exists between agricultural and industrial prices, between the prices of consumer goods and producer goods, between import and export prices, and among various regions. The differentiations are partly inherited from the historical price structure, but they mostly reflect government policy objectives.

### *Price Differentiation*

*Agricultural Versus Industrial Prices.* In the early years, the Chinese government followed the Soviet practice by adopting a "scissor-gap" policy to lower agricultural prices in relation to industrial prices. During World War II, the "scissors" had already opened against rural interests, and in 1950, the terms of trade (the index of the retail prices of industrial goods in rural areas divided by the index of the procurement prices of agricultural products) were estimated at 131.8, with 1931-1936 as the base.[25]

Although the scissor-gap policy helped to keep down food costs for urban workers and raw material costs for industries, it reduced the incentives for farmers. Thus, since 1953, policies have sought to close the agricultural-industrial gap. Official statistics show that between 1950 and 1964, government purchasing prices of farm and sideline products doubled while prices of certain industrial goods for daily use dropped by 80 percent.[26] As a result, the terms of trade have gradually moved in favor of agricultural products. By 1958, the price ratio had reached parity (100), and by 1964, it had dropped to 88.[27] The continuance of this trend since 1964 signals a substantial improvement in agricultural product prices when compared with industrial product prices (see Table 8.1).

The reversal of the terms of trade after 1953 was partly designed to correct the historical bias in favor of industrial products, but it also reflects the divergent growth rates of agriculture and industry during the period. Between 1958 and 1977, the average annual growth in grain production was only 2 percent, which barely kept pace with population growth, while industrial output grew at 9.1 percent a

Table 8.1
Agricultural and Industrial Price Indexes, 1950-1978

| Year | Purchase prices of farm and sideline products | | Rural retail price of industrial products | | Terms of trade industrial for agricultural products | |
|---|---|---|---|---|---|---|
| | 1952=100 | 1936=100 | 1952=100 | 1936=100 | 1952=100 | 1936=100 |
| 1950 | 82.2 | 164.4 | 91.2 | 228.0 | 111.0 | 188.7 |
| 1951 | 98.3 | 196.6 | 100.5 | 251.2 | 102.2 | 127.8 |
| 1952 | 100.0 | 200.0 | 100.0 | 250.0 | 100.0 | 125.0 |
| 1953 | 110.1 | 220.2 | 98.5 | 246.3 | 89.5 | 111.9 |
| 1954 | 113.8 | 227.6 | 100.2 | 250.5 | 88.1 | 110.1 |
| 1955 | 113.2 | 226.4 | 101.4 | 253.5 | 89.6 | 112.0 |
| 1956 | 116.6 | 233.2 | 100.4 | 251.0 | 86.1 | 107.6 |
| 1957 | 122.4 | 244.8 | 101.6 | 254.0 | 83.0 | 103.8 |
| 1958 | 125.1 | 250.2 | 101.0 | 252.5 | 80.7 | 100.9 |
| 1959 | 129.0 | 258.0 | 101.0 | 252.5 | 78.0 | 97.9 |
| 1963 | 154.7 | 309.4 | 114.3 | 285.8 | 73.8 | 92.4 |
| 1971 | 156.2 | 312.4 | 104.0 | 260.0 | 66.6 | 83.2 |
| 1974 | 164.4 | 238.8 | 97.8 | 244.5 | 59.5 | 74.4 |
| 1978 | 170.3 | 340.3 | 100.1 | 250.3 | 58.8 | 73.6 |

Sources: Base figures for 1952 from Peter Schran, "China's Price Stability: Its Meaning and Distributive Consequences," Journal of Comparative Economics No. 1 (1977), p. 375. Base figures for 1936 derived from the information that agricultural prices were double that in 1936; industrial prices were 2.5 times that in 1936. Tongji gongzuo (Statistical work) No. 1 (1957). Figures for 1978 derived from information contained in Zhang Guofan, "Some Questions on Industrial and Agricultural Scissor Prices," Jianghan luntan (Chiang-Han tribune) (Bi-monthly, published by the Hubei Academy of Social Sciences, Hankou) No. 2 (March 15, 1980), pp. 14-17.

year.[28] Since the growth of industrial output far exceeded that of agriculture, it was quite natural for the terms of trade to shift in favor of agriculture.

Despite the continuous shift of the terms of trade in favor of agriculture, many leading Chinese economists still think that 1980 agricultural procurement prices are too low to stimulate peasant enthusiasm, and they suggest the need for further increases.[29] Price differences among various agricultural products also need adjustment. For instance, the current exchange rate between cotton and wheat in China stands at 1:12.3. Compared with 1:15 in the United States, the Chinese exchange rate is still unfavorable to the cotton planters. Consequently, cotton output in China has been stagnant for more than a decade. In recent years, as China has stepped up its textile production, it has had to import more than 10 million bales of cotton a year from the United States and has become the largest customer for U.S. cotton.[30]

*Prices of Producer Goods Versus Prices of Consumer Goods.* Price differences between producer and consumer goods are relatively small as compared with the discrepancies between corresponding Soviet prices for 1926/27–1950. The 1948 prices of all Soviet consumer goods weighted by quantity were close to thirty times those of the 1926/27 base while the weighted prices of all producer goods fully free of turnover tax were only twice those of the 1926/27 level.[31] The Russians set producer goods prices relatively low, approximately 3 to 5 percent above the average cost for the industry. That policy resulted in a complex system of subsidies. At the same time, it imparted a producer goods bias to the industrial production process.

In contrast, China's producer goods prices were very high in the 1950s, and since they included a high ratio of profit, they remain very high today. As mentioned above, the average profit rate for heavy industry, on the basis of production costs, was 40 percent in 1955. On the other hand, the Chinese government relied more upon other measures, notably rationing, to control consumption, so the prices of consumer goods were kept at a more stable level. In the early years (1949–1952), prices of producer goods rose slightly more than those of consumer goods, but in the 1952–1957 period, consumer prices rose more than those of producer goods, resulting in a minor discrepancy between the price indexes of the two sectors (see Table 8.2).

In the 1970s, under the policy of industry supporting agriculture, the prices of several producer goods, such as agricultural machinery and chemical fertilizers, dropped quite substantially, thus further

Table 8.2
Deflators of Net Domestic Material Product (NDMP),
Accumulation, and Material Consumption, 1952-1957

| Year | Net Domestic Material Product | | | Accumulation | | | Material Consumption | | |
|---|---|---|---|---|---|---|---|---|---|
| | Billion yuan at current prices | Billion yuan at 1952 prices | Implicit deflator[a] | % of NDMP, current prices | % of NDMP, 1952 prices | Implicit deflator[a] | % of NDMP, current prices | % of NDMP, 1952 prices | Implicit deflator[a] |
| 1952 | 61.13 | 61.13 | 100.0 | 18.2 | 18.2 | 100.0 | 81.8 | 81.8 | 100.0 |
| 1953 | 72.33 | 70.04 | 103.3 | 21.4 | 22.4 | 98.7 | 78.6 | 77.6 | 104.6 |
| 1954 | 77.40 | 73.88 | 104.8 | 22.3 | 23.5 | 99.4 | 77.7 | 76.5 | 106.4 |
| 1955 | 81.84 | 78.80 | 103.9 | 20.9 | 22.9 | 94.8 | 79.1 | 77.1 | 106.6 |
| 1956 | 91.61 | 88.75 | 103.2 | 22.5 | 26.1 | 89.0 | 77.5 | 73.9 | 108.2 |
| 1957 | 95.00 | 92.95 | 102.2 | 21.0 | 24.0 | 89.4 | 79.0 | 76.0 | 106.2 |

[a] 1952=100

Source: Peter Schran, "China's Price Stability: Its Meaning and Distributive Consequences," Journal of Comparative Economics No. 1 (1977), p. 369.

widening the gap between the price indexes of the two sectors. Since consumer goods products are now in short supply and many capital goods are in surplus, a further reduction of capital goods prices in the 1980s is almost inevitable.[32]

*Import and Export Prices.* A unique feature of Chinese price policy is the total separation between domestic and international prices. By virtue of the state monopoly on foreign and domestic commerce, the government sets the prices of commodities handled by its foreign trade departments without any reference to international markets.[33] The procedure is somewhat complex. The state export corporations purchase goods for export from farmers and industrial enterprises at unified purchase prices (expressed in yuan) and sell them on the international market for foreign currencies. The foreign exchange revenue, however, must then be submitted to the People's Bank to be converted into yuan at the official exchange rate before it becomes the revenue of the export corporations.

For China's imports, the state import companies commonly use yuan to buy foreign exchange from the bank at the same official exchange rate. The companies then sell the imported product to state domestic trade companies at a price prevailing in the domestic market. The foreign exchange rate of the Renminbi (yuan) is thus the key to import and export prices.

Since 1950, the Chinese government has arbitrarily divorced foreign exchange rates from purchasing-power parities. Before 1960, the yuan was appreciably overvalued in relation to the U.S. dollar but highly undervalued in relation to the Russian ruble. According to official statistics, commodity prices in the Sino-Soviet trade were kept constant during 1950–1957, and the exchange rate was fixed at one ruble to 0.975 yuan. The official exchange rate was 2.24 yuan to one dollar in 1952 and 2.62 yuan to one dollar in 1953–1960.[34] Between 1950 and 1960, the official exchange rate was 4 rubles to one dollar. If one uses the 0.975 ruble-yuan rate, the dollar-yuan rate should be 1:3.9 ($0.975 \times 4 = 3.9$) instead of 2.24 or 2.62. On the other hand, if one uses the 2.24 to 2.62 yuan-dollar rates, the yuan-ruble rate should be one ruble equals 0.56 or 0.655 yuan rather than 0.975 yuan. Since exchange rates are arbitrarily set, China's exports usually incur a loss and its imports make a high profit. Import profits have been used to cover export losses.[35]

In recent years, as the value of the U.S. dollar depreciated, the exchange rate between Renminbi and dollars appreciated considerably. By June 1980, the exchange rate fluctuated around 1.5 yuan to the dollar, substantially higher than the 2.62 yuan rate in the 1960s.

The separation of domestic prices from the international market insulates China from the influence of the world market. However, it also severely distorts the price structure between exports and imports.

*Regional Price Differentiations.* The prices of some commodities vary greatly from region to region, depending on transportation costs and available supplies. In general, prices of centrally determined, nationally traded goods show relatively minor regional differences, and prices of locally traded commodities vary considerably from place to place. Raw materials usually have lower prices in the hinterland than in the coastal areas, and the prices of industrial products are usually lower in the coastal areas than in the hinterland. Information available in Hong Kong has revealed that as of 1974, the whole country was divided into twelve cost-of-living regions.[36] To reduce regional differences, the Chinese government has set uniform retail prices on many manufactured goods, regardless of the distance between factory and retail market. For instance, the prices of pharmaceuticals, matches, and wristwatches are identical in all parts of the country. The state also fixes the purchase and sale prices of grains, cotton, edible oils, cotton cloth, and animal by-products. Grain storage expenses, transportation expenses, and losses are covered by the state. These subsidies have lessened the price disparity between the coastal and interior regions.[37]

### *Price Stability*

Although various differentiations persist in the price system, the fundamental policy has been to keep prices as stable as possible. Since 1950, all government efforts have sought to forestall any recurrence of the severe price fluctuations of the post–World War II hyperinflation years. These efforts have been quite successful. Official statistics show that retail price indexes went up only 15 percent between 1950 and 1974, with an annual inflation rate of 0.6 percent (see Table 8.3). According to official sources, several factors account for the long period of price stability. They are planned adjustments of currency in circulation, unified management of prices, and isolation from the international market.[38]

The most significant factor contributing to price stability, however, has been the rationing system, which has enabled the government to control the aggregate demand for basic necessities–notably food grains, vegetable oils, and cotton cloth–which compose the bulk of consumer expenditures. Rationing has also effectively reduced con-

Table 8.3
Retail Price Indexes, 1950-1980 (1952=100)

| Period | Retail prices in 8 cities | | Retail prices in the nation |
|---|---|---|---|
| March 1950 | 112.6[a] | 106.7[b] | |
| 1950 | 88.6[a] | | |
| 1951 | 99.1[a] | 101.0[b] | 100.1[b] |
| 1952 | 100.0[a] | 100.0[b] | 100.0[b] |
| 1953 | 103.7[a] | 104.9[b] | 103.2[b] |
| 1954 | 104.1[a] | 106.9[b] | 105.5[b] |
| 1955 | 105.5[a] | 107.9[b] | 106.3[b] |
| 1956 | 105.8[a] | 107.8[b] | 108.6[b] |
| 1957 | 107.7[a] | 109.1[b] | 108.3[b] |
| 1958 | | 108.2[b] | 108.3[b] |
| 1963 | | 118.5[c] | |
| 1974 | | 115.0[d] | 115.0[d] |
| 1979 | | | 121.7[e] |
| 1980 | | | 129.0[f] |

Sources: Peter Schran, "China's Price Stability: Its Meaning and Distributive Consequences," Journal of Comparative Economics No. 1 (1977), p. 372. (a) The 1957 figures are from Tongji gongzuo (Statistical work) No. 11 (1957), p. 5. (b) The 1959 figures are from P.R.C. State Statistical Bureau, Ten Great Years (Beijing: Foreign Languages Press, 1960), p. 174. (c) Based on the information that prices in 1963 were 111 percent of March 1950 (Peking Review 7:47 /November 24, 1964/, p. 7). (d) 97.1 percent of 1963 (Far Eastern Economic Review, November 14, 1975, p. 41). (e) Beijing Review 23:20 (May 19, 1980), p. 21, assuming prices remained unchanged between 1974 and 1978. (f) Beijing Review 24:12 (March 23, 1981), p. 24.

sumer spending and forced savings. This explains why per capita income in China has been so low even though personal savings in the People's Bank have risen considerably since 1955. Between 1953, the year when rationing started, and the end of 1973, total personal savings in the bank reportedly increased by 800 percent, with an average annual growth rate of 11.6 percent, which was substantially higher than the growth rate of per capita income (4 percent) during the same period.[39] By the end of February 1980, total bank deposits had exceeded 30 billion yuan (30 yuan per capita).[40]

Another significant factor contributing to price stability has been the government stabilization of consumer prices for food grains. Despite the continuing rise in the purchase prices of farm and sideline products, their selling prices remained virtually unchanged between 1953 and 1978. The difference between the purchasing and selling prices was recorded as a net loss of the state companies and was financed by state subsidies. Normally, the state picks up transport and distribution expenses. This policy is in sharp contrast with the Stalinist policy of pricing essential consumer goods well above average production costs. Included in the state-subsidized list in China are food grains, vegetables, meat, and eggs. State subsidies for those items were said to run up to several thousand million yuan every year.[41] Other consumer goods receiving state subsidies are tea bricks and leather boots, two major items for the minority nationalities. The subsidy measures undoubtedly helped to stabilize consumer prices.

The long period of price stability came to an end in 1979. In recent decades, procurement prices have fallen below production costs, and agricultural production has stagnated. In March 1979, in order to stimulate peasant initiative, the government sharply raised the purchase prices of the main farm produce and sideline products, including grain, oil-bearing crops, cotton, hemp, hogs, cattle, sheep, fish, eggs, sugarcane, beetroot, and silkworm cocoons. The total purchase price index of farm produce and sideline products went up 22.1 percent over the previous year. Beginning in November 1979, to compensate for the rise in procurement prices, the state also raised the retail prices of pork, beef, mutton, poultry, eggs, aquatic products, and milk. The price hikes ranged between 32 and 33 percent, an unprecedented jump. As a result, in December 1979, the overall level of retail prices (including the list prices of state commercial units, negotiated prices, and prices at rural fairs) rose 5.8 percent over the corresponding period in 1978.[42] Developments in 1980 pointed to a continuous upward movement of retail prices. The era of consumer prices remaining unchanged for many years may be gone forever.

*Profit and Price Formation.* The basic price formula in Chinese industry—the average cost-plus method—has the advantage of simplicity, but it does generate many adverse effects on the use of capital. It has become a subject of controversy among Chinese economists during the past two decades.

The concept of prime cost in Chinese price formulation is quite similar to that of the Soviet system. It includes wages, raw materials, interest on working capital borrowed from the bank, and depreciation on fixed capital but excludes fixed capital costs, rent, and interest on working capital, which are included in the budget. In the official planning and accounting system, industrial capital comprises two components: fixed assets and working capital. Fixed assets for industrial production include: (a) factories, official buildings, and warehouses; (b) structure; (c) equipment, instruments, and tools. Working capital refers to funds required in the production process – such as funds for raw materials, fuel, and goods in process – as well as funds required in the circulating process – including cash, bank deposits, accounts receivable, notes paid in advance, and finished products in stock.[43]

According to official sources, of the total capital used in all industry in 1955, 24 percent was working capital and 76 percent was fixed assets.[44] Despite the importance of fixed capital in total capital, only the depreciation charges, which usually were fixed at 4 percent of fixed assets, were included in the production costs. (In the United States, depreciation charges generally run at about 10 percent of fixed assets.)

The prevailing method of reckoning profit on each industrial product is based on the branchwide average cost of each product. Price is the sum of cost plus a certain amount of profit calculated by the profit-cost ratio. Thus:

$$p = c + v + (c + v)\,\frac{S}{C+V}$$

where

- $p$ denotes the price of the product concerned
- $c$ stands for branch average cost of material inputs (including depreciation of plant and equipment) per unit of the product
- $v$ represents branch average wage cost per unit of the product
- $S$ represents total profit in the economy
- $C$ represents cost of material inputs in the economy
- $V$ denotes total wage bill in the economy

So that, $S/(C + V)$ represents the average profit rate of the economy and $(c + v)\,S/(C + V)$ represents the average profit rate of a particular product.[45]

The prevailing method of calculating profit on the basis of average cost tends to discourage cost-reduction efforts by managers, because it is in the interest of the individual enterprise and its ministry to maximize profit since they are entitled to a fixed proportion of total profits for certain specific purposes. Many modern enterprises with advanced equipment always turn out high-cost products. The output-capital ratio (or capital productivity) is in many cases lower for large industrial plants and higher for small industrial plants (see Table 8.4).

Since 1962, a fierce debate has raged among Chinese economists

Table 8.4
Output-Capital Ratio, by Plant Size, 1953-1955

| Fixed assets per worker (in 1000 yuan) | 1953 | 1954 | 1955 |
|---|---|---|---|
| Large industrial plants | 6.06 | 7.16 | 8.00 |
| Small industrial plants | 0.50 | 0.73 | 0.79 |
| Large plant as multiplier of small plant | 12.12 | 9.81 | 10.13 |
| Output/capital ratio (yuan) | | | |
| Large industrial plants | 1.07 | 1.01 | 0.99 |
| Small industrial plants | 14.63 | 13.10 | 13.41 |
| Small plant as multiplier of large plant | 13.67 | 12.97 | 13.55 |

Source: Fan Ruoyi, "A Brief Discussion of the Rate of Capital-Profit and the Policy of Construction with Quicker Tempo and with More Economy," Jihua jingji (Planned economy) No. 8 (August 1958), p. 22.

concerning the proper price formation method. One group of economists has advocated calculating the rate of profit on the basis of capital, rather than on the basis of total cost. They have advocated a different formula, defining *p, c, v,* and *S* as before but with *k* representing the average amounts of fixed and working capital per unit of the commodity and *K* the total fixed and working capital used in the whole economy. Thus:

$$p = c + v + k \frac{S}{K}$$

Members of this school have argued that prices so constructed would help the planner to evaluate investment more precisely and, hence, to make better decisions on investment allocations among various industries and projects, thus ensuring investment efficiency and helping save scarce capital.[46]

A second group of economists has rejected the adoption of a capital-profit ratio in a socialist system. According to them, there are great variations in the rate of profit to capital among different enterprises within one industrial department. For example, uniform railroad-freight rates or uniform wholesale prices for coal, petroleum, and steel do not reflect regional differences in natural resources. An equal amount of capital does not yield an equal amount of profit. There can be no equalization of the capital-profit ratio. Moreover, to accept the fact that the average profit rate of capital has an economic role to play in socialism is to imply that prices should fluctuate with demand and supply and that investment should shift constantly with the change in profitability. That approach has been seen as conflicting with the socialist system.[47]

To provide an alternative approach, some economists outside of those two schools have suggested that commodity prices should be determined by their value ($c + v$) plus profit reckoned by multiplying the wage-profit ratio ($S/V$). Thus:

$$p = c + v + v\frac{S}{V} = c + v\left(1 + \frac{S}{V}\right)$$

This last approach maintains the orthodox Marxist position, relating the surplus product markup to labor cost (wage bill) in order to obtain prices that are truly based on labor value, as Marx advocated.

The debates reached no consensus in the 1960s, and profit, which is a component of price, continued to be calculated on the basis of production cost. Since the beginning of 1978, there has been renewed interest in several economic issues, including the problem of fixing profit on the basis of wages, costs, or capital. Sun Yefang, the most outspoken critic of the cost-profit approach, appealed to the country to restore the "reputation of the capital/profit ratio" and advocated that the administration fix industrial prices on the basis of the capital-profit ratio without further delay. To eliminate the effect of differences in natural endowment on the profitability of each enterprise, Sun suggested an additional tax on plants with an above-normal endowment, a sort of quasi rent, to equalize the factor contribution.[48]

Despite these new arguments, the government has given no hint of immediate reform. As the Chinese economist Yu Lin pointed out in 1964, a universal profit ratio would encourage wasteful expenditures on the item (wages, total current costs, or capital) that forms its base. He suggested the use of different profit ratios for different industries. Fixed prices in industries on approximately the same technical level should use the same wage-profit ratio. Where technical levels differ widely, the capital-profit ratio would probably be more appropriate. The use of the cost-profit ratio would be justified on empirical grounds. In most circumstances, the level of cost-profit would frequently fall between those of wage-profit and capital-profit ratios.[49] Yu's article outlined the complexities of profit determination and the reasons for the government's hesitancy about making changes. Now that China is embarking on large-scale capital construction, however, the allocation of capital for investment according to profits on capital would seem to be the most logical and efficient method. Sun Yefang's arguments may gain more support in the years ahead.

## WAGE STRUCTURE AND POLICIES

Like the prices of producer goods, wages in China perform only a limited allocative function. Administrative assignment directs the horizontal movements of the labor force among different regions, sectors, industries, and plants. New workers are assigned jobs upon graduation from middle or technical schools or universities by the government bureau in charge of planning and balancing labor, most frequently, the municipal labor bureau. When workers receive promotions, enterprises will raise wages and salaries. In general, a combination of administrative order and wage differentiation regulates the allocation of labor in China.

The wage system in China comprises three primary elements: basic wages, bonuses and supplements, and welfare benefits (see Figure 8.1). Before and after the Cultural Revolution, bonuses accounted for roughly 12 percent of basic wages, and welfare benefits approximated 15–20 percent of the total wage fund. Since the wage reform in 1956, the complicated system of wage grades in industry has been consolidated and simplified into an eight-grade system with grade one as base. Coefficients attach to grades two to eight, and the wage rates for the higher grades are the wage for grade one multiplied by the appropriate coefficient. The coefficient assigned to each grade depends on (a) the difficulty of the job, (b) the working environment, (c) rank, and (d) industrial sector. The coefficients attached to each grade vary from one industry to another, and there may be small variations within the same industry (see Table 8.5). The eight-grade system was still in effect as of June 1980.

As shown in Table 8.5, the least skilled production worker in heavy industry receives about one-third the wage of the most skilled worker. In the light industry and service sectors, the wage spread is narrower. Classified according to various levels of management, the lowest and highest wages in 1974 in China ranged from a ratio of 2.44 for local industries to 2.73 for state-controlled industries (see Table 8.6).

Technical personnel in industry, including engineers and techni-

Figure 8.1
Wage System in China as of June 1980

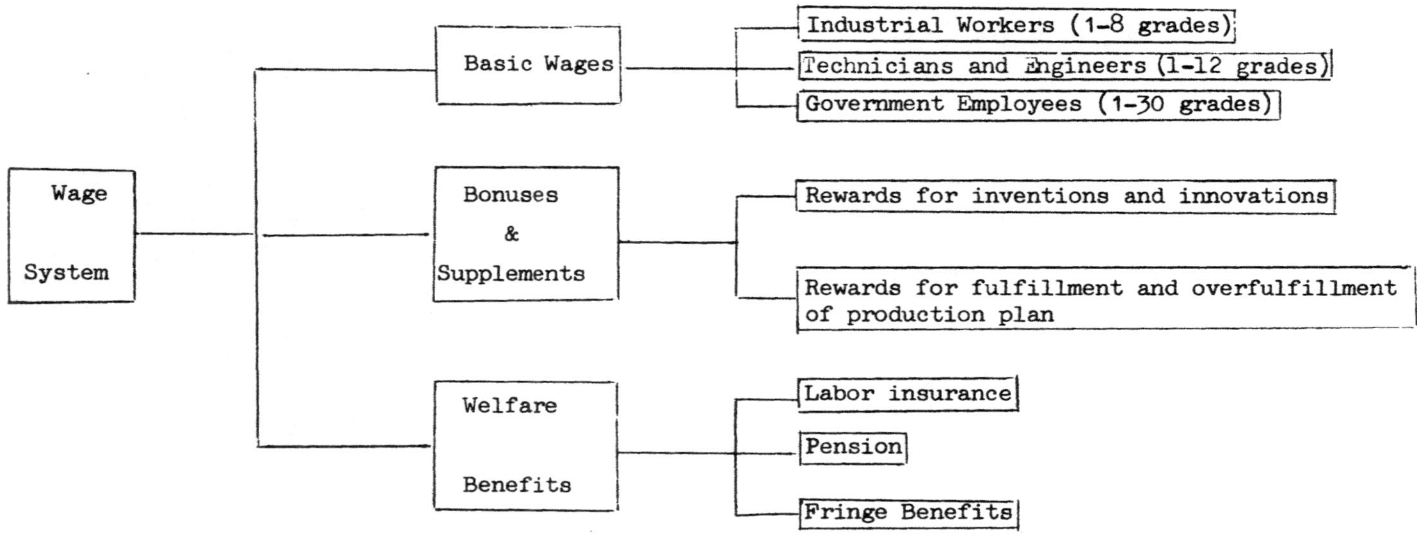

Table 8.5
Basic Wage Scales and Coefficients for Industrial Production Workers in Three Plants, 1972-1973
(Basic wage in yuan per month)

| Labor grade | Beijing No. 1 Machine-tool Plant | | Rough Rolling Mill in Anshan Steel Plant | | Shenyang No. 1 Machine-tool Plant | |
|---|---|---|---|---|---|---|
| | Basic Wage | Coefficients | Basic Wage | Coefficients | Basic Wage | Coefficients |
| 1 | 34.00 | 1.00 | 34.50 | 1.00 | 33.00 | 1.00 |
| 2 | 40.10 | 1.18 | 40.00 | 1.16 | 38.90 | 1.18 |
| 3 | 47.50 | 1.40 | 48.13 | 1.40 | 45.80 | 1.39 |
| 4 | 55.00 | 1.62 | 56.82 | 1.65 | 54.00 | 1.64 |
| 5 | 61.10 | 1.80 | 67.10 | 1.94 | 63.60 | 1.93 |
| 6 | 77.10 | 2.27 | 79.25 | 2.30 | 74.90 | 2.27 |
| 7 | 90.90 | 2.67 | 84.50 | 2.45 | 88.20 | 2.67 |
| 8 | 107.10 | 3.15 | 110.00 | 3.19 | 104.00 | 3.15 |
| Ratio of Maximum to Minimum | | 3.15 | | 3.2 | | 3.2 |

Source: Carl Riskin, "Workers' Incentives in Chinese Industry," in U.S. Congress, Joint Economic Committee, China: A Reassessment of the Economy (Washington, D.C.: Government Printing Office, 1975), pp. 216-217.

cians, are generally classified into twelve categories. Their wage scales are ranked according to three types of enterprises–heavy, intermediate, and light industries (Classes A, B, and C in Table 8.7). On the basis of Table 8.7, the highest-paid chief engineers received about four times the wage of average workers, 2.4 times that of average technical personnel, and 1.4 times that of average engineers.

Scientists and university professors are in the highest income bracket in China. According to information supplied by a former member of the Chinese Academy of Sciences, their salaries are divided according to the thirteen grades (see Table 8.8). Government administrative personnel are classified into thirty grades. Salaries of government employes in 1974 ranged from 400 yuan per month for the chairman of the People's Republic to 30 yuan for a grade-thirty clerk.[50]

Most of the wages are calculated on a time rate, but piece rates prevailed in the 1950s and reached a peak in 1956 when they covered some 42 percent of the work force. Piece rates varied widely, but most

Table 8.6
Minimum and Maximum Basic Monthly Wages of Production Workers by Management, 1974

| Industry | Basic Wage (yuan) | | Ratio |
|---|---|---|---|
| | Minimum | Maximum | |
| Industries under central state management | 39 | 107 | 2.73 |
| Industries under provincial management | 37 | 97 | 2.62 |
| Industries under county management | 34 | 83 | 2.44 |
| Industries under authorities below county level | 30 | 77 | 2.57 |

Source: China News Analysis (Hong Kong) No. 966 (July 13, 1974), p. 6.

were connected with the system of standard wage grades and paid more or less than a worker's grade depending on the quantity and quality of the work. Maoists criticized the piece rate system during the Great Leap Forward but were nevertheless still applying it to 35 percent of the work force in 1959. The system came under severe attack during the Cultural Revolution as a prime example of "economism." Largely abandoned at that time, it has gradually revived since the fall of the radicals in October 1976.

In addition to regular wages and salaries, workers, engineers, and scientists have also received bonuses, rewards, and retirement pensions. Various bonuses were instituted between 1950 and 1966. According to Barry Richman, most of the thirty industrial factories he surveyed in China in 1966 had bonus funds equal to 5 to 15 percent of total wages and salaries; about 20 percent of the eligible personnel received the maximum allowable bonuses, and 10 to 15 percent received no bonus at all.[51] The awarding of bonuses depends on various criteria, including fulfillment of output quotas, cost reduction, and so on. To motivate scientific and technical personnel, the government's May 1954 Regulations on Technical Improvements and Ra-

Table 8.7
Monthly Wages of Engineers, Technicians, and Management Personnel, by Job Titles and Wage Class, 1965

| Job Title | Monthly Wages in (yuan) | | |
|---|---|---|---|
| | Class A | Class B | Class C |
| Director, Deputy Director, Chief Engineer | 155–263 | 143–240 | 132–218 |
| Deputy Chief Engineer, Chief Mechanic, Chief Designer | 135–223 | 133–200 | 128–190 |
| Chief of major workshop, Chief of important section (*ko*) | 115–181 | 108–169 | 99–158 |
| Deputy Chief of Workshop, Secretary to the Director, Section (*ko*) Chief | 103–152 | 96–143 | 89–133 |
| Chief of Work Section | 77–147 | 72–136 | 70–126 |
| Engineers in responsible positions | 118–181 | 117–169 | 116–158 |
| Technicians in responsible positions | 103–166 | 96–156 | 89–145 |
| Technical Personnel | 64–102 | 64–102 | 64–102 |
| Economists in responsible positions | 103–166 | 96–156 | 89–145 |
| Chief Accountants, Chief Quota Adjustors | 74–126 | 73–123 | 72–109 |
| Accountants, Wage Clerks, Planning Personnel | 62–105 | 62–105 | 62–105 |
| Statisticians, Clerks for Technical Data Files | 50–89 | 50–89 | 50–89 |

Source: Chu-yuan Cheng, *Scientific and Engineering Manpower in Communist China, 1949–1963* (Washington, D.C.: National Science Foundation, 1966), p. 151.

tionalization Proposals provided that an inventor could receive a bonus that reflected the economic effect of his proposal. For an invention that could save 100,000 yuan, the inventor was to receive 2 percent of the savings plus 1,731 yuan in cash. The maximum bonus for inventions in a one-year period was 50,000 yuan, and the minimum was 20 yuan. The maximum and minimum bonuses for technical improvement in a one-year period were set at 20,000 and 10 yuan, respectively, and for management improvement, 10,000 yuan and 5 yuan, respectively.[52]

A new set of Regulations on Rewards for Technical Improvements

Table 8.8
Monthly Salaries of Scientists and Professors, 1978

| Grade | Research Institution | Educational Institution | Monthly Salary (yuan) |
|---|---|---|---|
| 1-3 | Researcher | Professor | 260-380 |
| 4-6 | Associate researcher | Associate Professor | 120-260 |
| 7-9 | Assistant researcher | Lecturer | 90-120 |
| 10-12 | Research Assistant | Instructor | 50-90 |
| 13 | Trainee | | 50 |

**Source:** Chou Hsin, "Research Works in Social Sciences in China: Current Situation and Prospects," Chi-shih nien-tai (The seventies) (Hong Kong), December 1978, p. 46.

was promulgated by the State Council in November 1963 but not put into effect until November 1978. Unlike the 1954 regulations, which emphasized inventions, the new regulations focus on technical improvements. Cash rewards ranging from 100 to 1,000 yuan depend on the contribution to annual value resulting from increased production.[53]

Like the piece rate system, bonuses and rewards came under attack during the Cultural Revolution and were mostly abandoned at that time. In 1972, many enterprises divided bonus funds equally among all workers as an automatic addition to their basic wage. Since April 1978, bonuses have been reinstituted throughout China. They constitute 12 to 14 percent of general wages and have become a significant component of the current material incentive system.[54]

Social welfare and labor insurance have been established since the 1950s and differ from wages and bonuses because they are paid on the basis of need rather than work. The government's Provisional Regulation on Retirement for Workers and Employees of November 16, 1957, applied to workers and staff members of state-operated semiprivate enterprises, business units, government agencies, and people's organizations. Under the regulations, male workers and staff members over the age of sixty and female workers and staff members over the age of fifty-five were eligible for retirement. They were also eligible for a monthly pension for life. Those with more than five but fewer than ten years of continuous service were to receive 50 percent of their wages as pensions; those with more than ten but fewer than fifteen years of service were to receive pensions amounting to 70 percent of their wages.

Other more recent workers' benefits include fifty-six days' maternity leave for female workers, full pay during two months of certified illness, full pay during a period of disability caused by a job-related injury, and free physical checkups once a year. In general, labor insurance and social welfare represent 15 to 20 percent of the total wage bill.[55]

The Chinese wage policy has been designed to attain three interrelated objectives: (1) to provide workers with incentives to work harder and to improve their skills; (2) to allocate the labor force among different occupations, industries, and regions; and (3) to control the total wage bill so as to assure price stability. Since most of the labor force allocations have resulted from administrative orders, wage policy has mainly been concerned with incentives and stability. In the early years of Communist control, there was more emphasis on incentives. This was reflected in the introduction of piece rate wages, bonuses, and raises at an average of 7.4 percent annually between 1953 and 1957. During the Great Leap in 1958, emulation campaigns and nonmaterial rewards replaced material incentives as the chief stimuli to motivate the workers. Since then, the maintenance of low wages has become the prime goal of wage policy. Between 1963 and 1976, the wage levels for workers and technical and managerial employees, except for some minor adjustments, were virtually frozen. The bonus system was reviled by the radicals as "the thin end of the capitalist wedge," and even wage differentiations were termed part of the "bourgeois right" and doomed for elimination.[56] Under the influence of the egalitarian Maoist ideology, wages were kept unabashedly low. Since wages are a vital component of production cost, the low-wage policy enabled state industrial enterprises to secure a high level of accumulation.

The low-wage policy has also contributed significantly to the stability of prices during the past two decades by restraining purchasing power in the household sector and maintaining low living standards, thus helping to relieve pressures on the consumer goods market. As Deng Xiaoping admitted to visiting overseas Chinese in October 1974, wages are low, and the living standard is not high. The Chinese only get enough clothing and a full stomach. To develop the economy, this situation must be maintained for some time to come.[57]

The persistence of low wages for such a long stretch of time is bound to affect workers' motivation. As Hu Qiaomu has observed, during the First Five-Year Plan period, when workers' wages increased at an average rate of 7.4 percent annually, labor productivity advanced at an average annual rate of 8.7 percent, and gross industrial production increased at an annual rate of 18 percent. During that period, rising labor productivity accounted for 59 percent of the industrial growth, with the remaining 41 percent coming from the increase in the size of the labor force. After 1958, as wages failed to rise in due time, growth of labor productivity stagnated. Consequently, the growth of industrial output depended entirely, or for the most part, on increasing the number of workers. Had the growth of labor productivity been maintained at 8.7 percent per annum, the 1977 labor productivity for workers in the industrial, capital construction, and communications and transportation sectors would be three times the current rate.[58]

Hu's comments indicate that the low-wage policy underlies the long-term stagnation in labor productivity. In a country where labor is the most important factor of production, the time has come for the leadership to pay special attention to nurturing human motivations if the ambitious goal of modernization is to be achieved.

## CONSEQUENCES OF CHINA'S WAGE-PRICE SYSTEM AND RECENT REFORMS

At a time when most of the Western world is suffering from chronic inflation, many Western economists have praised China's price stability. The Chinese government has also frequently expressed its pride in this achievement. To many economists inside China, however, the existing price system involves several defects that require radical reforms.

First, many leading Chinese economists believe that agricultural procurement prices have not properly reflected value in the Marxist sense of socially necessary labor. The prices of many agricultural products, particularly livestock and cotton, have not covered the cost of production. As Tong Dalin, one of China's leading agricultural economists, pointed out in 1978, it takes approximately 14,000 catties of fodder to raise a cow. At 0.038 yuan per catty, it costs the farmer 530 yuan to raise a cow. Yet the 1978 procurement price of a cow was less than 300 yuan. The same situation applies to the raising of sheep.[59] Tong's statistics relate the long-term stagnation of the livestock industry in China to the unrealistic price-fixing practices that existed for three decades. Procurement prices for many agricultural products such as cotton, tung oil, vegetable oils, rapeseed, sugarcane, hogs, and silkworms have also been far below the general price level. As a result, the peasants' incentive for producing those products has been severely damaged.

Second, the use of costs rather than capital as the basis for computing industrial profit has understated the contribution of capital. As of 1980, the production costs of an enterprise included only a tiny portion of the capital used by the enterprise, that is, circulating capital plus depreciation of fixed assets. In contrast to Western economies, depreciation in China has accounted for only 4 percent of the capital appropriated to enterprises by the state budget. According to many Chinese economists, the exclusion of huge portions of fixed assets from cost accounting has led enterprise managers to waste capital. They "always budgeted liberally and spent sparingly." "They requested large budgets for equipment but made little use of it."[60] As was shown in Table 8.4, the output-capital ratios (or capital productivity) have been lower for large industrial plants and higher for small plants in many cases.

Third, many economists view the bonus system as harmful. As long as an enterprise fulfills its production plans, it can draw bonuses at a fixed proportion of its total wages, regardless of whether it has overfulfilled its plans and irrespective of the size of any surplus. An overlapping and overstaffed enterprise with a huge wage bill can offer sizable bonuses, while a productive enterprise with a simple administrative structure and a low wage bill can provide only minimal bonuses. This system damages the government's efforts to improve management, simplify administrative structure, and increase labor productivity.[61]

The root of these problems, according to Sun Yefang and other economists, lies in the discrepancy between prices and value. Because pricing practices have not reflected the cost of labor, there has been no objective criterion of economic accounting.[62]

Since the second half of 1977, various proposals have been advanced to deal with shortcomings in the price system and in wages and bonuses. Some have already been put into effect; others are still under consideration. The first major change was the emphasis on wage reform and the overt repudiation of egalitarianism. In October 1977, the leadership granted a general round of wage increases for about 60 percent of the industrial and administrative workers, most of whom were in the lower income brackets. Those who earned more than ninety yuan (fifty-four dollars) per month were not included.[63] The increase in wages was accompanied by promotions for some staff employees and workers. Under the new system, those who had begun to work before 1966 had more than twelve years of experience, and whose wages were below the third grade were promoted to the third grade. Those who had begun to work before 1971, had more than seven years of experience, and whose wages were below the second grade were eligible for selection by the mass organizations to receive the second-grade wage. Each promotion resulted in an increase of two to four yuan per month, a 15 to 17 percent raise.[64] In 1978, 2 percent of the workers and employees were granted a wage hike. The third round of wage increases since 1976 was announced in 1979, and in November 1979, 40 percent of the urban working force received a raise.

An official denunciation of egalitarianism has accompanied the wage hikes. The Chinese authorities now recognize that granting equal rewards to the indolent and the industrious encourages the former and disheartens the latter. Since 1978, bonuses and piecework have gradually been incorporated into the wage system. Different areas have experimented with various formulas. In Sichuan, where 100 major enterprises have been assigned to be experimental bases for the country's new management reform, some enterprises link bonuses to the merits of the individual worker, which are determined by work attitude, technical proficiency, and, most important, contribution to the unit. Other enterprises calculate bonuses on the basis of profit. Many state enterprises engage in some sort of profit sharing between enterprises and the state and link individual bonuses to enterprise profit.[65] A unified bonus system has not yet been established, however.

Another major reform has been the government decision to raise procurement prices for agricultural products on a continuing basis to reduce the disparity between industrial and agricultural prices. Starting with the marketing of summer grains in 1979, grain purchase prices have been raised by 20 percent, with an additional 50 percent raise for above-quota purchases. Procurement prices for cotton, edible oils, sugar, animal by-products, aquatic and forestry products, and other farm and sideline products were also raised by 21 to 50 percent.[66] At the same time, the government also cut the factory and market prices of farm machinery, chemical fertilizers, insecticides, plastics, and other manufactured goods for farm use by 10 to 15 percent.[67]

Furthermore, in a continuing deviation from Maoist policy, a decontrol of prices for more than 10,000 items has been announced. Most of the products at issue represent the output of small-scale rural and cottage industries – ink, brushes, scissors, fruits, and so on. The prices of those commodities will now change according to market supply and demand. Controls on such items had been in effect since 1957.

These adjustments, although unprecedented, fall far short of correcting the distortions that have accumulated over the past three decades. Countless problems still plague the price and wage system. The foremost problem is the failure of the existing price system to correspond to production costs and to market supply and demand. Procurement prices are still too low to provide incentives to the peasants. In Hebei Province, for instance, the profit rate for producing food grains averaged only 1.1 percent in 1976, and for cotton, there was a net loss of 15.1 percent.[68] Even with the 1979 20 percent rise in procurement prices, peasants still find it more profitable to engage in sideline products than to produce grains and cotton. In the capital goods industry, the prices set for coal have been too low to cover costs, rendering a loss instead of a profit. In 1978, the average rate of profit was 40 percent for petroleum industries, 21 percent for power, 13 percent for metallurgy, and only 1 percent for coal enterprises. Due to irrational price fixing, the 33,000 workers at Beijing's Yanshan Petrochemical Corporation turned over 1 billion yuan in profits to the state in 1958, more than the total profit remittances contributed by China's 2 million coal miners.[69] Because the levels of reinvestment, bonuses, and worker fringe benefits are now linked directly or indirectly to profits, which are determined by price, the management reforms are bestowing the fattest profits upon those enterprises that enjoy arbitrarily high fixed prices and not necessarily upon the enterprises that are well managed. Without a further adjustment of the price structure, the efforts to modernize China's enterprise management will prove to be ineffective.

Yet a substantial rise in agricultural procurement prices and in prices for coal and other extractive industries would have great implications for capital formation, industrial structure, and production costs in other industries. As noted previously, the high rate of capital investment during the past three decades stemmed mainly from the continued squeeze of the agricultural sector. Low agricultural prices helped to keep down food costs for the urban population and raw material costs for the industries. That situation, in turn, tended to augment the profits of state enterprises, which were plowed back into investment. The same is true for the price of coal, which constitutes 70 percent of China's prime energy. As a result of increases in the procurement prices of farm products, retail food prices rose dramatically all over China in November 1979 and were responsible for inflationary pressures throughout the entire economy. As the government has tightened price controls, "disguised price increases" have spread everywhere in China. Sellers substitute substandard products or package less than the specified product weight. As procurement prices for raw materials rise and prices of industrial products remain unchanged, the profits of state enterprises will inevitably suffer. In 1979, the final state accounts were 17 billion yuan ($11 billion) in the red, and the deficit in 1980 was 12.1 billion yuan ($8.12 billion). The huge fiscal deficit was met by increasing bank-note insurance, which resulted in high inflation. Official statistics show a 6 percent increase in retail prices in 1980 and a 13.8 percent increase in the prices of nonstaple foods,[70] but unofficial sources put the 1980 inflation rate at more than 20 percent,[71] the highest in thirty years.

Thus, the Chinese economy is caught in a dilemma. The scissor price policy of the past, which facilitated capital accumulation, caused widespread discontent among the peasantry. By increasing the procurement prices of agricultural products and reducing the prices of industrial products, the new policy has caused a sharp decline in capital accumulation and high rate of inflation, which in turn would be detrimental to the industrialization drive.

## NOTES

1. For price systems in the Soviet Union, see Morris Bornstein, "Soviet Price, Theory and Policy," in U.S., Congress, Joint Economic Committee, *New Directions in the Soviet Economy* (Washington, D.C.: Government Printing Office, 1966), pp. 65–66; also Alec Nove, *The Soviet Economic System* (London: Allen and Unwin, 1977), chap. 7.

2. For a more detailed analysis of this topic, see Dwight H. Perkins, *Market Control and Planning in Communist China,* pp. 32–38.

3. Chen Boyuan and Wang Min, "The Role of the Law of Value in Cotton Production," *Guangming ribao* (Beijing), December 9, 1978, p. 3.

4. Dwight H. Perkins, *Market Control,* p. 113.

5. *Peking Review* 15:40 (October 6, 1972), p. 21, and 18:19 (May 9, 1975), p. 18.

6. Ibid.

7. Peter Schran, "China's Price Stability: Its Meaning and Distributive Consequences," *Journal of Comparative Economics* 1:4 (December 1977), pp. 381-385; also, Xiao Zhuoji, "The Laws of Price Changes in China," *Zhongguo shehui kexue* [Social sciences in China] No. 3 (May 1980), pp. 41–52.

8. Jan S. Prybyla, "Role and Determination of Prices in Mainland China," in *Proceedings of the Fifth Sino-American Conference on Mainland China* (Taipei: Institute of International Relations, 1976), pp. 513–514.

9. Chi Ti, "Stable Prices and the Reasons," *Peking Review* 18:19 (May 8, 1975), p. 19.

10. Hubei University, Department of Planning and Statistics, *Gongye tongji xue* [Industrial statistics] (Wuhan: Hubei Renmin Chubanshe, 1960), pp. 388–390.

11. Zhang Wen and Zhao Liguang, "An Analysis of the Factors Forming Commodity Prices Under Socialism," *Xin jianshe* No. 13 (December 20, 1963), pp. 28–35.

12. Audrey Donnithorne, *China's Economic System,* p. 315.

13. Yang Jianbai and Li Xuezeng, "China's Historical Experience in Handling the Relations Between Agriculture, Light Industry, and Heavy Industry," *Zhongguo shehui kexue* (Beijing) No. 3 (May 1980), pp. 20–22.

14. For details, see Tian Qi, "Several Problems in Revising the 1952 Constant Prices of Industrial Products," *Tongji gongzuo* No. 1 (January 1957), pp. 15–17.

15. Ibid.

16. For example, Fan Ruoyi, "The Pricing Policy for Products of Heavy Industry," *Jingji yanjiu* No. 3 (March 1957), pp. 54–67; and Choh-ming Li, *Economic Development of Communist China* (Berkeley and Los Angeles: University of California Press, 1959), p. 36.

17. The gross output values of industry and agriculture at 1952 constant prices and 1957 constant prices are from P.R.C., State Statistical Bureau, *Ten Great Years,* p. 16. The gross output values of industry and agriculture at 1970 constant prices are derived from Yang Jianbai and Li Xuezeng, "China's Historical Experience in Handling the Relations Between Agriculture, Light Industry, and Heavy Industry," p. 20.

18. Niu Zhonghuang, *Woguo guomin shouru de jilei he xiaofei* [Accumulation and consumption in the national income of our country] (Beijing, Zhongguo Qingnian Chubanshe, 1959), p. 89.

19. *Renmin shouce 1957* [People's handbook 1957] (Beijing: Da Gong Bao, 1957), p. 159.

20. Chi Hsin, "China Completed a Sharp Turn," *Chi-shih nien-tai* No. 2 (February 1979), p. 16.

21. Audrey Donnithorne, *China's Economic System,* p. 450.

22. Tong Dalin and Bao Tong, "Some Views on Agricultural Modernization," *Renmin ribao,* December 8, 1978, p. 3.

23. Nai-Ruenn Chen, *Chinese Economic Statistics* (Chicago: Aldine, 1967), pp. 80–81.

24. Yao Jinguan, "Several Problems Relating to the 'Scissors' Difference Between the Prices of Industrial and Agricultural Products," *Jingji yanjiu* No. 12 (December 1978), p. 34.

25. *Tongji gongzuo* No. 17 (September 14, 1957), p. 4.

26. *Peking Review* 18:19 (May 9, 1975), pp. 17–18.

27. Sung Kuang-wei, "Factors Behind Price Stability," *China Reconstructs* 15:7 (July 1966), p. 48.

28. Arthur G. Ashbrook, Jr., "China: Shift of Economic Gears in Mid-1970s," in U.S., Congress, Joint Economic Committee, *Chinese Economy Post–Mao,* p. 227.

29. Xue Muqiao, *Study of China's Socialist Economic Problems,* p. 134.

30. Li Debin, "Cotton Prices and Cotton Production During the Post-Liberation Period," *Beijing Daxue xuebao* [Journal of Peking University] No. 2 (April 20, 1980), pp. 49–54.

31. Naum Jasny, "The Soviet Price System," *American Economic Review* 40:9 (December 1950), p. 849.

32. Xue Muqiao, *Study of China's Socialist Economic Problems,* p. 13G.

33. For a detailed discussion, see Chu-yuan Cheng, "A Preliminary Study on Sino-Soviet Trade," *Democratic Review* (Hong Kong) 9:9 (May 1958), pp. 245–248; and Kang Chao, "Yuan-Dollar Price Ratios in Communist China and the United States," in Center for Chinese Studies, *Occasional Paper No. 2* (Ann Arbor: University of Michigan, July 1963), pp. 13–21.

34. Zhao Yiwen, *Xin Zhongguo de gongye* [Industry in new China] (Beijing: Tongji Chubanshe, 1957), pp. 106–107.

35. Ye Jizhuang, former minister of foreign trade, "Report on China's Foreign Trade," *Xinhua banyuekan* No. 16 (August 1957), pp. 92–93.

36. *China News Analysis* (Hong Kong) No. 966 (July 12, 1974), p. 5.

37. "China Practices Preferential Price Policy in Minority Nationality Areas," NCNA-Hohhot, June 14, 1977.

38. Chi Ti, "Stable Prices and the Reasons," pp. 17–20.

39. Cheng Shih, *A Glance at China's Economy* (Beijing: Foreign Languages Press, 1974), p. 39.

40. *Beijing Review* 23:15 (April 14, 1980), p. 6.

41. Chi Ti, "Stable Prices and the Reasons," p. 18.

42. *Beijing Review* 23:20 (May 19, 1980), p. 21.

43. Chu-yuan Cheng, *The Machine-Building Industry in Communist China,* pp. 273–274.

44. *Tongji gongzuo,* Reference Office, "A General Survey of National Industrial Capital," *Tongji gongzuo* No. 1 (1957), p. 32.

45. Sun Yefang, "It Is Necessary Righteously and Confidently to Grasp Socialist Profit," *Jingji yanjiu* No. 9 (September 20, 1978), p. 11.

46. See Yang Jianbai, He Jianzhang, and Jiang Lin, "On Prices of Production in the Socialist Economy," *Jingji yanjiu* No. 5 (May 1964), pp. 12–20; and, more recently, Sun Yefang, Liang Wensen, and Dian Jiangxi, "On Examination of Investment Result – With Respect to the Adoption of Capital Profit Rate as an Indicator," *Jingji yanjiu* No. 9 (September 20, 1978), pp. 26–31.

47. *Jingji yanjiu* No. 9 (September 15, 1964), pp. 1–11.

48. Sun Yefang, "It Is Necessary Righteously and Confidently to Grasp Socialist Profit," p. 12.

49. Yu Lin, "The Correct Manner of Determining Prices of Different Kinds of Products," *Jingji yanjiu* No. 5 (May 1964), pp. 1–16. For other discussions of this subject, see Nai-Ruenn Chen, "The Theory of Price Formation in Communist China," pp. 33–53, and Audrey Donnithorne, *China's Economic System,* chap. 16.

50. *China News Analysis* (Hong Kong) No. 966 (July 12, 1974), p. 6.

51. Barry M. Richman, *Industrial Society in Communist China,* pp. 812–813.

52. *Renmin shouce 1955* [People's handbook 1955] (Tianjin: Da Gong Bao, 1955), pp. 496–497.

53. NCNA-Beijing, November 24, 1978.

54. According to a State Council directive, bonuses should not exceed 12 percent of wages, but the average bonus in Sichuan in 1979 was 17 percent (*Jingji guanli* No. 1 [January 15, 1980], p. 13).

55. Jan S. Prybyla, *The Chinese Economy*, p. 128.

56. See Yao Wenyuan, "On the Social Basis of the Lin Biao Anti-Party Clique," *Hongqi* No. 3 (March 1975).

57. *Chi-shih nien-tai* No. 12 (December 1974), pp. 15–17.

58. Hu Qiaomu, "Act in Accordance with Economic Laws, Step Up the Four Modernizations."

59. Tong Dalin and Bao Tong, "Some Views on Agricultural Modernization," p. 3.

60. Sun Yefang, "It Is Necessary Righteously and Confidently to Grasp Socialist Profit," p. 11.

61. Xiao Liang and Zhang Wennian, "Improve the Bonus System, Give Full Play to the Role of Bonuses," *Guangming ribao*, November 11, 1978, p. 4.

62. Sun Yefang, "It Is Necessary Righteously and Confidently to Grasp Socialist Profit."

63. *Wen wei po* (Hong Kong), November 11, 1977, and *Peking Review* 21:18 (May 15, 1978), p. 13.

64. Chen Ting-chung, "The Pay Raise Program in Mainland China," *Issues and Studies* 14:2 (February 1978), pp. 5–6.

65. Wang Xiangjia, "Bonus System in 100 Enterprises Under Experiment in Sichuan Province," *Jingji guanli* No. 1 (January 15, 1980), pp. 11–14.

66. In Xinjiang, the purchase price for hogs rose 24 percent, for oxen 36 percent, goats 24 percent, eggs 30 percent, sugar beets 25 percent, silkworm cocoons 21 percent, and cashmere 50 percent (*China Business Review* [November–December 1979], p. 55).

67. *Peking Review* 21:52 (December 29, 1978), pp. 5–10.

68. Yao Jinguan, "Several Problems Relating to the 'Scissors' Difference Between the Industrial and Agricultural Products," p. 34.

69. *Honggi* No. 10 (October 2, 1979), p. 55.

70. Liu Guangdi, "Why Is China Striving to Wipe Out Its Deficit?" *Beijing Review* 24:15 (April 13, 1981), p. 21.

71. Reuter-Beijing, April 28, 1981.

# 9

# The Strategies of Development

Economic development requires the establishment of a set of fairly well-conceived and well-articulated policies in pursuit of a particular objective. In modern economic history, both Meiji Japan and the Soviet Union under Stalin formulated consistent developmental policies that guided their long-term development.

In the case of China, despite several pronounced goals such as a high rate of economic growth, self-reliance, and regional balance, no single consistent development strategy has prevailed throughout the Communist period. Since the 1950s, economic policies have shifted constantly from one period to another. Consequently, the pattern of resource allocation, sectoral priorities, and the choice of technique and scale also have swung frequently.

The frequent shift of developmental strategies results from the interplay of many factors. Among them are changes in international relations, oscillations between pragmatic and radical ideological approaches, and changing economic conditions. After discussing the Soviet and Japanese models of development, this chapter will delineate the fundamental Chinese policies at various stages, inquiring into the causes and consequences of those policy changes, and then examine the implications of those strategies for China's development prospects.

## CHOICE OF DEVELOPMENT STRATEGY

In late 1952 and early 1953, when the rehabilitation of the national economy was basically complete, Chinese leaders began to contemplate the choice of a strategy for a large-scale industrialization program. The question confronting the leadership was what kind of development model to pursue. At that juncture, at least two models seemed to be relevant to Chinese development. The Soviet model under Stalin's rule had proved remarkably successful in raising the Soviet Union to the status of a major power. The Japanese model, from the Meiji Restoration until World War II, also appeared to be a triumphant one.

The main features of the Soviet model consisted of (1) a strong commitment to a high rate of economic growth; (2) an exceptionally high rate of capital formation to sustain growth; (3) a high priority on the expansion of industry, particularly the capital goods industry; (4) a preference for concentrating investment in large plants with capital-intensive techniques; (5) the continuous channeling of agricultural surplus into the modern sector; and (6) an institutional transformation in the agricultural sector to facilitate an intersectoral capital flow.[1]

During the early years of Soviet industrialization (1928–1937), the rate of capital formation was as high as 20–25 percent, substantially higher than the "take-off" investment rate (10 percent) suggested by W. W. Rostow.[2] Of the total investment during the Soviet First Five-Year Plan period, 41 percent was allocated to industry, and 82 percent of that went to the capital goods industry. In the choice of technique and scale, the Soviet strategy was to invest heavily in relatively large capital-intensive projects. Apparently, this policy was the combined result of the Soviet leaders' neglect of interest charges in choosing among alternate projects, their obsession with technical rather than economic efficiency, and their "gigantomania," which identified large size with economies of scales.[3]

The Stalin model achieved impressive results. During the first two five-year plans (1928–1937), the Soviet Union achieved rapid industrialization, speedy growth, and marked structural transformation in its economy. By the end of the Second Five-Year Plan, Soviet industrial output had surpassed that of Western Europe, and the Soviet Union had successfully withstood the Nazi onslaught, becoming a military power second only to the United States.

The Soviet model, however, entailed rather high costs. The continuing squeeze on the agricultural sector to support the modern sector caused the long-term stagnation of agriculture. The policy set up its own vicious circle. Because agricultural development was sluggish while the demand for farm products grew—owing to increased population, urbanization, and exports—the regime was forced to extract a rising proportion of farm output to meet the demand. This need led to collectivization and compulsory procurement, which in turn further retarded agricultural development. The Stalin model also required prolonged sacrifices of personal consumption in order to maintain a high rate of capital formation and a totalitarian political framework to ensure resource allocation in line with the planners' preference.

In contrast to the Soviet model, the Japanese development experience after the Meiji Restoration in 1868 represented a more balanced growth path. During the early stage of industrialization between 1888 and the end of World War I, Japan's development strategy consisted of the following features:

1. a relatively low rate of investment
2. a more balanced development of agriculture and industry and of consumer goods and capital goods
3. the maximum use of abundant labor of adopting labor-intensive techniques
4. the concentration of investment in overhead capital instead of in direct production activities

Japanese records show that the rate of investment was only 12.6 percent between 1896 and 1919 as compared with 20–25 percent in the Soviet Union during its first two five-year plans.[4] During the early stage of industrialization, more than 70 percent of Japanese industrial production still consisted of consumer goods.[5] Moreover, at the very outset, Japan placed great emphasis upon agricultural development. This was attained chiefly through the introduction of Western technology and most especially through large applications of imported fertilizers.[6] Although the annual growth rate of GNP (in constant prices) between 1885 and 1919 was only 3.4 percent,[7] less than half of the Soviet growth rate between 1928 and 1937, the Japanese model did not demand sacrifices in personal consumption. Nor did it require agricultural collectivization and a totalitarian political structure as the Soviet model did.

In comparing the natural endowment and initial conditions of China, Japan, and the Soviet Union, China comes closer to Japan than to the Soviet Union. The Chinese economy of 1952 was at a stage of development roughly comparable to that of Meiji Japan but was much more underdeveloped than the Soviet economy on the eve of its FFYP in 1928 (see Table 9.1). The most striking difference between China and the Soviet Union was the demographic setting. In 1952, China's population was 567 million, almost four times that of the Soviet Union in 1928, and the population was growing at a rate of more than 2 per-

Table 9.1
Comparative Levels of Development: China, Soviet Union, and Japan in Each One's Initial Year of Industrialization

| Development Category | China (1952) | USSR (1926-28) | Japan (1872-82) |
|---|---|---|---|
| GNP | | | |
| (in billion US dollars) | $30.00 | $35.00 | $2.20 |
| GNP per head | | | |
| (in 1952 US dollars) | 50.00 | $240.00 | $65.00 |
| Population | | | |
| (million persons) | 567 | 150 | 35.36 (1875) |
| % of population in agriculture & fishing | 80 | 76.5 (1926) | 84.8 (1872) |
| Persons per acre of cultivated land | 1.90 | 0.20 | 2.0 |
| Output of grain per head | | | |
| (kg. per person) | 311 | 566 | NA |
| Industrial output | | | |
| (million metric tons) | | | |
| Coal | 53 | 40.1 | 0.6 (1875) |
| Pig iron | 1.6 | 3.3 | 0.01 (1877) |
| Crude steel | 1.2 | 4.3 | none |
| Electric power generating capacity in 1000 KW | 2,850 | 1,900 | none |
| Industrial output per capita | | | |
| (kg. per capita) | | | |
| Coal | 96 | 273 (1929) | 17 (1875) |
| Pig iron | 2.75 | 22 | 0.2 (1877) |
| Crude steel | 2.00 | 29 | none |
| Electric power generating capacity (KW per capita) | 0.005 | 0.01 | none |

Sources: Alexander Eckstein, China's Economic Development (Ann Arbor: University of Michigan Press, 1975), p. 214. K. C. Yeh, "Soviet and Communist Chinese Industrialization Strategies," in D. W. Treadgold, ed., Soviet and Chinese Communism: Similarities and Differences (Seattle: University of Washington Press, 1967), pp. 327-363.

cent per annum. Russian territory was three times that of the Chinese, and the crop area per head of rural population was 2.3 acres per person for the Soviet Union in 1928 but only 0.7 acre for China in 1952. Consequently, per capita output of food grains in the Soviet Union was 566 kilograms as compared with only 311 kilograms in China.[8]

The implications of these differences for resource allocation are profound. In the first place, because of China's greater population demand for consumption, it was much more difficult for China than it was for the Soviet Union to maintain a high ratio of savings to income. Moreover, a huge population with a high fertility rate creates employment problems. The Stalin model of squeezing agricultural surplus to feed industry and of concentrating resources on capital-intensive projects was unsuitable for China, given China's natural endowment.

In contrast to the Soviet model, Japan's initial conditions were much more encouraging from the Chinese point of view. As Alexander Eckstein has rightly pointed out, Meiji Japan was at about the same level or lagged behind 1952 China in terms of all major indicators. Japanese per capita product and degree of population pressure were just about the same as in China. On the other hand, Japan possessed practically no factory industry and had a much poorer mineral resource base.[9]

Despite the backward state of Meiji Japan's economy and that country's poor natural endowment, the GNP rose roughly tenfold between 1880 and 1940.[10] If China's economy were to continue to grow at about the same rate as that of Japan, China's GNP would attain the Japanese level around 1980, and the 1952 U.S. level would be reached around 2010.[11]

The Chinese leaders probably selected the Soviet model for the following reasons. First, the Soviet model was the only one at once available, ideologically acceptable, and already tested in practice. The Japanese economy was operating within a market system, and China's commitment to a socialist system automatically precluded adoption of the Japanese model. Second, China anticipated Soviet aid. The expectation of that aid led to the formulation and implementation of Mao's "lean-to-one-side" foreign policy, thereby excluding U.S. and Western European financial and technical assistance.[12] The technical assistance that the Soviet Union was capable of giving was geared to long experience with the Stalinist model. Finally, the Chinese Communist leaders in power when China's industrialization program was launched do not appear to have had a workable alternative of their own. Most of them lacked experience in ruling a vast economy. For these reasons, China's development strategy in its First Five-Year Plan was almost a duplicate of the Stalinist model.

## EVOLUTION OF CHINA'S DEVELOPMENT STRATEGIES

The initial adoption of the Soviet model of development has been followed by three decades of incessant change. In terms of the pattern of resource allocation, sectoral priorities, and choice of production techniques, the development process can be roughly divided into six stages.

*The Unbalanced Growth Strategy (1953–1957)*

China's early commitment to the Soviet model was reflected in the First Five-Year Plan. China's plan closely followed the Stalinist unbalanced growth strategy of rapid expansion of the capital goods industry at the expense of agriculture. To achieve high rates of growth, the ratio of gross investment to gross domestic product in 1952 prices was raised to about 24 percent, as compared with only 6 percent in the pre–World War II era.[13] This was an extremely high rate for a country with a low per capita income.

As in the case of the Soviet Union, 48 percent of China's capital investment during the FFYP was allocated for industry, of which 85 percent was for heavy industry, including 25 percent for the machine-building industry alone. Only 7.6 percent of the state's capital investment went to agriculture. Even including investment made by agriculture collectives, the share for agriculture stood at only 14.9 percent (see Table 9.2). Table 9.2 shows that China closely followed the Soviet pattern of investment by concentrating the bulk of its resources on developing industry. The share that went to agriculture was even smaller than in the Soviet Union. Since agriculture produced the lion's share of the total savings, the essence of this development policy was a continuous squeeze of the agricultural sector to support industry, especially the capital goods and defense industries (mostly under the covert heading of machine-building industry).

In the choice of techniques and scale, the Chinese planners also imitated the Stalinist model by investing in relatively large and capital-intensive projects. More than 85 percent of the investment in the modern sector was allocated to 694 "above-norm" industrial projects,[14] leaving only 15 percent of the investment for more than 10,000 small projects.[15] Of the 694 above-norm projects, the major ones were 156 large modern projects that were designed and built with the aid of the Soviet Union, which absorbed approximately half of the investment in modern industry.[16]

The Soviet model proved to be useful in the initial stage of China's industrialization, and the capacity of basic industry expanded rapidly. The output of steel tripled, rising from 1.35 million tons in 1952 to 5.35 million tons in 1957. In the same period, the output of electric power rose 166 percent from 7.26 billion kilowatt-hours to 19.3 billion kilowatt-hours. A new machine-building industry took shape and was able to manufacture automobiles, jet aircraft, and a wide variety of

Table 9.2
Distribution of Public Capital Investment by Economic Sectors, USSR (1928/29-1937) and China (1953-1959)
(in percent)

| Sector | USSR | | China | | |
|---|---|---|---|---|---|
| | 1928/29 | 1933-37 | 1953-57 | | 1958-59 |
| Industry | 40.9 | 39.3 | 47.9 | (52.0) | (65.1) |
| Agriculture | 19.2 | 15.5 | 14.9 | ( 7.6) | ( 8.7) |
| Transportation & Communications | 18.4 | 16.7 | 15.1 | (16.4) | (14.3) |
| Others | 21.5 | 28.6 | 22.1 | (24.0) | (11.9) |
| (Housing) | (9.0) | (8.8) | (7.3) | --- | --- |
| Total | 100.0 | 100.0 | 100.0 | (100.0) | (100.0) |

Note: Underlying data are in current prices. Figures in parentheses do not include investment by collective farms; they present state investment alone. For instance, state investment in agriculture accounted for only 7.6 percent of the state's capital investment in 1953-1957. But if investment by agricultural collectives is included, investment in agriculture reached 14.9 percent.

Source: K. C. Yeh, "Soviet and Communist Chinese Industrialization Strategies," in D. W. Treadgold, ed., Soviet and Chinese Communism: Similarities and Differences (Seattle: University of Washington Press, 1967), p. 334.

machinery and equipment. The annual growth rate of industrial output during the FFYP was officially reported as 18 percent and that for the producer goods industry as more than 30 percent. The annual growth rate of the GNP was 8.9 percent according to official statistics and 6-7 percent according to independent estimates.[17]

However, the unbalanced growth strategy created serious bottlenecks in the economy. One major drawback was the lower rate of growth in the agricultural sector. According to official statistics, agricultural output during the FFYP period rose at an annual rate of 4.5 percent per annum, and the output of food grains advanced by 3.7 percent per year. Independent studies put the growth rate of food grains at a much lower rate, ranging from 0.92 percent to 2.33 percent per annum.[18] If the nonofficial estimates are accepted, the output of food grains in this period barely kept pace with the population growth, which was officially reported as 2.2 percent per annum. Starting in 1953, the first year of the plan, food prices began to soar because of the growth of the nonagricultural labor force and rising monetary income in the urban areas. As a result, inflationary pressure appeared in the second half of that year. This led to the institution of the planned purchase and planned supply system in the autumn of 1953 and a nationwide uniform rationing system in 1955 (see Chapter 7).

The sluggishness of agricultural output also caused shortages of raw materials for light industries, which meant that many of them could not operate at full capacity. Official statistics show that in 1957, due to shortages of raw materials, the rates of operation were 85 percent for the textile industry, 66 percent for sugar making, 75 percent for oil pressing, 52 percent for tobacco processing, 68 percent for flour production, and 53 percent for canned foods.[19]

The concentration of investment in large-scale and capital-intensive projects resulted in a low absorption of labor. Between 1952 and 1957, the total labor force rose by 20 million (or about 4 million a year), but employment in the industrial sector increased only 1.78 million (an average of 0.36 million a year), which accounted for only 9 percent of the addition to the labor force.[20] Moreover, the increase of employment in the modern sector was partially offset by the decline of employment in handicrafts. Under this situation, the size of the rural population did not materially decline. Its proportion of the total population stood at 86.8 percent in 1953 and 85.7 percent in 1957. This would suggest that despite the sharp increase of capital investment in the modern sector, the distribution of population between urban and rural areas remained basically unchanged. As the economy faced the double pressure of raw material shortages and unemployment, the Stalinist model rapidly lost its attraction.

Prior to 1956, the applicability of the Soviet model to China was rarely questioned. In September 1956, the Eighth Party Congress, apparently still under Soviet influence, adopted a preliminary proposal for the Second Five-Year Plan (1958–1962). In broad outline, the proposal was similar to the first plan. Its main features included: (a) a rise in the rate of investment to 25 percent of GNP, with total capital investment double that of the first plan; (b) increases in the shares of capital investment allocated to industry and agriculture but with a very modest increase planned for agriculture, rising only from 7 to 10 percent of the total, and top priority still assigned to the development of heavy industry; and (c) a renewed emphasis on modern capital-intensive techniques, which would allow for the absorption of no more than 6 million to 7 million new workers and employees during 1958–1962.[21] The proposal, if put into effect, would have been a continuation of the Stalinist model.

As the problems of agricultural sluggishness and rising unemployment became acute, however, the Chinese leaders began to doubt the merits of the Soviet model. In December 1956, the Party's organ, *Renmin ribao,* commented that "all the experience of the Soviet Union, including its fundamental experience, is bound up with definite national characteristics and no other country should copy it mechanically."[22] This was the first straw in the wind. Thereafter, many economists and government planners openly advocated a more balanced growth strategy that would pay more attention to agricultural development. Ma Yinchu, the leading economist and former president of Beijing University, published two long essays in December 1956 and May 1957 criticizing the lopsided development of industry at the expense of agriculture.[23] Under Ma's influence, the pace of development in 1957 slowed down, and capital investment was curtailed by 7.4 percent. The retrenchment, however, aggravated the unemployment problems. A new approach, known as the Great Leap Forward, was introduced in 1958.

### *The Great Leap Forward (1958–1960)*

The general idea behind the new strategy was to accelerate simultaneously the growth of both agriculture and industry through the use of a technological dualism officially labeled the "walking on two legs" approach. The economy was envisaged as consisting of two broad sectors, one modern and one traditional. Although the modern sector would continue to use capital-intensive techniques and large-scale methods of production, the traditional sector would adopt labor-intensive and small-scale methods. The country's financial resources and technical manpower would continue to concentrate on further expansion of the modern sector, but China's increasing manpower could be transferred into capital by engaging in irrigation, flood control, and small-scale industrial production in the countryside. In the case of the Stalin model, the Russians had transformed agricultural surplus into industrial capital. In the case of the Great Leap, the Chinese leaders hoped to substitute surplus labor for capital or to use surplus labor for capital formation. The whole concept came very close to Ragnar Nurkse's proposal, which also focused on labor absorption or the employment-generating effects of industrialization.[24]

The new policy started with large-scale water conservation projects, which mobilized more than 100 million peasants in late 1957 and early

1958. According to official claims, 11,000 new irrigation projects were built in 1958 alone, as compared with the five-year total of 14,000 built in 1953–1957. That same year accounted for almost ten times as much earthwork as 1953–1957, and almost seven times as many man-days were spent in 1958 as in 1953–1957.[25] Such a large-scale mobilization of rural manpower was unprecedented in Chinese history.

The most dramatic aspect of the new policy, however, was the mushrooming of millions of small plants all over the country. Some 60 million persons were mobilized to build more than 1 million small backyard blast furnaces, using primitive production methods. The rationale behind the new drive was that the small workshops would have very low ratios of capital to labor (K/L) but very high ratios of labor to output (L/O), thus solving the problem of unemployment.[26]

It seems that remarkable results were achieved during the first year of the Great Leap. Not only was all surplus labor in the countryside eliminated but, in fact, a critical shortage of manpower in the agricultural sector was created. This shortage led to the establishment of the rural communes as a means of releasing peasant housewives from household chores so that they could participate in productive activities.[27] Official reports at the time painted a rosy picture of both industrial and agricultural development. The output of food grains was officially given as rising from 185 million tons in 1957 to 250 million tons in 1958, an increase of 35 percent; the output of cotton surged from 1.65 to 2.1 million tons, rising 28 percent; the output of steel was said to have leaped from 5.35 to 10 million tons, an increase of 100 percent; and the output of coal was supposed to have increased from 130 to 270 million tons, more than doubling in one year.[28]

Most of those miracles proved to be illusory, however. As the zeal diminished, the government admitted that many of the earlier statistics had been highly inflated by local cadres. Most of the small workshops and backyard furnaces built in 1958 lacked technical equipment and skilled labor and turned out unusable products at exceedingly high costs. The diversion of resources from modern industry to support local small plants cut output in the modern sector. According to Peng Dehuai, former minister of national defense, the waste in material caused by the backyard furnace campaign during the 1958–1959 period alone was estimated at 2 billion yuan (or $800 million at prevailing official exchange rates).[29] In April 1981, the Party's organ, *Renmin ribao,* carried a sober assessment of the Great Leap and blamed the rash campaign for a loss or waste of over 100 billion yuan ($66 billion) during the three years of the Great Leap Forward.[30]

The most detrimental effect, however, was upon the agricultural sector. Misled by false reports of fantastically high yields in 1958, the Chinese leaders believed that they had solved the agricultural problem. Later in the same year, Mao Zedong advocated the utopian prospect of transforming the whole country into a vast garden. Claiming that the area of sown land could be reduced by two-thirds by employing intensive methods of cultivation, Mao introduced the "three-three" system of cropping. It provided that all arable land would be divided into three parts: one to be planted, one to lie fallow, and the third to be afforested. Mao's new theory was formally adopted by the Eighth CCP Central Committee at its Sixth Plenum in December 1958, and a new policy of "plant less and reap more" was implemented.[31] The sown acreage for 1959 was deliberately cut down from 1.8 billion mu to 1.6 billion mu.[32] However, the illusion that had prompted the new policy was quickly dispelled by the discovery in mid-1959 that the 1958 harvest had been grossly exaggerated and that the 1958 grain output had increased only 2.5 percent. The new policy was hurriedly reversed, but it had already damaged the summer harvest of 1959.[33]

A more fundamental cause of the agricultural crisis was the ineffectual remuneration system in the early stage of the commune system, which dampened the peasants' initiative. Under the 1958 commune system, private plots were confiscated, rural free markets were abolished, and food grains were distributed on a more or less egalitarian basis. Peasants lost their enthusiasm for farming. When the intensive care necessary for China's garden-type farming was not forthcoming, agricultural output fell precipitously in 1959 and 1960.

The large-scale irrigation campaign also turned out to be destructive. Because many of the canals and reservoirs had been built without any proper geological survey or technical design, the new projects not only destroyed the natural irrigation system and hindered the regular functions of the main rivers, particularly the Huang He, but they also turned roughly a million acres of arable land into alkaline soil.[34]

When agricultural output registered a continuous drop, the economy soon reached its limit of tolerance. The 1960 grain output declined to only 143.5 million tons, a drop of 20 percent from 1957–the year before the Great Leap began. Per capita food supply dropped from 203 kilograms in 1957 to only 163.5 kilograms in 1960.[35] A severe food crisis developed, and famine became widespread. According to Sun Yefang, a leading economist in the P.R.C., Chinese demographic records show that the number of deaths in China in 1957, the year before the Great Leap, was 7.5 million people. In 1960, the number of deaths suddenly jumped to 17.8 million. The 10-million increase in the number of deaths probably was because of the famine caused by the agriculture failures in 1959 and 1960.[36] For the first time since it came into power, the regime had to import grains on a sizable scale. The Great Leap Forward, instead of moving the economy forward, brought it to the brink of collapse.

*The Readjustment (1961–1965)*

The economic crisis was exacerbated in August 1960 when the Soviet government suddenly withdrew all Soviet technicians working in China and suspended all technical aid to China. These moves dealt a severe blow to China's already weakened economy. In order to alleviate the crisis, China drastically revised its strategy of development, quietly abandoning the basic tenets of the Great Leap. A new policy of "readjustment of the pace of development, consolidation of existing plants, reinforcement of the weak links, and improvement of the quality of products" was decided upon at the Ninth Plenum of the Eighth CCP Central Committee in January 1961.[37] The major features of the new policy were as follows.

1. A balanced growth approach became the new guideline of development. Zhou Enlai announced that the rate of industrial growth would be determined by and coordinated with the amount of marketable grains and industrial raw materials made available by agriculture.[38] In other words, industrial development was to be a function of agricultural growth. This policy represented a new understanding of the constraints on Chinese economic development. Under the new guideline, capital investment in 1961–1962 dropped by 50 percent from 1960,[39] and most of the small workshops constructed during the Great Leap period were shut down. The economy entered a period of retrenchment.

2. Sectoral priorities were totally reversed. The new official slogan stated, "Agriculture is the foundation, and industry is the leading factor." In a speech before the National People's Congress in 1962, Zhou Enlai announced that investment priorities would be changed, with agriculture assigned first place, consumer goods coming next, and capital goods relegated to the lowest priority. A host of additional measures lent credibility to the new priorities. Some 20 million workers and urban dwellers were dispatched to the countryside to reinforce the agricultural front. Industrial investment was concentrated in areas that could support the agricultural sector, notably chemical fertilizers and agricultural machinery. The new strategy involved a strong commitment to the technical transformation of agriculture. The Tenth Plenum of the Eighth Central Committee, con-

vened in September 1962, determined "to give agriculture and the collective economy of the people's communes every possible material, technical, and financial aid."[40] The "agriculture first" policy has since become one of China's guiding principles, although it has never been fully implemented.

3. In response to the suspension of Soviet economic and technical aid in the summer of 1960, "self-reliance" became a new catchword. Trade relations underwent a fundamental change from "lean to one side" (the side of the Soviet bloc) to "lean to all sides" with countries around the world. Petroleum extraction and refining were greatly expanded to eliminate China's dependence on imports of strategic significance. Defense production was also greatly stepped up. From September 1963 to December 1964, four ministries of machine-building industry were set up to take charge of electronics, heavy weapons and artillery, naval equipment and shipbuilding, and aircraft and missiles.[41] In December 1964, China exploded its first nuclear bomb and became one of the world's nuclear powers.

4. A recognition of the growing pressure of population on agriculture also led to renewed efforts to control population growth. Prior to 1961, all Chinese leaders had emphasized the positive effect of a large population on production and accumulation. A large population had been considered an asset rather than a liability,[42] and a birth control campaign had been abruptly called off in May 1958. The failure in agriculture and the emergence of the food crisis brought a fundamental change in the leaders' notion of the relationship between population growth and economic development. Early marriages were openly discouraged, and the ideal family was put forth as one with only two children. Contraceptive methods were openly discussed in the Party's newspapers, indicating that the regime had abandoned its ideological dogma in favor of a more realistic policy for population control.

The new strategy signified a complete reversal of the unbalanced growth of the first period and also departed significantly from the labor-absorption strategy of the Great Leap. To accelerate recovery, material incentives were reemphasized, and a nationwide increase in salaries and wages was granted to workers and employees in 1963. The commune system underwent continuous revision. Private plots of land were redistributed to individual households, and farm markets were reopened. Major steps were also taken to restore managerial prerogatives and to provide management with incentives. Under Liu Shaoqi's aegis, the CCP promulgated the Sixty-Point Charter for Agriculture and the Seventy-Point Charter for Industry, which laid down the ground rules for agriculture and industry. As a result of these measures, agricultural output began a slow but steady recovery. In 1964, grain output again reached the 1957 level, and by 1965, most of China's industrial output had attained the 1958–1959 level. The Great Leap thus cost China roughly seven years of development.

The stress on material incentives and on technological progress from 1961 to 1965 caused widespread "capitalist tendencies" in the rural areas and among the workers and intellectuals. Party bureaucrats, central planners, and economists seemed to favor a revisionist line similar to that prevailing in the Soviet Union. From 1963 to 1965, articles on the subjects of material incentives and profits appeared in increasing numbers in government economic journals. Several leading economists within the Party, led by Sun Yefang, openly advocated that profit constitute a positive indicator in investment decisions. Leaders in charge of Party affairs and economic planning apparently agreed and contended that industrialization could only be achieved by economic means. Both material incentives and profits were indispensable for running the economy, regardless of differences in social structure. Liu Shaoqi was quoted as saying, "A factory must make money, otherwise, it must be shut down." He was also said to have asserted that "the enthusiasm of a socialist people's democracy lies in the people's concern for their own economic life. They must be concerned with wages, living accommodations, food, transportation, etc., and only through the solution of those problems can political life be attractive."[43]

Although the bureaucratic leaders favored a continuation of this moderate, pragmatic approach, Mao prepared to launch an even more radical program to level his opponents. Thus, Mao initiated a new Socialist Educational Campaign in 1963, to revive his faltering revolutionary program. He began to groom Defense Minister Lin Biao as the chief propagator of his doctrine and as a potential replacement for Liu Shaoqi as Mao's successor. The ensuing backstage struggle between Mao and Lin on one side and Liu and Deng on the other led to the Great Proletarian Cultural Revolution of 1966.

### *The Modified Great Leap Scheme (1966–1976)*

Although the Cultural Revolution was primarily a struggle for power, the leadership's new emphasis on Maoist values and concepts did have significant effects on economic policies. Many measures similar to those of the Great Leap were reinstituted between 1966 and 1976.

First, material incentives, which had constituted the cornerstone of the post-Great Leap policy, were openly condemned as "economism." Maoists accused managers who raised workers' wages of being the class enemy and of attempting to buy the workers' support.[44] By reducing material incentives and enhancing Maoist values, the Maoists tried to infuse a spirit and a work ethic that would achieve the same objectives.

Second, mass participation in industrial management was reencouraged. College-trained engineers and technicians were downgraded. Many technical regulations were discarded, and production procedures were simplified. The intellectuals, particularly prominent scientists and scholars, were humiliated and tortured. They were denigrated and reduced to a classification that equated them with counterrevolutionaries or other equally bad elements.

Third, small-scale plants were in favor again. The switch to labor-intensive, small-scale industry linked to simple domestic technology was intended to use the surplus work force in each locality and to achieve regional self-sufficiency. In a 1969 directive, Mao decreed that "each locality should endeavor to build up an independent industrial system. Where conditions permit, coordination zones, and then provinces should establish their own relatively independent and varied industrial system."[45] With this new directive, small enterprises increased by leaps and bounds. By 1970, more than 90 percent of China's counties had erected networks of small plants that could produce small-sized power machines, farm implements and spare parts, chemical fertilizers, coal, cement, iron, and steel. Within a single countywide industrial network, iron and other metals were extracted and refined on the spot, using locally mined coal, and subsequently processed into mechanical implements designed to suit the county's agricultural needs. Thousands of water mills and miniature hydroelectric stations were installed to provide power for irrigation pumps, flour mills, and processing machinery.[46] In 1973, 1,400 small chemical fertilizer plants reportedly produced more than 50 percent of China's chemical fertilizers. Some 2,400 small plants turned out 50 percent of China's total cement output. There were nearly half a million small electronics plants throughout the country. The 1973 output of the small steel plants was four times that of 1969. The number of small hydroelectric power stations rose from 9,000 in 1960 to more than 50,000 in 1973.[47]

Fourth, in line with the drive to establish small plants in rural areas, there was a large-scale campaign in 1968 to persuade young intellectuals, urban dwellers, and medical workers to resettle in rural and border areas in order to balance the distribution of technical manpower between urban and rural areas and to relieve population pressure in the cities. As a result, more than 16 million people were sent to the countryside.[48]

The new strategy, although retaining some flavor of the Great Leap, contained two major modifications. First, in comparison to the Great Leap, the rural industrialization program in the late 1960s and early 1970s was less spontaneous but better planned. The small plants were generally equipped with certain types of machinery, and some plants on the county level became technically quite sophisticated.[49] According to later visitors, the productivity of the small plants is much higher than the backyard furnaces of 1958–1959, and the quality of their products is also superior.[50]

Second, the "agriculture first" policy of the post-Great Leap period was partly continued, and those branches of industry that supported agriculture still received high priority. The output of chemical fertilizers rose from 7.6 million tons in 1965, on the eve of the Cultural Revolution, to 28.8 million tons in 1975. From 1970 to 1973, the number of tractors and diesel engines supplied to agriculture reportedly surpassed that of the entire previous twenty years. In terms of capital investment, however, agriculture received only 10 percent of the total, compared with 60 percent for heavy industry (1970–1972).[51] In essence, the new strategy can be viewed as a combination of the Great Leap and the readjustment.

During the eleven years of the Cultural Revolution and radical reign (1966–1976), the pendulum of economic policy swung back and forth three times. In the early stages (1966–1969), the focus was on the Maoists' seizure of political power from the Party powerholders. Many Party leaders who had previously expressed opposition to Mao's policy were purged. Of the 23 members of the Politburo before the Cultural Revolution, only 9 retained membership. Approximately two-thirds of the members of the CCP Central Committee elected in 1956 were ousted. A large majority of the bureaucratic leaders who had exercised power during the first two decades of Communist rule were publicly disgraced, including Liu Shaoqi and Deng Xiaoping. The purge of the technocrats in the field of economic affairs was far reaching. One detailed study has indicated that as of January 1966, 316 known leaders held key positions in controlling agencies located in Beijing. By 1969, only one-fourth of them retained their positions. Of the highest-ranking 75 leaders in economic affairs (members of the CCP Central Committee), 70 had been ousted.[52]

The purges paved the way for a return of many of Mao's radical policies. Material incentives were denounced as the "ill wind of economism," and workers' bonuses were mostly abolished. In some areas, private plots were confiscated, and the free markets were banned. In industry, the director-responsibility system was abolished. Revolutionary committees composed of workers, cadres, and army representatives and technicians replaced administrative committees and performed the functions of the director. Many traditional work rules and regulations were discarded, and managerial personnel were downgraded. The consequences bordered on a management debacle.[53]

The radical policies caused output to decline. Industrial output dropped 13 percent in 1967, and by 1968, it was still 5 percent below that of 1966.[54] As the population continued to grow, per capita income declined in 1966-1968. To arrest the economic decline, Mao, with the support of the military leaders, charged Zhou Enlai in 1971 with the responsibility of reviving the ailing economy. Although Zhou had allied with Mao during the Cultural Revolution, his outlook and commitment were more closely akin to those of the purged leaders than to those of the radicals. Zhou took advantage of this opportunity to rehabilitate hundreds of experienced administrators, including Deng Xiaoping and Luo Ruiqing, two prominent targets of the Cultural Revolution. Between 1973 and April 1976, Zhou was stricken with terminal cancer, and Deng became the de facto premier. Firmly determined to eliminate the ultraradical elements, Deng put forward a set of programs that amounted to a total denial of the radicals' philosophy and a challenge to the ultraleftists led by Mao's wife Jiang Qing.

The new policy substantially revised the self-reliance doctrine advocated by Mao. During the 1973-1974 period, China contracted for the purchase of more than $2 billion worth of "complete plants" from Western Europe and Japan, in addition to large imports of machinery and equipment. Total imports of machinery and equipment in 1974 jumped to $1.7 billion, double that in 1973. In January 1975, Zhou presented the Fourth National People's Congress a program for developing the nation's economy through modernizing China's agriculture, industry, defense, and science and technology (the "four modernizations"). In this document, Zhou pointed out that China envisaged the development of the national economy in two stages. "The first stage is to build an independent and relatively comprehensive industrial and economic system in fifteen years, that is before 1990; the second stage is to accomplish the comprehensive modernization of agriculture, industry, national defense, and science and technology before the end of the century so that our national economy will be advancing in the front ranks of the world."[55] This proposal constituted the guideline for the 1976-1985 program.

The death of Zhou on January 8, 1976, triggered a new struggle between Deng and the radicals. The radicals described Deng's policy as a "philosophy of foreigners' slaves" that would sell out China's natural resources to the imperialists. As a result, imports of foreign plants and equipment dropped sharply in 1976.

During the period between Zhou's death and the demise of Mao on September 9, 1976, China was under the reign of the ultraleftists. They openly called for the abolition of wage differentials and placed restrictions on the legal rights of the "bourgeois."[56] In some provinces, a ceiling of 150 yuan per year ($75) was placed on the per capita income of each commune member.[57] Peasant resentment and worker unrest, as well as a managerial abdication of responsibility, became widespread. Industrial output suffered a deep decline. According to Hua Guofeng's report to the Fifth National People's Congress on February 26, 1978, between 1974 and 1976, the radicals had caused losses worth 100 billion yuan ($53 billion) in industrial output, 40 billion yuan ($21 billion) in state revenue, and 28 million tons of steel production. As a result, Hua indicated, "the national economy was on the brink of collapse."[58]

The fall of the radicals, signaled by the arrest of the Gang of Four in October 1976, paved the way for Deng's second comeback. At the Third Plenum of the CCP Tenth Party Congress convened in July 1977, Deng was restored to all his former posts. He immediately resumed the programs he had advocated in 1975. In February and March 1978, Hua Guofeng presented the four modernizations program, originally envisioned by Zhou but subsequently developed by Deng, to the Fifth National People's Congress.

Events up to the 1978 reforms demonstrate that the course of Chinese economic development since 1949 has not been a smooth or an uninterrupted process. The erratic twists and turns of development strategy suggest a policy of trial and error followed by overcorrection rather than the implementation of a set of consistent and well-conceived plans. The erratic policy changes are roughly depicted in Figure 9.1. Generally speaking, periods of radical experimentation have been succeeded by periods of retreat and adjustment in a series of pendulumlike oscillations of Chinese economic policy.

### *The Ephemeral Ten-Year Plan*

The overriding goal of the post-Mao leadership has been to recoup the economic losses attributed to the Cultural Revolution and to accelerate the growth of China's economy. The blueprint for this program was presented by Hua Guofeng to the Fifth National People's Congress in February 1978. Hua's announced target reiterated Zhou Enlai's 1975 proposal that "by the end of this century, the planned out-

## Figure 9.1
## Evolution of Developmental Strategies in P.R.C., 1953–1981

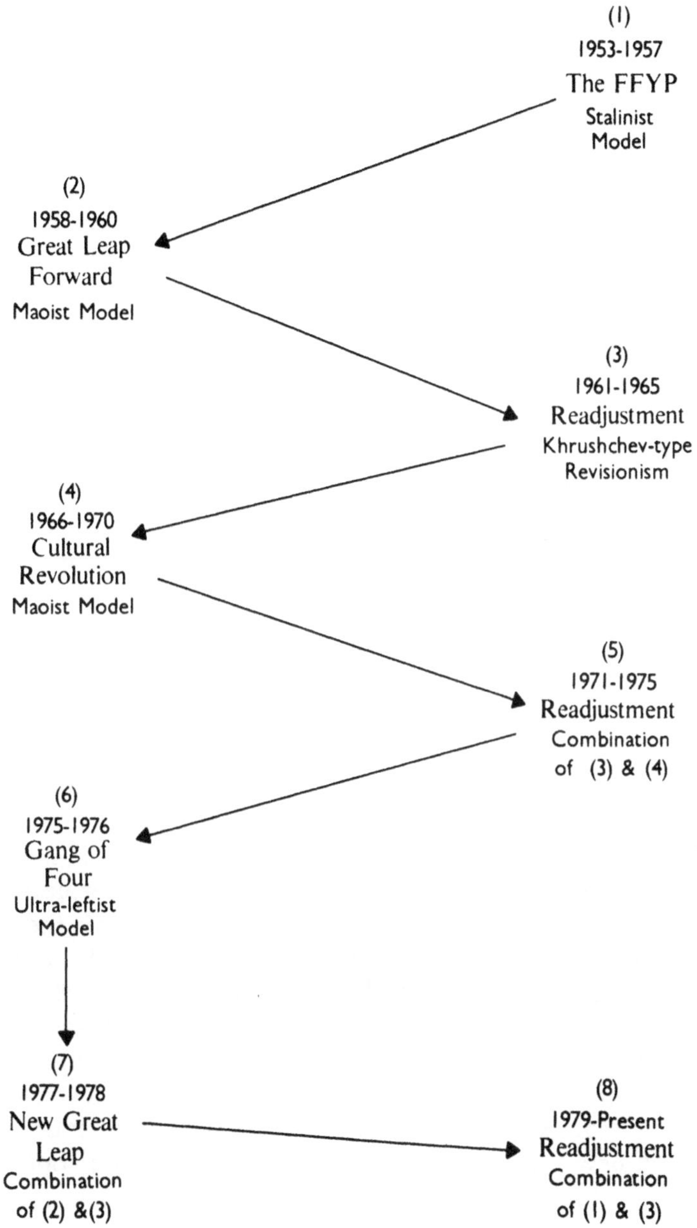

put of major agricultural products per acre is expected to reach or surpass that of advanced nations of the world, and the output of major industrial products to approach, equal, or outstrip that of the most developed capitalist countries." In order to accomplish those ambitious goals, Hua submitted a Ten-Year Plan of development for the 1976–1985 period.

According to the Ten-Year Plan, by 1985, the country would produce 400 million tons of grains and 60 million tons of steel, as measured against the 272 million tons and 20 million tons produced in 1976.[59] During the eight years 1978 to 1985, the value of agricultural output was to increase by 4 to 5 percent annually, twice the average growth rate since 1953. In the same time frame, industrial output was to increase at a 10 percent annual rate. State revenues and investments budgeted for capital construction were slated to equal the total for the previous twenty-eight years.[60] In view of the precarious state of China's economy in 1976, these targets were both ambitious and unrealistic.

To attain those ambitious goals, Hua Guofeng indicated that agricultural investment would be stepped up and that basic mechanization of agriculture would be achieved by 1980 in order to provide the impetus for overall economic development. On the industrial side of the ledger, the plan called for the building of 120 large-scale projects, including ten iron and steel complexes, nine nonferrous metal complexes, eight coal mines, ten oil and gas fields, thirty power stations, six new trunk railways, and five key harbors.

Two features distinguished the new plan from preceding plans and strategies. The first was the major role assigned to massive imports of Western equipment, complete plants, and technology. Whereas the First Five-Year Plan had focused on capital-intensive projects and had emphasized capital formation and Mao's Great Leap had stressed labor mobilization, the Ten-Year Plan emphasized the adoption of modern technology. In the four modernizations, the modernization of science and technology was regarded as a prerequisite for the other three. As Hua Guofeng noted, "To catch up quickly with the dramatic changes in modern science and technology and rapidly transform our backwardness in these fields are important and indispensable steps for the speedy development of our economy and the strengthening of our national defense."[61] This contrasts sharply with the low priority given to technological progress during the Cultural Revolution.

The second new feature of the Ten-Year Plan was a more open and liberal attitude toward foreign investment in China. Following the Sino-Soviet break in 1960, development policy was constrained by the heavy emphasis on self-reliance, which led China to give priority to projects that could be implemented without foreign assistance. This tended to reinforce the policy preference for labor-intensive as opposed to capital-intensive or technology-intensive projects. The large-scale development of small industrial plants was in line with that policy preference. Conversely, the post-Mao leaders have abandoned self-reliance in favor of fostering foreign trade and foreign investment as important avenues of technical infusion and financing. Western observers have labeled the open door policy for Western technology and capital the "Great Leap Outward";[62] it represents the most distinctive feature of the new development plan.

The technology-oriented and outward-looking strategy has been reflected in capital formation, technology infusion, technical manpower training, and foreign participation in industry.

1. In capital formation, in the 1950s and 1960s, China had relied on domestic resources, primarily the agricultural sector, to support the industrialization program. In the Ten-Year Plan, total investment was reportedly estimated at 1 trillion Renminbi, or $630 billion at the prevailing exchange rate.[63] According to Deng Xiaoping, China was about $300 billion short of the capital needed to fulfill the Ten-Year Plan.[64] To finance the development program, the leadership dropped its ideological opposition to borrowing from abroad. Prior to 1978, China had sought foreign bank loans on suppliers' credit for periods exceeding five years but still avoided accepting financial aid, investment by foreign countries, or joint ventures with other countries. This attitude has softened dramatically since 1978. During 1979 and 1980, Beijing accepted many arrangements unprecedented in P.R.C. history, including direct government-to-government loans. By June 1980, China had succeeded in negotiating foreign loans of $27 billion.[65]

2. Apart from direct foreign loans, Beijing has also encouraged joint ventures for the production of a wide range of industrial goods from textile to petroleum extraction. The most significant move was the promulgation on July 8, 1979, of China's first law on joint ventures, using Chinese and foreign investment. Under that law, foreign participation in a joint venture in China was to be at least 25 percent of the total investment. No upper limit was set. Apparently intended to attract badly needed foreign technology, management skills, and capital, the new law granted a two-to-three-year tax holiday for foreign investors who provided "up-to-date technology by world standards." In return for reinvesting part of this share of the profits in China, a foreign stockholder "may apply for the restitution of a part of the income taxes

paid."[66] Although the law has remained vague on many key issues, it represented a major step toward international cooperation.

3. In technology infusion, China has shown a voracious appetite for foreign technology and equipment since late 1977. In February 1978, an eight-year trade agreement was signed with Japan that called for an exchange of $10 billion worth of Chinese oil and coal for an equal amount of Japanese plants and equipment. Later in the year, Beijing and Tokyo agreed to extend the agreement for an additional five years. At midyear, a trade agreement was signed with the European Community that set up a framework for expanded trade. By the end of 1978, Beijing had been involved in negotiations involving about $40 billion for complete industrial plants, modern equipment, and related technology and had signed contracts amounting to $7 billion.[67] All these developments signaled the abandonment of traditional self-reliance policies in favor of foreign technology and equipment.

4. The influx of foreign equipment required the services of millions of technicians, engineers, managers, and scientists—another bottleneck in the Chinese economy. Although a sizable army of middle-level factory technicians had been spawned by China's "learning by doing" approach to industrial training, there was a serious shortage of experienced design and production engineers and other highly trained technicians essential in setting up and operating a modern factory. To tackle this problem, more than 5,000 students had been sent abroad for training in capitalistic countries by the end of 1980.

The major policy changes surveyed above form a general picture of China's economic strategy after Mao. In essence, the new strategy has aimed at using foreign capital and foreign technology on a large scale to push the production possibility curve outward.

### *The 1979–1981 Adjustment*

After Hua Guofeng enthusiastically announced the Ten-Year Plan in February 1978, the initial steps were reminiscent of the Great Leap Forward. During the first year of the new program, more than 100,000 construction projects of different sizes were launched. Capital investment for agriculture, industry, transportation, and public utilities totaled 61,970 million yuan, or approximately $40 billion, which represented a 50 percent increase over the preceding year. Adding other extrabudgetary construction investments undertaken by various departments and localities, the rate of accumulation in 1978 was officially stated as 36.6 percent of the national income, far exceeding the 24 percent rate during the First Five-Year Plan and close to the 40 percent accumulation rate during the disastrous Great Leap years.[68]

Because the scale of capital investment was beyond the reach of China's material and financial resources, the goals were overzealous. Lacking material and financial supplies, many projects failed to be completed on schedule, resulting in a frightful waste of manpower and materials. The annual waste of wages alone was put at 5 billion yuan, equivalent to the total average annual wage of 10 million workers.[69]

Moreover, although the Chinese leaders have insisted on the supremacy of agriculture over the past twenty years, that policy has never really been carried out in earnest. Investment in agriculture has been meager. In 1978, it amounted to only 10.7 percent of state capital investment, and the lion's share of investment was still poured into heavy industry, particularly the steel industry. Investment for heavy industry accounted for 54.7 percent of state investment in 1978, far exceeding the 46.5 percent ratio in the First Five-Year Plan when China pursued the Stalinist development model. The sectoral allocation policy not only hampered the progress of agriculture but also impeded the growth of light industry, the two sectors that provided the bulk of China's capital accumulation. The concentration of investment in heavy industry caused a steady decline of the overall profit rate in industry from 24 percent in 1966 to only 16 percent in 1978. This, in turn, prevented an increase in annual state revenue. During the 1958–1978 period, China's state revenue rose from 42 billion yuan to 112 billion yuan, representing an annual growth of 5.1 percent, which was significantly lower than the 12 percent growth rate achieved between 1952 and 1957.[70] The large-scale procurement of foreign equipment in 1978 created a $3-billion trade deficit and quickly drained the country's foreign exchange reserves.

Furthermore, in heavy industry, the development of the coal, electric power, petroleum, transportation, and building material industries failed to keep pace with the development of the metallurgical, machine-building, and processing industries. The economy has faced an acute energy crisis, too. In 1979, it was officially estimated that due to the shortage of electric power, about 30 percent of the nation's industrial capacity had not been tapped.[71]

In view of these problems, the Third Plenum of the Eleventh CCP Central Committee decided in December 1978 on a fundamental revision of the Ten-Year Plan, and a new guideline of "adjustment, reconstruction, consolidation, and raising of standards" was announced. Recognizing the size and nature of the gap between China's existing capabilities and its ambitions, the Chinese leadership became more concerned with the solution of short-term problems and the establishment of a firm foundation for modernization than with the attainment of long-term production goals. Therefore, the Ten-Year Plan was replaced by a three-year retrenchment plan (1979–1981). Official statements in early 1981 revealed that the period of adjustment is to extend to 1985. A new five-year plan (1981–1985) will replace the 1976–1985 plan.[72]

Under the 1979–1981 adjustment plan, capital investment in many areas was dramatically slashed. In March 1979, the National Construction Conference held in Beijing decided to immediately suspend those construction projects with uncertain resources and geological conditions, inadequate technology for the requirements of production, or no assured supply of fuel, power, or raw materials. It also ordered substantial investment cuts in the metallurgical, machine-building, and chemical industries. Investment as a percentage of state expenditure dropped from 40.2 percent in 1978 to 34.8 percent in 1979. In 1979, construction of 348 large- and medium-sized projects was halted, and 4,500 small projects were scrapped.[73] Of those projects suspended, the bulk were in the metallurgical, chemical, and machine-building industries. Total capital outlays for the metallurgical industry were slashed by 45 percent in 1979.

Despite those drastic curbs in capital investment, the economy in 1980 was still in a state of severe imbalance. Energy and raw material supplies fell short of the demand by existing industrial enterprises, and consumer goods supplies were lagging behind the increase of social purchasing power.[74] In April 1980, the State Capital Construction Commission called a national conference and demanded a further reduction in the scope of capital investment. In Shanghai, the country's leading industrial center, capital construction projects for 1980 were cut by one-third. Terminated or postponed were 234 large- and medium-sized industrial projects and 86 other individual projects, 64 percent of which were projects connected with machinery, chemical, and metallurgical industries. In some underdeveloped areas, such as Nei Monggol, capital construction investment in 1980 was trimmed by as much as 40 percent.[75]

The cut in steel and machinery investment represented a fundamental shift in development priorities. To correct the structural imbalance, the share of capital investment for agriculture was raised from 10.7 percent in 1978 to 14 percent in 1979 and 16 percent in 1980. The share of investment for textile and light industries rose from 5.4 percent in 1978 to 5.8 percent in 1979 and possibly reached 8 percent in 1980. Conversely, the share of investment for heavy industry decreased from 54.7 percent in 1978 to 46.8 percent in 1979. It might have fallen below 45 percent in 1980.[76]

The chief victim of the readjustment plan was the steel industry. For more than two decades, the Chinese leadership had regarded steel as the mainstay of modern industry. Investment in the steel industry alone had accounted for 1.5 times the total investment for textile and light industries. The entire industrial sector had taken steel as the "key link" and had planned for other industries to serve steel production. By 1978, the Chinese steel industry was officially estimated as having an annual production capacity of 55 million tons of steel. China turned out only 32 million tons in that year, however, due to the shortage of coal, coke, electricity, and iron ore.[77] In the 1976–1985 plan, ten major steel plants worth tens of billions of dollars were slated for construction. The output target was set at 60 million tons in 1985, almost doubling that in 1977. Under the 1979–1981 readjustment plan, the output of steel was to be reduced to only 45 million tons in 1985, and the 1980 output target was set at only 33 million tons, 1.4 million tons less than that of 1979.[78]

Other heavy industries bearing the brunt of cutbacks were machine-building and chemicals; in 1980, investment in the chemical industry was curtailed by 30 percent. Within the capital goods sector, petroleum, coal, construction materials, electric power, and railway construction still remained on the priority list.

The focus of the 1979–1981 readjustment plan was on textile and light industries, two long-neglected sectors. In 1979, many provinces and municipalities set up special organizations to promote textiles and light industries, and those industries received priority in the supply of raw and semifinished materials, fuel, power, and investment funds. In 1980, state loans for textile and light industries came to 2 billion yuan. In addition, $300 million were assigned for importing machinery and raw materials. As a result of increasing investment and material supplies, light industry scored a 9.6 percent growth rate in 1979, surpassing the 7.7 percent growth of heavy industry for the first time in more than a decade.[79] The shift of emphasis has gradually steered Chinese industry toward a more balanced growth between the capital goods and consumer goods sectors.

## IMPLICATIONS AND PROSPECTS

China's development evolution over the past three decades has been marked by sharp oscillations. For more than thirty years, China has been searching for a lasting development model, but no overall development strategy has lasted longer than six years. Few of the four major aspects of development strategy—sectoral priorities, choice of techniques, source of support, and incentive system—have remained

Table 9.3
Evolution of China's Developmental Strategies, 1953-1981

| Period | Sectoral Priorities | Choice of Technique | Source of Support | Incentive System |
|---|---|---|---|---|
| FFYP (1953-1957) | 1. Heavy industry<br>2. Light industry<br>3. Agriculture | Capital-intensive | Massive Soviet aid | Material incentives |
| Great Leap Forward (1958-1960) | 1. Heavy industry<br>2. Light industry<br>3. Agriculture | Labor-intensive | Soviet aid stopped in 1960 | Nonmaterial incentives |
| Readjustment (1961-1965) | 1. Agriculture<br>2. Light industry<br>3. Heavy industry | Capital- and labor-intensive | Self-reliance | Material incentives |
| Cultural Revolution (1966-1970) | 1. Heavy industry<br>2. Agriculture<br>3. Light industry | Labor-intensive | Self-reliance | Nonmaterial incentives |
| Adjustment (1971-1975) | 1. Heavy industry<br>2. Agriculture<br>3. Light industry | Labor-technology intensive | Resuming import of foreign equipment | Nonmaterial incentives |
| The Gang of Four (1975-1976) | 1. Heavy industry<br>2. Agriculture<br>3. Light industry | Labor-intensive | Self-reliance | Nonmaterial incentives |
| Four Modernizations (1976-1985) | 1. Heavy industry<br>2. Agriculture<br>3. Light industry | Technology-intensive | Outward-looking | Material incentives |
| a) Original plan 1978 | 1. Heavy industry<br>2. Agriculture<br>3. Light industry | Technology- and capital-intensive | Outward-looking | Material incentives |
| b) Adjustment (1979-1981) | 1. Agriculture<br>2. Light industry<br>3. Heavy industry | Technology- and labor-intensive | Outward-looking | Material incentives |

unchanged for a longer period (see Table 9.3). Although the table cannot mirror the content of the strategy for each period, it does display the shift of emphasis from one period to another. The shifts shown in Table 9.3 have a number of important implications. With regard to sectoral priorities, the Chinese experience suggests that the Stalinist model of squeezing the agricultural sector to feed heavy industry cannot be applied for a long period to a backward agrarian economy with a dense population. Although Beijing's initial emphasis on expanding capital goods industries in disregard of the country's natural or factor endowments did bring rapid growth in the capital goods and defense industries, the neglect of agriculture eventually had a dragging effect on the entire economy. For a short period, a country may be able to concentrate its scarce resources in a sector that is not in harmony with its factor endowment, but it cannot sustain the lopsided development for a long period.

As Hua Guofeng testified in his Ten-Year Plan report: "Agriculture is the foundation of the national economy. If agriculture does not develop faster, there will be no upswing in our industry and economy as a whole, and even if there is a temporary upswing, a decline will follow. There will be really serious trouble in the event of major natural calamities."[80] The fact that the shift from an emphasis on heavy industry during the 1953–1960 period to an emphasis on agriculture after 1960 was a shift in name only demonstrates how difficult it is to achieve the more desirable policy of a balanced growth between agriculture and industry.

In the choice of technique, Chinese agriculture and industry have pursued different paths. In agriculture, the emphasis has been on institutional changes and mass mobilization rather than on the increase of modern inputs. The two measures emphasized, however, produced very limited output growth. In more recent years, the choice has been to lean toward agricultural mechanization and an increasing supply of chemical fertilizer.

In industry, the FFYP strategy, emulating the Soviet model, placed priority on large-scale and fairly capital-intensive methods of production. It generated high rates of growth in industrial output at the expense of aggravating unemployment. By contrast, the "walking on two legs" approach during the Great Leap period generated a high rate of labor absorption, yet created waste and chaos.

The strategy of the 1976–1985 plan of 1978 apparently shifted back to more capital- and technology-intensive techniques by seeking the most advanced and sophisticated foreign technology and equipment. This shift suggests that industrialization cannot rely on labor-intensive techniques alone, no matter how effective mass mobilization may be.

With respect to source of support, China's industrialization started with a seven-year period of Soviet assistance. During those years, China received the most comprehensive technology transfer in its modern industrial history. The Russians not only helped China build a foundation for modern industry but provided guidance for scientific and technical education, project designs, and assistance from production engineering to the creation of a modern industrial organization.[81] The massive infusion of Soviet capital goods and know-how proved invaluable in China's subsequent development.

Soviet assistance, however, was patronizing and paternalistic; it evoked a sharp reaction in China, which led, for that and other reasons, to the total break between the two countries. After 1960, China pursued an inner-directed, go-it-alone policy, which enabled China to achieve some degree of technical and economic independence of the outside world. The self-reliance doctrine, however, widened the technology gap between China and the advanced countries. The trend of the late 1970s was a steady and highly visible drift away from the self-reliance structure toward an open and more flexible relationship with the outside world. This development signified that modernization could not be achieved with a strategy of autarky.

Concerning the incentive system, for years some Western economists have praised China's stress on egalitarianism and its success in equalizing living standards. Yet, in reality, the egalitarian policy was at the root of China's economic stagnation. The periods during which the Chinese economy experienced steady growth, such as the FFYP period and the readjustment periods, were the times when material incentives prevailed. In contrast, when material incentives were ignored and egalitarianism dominated—as in the Great Leap, the Cultural Revolution, and the Gang of Four periods—the economy usually suffered deeply.

The leadership in Beijing has sought to learn from the lessons of the past three decades. By adopting the capital/technology-intensive and outward-directed policies of the FFYP and the material incentives policies of the readjustment period, the 1976–1985 strategy promised to incorporate the best points of the two periods during which the Chinese economy registered steady growth. The execution of the new strategy, however, has proved to be a difficult task. Contradictions, barriers, and dilemmas exist on almost every level of the administration and the economic sectors, which make implementation a formidable job.

First, since the four modernizations program requires a huge infusion of foreign technology, China's ability to pay becomes a prerequisite for the plan's implementation. As of 1980, agricultural products and light industrial products still accounted for 70 percent of China's exports. As long as agriculture remains stagnant, the expansion of light industry will be beset with material shortages and capacity limitations, and rapid expansion of those items will be difficult. The Chinese government bases its hopes on China's huge petroleum resources as the key to the solution of its foreign exchange problems. But petroleum exploration, extraction, and refining will require a huge investment and will necessitate more foreign technology imports. This forms a vicious circle. Moreover, agricultural and industrial mechanization will greatly add to petroleum consumption. Since the crude oil output stagnated between 1979 and 1980 and may suffer a decline in 1981 and 1982, it will be extremely difficult for China to pay for the huge imports of machinery and equipment, estimated at $40 billion to $50 billion between 1978 and 1985.[82]

Second, since material incentives are a key component of Beijing's development strategy, success in bolstering economic growth depends heavily on China's ability to improve worker incentives and boost labor productivity. Government statements in 1980 ended any doubts about the leadership's determination to make a greater use of material incentives to arouse workers' enthusiasm. Wall posters and open peasant protests in Beijing during 1978 and 1979 convinced the leadership that the demand for improved living standards could no longer be postponed. The government must come up with a package of wage raises and bonuses that significantly increases income, and it must ensure the availability of consumer goods at prices that leave the workers with real gains. Unless wage increases are accompanied by parallel increases in the output of consumer goods, the effect will be inflationary. From 1980 to 1982, consumption increases can be achieved by tapping unused capacity in light industry and by restoring order to markets. Beyond 1982, and until the completion of the current investment program, more than a moderate gain in consumption seems unlikely. The expansion of exports will further compete with domestic consumption. The failure to satisfy rising consumer expectations may affect the productivity gains implicit in the development plan.

Finally, the pursuit of a technology-intensive strategy may aggravate the unemployment problem. During the 1950s, there was a constant stream of peasants migrating to the cities despite food and housing shortages, the lack of job opportunities, and government attempts to curb the migration. In the 1960s, the government sent more than 20 million city dwellers to the countryside, and since 1968, 16 million high school students have been resettled in villages. Visible symptoms of underemployment have surfaced almost everywhere. According to a report by Li Xiannian to a working conference of the CCP Central Committee on April 25, 1979, some 20 million people were then unemployed.[83] The closing of 25,000 to 50,000 units of marginal plants will put even more people out of work. The problem of rising unemployment will become the most difficult task the Chinese planners must tackle.

In view of these problems, a new set of development policies was enunciated in early 1980 by the Chinese authorities. The central theme of the new guideline is "act according to actual capabilities."[84] As the Party's organ, *Renmin ribao,* pointed out: "One major defect in our economic work is that for a long time we have exaggerated man's subjective initiative; acted only according to our subjective desire regardless of objective conditions and blindly sought after high speed and high quotas. . . . The result was not real progress but waste and disaster."[85] In a sharp departure from the earlier development strategies, the new guideline emphasizes the following points:

1. The goal of economic development is the improvement of people's lives, not a high rate of growth. Consumer welfare should be the fundamental premise of economic policy. That premise was elaborated in detail at the Second Session of the Fifth National People's Congress in June 1979, reiterated during the Fourth Plenum of the Eleventh CCP Central Committee in September 1979, and reemphasized by numerous government statements in 1980.[86] The new commitment to meet the long-suppressed popular demand for consumer goods and housing led to the decision for further reductions in the rate of accumulation, an adjustment of the mix of industrial production, and the reallocation of resources from heavy industry to agriculture and light industry.

2. With respect to the optimum rate of capital accumulation, the new consensus among Chinese economists and central planners is that the rate of accumulation in the forthcoming new Ten-Year Plan (1981–1990) should not exceed 25 percent of national income. Many leading economists have contended that China's economy scored steady growth when the rates of accumulation were not excessive, such as the 24.2 percent accumulation rate during the FFYP and the 22.7 percent accumulation rate of the 1963–1965 adjustment period. In contrast, the 40 percent accumulation rate during the Great Leap and the 33 percent accumulation rate between 1971 and 1975 resulted in a great waste of investment funds, an overstretching of the capital

construction front, a sharp decline in personal consumption, and severe damage to worker and peasant enthusiasm.[87]

3. Concerning the choice of production technique, the new policy seeks technology that is congruent with China's factor endowment, which is characterized by a huge population but limited capital. The Chinese planners have contemplated that at the present stage, the best technology should be oriented toward saving capital and using labor. Although the importation of modern technology and equipment will continue, attention is now focused on China's capacity to absorb and its ability to pay. Under this new guideline, mechanization is no longer the mainstay of the modernization of agriculture, and the renovations of the existing 350,000 plants are deemed more urgent than the construction of super modern plants.[88]

4. For regional development, the past policy of achieving regional balance by building a comprehensive industrial system for each province is now regarded as irrational and as totally ignoring the principle of comparative advantage. Under the new guideline, each province will develop its own industry according to its peculiar conditions. Thus, Guandong Province in South China will become an agricultural region that specializes in subtropical economic crops; Liaoning Province in Northeast China will concentrate on heavy industry; Shanghai will continue to be the country's comprehensive industrial base, specializing in high-grade, precision, and most-advanced industries; Hebei, Shandong, and Henan will become the country's cotton-producing regions, and Nei Monggol, Xinjiang, Qinghai, and Xizang will be built into animal husbandry regions. The main idea is to fully develop the superior conditions of each region instead of attaining regional self-sufficiency.[89]

The new policies highlighted above signal another twist in China's development strategy. The main focus of the new policies is not on pushing for ambitious, high-speed growth, but rather on remedying the conditions that have constrained rapid development for the previous two decades. Implementation of the new policies is bound to slow the pace of development, but it may sustain a steady advance within the boundaries of China's financial and technological capabilities.

## NOTES

1. For a detailed discussion of the Stalin development model, see K. C. Yeh, "Soviet and Communist Chinese Industrialization Strategies," in Donald W. Treadgold, ed., *Soviet and Chinese Communism: Similarities and Differences*

(Seattle: University of Washington Press, 1967), pp. 327–363; also Stanley H. Cohn, *Economic Development in the Soviet Union* (Lexington, Mass.: D.C. Heath, 1970), chap. 4.

2. W. W. Rostow, *The Stages of Economic Growth: A Non-Communist Manifesto* (Cambridge, Engl.: Cambridge University Press, 1961), p. 37.

3. K. C. Yeh, "Soviet and Communist Chinese Industrialization Strategies," p. 338; Gregory Grossman, "Scarce Capital and Soviet Doctrine," *Quarterly Journal of Economics* 67 (1953), pp. 311–343.

4. Lawrence Klein and Kazushi Ohkawa, eds., *Economic Growth: The Japanese Experience Since the Meiji Era* (Homewood, Ill.: Irwin, 1968), p. 22.

5. Ibid., p. 89.

6. Bruce F. Johnston, "Agricultural Productivity and Economic Development in Japan," *Journal of Political Economy* 59 (1951), pp. 498–513.

7. Lawrence Klein and Kazushi Ohkawa, *Economic Growth,* p. 10.

8. K. C. Yeh, "Soviet and Communist Chinese Industrialization Strategies," p. 343.

9. Alexander Eckstein, *China's Economic Development* (Ann Arbor: University of Michigan Press, 1975), p. 215.

10. Shigeto Tsuru and Kazushi Ohkawa, "Long-Term Changes in the National Product of Japan Since 1878," in *Income and Wealth,* series 3 (Cambridge, Engl.: Cambridge University Press, 1953), pp. 19–44.

11. Alexander Eckstein, *China's Economic Development,* p. 215.

12. Mao Zedong, "On People's Democratic Dictatorship," in *Selected Works,* vol. 4, p. 417.

13. K. C. Yeh, "Capital Formation," in Alexander Eckstein, Walter Galenson, and Ta-chung Liu, eds., *Economic Trends in Communist China,* p. 511.

14. A project is classified as above-norm when invested capital is above the norm figure. For example, in industry, the investment norm for the iron and steel, motor vehicle, tractor, and shipbuilding industries is 10 million yuan; for textiles, it is 5 million yuan; for other light industries, it is only 3 million yuan (see Chu-yuan Cheng, *The Machine-Building Industry in Communist China,* p. 29).

15. Yang Yingjie, "Coordinated Development of Newly Constructed and Existing Enterprises, Large and Medium or Small Enterprises," *Xuexi* No. 8 (1955), p. 8.

16. Chu-yuan Cheng, *Economic Relations Between Peking and Moscow, 1949–1963* (New York: Praeger, 1964), p. 27–28.

17. For official figures, see P.R.C., State Statistical Bureau, *Ten Great Years,* p. 20. The 6 percent figure was estimated by Ta-chung Liu and Kung-chia Yeh in *The Economy of the Chinese Mainland: National Income and Economic Development, 1933–1959* (Princeton: Princeton University Press, 1965), p. 66. A later Chinese official statement put the growth rate for the period at 7 percent (see *Tung-hsiang Monthly* [The trend] No. 1 [1979]).

18. The 0.92 percent figure is estimated in Ta-chung Liu and Kung-chia Yeh, *Economy of the Chinese Mainland,* p. 132. The 2.33 percent figure is from Kang Chao, *Agricultural Production in Communist China,* p. 227.

19. *Xuexi* No. 20 (1957).

20. P.R.C., State Statistical Bureau, *Ten Great Years,* pp. 180 and 183.

21. CCP, "Proposals for the Second Five-Year Plan for Development of the National Economy 1958–1962," *Xinhua banyuekan* No. 20 (1956), pp. 164–170.

22. Editorial Department, *Renmin ribao,* "More on the Historical Experience of the Dictatorship of the Proletariat," *Xinhua banyuekan* No. 2 (1957), p. 6.

23. See Ma Yinchu, *Wode jingji lilun zhixue sixiang he zhengshi lichang* [My economic theory, philosophical ideas, and political standpoint] (Beijing: Caizheng Chubanshe, 1958).

24. Ragnar Nurkse, *Problem of Capital Formation in Underdeveloped Areas* (Oxford: Oxford University Press, 1953), p. 49.

25. *Renmin ribao,* May 3, 1958.

26. Xu Lizhun, "On the Policy of Walking on Two Legs," *Hongqi* No. 6 (1959), pp. 9–11.

27. On the urgent need to liberate housewives from domestic chores for socialist construction, see Li Xiannian, former minister of finance, in *Cai zheng* [Public finance] No. 8 (August 15, 1958).

28. P.R.C., State Statistical Bureau, "On the Fulfillment of the 1958 State Economic Plan," *Renmin ribao,* April 15, 1959.

29. Peng Dehuai, "Letter to Chairman Mao," in *Union Research Institute, The Case of P'eng Teh-huai 1959–1968* (Hong Kong: Union Press, 1968), pp. 11–12. A more recent account of the loss is Lu Dingyi's article in *Renmin ribao,* March 8, 1979.

30. Commentator, "Straighten Out Guidelines for Economic Work—On Leftist Mistakes in Economic Construction," *Renmin ribao,* April 9, 1981, p. 5.

31. CCP, Central Committee, "Resolution on Some Questions Concerning the People's Communes," *Xinhua banyuekan* No. 24 (1958), p. 7.

32. *Renmin ribao,* February 17, 1959, p. 2.

33. *Renmin ribao,* June 11, 1959; also Chi Hsin, "The Left Deviation of Communization and the Great Leap Forward," *Chi-shih nien-tai* No. 10 (October 1978), pp. 30–37.

34. Two pedologists of the Chinese Academy of Sciences concluded that large areas of alkaline soil had resulted from improper irrigation (see Xiong Yi and Wang Zunji, "Must the River Be Drained on Alkaline Soil?" *Guangming ribao,* April 20, 1961).

35. Yang Jianbai and Li Xuezeng, "China's Historical Experience in Handling the Relations Between Agriculture, Light Industry, and Heavy Industry," p. 28.

36. *World Journal* (New York), April 24, 1981; *New York Times,* April 25, 1981.

37. *Renmin ribao,* January 21, 1961.

38. Zhou Enlai, speech of March 27, 1962, to the Third Session of the National People's Congress (*Renmin ribao,* April 16, 1962).

39. Kang Chao, *The Construction Industry in Communist China* (Chicago: Aldine, 1968), pp. 60–64. A later official source disclosed that investment for industry dropped from 10 billion yuan in 1960 to 6 billion yuan in 1961 (Hu

Ning-hui, "China Reforms Its Economy While Carrying Out Readjustment of It," *Chi-shih nien-tai* No. 6 [June 1979], p. 14).

40. CCP, Central Committee, "Communiqué of the Tenth Plenary Session of the Eighth Central Committee on the Chinese Communist Party," NCNA-Beijing, September 28, 1962.

41. Chu-yuan Cheng, *The Machine-Building Industry in Communist China*, pp. 12–14.

42. See Mao's speech, "On the Correct Handling of Contradictions Among the People," *Xinhua banyuekan* No. 13(1957), p. 9.

43. "Two Diametrically Opposed Lines in Building the Economy," *Renmin ribao*, August 25, 1967.

44. Chu-yuan Cheng, "The Cultural Revolution and China's Economy," *Current History* 53:313 (September 1967), pp. 148–177.

45. *Peking Review* 13:48 (November 27, 1970), p. 15.

46. For details, see Chu-yuan Cheng, "China's Industry: Advances and Dilemma," *Current History* 61:361 (September 1971), pp. 154–159.

47. Nai-Ruenn Chen, *Industrial Development in China*, Research Note no. 11 (Washington, D.C.: Trade Analysis Division, Bureau of East-West Trade, Department of Commerce, 1974), pp. 19–23; and Cheng Shih, *A Glance at China's Economy*, pp. 22–26.

48. *New York Times*, December 5, 1978.

49. Jon Sigurdson, *Rural Industrialization in China* (Cambridge, Mass.: Harvard University Press, 1977), pp. 75–120.

50. American Rural Small-Scale Industry Delegation, *Rural Small-Scale Industry in the People's Republic of China* (Berkeley: University of California Press, 1977), chap. 4.

51. *Zhongguo shehui kexue* No. 3 (1980), p. 25.

52. Richard Diao and Donald Zagoria, *The Nature of Mainland Chinese Economic Structure, Leadership, and Policy (1949–1969) and the Prospects for Arms Control and Disarmament*, ACDA YE-124 (Washington, D.C.: U.S. Arms Controls and Disarmament Agency, February 1972), pp. 181–183.

53. *Peking Review* 21:28 (July 14, 1978), p. 3.

54. U.S., Central Intelligence Agency, *China: Economic Indicators* (Washington, D.C., December 1978), p. 3.

55. *China Reconstructs*, Special Supplement 24:3 (March 1975), p. 21.

56. Yao Wenyuan, "The Social Basis of Lin Biao's Anti-Party Clique," *Hongqi* No. 3 (March 1975).

57. NCNA-Beijing, January 21, 1979, in FBIS, January 24, 1979, pp. E18–E19.

58. *Peking Review* 21:10 (March 10, 1978), p. 12.

59. The 1976 grain figure is based on estimates from the U.S. Department of Agriculture, *People's Republic of China, Agricultural Situation, Review of 1977 and Outlook for 1978* (Washington, D.C., May 1978), p. 8. The steel output figure is from *Chi-shih nien-tai* No. 9 (September 1978), p. 74.

60. Hua Guofeng, "Unite and Strive to Build a Modern, Powerful Socialist Country!" pp. 18–31.

61. Ibid.

62. U.S., Central Intelligence Agency, *China: The Continuing Search for a Modernization Strategy* (Washington, D.C., April 1980), p. 3.

63. Li Xiannian's interview with Daisaku Ikeda, president of the Japanese neo-Buddhist organization, *Kyodo*, September 19, 1978.

64. *New York Times*, February 8, 1979, p. A12.

65. *China Business Review* 7:1 (January–February 1980).

66. *Wen Wei Po, Law of the PRC on Joint Ventures Using Chinese and Foreign Investment* (Hong Kong: Wen Wei Po, July 1979).

67. U.S., Central Intelligence Agency, *China: The Continuing Search for a Modernization Strategy*, p. 4.

68. *Renmin ribao*, November 23, 1979.

69. *Jingji yanjiu* No. 15 (1979), p. 7.

70. The 1978 figures are derived from the budget report by Zhang Jingfu, minister of finance, to the Second Session of the Fifth NPC (NCNA-Beijing, June 21, 1979). The 1958 figures are from Go Zhida, *Guodushiqi de Zhongguo yusuan* [China's state budget during the transition period], (Beijing: Caizheng Chubanshe, 1956), p. 16.

71. Shi Zhengwen, "Readjusting the National Economy: Why and How?" *Beijing Review* 22:26 (June 29, 1979), p. 14.

72. Cheng Hsiang, "China Is Now Drawing Up a New Five-Year Plan," *Wen Wei Po* (Hong Kong), March 26, 1981, p. 1.

73. NCNA-Beijing, April 15, 1980.

74. It was reported that in early 1980, paper production met only two-thirds of domestic demand, one-third of the sugar supply depended on imports, supplies of detergents could only meet one-half of the demand, and per capita consumption of textile products was less than 40 percent of the world's average (see *Jingji yanjiu* No. 2 [1980], p. 27).

75. FBIS, December 27, 1979, p. R2.

76. The 1978 and 1979 figures are from *Xinhua yuebao*, November 6, 1979, p. 26. The 1980 agriculture figures are official, but the figures in light and heavy industries have been projected by the author.

77. *Ta kung pao* [Impartial daily] (Hong Kong), March 27, 1979, p. 1.

78. NCNA-Beijing, April 18, 1980.

79. NCNA-Beijing, April 8, 1980.

80. Hua Guofeng, "Unite and Strive to Build a Modern, Powerful Socialist Country," p. 20.

81. Hans Heyman, Jr., "Self-Reliance Revisited, China's Technology Dilemma," in Bryant G. Garth, ed., *China's Changing Role in the World Economy* (New York: Praeger, 1974), p. 18.

82. For details, see discussion in Chapter 14.

83. *Ming pao* [Ming daily] (Hong Kong), June 14, 1979, p. 4.

84. From May 26 to June 26, 1980, *Renmin ribao* published five editorials expounding this guiding principle. The most important ones appeared on May 26, June 12, and June 26.

85. Editorial, "Haste Makes Waste," *Renmin ribao*, June 12, 1980, p. 1.

86. The latest statement is by Zhao Zhiyang, NCNA-Beijing, June 18, 1980.

87. Zhang Renfu, "Inquire Into the Reasonable Rate of Accumulation for Our Country from Historical Experience," *Renmin ribao,* May 15, 1980; and Zhou Jin, "Further Economic Readjustment: A Break with 'Leftist' Thinking," *Beijing Review* 24:12 (March 23, 1981), pp. 23–25.

88. Editorial, "What Should Be Upheld and What Should Be Opposed," *Renmin ribao,* June 26, 1980, pp. 1 and 2.

89. Editorial, "Fully Develop the Superior Conditions," *Renmin ribao,* June 30, 1980, p. 1.

# 10

# Growth and Fluctuations in the National Economy

Economic fluctuations are generally identified as characteristics of market-oriented free enterprise systems. Marxists have regarded the periodic expansion and contraction arising from the market forces of supply and demand as the hallmark of the market economy and as one of the vital drawbacks of the capitalist system.[1]

The first nonmarket economy in the world was established in the Soviet Union, and central planning replaced the market mechanism as a means of resource allocation and coordination. By definition, economic planning implies a more ordered development and a more effective control over economic fluctuations than that provided by market forces. Nevertheless, post-1945 developments in the Soviet Union and in Eastern Europe suggest that economic fluctuations are also common phenomena in planned economies.[2] In the case of the People's Republic of China, the backwardness of the economy and tendency to emphasize politics over economics have resulted in periodic internal disruptions and great fluctuations in economic activities. Although central planning was inaugurated in 1953, the Chinese economy has not followed a consistent development course and has experienced a series of cyclical oscillations no less marked than those of market economies.

This chapter will discuss the reliability of statistics on the Chinese economy, examine the quantitative trends of the Chinese economy between 1949 and 1979, analyze the underlying causes and implications of its economic fluctuations, and explore the future pattern of Chinese economic growth.

## ECONOMIC DATA

Any quantitative study of the Chinese economy after 1949 encounters the problem of obtaining and evaluating statistics. The data problem, the major deterrent in Chinese economic studies, has been dealt with in detail elsewhere and will only be summarized here.[3] Primarily, it involves three dimensions: availability, consistency, and reliability.

### *Availability*

The availability of quantitative data for the Chinese economy varies considerably from period to period. Data were comparatively abundant between 1953 and 1960 but became basically absent during 1961–1964, the years following the failure of the Great Leap Forward. Statistics reappeared in fragmentary form in 1965–1966 when the economy recovered; disappeared again during the Cultural Revolution (1967–1970); and reemerged following 1970, in most instances in a selective and fragmentary form. Since 1979, the Chinese government has resumed publication of agricultural and industrial production data.

During the 1955–1960 period, several official publications contained a series of physical quantities and values for agriculture, industry, communications, transportation, trade, and other major economic sectors. The first important document was the First Five-Year Plan, which the government published in mid-1955. The FFYP not only provided detailed production and investment figures, but revealed a vast array of hitherto unpublished data. In 1955–1957, the State Statistical Bureau also made available many valuable, comprehensive statistical analyses, including population statistics for 1949–1956, data on socialist industrialization, statistics on living standards of workers and employers, and data on the composition of professional manpower. Several books dealing with national income and with capital formation and some general surveys of key industries from 1949 to 1955 were also released around this time.[4] By far the most comprehensive statistical volume was the *Ten Great Years*, first published by the State Statistical Bureau in 1959, which contains most of the statistical data for the 1950s.

An almost total statistical blackout of macroeconomic data was imposed by the Chinese authorities for the entire decade of the 1960s. In 1970, as the turbulence of the Cultural Revolution subsided, Zhou Enlai revealed some aggregative data to the late American journalist Edgar Snow.[5] Since then, the flow of statistical information has resumed, but on a much smaller scale than that of the 1950s.

Statistics published between 1970 and 1978 may be classified into three groups according to the level of aggregation. One, statistics pertaining to the economy as a whole are mostly expressed as percentage rates of growth for the preceding year and/or 1965, the year before the Cultural Revolution. Frequently, these percentages are given without bases and are extremely difficult for outsiders to translate into absolute numbers. Two, statistics relating to individual provinces, autonomous regions, and municipalities contain some absolute figures, but most of the production data are still given in percentage terms. Three, numerical information for cities, counties, factories, and communes is expressed mostly in absolute figures and is reported frequently in local and provincial broadcasts.[6]

On June 27, 1979, and April 30, 1980, the State Statistical Bureau issued two communiqués on the fulfillment of China's 1978 and 1979 national economic plans, revealing detailed output data for major industrial and agricultural products as well as data on capital construction, transportation, postal service and telecommunications, domestic and foreign trade, science, technology, education, culture, public health, people's livelihood, and population.[7] Although these data cover only two years, they form a basis for comparison with the previous periods.

Changes in the availability of statistical data in various periods reveal a basic tendency of the Chinese authorities to withhold unfavorable information and to mainly publish statistics that show success. In the 1960s, when the economy suffered great setbacks, most production data were not published. The statistical data published so far for the 1970s have covered mostly industries with high growth rates (petroleum, electronics, chemical fertilizers, and agricultural machines), and relatively few figures have been released for industries with only a mediocre performance.[8]

*Consistency*

The quality of Chinese statistics has been assessed by a number of writers. Several attempts have been made to check the consistency between aggregate and disaggregated data published in the 1950s, and to compare some of the statistics published in the 1970s with those issued in the 1950s. The general consensus is that although Chinese statistics suffer from many deficiencies, aggregative data are generally consistent with their components. For instance, in an effort to reconstruct the gross value of industrial output by province, Field, Lardy, and Emerson found an extremely close correspondence between the sum of provincial totals of the gross value of industrial output, pieced together from a large number of sources, and the reported national totals for 1952 and 1957.[9] Likewise, in my study of the petroleum industry in China, I used two official crude-oil output figures for 1965 and 1972 and conducted backward and forward derivations by applying percentage increases of crude oil in different years as revealed in various official sources. From crosschecks, it appears that most of the official data are consistent.[10]

Proof of internal consistency, however, does not preclude the possibility of outright fabrication. The Chinese government could maintain two sets of national statistics – one for planning and the other for propaganda – but most experts on the Chinese economy regard such a practice as unlikely. In an early study of the Chinese petroleum industry, K. C. Yeh detected no apparent falsification in official output data, since adverse information, such as the failure to reach the First Five-Year Plan target, had been openly admitted, which would have been unnecessary if the data had been falsified.[11] Yeh's observation is confirmed by my own study. Although the Chinese government tends to publish figures reflecting achievement, such as figures for 1965 and 1972, it has generally withheld data for adverse years, such as 1967 and 1968. This withholding of adverse data would further suggest that a double bookkeeping type of manipulation probably does not exist.

Nevertheless, statistical fabrication was and still is practiced by lower administrative echelons. Because the bonus system of each enterprise is related to its fulfillment of output targets, there is always a built-in tendency for local cadres to exaggerate achievement. For example, the official Xinhua News Agency reported in 1978 that the Party secretary of iron plants in the Anshan Iron and Steel Company had fabricated the output figures for the first quarter of 1978, with the Party's open sanction.[12] Another example was the false report by the Dazhai Brigade in Xiyang County, which was heralded by Mao Zedong and his successor as the country's model and showplace for agricultural development. The Dazhai Brigade was recently accused of giving false output figures every year since 1973, with an accumulated fraudulent figure of 270 million catties more than the actual grain output.[13] Such false reports have been common in Chinese newspapers. According to a careful study that appeared in the Party's *Renmin ribao* on July 24, 1979, there are three categories of false reports. The first is total fabrication, designed to present fabricated things as fact. The second is the transformation of a part into a whole – a point standing for an area or a local situation representing a general condition. The third category is reports of good news alone, with even shortcomings described as achievements.[14] The above practices render Chinese statistics unreliable, even though corrective measures have been taken by the central authorities.

The general usability of Chinese statistics is further limited by a number of methodological deficiencies and certain peculiar practices. As Nai-Ruenn Chen has pointed out:

> One of the major difficulties with Chinese statistics has to do with the definition of concept, coverage, and classification. They are often left unexplained. To the extent that they were explained, they were sometimes defined in a peculiar way. Frequently, definitional changes were made without corresponding corrections to the data. In some of the time series data, widely heterogeneous components were grouped together and treated as if they were homogeneous.[15]

With these reservations, the consensus of economists on China's economic data can be summarized as:

1. Official data for the 1952–1957 period are relatively consistent and reliable, while statistics for the 1958–1960 Great Leap period are highly inflated.
2. Official statistics understate agricultural output for the early years (1950–1952), due to incomplete coverage, and therefore overstate the rate of growth during later years.
3. The official factory reporting method leads to a significant double counting of industrial output, thus inflating the aggregate output value. The pricing system inflates the output value of capital goods and new industrial products, thus imparting an upward bias to the rate of growth of industrial production.
4. Official estimates of the GNP, by excluding some service sectors and by imparting the above biases, also inflate the annual rate of growth.[16]

For the period between 1960 and June 1979, there was a total lack of officially published systematic data. All indicators concerning economic trends in the 1960s and 1970s are necessarily based on highly fragmentary or circumstantial evidence. Strenuous efforts have been made in the United States to fill the data gap. In late 1960 and early 1970, the Committee on the Economy of China of the Social Science Research Council sponsored a series of monographs on China's construction, machine-building, and chemical fertilizer industries, agriculture, foreign trade, and industrial development in pre-Communist China.[17] The Joint Economic Committee of the U.S. Congress has also published four compendiums (1967, 1972, 1975, and 1978) on the Chinese economy.[18] In these publications, Western specialists have provided estimates of the food grain output, the agricultural production index, the industrial production index, foreign trade volume, the output of major industrial products, and GNP estimates from 1949 to 1979. These Western estimates constitute the primary data base of this chapter (see Table 10.1).

*Reliability*

How reliable are the Western estimates? Do they represent independent calculations in their corrections of such distortions as double-counting and the other methodological deficiencies mentioned above? Or are they using the fragmentary data available as a basis from which to interpolate or derive the missing figures? A random comparison of the six indexes in Table 10.1 with some official statistics reveals that the industrial output and agricultural output indexes come very close to official statistics but the Western GNP estimates show significant variations from the official statistics.

In the industrial output indexes, growth rates in the 1949–1959 period came very close to the official figures. Estimates for the 1965–1977 period are also based on official data. According to one official Chinese source, the average annual growth rate of industrial output (gross value) was 13.5 percent between 1949 and 1977, 11.7 percent during the Third Five-Year Plan (1966–1970), and 9.1 percent during the Fourth Five-Year Plan (1971–1975).[19] Growth rates for the 1966–1970 and 1971–1975 periods, derived from the estimated gross output data in Table 10.2, come out the same as those reported in official sources.

There are, however, variations between the estimated and official figures in certain years. The estimated series shows an increase of 8.8 percent in industrial output in 1968, but official data indicate a 5 percent decline. In 1970, when official data show a 30.7 percent increase, the estimated series registers only 18.7 percent growth. Between 1949 and 1978, official statistics show an average annual growth rate of 13.3 percent,[20] compared with the 12.8 percent growth rate in the estimated series.

With respect to agricultural output, during the 1949–1978 period, the average annual growth rate was 3.9 percent based on the estimated series, and 4.3 percent based on official data. Again, variations exist for several of the years (see Table 10.3). U.S. government estimates of China's GNP growth in the 1953–1959 period conflict with official statistics and with estimates made by T. C. Liu and K. C. Yeh (see Table 10.4).

Official records show that 1956 was a "big push" year. Total capital investment went up 21.3 percent, industrial capital investment soared 58.6 percent, nonagricultural employment rose 27 percent, and industrial output advanced 24 percent. In contrast, 1955 was a mediocre year, with only a 5.7 percent rise in capital formation, a 12 percent increase in industrial investment, a 14 percent increase in nonagricultural employment, and only a 3.7 percent rise in industrial output.[21] Yet the CIA estimated the GNP growth rate for 1956 at only 8 percent as against the 10 percent growth rate for 1955. These estimates are not only at odds with all the known records, but they also contradict other independent estimates.

According to Vice-Premier Chen Muhua, average per capita national income in terms of current U.S. dollars was $28 in 1950, $49 in 1955, $78 in 1965, $95 in 1970, and $139 in 1976.[22] These figures account for one-fifth to one-third of the per capita GNP estimated by the CIA for the corresponding years. The 1976–1979 national income figures in yuan can be derived from the communiqué on the fulfillment of the 1978 and 1979 national economic plans as 337 billion yuan for 1979, 315 billion yuan for 1978, 281 billion yuan for 1977, and 260 billion yuan for 1976. Divided by the official population data, per capita national income in yuan can be calculated as 347 yuan for 1979, 329 yuan for 1978, 297 yuan for 1977, and 278 yuan for 1976. When converted into U.S. dollars, the 1976–1979 per capita figures all fall substantially below the CIA estimated figures (see Table 10.5 and Table 10.6).

The discrepancies can be partly accounted for by differences in coverage. The CIA series is a measure of GNP that includes gross value added in all economic sectors, and the Chinese data are for national income (net of depreciation) earned in the production of "material goods." The sectors producing material goods are industry, agriculture, construction, trade, and transportation of goods. Passenger transportation and personal and government services are excluded from the Chinese material income statistics. The size of the difference in coverage was estimated by C. M. Li in the 1950s to be about 16 percent of net national product. The amount of depreciation excluded from Chinese national income is estimated by T. C. Liu and K. C. Yeh at about 5 percent of the gross product.[23] If those two items are added, the Chinese per capita income adjusted to the Western concept of GNP could increase by 21 percent. Earlier Chinese official statistics reported that national income per capita in 1978 was $188 (see Table 10.5). In 1981, the World Bank listed China's GNP per capita for 1978 as $230. Since the latter figure is "based on partial official information"[24] and the difference between the two figures is 22

Table 10.1
Major Economic Indicators of the P.R.C., 1949-1979

| Year | GNP (Billion 1979 US $) | Agricultural Production (Index: 1957=100) | Grain Output (Million Tons) | Industrial Production (Index: 1957=100) | Crude Steel (Million Tons) | Foreign Trade Volume (Billion Current US $) |
|---|---|---|---|---|---|---|
| 1949-52 Rehabilitation | | | | | | |
| 1949 | 64 | 53 | 111 | 20 | 0.16 | 0.8 |
| 1950 | 78 | 64 | 130 | 27 | 0.61 | 1.2 |
| 1951 | 91 | 72 | 141 | 38 | 0.90 | 1.9 |
| 1952 | 108 | 84 | 161 | 48 | 1.35 | 1.9 |
| 1953-57 First Five-Year Plan | | | | | | |
| 1953 | 114 | 84 | 164 | 61 | 1.77 | 2.3 |
| 1954 | 119 | 84 | 166 | 70 | 2.22 | 2.4 |
| 1955 | 131 | 94 | 180 | 73 | 2.85 | 3.1 |
| 1956 | 142 | 97 | 188 | 88 | 4.46 | 3.1 |
| 1957 | 151 | 100 | 191 | 100 | 5.35 | 3.0 |
| 1958-60 Great Leap Forward | | | | | | |
| 1958 | 179 | 107 | 206 | 142 | 11.08 | 3.7 |
| 1959 | 170 | 83 | 171 | 173 | 13.86 | 4.3 |
| 1960 | 165 | 74 | 156 | 181 | 18.66 | 4.0 |

| | | | | | | |
|---|---|---|---|---|---|---|
| 1961–65 Readjustment and Recovery | | | | | | |
| 1961 | 131 | 78 | 168 | 105 | 8 | 3.0 |
| 1962 | 143 | 87 | 180 | 111 | 8 | 2.7 |
| 1963 | 161 | 93 | 190 | 134 | 8 | 2.8 |
| 1964 | 179 | 98 | 194 | 161 | 9.6 | 3.3 |
| 1965 | 202 | 101 | 194 | 199 | 12.2 | 3.8 |
| 1966–70 Third Five-Year Plan | | | | | | |
| 1966 | 229 | 112 | 215 | 232 | 15 | 4.2 |
| 1967 | 220 | 118 | 225 | 202 | 10 | 4.0 |
| 1968 | 221 | 110 | 210 | 221 | 9 | 3.8 |
| 1969 | 246 | 112 | 215 | 266 | 16 | 3.9 |
| 1970 | 286 | 126 | 243 | 316 | 17.8 | 4.4 |
| 1971–75 Fourth Five-Year Plan | | | | | | |
| 1971 | 306 | 130 | 246 | 349 | 21 | 4.8 |
| 1972 | 320 | 126 | 240 | 385 | 23 | 6.0 |
| 1973 | 361 | 142 | 266 | 436 | 25 | 10.1 |
| 1974 | 375 | 146 | 275 | 455 | 21 | 14.1 |
| 1975 | 401 | 148 | 284 | 502 | 24 | 14.5 |
| 1976–80 Fifth Five-Year Plan | | | | | | |
| 1976 | 400 | 148 | 285 | 502 | 20.5 | 13.3 |
| 1977 | 433 | 144 | 283 | 574 | 23.7 | 15.2 |
| 1978 | 483 | 156 | 305 | 651 | 31.8 | 21.1 |
| 1979 | 514 | 160 | 315 | 703 | 34.4 | 27.1 |

Source: U.S. Central Intelligence Agency, China: Major Economic Indicators (Washington, D.C., February 1980).

Table 10.2
Estimated Industrial Production in the P.R.C., 1965-1979

| | Gross Value | | | Value Added | |
|---|---|---|---|---|---|
| Year | Billion 1957 yuan | Index (1965=100) | Annual Percentage Change | Index (1965=100) | Annual Percentage Change |
| 1965 | 139.3 | 100 | | 100 | |
| 1966 | 175.9 | 126 | 26.3 | 117 | 17.0 |
| 1967 | 147.2 | 106 | -16.3 | 102 | -12.8 |
| 1968 | 154.7 | 111 | 5.1 | 111 | 8.8 |
| 1969 | 197.3 | 142 | 27.5 | 134 | 20.7 |
| 1970 | 242.2 | 174 | 22.8 | 159 | 18.7 |
| 1971 | 267.5 | 192 | 10.5 | 175 | 10.1 |
| 1972 | 295.4 | 212 | 10.4 | 193 | 10.3 |
| 1973 | 326.0 | 234 | 10.3 | 219 | 13.5 |
| 1974 | 340.6 | 245 | 4.5 | 229 | 4.6 |
| 1975 | 374.3 | 269 | 9.9 | 252 | 10.1 |
| 1976 | 382.7 | 275 | 2.2 | 252 | 0 |
| 1977 | 436.3(372.8) | 313 | 14.0 | 287 | 13.9 |
| 1978 | 495.2(423.1) | 355 | 13.5 | 324 | 12.9 |
| 1979 | 534.8(459.1) | 383 | 8.0 | 350 | 8.0 |

Notes: Figures in parentheses are official data, from P.R.C. State Statistical Bureau, Communiqués on Fulfillment of China's 1978 and 1979 National Economic Plans, Beijing Review 22:27 (July 6, 1979), p. 37, and 23:19 (May 12, 1980), p. 12.

Sources: The gross value for 1965-1977 and value added for 1965-1975 are from Robert M. Field, Kathleen M. McGlynn, and William B. Ahnett, "Political Conflict and Industrial Growth in China: 1965-1977," in U.S. Congress, Joint Economic Committee, Chinese Economy Post-Mao (Washington, D.C.: Government Printing Office, 1978), p. 242. Gross value for 1978-1979 and value added for 1976-79 are estimated by the author.

percent, one might infer that the 21-22 percent discrepancy is due to the difference in coverage.

Another source of divergency stems from the different methods used to convert yuan to dollars. The CIA method uses a purchasing-power parity rate of 1.91 yuan per dollar in 1955, compared with the 2.59 yuan rate used by the Chinese.[25] Moreover, the CIA series is converted from 1955 dollars to 1979 dollars by using the implicit U.S. GNP price deflator. This approach does not take into account price changes in China and thus inflates the current dollar figure.

The Chinese 1979 per capita income figure accounts for only 43 percent of the CIA estimate. Since both figures are expressed in 1979 dollars, price change is not a factor. Even with coverage adjustment (adding 21 percent to the Chinese figure), the Chinese figure still accounts for only 52 percent of the CIA estimates.

There are two possible sources of upward bias in the CIA estimates. First, the GNP index employed by the CIA is a weighted average of industrial and agricultural output indexes, each of those in turn being weighted averages of product output. National product is a value-added concept, but the CIA index is based on gross output value and does not measure changes in the value added to the gross value ratio. If net-to-gross ratios in industry and agriculture have dropped in the past twenty-odd years, the CIA index will overstate real growth.[26] Official statistics show that in 1957, net national product (NNP) in China was 96.5 billion yuan and the combined gross output value of industry and agriculture was 138.74 billion yuan.[27] Thus, NNP accounted for about 70 percent of the combined gross output value of industry and agriculture in 1957. In 1978, the combined gross output value of industry and agriculture was officially reported as 569 billion yuan, and national income was 315 billion yuan. The net-to-gross ratio had dropped to 55 percent, representing a decline of 21.4 percent during the twenty-one-year period. The application to 1978 of the 1957 net-to-gross ratio inflates the 1978 GNP by at least 21 percent. Second, the CIA index assumes that the service sector would grow as rapidly as the weighted average of agriculture and industry. In fact, since the completion of socialization in the private sector in 1956, there has been a drastic curtailment of nonproductive services.

Despite the upward bias involved in the CIA estimates on the absolute size of the Chinese GNP, the average annual growth rates of the official and CIA series are very close. In the official yuan series, the index number for 1979 (with base 100 in 1955) is 432, and the comparable number in the CIA series is 392, a difference of only 10 percent. Because this chapter is mainly concerned with the changes in

Table 10.3
Estimates of Total and Per Capita
Grain Output in the P.R.C.
1949-1979

| Year | Grain Output (million metric tons) | | Population (mid-year) (million persons) | | Grain Output per Capita (Kilograms) | |
|---|---|---|---|---|---|---|
| 1949 | 111 | | 538 | | 205 | |
| 1950 | 130 | | 547 | (551.67) | 235 | (239.5) |
| 1951 | 141 | | 558 | | 250 | |
| 1952 | 161 | | 570 | | 280 | |
| 1953 | 164 | | 583 | | 278 | |
| 1954 | 166 | | 596 | | 275 | |
| 1955 | 180 | | 611 | (614.09) | 291 | (299.5) |
| 1956 | 188 | | 626 | | 297 | |
| 1957 | 191 | | 642 | | 294 | |
| 1958 | 206 | (200) | 657 | | 310 | |
| 1959 | 171 | | 672 | | 252 | |
| 1960 | 156 | | 685 | | 226 | |
| 1961 | 168 | | 696 | | 240 | |
| 1962 | 180 | | 706 | | 253 | |
| 1963 | 190 | | 720 | | 261 | |
| 1964 | 194 | | 736 | | 261 | |
| 1965 | 194 | (200) | 753 | (723.88) | 255 | (268.0) |
| 1966 | 215 | | 770 | | 276 | |
| 1967 | 225 | | 788 | | 282 | |
| 1968 | 210 | (216) | 808 | | 257 | |
| 1969 | 215 | | 828 | | 257 | |
| 1970 | 243 | | 849 | (825.13) | 283 | (294.5) |
| 1971 | 246 | | 870 | | 279 | |
| 1972 | 240 | | 891 | | 266 | |
| 1973 | 266 | (265) | 912 | | 288 | |
| 1974 | 275 | | 933 | | 292 | |
| 1975 | 284 | | 952 | | 295 | |
| 1976 | 285 | | 971 | (932.57) | 291 | (307) |
| 1977 | 283 | (283) | 987 | (946.73) | 284 | |
| 1978 | 305 | (305) | 1,002 | (958.09) | 302 | (317.5) |
| 1979 | 315 | (332) | 1,017 | (970.92) | 307 | (342) |

Note: Figures in parentheses are Chinese official data; others are U.S. government estimates.
Sources: U.S. government estimates are from U.S. Central Intelligence Agency, China: Major Economic Indicators (Washington, D.C., February 1980). Chinese official

Table 10.3 (continued)

figures are from (1) Xue Muqiao, "Thirty Years of Strenuous Efforts," Hongqi (Red flag) No. 10 (October 1979), pp. 40-49. (2) Yang Jianbai and Li Xuezeng, "China's Historical Experience in Handling the Relations Between Agriculture, Light Industry, and Heavy Industry," Zhongguo shehui kexue (Social sciences in China) No. 3 (May 1980), pp. 19-40. (3) The 1978-1979 population figures are from P.R.C. State Statistical Bureau, "Communiqué on Fulfillment of China's 1979 National Economic Plan," Beijing Review 23:19 (May 12, 1980), p. 14. The 1950, 1955, 1965, 1970, and 1976 populations and per capita grain output figures are derived from data in Chen Muhua's article "To Realize the Four Modernizations, Population Growth Must Be Controlled in a Planned Way," Renmin ribao (People's daily), August 11, 1979, p. 2.

growth rates over time, not with the absolute size of GNP, and because the CIA estimates provide the most complete and systematic data for analysis, this study uses them with some adjustments.

## GROWTH PATTERN

The 1950-1979 growth trend of economic activities in China, as illustrated in Figure 10.1 and summarized in Tables 10.7 and 10.8, displays three major cycles between 1950 and 1976, each of which has several smaller cycles. The 1977-1979 period can be considered as the beginning of a fourth major cycle.

The first major cycle started with the recovery process in 1950-1952. The increase in capital investment and the inflow of Soviet technical aid in 1953-1956 culminated in 1958, when the Great Leap Forward was launched. Benefiting from favorable weather conditions, grain output in 1958 showed a moderate rate of growth. Managers of industrial plants were ordered to meet greatly increased quotas at any cost, and machines and workers were driven mercilessly to meet those quotas, regardless of the effect on quality or on the balances of raw materials and finished goods. The results of the Great Leap in industry were a spectacular but unsustainable jump in industrial production in 1958-1959 and a quick collapse in 1961. The precipitous drop in agricultural output in 1959-1960 and the suspension of Soviet aid in 1960 caused a sharp decline in GNP. The 1959-1961 crisis was so profound that it not only slowed down the

Table 10.4
Comparison of Three Estimates of China's National Product, 1950-1959

| Year | Annual Growth Rates in Percent | | |
|---|---|---|---|
| | Chinese Official Data (National Income) | Liu-Yeh Estimates (Gross Domestic Product) | U.S. Government Estimates (Gross National Product) |
| 1950 | 18.6 | n.a. | 24.0 |
| 1951 | 17.0 | n.a. | 16.0 |
| 1952 | 22.3 | n.a. | 18.0 |
| 1953 | 14.0 | 5.9 | 7.0 |
| 1954 | 5.7 | 5.5 | 4.0 |
| 1955 | 6.5 | 3.9 | 10.0 |
| 1956 | 14.0 | 12.4 | 8.0 |
| 1957 | 4.6 | 3.6 | 6.0 |
| 1958 | 23.1 | 13.0 | 20.0 |
| 1959 | 8.2 | 16.7 | -5.0 |

Note: The coverage of these three sets of figures is not identical. The Chinese official figures refer to "National Income" which is defined as net output value of material-producing departments including industry, agriculture, building construction, communications, transport, and commerce. (See P.R.C. State Statistical Bureau, "Communiqué on Fulfillment of China's 1979 National Economic Plan," Beijing Review 23:19 (May 12, 1980), p. 12. The Liu-Yeh estimates include government administration, finance, personal services, residential rents, and work brigades. The U.S. government estimates, following the conventional concept of GNP, also include services.

Sources: (1) The Chinese official data for 1950-57 are from P.R.C. State Statistical Bureau, Ten Great Years (Beijing: Foreign Languages Press, 1960), p. 20; for 1958-69, from Yang Jianbai and Li Xuezeng, "China's Historical Experience in Handling the Relations Between Agriculture, Light Industry, and Heavy Industry," Zhongguo shehui kexue (Social sciences in China) No. 3 (May 1980), pp. 19-40. (2) The Liu-Yeh figures are from Ta-chung Liu and Kung-chia Yeh, The Economy of the Chinese Mainland: National Income and Economic Development, 1933-1959 (Princeton, N.J.: Princeton University Press, 1965), Table 8, p. 66. The 1958-59 figures are their conjectural estimates. (3) The U.S. government figures are derived from Table 10.1.

Table 10.5
Official Data on National Income, 1950-1979
(Selected Years)

| Year | National Income per Capita (U.S. $) | Population (million persons) | National Income (Billion U.S.$) | National Income (Billion yuan) | Exchange Rate (yuan per U.S. $) |
|---|---|---|---|---|---|
| 1950 | 28[a] | 551.96[e] | 15.45[g] | 42.46[h] | 2.75[k] |
| 1955 | 49[a] | 614.65[e] | 30.12[g] | 77.95[h] | 2.59[k] |
| 1965 | 78[a] | 723.88[f] | 56.46[g] | 138.89[i] | 2.46[k] |
| 1970 | 95[a] | 825.13[f] | 78.39[g] | 192.89[i] | 2.46[k] |
| 1976 | 139[a] | 932.57[f] | 129.63[g] | 260.00[j] | 2.01[k] |
| 1977 | 152[b] | 946.73[e] | 143.73[g] | 281.00[j] | 1.96[k] |
| 1978 | 188[c] | 958.09[e] | 180.30[g] | 315.00[j] | 1.75[k] |
| 1979 | 217[d] | 970.92[e] | 210.60[g] | 337.00[j] | 1.60[l] |

Sources: (a) Chen Muhua, "To Realize the Four Modernizations, Population Growth Must Be Controlled in a Planned Way," Renmin ribao (People's daily), August 11, 1979, p. 2. (b) Reported by P.R.C. United Nations delegation, Shih-chieh jih-pao, New York, October 1, 1979. (c) U.S. Central Intelligence Agency, China: A Preliminary Reconciliation of Official and CIA National Product Data (Washington, D.C., December 1979). (d) Derived from official yuan figure. (e) Official reported figures, see P.R.C. State Statistical Bureau, Communiqués on Fulfillment of China's 1978 and 1979 National Economic Plans, Beijing Review 22:27 (July 6, 1979), pp. 37-41, and 23:19 (May 12, 1980), pp. 12-15. (f) Calculated from Chen Muhua's grain per capita figures (grain production divided by grain per capita). (g) National income per capita times population. (h) China: A Preliminary Reconciliation. (i) National income in current dollars multiplied by the exchange rate. (j) The 1979 national income was officially reported as 337 billion yuan, which was 7 percent over 1978. The 1978 national income can be derived as 315 billion yuan (communiqué on fulfillment of 1979 plan); the 1978 national income was 12 percent over 1977; the 1977 national income should be 281 billion yuan. The 1977 national income was 8 percent more than 1976; the 1976 national income should be 260 billion yuan (communiqué on fulfillment of 1978 plan). (k) China: A Preliminary Reconciliation. (l) Current exchange rate.

Table 10.6
Comparison of Two Estimates of China's
Per Capita Income, 1950-1979
(in U.S. dollars)

| Year | U.S. Government Estimates | | Chinese official data in current dollars[g] |
|---|---|---|---|
| | in 1979 dollars[a] | in current dollars | |
| 1950 | 143 | | 28 |
| 1955 | 214 | 79[b] | 49 |
| 1965 | 268 | | 78 |
| 1970 | 337 | 146[c] | 95 |
| 1976 | 412 | | 139 |
| 1977 | 438 | 379[d] | 152 |
| 1978 | 482 | 443[e] | 188 |
| 1979 | 505 | 505[f] | 217 |

Sources: (a) U.S. Central Intelligence Agency, China: Major Economic Indicators (Washington, D.C., February 1980). (b) U.S. Central Intelligence Agency, China: A Preliminary Reconciliation of Official and CIA National Product Data (Washington, D.C., December 1979). (c) U.S. Congress, Joint Economic Committee, People's Republic of China: An Economic Assessment (Washington, D.C.: Government Printing Office, 1972), p. 47. (d) U.S. Congress, Joint Economic Committee, Chinese Economy Post-Mao (Washington, D.C.: Government Printing Office, 1978), p. 208. (e) China: Major Economic Indicators (Washington, D.C., September 1979). (f) China: Major Economic Indicators (Washington, D.C., February 1980). (g) From Table 10.5.

growth rate but resulted in absolute declines of 27 percent in GNP, 27 percent in agricultural output, 26 percent in industrial output, and 19 percent in foreign trade (1961 against 1958) (see Table 10.1). This contraction had many of the attributes of a classical depression, with considerable underutilization of plant capacity and large-scale industrial unemployment.

The first cycle reached its trough in 1961, and a steady recovery began. The readjustment policy for 1961–1965 achieved its objectives. With new investment in agriculture, farm production advanced steadily, and a number of priority industries grew rapidly in this period. By 1965, China had become self-sufficient in crude oil, and the armaments industry also greatly expanded. The second cycle peaked in 1966, with agricultural output and foreign trade returning to the 1958–1959 level. Industrial output surpassed the 1958–1959 peak, and GNP was 28 percent higher than in 1958.

Figure 10.1
Fluctuations of Industrial Output, Agricultural Output, and GNP in China, 1951–1979

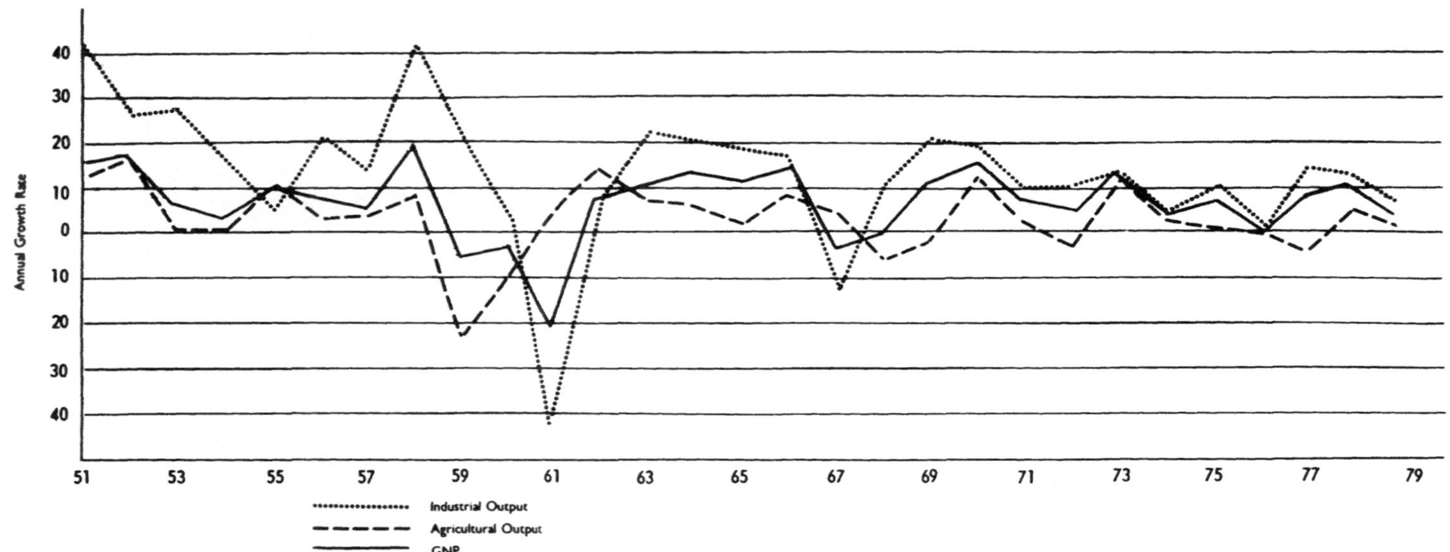


Source: Table 10.7

Table 10.7
Yearly Change in Selected Economic Indicators
1949–1979 (in percent)

| Year | Grain Output | Agricultural Output | Steel Output | Industrial Output | Gross National Product | Foreign Trade Value |
|---|---|---|---|---|---|---|
| 1949–50 | 17 | 21 | 281 | 35 | 22 (18.6) | 50 |
| 1950–51 | 8 | 13 | 48 | 41 | 17 (17.0) | 58 |
| 1951–52 | 14 | 17 | 50 | 26 | 19 (22.3) | 0 |
| 1952–53 | 2 | 0 | 31 | 27 | 6 (14.0) | 21 |
| 1953–54 | 1 | 0 | 25 | 15 | 4 ( 5.7) | 4 |
| 1954–55 | 8 | 12 | 28 | 4 | 10 ( 6.5) | 29 |
| 1955–56 | 4 | 3 | 56 | 21 | 8 (14.0) | 0 |
| 1956–57 | 2 | 3 | 20 | 14 | 6 ( 4.6) | -3 |
| 1957–58 | 8 ( 4.7) | 7 ( 2.4) | 107 (50) | 42 | 19 (23.1) | 23 |
| 1958–59 | -17 | -22 (-13.6) | 25 (67) | 22 | -5 ( 8.2) | 16 |
| 1959–60 | -9 | -11 | 35 (35) | 5 | -3 | -7 |
| 1960–61 | 8 | 5 ( -2.4) | -57 | -42 | -21 | -25 |
| 1961–62 | 7 | 12 | 0 | 6 | 9 | -10 |
| 1962–63 | 6 | 7 | 0 | 21 | 13 | 4 |
| 1963–64 | 2 | 5 | 20 | 20 | 11 | 18 |
| 1964–65 | 0 | 3 | 27 | 24 | 13 | 15 |
| 1965–66 | 11 | 11 ( 8.3) | 23 | 17 | 13 | 11 |
| 1966–67 | 5 | 5 ( 1.6) | -33 (-33) | -13 | -4 | -5 |
| 1967–68 | -7 (-4.0) | -7 ( -2.5) | -10 (-10) | 9 (-5) | 0.4 (-?) | -5 |
| 1968–69 | 2 | 2 ( 1.1) | 78 ( 44) | 20 | 11 | 3 |
| 1969–70 | 13 | 13 ( 11.5) | 11 ( 37) | 19 (30.7) | 16 | 13 |
| 1970–71 | 1 | 3 | 18 | 10 | 7 | 9 |
| 1971–72 | -3 | -3 | 10 | 10 | 5 | 25 |

| | | | | | | |
|---|---|---|---|---|---|---|
| 1972-73 | 11 | 13 | 9 | 13 | 13 | 68 |
| 1973-74 | 3 | 3 | -16 | 4 | 4 | 40 |
| 1974-75 | 3 | 1 | 14 | 10 (15.1) | 7 | 3 |
| 1975-76 | 0.3 ( .4) | 0 | -14 | 0 | -0.2 (-?) | -8 |
| 1976-77 | -0.7 (-1) | -3 | 16 | 14 | 8 (8) | 14 |
| 1977-78 | 7.7 (7.8) | 8.3 (8.9) | 34 | 13 (13.5) | 12 (12) | 39 (30.3) |
| 1978-79 | 3.3 (9.0) | 2.6 (8.6) | 8 (8.5) | 8 ( 8.5) | 6 (7) | 31 (28) |

Note: Figures in parentheses are Chinese official data; others are U.S. government estimates. The sign (-?) denotes a decline without specifying the magnitude.

Sources: U.S. government figures are derived from data in Table 10.1. Chinese official data are derived from information contained in the following sources: (1) Xue Muqiao, "Thirty Years of Strenuous Efforts," Hongqi (Red flag) No. 10 (October 1979), pp. 44-49. (2) Yang Jianbai and Li Xuezeng, "China's Historical Experience in Handling the Relations Between Agriculture, Light Industry, and Heavy Industry," Zhongguo shehui kexue (Social sciences in China) No. 3 (1980), pp. 19-40. (3) P.R.C. State Statistical Bureau, Communiqués on Fulfillment of China's 1978 and 1979 National Economic Plans, Beijing Review 22:27 (July 6, 1979), pp. 37-41, and 23:19 (May 12, 1980), pp. 12-15.

Table 10.8
Cyclical Fluctuations of the Chinese Economy, 1950-1979
(in percent)

| Major Cycles | | Average Annual Growth Rates | |
|---|---|---|---|
| | GNP | Agricultural Output | Industrial Output |
| First Major Cycle (1950-61) | | | |
| Recovery (1950-52) | 17.5 | 14.5 | 33.4 |
| Expansion (1953-57) | 7.2 | 4.5 | 13.2 |
| Peak (1958) | 19.0 | (23.1)7.0 (2.4) | 42.0 |
| Contraction (1959-60) | -4.0 | -15.5 | 12.7 |
| Trough (1961) | -21.0 | 5.0 (-2.4) | -42.0 |
| Second Major Cycle (1961-67) | | | |
| Recovery (1962-63) | 11.0 | 9.1 | 13.2 |
| Expansion (1964-65) | 11.9 | 4.5 | 22.0 |
| Peak (1966) | 13.0 | 11.0 (8.3) | 17.0 |
| Contraction (1966-68) | -3.0 | -2.0 | -2.5 |
| Trough (1967) | -4.0 | 5.0 (1.6) | -13.0 |
| Third Major Cycle (1967-76) | | | |
| Recovery (1969-70) | 13.6 | 7.2 | 19.6 |
| Expansion (1971-73) | 8.7 | 4.4 | 11.3 |
| Peak (1973) | 13.0 | 13.0 | 13.0 |
| Contraction (1974-75) | 5.4 | 2.0 | 7.2 |
| Trough (1976) | -0.2 | 0 | 0 |
| Fourth Major Cycle (1977-) | | | |
| Recovery (1977-79) | 8.7 | 4.9 | 10.5 |

Note: Figures in parentheses are Chinese official data from Yang Jianbai and Li Xuezeng, "China's Historical Experience in Handling the Relations Between Agriculture, Light Industry, and Heavy Industry, Zhongguo shehui kexue (Social sciences in China) No. 3 (May 1980), pp. 19-40. Other figures are derived from data in Table 10.1.

The upward trend was disrupted again by the Cultural Revolution. As a result of widespread turmoil, industrial output declined by 13 percent in 1967. Foreign trade dropped 5 percent in the same year, and GNP fell 4 percent. According to U.S. government estimates, the industrial output lost between 1967 and 1969 amounted to 100.6 billion yuan or 16.8 percent of potential output.[28]

The degree of economic disruption, however, was less catastrophic than that of the Great Leap Forward. The upward trend soon resumed and reached a new high in 1973. In that year, grain and industrial outputs, GNP, and foreign trade all registered a solid advance. The succession struggle between 1974 and 1976 again caused disruptions in economic growth, but the loss of industrial output was less serious than that of the 1967–1969 period. After the purge of Deng Xiaoping in 1976 and the launching of the divisive campaign to discredit him, however, the disruption intensified.

The purge of the Gang of Four in October 1976 set the economy on the track of recovery. The new leadership took steps to restore order to the economy and jettisoned institutional and ideological baggage that stood in the way of improved efficiency and higher productivity. The process of recovery was slow in 1977 but accelerated in 1978. Although industrial output averaged 13.5 percent annual growth in those two years, agricultural output rose only 2.5 percent, barely ahead of population growth. Although the Chinese leaders announced an ambitious Ten-Year Plan (1976–1985) in 1978, an official statement in June 1979 indicated that the years 1979 through 1981 "would be a time of adjustment, recovery, and improvement,"[29] and in March 1981, the period of adjustment was extended to 1985. The extension implies that the Chinese economy remained in a recovery phase during 1977–1981 and that a new peak would probably not arrive until after 1985, when the new expansion would start.

Apart from cyclical fluctuations, the growth pattern in the 1952–1978 period exhibited two salient features. First, when the growth rates between the peaks and troughs are compared, the degree of variation was much more severe in the first cycle than in the second or third. The change in the growth rate of GNP between 1958 and 1961 was more than 40 percent, but the change between 1966 and 1967 was only 17 percent; in the third cycle, the variation was only 13 percent. This would suggest that the Chinese economy was less volatile in the 1970s than it was in the 1950s. One major factor causing this moderation was the steadily rising importance of the industrial sector in relation to agriculture. In the early 1950s, agricultural gross output value accounted for more than 60 percent of the combined gross output value for industry and agriculture, but its relative share has shown a steady decline. The agricultural gross output value dropped to only 36.4 percent of the combined value in 1958 and to only 25.6 percent in 1978.[30] As the share of industrial output in GNP continuously advanced, variations of the growth rate in GNP were less affected by agricultural performance and thus became more stable.

Second, a computation of the growth rates for grain output, industrial output, GNP, and foreign trade over five-year intervals, ten-year intervals, and twenty-five-year intervals shows that there was no clear trend of growth over a five-year period but that the overall growth rates of 1962-1972 generally more than doubled those of 1952-1962 (see Table 10.9). Despite high fluctuations, the general trend of the Chinese economy is moving upward rather than downward.

Table 10.9
Growth Rates for Grain Output, Industrial Output, GNP, and Foreign Trade in P.R.C., 1952-1977
(in percent)

| Year | Grain Output | Industrial Output | GNP | Foreign Trade |
|---|---|---|---|---|
| | Percentage Increase or Decrease | | | |
| Five-year Interval | | | | |
| 1952-57 | 18.6 | 108.3 | 39.8 | 57.9 |
| 1957-62 | -5.8 | 11.0 | -5.3 | -10.0 |
| 1962-67 | 25.0 | 82.0 | 53.8 | 48.1 |
| 1967-72 | 6.7 | 90.6 | 45.5 | 50.0 |
| 1972-77 | 17.9 | 49.1 | 35.3 | 153.3 |
| Ten-year Interval | | | | |
| 1952-62 | 11.8 | 131.3 | 32.4 | 42.1 |
| 1962-72 | 33.3 | 246.8 | 123.8 | 122.2 |
| 25-year Interval | | | | |
| 1952-77 | 75.8 | 1,095.8 | 300.9 | 700.0 |
| | Annual Rates of Growth | | | |
| Five-year Interval | | | | |
| 1952-57 | 3.5 | 15.8 | 6.9 | 9.6 |
| 1957-62 | -1.2 | 2.1 | -1.1 | -2.0 |
| 1962-67 | 4.6 | 12.7 | 9.0 | 8.2 |
| 1967-72 | 1.3 | 13.8 | 7.8 | 8.5 |
| 1972-77 | 3.3 | 8.3 | 6.2 | 20.4 |
| Ten-year Interval | | | | |
| 1952-62 | 1.1 | 8.7 | 2.8 | 3.6 |
| 1962-72 | 2.9 | 13.3 | 8.4 | 8.3 |
| 25-year Interval | | | | |
| 1952-77 | 2.3 | 10.4 | 5.7 | 8.7 |

Source: Derived from data in Table 10.1.

## UNDERLYING CYCLES

The incessant fluctuations in the Chinese economy under a central planning system have drawn attention from economists in Chinese studies. The phenomenon was first analyzed by this author in 1963 in an analysis of three small cycles that occurred during the 1949–1959 period. Two important factors were pinpointed as the prime causes of the cyclical fluctuations–the harvest cycle and the confiscation of private property and the effect of the latter on capital formation and the growth of national product.[31]

A more detailed study was undertaken by Alexander Eckstein in 1968.[32] He identified four to five short cycles in the 1950–1965 period, each of two or three years' duration. He suggested that the cyclical fluctuations in China's economic policy and in the rates of economic expansion could be viewed as a function of the deep-seated conflict between the Maoist vision and the realities of the country's economic and technical backwardness. He agreed that an underlying cause of the fluctuations was the harvest cycle, but he saw that cycle as not merely a function of weather variations but also as the outcome of the ebb and flow of Party policy toward the agricultural sector. His analysis thus dealt with two separate but closely related movements–a harvest cycle and a policy cycle.

Although Eckstein's study sheds some new light on the problem, his analysis focuses mainly on the first decade of development, when the policy cycle involved farming policies primarily. During the 1970s, the role played by agriculture in the Chinese economy gradually diminished. In 1958–1959, when agricultural output dropped 22 percent, the GNP dropped 5 percent despite a 22 percent gain in industrial output. Yet in 1971–1972, even with a 3 percent decline in agricultural output, the GNP still showed a 5 percent increase thanks to a 10 percent rise in industrial output. Any analysis of cyclical fluctuations, therefore, has to incorporate nonagricultural factors, including population policy and what Dwight Perkins has called the "implementation cycles" of economic plans.[33]

### *The Harvest Cycle*

Despite the diminishing role of agriculture in the 1970s, the relationship between agricultural output and other economic activities remains extremely close in China. Until 1957, in terms of net value added, agriculture still accounted for more than 40 percent of national income. About 80 percent of the raw materials for light industry and 50 percent of those for industry as a whole were derived from agriculture. Approximately half the government's total fiscal revenue came directly or indirectly from agriculture. Farm products in raw or processed form accounted for more than 70 percent of China's exports.[34] Even in 1978, agriculture still represented 43.3 percent of national income, as compared with 56.7 percent for industry.[35]

As Table 10.9 suggests, the levels of industrial output, foreign trade, and GNP were closely related to food grain output until 1967. When food grain output grew at 18.6 percent between 1952 and 1957, industrial output spurted by 108.3 percent, GNP by 39.8 percent, and foreign trade by 57.9 percent. In contrast, in the 1957–1962 period, food grain output declined by 5.8 percent, and industrial output growth slowed to only 11 percent, while GNP and foreign trade dropped 5.3 and 10 percent, respectively. When food grain output rebounded in the 1962–1967 period, industrial output, foreign trade, and GNP all showed steady growth. The growth rate for agriculture was 25 percent as compared with 82 percent for industry, 53.8 percent for GNP, and 48.1 percent for foreign trade.

The 1967–1972 period heralded a new relationship between food grain output and other sectors of the economy. Despite near stagnation in food production (up only 6.7 percent in five years), industrial output rose 90.6 percent, GNP gained 45.5 percent, and foreign trade 50 percent. This new trend, if continued, would suggest that in the future, food production may have a diminishing influence on China's general economic development.

Between 1952 and 1960, available statistics show that changes in agricultural output, particularly grain output, invariably induced an investment cycle with roughly a one-year lag.[36] The effects of agricultural production on the national economy, based on available official data, are summarized in Table 10.10. From that table, it can be seen that the two small cycles in the first major cycle are the result of agricultural fluctuations. The fairly high rates of GNP in 1953 and 1956 were the outcome of bumper harvests in 1952 and 1955. The Great Leap in 1958–1959 did not follow a bumper harvest in 1957. It was somewhat artificially stimulated and caused disastrous effects in the following years.

In 1965, a new policy of crop diversification was implemented. In North China, where grain is very vulnerable to droughts, floods, and insects, efforts have been made to expand industrial crops that are more suited to local conditions. Although staple food production has suffered a decline, vegetables, fruits, sugarcane, tobacco, and livestock have achieved continuous advances.

A new factor that may explain recent changes in the relationship be-

Table 10.10
The Effects of Agricultural Production on the National Economy of the P.R.C.
1949-1960

| Year | Increase Rate of Agricultural Output in Current Year | Effect on Economic Development of the Following Year | | | | |
|---|---|---|---|---|---|---|
| | | | | Increase Rate of Industrial Output | | |
| | | Year | Increase Rate of National Income | Whole Industry | Light Industry | Increase Rate of State Revenue |
| 1950 | 17.7 | 1951 | 17.0 | 37.9 | 32.6 | 98.5 |
| 1951 | 9.4 | 1952 | 22.3 | 30.3 | 23.8 | 35.5 |
| 1952 | 15.3 | 1953 | 14.0 | 30.2 | 26.7 | 24.0 |
| 1953 | 3.1 | 1954 | 5.7 | 16.3 | 14.2 | 20.5 |
| 1954 | 3.3 | 1955 | 6.5 | 5.6 | -0.03 | 3.7 |
| 1955 | 7.7 | 1956 | 14.0 | 28.2 | —— | 5.9 |
| 1956 | 4.9 | 1957 | 4.6 | 11.4 | 5.6 | 7.9 |
| 1957 | 3.5 | 1958 | 23.1 | 66.2 | 34.0 | 8.0 |
| 1958 | 2.4 | 1959 | 8.2 | 39.3 | 34.0 | 29.4 |
| 1959 | -13.6 | 1960 | —— | 29.0 | —— | —— |

Notes: Figures in this table are not consistent with those in Table 10.1 because Table 10.1 is estimated while figures in this table are official statistics.

Sources: Agricultural Increase Rate: 1950-57 from P.R.C. State Statistical Bureau, Ten Great Years (Beijing: Foreign Languages Press, 1960), p. 118; 1958-59 figures from Yang Jianbai and Li Xuezeng, "China's Historical Experience in Handling the Relations Between Agriculture, Light Industry, and Heavy Industry," Zhongguo shehui kexue (Social sciences in China) No. 3 (May 1980), p. 21. Industrial Increase Rate: Ten Great Years, p. 89. National Income Increase Rate: 1951-57 Ten Great Years, p. 20; 1958-59 Yang Jianbai and Li Xuezeng, ibid., p. 21. State Revenue Increase Rate: Ten Great Years, p. 21; Light Industry: Hongqi (Red flag) No. 6 (March 16, 1961).

tween agriculture and industry is the growth of small industries in the countryside. The revival of the "walking on two legs" policy has resulted in the building of tens of thousands of small iron and steel plants, small hydroelectric stations, small chemical fertilizer plants, and small cement and farm machinery plants, most of which use inputs of nonagricultural materials.[37]

The expansion of industrial crops and the growth of small industries have helped reduce the impact of food grain output on the national economy. Thus, the harvest cycle, which affected the early economic fluctuations, cannot alone explain the fluctuations in more recent years.

### *Farm Policy Cycles*

Agricultural output is affected by a number of factors, most particularly weather conditions and the Party's policy toward the peasants. The weather remains an unpredictable and a largely uncontrollable variable, despite a continuous drive to improve water conservation. The three good harvest years in the first cycle—1950, 1952, and 1955—were to a great extent the result of favorable weather. In some cases, good weather conditions were offset and bad weather conditions aggravated by the Party's policy toward the peasants, including the degree of agricultural collectivization, the terms of trade between agricultural and industrial products, and the incentive system.

As a rule, when agricultural production is high, peasants' cash income rises and so does their interest in farm trade, as this brings a higher rate of return in a relatively shorter period. Furthermore, farm trade among peasant households is a means of avoiding government taxation and procurement quotas. Mao viewed this kind of "spontaneous tendency toward capitalism" as a potential threat to the socialist system[38] and sought to control it by speeding up collectivization or by making the terms of trade unfavorable to the peasants. Such measures in 1953, 1956, 1964, and 1967 dampened peasant incentives and led to a decline in output. Thus, although 1953 was a normal weather year, agriculture suffered the lowest growth rate in five years (3.1 percent according to official statistics and zero growth according to U.S. government estimates). In the beginning of that year, large-scale agricultural cooperatives were introduced, and in the middle of that year, the compulsory purchase of food grains was instituted.

The low agricultural output in 1959–1961 can probably be attributed, in large part, to the regimentation of peasant households into communes. The egalitarian approach to income distribution, the wholesale transfer of private property to communal ownership, the drastic changes in family life, and the tremendous difficulties involved in commune management had a negative effect on agricultural production.

The slow and steady recovery of agricultural output after 1962 was partly due to normal weather but more significantly stemmed from new economic policies toward the peasants. Under the guideline of readjustment (later identified by the Maoists as Liu Shaoqi's revisionist program), the commune system was greatly modified. Not only were communes reduced in size by two-thirds (which increased the number of communes from 24,000 in 1959 to 74,000 in 1963), but controlling power was delegated to lower production units. Moreover, peasant households were permitted to retain small private plots and engage in sideline occupations.

Peasant incentives were gradually revitalized under the policy of *san zi yi bao* ("three selfs and one guarantee")–increasing the size of private plots, increasing the number of free markets, and increasing the number of small enterprises with sole responsibility for their own profits and losses while fixing output quotas on the household level.

Apart from the shift in incentive policy, there has also been a shift in emphasis, with agriculture assigned first priority in development since 1962. This new emphasis has brought a steady growth in manufactured inputs for farming. Between 1957 and 1965, the annual output of farm machinery and equipment more than tripled, and the output of chemical fertilizers grew from less than 1 million tons in 1957 to more than 16 million tons in 1971. Largely as a consequence of these policy changes, agricultural output rose steadily after 1962, despite several years of adverse weather and the disruptions of the Cultural Revolution.

China's farm policy is essentially one of "the carrot and the stick," with more stringent measures imposed during periods of improved output and an easing up during periods of agricultural difficulties.[39]

### *The Confiscation Cycle*

Fluctuations in the growth rates of the nonagricultural sectors, particularly industrial output, are primarily affected by the volume of investment. The high growth rates of 1952, 1953, 1956, and 1958 are directly correlated with high state investment outlays (see Table 10.11).

Until 1960, rates of investment could be correlated with the size of the preceding year's harvest, because agricultural surplus constituted the main source of accumulation. Rates of investment were also af-

Table 10.11
Indexes of GNP, Industrial Output, and Net Domestic Investment, 1952-1965
(Annual Rate in Percentage)

| Year | GNP | Industrial Output | Net Domestic Investment |
|---|---|---|---|
| 1952 | 19 | 26 | — |
| 1953 | 6 | 27 | 34 |
| 1954 | 4 | 15 | 7 |
| 1955 | 10 | 4 | 5 |
| 1956 | 8 | 21 | 21 |
| 1957 | 6 | 14 | -12 |
| 1958 | 19 | 42 | 30 |
| 1959 | -5 | 22 | -15 |
| 1960 | -3 | 5 | -15 |
| 1961 | -21 | -42 | -9 |
| 1962 | 9 | 6 | 0 |
| 1963 | 13 | 21 | 7 |
| 1964 | 11 | 20 | 8 |
| 1965 | 13 | 24 | 7 |

Note: Investment in this table differs from the official figures. According to P.R.C. State Statistical Bureau, Ten Great Years (Beijing: Foreign Languages Press, 1960), p. 55, the growth rate was 83.5 percent for 1953, 13.4 percent for 1954, 2.5 percent for 1955, 59 percent for 1956, -6.4 percent for 1957 and 93 percent for 1958. Figures in the third column of this table are independent estimates. Although the growth rates are much smaller than official statistics, the correlations between investment and the two other growth rates remain fairly close.

Sources: GNP and Industrial Output from Table 10.7. Net Domestic Investment from Kuan-I Chen, "Economic Fluctuations in a Planned Under-Developed Economy--A Case Study of Mainland China 1952-1965," Asian Survey 12:4 (April 1972), Table p. 359.

fected by the confiscation of private properties, with such measures employed at roughly two-year intervals between 1949 and the Great Leap.[40] From the macroeconomic point of view, such measures only transfer property from the private sector to the public sector without creating any new wealth for society. Yet, because they perform the function of resource reallocation, they can considerably increase the rate of investment in a given area.

In 1949–1950, Beijing confiscated properties of capitalists who had previously had connections with the Nationalist government. In the rural areas, properties belonging to landlords and rich peasants were also confiscated, as well as the property of people classified as "reactionaries." The "five-anti" campaign of 1952 was directed at firms that had profited during the Korean War, and some 340,000 private enterprises were ordered to pay large fines totaling about $2 billion.[41] This sum was a chief source of the capital investment in 1953 when state investment outlays soared 84 percent over the preceding year. In late 1955 and early 1956, a new drive was undertaken to incorporate some 112,000 private industrial establishments into joint state-private operations. The share of profits that usually went to the owners was channeled into the state treasury, and investment rose that year by 59 percent.

The same situation prevailed in 1958 when communes were established and private property in rural areas was further expropriated. The state was able to launch the Great Leap Forward without the usual support of a bumper harvest the preceding year. The amount of property transferred to the government in 1958 can be roughly measured by the sharp increase in extrabudgetary investment—that is, investment that was not included in the original state capital construction plan. Official statistics showed a spectacular rise in extrabudgetary investments amounting to 5.3 billion yuan, or approximately $2 billion, a sum almost equal to the extrabudgetary investments of the entire First Five-Year Plan period.[42] The four large-scale confiscations, which transferred roughly $10 billion from the private sector to the public sector, were a significant source of state capital investment during the 1952–1959 period.

By 1960, most vestiges of private property had been confiscated. Since then, three other methods have been used to bring about the growth of industrial output. The first has been a fuller utilization of capacity built during the 1952–1959 period. Fragmentary reports in recent years indicate that output in some major industrial plants may exceed their design capacity two to three times.[43] The second has been a steady rise in the level of expertise and technology. Thirty years of training and practice have created a more experienced work force in the modern sector, and this has helped push the production-possibility curve outward. The third means of increasing production has been the adoption of labor-intensive techniques. The proliferation of small-scale industry in the Chinese countryside since 1966 has substantially reduced the capital-output ratio. This orientation makes it possible to increase industrial output with relatively little increase in capital. For example, in 1965, small plants accounted for only 12 percent of production capacity in the chemical fertilizer industry. That percentage rose to over one-third in 1968 and to 43 percent in 1969.[44] Of the 14 million tons of chemical fertilizers reportedly produced in 1970, some 6 million tons were from small plants. The establishment of small plants also resulted in a 48 percent increase in the amount of iron ore processed in 1970. Pig iron produced by small local plants in 1970 was said to be 2.8 times that of 1969.[45]

*The Population Policy Cycle*

Another factor relevant to this discussion is the official birth control policy. Changes in Beijing's attitude toward population control have coincided with the ups and downs of the food supply. In the early years (1949–1953), when agricultural output enjoyed a steady recovery, the Party leadership rejected any suggestion of population planning, upholding the Marxist contention that overpopulation is a problem of capitalism that does not exist in a socialist system.

The 1953 census put China's population close to 600 million, however, instead of the often quoted 400 million. This figure, combined with a slower rate of growth in food production, made population pressures more apparent. A Party policy favoring population control was formally announced in June 1956 by Li Dequan, then minister of public health, and approved by Zhou Enlai in a major speech before the Eighth Party Congress in September 1956.[46] A clause advocating birth control in rural areas was included in the second version of the twelve-year development plan for agriculture, and Mao is said to have favored birth control in the original (February 1957) version of his speech "On the Correct Handling of Internal Contradictions Among the People."[47]

Following these policy statements, a mass campaign to promote birth control began to take shape. In April 1957, a national committee on technical guidance was established under the auspices of the Chinese Medical Association. Guidance and counseling clinics were set up, birth control cadres were trained, and the manufacture and distribution of contraceptives was expanded.

The program was quietly terminated in 1958, when the Great Leap Forward and commune movement were in full swing. False reports of tremendous increases in food grain production in 1958–1959 and a widespread labor shortage in the rural areas due to the backyard furnace drive created the impression that the problem of food supply and population size had been solved. Leading economist and birth control advocate Professor Ma Yinchu came under severe criticism. He was condemned as a Malthusian and removed from his post as president of Beijing University.[48]

Following the severe agricultural failures of 1959–1961, the birth control program was reactivated in the spring of 1962. The media urged young people to delay marriage and couples to limit the size of their families. The campaign was temporarily slowed down in mid-1963 and again during the Cultural Revolution. As a result of the policy fluctuation, China's population growth has never been effectively checked, and official statistics reveal that natural increase per thousand people in 1971 was as high as 23.4, almost the same as in 1954 when the birth control program was initiated.[49]

The steady growth in the population was a major drag on the economy, a burden upon the educational system, and a contributor to rising unemployment. As the country's population approached the 1 billion mark, the new leadership committed itself to reducing the population growth rate. Starting in the summer of 1979, a new scheme of family planning was launched. This program uses differential taxation, educational opportunity, and job assignment as sanctions to households with more than two children and as rewards to those with only one child.[50] In mid-July 1979, the renowned economist Ma Yinchu, who had strongly advocated birth control in the early 1950s and was later labeled a Malthusian, was rehabilitated at the age of ninety-eight.[51]

Again, the evolution of population policy points to a trial-and-error approach. Had the Chinese leaders accepted the need to limit population growth from the beginning, a significant economic burden might have been lightened. There would have been less pressure on the food supply and possibly a saving of billions of dollars in food grain imports. This, in turn, could well have accelerated the rate of capital accumulation and the growth rate of the GNP.

### *Economic Policies and Political Stability Cycles*

A more fundamental factor causing economic fluctuations has been the incessant shifts of development policies and the changing attitudes toward economic planning and management. The erratic twists and turns of development strategy (see Chapter 9) suggest a policy of trial and error followed by overcorrection rather than the implementation of a set of consistent and well-conceived plans. Which policy was in effect was in part the result of which particular political forces were in control of the Party. Generally speaking, periods of radical experimentation were succeeded by periods of retreat and adjustment. In contrast to a market economy, in which economic policymaking is somewhat independent of politics, economic policy changes in China have been closely tied to leadership changes.

From 1949 to 1957, despite policy differences, the Chinese leadership showed no signs of open split. The economy grew steadily, and Chinese planners made systematic efforts to regulate enterprise behavior. The turning point came in 1958 when the Great Leap program and rural communes replaced the orderly development plan. Those two radical measures were Mao's first major steps to combat institutional complacency and to promote novel experiments. The new measures aroused open opposition from other Party leaders, however, and signaled the crack in the Party's solidarity. Since then, China has been entangled in a power struggle that has severely disrupted economic development.

When the radical element was in control, as in 1958–1960 and 1966–1976, virtually all formal rules were abandoned, and the resulting anarchy caused economic failure. The damage caused by the Great Leap and the Cultural Revolution underlay the three trough years of 1961, 1967 and 1976. As Sun Chingwen, minister of the chemical industry, observed in March 1979, the three periods of relative stability were those of the First Five-Year Plan, the three years of readjustment (1963–1965), and the years after the smashing of the Gang of Four. "These were the times during which our country's economy developed relatively rapidly. When stability and unity were torpedoed, production invariably suffered setbacks."[52] The ups and downs of economic activities thus can be explained to a large extent as the outcome of shifts in politics and leadership.[53]

## APPRAISALS AND PROJECTIONS

China's economic experiences since 1949 suggest several generalizations concerning economic planning and development. First, despite Marxist claims that a centrally planned socialist economy is free of fluctuations, no planning mechanism can control at least two vital factors: the motivation of the peasants and the whims of nature. And, because agriculture remains the most significant component of China's national product, economic development will continue to be subject to periodic oscillations. Until China can achieve a breakthrough in industrial development, fluctuation will remain the main feature of its economy.

Second, the original idea of a centrally planned economy presupposed that the planning authority obtain three types of information in order to formulate its commands: (1) knowledge of the country's physical capacity – labor, land, capital, and raw materials; (2) information about the production functions of each commodity – the number and kind of inputs necessary for the production of each output and the possibilities of substituting one input for another in production; and (3) a preference function indicating the possibilities of substituting one type of output for another in order to maximize satisfaction. Such a "perfectly visible hand" does not exist in the real world, however. In the case of China, the plan often reflected the planners' subjective judgment, which did not always correspond to objective economic conditions, so there were always imbalances between savings and investment, between the targeted output and the inputs it required, and between the products produced and the products needed. In a market economy, in which numerous consumers and producers make separate decisions, the market mechanism can correct such imbalances. The correction of a mistake in a centrally planned system, however, not only takes time but requires a fine hand, for excessive tuning can cause severe vibrations.

Despite the continuous fluctuations, the long-term growth rate of the Chinese economy is still quite impressive. Using U.S. government estimates and 1952 as the base, Table 10.12 shows the 1952–1979 growth rates of GNP, per capita income, agricultural output, and industrial output. As that table shows, China's long-term GNP growth rate was 5.9 percent per year, and per capita income grew at an annual rate of 3.7 percent.[54] The growth rates of agriculture and industry differ greatly, being 2.4 percent for the former and 10.5 percent for the latter. Agricultural production has barely kept pace with population growth (2.2 percent) in the same period. As a result, food grain output per capita grew at merely 0.2 percent per year.

Within the industrial sector, crude oil registered a spectacular 23 percent annual growth rate. Although electric power and crude steel achieved growth rates well above the average, the growth rate for coal was below the average, and that of cotton cloth, at 4.4 percent, was less than half the growth rate for industry as a whole. The imbalance between the growth rates of the producer and consumer goods industries has constrained the growth of per capita consumption.

Compared with its neighbors, China's 1960–1976 growth rate in per capita GNP was lower than that of Japan, Taiwan, South Korea, Singapore, Thailand, Malaysia, North Korea, and Hong Kong but higher than that of India, Pakistan, the Philippines, Burma, and In-

Table 10.12
China's Long-term Growth Rates, 1952-1979

| Category | 1952 | 1979 | 1979 as % of 1952 | Annual Growth Rate (%) |
|---|---|---|---|---|
| National Income (billion current yuan) | 58.9 | 337 | 572 | 6.6 |
| GNP (billions of 1979 dollars) | 108.0 | 514 | 476 | 5.9 |
| Per Capita GNP (1979 dollars) | 190 | 505 | 266 | 3.7 |
| Population (millions) | 570 | 1,017 | 178 | 2.2 |
| Agricultural Production (index 1957=100) | 84 | 160 | 190 | 2.4 |
| Grain Output (million metric tons) | 161 | 332 | 206 | 2.7 |
| Grain Output Per Capita (kg.) | 283 | 307 | 108 | 0.2 |
| Cotton (million metric tons) | 1.3 | 2.2 | 169 | 2.0 |
| Industrial Production (index 1957=100) | 48 | 703 | 1,465 | 10.5 |
| Electric Power (billion KWH) | 7.3 | 282 | 3,863 | 14.5 |
| Coal (million metric tons) | 66.5 | 635 | 955 | 8.7 |
| Crude Oil (million metric tons) | 0.4 | 106 | 26,500 | 23.0 |
| Crude Steel (million metric tons) | 1.3 | 34.5 | 2,654 | 12.9 |
| Cotton Cloth (billion linear meters) | 3.8 | 12.2 | 321 | 4.4 |

Sources: The 1952 National Income is from Yang Jianbai and Li Xuezeng, "China's Historical Experience in Handling the Relations Between Agriculture, Light Industry, and Heavy Industry," Zhongguo shehui kexue (Social sciences in China) No. 3 (May 1980) p. 19. The 1979 figures are from P.R.C. State Statistical Bureau, "Communiqué on Fulfillment of China's 1979 National Economic Plan," Beijing Review 23:19 (May 12, 1980), p. 12. Others are from Table 10.4 and Table 10.5.

Table 10.13
Comparison of Average Annual Growth Rates for GNP and GNP Per Capita: China and Other Asian Countries, 1960–1976

| Countries | Growth rate of GNP | Growth rate of GNP Per Capita |
|---|---|---|
| China, People's Republic of | 5.7 | 3.6 |
| India | 3.5 | 1.2 |
| Japan | 9.1 | 8.0 |
| Pakistan | 6.1 | 3.2 |
| Philippines | 5.4 | 2.4 |
| Korea, Republic of | 9.6 | 7.3 |
| Burma | 2.9 | 0.7 |
| China, Republic of (Taiwan) | 9.0 | 6.2 |
| Malaysia | 6.7 | 3.9 |
| Thailand | 7.7 | 4.6 |
| Singapore | 9.5 | 7.5 |
| Hong Kong | 8.7 | 6.4 |
| Indonesia | 5.2 | 3.1 |
| Korea, Democratic People's Republic of | 8.0 | 5.2 |

Sources: Data for China are from Table 10.1. Data for other countries are derived from 1978 World Bank Atlas (Washington, D.C.: World Bank, 1978), pp. 16 and 23. All figures are in 1976 prices.

donesia (see Table 10.13). In 1976, China's GNP of $323.7 billion (U.S. government estimate in 1976 dollars) amounted to 53 percent of Japan's GNP, 43 percent of Soviet Russia's, and only 18 percent of that of the United States.

Looking forward, will the Chinese economy continue to grow at more or less the pace of the past three decades, or will it enter a new era of accelerating growth? Although the 1978 Ten-Year Plan for 1976–1985 set annual growth rates for industrial output at more than 10 percent and those of agriculture at 4 to 5 percent, recent adjustments have significantly reduced the pace of growth.

Between 1949 and 1978, based on data in Table 10.1, the multiple regression coefficients between the growth rate of GNP and the growth rates of agricultural output and industrial output have been estimated using the following formula:

$Y = \alpha + B_1X_1 + B_2X_2$ Where Y denotes the growth rate of GNP
$X_1$ stands for the growth rate of agricultural output
$X_2$ denotes the growth rate of industrial output
and $\alpha$ = the constant term, while $B_1$ and $B_2$ are the coefficients for agricultural and industrial output, respectively.

The results can be summarized as follows:

| $\alpha$ | $B_1$ | $B_2$ | $R^2$ | F-ratio | N |
|---|---|---|---|---|---|
| 0.099 | 0.5174 | 0.4150 | 0.95103 | 123.1 | 29 |
| (0.01216)* | (7.911) | (12.04) | | | |

*figures in parentheses are T-ratios

Since the coefficient of multiple regression is 0.95103, the change in the growth rate of GNP is significantly correlated to the change in the growth rates of agricultural and industrial output. Assuming that the resource base and economic system in China remain basically unchanged, a 10 percent growth in industry and a 4.5 percent growth in agriculture would result in a 6.5 percent increase in GNP ($Y = 0.099 + 0.5174 \times 4.5 + 0.4150 \times 10 = 6.5$). That growth rate would be 14 percent higher than that actually achieved in the past twenty-six years.

The attainment of the higher growth rate will largely depend on substantial improvements in agricultural production. China's agricultural output grew at only 2.3 percent a year during the 1952–1978 period, barely keeping pace with population growth but falling short of supporting a large-scale industrialization program. With less than 8 percent of the world's cultivated land, Chinese peasants have to support approximately one-fourth of the world's population. Given the available area of cultivatable land, its location, and its inherent fertility, doubling the agricultural growth rate from 2.3 percent to 4.5 percent is a formidable task that will require not only a much higher rate of capital investment in the agricultural sector, but also a thorough reform of the agricultural management and incentive system, which current Chinese authorities are unlikely to want to do. As a result, a breakthrough in agriculture is not yet in sight. Agricultural growth will more than likely continue at the pace of 2 to 3 percent and remain the major constraint on China's economic growth.[55]

In the industrial sector, a 10 percent growth rate will also require increased investment. The significant industrial growth since 1949 was made possible by a very high rate of investment in physical capital. Despite the claim made by Hua Guofeng that total investment in the 1978–1985 period will exceed that of the entire previous twenty-eight years, official statements in 1980 suggested that China has already had great difficulty in maintaining that high rate of investment. In 1979, total investment in capital construction was maintained at the scale achieved in 1978.[56] The thousands of construction projects that have been halted or postponed will affect the growth rate of industry. In fact, industrial output rose by only 8.5 percent in 1979 and 8.4 percent in 1980. The target for 1981 was set at only 3 to 4 percent.[57] With the new adjustment, it seems unlikely that the growth rate of industrial output during the 1978–1985 period will exceed 7 percent a year.

Assuming that the growth rate of agricultural output in the 1977–1985 period averages about 4 percent instead of 4.5 percent and that the growth rate of industrial output is 7 percent instead of more than 10 percent, the growth rate of GNP will be around 5 percent a year, slightly lower than the growth rate in the 1960–1976 period. For the period 1986–2000, as the economic base becomes larger, the probable ranges for annual growth rates are expected to decline to 2.5 to 3 percent for agriculture and 5 to 6 percent for industry, resulting in a GNP growth rate of 4 to 4.5 percent a year.

Those ranges of estimates for 1985 to 2000 are conjectural in nature, but they represent reasonable expectations of the impact of the current modernization efforts on GNP levels. An attainment of levels significantly below the lower estimates would indicate the failure of the modernization program. On the other hand, the probability of achieving levels considerably above the higher estimates will be small unless there are major ideological modifications, institutional reforms, large-scale foreign aid, and technological breakthroughs.[58]

To gain some perspective on China's future economic position in relation to the major industrial countries, the projected Chinese GNP in 1985 and 2000 may be compared to those for the United States, the Soviet Union, Japan, and the countries of the European Economic Community. During the 1960–1976 period, GNP growth rates averaged 4.9 percent for the Soviet Union, 9.6 percent for Japan, 3.5 percent for the United States, and 4.2 percent for the European Economic Community.[59] Assuming that the growth rates of those four economic powers will be scaled down as their economies mature, the estimated growth rate of GNP for the Soviet Union during 1977–1985 would be 4.5 percent; for the United States, 3.5 percent; for Japan, 7 percent;

and for the European Economic Community, 4 percent. In the 1986–2000 period, the growth rates are expected to be 3 percent for the United States, 6 percent for Japan, and 4 percent for the Soviet Union and the European Economic Community. The projected GNP for China at the end of this century will depend on which GNP figure is used as base. If the CIA estimate of $323.7 billion (1976 dollars) is used for 1976, China will enhance its relative share slightly from 6.7 percent of the total GNP of the five major powers in 1976 to about 7.5 percent in 2000 (see Table 10.14). By the year 2000, China's per capita income will be around $810–880 (1976 value), depending on the size of population, which is projected to be 1.1 billion to 1.2 billion persons.[60]

On the other hand, by using the Chinese official national income data ($129.63 billion in 1976) and adjusting to the Western GNP concept by adding 5 percent of capital depreciation and 16 percent of services, the 1976 GNP would be only $156.9 billion. In that case, China's

Table 10.14
Projected GNPs of China and Four Major Powers, 1985 and 2000
(in billions of 1976 U.S. dollars)

| Economy | 1976 | | 1985 | | 2000 | |
|---|---|---|---|---|---|---|
| | GNP | % | GNP | % | GNP | % |
| U.S.A | 1,691.6 | 34.8 | 2,306 | 32.2 | 3,592 | 27.6 |
| E.E.C. | 1,380.0 | 28.3 | 1,964 | 27.5 | 3,537 | 27.2 |
| U.S.S.R. | 921.7 | 18.9 | 1,370 | 19.2 | 2,467 | 19.0 |
| Japan | 550.2 | 11.3 | 1,012 | 14.1 | 2,425 | 18.7 |
| China | 323.7 | 6.7 | 502 | 7.0 | 971 | 7.5 |
| Total | 4,867.2 | 100.0 | 7,154 | 100.0 | 12,992 | 100.0 |

Notes and Sources: 1976 GNP figures are based on U.S. Central Intelligence Agency, Handbook of Economic Statistics 1977 (Washington, D.C., 1977), p. 31. Average annual growth rates of GNP for 1977–1985 are assumed to be 3.5 percent for the United States, 4 percent for the European Economic Community, 4.5 percent for the Soviet Union, and 7 percent for Japan. For the 1986–2000 period, annual growth rates are assumed to be 3 percent for the U.S., 4 percent for the E.E.C., 4 percent for the U.S.S.R., and 6 percent for Japan.

The GNPs for China are projected by assuming an average annual growth rate of 5 percent for 1977–1985 and 4.5 percent for 1985–2000. The rationales for the selection of these growth rates are explained in the text.

relative share in the total GNP of the five major powers would be only 3.8 percent at the end of this century, with a per capita income of \$400–\$430 (1976 dollars), a level achieved by most Third World countries in 1976.

## NOTES

1. Karl Marx and Friedrich Engels, *Manifesto of the Communist Party* (New York: International Publishers, 1948), pp. 14–15.
2. George J. Staller, "Fluctuations in Economic Activity: Planned and Free-Market Economies in 1950–1960," *American Economic Review* 54:3 (June 1964), pp. 385–395.
3. See Choh-ming Li, *The Statistical System of Communist China;* Nai-Ruenn Chen, *Chinese Economic Statistics;* Chu-yuan Cheng, *Communist China's Economy, 1949–1962,* Appendix; Ta-chung Liu and Kung-chia Yeh, *The Economy of the Chinese Mainland;* and Alexander Eckstein, *Communist China's Economic Growth and Foreign Trade* (New York: McGraw-Hill, 1966), Appendix A.
4. The most important works are Zhao Yiwen, *Xin zhongguo de gongye* [Industry in new China]; Niu Zhonghuang, *Woguo guomin shouru de jilei he xiaofei* [Accumulation and consumption in the national income of our country]; and P.R.C., State Statistical Bureau, *Woguo gangtie dianli meitan jixie fangzhi zaozhi gongye de jinxi* [The present and past of China's iron and steel, electrical power, coal, machinery, textile, and paper industries] (Beijing: Tongji Chubanshe, 1958).
5. Edgar Snow, "Talks with Chou En-lai: The Open Door," *New Republic* 164:13 (March 27, 1971), p. 20.
6. Nai-Ruenn Chen, "An Assessment of Chinese Economic Data: Availability, Reliability, and Usability," in U.S., Congress, Joint Economic Committee, *China: A Reassessment of the Economy,* pp. 54–55.
7. The English version of these two communiqués appeared in *Beijing Review* 22:27 (July 6, 1979), and 23:19 and 20 (May 12 and May 19, 1980).
8. Nai-Ruenn Chen, "An Assessment of Chinese Economic Data," p. 60.
9. Robert Michael Field, Nicholas Richard Lardy, and John Phillip Emerson, *A Reconstruction of the Gross Value of Industrial Output by Province in the People's Republic of China, 1949–1973* (Washington, D.C.: Foreign Diplomatic Analysis Division, Bureau of Economic Analysis, Department of Commerce, 1976).
10. Chu-yuan Cheng, *China's Petroleum Industry,* pp. 18–19.
11. K. C. Yeh, *Communist China's Petroleum Situation* (Santa Monica, Calif.: Rand Corporation, 1962), p. 1.
12. NCNA-Beijing, August 4, 1978.
13. Commentator, "A Warning Against Liars," *Renmin ribao,* July 8, 1980.
14. Commentator, "Defend Truth, Oppose False Reports," *Renmin ribao,* July 24, 1979, pp. 1–2.

15. Nai-Ruenn Chen, "An Assessment of Chinese Economic Data," p. 68.

16. For a detailed discussion, see Kang Chao, *The Rate and Pattern of Industrial Growth in Communist China* (Ann Arbor: University of Michigan Press, 1965); Alexander Eckstein, *The National Income of Communist China* (New York: Free Press, 1961); Ta-chung Liu and Kung-chia Yeh, *The Economy of the Chinese Mainland;* and Leo A. Orleans, "Chinese Statistics: The Impossible Dream," *American Statistician* 28:2 (May 1974), pp. 47–52.

17. Special studies dealing with important aspects of the Chinese economy are (1) Dwight H. Perkins, *Agricultural Development in China, 1368–1968* (1969); (2) Kang Chao, *The Construction Industry in Communist China* (1968); (3) Chu-yuan Cheng, *The Machine-Building Industry in Communist China* (1971); (4) John K. Chang, *Industrial Development in Pre-Communist China* (1969); and (5) Feng-hwa Mah, *The Foreign Trade of Mainland China* (1971). All these studies were published by Aldine in Chicago in the years indicated.

18. The four volumes are (1) *An Economic Profile of Mainland China,* 2 vols. (Washington, D.C.: Government Printing Office, 1967); (2) *People's Republic of China: An Economic Assessment* (Washington, D.C.: Government Printing Office, 1972); (3) *China: A Reassessment of the Economy* (Washington, D.C.: Government Printing Office, 1975); and (4) *Chinese Economy Post-Mao* (Washington, D.C.: Government Printing Office, 1978).

19. Liu Guoguang, "On Sustained High Rate of Growth," *Jingji yanjiu* No. 2 (February 1978), pp. 7–13.

20. Yang Jianbai and Li Xuezeng, "China's Historical Experience in Handling the Relations Between Agriculture, Light Industry, and Heavy Industry," p. 20.

21. Information for these two years is from P.R.C., State Statistical Bureau, *Ten Great Years,* pp. 57 and 159, and from Kang Chao, "Policies and Performance in Industry," in Alexander Eckstein, Walter Galenson, and Ta-chung Liu, eds., *Economic Trends in Communist China,* p. 580.

22. Chen Muhua, "To Realize The Four Modernizations, Population Growth Must Be Controlled in a Planned Way," *Renmin ribao,* August 11, 1979, p. 2.

23. Choh-ming Li, *Economic Development of Communist China,* pp. 102–107, and Ta-chung Liu and Kung-chia Yeh, *Economy of the Chinese Mainland,* p. 66.

24. World Bank, *1980 World Bank Atlas* (Washington, D.C., 1981), p. 6.

25. U.S., Central Intelligence Agency, *China: A Preliminary Reconciliation of Official and CIA National Product Data* (Washington, D.C., December 1979), p. 3.

26. Ibid.

27. The combined gross output value figure is from P.R.C., State Statistical Bureau, *Ten Great Years,* p. 16, and the NNP figure is from *Tongji yanjiu* No. 1 (January 1958), p. 11.

28. Robert Michael Field, Kathleen M. McGlynn, and William B. Abnett, "Political Conflict and Industrial Growth in China, 1965–1977," in U.S., Congress, Joint Economic Committee, *Chinese Economy Post-Mao,* p. 258.

29. Shi Zhengwen, "Readjusting the National Economy: Why and How?" *Beijing Review* 22:26 (June 29, 1979), pp. 13–18.

30. The 1958 figure is from P.R.C., State Statistical Bureau, *Ten Great Years,* p. 17, and the 1978 figure is from *Beijing Review* 22:27 (July 6, 1979), p. 37.

31. Chu-yuan Cheng, *Communist China's Economy, 1949–1962,* pp. 160–165.

32. Alexander Eckstein, "Economic Fluctuations in Communist China's Domestic Development," in Ping-ti Ho and Tang Tsou, eds., *China in Crisis,* vol. 1, bk. 2, pp. 691–729.

33. Dwight H. Perkins, "Plans and Their Implementation in the People's Republic of China," pp. 234–240.

34. Liu Rixin, "On the Relationship Between Agriculture and Heavy Industry," *Da gung bao* (Beijing), February 2, 1961.

35. Yang Jianbai and Li Xuezeng, "China's Historical Experience," p. 21.

36. This one-year lag was also observed by an economist in the P.R.C. (see Su Xing, "The Two-Way Struggle Between Socialism and Capitalism in China's Rural Areas After the Land Reform," *Jingji yanjiu* No. 7 [July 1965], pp. 5–15).

37. For details, see Chu-yuan Cheng, "Food and Agricultural Problems in Communist China," *Current History* 11:9 (September 1973), pp. 120–121.

38. Mao Zedong, "On the Question of Agricultural Cooperativization," in *Selected Works,* vol. 5, pp. 168–191.

39. For a study of cyclical evolution in farm policy during the 1950s, see G. William Skinner and Edwin A. Winckler, "Compliance Succession in Rural Communist China: A Cyclical Theory," in Amitai Etzioni, ed., *A Sociological Reader on Complex Organizations* (New York: Holt, 1969), pp. 410–430.

40. Chu-yuan Cheng, *Communist China's Economy, 1949–1962,* pp. 163–164.

41. Ibid., pp. 67–68.

42. Ibid., pp. 163–165.

43. For example, output at the Preliminary Rolling Plant of the Anshan Steel Complex in 1972 exceeded its designed capacity three times (*Hongqi* No. 8 [August 1973], p. 66). Truck production at the Changchun No. 1 Automobile Plant exceeded its designed capacity in 1966 (see Chu-yuan Cheng, "China's Machine-Building Industry," *Current Scene* 11:7 [July 1973], p. 5).

44. *Renmin ribao,* April 13, 1969.

45. *Peking Review* 14:3 (January 15, 1971), p. 10.

46. For a detailed discussion of this problem, see Kenneth Walker, "Ideology and Economic Discussion in China: Ma Yin-chu on Developmental Strategy and His Critics," *Economic Development and Cultural Change* 11:2 (January 1963), pp. 113–133. See also P. C. Chen, "Population Planning in China: Policy Evolution and Action Program" (Paper presented to the Conference on Public Health in the P.R.C., Ann Arbor, May 1972).

47. Kenneth Walker, "Ideology and Economic Discussion in China," pp. 117–118.

48. Ibid.

49. *New York Times,* August 13, 1979.

50. *Beijing Review* 22:31 (August 3, 1979), pp. 3–4.

51. "Economist Ma Yinchu Rehabilitated," *Beijing Review* 22:31 (August 3, 1979), p. 3.

52. Yu Youhai, "Use History as a Mirror, March Toward the Four Modernizations," FBIS, March 27, 1979, pp. 7-8.

53. For details of this subject, see Chu-yuan Cheng, "Leadership Changes and Economic Policies in China," *Journal of International Affairs* 32:2 (Fall/Winter 1978), pp. 255-273.

54. These growth rates are derived from GNP estimates by the U.S. government. Compared with other Chinese statistics, the figures may contain an upward bias.

55. The same conclusion was argued by Robert F. Dernberger and David Fasenfest, "China's Post-Mao Economic Future," in U.S., Congress, Joint Economic Committee, *Chinese Economy Post-Mao,* pp. 21-26.

56. Vice-Premier Yu Qiuli's report to the NPC, *Beijing Review* 22:26 (June 29, 1979), p. 9.

57. Xue Muqiao, "Adjust the National Economy and Promote Overall Balance," *Jingji yanjiu* No. 2 (February 1981), pp. 25-31.

58. Analysis in this section has greatly benefited from Nai-Ruenn Chen's work, "Economic Modernization in Post-Mao China: Policies, Problems, and Prospects," in U.S., Congress, Joint Economic Committee, *Chinese Economy Post-Mao,* pp. 202-203.

59. World Bank, *1979 World Bank Atlas* (Washington, D.C., 1979), pp. 16, 18, and 20.

60. According to Chinese government estimates, even if the natural population growth rate falls to zero by the year 2000, China's population will still reach 1.2 billion people (Editorial, "It Is Imperative to Control Population Growth in a Planned Way," *Renmin ribao,* February 11, 1980).

# 11

# The Industrialization Program

Of all the national goals pursued by the P.R.C. since 1949, the overriding one has been rapid industrialization. In the early 1950s, Mao Zedong emphatically asserted that "without industry, there can be no solid national defense, no people's welfare, and no national prosperity and power."[1] When China announced its First Five-Year Plan in 1955, the long-range objective was to establish a modern economy through "socialist industrialization."[2] In January 1975, Zhou Enlai called for the nation to embark on a two-stage modernization scheme so as to build China into a powerful modern socialist state by the end of this century. The pursuit of power status requires rapid industrialization. Apparently, both Mao and Zhou envisaged the establishment of an independent and relatively comprehensive industrial system as a prerequisite for the modernization of agriculture, national defense, science, and technology.[3]

This chapter will survey the process of industrialization in China during the past three decades and discuss the goals and priorities of industrialization; the path of expansion of modern industry; the performance of the industrial sector on the aggregate and subsectoral levels with regard to rate of output growth, productivity, and technological progress; the development program outlined by Hua Guofeng in February 1978 and the subsequent readjustment program adopted by the National People's Congress in June 1979 and August 1980; and the prospects for industrial development.

## GOALS AND PRIORITIES OF INDUSTRIALIZATION

The Chinese Communist leaders conceive of industrialization as "the marshalling of all efforts and resources for an industrialized state and a modernized national defense."[4] Although official statements often mention improvement in consumers' welfare, that assumes only a secondary place in the scale of priorities and is promised either as a distant goal or as a natural consequence of industrialization. Mechanization of agriculture is also expected to develop much more slowly than the rest of the industrialization process. Since 1949, the specific goals for industrialization can be ranked in the following order:

1. establishment of a comprehensive industrial base capable of producing machinery and equipment for industrial development
2. provision of military goods for national defense
3. building a technological base to catch up with advanced countries
4. production of machinery and equipment for agricultural mechanization

Not all of these tasks are always consistent or simultaneously feasible, and the emphasis has shifted from one to another in different periods and under different circumstances.

Throughout the entire period, the establishment of a comprehensive industrial system has underlain the industrialization program. The commitment to this goal stems from China's historical past. Between the Opium War in 1840 and the Communist victory in 1949, the Chinese economy was under the influence of Western industrial powers, and the industrial system was characterized by uneven geographical distribution and a high concentration on consumer goods production. Because of the lack of tariff protection, inadequate financial facilities, excessive internal levies, and insufficient technical know-how, Chinese industrialists could hardly compete with the foreign entrepreneurs. In 1936, about 42 percent of the industrial capital in China was owned by foreigners.[5] Since most foreign capital was invested only in the treaty ports, industries were clustered in the coastal provinces, which compose only 10 percent of the total land area but produced 77 percent of the gross value of factory output in 1949.[6] Prior to the Sino-Japanese War (1937–1945), nearly 92 percent of the industrial capital of China was invested in consumer goods industries, and in 1933, almost 85 percent of the gross value of industrial output was created by those industries. China had to rely on foreign supply for almost all of its producer goods and military products.

Determined to correct this lopsided development, the Chinese planners allocated the bulk of capital investment to producer goods in the First Five-Year Plan and the ensuring plans. As Li Fuchun, then chairman of the State Planning Commission, stated pointedly in 1955, "The purpose of industrialization is to achieve economic and political independence so that China can produce all the producer goods she needs and thereby free herself from relying on imports."[7]

To build a comprehensive industrial system, strenuous efforts were made to establish new industries and to strengthen weak links. The focus was on the iron and steel, chemical, metal-processing, and machine-building industries. Of the investment in industry during the First Five-Year Plan, 88.8 percent was allocated to heavy industry, leaving only 11.2 percent for light industry. Despite incessant changes in development strategies, the investment pattern remained unchanged. In 1979, 90 percent of industrial investment still went to heavy industry and only 10 percent to light industry.[8]

Within the sphere of heavy industry, the defense industry received high priority. In August 1952, the Second Ministry of Machine-Building Industry was inaugurated to supervise the defense industry, primarily the nuclear weapons program. Between 1952 and 1957, some forty major plants in the defense industry were built or expanded with Soviet aid. In 1958, in addition to strengthening the nuclear weapons program, the production of conventional weapons was accelerated. A Third Ministry of Machine-Building Industry was set up in September 1960 to undertake conventional weapons production. From May 1963 to December 1965, four new ministries of machine-building were added to supervise the production of a wide range of modern defense equipment, including electronics, telecommunications, and radio; artillery; submarines; missiles; and aircraft. Significant progress has been made in the rocket and missile program. In 1980, of the seventeen industrial ministries under the State Council, seven specialize in defense products.

The third major goal of industrialization is the acquisition and development of the latest technology. A two-pronged effort has been made: first, to set up new industries, such as instruments and meters, measuring and cutting tools, electronic equipment, computers, mining and petroleum equipment, petrochemicals, and a wide variety of industry previously nonexistent in China; and, second, to exploit foreign technology.

During the 1950s, new technology and equipment were imported on a large scale from the Soviet Union and Eastern Europe. In the 1960s, as the Sino-Soviet relationship deteriorated, China turned to Japan and Western Europe for know-how and industrial plants. Since 1978, in order to jump over intermediate stages of development, Beijing has undertaken a massive, broad-brush approach to industrialization by attempting to acquire Western technology and machinery to help modernize China's backward industrial base. That effort is to run through the remainder of the century. Specific weak sectors to be fortified by 1985 include steel, electric power, coal, petroleum, petrochemicals, electronics, transportation, and communications. In order to achieve self-reliance, China first has to establish a technological base.

The last major goal of industrialization is to furnish equipment for agricultural mechanization. In 1955, Mao Zedong declared that "without the realization of agricultural mechanization, China cannot solve the contradiction between the ever-increasing demand for marketable grain and industrial raw materials and the present generally low yield of staple crops."[9] In May 1958, the CCP Central Committee called on the whole country to work toward the mechanization of agriculture in three consecutive steps: a small-scale solution in five years, with 10 percent of the cultivated land being mechanized; a medium-scale solution in seven years, with half of the arable land being mechanized; and a large-scale solution in ten years, with most of the land being farmed with mechanical power. The new program created a tremendous demand for agricultural machinery and chemical fertilizers. Based on the historical experience of the Soviet Union, Japan, and the United States, the planners in Beijing mapped out tentative norms for the realization of agricultural mechanization, which required some 130 million horsepower for agricultural machinery, 800,000 to 1 million tractors, 400,000 heavy trucks, 20 million horsepower for irrigation machines, 24 million tons of chemical fertilizers, and 8 billion kilowatt-hours of electricity for rural consumption.[10] To meet these demands, a Ministry of Agricultural Machinery Industry was set up, and hundreds of machine-building plants were assigned to the production of farm tools and machines. By 1979, 1,600 agricultural machinery plants had been established in China. Almost every province, municipality, and autonomous region had built tractor and motor plants, and 98 percent of the counties in the country now have their own farm-machinery repair plants. Nevertheless, farm machinery is still inadequate – for example, official statistics in April 1980 show that there were only about 667,000 large and medium-sized tractors in the country[11] – and the output of chemical fertilizers in 1979 reached only about 10.65 million tons (plant nutrient content). The mechanization program appears to be far behind schedule.

Those four major goals of industrialization have dictated the direction of Chinese industrial development during the past three decades and are expected to guide its growth in the years ahead.

## PROCESS OF INDUSTRIAL EXPANSION

In 1952, on the eve of the First Five-Year Plan, industrial output in China accounted for only 18 percent of national income, as compared with agriculture, which accounted for 59.2 percent.[12] Of the combined gross output value of industry and agriculture, the share was 41.5 percent for industry and 58.5 percent for agriculture.[13] In 1979, industrial output represented 74.3 percent of the combined gross output value as against 25.7 percent for agriculture.[14]

The expansion of the industrial sector has followed different paths—the construction of large, integrated, and capital-intensive plants with foreign equipment and technology; the renovation of inherited enterprises in the coastal areas; and the erection of hundreds of thousands of labor-intensive small plants in the countryside.

The mainstay of industrialization is the construction and expansion of approximately 1,500 major integrated plants using foreign technology and equipment. In the 1949–1959 period, the 156 major industrial projects build with Soviet aid constituted the backbone of China's modern industry. Those 156 projects, together with 143 ancillary projects, absorbed over half of all industrial investment during the FFYP period. They included giant iron and steel complexes, nonferrous metallurgical enterprises, coal mines, oil refineries, chemical plants, power stations, and factories for the production of heavy machinery, precision instruments, automobiles, aircraft, and tractors. According to official Chinese reports, 50 to 70 percent of the equipment required for the 156 key projects was supplied by the Soviet Union. The three major iron and steel complexes in Anshan, Wuhan, and Baotou were all equipped with Soviet machinery. In the nonferrous metal industry, Soviet equipment was supplied for the construction of a tungsten plant in Anyang in Henan, a tin combine in Gejiu in Yunnan, an aluminum plant in Fushun in Liaoning, and a rolled aluminum plant in Harbin.

The most significant development in the 1949–1959 period, however, was the expansion of the machine-building industry. Originally merely a repair and assembling business, machine-building has become the foundation of modern Chinese industry. The Soviet aid to this industrial sector was comprehensive and extensive. Of the 156 Soviet aid projects, 63 units (or 40 percent) were for machine-

Table 11.1
Thirty-two Identifiable Machine-Building Plants Built with Soviet Aid, 1949–1959, by Fields

Machine Tools (4)
1. Shenyang first machine-tool plant
2. Wuhan heavy machine-tool plant
3. Shanghai machine-tool plant
4. Qiqihar No. 1 machine-tool plant

Tools (1)
5. Harbin measuring and cutting tool plant

Heavy Machinery (3)
6. Taiyuan heavy machinery plant
7. Fularki heavy machinery plant
8. Luoyang mining machinery plant

Ball Bearings (2)
9. Luoyang ball bearing plant
10. Harbin ball bearing plant

Radio and Electronics (4)
11. Southwest radio appliance plant in Chengdu
12. Chengdu radio plant
13. Beijing electronic tube manufacturing plant
14. Beijing wired communication equipment plant

Automobiles (1)
15. Changchun first automobile plant

Tractors (1)
16. Luoyang first tractor plant

Power Equipment (4)
17. Harbin steam turbine plant
18. Harbin boiler plant
19. Wuhan boiler plant
20. Harbin power equipment plant

Electrical Machinery (6)
21. Harbin electric instrument and meter plant
22. Shenyang cable and wireless plant
23. Shenyang transformer plant
24. Xian switch and rectifier plant
25. Xian voltage equipment plant
26. Xian high-voltage ceramics plant

Table 11.1 (continued)

Petroleum and Chemical Equipment (2)
27. Lanzhou petroleum equipment plant
28. Lanzhou petroleum and chemical equipment plant

Shipbuilding (2)
29. Wuchang shipbuilding plant
30. Dalian shipbuilding plant

Textile Machinery (1)
31. Yuci Jingwei textile machinery plant

General Machinery (1)
32. Shenyang pneumatic tool plant

Source: Chu-yuan Cheng, The Machine-Building Industry in Communist China (Chicago: Aldine, 1971), pp. 190-191.

building; 32 of those 63 projects were for civilian products, and the rest were for military products. The distribution of the 32 identifiable machine-building plants illustrates the Chinese effort to establish a comprehensive industrial base (see Table 11.1).

In energy, the Soviets helped China reconstruct the giant Fengman hydroelectric power plant near Jilin and designed and equipped the great Sanmenxia project in Northwest China. In the coal industry, the major construction works in Fuxin, Jiamusi, Fengfeng, Jixi, Huainan, and Fushun were all equipped with Soviet machinery.

The massive infusion of Soviet equipment and know-how proved invaluable in China's subsequent development. For almost ten years after the 1960 Soviet suspension of technical aid, China adopted an inner-directed, go-it-alone approach. Imports of whole plants from abroad dropped to negligible levels. During this period, the renovation of older industrial plants inherited from the pre-1949 era made great contributions to Chinese industrial growth.

Despite their low priority in Chinese investment policy and, hence, their lack of advanced capital equipment, the older plants – clustered in Shanghai, Tianjin, and other centers of China's prewar industrial development – formed the cutting edge of China's technological advance. Their primary function was to respond to shifts in domestic demand by providing an appropriate mixture of technical change drawn from both foreign and domestic progress. The petroleum equipment industry and the chemical fertilizer industry, two rapidly growing branches of China's modern industry during the self-reliance period, demonstrate the contribution of the old firms.

Prior to 1949, with the exception of a few factories making maintenance equipment and parts, virtually no plants specialized in the manufacture of petroleum equipment. Between 1949 and 1952, most of the needed equipment was supplied by the Soviet Union. Extensive geological surveying and prospecting during the FFYP period rapidly increased the demand for drilling machines and tools. In 1954, a number of small textile machinery plants in Shanghai were converted to produce relatively unsophisticated oil-extracting machines, drilling tools, oil pumps, and small compressors.

The opening of the Daqing oilfield in 1960 and the withdrawal of Soviet aid in the same year provided a new impetus for petroleum equipment manufacturing, and several dozen specialized plants and a few multiple-product factories were established in Shanghai, Harbin, and Tianjin. These plants produced large quantities of drilling rigs with 1,000–1,200 meter capacity. Experimental prototypes were built, and trial attempts to produce tower facilities for refineries were conducted. Most of the petroleum equipment was manufactured in general machinery plants build in prewar years. The first fractional distillation tower was successfully built by the Xinjian Machinery Plant in 1964, originally a small shipyard in Shanghai. A wing-type heat exchanger, another key piece of refining equipment, was produced at the Sifang boiler plant, also an old Shanghai factory. By 1964, the industry was capable of producing coke towers to decompose heavy oil into light petroleum, main-column extracting installations to make lubricating oil, heat exchangers, and various oil pumps. A large vacuum fractionating tower 27 meters high, 290 tons in weight, and 6.4 meters in diameter was produced in Shanghai during this period. With these developments, the petroleum equipment industry began to acquire meaningful proportions.

Since 1965, the petroleum equipment sector has tended to outperform the machine-building industry as a whole. Although unable to produce offshore drilling rigs, some petrochemical equipment, and a few of the more sophisticated instruments, the Chinese petroleum equipment industry now manufactures a wide range of products that can satisfy nearly 80 percent of the country's prospecting and exploration needs.[15]

The case of chemical fertilizers, in which output (in terms of nutrient content) rose from 0.2 million to 10.65 million tons between 1957 and 1979, again with little reliance on foreign equipment, provides even clearer evidence of the role of older firms. Beginning in

1962, fertilizer equipment was produced in Shanghai in quantity. In 1965, Shanghai turned out China's first equipment for urea manufacturing. Small fertilizer plants, which have provided the bulk of output growth since 1965, relied heavily on the old firms in Shanghai to supply the main equipment. Between 1970 and 1972, a group of more than 400 plants supplied more than 300 sets of equipment for synthetic-ammonia plants.[16]

In general, those older firms possessed not only a technical labor force with long years of experience but also a wide range of modern industrial departments, which could turn out a wide variety of products with relatively higher quality and a higher rate of return to capital than the Soviet-aided plants. During the FFYP period, not a single new major project of the machine-building industry was constructed in Shanghai, but the city still continuously increased its leading position for the trial manufacturing of heavy-duty and precision machinery and contributed the greatest share of capital accumulation to the state. In 1953–1957, Shanghai accumulated enough capital funds to account for one-third of the nation's total capital investment in industrial construction.[17]

Supplemental to the large modern and medium-sized plants are 350,000 small plants in cities, county seats, and rural areas. The initial impetus toward the expansion of rural industry came under the policy of "walking on two legs," which was advocated by Mao Zedong during the Great Leap Forward period. The collapse of the Great Leap led to the wholesale closing of most small plants. Then, as agricultural conditions stabilized and the opportunity cost of rural industrial ventures declined, official policy once again encouraged local industrial development. The volume of resources devoted to small factories has expanded steadily since 1963. During the Cultural Revolution, new guidelines urged the speeding up of the development of labor-intensive small-scale industry, which could link to simple domestic technology and could use the surplus labor in each locality. By 1972, 92 percent of the *xian* in the nation had erected networks of small plants capable of producing small-sized power machines, farm implements, and spare parts.[18] The large-scale expansion of small plants has enhanced their relative importance in several industrial sectors. In 1970, small coal mines reportedly turned out one-third of China's coal production, small chemical plants produced 43 percent of the chemical fertilizers, and small cement plants manufactured 40 percent of the cement output.[19]

In terms of ownership and technology, small-scale industry has comprised two separate segments: the more advanced state-owned sector and the primitive collective sector. The state-owned plants have consisted mainly of enterprises operated on the *xian* level. These plants derive fixed assets from the state budget and remit most of their profits to the state. The average size of the county plants, based on a sample study by the American Rural Small-Scale Industry Delegation, which toured China in 1975, was 379 workers.[20] The plants operate large quantities of machinery, sometimes including items obtained from leading national-level plants, and have their own machine shops, which produce considerable quantities of equipment for their own use. The bulk of the small-plant output comes from the county plants. The collective sector consists of enterprises that are owned, financed, and managed by communes, brigades, and teams. Most of those enterprises engage in the processing of grains, cotton, and other farm products; handicrafts; the repair of farm machinery; carpentry; and other sideline ventures. In 1973, official sources revealed that collective industry accounted for 3 percent of the fixed assets, 36.2 percent of industrial labor, and 14 percent of the industrial output value.[21] These statistics include collective enterprises in both urban and rural areas. According to an estimate by Thomas Rawski, the five major sectors of rural small plants (chemical fertilizers, cement, machinery, coal, and steel) accounted for only 6.3 percent of the estimated 1972 industrial output.[22] This figure would indicate that despite their large numbers, small plants provide only a fraction of the overall industrial output.

One rationale behind the construction of small-scale factories in the rural areas is the inadequacy of China's rural transport and marketing systems. Because of the expense, the only goods worth transporting between urban and rural locations are items of high initial price, low bulk, and easy transportability. The list of such goods generally does not include processed food or chemical fertilizers,[23] and those two items are more economically produced locally. A second reason for small-scale factories in the rural areas is the availability of local resources that are not being exploited by large-scale enterprises. Since small rural plants are closer to their markets than large urban enterprises are, they can better understand and meet the needs of their customers. Moreover, the Chinese planners hope that the small plants can bring modern technology to the countryside and thus gradually eliminate the gap between rural areas and city.

The development of rural small-scale industry is not conceived of as a substitute for urban-based large- and medium-scale industrialization, however. Between 1964 and 1974, an estimated 1,100 large modern enterprises were built in China. Official statistics show that the 1973 gross values of industrial output in Shanghai and Tianjin were more than double the levels of 1965, and in Beijing the value tripled.[24] In 1972, the political turbulence of the Cultural Revolution subsided, and China began to search for foreign technology again. Between January 1972 and May 1974, a total of 149 complete plants were purchased from abroad. Compared with the 1949–1959 period, several new trends marked China's renewed effort to expand modern industry. First, unlike the early development, which concentrated on machine-building and military products, the acquisitions of the 1970s centered on the areas of petroleum exploration and petrochemical and chemical fertilizer plants. Of the 149 complete plants imported, those three groups accounted for 66 percent of the plants and 60 percent of the cost.[25] The imported equipment will add a total annual production capacity of 13 million tons of fertilizer, 390,000 tons of synthetic fiber, and 4 million tons of sheet steel.[26] Second, in contrast to the 1950s when the Soviet Union supplied most of China's turnkey plants, Japan and Western Europe are now the chief suppliers of such plants. Third, most Soviet-aided plants of the 1950s were comparatively less efficient than the equipment then available in the West. The plants delivered in the 1970s were ultramodern and represented high-technology production equipment in terms of efficiency and quality.

In summary, the expansion of Chinese industry in the past three decades has followed three different paths. The large integrated plants built between 1949 and 1959 with Soviet technology and the new plants built in the 1970s with Japanese and Western equipment form the backbone of modern Chinese industry. The medium-sized and small industrial plants inherited from the pre-1949 era have been significant technical innovators and have been highly responsive to changing demands. They act as technological intermediaries between the bulk of the Chinese producers and the outside world. They have also provided millions of skilled workers for the newly established industrial centers. The small-scale industrial plants spread over the countryside have developed rudimentary facilities to support agriculture. Although they have performed a supplementary function for the urban industrial sector, they are not in the mainstream of China's industrialization.

## INDUSTRIAL PERFORMANCE

The paucity of systematic statistical data has made it difficult to assess the performance of Chinese industrial development. Official statistics for gross output value and for physical volumes of major products are available only for the years 1949–1959 and 1977–1980, and all data for the years 1960 to 1976 are fragmentary and sometimes inconsistent. To fill the statistical gap, one has to use independent estimates made by Western economists. The following analysis of China's industrial performance will focus on the aggregate growth rate, the output of selected industries, labor productivity, and technological progress.

*Aggregate Growth Rates*

Chinese statistics on industrial growth are expressed in gross output value, and the gross output data are collected by the factory reporting method. Under that system, each enterprise reports the gross value of its output in constant prices. The gross value is the net of intraenterprise transfers but includes the costs of purchased raw materials and semifinished inputs. In other words, the semifinished inputs produced within an enterprise are not included in the gross output value, but those purchased from other enterprises are counted as a part of the gross value. This method introduces a substantial amount of double-counting and tends to inflate the share of gross output value of industry in relation to agriculture. In 1978, calculated in gross output value, the relative share of industry and agriculture in their combined gross value was 74.4:25.6. The use of net output value, however, changes that ratio to 56.7:43.3.[27]

Despite that defect, the gross output value figures constitute the only official comprehensive data for both civilian and defense sectors that can partly reflect the progress of industry as a whole. The annual growth rates of industrial output between 1949 and 1979 shown in Table 11.2 have been derived from official Chinese data.

As an alternative, the U.S. government has constructed a value-added index based on physical data for forty-two commodities produced by eleven branches of industry. The results are summarized in Table 11.3. The value-added index represents only the civilian sector, since published sources reveal no data on defense products. Because of the divergent coverage, the indexes in Tables 11.2 and Table 11.3 are not comparable.

Together, those two tables reveal a pattern of Chinese industrial growth. First, like the general trend of the national economy, aggregate industrial growth has displayed sharp fluctuations since 1949. Almost uninterrupted progress between 1949 and 1966, with rapid growth in 1949–1952 and 1958–1960, was followed by a sharp decline in industrial output due to the failure of the Great Leap. The retrenchment reached a trough in 1961. Steady growth resumed in 1962–1966, and by 1965, industrial output had surpassed that of 1960. After 1966, industrial output again declined because of the disruption caused by

Table 11.2
Growth of Gross Value of Industrial Output,
1949-1979 (at 1957 constant prices)

| Year | Gross Output Value (in million yuan) | Indexes 1952=100 | Indexes 1957=100 |
|---|---|---|---|
| 1949 | 12,590 | 41 | 18 |
| 1950 | 17,170 | 56 | 24 |
| 1951 | 23,662 | 77 | 34 |
| 1952 | 30,828 | 100 | 44 |
| 1953 | 40,140 | 130 | 57 |
| 1954 | 46,670 | 151 | 66 |
| 1955 | 49,273 | 160 | 70 |
| 1956 | 63,183 | 205 | 90 |
| 1957 | 70,400 | 228 | 100 |
| 1958 | 117,000 | 380 | 166 |
| 1965 | 139,400 | 452 | 198 |
| 1976 | 326,160 | 1,058 | 463 |
| 1977 | 372,800 | 1,210 | 530 |
| 1978 | 423,100 | 1,372 | 601 |
| 1979 | 459,100 | 1,489 | 652 |

Annual Growth Rates (%)

| | | | |
|---|---|---|---|
| 1949-1958 | 28.1 | 1949-1977 | 12.8 |
| 1949-1979 | 12.7 | 1957-1977 | 8.7 |
| 1952-1958 | 24.9 | 1952-1978 | 10.6 |
| 1952-1979 | 10.5 | 1957-1978 | 8.9 |
| 1957-1979 | 9.3 | 1965-1978 | 8.9 |
| 1965-1979 | 8.9 | | |

Sources and Notes: 1949-1958 figures are from P.R.C. State Statistical Bureau, Ten Great Years (Beijing Foreign Languages Press, 1960), p. 87. The original figures for 1949-1956 are expressed in 1952 prices. They are converted into 1957 prices by using a coefficient of 0.898.

1965 figures are based on U.S. Central Intelligence Agency, China: Economic Indicators (Washington, D.C., December 1978), p. 17. This figure is a reconstruction of the official index that is based on provincial data.

1976-1978 figures are derived from Yu Qiuli, "Report on Draft of the 1979 National Economic Plan," Xinhua yuebao (New China monthly) No. 6 (June 1979), p. 22. The 1979 figure is from P.R.C. State Statistical Bureau, "Communiqué on Fulfillment of China's 1979 National Economic Plan," Beijing Review 23:19 May 12, 1980), p. 13.

Table 11.3
Indexes of Chinese Industrial Growth: Gross Output Values vs. Net Value Added, 1949-1977

| Year | Value Added in Industrial Production | | | Gross Value of |
|---|---|---|---|---|
| | Total | Producer Goods | Consumer Goods | Industrial Output |
| 1949 | 20 | 14 | 28 | 49 |
| 1950 | 27 | 21 | 36 | 50 |
| 1951 | 38 | 30 | 48 | 51 |
| 1952 | 48 | 39 | 60 | 52 |
| 1953 | 61 | 51 | 73 | 53 |
| 1954 | 70 | 62 | 82 | 66 |
| 1955 | 73 | 66 | 81 | 70 |
| 1956 | 88 | 84 | 94 | 90 |
| 1957 | 100 | 100 | 100 | 100 |
| 1958 | 142 | 161 | 117 | — |
| 1959 | 173 | 204 | 131 | — |
| 1960 | 181 | 232 | 114 | — |
| 1961 | 105 | 123 | 80 | — |
| 1962 | 111 | 132 | 83 | — |
| 1963 | 134 | 153 | 109 | — |
| 1964 | 161 | 180 | 135 | 164 |
| 1965 | 199 | 211 | 183 | 198 |
| 1966 | 232 | 251 | 206 | 250 |
| 1967 | 202 | 208 | 196 | — |
| 1968 | 221 | 226 | 215 | 220 |
| 1969 | 266 | 290 | 233 | 280 |
| 1970 | 316 | 350 | 272 | 344 |
| 1971 | 349 | 407 | 272 | 380 |
| 1972 | 385 | 452 | 295 | 420 |
| 1973 | 436 | 513 | 334 | 463 |
| 1974 | 455 | 536 | 347 | 484 |
| 1975 | 502 | 602 | 368 | 532 |
| 1976 | 502 | — | — | 544 |
| 1977 | 574 | — | — | 620 |
| Annual Growth Rate (%) | | | | |
| 1949-1977 | 12.7 | | | |
| 1957-1977 | 9.1 | | | |

Sources and Notes: The indexes of value added are based on physical output series, whereas the gross value index is a reconstruction of the official index that is based on provincial data. See U.S. Central Intelligence Agency, China: Economic Indicators (Washington, D.C., December 1978), p. 17, and U.S. Central Intelligence Agency, China: A Statistical Compendium (Washington, D.C., July 1979), p. 3.

the Cultural Revolution; that decline was arrested in 1969. A new upsurge, mainly in the producer goods sector, brought the index to a new high in 1975. The rampage of the ultraleftists and the severe Tangshan earthquake in July 1976 dealt a blow to industry, and output declined again. The years 1977-1979 were considered by official sources to be a recovery period from that disruption. The average annual growth rate for those three years was 12 percent, much higher than the 8.7 percent achieved during 1957-1977. Second, there has been a large disparity between the growth in producer goods and that in consumer goods. Between 1952 and 1978, when the producer goods industry grew at an annual rate of 13.7 percent, consumer goods went up at an annual rate of only 9.1 percent. Third, the annual growth rate of industrial output has diminished as the industrial base has been enlarged. Taking 1949 as a base year, the growth rate was 28.1 percent between 1949 and 1958 and only 12.7 percent between 1949 and 1979. When the base year shifted to 1952, the growth rate was 24.9 percent between 1952 and 1958 and 10.5 percent between 1952 and 1979. The growth rate diminished to only 9.3 percent between 1957 and 1979 and fell to only 8.9 percent between 1965 and 1979. In 1980, the growth rate was 8.4 percent, and the growth rate for 1981 dropped to only 3-4 percent. If past records can serve as an indicator for the future, the growth rate of Chinese industry in the 1981-1985 period may be around 7 percent a year.

### *Subsectoral Growth Rates*

The physical outputs of twenty-five major civilian industries in various years are shown in Table 11.4 and Table 11.5. The figures are derived from official sources and provide a more detailed and tangible picture of China's industrialization than do the general indexes discussed above. These output figures generally conform with the growth pattern of the industry as a whole. First, the growth rates for 1952-1979 were generally higher than those for 1957-1979, which in turn were higher than those for 1965-1979, indicating a diminishing rate of growth for most industrial products. Second, with some exceptions – particularly coal, soda ash, and timber – the output of producer goods scored higher growth rates than the average of industry as a whole, but the growth rates for consumer goods – particularly cotton cloth, cotton yarn, processed sugar, and salt – were much lower than the average growth rate. Some new products – such as watches, bicycles, and sewing machines – did register an above-average growth rate, however.

Table 11.4
Production and Growth Rates of Major Producer Goods, 1952-1979

| Products | Physical Output | | | | Annual Growth Rates (%) | | |
|---|---|---|---|---|---|---|---|
| | 1952 | 1957 | 1965 | 1979 | 1952-1979 | 1957-1979 | 1965-1979 |
| Electric Power (million KWH) | 7,300 | 19,300 | 62,000 | 281,950 | 14.5 | 13.0 | 11.4 |
| Crude Oil (million metric tons) | 0.436 | 1.458 | 11,374 | 106.15 | 22.6 | 21.5 | 17.3 |
| Natural Gas (million cubic meters) | negl. | 600 | 9,200 | 14,510 | — | 15.6 | 3.4 |
| Coal (million metric tons) | 66.5 | 130.7 | 232.2 | 635 | 8.7 | 7.5 | 7.5 |
| Pig Iron (thousand metric tons) | 1,929 | 5,936 | 13,800 | 36,730 | 11.5 | 8.5 | 7.2 |
| Crude Steel (thousand metric tons) | 1,349 | 5,350 | 2,200 | 34,480 | 12.8 | 8.8 | 7.7 |
| Finished Steel (thousand metric tons | 1,110 | 4,290 | 9,100 | 24,970 | 12.2 | 8.4 | 7.5 |
| Chemical Fertilizer (thousand metric tons) | 194 | 803 | 7,600 | 53,530 | 23.2 | 21.0 | 15.0 |
| Sulfuric Acid (million metric tons) | 0.2 | 0.6 | — | 7.0 | 14.1 | 10.3 | — |
| Soda Ash (million metric tons | 0.2 | 0.5 | — | 1.5 | 7.7 | 5.1 | — |

| | | | | | | | |
|---|---|---|---|---|---|---|---|
| Caustic Soda (million metric tons) | 0.08 | 0.2 | — | 1.8 | 22.8 | 10.5 | — |
| Cement (thousand metric tons) | 2,860 | 6,860 | 16,280 | 73,900 | 12.8 | 11.4 | 11.4 |
| Timber (thousand metric tons) | 11,200 | 27,870 | — | 54,390 | 6.0 | 3.1 | — |
| Machine-made Paper (thousand metric tons) | 371.8 | 913 | — | 4,930 | 10.0 | 8.0 | — |
| Electric Generators (thousand kilowatts) | 29.7 | 312.2 | 800 | 6,212 | 21.9 | 14.5 | 15.7 |
| Mainline Locomotives (units) | 20 | 167 | — | 573 | 13.2 | 5.8 | — |
| Freight Cars (units) | 5,792 | 7,300 | — | 16,042 | 3.9 | 3.6 | — |
| Trucks (units) | 0 | 7,500 | — | 186,000 | — | 15.7 | — |

Sources and Notes: Figures for 1952-1957 are from P.R.C. State Statistical Bureau, Ten Great Years (Beijing: Foreign Languages Press, 1960), pp. 95-100. Figures for chemical fertilizer and machine-made paper are adjusted from U.S. Central Intelligence Agency, China: A Statistical Compendium (Washington, D.C., July 1979), pp. 8-9; also 1965 figures. Figures for 1979 are from P.R.C. State Statistical Bureau, "Communiqué on Fulfillment of China's 1979 National Economic Plan," Beijing Review 23:19 (May 12, 1980), p. 13.

Table 11.5
Production and Growth Rates of Major Consumer Goods, 1952-1979

| Products | Physical Output | | | | Annual Growth Rates (%) | | |
|---|---|---|---|---|---|---|---|
| | 1952 | 1957 | 1965 | 1979 | 1952-1979 | 1957-1979 | 1965-1979 |
| Cotton Cloth (billion linear meters) | 3.8 | 5.0 | 5.8 | 12.15 | 4.4 | 4.1 | 5.4 |
| Cotton Yarn (million bales) | 2.7 | 4.7 | 7.3 | 14.67 | 6.5 | 5.3 | 6.0 |
| Processed Sugar (million metric tons) | 0.5 | 0.9 | 1.5 | 2.5 | 6.1 | 4.7 | 4.4 |
| Salt (million metric tons) | 4.9 | 8.3 | — | 14.77 | 4.2 | 2.7 | — |
| Bicycles (thousand units) | 80 | 806 | 1,792 | 10,090 | 19.6 | 12.2 | 15.5 |
| Watches (thousand units) | — | — | 1,200 | 17,070 | — | — | 24.8 |
| Sewing Machines (thousand units) | 84 | 267 | 1,571 | 5,870 | 17.0 | 15.0 | 11.6 |

Sources: Figures for sewing machines in 1952 and 1957 are from Chu-yuan Cheng, The Machine-Building Industry in Communist China (Chicago: Aldine, 1971), p. 263. Others are from the same sources as Table 11.4

*Labor Productivity*

During the First Five-Year Plan period, official statistics show that labor productivity in industrial enterprises went up by 51 percent, with an average annual growth rate of 8.7 percent.[28] In 1978, an official statement revealed that the increase of labor productivity in the 1952–1957 period accounted for 59 percent of industrial growth while increases of labor input accounted for the remaining 41 percent.[29]

The increase in labor productivity in the early years stemmed from two sources. First, there was a steady rise in the capital-labor ratio. According to a study by Robert M. Field, the number of workers in the 1952–1957 period increased by 49.5 percent while the net value of industrial capital rose by 131.9 percent (see Table 11.6). As a result, the capital-labor ratio increased by 55.1 percent.

Since output per unit of labor (labor productivity) equals output per unit of capital (capital productivity), multiplying capital per unit of labor (capital-labor ratio), algebraically, the relationship is:

$$\frac{Q}{L} = \frac{Q}{K} \times \frac{K}{L}$$

($Q$ represents quantity of output, $K$ represents capital, and $L$ represents the average number of workers.) As capital investment increased, the mix of factor inputs changed, and by 1957, considerably more capital was used per worker than had been used in 1952. Real capital stock not only increased faster than the average number of workers, but after 1953, it also increased faster than output. As a result, substantial increases in labor productivity were accompanied by a steadily increasing capital-labor ratio and some decreases in the productivity of capital.[30]

Second, although industrial output had returned to its pre–World War II level by 1952, industrial capacity was not fully used in that year. A more intensive use of existing capacity was another important factor contributing to the growth of labor productivity during the FFYP period.

After 1958, however, the growth of labor productivity diminished. During the three years of the Great Leap, the number of workers in heavy industry rose sharply. Consequently, the number of workers and employees in the industrial enterprises owned by the state rose from 7.48 million in 1957 to 23.16 million in 1958; the number decreased slightly to 21.44 million in 1960. Since then, the total number of workers and employees has continued to rise, reaching more than

Table 11.6
Indexes of Output, Labor, Net Capital, and Productivity in Chinese Industry, 1952-1957

| | 1952 | 1953 | 1954 | 1955 | 1956 | 1957 |
|---|---|---|---|---|---|---|
| Output | | | | | | |
| Index (1952=100) | 100.0 | 120.7 | 138.6 | 146.2 | 190.4 | 209.6 |
| Annual % change | | 20.7 | 14.8 | 5.5 | 30.2 | 10.1 |
| Labor | | | | | | |
| Index (1952=100) | 100.0 | 115.7 | 124.2 | 121.0 | 133.9 | 149.5 |
| Annual % change | | 15.7 | 7.3 | -2.6 | 10.7 | 11.6 |
| Capital | | | | | | |
| Million 1952 yuan | 9,942 | 10,844 | 12,480 | 14,718 | 18,124 | 23,056 |
| Index (1952=100) | 100.0 | 109.1 | 125.5 | 148.0 | 182.3 | 231.9 |
| Labor Productivity | | | | | | |
| Index (1952=100) | 100.0 | 104.3 | 111.5 | 120.8 | 142.2 | 140.2 |
| Annual % change | | 4.3 | 6.9 | 8.3 | 17.7 | -1.4 |

Notes: Labor productivity calculated in this table is lower than the official figure. Official output indexes are gross output value; in this table, the output indexes are value added.

Source: Robert M. Field, "Labor Productivity in Industry," in Alexander Eckstein, Walter Galenson, and Ta-chung Liu, eds., Economic Trends in Communist China (Chicago: Aldine, 1968), pp. 647, 656, and 658.

40 million by 1978.[31] Between 1957 and 1978, the gross value of industrial output (based on official statistics) increased 500 percent, and the number of workers and employees in industry went up 435 percent. As a result, labor productivity in those twenty-one years rose only 15 percent, with an annual growth rate of 0.7 percent, substantially less than that achieved during the FFYP period (see Table 11.7).

The sharp decline in labor productivity in the post-1957 period is

Table 11.7
Labor Productivity of Full-Time Workers and Employees in the State-Owned Industrial Enterprises
(in 1970 constant prices)

| Period | Annual Average Growth Rates (%) |
|---|---|
| Rehabilitation Period (1949-52) | 11.5 |
| First Five-Year Plan (1953-57) | 8.7 |
| Second Five-Year Plan (1958-62) | -5.4 |
| Adjustment (1963-65) | 23.1 |
| Third Five-Year Plan (1966-70) | 2.5 |
| Fourth Five-Year Plan (1971-75) | 1.3 |
| Fifth Five-Year Plan (1976-78) | 1.7 |
| 1950-1978 | 4.6 |
| 1957-1978[a] | 0.7 |

Sources: (a) From text. Other figures are from Yang Jianbai and Li Xuezeng, "China's Historical Experience in Handling the Relations Between Agriculture, Light Industry, and Heavy Industry," Zhongguo shehui kexue (Social sciences in China) No. 3 (May 1980), p. 29.

due to several factors. First, unlike the orderly and steady growth of output during 1949–1957, industrial production fell back in the wake of the Great Leap Forward and again during two phases of the Cultural Revolution, thereby slowing the growth rate for industrial output. Second, as one top Chinese leader pointed out, during those twenty-one years, wages and salaries for most workers and employees were virtually frozen.[32] Since remuneration did not correspond to individual contribution, workers' incentives were impaired. Third, between 1950 and 1978, although fixed assets of industry increased more than twenty-five times[33] and the number of workers increased only thirteen times, the productivity of capital declined dramatically. Official statements have revealed that a large portion of productive fixed assets have lain idle or been wasted. In 1978, idle capacity amounted to one-third of the total capital construction investment in that year. Even for equipment in use, the rate of utilization was extremely low. In many machine-building enterprises in the Beijing area, the rate of utilization of machinery and equipment fell below 30 percent of capacity. The productivity of capital in the 1970s reportedly was only one-half to one-third of that during the FFYP.[34] In recent decades, the sharp decline of capital productivity and the near stagnation of labor productivity have become the most serious stumbling blocks for China's industrialization.

*Technological Progress*

Despite a slowdown in production growth, the technical level of Chinese industry has made impressive progress since 1949. First, there has been a constant evolution in the product mix, so the output composition of the 1970s differed significantly from that of the 1950s. This change is particularly evident in the machine-building industry, the core of China's industrialization. In 1979, the machine-building industry was no longer merely a repair or an assembly business but a major manufacturing sector of more than twenty branches. It was turning out fairly sophisticated machinery and equipment, including blast furnaces with a capacity of 1,513 cubic meters and an annual production capacity of over 800,000 tons of iron; open-hearth furnaces with a daily output of 500 tons; prerolling machines with a diameter of 1,150 millimeters; 100,000-ton-class ocean freighters; petroleum extracting and refining equipment; computers; and many precision machine tools. By 1979, China was producing 1,600 different kinds of machine tools, which could satisfy 99 percent of domestic demand.[35] Similarly, the Chinese metallurgical industry has trial manufactured many new kinds of steel alloys by using paragenetic iron ores containing copper, vanadium, titanium, and crystallites and by using manganese, silicon, molybdenum, and boron. Some 500 new steel products were indispensable for the development of petroleum equipment, power-generating equipment, precision instruments, automobiles, tractors, and shipbuilding. By 1979, the metallurgical industry could produce more than 20,000 varieties of steel products.[36] The continuous addition of new products changed the structure of the steel industry. In 1958, the petroleum industry could produce only 79 varieties of products, and most high-grade products had to be imported. By 1979, China was producing more than 600 kinds of petroleum products, significantly improving its production mix.[37]

Second, China has acquired an impressive amount of new technology and has filled many gaps in its modern industry. The establishment of automobile, tractor, aircraft, and electronics industries; the development of rockets, ballistic missiles, satellites, and a nuclear industry; and the expansion of the petrochemical industry have significantly raised the country's technological level.

Starting from almost no base at all, phenomenal progress has been made in the aerospace industry, which depends heavily on advanced electronics, computers, chemical fuels, and telecommunications. Visible achievements in the aerospace industry are good indicators of the level of advanced technology developed in a country. The aerospace industry now provides China with strategic delivery systems for its nuclear weapon and defense systems. Chinese medium-range ballistic missiles (MRBMs) first became operational in 1966. In 1970, China began to develop intermediate-range ballistic missiles (IRBMs) to cover 3,219–5,633 kilometers in a multistage configuration. In May 1980, China launched its first intercontinental ballistic missile (ICBM) from Xinjiang, sending it some 9,656 kilometers to a target zone near the Solomon Islands in the Pacific.[38] On April 24, 1970, China successfully orbited an earth satellite, and by June 1980, seven more satellites had been placed in orbit. In 1980, official sources indicated that China was on the brink of launching a manned satellite. All of those developments signify advancing technology.

In general, China's technological level in 1980 was still fifteen to twenty years behind that of the United States, Japan, and Western Europe in basic industries such as energy, steel, and machinery. In some specific fields, such as the aircraft and automotive industries, the technological gap between China and the advanced countries may be twenty to thirty years.

The low level of technology reflects extremely low efficiency in the utilization of energy and raw materials. In 1978, the aggregate nationwide conversion efficiency of primary energy (fossil fuels and hydroelectricity) was just 28 percent, compared with 51 percent in the United States, 57 percent in Japan, and 40 percent in Western European countries. In the power industry, the average 1978 coal consumption by large thermal power plants in China was 433 grams of standard coal (or 3,031 kilocalories) per kilowatt-hour, compared with 360 grams in the United States and 330 grams in the Soviet Union. Because of backward technology and poor management, electricity consumption per ton of steel in the Chinese metallurgical industry had risen steadily from 665 kilowatt-hours in 1965 to 1,102 kilowatt-hours in 1977, compared with 400 in the United States and between 300 and 500 kilowatt-hours in most industrialized nations.[39] In 1979, China's total consumption of energy was comparable to that of Japan, but its industrial output value was only one-fourth that of Japan's. That fact indicates the extent of the inefficiency in Chinese industry.

## MODERNIZATION PROGRAM

In view of China's productivity stagnation and technological backwardness, the industrial modernization program adopted in February 1978 was an ambitious one. Basic industries such as steel, coal, petroleum, electric power, and nonferrous metals received first priority; in 1978, capital investment in light industry accounted for a mere 10 percent of industrial investment. Although light industry's share increased to 12 percent in 1979 and 15 percent in 1980, heavy industry still forms the core of the current modernization program.

### *Steel Industry*

For years, Chinese Communist leaders have termed the steel industry the "key link" in industrial development. In the first decade of the People's Republic, that industry achieved rapid progress. The Soviet Union helped with the expansion of the Anshan Iron and Steel Company in Liaoning and with the construction of two steel complexes in Wuhan and Baotou. By 1952, production of crude steel had already surpassed pre-1949 highs. In 1957, the output of crude steel was four times that of 1952, rising from 1.35 to 5.35 million tons. During the Great Leap Forward, small iron and steel backyard furnaces were built by the hundreds of thousands, giving rise to exaggerated claims of huge increases in iron and steel production. Because those plants were using large amounts of valuable raw materials and labor to produce a nearly useless product, many of them had to be closed down in 1959.

In the meantime, the large modern sector of the steel industry continued to expand. Installation of new equipment was speeded up, and an attempt was made to increase production by using equipment around the clock with practically no shutdown for maintenance and repair. That attempt, together with the introduction of poor grades of iron in the modern plants, reduced quality and damaged equipment. Nevertheless, useful production did increase considerably, though not as much as the government announced. The claimed increase in steel production from modern plants more than doubled from 5.35 million tons in 1957 to 12.45 million tons in 1960. The total steel output, including that of both modern and small plants, amounted to 18.67 million tons in 1960[40] (see Table 11.8).

During the retrenchment period following the Great Leap, almost all of the small plants were closed down. Production of steel fell sharply to only 8 million tons in 1961 and did not recover the level claimed for 1960 until 1970, when 17.8 million tons were produced. Since 1970, small and medium steel plants have again played an increasing role. Steel output reached 25 million tons in 1973. After 1974, rising political turmoil led to work stoppages in major steel centers, and the steel output dropped to 20.5 million tons in 1976. The 1960–1976 period was one of sharp fluctuations with only small gains in output. Capacity utilization in 1976 was less than 70 percent, with almost 10 million tons of operable steel-making capacity lying idle. In late 1977, moreover, 3 million to 4 million tons of new capacity came on line with the completion of 1.5-million-ton blast furnaces at Anshan and the activation of new steel-making facilities at Wuhan and Benxi. These additions boosted total capacity to about 34 million tons in 1978.[41]

The spurt in production in 1978 lifted China to the fifth largest producer of steel in the world–behind the Soviet Union, the United States, Japan, and West Germany. On a per capita basis, however, China was the second lowest of thirteen major steel-producing countries. Its per capita output of 31.6 kilograms in 1978 was only about 5 percent of the U.S. per capita output and 4 percent of Japan's (see Table 11.9).

In the 1976–1985 development plan of 1978, the Chinese leaders placed great emphasis on modernizing the steel industry, and ten steel projects that were called for involved the construction of two brand new integrated steel complexes. One was to be constructed at Baoshan, a northern suburb of Shanghai, at a planned cost of $20 billion and with a designed capacity of 6 million tons of steel per year.[42] Another was to be built in eastern Hebei Province with a projected capacity of 10 million tons. The Nippon Iron and Steel Com-

Table 11.8
China's Production of Crude Steel, 1949–1980

| Year | Million Metric Tons | Index (1957=100) | Year | Million Metric Tons | Index (1957=100) |
|---|---|---|---|---|---|
| 1949 | 0.158 | 3 | 1965 | 12.2 | 228 |
| 1950 | 0.606 | 11 | 1966 | 15 | 280 |
| 1951 | 0.896 | 17 | 1967 | 10 | 187 |
| 1952 | 1.349 | 25 | 1968 | 9 | 168 |
| 1953 | 1.774 | 33 | 1969 | 16 | 299 |
| 1954 | 2.225 | 42 | 1970 | 17.8 | 333 |
| 1955 | 2.853 | 53 | 1971 | 21 | 393 |
| 1956 | 4.465 | 83 | 1972 | 23 | 430 |
| 1957 | 5.35 | 100 | 1973 | 25 | 467 |
| 1958 | 11.08 | 207 | 1974 | 21 | 393 |
| 1959 | 13.35 | 250 | 1975 | 24 | 449 |
| 1960 | 18.67 | 349 | 1976 | 20.5 | 383 |
| 1961 | 8 | 150 | 1977 | 23.7 | 443 |
| 1962 | 8 | 150 | 1978 | 31.7 | 593 |
| 1963 | 9 | 168 | 1979 | 34.5 | 645 |
| 1964 | 9.6 | 179 | 1980* | 33 | 617 |

* Planned Figures

Sources: 1949-1958 -- P.R.C. State Statistical Bureau, Ten Great Years (Beijing: Foreign Languages Press, 1960), p. 95. 1959-1963 -- Alfred H. Usack, Jr., and James D. Egan, "China' Iron and Steel Industry," in U.S. Congress, Joint Economic Committee, China: A Reassessment of the Economy (Washington, D.C., 1975), p. 276. 1964-1978 -- U.S. Central Intelligence Agency, China: The Steel Industry in the 1970s and 1980s (Washington, D.C., May 1979), p. 3. 1979 -- P.R.C. State Statistical Bureau, "Communiqué on Fulfillment of China's 1979 National Economic Plan," Beijing Review 23:19 (May 12, 1980), p. 13.

pany was to supply equipment for the first plant, and West Germany was to provide equipment for the second. However, the second project was canceled in December 1978. Other major projects in the Ten-Year Plan adopted in 1978 included the continued construction of the Banzhihua plant in southern Sichuan and the expansion and renovation of existing major plants in Anshan, Wuhan, Baotou, Beijing, Benxi, and Maanshan. The 1985 target, originally set in 1978, was a steel output of 60 million tons, with further expansion to approxi-

Table 11.9
Comparison of Steel Production in Selected Countries, 1978

| Countries | Steel Production (million metric tons) | Per Capita Production (kilograms) |
|---|---|---|
| USSR | 151.0 | 577.7 |
| United States | 124.0 | 567.8 |
| Japan | 102.1 | 887.8 |
| West Germany | 41.2 | 670.0 |
| China | 31.7 | 31.6 |
| Italy | 24.3 | 428.6 |
| France | 22.8 | 427.0 |
| United Kingdom | 20.3 | 363.1 |
| Poland | 19.3 | 551.4 |
| Czechoslovakia | 15.3 | 1,013.2 |
| Brazil | 12.1 | 104.9 |
| India | 9.5 | 14.4 |
| Mexico | 6.4 | 97.3 |

Sources: U.S. Central Intelligence Agency, China: The Steel Industry in the 1970s and 1980s (Washington, D.C., May 1979), p. 3.

mately 180 million tons in 1999 at the conclusion of the twenty-three-year grand plan.[43]

In early 1979, the Chinese authorities admitted that the original plan was "overambitious" and substantially revised it. It was estimated that the proposed expansion program would have cost $40 billion, or 8 percent of the total capital investment for the Ten-Year Plan. Moreover, since 1957, China has been able to add, on the average, only 1.3 million tons of new steel-making capacity annually. A production goal of 60 million tons by 1985 would have required an additional 4 million tons of capacity each year for seven years – an unrealistic target under the best of circumstances. The Chinese leaders decided to slash the output goal for 1985 to 45 million tons.[44]

In 1979 and 1980, the steel industry bore the brunt of the economic readjustment plan, and the construction of thirty-eight large and medium-sized steel projects was terminated. More than 240 small iron-smelting plants and small mines were also eliminated. Total capital outlays for the metallurgical industry in 1979 were slashed by 45 percent. China produced 37 million tons of steel in 1980, 7.6 percent more than that in 1979. In 1981, as the policy shifted from developing heavy industry to light industry, the steel output target was set at 33 million tons, 11 percent less than in 1980.[45] The goal of 60 million tons will probably not be reached until 1990 or later.[46]

*Petroleum Industry*

Large outlays for new industrial plants create an enormous demand for foreign exchange, and the petroleum industry is expected to play a critical role in that area. Originally identified as the weakest link in China's modern industry, China's petroleum industry enjoyed a spectacular growth between 1960 and 1978. In 1957, China produced a mere 1.46 million tons of crude oil per year, which only met 45 percent of domestic needs. A dramatic change began in 1965 when the Daqing oilfield in Heilongjiang Province began to operate on a large-scale basis. Subsequently, the Shengli oilfield on the Shandong Peninsula and the Dagang oilfield in the Tianjin area were opened (see Figure 11.1). China's output of crude oil doubled between 1960 and 1965, doubled again by 1969, and by 1980 equaled 2.1 million barrels a day, or 106 million tons a year, nineteen times China's 1960 output and seventy times its 1957 output. In crude oil output, China ranked eighth in the world in 1978.

The rapid growth in China's crude oil output in recent decades has raised hopes that China might become a major oil exporter, and the policy of exporting crude oil in exchange for foreign equipment and technology was the backbone of the 1976–1985 modernization plan. In May 1977, Hua Guofeng announced that China would build ten new oilfields comparable in size to Daqing, which produced 50 million tons, or half of China's crude oil output, in 1977. Although Hua did not announce the output target for crude oil production, a later official source gave an output target of 250 million tons of crude oil by 1985.[47]

During the 1977–1980 period, seven new oilfields were officially begun, and several offshore oilfields were under preliminary exploration.

1. The Renqiu oilfield on North China's central Hebei Plain, with an estimated annual output of 10 million tons of crude oil in 1979.
2. The Dongpu oilfield in the border area of Shandong and Henan provinces along the lower reaches of the Huang He. Still in the initial stages of development, this oilfield is an extension of the Shengli oilfield.

Figure 11.1
China's Major Oilfields and Crude Oil Production

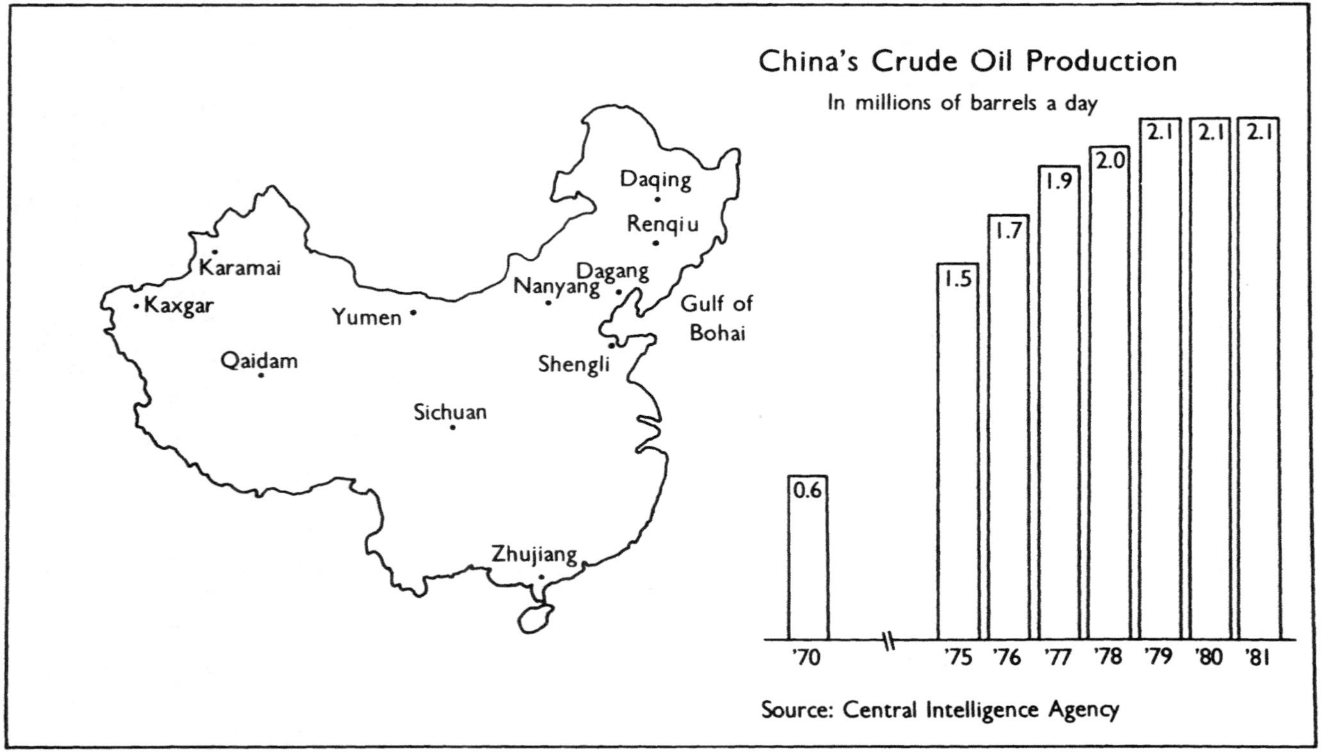

3. The Nanyang oilfield in southern Henan Province, with an estimated output of 3.7 million tons by 1980.[48]
4. The Liaohe oilfield in Liaoning Province, with an annual output of 5 million tons in 1980.
5. The Zhenwu oilfield in northern Jiangsu Province. This field is in the early stages of development.
6. The Nanjiang oilfield in the southern part of Xinjiang Autonomous Region.
7. The northern Daqing oilfield bordering Daqing, with deposits expected to produce 3 million tons of crude oil a year.[49]

The operation of these new oilfields added about 20 million tons of crude oil a year, but not the 150-million-ton increase anticipated by the Chinese leaders. More promising are the offshore oil reserves from the Huang Hai to the Nan Hai, including the Bohai oilfield in the Bohai Wan of the Huang Hai; the Nahai oilfield close to Guangzhou; the Zhujiang oilfield at the mouth of the Zhu Jiang; and the Beibuwan oilfield in the Gulf of Tonkin. An estimated 4 billion to 7 billion tons of crude oil may lie in petroliferous regions off China's extensive coastline.[50]

Oilfield construction requires tremendous outlays of capital to procure the massive drilling rigs and sophisticated equipment necessary to extract large quantities of oil. China will also need to build tens of thousands of kilometers of pipelines to transport the crude oil to export terminals. Between 1953 and 1974, China invested some $9 billion in its petroleum industry, half of which was for purchase of foreign equipment.[51] To increase crude oil production from 92 million tons in 1977 to 250 million tons in 1985, based on the capital-output ratio of the past twenty-one years and taking into account the rising cost of foreign machinery, China would have to invest $40 billion to $50 billion in the petroleum industry, a figure approximating 7 percent of the total investment in the original 1976–1985 modernization plan.

Extensive geological surveys will also be needed for most of these oilfields. Western oil experts regard China's seismic surveys as "unmethodical and of only moderate quality."[52] A low technological level and poor management have resulted in many accidents. Official reports disclosed that more than 1,000 offshore oil accidents have occurred since 1975, killing more than 100 people. The most severe accident involved the sinking of an offshore oil rig in November 1979 in the Bohai Wan, causing the death of 72 crew members and the loss of a $34-million offshore drilling platform imported from Japan.[53]

To solve the financial and technical difficulties, China dropped its established policy of self-reliance and invited Japanese and Western oil companies to participate in China's oil development. By the autumn of 1979, many Western oil companies were carrying out seismic surveys in about eight concession areas spread across the Huang Hai and the Nan Hai. Under risk contracts, the companies bear 100 percent of the cost, hoping eventually to negotiate drilling and production contracts.

The first joint venture, signed on December 6, 1979, provided for joint Sino-Japanese development of the Bohai Wan. A consortium led by the Japan National Oil Company assumed exploration costs of $120 million for 24,500 square kilometers in the southern and western Bohai Wan. Development costs are to be shared – 51 percent assumed by China and 49 percent by Japan. Over a fifteen-year period, 15 percent of the produced oil will go to China, and the remaining 85 percent will be divided equally. In effect, China will retain 57.5 percent of production, and 42.5 percent will go to Japan. If everything works out as expected, production could begin by early 1984.

Unless foreign oil companies participate heavily in developing China's petroleum industry, the growth rate of China's crude oil output may continue to decline. During 1973–1975, the average annual growth rate of the crude oil output was 20 percent. The rate fell to 13 percent in 1976, 8 percent in 1977, rose slightly to 11 percent in 1978, and dropped to only 1.9 percent in 1979, with zero growth in 1980. The 1981 output target was set at only 100 million tons, 6 percent below the 1980 output. This slowdown in the rate of growth would seem to reflect difficulties in exploiting the existing fields and the obsolescence of much of China's exploration, production, and refining equipment. Until China can utilize its offshore oil resources, the annual growth rate of crude oil production is unlikely to exceed 4 percent. By 1985, the total crude output may reach only 120 million tons instead of the 250 million tons that is planned.

### *Coal Industry*

In contrast to the rapid growth of the petroleum industry, the coal industry, which provides 70 percent of China's primary energy, has experienced an erratic rate of growth, trending downward from 14 percent growth per year in 1952–1957 to 7.7 percent per year in 1957–1978. Two factors are primarily resonsible for the diminishing rate of increase: the geographic disparity between the regions needing coal and those with coal reserves, and the relatively small investment in the coal industry over the past two decades. Although Manchuria has ranked highest in regional coal production, it possesses only small coal reserves. In 1970, Manchuria produced 30 percent of China's total coal, although it possessed but 2.7 percent of the estimated coal reserves. Since the rich coal mines near the major metallurgical centers in southern Liaoning, such as Benxi and Fushun, have been mined for more than half a century, the most-accessible and best-situated coal veins have already been depleted. Recovery costs will rise, making it difficult to sustain the former high rates of growth.

Inadequate investment in the construction of new coal mines has also caused the stagnation in coal production. Since 1960, the priority in energy development has apparently shifted from coal to oil, with a sharp curtailment in the funds available for the development of the coal industry. Increases in coal production have therefore relied heavily on small, locally run mines instead of on the development of large-scale major shafts. In 1977, small mines were said to have produced 33 percent of China's coal. By relying on small mines, the Chinese planners opted for a short-term solution to a long-term problem.

In the 1976–1985 modernization program, Beijing planned to double coal production between 1978 and 1987, with a targeted output of more than 1 billion tons per year in 1987. This target implies an average annual growth rate of 7.2 percent compared with the 6.6 percent average growth rate achieved by the large mines during the early 1970s. The ambitious goal reflects the growing energy requirements of the modernization plan as well as China's decision to halt the substitution of oil for coal in order to save oil for export.

Because Beijing envisages industrial expansion more in terms of large-scale than small-scale enterprises, most of the mammoth increase in coal production will have to come from the large mines. The original Ten-Year Plan calls for the opening of eight major coal centers, each with a designed capacity of more than 10 million tons. Those eight coalfields reportedly have a verified aggregate reserve of 120 billion tons, and about 100 million tons of output is expected to come from the new coal bases by 1987. The three major coalfields under construction are:

1. The Huainan and Huaibei coalfields in East China, which have proven deposits of well over 22,000 million tons. These fields are stepping up construction of seven pairs of pit shafts, with an aggregate capacity of 14.1 million tons.
2. The Yanzhou mining area on the southwestern plain in Shandong. This area will add two modern coal pits, each with an annual production capacity of 3 million tons.

3. A new coalfield with an annual capacity of 20 million tons to be constructed at Huolinhe on the Horqin grasslands in Nei Monggol. The opencast mine, one of China's biggest, was designed by two West German corporations. A new 400-kilometer railway from Tongliao in Nei Monggol to the coalfield has been constructed.

Other major coal centers under construction or being expanded include the Kailuan coal mines in Hebei Province, the Datong coal mines in Shanxi Province, the Pingdingshan coal mines in Henan Province, the Xuzhou coal mines in Jiangsu Province, and the Liupanshui coal mines in Guizhou Province.[54] A large part of the output increase, however, will come from the mechanization of existing coal mines. According to Xiao Han, minister of the coal industry, one-third of the increments in coal production through 1985 will spring from increased mechanization, and the rest will come from minor investment projects and a more intensive use of existing capacity.

Since the construction of new mines and the mechanization of existing ones are the keys to achieving coal targets, a rapid expansion of domestic manufacturing of mining equipment and massive imports of foreign facilities are essential to solve basic extraction problems and to increase coal production. Because of the industry's low priority in the past, domestic manufacturers of mining equipment have concentrated on the needs of other extractive industries, notably the ferrous and nonferrous metals industries. It will be difficult for those manufacturers to convert to the production of coal mining equipment. On the other hand, the availability of foreign exchange and foreign credit acts as a constraint on imports of foreign equipment. In addition, China's lack of recent experience will mean long lead times to bring new mine facilities on stream. Given these limitations, it appears very unlikely that China can double its coal output over the next decade.

### *Electric Power Industry*

Electric power constitutes another bottleneck for China's industrial modernization. Between 1949 and 1979, some 100 major power stations and more than 86,000 small-scale stations were constructed in various parts of the nation.[55] Installed capacity in September 1979 was officially reported as more than 50 million kilowatts, thirty times the capacity in 1952.[56] In 1979, electric power production in China reached 282 billion kilowatt-hours, making China the sixth largest electric-power-generating country in the world. The official statistics put annual growth at 15 percent between 1949 and 1979 but only at 13 percent between 1957 and 1979. In the 1971–1975 period, the average annual growth rate was only 11 percent. Consequently, there exists a widespread shortage of electric power, which has adversely affected the economy. A 10 percent rate of industrial growth per year would require a 13 to 14 percent annual growth rate in the power industry. The 1976–1985 plan called for the construction of thirty major power stations, twenty of which were to be hydropower stations.

China's emphasis on hydroelectric power stems from the fact that the country possesses a potential hydropower capacity of 680 million kilowatts. If fully exploited, this potential could generate electric power equivalent to 14 billion tons of coal. In 1980, only 2.4 percent of the potential was being exploited,[57] but eleven large hydroelectric stations, with a total designed capacity of 10.94 million kilowatts, are under construction. The largest project is the Gezhouba hydropower stations in the middle reaches of the Chang Jiang. The project consists of two hydroelectric power plants with a combined capacity of 2.71 million kilowatts and is located near Yichang in Hubei Province. Upon completion, the two stations will supply 13,800 million kilowatt hours of electricity a year, approximately 5 percent of the 1979 electricity output.[58]

The second largest hydropower station is the 1.6-million-kilowatt Longyang Gorge station on the upper reaches of the Huang He near Xining, capital of Qinghai Province. Within a stretch of 900 kilometers east of the Longyang Gorge, six other hydroelectric power stations, with an aggregate capacity of 2.4 million kilowatts, are already in operation. Those seven stations, with a total capacity of about 4 million kilowatts, will form the hub of a power grid for Northwest China.[59]

Other major hydroelectric stations being planned or under construction are

- the Wuqiangxi station in Hunan Province, with a capacity of 1.5 million kilowatts
- the Gongzui station on the Dadu He in Sichuan Province, with a capacity of 750,000 kilowatts
- the Xierhe station in Yunnan Province, with a capacity of 255,000 kilowatts
- the Wujiangdu station in Guizhou Province, with a capacity of 630,000 kilowatts
- the Baishan station on the Songhua Jiang in Jilin Province, with a capacity of 900,000 kilowatts
- the Dahua station in Guangxi Province, with a capacity of 400,000 kilowatts

the Manas He station in Northwest Xinjiang Province and the Yangbajain geothermal power station in Tibet, each with a capacity of 600,000 kilowatts[60]

Apart from the construction of hydropower stations, coal-fired power plants are to be built at the Datong coal mines in Shanxi Province, with a capacity of 1.2 million kilowatts, and at the coal centers of Huainan and Huaibei in East China, with a capacity of 2 million kilowatts. A number of large and medium-sized steam power plants are also being built or expanded in several major industrial cities and coastal areas. These projects, when completed, should enable China to expand its capacity by 6 million to 8 million kilowatts per year, compared with a 5-million-kilowatt average annual increase in recent years. Even assuming the completion of these projects, however, the electricity supply will still have difficulty keeping pace with the rising demand. As Yu Qiuli pointed out at the national work conference on the coal industry in July 1980: "It takes heavy investment and a long time to complete hydropower generating projects. These projects may not soon supply enormous amounts of energy. The energy needed for developing the national economy will mainly rest on the coal industry for some time."[61]

### *Machine-Building Industry*

Although the machine-building industry was not singled out for expansion in the 1976–1985 plan, it has played a crucial role in China's industrialization. In official statements, the industry is often referred to as the basis for technological transformation of the national economy and the pillar of national defense. In 1949, machinery accounted for only 2.7 percent of the nation's gross industrial output value. Since 1952, however, the industry has been given a high priority in development plans, and by 1966, its relative share in the total gross industrial output value had increased to 12 percent.[62] By 1980, the machinery industry's share of the total had risen to 25 percent, making it one of the most dynamic branches of Chinese industry.

Compared with other industrial sectors, the growth rate of the machinery industry was 21 percent between 1949 and 1975 and 14.5 percent between 1957 and 1975. The growth rate has increased more rapidly than total producer goods output and twice as rapidly as overall industrial output.[63]

Investment priorities in machine-building industries have changed according to the objectives of whatever five-year plan happens to be in force. In the First Five-Year Plan period, new investment was mostly in two new sectors: power-generating equipment and transportation equipment. During 1958–1960, in order to meet the rising demand created by the large-scale expansion of the iron and steel industry, the manufacturing of metallurgical and mining equipment developed rapidly. Between 1963 and 1966, emphasis was placed on the manufacture of chemical and petroleum equipment. In more recent years, agricultural machinery appears to have had the highest priority. The 1976–1985 plan stipulated that 70 percent of all major farm processes should be mechanized by 1980, and 85 percent by 1985. In early 1979, the Ministry of Agricultural Machinery was restored. To greatly expand agricultural machinery production during 1978–1980, the state planned to supply 50 percent more steel for the manufacture and repair of farm machines than it had during the previous three-year period. Nevertheless, because the agricultural machinery industry still confronts numerous problems—such as poor machine quality, the lack of standardization, and a limited range of available equipment and accessories—the content of the mechanization program has been dramatically cut back, and quantitative targets have been quietly abandoned.

Other machinery areas slated for expansion in the 1976–1985 plan were heavy machinery for coal mines and the petroleum and electrical industries. The mechanization of coal mines requires large quantities of hoists, winches, drilling rigs, and refining facilities. For electric power, China is now producing 200,000-kilowatt steam turbine generating units and 200,000- to 300,000-kilowatt hydraulic turbine generating units. Efforts are being made to produce 300,000-kilowatt steam turbine generating units.[64]

In the defense sector, strenuous efforts have been made in recent years to manufacture turbofan jet engines based on the Rolls-Royce Spey designs. The development of a Chinese ICBM also commanded a high priority for the machine-building industry. In September 1979, an Eighth Ministry of Machine-Building was added, raising the number of machinery ministries in charge of defense products to seven. The number of such ministries would indicate that in the modernization of national defense, the machine-building industry plays a critically important role.

### *Light Industry*

Light industry, which consists of the textile, food processing, paper-making, sugar refining, and a wide array of consumer goods industries, was the backbone of China's modern industry in 1949, when it accounted for 75 percent of the gross output value of industry. In the years since 1949, light industry has been accorded a very low priority, receiving only 5 percent of total capital investment and achieving a moderate rate of growth. Between 1952 and 1978, when the gross output value of heavy industry surged by 26.8 times, light industry registered only an 8.7-fold increase.[65]

Despite its relatively slow progress, light industry still represented 46.7 percent of China's gross industrial output value in 1980, and it has played an important role in capital formation and employment. During the past thirty years, one-fifth of China's state revenue, or 44 percent of the capital investment fund, came from profits of and taxes paid by light industry.[66] The products of textile and other light industries constituted more than one-half of the nation's total volume of retail trade, and more than 10 million workers were employed in light industry in 1979. Of China's 350,000 industrial enterprises in 1980, 60,000 were engaged in light industrial productions.

In an attempt to correct the structural imbalance of industry, the Chinese planners shifted the focus from heavy to light industry in the 1979–1981 readjustment plan. In 1979, many provinces and municipalities set up special organizations to promote textile and light industries, and priority was given to the needs of the textile and light industries for supplies of raw and semifinished materials, fuel, power, and funds. The share of capital investment for light industry increased from 5.4 percent in 1978 to 5.8 percent in 1979 and about 8 percent in 1980. In 1980, state loans for textile and light industries came to 2 billion yuan. In addition, $300 million were assigned for importing machinery and raw materials. As a result of increasing investment and material supplies, light industry output in 1979 scored a 9.6 percent growth, surpassing the 7.7 percent growth of heavy industry for the first time in almost two decades. In 1980, the output value of light industry registered a 17.4 percent jump over the corresponding period of 1979, compared with a mere 1.6 percent increase for heavy industry.[67]

The mainstay of light industry in China is the textile industry, which has been one of the most significant sectors in modern Chinese industry. In the 1950s, the number of spindles added far exceeded the total accumulated during the fifty years before 1949. After 1958, the textile industry shared the same fate as other light industries and suffered from many problems. As the bulk of capital investment was concentrated in heavy industry, very little went to textile and other light industries. Most of the facilities were built in the 1930s and early 1940s and have become obsolete. In Shanghai, 75 percent of the textile machines and 90 percent of the papermaking machines are of pre-1949 vintage. Productivity is low, and the consumption of fuel and raw materials is very high, resulting in extremely high costs of production.[68] Moreover, most light industries rely heavily on agriculture for raw materials. In 1978, 68.4 percent of the raw materials for textile and other light industries came from agricultural products. The stagnation of agriculture therefore hinders the growth of light industry.

To remedy these drawbacks, the Chinese authorities have carried out some important reforms in recent years. One new measure is to expand the supplies of nonagricultural raw materials. During the past few years, China has imported four big modern chemical fiber plants. The Jinshan General Petrochemical Works in Shanghai, capable of producing 100,000 tons of synthetic fiber per annum, was completed in 1979. Two new plants have been constructed in Liaoning and Sichuan, and the fourth is under construction in Tianjin. By 1985, chemical fibers will account for around 40 percent of textile raw materials, thus gradually releasing light industry from the constraints of agriculture.[69]

Another major measure is an increase in the production of high-value consumer goods. Plans are being contemplated for the production of over 300 kinds of durable consumer goods, such as quartz watches, high-frequency automatic double-calendar watches, multigear bicycles, multipurpose electric sewing machines, color television sets, and washing machines. China's first color television kinescope plant is under construction in the suburbs of Xianyang in Shaanxi Province. Equipped with Japanese machinery, the plant will produce 960,000 self-convergent color kinescopes.[70] In recent years, television-set manufacturing has become a shining star in the Chinese consumer goods industry. In 1980, the production target was set for 2 million television sets, up 53 percent from 1979 and 135 percent from 1978.

Taken as a whole, light industry remains rather backward in China. The technical levels of many products still remain at the 1940 and 1950 level. Products are poor in quality, design, and packing, which renders them far from satisfactory in meeting both domestic demand and international competition.

### *Railroads and Harbors*

Besides developing the manufacturing and energy-related industries, the 1976–1985 development program called for the expansion of China's railroad system and the expansion and construction of harbors. China's railroads increased from 24,500 kilometers in 1949 to 51,300 kilometers in 1978, with an average increase of 900 kilometers per year. About 75 percent of the new railroads were built in western China, which used to have almost no railroads. The 1976–1985 plan called for the completion of six new trunk railroads. Major lines that have been completed recently or are under construction include:

1. The Southern Xinjiang Railroad, which extends from Turfan to Korla in Xinjiang Uygur Autonomous Region.[71]
2. The Qinghai-Xizang Railroad between Xining, capital of Qinghai, and Lhasa, capital of Xizang. The section between Xining and Golmud, both in Qinghai Province, is now under construction.
3. The Anhui-Jiangxi Railroad is a 560-kilometer trunk line that links the southern provinces and the lower reaches of the Chang Jiang with the northern network.
4. The Beijing–Nei Monggol Railroad connects Beijing with Tungliao in Nei Monggol. This 400-kilometer trunk line will bring coal from the Huolinhe colliery to North China.
5. The new north-south railroad network starts at Taiyuan in Shanxi Province, passes through Jiaozuo in Henan Province and Zhicheng in Hubei Province, and terminates at Liuzhou in Guangxi-Zhuang Autonomous Region. This new trunk line runs parallel to the Beijing-Guangzhou Railroad and links Taiyuan in the North with Liuzhou in the South. From Taiyuan, the new line will connect with the Beijing-Baotou Railroad in the north at Datong. From Liuzhou, it will link with the Hunan-Guangxi and Guizhou-Guangxi Railroads.[72]

Since most of the new railroads are in western China while China's industry is still concentrated in the eastern coastal areas and in the Northeast where railroads were built before 1949, the volume of cargo handled by the older railroads still accounts for 85 percent of the total. Several major trunk lines, such as the 1,760-kilometer east-west trunk line extending from the coastal city of Lianyungang in Jiangsu to Lanzhou in Gansu Province and the 2,000-kilometer north-south trunk line from Beijing to Guangzhou, are overburdened. Therefore, a second objective of the 1976–1985 plan was to double-track eight trunk lines and to electrify five lines. These two measures, when completed, are expected to expand transport capacity between 50 and 100 percent.[73]

To facilitate imports and exports, major harbors along the eastern coast will be renovated, expanded, and mechanized. Noteworthy harbors along China's coast, from north to south, include Dalian, Qinhuangdao, Tianjin, Qingdao, Shanghai, Huangpu, and Zhanjiang. Dalian, the biggest deep-water harbor in the Northeast, is the leading oil terminal in China. The terminal went into operation in July 1976 and can handle 100,000-ton-class tankers. In the 1970s, the harbor was accommodating an average of 700 to 800 oil tankers annually, and further construction will enable the port to accommodate tankers of more than 100,000 tons.[74] The port of Qinhuangdao, west of Dalian, is northwest of the Bohai Wan, and a huge oil wharf is under construction there. Tianjin harbor lies at the western tip of Bohai Wan and is the site of the Dagang oilfield. These three northern harbors will become the main terminals for shipping crude oil from the Daqing and Dagang oilfields to Japan, the Philippines, and other coastal industrial centers.

Qingdao harbor in Jiaozhou Wan of Shandong Peninsula has oil storage facilities under construction. Shanghai, China's biggest trade port, has built or rebuilt berths to accommodate ships of up to 50,000 tons. Zhanjiang harbor, which lies in Leizhou Wan in southern China, is the dispersal point for the crude oil produced by the Maoming Shale Combine and was the first Chinese port capable of handling 50,000-DWT (deadweight ton) tankers. In recent years, an oil bunkering wharf has been constructed. Chinese oil exports to Hong Kong and Southeast Asia must come from Zhanjiang harbor.

## PROBLEMS AND PROSPECTS

As of the end of 1980, the modernization programs outlined above were still in a process of adjustment, and many of them may be suspended or canceled. Although the long-term prospects for Chinese industrial development appear quite promising, the short-term outlook is less sanguine. Many formidable problems remain to be solved.

A basic dilemma stems from the trade-off between employment and efficiency. Since 1949, the Chinese government has pursued a policy of maintaining high employment at the expense of efficiency. The result was overstaffing, underemployment, and a steady decline in labor productivity. As a part of the modernization program, Beijing has adopted a new policy emphasizing improved efficiency. The large-scale acquisition of Western technology and equipment will reduce labor input in production, and under the new management system, enterprises are encouraged to trim excessive personnel and use part of the wage bill saved for worker and staff bonuses, provided production quotas are fulfilled. An official study has revealed that the modernization of industry may mean a 50 percent reduction in China's 50 million workers and employees in industry and the relocation of some 25 million people.[75] As population growth continues, the urban labor force is expected to increase by 25 million people between 1980 and 1985, but there is still no feasible outlet for the transferred and new labor forces. Thus, the industrial modernization drive may create an explosive unemployment problem.

Moreover, the purposes of the current readjustment are to correct the serious imbalances between heavy industry and light industry, and between raw materials industries and processing industries and to reduce the scale of capital construction. Unless there is considerable tightening up on the capital construction front, it will be impossible to guarantee the supply of the materials urgently needed by agriculture and light industry. Official surveys in mid-August 1980 revealed that the readjustment plan had confronted sturdy resistance and had made little progress. Many people paid lip service to curtailing and readjusting capital construction, but in fact they were trying in every possible way to save their projects and keep them intact. The "departmentalism" was so prevalent that a check-up made in China's five major economic regions showed that most of the projects canceled or postponed were small, local ones that would save very little in funds or materials.[76] The effort to correct the existing imbalances may not succeed.

Furthermore, there are many structural weaknesses in almost every major industry. The steel industry has been characterized by pronounced imbalances between iron making, steel making, and steel finishing. The output of pig iron lags behind the needs of the steel furnaces, and blast furnace requirements for iron ore are not being met. Similarly, China's steel-finishing sector lags behind the outflow of crude steel. In 1978, finished steel production amounted to about 21 million tons, only two-thirds of the crude steel output. In the same year, China had to import 8 million tons of finished steel.[77] The coal industry not only faces shortages of modern mining equipment and trained personnel, but also the chronic problem of providing the proper assortment of coal to the economy. The bulk of China's coking coal deposits are of low quality and require extensive blending of low- and high-grade coking coals to suit key metallurgical applications. Most of China's coal is carried by railroads, and expanding coal sup-

Table 11.10
Actual, Planned, and Projected Output of Five Major Industries, 1977-1985

| Industry | Actual Output | | | Original Planned Output | Author's Projected Output |
|---|---|---|---|---|---|
| | 1977[a] | 1978[a] | 1979[b] | 1985[c] | 1985[d] |
| Steel (million tons) | 23.7 | 31.8 | 34.5 | 60 | 40 |
| Coal (million tons) | 550 | 618 | 635 | 900 | 745 |
| Crude Oil (million tons) | 93.6 | 104 | 106.2 | 250 | 120 |
| Electricity (billion kwt.) | 223.6 | 256.6 | 282 | n.a. | 420 |
| Cement (million tons) | 55.7 | 65.2 | 73.9 | 100 | 90 |

Sources and Notes: (a) 1977 and 1978 figures are from P.R.C. State Statistical Bureau, "Communique on the Fulfillment of China's 1978 National Economic Plan," Beijing Review 22:27 (July 6, 1979).
(b) 1979 figures from P.R.C. State Statistical Bureau, "Communique on the fulfillment of China's 1979 National Economic Plan," Beijing Review 23:19 (May 12, 1980), p. 14. (c) For the original plan figures, see Chu-yuan Cheng, "The Modernization of Chinese Industry," in Richard Baum, ed., China's Four Modernizations: The New Technological Revolution (Boulder, Colo.: Westview Press, 1980), p. 44. (d) The projected figures are based on the following assumptions: (1) an annual average growth rate of 5 percent between 1981-1985 for steel and cement; (2) a 4 percent growth rate for coal and crude oil; and (3) a 7 percent growth rate for electricity.

plies would severely strain the rail system. In the petroleum industry, an imbalance exists between extraction and exploration. For years, the administration's eagerness to increase the current year's output resulted in underexploration and overextraction. This explains why productions of crude oil stagnated in 1979 and 1980 and will decline in 1981 and 1982.[78]

The machine-building industry encounters numerous structural hindrances. More than forty industrial departments and commissions throughout the country have their own machine works, which are supervised by Party organs on different levels. There is virtually no coordination among them. Official statistics in 1981 show that about 80 percent of the 6,000 enterprises under the First Ministry of Machine-Building Industry are "comprehensive complexes." Each produces from accessory parts to machine tools within its own plant, which results in problems that seriously hinder specialization and technical improvement.[79]

China's textile industry is seriously hampered by weak technical and logistical support and an inadequate supply of fitting and replacement parts. For example, Henan Province, one of China's major textile industry areas, has more than 1 million spindles and 32,000 looms. Each year it needs to have 17,000 kinds of spinning and weaving machine parts available in the province. Some parts available locally are inferior in quality and are not up to specifications. The insufficient supply of parts not only frequently idles machines but also accelerates their deterioration.[80] These examples illustrate the host of problems confronting industrial modernization. Most of the target goals proclaimed in February 1978 face further reductions by 1985. On the basis of new adjustments and progress reports revealed by official sources in 1980, electricity and cement production may come close to the mark, but the outputs of steel, coal, and crude oil are likely to be substantially below the targeted goals (see Table 11.10).

The longer-term prospects of Chinese industrial development are more favorable, however. If China can solve the shorter-term problems and can complete most of the 120 major projects as planned, the infrastructure of Chinese industry will significantly improve. During the 1949–1979 period, fixed assets for industrial enterprises under state control reached a total of 320 billion yuan, or $200 billion at the prevailing exchange rate.[81] The completion of the new development plan should double China's industrial fixed assets of 1978. With abundant coal, hydropower, and mineral resources, the country should be able to move into a stronger position among the world's industrial powers.

## NOTES

1. Quoted in P.R.C., State Planning Commission, *The First Five-Year Plan for the Development of the National Economy, 1953–1957* (Beijing: Foreign Languages Press, 1956), p. 15.
2. Editorial, *Renmin ribao,* April 5, 1955.
3. *Peking Review* 18:4 (January 26, 1975), p. 23.
4. Li Fuchun, "The First Five-Year Plan," *Da gong bao* (Tianjin), September 16, 1953.
5. Zhao Yiwen, *Xin Zhongguo de gongye* [Industry in new China], pp. 8–9.
6. *Tongji gongzuo tungxun,* Data Office, "Several Problems of Socialist Industrialization in China," *Xinhua ban yuekan* (Beijing) No. 1 (January 1957), pp. 67–71.
7. P.R.C., State Planning Commission, *First Five-Year Plan,* p. 165.
8. "China's National Economy (1978–79)," *Beijing Review* 22:6 (June 29, 1979), p. 10.
9. Mao Zedong, "On the Question of Agricultural Cooperativization," in *Selected Works,* vol. 5, pp. 168–191.
10. Liu Rixin, "Agricultural Mechanization and Industrialization," *Da gong bao,* July 15, 1963.
11. P.R.C., State Statistical Bureau, "Communiqué on Fulfillment of China's 1979 National Economic Plan," *Beijing Review* 23:19 (May 12, 1980), p. 14.
12. *Tongji yanjiu* No. 1 (January 1958), p. 11.
13. P.R.C., State Statistical Bureau, *Ten Great Years,* p. 17.
14. P.R.C., State Statistical Bureau, "Communiqué on Fulfillment of China's 1979 National Economic Plan," *Beijing Review* 23:19 (May 12, 1980), and 23:20 (May 19, 1980).
15. Chu-yuan Cheng, *China's Petroleum Industry,* pp. 111–114.
16. Thomas G. Rawski, *Economic Growth and Employment in China* (New York: Oxford University Press, 1979), p. 59.
17. Sun Jingzhi et al., eds., *Huadongdiqu jingjidili* [Economic geography of eastern China] (Beijing: Kexue Chubanshe, 1959), p. 84.
18. *Peking Review* 15:48 (November 28, 1972), p. 17.
19. *Peking Review* 14:3 (January 17, 1971), p. 10.
20. American Rural Small-Scale Industry Delegation, *Rural Small-Scale Industry in the People's Republic of China,* chap. 4.
21. Zhang Chunqiao, "On Exercising All-Round Dictatorship over the Bourgeoisie," *Peking Review* 18:14 (April 4, 1975), p. 6.
22. Thomas G. Rawski, *Economic Growth and Employment in China,* p. 63.
23. American Rural Small-Scale Industry Delegation, *Rural Small-Scale Industry,* p. 5.
24. Ibid., p. 9.
25. Hans Heymann, Jr., "Self-Reliance Revisited: China's Technology Dilemma," in Bryant G. Garth, ed., *China's Changing Role in the World Economy,* p. 18.
26. *China Reconstructs* 28:1 (January 1979), p. 27.

27. Yang Jianbai and Li Xuezeng, "China's Historical Experience in Handling the Relations Between Agriculture, Light Industry, and Heavy Industry," pp. 20–21.
28. P.R.C., State Statistical Bureau, *Ten Great Years*, p. 86.
29. Hu Qiaomu, "Act in Accordance with Economic Laws, Step Up the Four Modernizations."
30. Robert M. Field, "Labor Productivity in Industry," in Alexander Eckstein, Walter Galenson, and Ta-chung Liu, eds., *Economic Trends in Communist China*, p. 646.
31. Yang Jianbai and Li Xuezeng, "China's Historical Experience," p. 28.
32. Hu Qiaomu, "Act in Accordance with Economic Laws."
33. *Jingji yanjiu* No. 4 (April 15, 1979), p. 17.
34. Ibid., pp. 17–18.
35. *Hua-chiao jih-pao* (New York), September 24, 1979, p. 3.
36. *Shih-tai pao*, September 16, 1979, p. 1.
37. *Hua-chiao jih-pao*, September 15, 1979.
38. *Time* 115:22 (June 2, 1980), p. 49.
39. Vaclav Smil, "Deep Structural Deficiencies," *China Business Review* 7:1 (January–February 1980), p. 64; also, He Jianzhang, "How to Increase Economic Results," *Guangming ribao*, May 9, 1980, pp. 1 and 3.
40. Alfred H. Usack, Jr., and James D. Egan, "China's Iron and Steel Industry," in U.S., Congress, Joint Economic Committee, *China: A Reassessment of the Economy*, p. 276.
41. U.S., Central Intelligence Agency, *China: The Steel Industry in the 1970s and 1980s* (Washington, D.C., May 1979), p. 3.
42. *Beijing Review* 22:12 (March 23, 1979), pp. 14–16.
43. *Hua-chiao jih-pao*, February 17, 1979.
44. *Los Angeles Times*, May 10, 1979.
45. Xinhua-Beijing, March 31, 1981.
46. With the steel output for 1981 being set at 33 million tons and assuming a 5 percent annual growth between 1982 and 1990, output in 1990 will be around 50 million tons.
47. Commentator, "Straighten out Guidelines for Economic Work – On Leftist Mistakes in Economic Construction," *Renmin ribao*, April 9, 1981, p. 5.
48. "More Oil from More Fields," *China Reconstructs* 24:1 (January 1980), p. 15.
49. *New York Times*, May 1, 1980.
50. Kevin Fountain, "The Development of China's Offshore Oil," *China Business Review* 7:1 (January–February 1980), p. 23.
51. Chu-yuan Cheng, *China's Petroleum Industry*, pp. 112–113.
52. "China: A New Frontier for the Oil Industry," *World Business Weekly* (London), September 3, 1979, pp. 20–21.
53. *Gongren ribao* [Workers' daily] (Beijing), July 22, 1980.
54. Xinhua-Beijing, September 15, 1979; FBIS, September 17, 1979, pp. L15–L15.
55. "What About Energy in China?" *China Reconstructs* 23:4 (April 1979), p. 10.

56. Xinhua-Beijing, September 7, 1979; FBIS, September 7, 1979, p. L4.

57. In 1980, hydroelectric power stations throughout the country produced only 16.05 million kilowatts (*Beijing Review* 23:31 [August 4, 1980], pp. 5-6).

58. Xinhua-Beijing, September 7, 1979.

59. *Hua-chiao jih-pao,* September 29, 1979.

60. *Peking Review* 18:15 (April 13, 1975), p. 5, and 23:31 (August 4, 1980), pp. 5-6.

61. Xinhua-Beijing, July 27, 1980; FBIS, July 28, 1980, p. L3.

62. Chu-yuan Cheng, "Growth and Structural Changes in the Chinese Machine-Building Industry, 1952-1966," *China Quarterly* No. 41 (January-March 1970), pp. 26-57.

63. U.S., Central Intelligence Agency, *China: Economic Indicators,* pp. 16-17.

64. Xinhua-Beijing, September 7, 1979.

65. Li Qianheng and Zhang Yongtao, "Several Problems Relating to the Aim of Socialist Production," *Nanjing Daxue xuebao* [Journal of Nanking University] (Nanjing) No. 1 (1980), p. 4.

66. Editorial, *Renmin ribao,* March 14, 1981, p. 1.

67. Yao Yilin, "Report on the Readjustment of the 1981 National Economic Plan and State Revenue and Expenditure," *Beijing Review* 24:11 (March 15, 1981), p. 14.

68. Li Songlin, "Acceleration of Renovation for Fixed Assets Is the Basic Way to Promote Labor Productivity in Existing Enterprises," *Nanjing Daxue xuebao* No. 1 (1980), p. 38.

69. Fang Yen, "China's Textile Industry," *China's Foreign Trade* No. 2 (February 1979), pp. 4-5.

70. *Beijing Review* 23:23 (June 8, 1980), p. 38.

71. *Beijing Review* 22:12 (March 23, 1979), p. 16.

72. "A New North-South Railway Line," *Beijing Review* 22:2 (January 12, 1979), pp. 8-9.

73. Statement by Guo Weicheng, minister of railroads, Xinhua-Beijing, September 6, 1979.

74. Xinhua-Beijing, August 14, 1979.

75. Xinhua-Beijing, August 5, 1979; FBIS, August 7, 1979, p. L10.

76. Li Zhengrui, "We Can Accomplish Something Only by Refraining from Doing Some Other Things," *Renmin ribao,* June 5, 1980, p. 5.

77. Xue Muqiao, *Zhongguo shehuizhuyi jingji wenti yanjiu* [Study of China's socialist economic problems], p. 178.

78. Xue Muqiao, "Adjust the National Economy and Promote Overall Balance," *Jingji yanjiu* No. 2 (February 1981), pp. 25-31.

79. Wen Tsai, "An Initial Look at the Prospects for China's Machine-Building Industry," *Wen wei po* (Hong Kong), April 18, 1981, p. 3.

80. Xinhua-Beijing, September 5, 1979.

81. Ye Jianying's speech in honor of the thirtieth anniversary of the founding of the P.R.C. (*Hua-chiao jih-pao,* October 4, 1979).

# 12
# Agricultural Development

Agriculture, the mainstay of the Chinese economy for several thousand years, has had a relatively low priority in the overall development plans since the founding of the People's Republic. Although agriculture has fed the growing population, provided industrial raw materials, and earned foreign exchange, it has received only a minor share of the total state investment since 1949. Consequently, the growth rate of agriculture has lagged far behind that of industry, and food grain output has only slightly exceeded population growth. In 1980, agriculture loomed very large in the Chinese economy. It employed more than 75 percent of the labor force, supplied 60 to 70 percent of the industrial raw materials, provided 60 percent of the products for foreign trade, furnished 50 percent of state revenue, and generated 30 percent of the gross national product. In domestic markets, 80 percent of China's consumer goods were derived from agricultural products.

The sluggishness of agriculture has become a severe drag on Chinese economic growth. In the current four modernizations program, Chinese leaders view agricultural modernization as a necessary condition for the achievement of other economic goals. The success or failure of agricultural modernization will have a profound impact on the economy and on the people's standard of living in the 1980s.

This chapter examines several major aspects of China's agricultural development. It starts with a summary analysis of the major policy changes in agriculture since 1949 and then assesses the performance of the agricultural sector in terms of output growth, structural changes, and productivity and analyzes the factors that affect agricultural production. It also discusses and evaluates the essential features of the current modernization program and the outlook for China's agricultural development.

## EVOLUTION OF AGRICULTURAL DEVELOPMENT POLICIES

The agricultural system that the Chinese Communists inherited in 1949 was characterized by intensive inputs of labor on a limited supply of arable land. In the early years of the P.R.C., the Chinese Communist leaders attempted to solve agricultural problems by means of institutional changes and a large-scale mobilization of peasant labor to raise crop yields. Little effort was made to increase the supply of modern inputs.

The early policy stemmed partly from the Communist leaders' socialist ideology and partly from the constraints of Chinese endowments. Most socialists throughout the world believe that the socialization of agricultural production will lead to more effective mobilization of peasants' labor power and unleash the productive power of the peasants. Moreover, since the Chinese peasants' income was very low, the capacity of the agricultural sector to absorb new industrial input was still rather limited. But perhaps the most important factor was that in the view of Chinese leaders, the key to agricultural growth was collectivization and not state investment.[1] Based on these perceptions, supplies of modern inputs (chemical fertilizers, machinery, new seeds, and so on) were kept at extremely low levels in the expectation that a more effective use of traditional means alone would be sufficient to raise farm yields. During the First Five-Year Plan, agriculture received only 7.6 percent of the state capital investment, as compared to 58 percent for industry and 19 percent for transportation and communication.[2]

In 1956, as the first step toward a long-term development plan, the National Program for Agricultural Development, 1956–1967, was adopted. The program, containing forty articles, touched almost every Chinese agricultural problem.[3] It not only set production targets for grains and ginned cotton in various regions, but also specified the average multiple-crop index for various areas and concrete measures to achieve the targets. Among the most important targets were the goals for grain output. By 1967, the main agricultural areas north of the Huang He were to attain annual grain yields of 1.2 tons per acre; between the Huang He and the Huai He, 1.5 tons per acre; and south of the Huai He, 2.43 tons per acre. All of these targets were substantially higher than actual production in 1955.

The twelve-year development program was sidelined in 1958,

however, as the Chinese leaders, aiming at even more ambitious targets, launched the Great Leap Forward; its excesses pushed the economy toward the brink of total collapse. In the ensuing crisis, the Chinese leadership realized that institutional reorganization alone could not solve China's agricultural problems and that industrial development could not proceed without agricultural development. The pragmatic leaders within the Party adopted a new development policy, and it differed from past ones in several respects. First, there was a subtle shift of emphasis toward agriculture. Agriculture was to be the foundation of the economy, whereas industry was to be the leading sector. Accordingly, acceleration of agricultural development became the central task. All other sectors were to support agriculture. Second, within the agricultural sector, the focus was to be on grain. Another new guideline, "taking grain as the key link," has dominated Chinese agricultural development since 1962.[4]

Third, the "agriculture first" policy provided for the allocation of a larger share of state investment to agriculture than before and directed the industrial sector to provide more inputs for agriculture. A new program called for moderate farm mechanization in four years (beginning in 1959), semimechanization by 1967, and complete mechanization by 1970 (goals that were not implemented on schedule).[5] Imports of chemical fertilizers increased considerably. The supply of chemical fertilizers rose from 2.7 million tons in 1958 to 9.5 million tons in 1967, a 250 percent increase in ten years.

As agriculture gradually recovered, the Party leadership debated two diametrically opposed views on how to organize rural economic activities so as to generate and sustain agricultural growth. Mao was adamant about the "correctness" of the commune and the Great Leap and insisted that organization rather than technology, indigenous inputs rather than modern industrial inputs, and labor rather than capital were the keys to agricultural development. In contrast, Liu Shaoqi, Deng Xiaoping, and Bo Yipo favored mechanization before collectivization, the extensive use of chemical fertilizers, and heavy reliance on modern technology.

To accentuate his views, Mao personally initiated another new movement in 1964 – "In agriculture, learn from Dazhai." Mao selected Dazhai, a small production brigade in a very backward area of Northwest China, as the symbol of self-reliance and hard struggle to improve the peasants' lot. Dazhai was also very advanced in "socialist style." It had eliminated all private plots, had taken the brigade instead of the production team as the basic unit of accounting, and had developed an incentive system in which income was distributed on the basis of group instead of individual work efforts.

During the ten years of the Cultural Revolution, the exhortation to emulate Dazhai became a national ritual, and millions of peasants from all over the country visited Dazhai each year. The campaign reached its apex in September 1975 with the convening of the First National Conference on Learning from Dazhai. The conference, which was chaired by Hua Guofeng and attended by 3,700 delegates, including most of the top Party leaders, set several major agricultural targets for 1980, one of which was to transform at least one-third of the country's 2,100 counties into Dazhai-type counties.[6]

The fall of the radicals in October 1976 did not bring about a fundamental change in agricultural policy. At the Second National Conference on Learning from Dazhai, held in Beijing December 10–27, 1976, Hua Guofeng called the movement to learn from Dazhai 'a strategic step toward the four modernizations" and reiterated that "the whole nation should strive to build more than one-third of the counties into Dazhai-type by 1980."[7]

Early in 1978, however, Chinese agricultural development policy entered a new era with the announcement of the 1976–1985 plan. Agriculture's important role in China's development was stressed in Vice-Premier Yu Qiuli's speech to the Third National Conference on Agricultural Mechanization in January 1978. In February, Hua Guofeng presented a detailed plan for agricultural development in 1978–1985 to the National People's Congress.[8] Two aspects of the plan represented new departures. First, its stress on the importance of modern inputs reversed the focus of the 1950s and the Great Leap period on institutional changes and labor mobilization. By 1980, the output of chemical fertilizers was to increase 58 percent over the 1977 level, and basic mechanization was to be in effect in 70 percent of the major operations in agriculture, forestry, animal husbandry, sideline production, and fisheries.[9] Second, in contrast to the self-reliance embodied in the "learn from Dazhai" campaign, the new program emphasized financial support for local communes. In 1978, state banks and credit cooperatives provided an unprecedented 25 billion yuan in credits to production brigades.

In February 1979, the Agricultural Bank of China reopened and was put in charge of issuing loans to rural communes. During 1979 and 1980, loans released by banks to support agriculture amounted to more than 13 billion yuan.[10] In state capital investment, the share allocated to agriculture rose from 10.7 percent in 1978 to 14 percent in 1979.

Despite these changes, economic policies and institutions were still not conducive to agricultural development. Procurement prices remained too low, and material incentives to arouse the peasants' enthusiasm were far from adequate. When the Third Plenum of the Eleventh CCP Central Committee met in December 1978, agriculture was singled out as the most pressing issue facing China. The session approved two significant guidelines for Chinese agricultural development in the forthcoming decade: the Decisions on Some Questions Concerning the Acceleration of Agricultural Development and the (Draft) Regulations on the Work in the Rural People's Communes (the new Sixty Articles on Rural Communes).[11] The two documents repudiated Mao's policies and returned to those advocated by Liu Shaoqi, Deng Xiaoping, and Chen Yun during the post-Great Leap period. More specifically, the documents recognized that political stability, instead of class struggle, was a prerequisite for the modernization of agriculture and made the prevention of a revival of left deviationism the main task of the peasants at the current stage. Second, the documents established that the Party's new agricultural line stressed improved agricultural technology and equipment instead of reorganization. Third, the documents described material incentives and democratic rights as the two most important means of stimulating peasant initiative. Only with the full exercise of peasant initiative could the state's material and technical support be fully exploited.

The spring of 1979 saw a large-scale expansion of government organization in the agricultural sector. A State Agricultural Commission, on a par with the State Planning Commission, was established in February 1979 and five ministries are under its jurisdiction—agriculture, forestry, agricultural machinery, water conservancy, and state farms and land reclamation. Most of them had been abolished or had merged during the 1965–1978 period. Many changes providing better material incentives to agricultural producers were put into effect. The new program stressed economic laws and a specialization of production according to local conditions, and exhortations to emulate Dazhai disappeared from the news media. Indeed, Dazhai was condemned for a misuse of agricultural machinery, falsification of production records, low labor productivity, and low commercial grain rates.[12]

In summary, agricultural development policy in the P.R.C. during the past three decades has undergone a gradual shift of emphasis from institutional change and the intensified use of traditional techniques to material incentives and modern techniques. Both the National Program for Agricultural Development (1956–1967) and Mao's Eight-Point Charter of 1956 stressed the intensive use of traditional techniques.[13] In the aftermath of the Great Leap and the dislocation of the early stages of the commune movement, the leadership realized that traditional technology and an intensive use of labor could not bring about a major breakthrough in agriculture without substantial increases of modern inputs. With the emergence of the "agriculture as the foundation" policy in 1962, there was a definite shift toward modern technology, and neither the campaign to "learn from Dazhai" nor the Cultural Revolution halted the trend. The 1976–1985 plan called for an intensification of the modernization process. Despite persistent constraints and obstacles, this new policy may provide a favorable basis for a more rapid transformation of Chinese agriculture.

## AGRICULTURAL PERFORMANCE

The performance of the agricultural sector cannot be assessed by any single indicator. The official gross agricultural output value reveals very little about the progress or stagnation of individual products. Conventional appraisals tend to focus on the growth of the grain output, but since agriculture consists of farming, forestry, animal husbandry, sideline occupations, and fishery, grain output alone is no gauge of agricultural performance. Thus, this section will evaluate three aspects of China's agricultural progress: the growth rate for grains, industrial crops, and livestock between 1952 and 1979; changes in output structure; and the growth in productivity.

### *Growth of Agricultural Output*

According to Chinese official statistics in 1980, the net value of agricultural output grew at an average annual rate of 4.5 percent between 1952 and 1979, as compared to 10.1 percent for the net value of industrial output in the same period. During that time span, food grains (including soybeans) increased from 164 million tons in 1952 to 330 million tons in 1979, representing an annual growth rate of 2.6 percent. The gross output value of agriculture went up from 63,217 million yuan in 1952 to 158,400 million yuan in 1979 (all expressed in 1970 constant prices), with an annual growth rate of 3.5 percent, compared with 9.1 percent for light industry and 13.7 percent for heavy industry (see Table 12.1).

The output of major agricultural products and their growth rates in various periods, based on official statistics, are summarized in Table 12.2. Although the eleven major products all show an upward trend, sharp variations have occurred in different periods. In the case of food grains, the sharpest increase occurred between 1949 and 1952, when

Table 12.1
Gross Value of Agricultural Output, 1949-1979

| Year | Gross Output Value (in million 1957 yuan) | Gross Output Value (in million 1970 yuan) | Index (in 1970 prices) 1949=100 | Index (in 1970 prices) 1952=100 |
|---|---|---|---|---|
| 1949 | 28,999[a] | 42,765[c] | 100 | 67 |
| 1952 | 43,057[a] | 63,217[c] | 148 | 100 |
| 1957 | 53,700[a] | 78,939[c] | 185 | 125 |
| 1964 | 51,500[b] | 75,705[c] | 177 | 120 |
| 1970 | 72,000[b] | 105,840[c] | 248 | 167 |
| 1974 | 77,700[b] | 114,219[c] | 267 | 181 |
| 1977 | | 133,980[d] | 313 | 212 |
| 1978 | | 145,400[e] | 340 | 230 |
| 1979 | | 158,400[f] | 370 | 251 |

| | | |
|---|---|---|
| Growth rate | 1949-1979 | 4.5% |
| | 1952-1979 | 3.5% |
| | 1957-1979 | 3.2% |

Notes and Sources: (a) P.R.C. State Statistical Bureau, Ten Great Years (Beijing: Foreign Languages Press, 1960), p. 16. Original figures for 1949 and 1952 are in 1952 prices. They are converted into 1957 prices by multiplying by a factor of 0.8898. (b) From Dwight H. Perkins, "Constraints Influencing China's Agricultural Performance," in U.S. Congress, Joint Economic Committee, China: A Reassessment of the Economy (Washington, D.C.: Government Printing Office, 1975), p. 351. (c) The 1957 yuan are converted into 1970 yuan by multiplying by a factor of 1.47. This figure is derived from the comparison of data in Ten Great Years with statistics provided by Yang Jianbai and Li Xuezeng, which are expressed in 1970 prices (see "China's Historical Experience in Handling the Relations Between Agriculture, Light Industry, and Heavy Industry," Zhongguo shehui kexue /Social sciences in China/ No. 3 /May 1980/, p. 20). (d) Yu Qiuli, "Report on Draft of the 1979 National Economic Plan," Xinhua yuebao (New China monthly) No. 6 (June 1979), p. 21. (e) Yang Jianbai and Li Xuezeng, op. cit. (f) P.R.C. State Statistical Bureau, "Communiqué on Fulfillment of China's 1979 National Economic Plan," Beijing Review 23:19 (May 12, 1980), p. 13.

Table 12.2
Production and Growth Rates of China's Eleven Major Agricultural Products, 1949-1979

| Product | Production | | | | | Annual Growth Rates | | |
|---|---|---|---|---|---|---|---|---|
| | 1949 | 1952 | 1957 | 1978 | 1979 | 1952-57 | 1952-79 | 1957-79 |
| Grains (million tons) | 113.2 | 163.9 | 195 | 304.8 | 332.1 | 3.6 | 2.6 | 2.4 |
| Cotton (1,000 tons) | 445 | 1,304 | 1,640 | 2,167 | 2,207 | 4.7 | 2.0 | 1.4 |
| Peanuts, Sesame & Rapeseed (1,000 tons) | 2,328 | 3,729 | 3,800 | 4,568 | 5,641 | 0.4 | 1.5 | 1.8 |
| Sugar Cane & Beetroot (1,000 tons) | 2,833 | 7,595 | 11,894 | 23,819 | 24,614 | 9.4 | 4.5 | 3.4 |
| Jute, Ambary Hemp (1,000 tons) | 37 | 306 | 500 | 1,088 | 1,089 | 3.3 | 4.8 | 3.6 |
| Silk Cocoons (1,000 tons) | 43 | 123 | 113 | 228 | 271 | -1.6 | 3.0 | 4.0 |
| Tea (1,000 tons) | 41 | 83 | 112 | 268 | 277 | 6.3 | 4.6 | 4.2 |
| Large Draft Animals (1,000 head) | 60,020 | 76,460 | 83,820 | 94,000 | 94,591 | 1.8 | 0.7 | 0.6 |
| Sheep, Goats (1,000 head) | 42,350 | 61,780 | 98,580 | 169,940 | 183,142 | 9.8 | 4.1 | 2.8 |
| Hogs (1,000 head) | 57,750 | 89,770 | 145,900 | 301,290 | 319,705 | 10.2 | 4.8 | 3.6 |
| Aquatic Products (1,000 tons) | 450 | 1,670 | 3,100 | 4,660 | 4,305 | 13.2 | 3.6 | 1.5 |

Sources: 1949, 1952, and 1978 figures are from Beijing Review 22:40 (October 5, 1979), p. 13. 1957 figures are from P.R.C. State Statistical Bureau, Ten Great Years (Beijing: Foreign Languages Press, 1960), pp. 118-132. 1979 figures are from P.R.C. State Statistical Bureau, "Communiqué on Fulfillment of China's 1979 National Economic Plan," Beijing Review 23:19 (May 12, 1980), p. 13.

Notes: Large animals, sheep, goats, and hog figures are year-end figures. Food grain production includes soy beans.

Chinese agriculture recovered from the ravages of a decade of war. By 1952, most food crop production had reached or surpassed its prewar level. Production continued to improve during the First Five-Year Plan period, despite a low level of investment. Between 1952 and 1957, grain output rose 19 percent, with an annual growth rate of 3.6 percent – a modest but respectable record when compared to the decline in the Soviet Union during its First Five-Year Plan period.[14] The growth rate in this period may be somewhat inflated due to an underreporting of the grain output in 1952. Even if some allowance is made for underreporting in early years, however, grain output still grew faster than the population.

China's agriculture entered a period of stagnation between 1958 and 1965. In 1958, the first year of the Great Leap, grain output increased by only 2.5 percent, from 195 million tons to 200 million tons, compared to the earlier official exaggerated claims of 250 million tons, or an increase of 35.1 percent.[15] Grain output fell sharply in 1959–1961 and began a slow recovery in 1962–1964. By 1965, it still hovered below the 200-million-ton mark attained in 1958.[16] Thus, there was no growth in grain production in the eight years between 1958 and 1965.

Grain output resumed an upward trend in the Third Five-Year Plan period (1966–1970) and reached 240 million tons in 1970, with an annual growth of 3.7 percent, slightly higher than that in 1952–1957. Between 1970 and 1979, with the exception of 1977, grain output continued to rise, reaching 265 million tons in 1973, 305 million tons in 1978, and 332 million tons in 1979. However, due to a serious flood in the South and a serious drought in the North, grain output dropped to 316 million tons in 1980, with an average annual rate of 2.8 percent for those ten years (see Table 12.3).

Growth rates for other crops have been uneven: higher for sugarcane, beetroot, and tea but lower for cotton and oilseeds. Among the nongrain crops in China, cotton has paramount importance as it is the prime source of raw material for the textile industry, which accounted for 11 percent of China's industrial output in 1978. Before the Sino-Japanese War, China produced about 10 percent of the world's cotton. Cotton output touched 850,000 tons in 1937, dropped to 445,000 tons in 1949, but rapidly rose to 1.3 million tons in 1952. By 1957, China's cotton output had reached 1.64 million tons, with an annual growth rate of 4.7 percent for the five-year period. Since then, the pressure to produce more food grains has resulted in a decrease in the amount of land devoted to cotton. Cotton output since 1958 has shown little progress, leveling off for the four-year period, 1973–1976. In 1979, output was up only slightly over 1978 but still lagged behind the 1973 level. A

Table 12.3
The Output of Grains and Cotton, 1949-1980
(million metric tons)

| | 1949 | 1952 | 1957 | 1958 | 1965 | 1970 | 1973 | 1977 | 1978 | 1979 | 1980 |
|---|---|---|---|---|---|---|---|---|---|---|---|
| Grains | 113.2 | 163.9 | 195 | 200 | 196 | 240 | 265 | 283 | 304.8 | 332.1 | 316 |
| Cotton | 0.45 | 1.30 | 1.64 | 1.70 | 1.65 | 2.00 | 2.55 | 2.00 | 2.17 | 2.20 | 2.60 |

Growth Rates in Various Periods (in %)

| | Grains | Cotton |
|---|---|---|
| 1949-1952 | 13.1 | 42.4 |
| 1952-1957 | 3.6 | 4.7 |
| 1958-1965 | -0.5 | -0.4 |
| 1965-1970 | 3.7 | 3.9 |
| 1970-1980 | 2.8 | 2.6 |
| 1952-1980 | 2.4 | 2.5 |

Sources: 1949, 1952, 1957, 1978, and 1979 figures from Table 12.2. Other years are from Xue Muqiao, "Thirty Years of Strenuous Efforts," Hongqi (Red flag) No. 10 (October 1979), pp. 46-47. 1980 figures are from Yao Yilin, "Report on the Readjustment of the 1981 National Economic Plan and State Revenue and Expenditure," Beijing Review 24:11 (March 16, 1981), p. 14.

bumper harvest was registered in 1980, when 2.6 million tons was produced, an increase of 20 percent over the previous year.

The primary oilseed crops in China are peanuts, rapeseed, and sesame. Oil is also extracted from cottonseeds and soybeans, but they are not counted as oilseeds in Chinese agricultural statistics. The production of oilseeds fell short of the target set in FFYP, largely because of the unreasonably low price set by the government in procuring oil-bearing materials from the farmers. The long-term growth rate for oil-bearing crops between 1952 and 1979 was only 1.5 percent, which was below the population growth rate. The result was a chronic shortage of edible oils throughout the entire period.

The progress of the livestock sector has also been very uneven. Long-term growth rates are more favorable for hogs and sheep than they are for draft animals. Hogs are China's most significant meat producers and are also the chief suppliers of organic fertilizer. During the 1950s, the number of hogs fluctuated depending on government policy toward private hog raising and procurement. Toward the end of the period, their numbers increased sharply, but with the drive to organize agricultural producers into communes, the number began to fall. There was a steep decline in hog production during the agricultural crisis of 1959–1961. In the early 1960s, the government provided various incentives to the peasants to stimulate hog raising. By the end of 1964, the number of hogs was officially reported to have surpassed the previous record.[17] During the remainder of the 1960s and the early 1970s, hog production rose considerably. In the twenty-two years between 1957 and 1979, the annual growth rate in hog production averaged 3.6 percent, 50 percent higher than that of food grains.

In contrast to the increase in hog production, the number of large draft animals (horses, cows, donkeys, and camels), which compete for grains with humans and hogs, registered a very slow increase. As more heavy farm tasks are mechanized in the future and the need for draft animals tapers off, the number of draft animals is likely to increase even more slowly, if at all.

In summary, agricultural production during the first thirty years of the P.R.C. fluctuated widely. Although the output of food grains and hogs, two important components of the Chinese diet, grew faster than the population, the production of cotton and oil-bearing crops lagged behind population growth. In general, China has not yet broken out of the range of subsistence-level production. Since the early 1960s, China has been a net importer of grains, soybeans, and raw cotton. Compare China's recent performance with that of other Asian countries: the 2.4 percent rise in grain output per annum in the 1952–1980 period is below the 3 percent average achieved in Asia as a whole.[18] Yet, compared with the long-term growth rate of 1.1 percent that China had achieved in the past (1930s–1974),[19] the recent record still shows considerable improvement.

*Structural Changes in Agriculture*

The relative shares of farming, forestry, livestock, fishery, and subsidiary products in a country's agricultural sector reflect the degree to which the nation has modernized. In modern agriculture, the roles of livestock and forestry often equal or even surpass that of farming. In 1978, livestock accounted for 57 percent of the agricultural output in West Germany, 60 percent in the United States, 63 percent in Canada, and 90 percent in Denmark.[20] In a country like China, animal husbandry not only provides meat, dairy, and other animal products, but also generates indispensable organic fertilizer. Forestry not only produces timber but also helps to retain water and soil, regulate weather, provide shelter against wind, and check moving sand.

For 2,000 years, grain has been the key factor in China's agriculture and the principal source of food. People must consume large quantities in order to obtain adequate calories, which constantly strains the grain supply. Since 1949, the structural imbalance of farming, forestry, and animal husbandry has deepened. Under the guideline of "taking grain as the key link," agricultural production has become structurally concentrated in farming to the neglect of the other categories. A statement from the Party organ, *Renmin ribao,* in March 1979, described the situation.

> For almost two decades, the amount of grain purchased became the sole criterion in judging the farm work of a locality. Under this circumstance, many pastoral areas were converted from raising animals to growing grains. The forests were destroyed to bring more land under cultivation, and even lakes and ponds were filled to grow grains. The ecological equilibrium of nature was destroyed as trees were felled and grasslands opened up for crops.[21]

As a result of the one-sided emphasis on grain production, the share of livestock had dropped to 13.2 percent of the agricultural output by 1978, as against 16 percent in the early 1950s (see Table 12.4).

Since hilly land accounts for 60 percent of China's total land area and grasslands make up another one-fifth, the potential for forestry and livestock is very high. Their minute shares of the total agricultural output indicate that much of the country's valuable agricultural

Table 12.4
Structure of China's Agricultural Production
1977-1978

| Categories | Percent of Gross Agricultural Output Value | |
|---|---|---|
| | 1977 | 1978 |
| Farming | 67.5 | 67.8 |
| Forestry | 3.1 | 3.0 |
| Animal Husbandry | 13.7 | 13.2 |
| Fishery | 1.5 | 1.4 |
| Subsidiary Occupations | 3.0 | 2.9 |
| Small Industries* | 11.2 | 11.7 |
| Total | 100.0 | 100.0 |

Sources: 1977 figures from Go Qingyun, "Animal Husbandry Must Be Expanded Rapidly," Guangming ribao (Enlightenment daily), September 7, 1979. 1978 figures from Tong Dalin, "Transforming China's Agricultural Components," Beijing Review 23:4 (January 28, 1980), p. 20.

* Includes output value of brigade-run small industries but excludes output value of commune-run industries, which are counted as industrial output value.

resources are not being properly used. In 1979, only 12.7 percent of the land in China was forested, compared with 68 percent in Japan, 57 percent in Sweden, 35 percent in Canada, and 34 percent in the United States. China's state investment in livestock in 1979 was less than 1 percent of the total state capital investment, or about 7 percent of the agricultural investment.[22] The miniscule share of fishery products was attributed to the large-scale transfer of lakes and ponds into farmland. The lake area in Hubei, Central China, traditionally the "thousand lakes" province, had been reduced by two-thirds by 1979, from an original 12.4 million mu to only 4.3 million mu (15 mu equal 2.47 acres). Dongting Hu, one of the biggest in China, shrank from 6.52 million mu to merely 2.2 million mu in 1979.[23] During the 1957-1979 period, the annual growth rate of aquatic products was only 1.5 percent, among the lowest of the eleven major agricultural products. Unless there is a fundamental change in policy, the imbalances among farming, livestock, forestry, and fishery seem likely to persist in the near future.

Within the farming sector, more than two-thirds of the sown area is devoted to grains. If soybeans are counted as a food grain rather than as an oil-bearing crop, the sown area for grains amounted for 84.2 percent of the total sown area during 1957–1965 (see Table 12.5).

Data on sown areas for various crops are fragmentary after 1965. Based on scattered reports, the sown areas for cotton and soybeans shrank continuously in the 1970s. For example, Shaanxi Province, a major cotton-producing area, registered annual decreases in cotton acreage of 200,000 mu to 300,000 mu for the decade. Under the policy of "taking grain as the key link," food rations for some cotton-producing areas were not guaranteed, which compelled the peasants in those areas to switch to producing grains.[24] In Shandong, a major cotton-producing area, the highest annual production was 270,000 tons in 1970. In 1979, its output fell below 200,000 tons, a decline of 30 percent. The most dramatic drop, however, occurred in Hebei, the leading cotton-producing province in the mid-1950s. Between 1957 and 1977, Hebei's cotton land shrank by 58 percent, and its cotton output fell 68 percent.[25]

In grain output during the 1949–1957 period, there was a sharp increase in high-yielding crops, such as potatoes and corn, as substitutes for lower-yielding crops, such as millet and soybeans. Since 1957, the structure of the grain output has remained quite stable. Rice accounts for 43–45 percent of the total output of grain, and wheat accounts for 11–12 percent; soybeans registered a steady decline from 6 percent in 1952 to only 3 percent in 1974. The remaining 42 percent consisted of potatoes and other coarse grains. Since 1973, China has had to import vegetable oils and soybeans from the United States, France, and Brazil.

### *The Productivity Trend*

Traditionally, Chinese agriculture has been characterized by a high yield per acre but a low yield per farmer. In the pre–World War II era, the labor requirements of Chinese agriculture were much higher than those of the advanced countries. It took 244 man-hours per year to cultivate an acre of wheat in China, compared with 7 in the United States and 30 in the U.S.S.R.; an acre of cotton required 657 man-hours in China, compared with 88 in the United States and 330 in the U.S.S.R.[26]

The use of labor-intensive farming inevitably resulted in a low output per farmer. During 1929–1933, Buck's estimates show that a Chinese farmer working a full year produced only 1,400 kilograms (1.4 tons), compared with 20,000 kilograms (20 tons) in the United States.[27] Chinese yields per acre, however, were higher in the 1930s

Table 12.5
Distribution of Sown Areas for Various Crops, 1957-1965

| Year | Total all crops | Grain | Soybean | Other non-grain crops | Cotton | Other technical crops | Green manure |
|---|---|---|---|---|---|---|---|
| 1957 | 2,343 | 1,798 | 191 | 109 | 87 | 107 | 51 |
| 1958 | 2,344 | 1,819 | 147 | 110 | 86 | 119 | 63 |
| 1959 | 2,222 | 1,669 | 142 | 110 | 84 | 151 | 66 |
| 1960 | 2,203 | 1,721 | 140 | 110 | 73 | 90 | 69 |
| 1961 | 2,168 | 1,725 | 137 | 110 | 55 | 69 | 72 |
| 1962 | 2,155 | 1,723 | 129 | 110 | 53 | 65 | 75 |
| 1963 | 2,131 | 1,687 | 120 | 110 | 61 | 75 | 78 |
| 1964 | 2,146 | 1,685 | 115 | 110 | 69 | 85 | 82 |
| 1965 | 2,146 | 1,661 | 115 | 110 | 71 | 87 | 102 |
| Percentage (1957-65) | 100 | 78 | 6.2 | 5.0 | 3.2 | 4.3 | 3.3 |

**Source: Kang Chao, Agricultural Production in Communist China (Madison: University of Wisconsin Press, 1970), pp. 306-308. Other nongrain crops consist of vegetables and fruits. Other technical crops include tobacco, sugarcane, sugar beets, jute, flax, peanuts, rapeseeds, and sesame.**

than those of most countries, including those of many advanced countries.[28]

The combination of low output per farmer and high yield per acre has not changed much since 1949. In 1952–1957, the average yield for the four major grain crops (rice, wheat, potatoes, and other coarse grains) fell short by varying degrees of the corresponding prewar estimates. The average yield per unit picked up sharply in the 1970s as more modern inputs and labor were invested. In 1977, official statistics reveal that rice yields per hectare were 3,473 kilograms (1,406 kilograms per acre), corn yields were 2,505 kilograms per hectare (1,014 kilograms per acre), and wheat yields were 1,770 kilograms per hectare (717 kilograms per acre).[29]

The 1977 rice yield was 40 percent higher than that of 1952–1957 but only 5 percent over that of 1929–1933 (see Table 12.6). The 1977 wheat yield was more than double that of 1952–1957 and about 50 percent higher than that of 1929–1933. Compared with other countries, China's rice yield of 3.5 tons per hectare (1,406 kilograms per acre) in 1977 was on a par with South Korean and Taiwanese yields of the early and mid-1960s and with Japan's prewar standard,[30] but it ac-

Table 12.6
Grain Yields Per Mu in 1929–1933, 1952–1957, and 1977
(in catties per mu)

| Crop | | 1929–1933[1] | 1952[2] | 1957[2] | 1952–1957[2] | 1977[3] |
|---|---|---|---|---|---|---|
| Rice<br>(Glutinous rice) | | 447<br>433 | 321 | 359 | 336 | 463 |
| Wheat | (winter)<br>(spring) | 141<br>152 | 98 | 114 | 106 | 236 |
| Potatoes | (sweet)<br>(Irish) | 264<br>213 | 251 | 278 | 246 | |
| Coarse Grains | | 151 | 136 | 139 | 134 | 334<br>(corn) |

Sources: 1) John Lossing Buck, Land Utilization, vol. 1 (New York: Council on Economic and Cultural Affairs, 1956), p. 209. 2) P.R.C. State Statistical Bureau, Ten Great Years (Beijing: Foreign Languages Press, 1960), p. 121. 3) Renmin jiaoyu (People's education) No. 9 (1978), p. 58.

Note: One mu = $\frac{1}{15}$ hectare; one catty= $\frac{1}{2000}$ ton.

counted for only 56 percent of the Japanese rice yield in 1977 (6.1 tons per hectare). China's corn yield in 1977 amounted to 41 percent of the U.S. yield in the same year (6 tons per hectare); its wheat yield in 1977 accounted for only 31 percent of the 5.7 tons achieved in the Netherlands. Two Chinese economists observed that if China could attain advanced world levels in per unit yields of rice, wheat, and corn, it could harvest 450 million tons on the existing sown land.[31]

China's yield per farmer has been severely constrained by a decrease in cultivated land and a rapid increase in the labor force. Between 1957 and 1978, the amount of cultivated land fell from 276 million acres (111.8 million hectares) in 1957 to only 247 million acres (100 million hectares) in 1978[32] as a result of capital construction and the alkalinization of farmland. During the same period, the labor force engaged in agriculture leaped from less than 200 million people to 300 million people,[33] an increase of 50 percent. Although yield per acre has increased only moderately, the rapid growth of farm labor has reduced the output per farmer. In 1978, grain output per farmer averaged only 1,040 kilograms, compared with 1,400 kilograms in the 1929–1933 period and 95,352 kilograms for the U.S. farmer.[34] The grain output per Chinese farmer in 1978 amounted to only a little more than 1 percent of that of the U.S. farmer, as against 7 percent in the 1930s (see Table 12.7). The gap between China and other advanced countries has thus been growing instead of narrowing.

In summary, the performance of Chinese agriculture since 1949 has

Table 12.7
Comparison of Crop Yields Per Agricultural Worker in China, U.S.S.R., West Germany, France, United Kingdom, and U.S.A., 1978

| Country | Annual Output Per Worker (kg.) | China = 1 |
|---|---|---|
| China | 1,040 | 1.00 |
| U.S.S.R. | 10,265 | 9.87 |
| West Germany | 18,877 | 18.15 |
| France | 20,155 | 19.38 |
| United Kingdom | 32,609 | 31.35 |
| U.S.A. | 95,352 | 91.68 |

Source: <u>Xinhua yuebao</u> (New China monthly) (Beijing) No. 4 (April 1980), p. 63.

shown only moderate gains. The strong government emphasis on grain output has slowed progress in forestry, livestock, and fishery. Although the growth in food grains has slightly exceeded population growth, supplies of cooking oil, soybeans, and other components of the Chinese diet are chronically short. Because the amount of cultivated land has shrunk, increases in input cannot increase output proportionately. Both land productivity and labor productivity show signs of deterioration. Should labor productivity remain unchanged, China would have to expand its labor force from 300 million to 400 million in order to produce 400 million tons of grain by 1985. The expansion of the labor force would bring no improvement in the standard of living. The future of Chinese agriculture, therefore, depends on a rapid increase in per unit yield and the promotion of labor efficiency.[35]

## FACTORS AFFECTING AGRICULTURAL GROWTH

Prior to 1957, the rise of agricultural output in China was mostly due to increased land, labor, capital, and current inputs (such as seeds, chemical and traditional fertilizers, and insecticide). Technological change, whether from improved equipment, better methods of cultivation, or new crops and new seeds, played no significant role. Since 1957, increases of labor and current inputs have been the most important factors contributing to agricultural growth.

During the 1952–1957 period, Chinese agricultural production increased by 25 percent. Anthony Tang cited several sources for this growth: increases of labor contributed five percentage points (20 percent) of the output increment; land, three percentage points (12 percent); capital, two percentage points (8 percent); current inputs, sixteen percentage points (64 percent); and productivity change, a loss of one percentage point (−4 percent).

Tang's study assumed that water conservation projects, reclamation works, and other capital construction in agriculture led to increased acreage and its more intensive use. Although the current-inputs category scored the highest growth rate among the four components, its relative share remained rather small[36] (see Table 12.8).

That fact means that despite a rapid rise in current inputs, primary reliance was still placed upon traditional sources of growth, which have a limited capacity for generating new growth. By 1957, the traditional sources appeared to be drying up. Between 1957 and 1978, the land area under cultivation, instead of expanding, decreased by 12 percent. Official explanations for the decline include the appropria-

Table 12.8
Relative Input Weights of Selected Countries and China

| Country | Relative Input Weights | | | |
| --- | --- | --- | --- | --- |
| | Labor | Land | Capital | Current Inputs |
| Taiwan (1952-1956) | 0.45 | 0.25 | 0.11 | 0.19 |
| Japan (1933-1937) | 0.52 | 0.26 | 0.08 | 0.14 |
| India (1945-1948) | 0.34 | 0.25 | 0.30 | 0.11 |
| U.S.A. (1949) | 0.33 | 0.19 | 0.48 | a |
| China (1952-1957) | 0.55 | 0.25 | 0.09 | 0.11 |

a. Classification does not permit separation into capital and current inputs.

Source: Anthony M. Tang, "Policy and Performance in Agriculture," in Alexander Eckstein, Walter Galenson, and Ta-chung Liu, eds., Economic Trends in Communist China (Chicago: Aldine, 1968), p. 483.

tion of agricultural land for industrial, transportation, and military uses; water conservancy projects; and urbanization.[37] In addition, the mismanagement of irrigation projects created areas of alkaline and saline soils, which made some land sterile. As cultivated land declined, increases in agricultural output could come only from raising yields on existing cultivated land. During the 1960s and 1970s, efforts were made in three major areas: increased supplies of fertilizer, the expansion of irrigation and drainage facilities, and the increase of agricultural machinery.

### *Increase of Fertilizer Supply*

Chinese agriculture has long depended on enormous supplies of organic fertilizer for the maintenance of yields. Since 1949, the application of both organic and chemical fertilizers has shown a steady increase, yet the bulk of the fertilizer nutrients continue to come from organic sources. In 1957, the average chemical fertilizer consumption amounted to only 4 kilograms per hectare (1.6 kilograms per acre) in nutrient weight–or less than 20 kilograms per hectare (8.2 kilograms per acre) in gross weight–and the organic fertilizer consumption per hectare was estimated at 36 kilograms (14.6 kilograms per acre).[38] The three years of agricultural crisis (1959–1961) and the resultant sharp decline in livestock launched a vicious cycle in which the loss of livestock reduced the supply of organic fertilizer, which contributed to a drop in crop yields, which further reduced feed for livestock, and so on. To break this cycle, the Chinese government has, since 1962, increased the production and importation of chemical fertilizers.

In 1962, the supply of chemical fertilizers was less than 1 million tons in nutrient weight (or less than 5 million tons in gross weight), and it represented less than 7 percent of the total supply of nutrient from both chemical and organic fertilizers. Between 1962 and 1975, however, the supply of chemical fertilizers increased at an average annual rate of 17 percent, due in large part to imports of chemical fertilizers, which accounted for 40 percent of domestic production during 1962–1970. In the early 1970s, because of the tight world fertilizer market and the prospect of increasing oil and natural gas supplies in China, the Chinese government purhased thirteen complete fertilizer plants from abroad to rapidly increase domestic production. Until then, small plants had produced most of China's domestic chemical fertilizers. In 1977, of the 9.1 million tons (plant nutrient content) of chemical fertilizers produced in China, 60 percent still came from small plants. Those fertilizers were low-quality and low-nutrient products and therefore contained a lower percentage of plant nutrient per unit of weight than those produced in larger plants or imported from abroad. Based on pre–World War II data, Owen L. Dawson has suggested that approximately one ton of gross chemical fertilizer means a yield of two tons for all food grains. But calculated at plant nutrient, the ratio becomes 1:8.[39] Table 12.9 estimates the 1949–1977 supply of chemical fertilizers (converted into nutrient content).

As shown in that table, the amount of chemical fertilizer supplied per hectare of farmland increased from one-third of one gram in 1950 to 0.09 metric tons in 1977 (calculated on the basis of 100 percent effectiveness). At an input-output ratio of 1:8, this would increase grain output by 72 million tons, or 46 percent of the 156-million-ton increment of food grains between 1950 and 1977.

### *Irrigation and Drainage Facilities*

The effectiveness of chemical fertilizers, however, depends to a great extent on the adequacy of the water supply. The provision and use of irrigation facilities began in China more than 2,000 years ago. Most irrigation facilities in the past were concentrated in the rice growing region of the South; by 1930, it was estimated that 69 percent of the cultivated land in the rice region was irrigated. During the 1950s, irrigation facilities were restored and expanded on a wide scale. At their peak in that decade (1958), they covered about one-third of China's cultivated acreage. During 1959–1961, countless irrigation facilities

Table 12.9
Supply of Chemical Fertilizers in
Nutrient Content (1,000 metric tons)

| Year | Total | Production | | | Imports |
|---|---|---|---|---|---|
| | | Nitrogen | Phosphorous | Potassium | |
| 1949 | 5 | 5 | 0 | 0 | 0 |
| 1950 | 34 | 14 | 0 | 0 | 20 |
| 1951 | 67 | 27 | 0 | 0 | 40 |
| 1952 | 79 | 39 | 0 | 0 | 40 |
| 1953 | 133 | 53 | 0 | 0 | 80 |
| 1954 | 205 | 69 | 0 | 0 | 136 |
| 1955 | 243 | 84 | 1 | 0 | 158 |
| 1956 | 401 | 117 | 14 | 0 | 270 |
| 1957 | 429 | 137 | 22 | 0 | 270 |
| 1958 | 626 | 202 | 64 | 0 | 360 |
| 1959 | 639 | 275 | 94 | 0 | 270 |
| 1960 | 710 | 345 | 150 | 0 | 215 |
| 1961 | 589 | 280 | 84 | 0 | 225 |
| 1962 | 788 | 444 | 104 | 0 | 240 |
| 1963 | 1,297 | 542 | 215 | 0 | 540 |
| 1964 | 1,485 | 712 | 416 | 0 | 357 |
| 1965 | 2,120 | 902 | 578 | 0 | 640 |
| 1966 | 2,604 | 1,046 | 800 | 36 | 722 |
| 1967 | 2,763 | 883 | 658 | 68 | 1,154 |
| 1968 | 3,128 | 1,040 | 761 | 92 | 1,235 |
| 1969 | 3,558 | 1,180 | 963 | 100 | 1,315 |
| 1970 | 4,266 | 1,562 | 1,103 | 116 | 1,485 |
| 1971 | 4,820 | 1,900 | 1,300 | 140 | 1,480 |
| 1972 | 5,494 | 2,345 | 1,447 | 152 | 1,550 |
| 1973 | 6,435 | 2,930 | 1,819 | 168 | 1,518 |
| 1974 | 6,106 | 3,165 | 1,612 | 180 | 1,149 |
| 1975 | 6,935 | 3,661 | 1,866 | 207 | 1,201 |
| 1976 | 5,851 | --- | --- | --- | 1,009 |
| 1977 | 9,088 | 4,830 | 2,462 | 273 | 1,523 |

Note: Domestic production figures in terms of standard weights are converted into nutrient content by the following coefficients: 20 percent for one nitrogen unit; 18.7 percent for one phosphoric acid unit; and 40 percent for potassium oxide.

Source: U.S. Central Intelligence Agency, China: Economic Indicators (Washington, D.C., December 1978), p. 14.

were washed out by floods, and the amount of irrigated acreage did not regain its previous peak level until the mid-1960s. Since the early 1960s, much of the expansion of irrigated areas has been on the North China Plain, where rainfall is both sparse and unevenly distributed throughout the year. During the 1970s, acreage under irrigation expanded at an average rate of about 3.95 million acres per year.[40] Official statistics reveal that between 1949 and 1979, China built 84,500 water reservoirs of various sizes, with a total capacity of 400 billion cubic meters. In addition, the Chinese peasants have dug 2.2 million tube wells. By 1979, 116 million acres (700 million mu) of the 247 million acres of Chinese farmland had reportedly been irrigated. Irrigated land now accounts for nearly one-half of China's cultivated land, compared to less than 10 percent in the United States, the U.S.S.R., and most European countries.

The expansion of irrigation and drainage facilities has helped to improve productivity and has turned more farmland into high- and stable-yield areas. As of 1979, those areas amounted to 81.5 million acres (500 million mu), or one-third of China's cultivated land.[41]

### *Agricultural Machinery*

Despite the government's repeated emphasis on agricultural mechanization, progress has been slow. Since 1961, mechanization has been gradually introduced, with the more power-consuming and labor-intensive operations being mechanized first. The priorities seem to fall in the following order:

1. water conservation and irrigation
2. food and fodder processing
3. threshing
4. land preparation
5. paddy transplanting and harvesting of crops

According to 1980 statistics, in 1979 China produced 126,000 tractors (15-horsepower units) and 318,000 hand tractors. The tractors in use in 1980 consisted of 670,000 large and medium-sized (20-horsepower and up) tractors and 1.67 million hand tractors. There were also 18,900 combined harvesters and 70,000 trucks for rural use. The total stock of power-driven drainage and irrigation machinery for rural use reached 71.22 million horsepower in 1979.[42] In that year, the country possessed 1,900 agricultural machinery manufacturing plants and more than 2,000 maintenance and repair plants. There were 10 million operators of agricultural machinery in the countryside.

This quite impressive record did not alter the agricultural scene much, however. A visitor to China during transplanting, harvesting, or threshing seasons will see that manual labor and draft animals continue to be the main source of power all over China. According to a 1974 estimate made by the Wheat Studies Delegation of the National Academy of Sciences, the number of workdays per year for the average Chinese peasant has approximately doubled in comparison with both the 1930s and the early 1950s.[43] Some of the increased labor per agricultural worker is devoted to the cultivation of crops, but much of it has gone into irrigation projects, multiple-cropping, fertilizing, and farmland construction.

The increase in the level of inputs has failed to raise output significantly, however. According to Robert Dernberger, between 1952 and 1975, the annual growth in the agricultural labor force was 1.73 percent; in sown areas adjusted for changes in irrigation, it was 0.95 percent; in livestock, 2.8 percent; and in fertilizers, 4.55 percent. These four items can be taken as representative of the increases in labor, land, capital, and current inputs, respectively. Using weights of 0.55 for labor, 0.25 for land, 0.09 for capital, and 0.11 for current inputs (see Table 12.8), Chinese peasants increased total inputs in agriculture by approximately 1.94 percent a year. During the same period, 1952–1975, the gross value of agricultural production was estimated to have increased by 2.9 percent, but its growth in value added was only 1.1 percent.[44] In other words, the average annual rate of increase of the gross value-added product in the Chinese agricultural sector during 1952–1975 was almost 1 percent less than the average annual rate of increase of the total quantity of inputs.

The low value added was due to the significant and steady increase of current inputs as a share of the gross value of output over the entire period, from 8 percent in 1952 to 38 percent in 1978, which resulted in higher costs of production. During the Cultural Revolution, the abolition of regulations led to the deterioration of product quality, and the utility of many industrial products, such as agricultural machinery and chemical fertilizers, declined. As a result, the cost of agricultural production mounted.[45] An investigation made by the Ministry of Agriculture of 2,162 agricultural production teams throughout China showed that average yields per acre for six food grains rose from 1,740 kilograms in 1965 to 2,370 kilograms in 1976 (705 to 960 kilograms per acre), an increase of 36 percent; yet the production costs per hectare increased from 393 yuan to 606 yuan, a rise of 54 percent. Consequently, net production suffered a decline, and the value of a peasant's average workday fell by 20 percent.[46]

As Dernberger observed, the developments in the input-output relationship in agricultural production signal future difficulties in sustaining an average rate of growth in total output of almost 3 percent within the framework of traditional Chinese agriculture.[47] For a breakthrough in agricultural production, further modernization becomes imperative.

## REFORMS AND PROSPECTS

By 1980, two conflicting forces were affecting Chinese agriculture. On the one hand, the material basis for higher productivity had been gradually formed over several years. But on the other hand, Chinese agriculture was being held back by severe problems of disincentives, maladministration, and poor planning, which remained unresolved after three decades.

Among the factors favoring agricultural advance, the most significant is the increase of chemical fertilizer production. As thirteen major urea-ammonia complexes constructed with foreign technology come on stream, domestic chemical fertilizer supplies will enjoy a quantum jump. The addition of some 3.5 million tons of nitrogen to the 7 million tons produced in 1977 will help the country increase production by 15 million tons of food grains a year. In irrigation development, the main thrust is to improve the utilization of existing facilities, which are currently exploited at well below designed capacity. The completion of auxiliary facilities to existing projects can immediately bring 20 million acres under irrigation (about 16 percent of the currently irrigated acreage).

Among the adverse factors for Chinese agriculture, the major one is the disruption of the ecological balance. As a result of large-scale destruction of forests and the blind conversion of vast stretches of grassland into farmland, huge mountain areas in the Northeast and Southwest have been denuded of vegetation, and each year erosion has stripped away topsoil and dumped millions of tons of silt into the Huang He and Chang Jiang. A survey by the Chinese Academy of Sciences reveals that since 1960, more than 3.5 million acres of farmland (cropland and grassland) have turned into desert each year. The water table of many major rivers and lakes has dropped drastically, and steady declines in rainfall in the Northeast and the North threaten agricultural growth in those regions.[48] Many geologists are concerned that before long the Chang Jiang will become silt-laden like the Huang He.[49]

The lopsided concentration on grain production has had several negative effects on Chinese agriculture. With farmland averaging out to a shade more than one-quarter of an acre per capita, food grains, cotton, and edible oils are all in short supply. A policy of regional self-sufficiency has prevented any specialization in agricultural production. Because arable land suitable for producing high-yield cotton, soybeans, or sugarcane has been used for grain, China has had to import not only increasing quantities of grain but cotton, edible oils, and sugar as well. Between 1960 and 1978, the reclamation of land for food production has shrunk the size of lakes and caused a 17 percent decline in the supply of freshwater fish, and the number of milk cows in 1978 was no larger than in 1963. An increasing population has meant a steady decline in the per capita supply of fish, meat, and dairy products.

In view of these problems, in late 1979, the central planners introduced new guidelines for agricultural modernization. The new plan made several important revisions in the program that Hua Guofeng had announced in February 1978. In the first place, diversification and all-around rural development have replaced the increase in food grains as the main goal of agricultural development. One consensus reached by Chinese leaders and agro-economists was that the traditional policy ("taking grain as the key link") must be altered. This historic shift of emphasis will require a step-by-step restructuring of the small peasant economy, with its focus on grains, into a modern agricultural production system, with an all-around development of forestry, livestock breeding, fisheries, and the cultivation of grains and cash crops. Moreover, agricultural development should combine with industry and commerce. Thus, people freed by machines would move into diverse occupations, including afforestation, horticulture, stock breeding, fisheries, transport, small industrial enterprises, and service trades.

The mechanization program has been drastically cut back, and quantitative targets have been quietly abandoned. In the spring of 1978, it was officially announced that the country would achieve 70 percent mechanization of all major farm processes by 1980 and 85 percent mechanization by 1985. The Decisions on Some Questions Concerning the Acceleration of Agricultural Development of December 1978 dropped the goal of mechanization. In early 1980, Zhao Ziyang, the new premier of the State Council, openly argued that, given China's huge population, mechanization was not an urgent task to which great resources should be devoted. He recommended that in the short-run, China stress the application of modern science and technology to agriculture by improving seed strains, sprinkler irrigation, and composite feed for poultry and pigs. Moreover, Zhao contended that the emphasis in mechanization should be on rural transportation not on the increase of tractors, since peasants had been using their tractors on the roads instead of in the fields.[50] Zhan Wu, president of the Institute of Agricultural Economy of the Chinese Academy of Social Sciences, added that for a long period, mechanization, semimechanization, and manual labor would exist side by side. Full mechanization could only be a long-term goal. For South China, he recommended an increased use of irrigation and drainage machines to raise yields in low-lying rice-producing areas. In the North, where summer rains damage mature wheat crops, harvesting and drying machines were urgently needed. In short, the old policy of identifying tractors with agricultural mechanization has been abandoned.

The promotion of peasant incentives and the reform of farm institutions were also a part of the package designed to accelerate agricultural development. The 1978 campaign to relieve the peasants of unreasonable burdens and arbitrary exactions exposed a host of abuses that had reduced peasant incentives to improve production. The three major causes of peasant apathy and resistance were the high costs of agricultural inputs, unduly low procurement prices, and the lack of a direct connection between work and reward. Because of an overconcentration of power in local goverment and because production teams had not been allowed to make their own decisions, farming in many areas was carried out in such a way "as to fit the restrictive, petty and multifarious regulations formulated by high-ups who are divorced from reality."[51]

Aware of these problems, the government announced in early 1979 a general producer's price increase of 20 percent for within-quota grain and of 50 percent for above-quota grain, to begin in the summer of 1979, together with a gradual decrease of 10–15 percent in prices of industrial inputs sold to the peasants. These changes raised the fertilizer-to-grain price ratio for above-quota sales to a level somewhat equal to that prevailing in Taiwan but still well below those in South Korea and Japan.[52]

Improved incentives require changes in the income distribution system. From 1958 to 1978, the communes apportioned income largely on a per capita basis, with work points accounting for only 10 percent in the calculation. This egalitarian policy weakened peasant motivation. To promote initiative, a new system was introduced in the fall of 1979, wherein work points count for 30 percent in the income distribution, and the other 70 percent of income is distributed on an equal per capita basis. Moreover, larger private plots were permitted. Previously, only 5 percent of the cultivated land had been alloted as private plots, but under the new system, commune members may contract to farm small plots of outlying and barren land in addition to the regular plots assigned to each household. Any additional income derived from increased output as a result of soil improvement and good management belongs to the individual commune member. Private plots and this type of contract plot can account for 15 percent of the cultivated area of a production team.[53]

By far the most dramatic reform was the breaking up of the production team (previously the smallest unit of the commune organization) into groups of families or individuals. The teams still own the land and means of production, but the work groups have become the real operation units. They sign contracts with their teams specifying what they are expected to produce. Quotas assigned to work groups are based roughly on an average of the three previous years' crops yields but are set low enough to let hard-working peasants overfulfill their quotas. Any excess goes to the work groups.[54] Official reports indicate that by June 1980, some 80 percent of the rural production teams had adopted the new system.[55]

Another reform under consideration would change the current procurement system into a contract system. Under this arrangement, the state would only propose production quotas, purchase quotas, and planting plans to the communes, brigades, and teams. Each commune would then decide if it wished to specialize in certain crops. If it decided to specialize, it could exchange its products with other communes on a contract basis.[56]

The reforms are intended to correct institutional impediments to agricultural development. It remains to be seen, however, how well the new government policy will be carried out. Most rural cadres have joined the Party and/or government since the Cultural Revolution and may not share the national and provincial leaders' enthusiasm for the new policies. Local reports have indicated widespread resistance among commune directors and county Party secretaries.[57] Even the peasants are very skeptical about the durability of the new policies.

In the near future, agricultural progress will depend on two crucial variables: strict control of rural population growth and high peasant motivation. In contrast to other developing countries, where economic growth has generally accompanied a steady decline in agricultural labor, China's industrialization has failed to reduce the country's agricultural population. The nation's labor force has increased by 13 million people per annum since 1970, but fewer than 2 million of them have been absorbed into the modern sector. Consequently, the growth of the rural population has meant a steady decline in per capita output and consumption. Between 1957 and 1978, the per capita consumption of staples in the rural areas declined steadily. According to recent official statistics, over those twenty years, there was a drop of 5.9 percent in food grain consumption, 5.7 percent in cotton cloth consumption, and a sharp drop of 43.2 percent in edible oil consumption. In 1978, peasant income from the commune averaged only 73.9 yuan, or $47 per capita. Total cash and food grain reserves for the entire commune system amounted to only 8 billion yuan ($5 billion), with an average of $6 per capita.[58] This low level of rural consumption and capital accumulation makes strict control of rural population growth imperative. Without an effective rural birth control program, the land-population ratio can only deteriorate. Moreover, since the flow of capital into the agricultural sector will remain very limited, the key to agricultural development lies in motivating the 300 million rural laborers to increase production. Records over the past thirty years show an inverse relationship between peasant enthusiasm and the degree of collectivization. The disincentive effect of socialized farming has been confirmed by the experiences of the Soviet Union and Eastern Europe. If self-interest is indeed a basic human drive, the relegation of control from production teams to small working groups, the increased size of private plots, and the relaxation of control over farm markets may help unleash the productive potential of China's 800 million rural people.

## NOTES

1. P.R.C., State Planning Commission, *The First Five-Year Plan for the Development of the National Economy, 1953–1957,* p. 82.
2. Ibid., p. 23.
3. The Chinese version was published in *Renmin ribao,* January 26, 1956. The English version was issued by the Foreign Languages Press in Beijing in 1956.
4. NCNA-Beijing, September 7, 1979; FBIS, September 12, 1979, p. L14.
5. *Jihua yu tongji* [Planning and statistics] No. 4 (April 1960), p. 9.
6. Hua Guofeng, "Mobilize the Whole Party, Make Greater Efforts to Develop Agriculture, and Strive to Build Dazhai-Type Counties Throughout the Country," *Renmin ribao,* October 21, 1975.
7. Hua Guofeng, "Speech at the Second National Conference on Learning from Dazhai in Agriculture," *Renmin ribao,* December 24, 1976; *Peking Review* 20:1 (January 1, 1977), pp. 31–44.
8. For details, see Hua Guofeng's February 26, 1978, speech, "Unite and

Strive to Build a Modern, Powerful Socialist Country!" p. 7.

9. Yu Qiuli's speech to the Third National Conference on Agricultural Mechanization, January 25, 1978 (FBIS, January 31, 1978, pp. E6–E25).

10. Xinhua-Beijing, August 2, 1980.

11. The English text of these two documents appeared in *Issues and Studies* 15:7 (July 1969) and 15:8 (August 1979).

12. Yin Ta-keng, "Will the Banner of Dazhai Fall?" *Tung-hsiang* [Trends] No. 1 (October 20, 1978), pp. 22–25; and Commentator, "A Warning Against Liars," *Renmin ribao*, July 8, 1980.

13. The Eight-Point Charter advocated by Mao included eight important measures to improve agricultural production: water, fertilizer, soil conservation, seed selection, close planting, plant protection, implements, and field management.

14. D. Gale Johnson and Arcadius Kahan, "Soviet Agriculture: Structure and Growth," in U.S., Congress, Joint Economic Committee, *Comparisons of U.S. and Soviet Economies*, Part 1 (Washington, D.C.: Government Printing Office, 1959), p. 204.

15. The figure of 250 million tons is reported in P.R.C., State Statistical Bureau, *Ten Great Years*, p. 119. The figure of 200 million tons is revealed in Xue Muqiao, "Thirty Years of Strenuous Efforts," *Hongqi* No. 10 (October 1979), p. 46.

16. Xue Muqiao, "Thirty Years of Strenuous Efforts," p. 46.

17. *Peking Review* 8:29 (July 16, 1965), p. 20.

18. Christopher Howe, *China's Economy: A Basic Guide* (New York: Basic Books, 1978), p. 81.

19. Ibid., p. 73.

20. *Jingji yanjiu* No. 12 (December 1978), p. 22.

21. "China to Speed Up Agricultural Development," *Beijing Review* 22:11 (March 16, 1979), pp. 14–15.

22. *Jingji yanjiu* No. 2 (February 1979), pp. 31 and 43, and No. 7 (July 1979), p. 21.

23. *Guangming ribao*, December 8, 1979.

24. Xian Shaanxi Provincial Services, March 23, 1979.

25. FBIS, January 9, 1980, pp. O1–O2; and *Guangming ribao*, December 8, 1979.

26. Colin Clark, *The Condition of Economic Progress*, 3d ed. (London: Macmillan, 1960), Table XXIII.

27. John Lossing Buck, *Land Utilization in China*, vol. 1 (New York: Council on Economic and Cultural Affairs, 1956), p. 15.

28. Nai-Ruenn Chen and Walter Galenson, *The Chinese Economy Under Communism*, p. 6.

29. *Renmin jiaoyu* [People's education] No. 9 (September 1978), p. 58.

30. Henry J. Groen and James A. Kilpatrick, "China's Agricultural Production," in U.S., Congress, Joint Economic Committee, *Chinese Economy Post-Mao*, p. 646.

31. *Renmin ribao*, December 8, 1978, p. 3.

32. Editorial, *Renmin ribao,* March 6, 1979.
33. *Jingji yanjiu* No. 2 (February 1979), p. 37.
34. Ibid., p. 39.
35. Tong Dalin and Bao Tong, "Some Views on Agricultural Modernization."
36. Anthony M. Tang, "Policy and Performance in Agriculture," in Alexander Eckstein, Walter Galenson, and Ta-chung Liu, eds., *Economic Trends in Communist China,* p. 492.
37. Editorial, *Renmin ribao,* March 6, 1979.
38. Kang Chao, *Agricultural Production in Communist China,* p. 156.
39. U.S., Congress, Joint Economic Committee, *People's Republic of China: An Economic Assessment,* pp. 47–51.
40. *Peking Review* 20:9 (February 25, 1977), p. 15.
41. *Zhongguo xinwen,* September 30, 1979, p. 2.
42. P.R.C., State Statistical Bureau, "Communiqué on Fulfillment of China's 1979 National Economic Plan," *Beijing Review* 23:19 (May 12, 1980), p. 14.
43. Robert F. Dernberger, "The Progress of Agricultural Transformation in Mainland China," *Issues and Studies* 14:10 (October 1978), pp. 80–81.
44. Ibid.
45. *Xinhua yuebao* No. 2 (February 1980), p. 69.
46. "Strengthening Study on the Technological Economy of Agricultural Mechanization," *Jingji yanjiu* No. 12 (December 1978), pp. 17–18.
47. Robert F. Dernberger, "Progress of Agricultural Transformation."
48. *Renmin ribao,* October 16, 1979, and *Beijing Review* 23:4 (January 28, 1980), pp. 24–26.
49. *Renmin ribao,* September 4, 1979.
50. Zhao Ziyang, "Study New Conditions and Implement the Principle of Readjustment in an All-Round Way," *Hongqi* No. 1 (January 1980), pp. 15–20.
51. Xinhua-Beijing, November 22, 1978; FBIS, November 22, 1978, p. K2.
52. According to an official study, in Japan 1 jin (0.5 kilogram) of rice is worth 3 jin of diesel oil, but in China 1 jin of rice can buy only 0.5 jin of diesel oil. In Japan, a 20-horsepower tractor costs 11,000 jin of rice; in China, a 28-horsepower tractor costs 91,000 jin of rice. In Japan, 1 jin of rice can buy 8.5 jin of phosphorus fertilizer; in China, 1.5 jin of rice is worth only 1 jin of phosphorus fertilizer (*Jingji yanjiu* No. 12 [December 1978], pp. 20–21).
53. Zhao Ziyang, "Study New Conditions," pp. 15–20.
54. Xinhua-Beijing, February 4, 1980; FBIS, February 5, 1980, pp. L7–L8.
55. Xinhua-Beijing, June 27, 1980; FBIS, July 2, 1980, p. L12.
56. Yu Guoyao, "Applying Economic Means to Readjusting the Irrational Structure of Agriculture," *Guangming ribao,* January 17, 1980, p. 2.
57. See Editorial, *Renmin ribao,* September 17, 1979; *Renmin ribao,* October 4, 1979, p. 2; *Renmin ribao,* October 14, 1979, p. 2; Xinhua-Beijing, June 27, 1980; FBIS, July 2, 1980, p. L13.
58. Wang Jingjin, "Socialist Reconstruction Must Respect the Law – Agriculture as the Foundation of the National Economy," *Jingji yanjiu* No. 12 (December 1979), p. 37.

# 13

# Changes in the Structure of the Economy

Economic development has two major components: growth of national output and changes in the structure of the economy. The previous three chapters discussed the growth of GNP, industrial output, and agricultural output. This chapter will focus on changes in the structure of the economy.

Many developed countries have displayed a general pattern of change as their economies modernized and grew. First, a long-term increase in per capita output has generally been accompanied by a continuous decline in the proportion of GNP supplied by agricultural and related primary industries. This shift in favor of the nonagricultural sector is evident in its shares of the labor force, capital stock, and national product. In the century between 1850 and 1950, the share of agricultural employment in the U.S. labor force dropped from more than 70 percent to less than 10 percent. As Simon Kuznets has observed, "One of the major requirements of economic growth is the capacity of society to undergo these rapid internal shifts, to make feasible this continuous mobility and redistribution of the labor force and population among the various sectors of the country's economy."[1] Second, shifts in the industrial structure and the acceleration of urbanization have required a significant rise in capital formation, In many developed countries, net capital formation in the process of industrialization rose from less than 5 percent of GNP to about 15 percent, and gross capital formation rose from less than 10 percent to about 25 percent of GNP.[2]

Third, within modern industry, a marked change has also occurred in the pattern of manufacturing output. According to W. G. Hoffmann, in the first stage of industrialization, the net output of consumer goods industries is, on the average, five times that of capital goods. In the second stage, the ratio is reduced to about 2.5 to 1, and in the third stage, the net output of the two groups is approximately equal.[3] Fourth, apart from changes in the industrial structure, modern economic growth has spread capital and technology from the industrial centers to the less developed regions, bringing about a more balanced development of the entire country. Although these general trends may not fit every economy, they represent generally accepted criteria by which to gauge modern economic development.

Over the past thirty years, the structure of the Chinese economy has undergone dramatic changes in terms of sectoral structure, relationships between investment and consumption, industrial structure, and geographic distribution of production facilities. This chapter will explore China's progress in these four areas and assess the impact of the structural changes on economic growth. Since the systematic information required for an in-depth study is extremely scarce, the analysis relies quite heavily on sketchy evidence. Most of the findings must therefore be taken as illustrative rather than as conclusive, but, in my opinion, the central tendencies are basically borne out by the facts.

## CHANGES IN SECTORAL CONTRIBUTIONS TO NATIONAL PRODUCT

The most distinctive feature of modern economic development is the shift of product and labor force from agriculture into manufacturing. In twelve of the thirteen countries surveyed by Kuznets, the share of the agricultural sector in total product declined with modernization. The premodern shares of agriculture were near 50 percent and fell to 10–20 percent with industrialization. The proportion of the labor force engaged in agriculture fell from approximately 65 percent to 10 percent. During the process, the share of manufactured products in the GNP rose from 20–30 percent (premodern) to 40–50 percent. The proportion of the labor force in manufacturing also rose, but to a lesser degree. Economic development produced no marked trends, however, in the service sector's share of total product or labor force.[4]

In pre–World War II years, agriculture supplied the overwhelming share of China's national product. As Table 13.1 shows, in 1933, calculated in 1952 constant prices, agriculture accounted for 56.9 percent of net domestic product (NDP), and the modern nonagricultural sector accounted for only 20.9 percent, the traditional nonagricultural sector contributed 19.8 percent, and government administration, 2.4 percent. In 1952, on the eve of China's First Five-Year Plan, agriculture still represented 47.9 percent of China's NDP. Table 13.1 shows the sectoral division of NDP in the three landmark years of 1933, 1952, and 1957.

Between 1933 and 1952, the share of agricultural products in the NDP dropped 9 percentage points, and that of the nonagricultural modern sector rose 7.9 percentage points. When the new government began its FFYP in 1953, a large share of new investment was concentrated on industrial development. Consequently, agriculture's share of NDP dropped another 8.9 percentage points (almost equaling the decline of 1933–1952), and that of the modern nonagricultural sector

Table 13.1
Percentage Distribution of Net Domestic Product
by Modern and Traditional Sectors
(in percent)

| Sector | In Constant 1933 Prices | | | In Constant 1952 Prices | | |
|---|---|---|---|---|---|---|
| | 1933 | 1952 | 1957 | 1933 | 1952 | 1957 |
| Agriculture | 65.0 | 56.6 | 49.3 | 56.9 | 47.9 | 39.0 |
| Modern non-agricultural sector | 12.6 | 18.1 | 26.9 | 20.9 | 28.8 | 41.2 |
| Traditional nonagricultural sector | 19.6 | 19.6 | 16.5 | 19.8 | 18.7 | 14.5 |
| Government administration | 2.8 | 5.7 | 7.3 | 2.4 | 4.6 | 5.3 |

Notes: The modern nonagricultural sector includes factories, mines, utilities, construction, modern transportation and communications, trading stores, restaurants, and modern financial institutions.

The traditional nonagricultural sector includes handicrafts, old fashioned transportation, peddlers, traditional financial institutions, personal services, rent, and work brigades.

Sources: Ta-chung Liu and Kung-chia Yeh, The Economy of the Chinese Mainland: National Income and Economic Development, 1933-1959 (Princeton, N.J.: Princeton University Press, 1965), p. 89.

gained 12.4 percentage points. This indicates that China was industrializing fairly rapidly during the FFYP period.

To facilitate a comparison of Chinese modernization efforts in 1953–1957 with those of the Soviet Union in 1928–1940 (the first two five-year plans of the U.S.S.R.), Table 13.2 segregates the Chinese NDP into three sectors: agricultural (A sector), including farming, fishery, and forestry; modern (M+ sector), including manufacturing, mining, construction, transportation and communications, and utilities; and the rest of the economy (S– sector), mainly the service sector.

Both China and the U.S.S.R. started their respective FFYPs with about half of their total product coming from agriculture, a little more than a quarter from the modern sector, and slightly less than a quarter from the remaining sector. The decline in the share of agriculture oc-

Table 13.2
Shares of Major Sectors in Net Domestic Product and Labor Force and Relative Product Per Worker in China and U.S.S.R.

| Share | China (in 1952 prices) | | | | U.S.S.R. | |
|---|---|---|---|---|---|---|
| | Official data reconstructed on Western concept | | Liu-Yeh estimates | | | |
| | 1952 | 1957 | 1952 | 1957 | 1928 | 1940 |
| Share in NDP (%) | | | | | | |
| A Sector | 46.1 | 38.6 | 47.9 | 39.0 | 49.2 | 28.9 |
| M+ Sector | 29.0 | 37.9 | 28.2 | 38.7 | 27.9 | 44.8 |
| S-Sector | 24.9 | 23.5 | 23.9 | 22.3 | 22.9 | 26.3 |
| Share in Labor Force (%) | | | | | | |
| A Sector | 69.9 | 73.1 | 72.9 | 72.9 | 70.9 | 50.9 |
| M+ Sector | 17.1 | 16.4 | 15.5 | 16.6 | 17.6 | 29.4 |
| S-Sector | 13.0 | 10.5 | 11.6 | 10.5 | 11.5 | 19.7 |
| Relative Product Per Worker | | | | | | |
| A Sector | 0.66 | 0.53 | 0.66 | 0.53 | 0.69 | 0.57 |
| M+ Sector | 1.70 | 2.31 | 1.82 | 2.33 | 1.59 | 1.52 |
| S-Sector | 1.92 | 2.24 | 2.06 | 2.12 | 1.99 | 1.34 |

Source: Ta-chung Liu, "Quantitative Trends in the Economy," in Alexander Eckstein, Walter Galenson, and Ta-chung Liu, eds., Economic Trends in Communist China (Chicago: Aldine, 1968), pp. 124-125.

curred at almost the same speed in China during 1952–1957 as in the U.S.S.R. during 1928–1940, roughly 17 percentage points per decade. The expansion of the modern sector was more rapid in China, however—23 percentage points per decade as against only 14 percentage points for the U.S.S.R. The rest of the economy declined in China but expanded a little in the U.S.S.R.[5]

Although the changes in product composition were very striking, the structure of the Chinese labor force remained virtually unchanged between 1952 and 1957, whereas the proportion of the Soviet labor force in agriculture had dropped 17 percentage points in one decade. These statistics suggest that in 1952–1957, the Chinese agricultural sector had either experienced massive underemployment or had failed to achieve an increase in labor productivity. The data also show that approximately 70 to 73 percent of China's labor force was responsible for only 40 to 50 percent of NDP in 1952–1957.

National income data became extremely scarce after the collapse of the Great Leap in 1960. Starting with scanty evidence and differing assumptions, Ta-chung Liu and K. C. Yeh, Robert Dernberger, and Nai-Ruenn Chen made separate estimates of the sectoral contributions to China's national income for different years. Table 13.3 summarizes these estimates, although the results are not strictly comparable. Nevertheless, the trend shown in the table is consistent with the changes in relative shares between agricultural gross output value and industrial gross output value as reported by official Chinese sources (see Table 13.4).

Table 13.4 illustrates the sharp decline of agriculture's contribution to the combined agricultural and industrial gross output value from about two-thirds in 1949 to approximately one-fourth in 1979. But the figures do not reflect the real importance of those two sectors, since they are gross output values and are subject to different degrees of double-counting. Official statistics reveal that the net to gross ratio (net output value divided by gross output value) in 1956 was 73.56 percent for agriculture, 48.65 percent for producer goods, and only 20 percent for consumer goods.[6] Of industrial consumer goods, four-fifths embody raw materials. If calculated on a net basis, by deducting intermediate goods from gross value, the agricultural share still looms very large. For instance, when calculated in gross value, agriculture accounted for only 25 percent of the combined agricultural-industrial gross output value in 1977. Yet when net value is reckoned, agriculture contributed 42 percent and industry 58 percent.[7] Despite these distortions, the decline of the agricultural share and the rise of the industrial share are beyond dispute.

Table 13.3
Sectoral Contribution to China's National Product
in Selected Years
(in percent)

| Year | Independent Estimates | | | Official Statistics | | |
|---|---|---|---|---|---|---|
| | Agriculture | M+ Sector | Service | Agriculture | M+ Sector | Service |
| 1949 | N.A. | N.A. | N.A. | 68.4[e] | 12.6[e] | 19.0[e] |
| 1952 | 47.9[a] | 28.2[a] | 23.9[a] | 57.7[e] | 19.5[e] | 22.8[e] |
| 1957 | 39.0[a] | 38.7[a] | 22.3[a] | N.A. | N.A. | N.A. |
| 1965 | 30.0[b] | 42.0[b] | 28.0[b] | N.A. | N.A. | N.A. |
| 1970 | 29.0[b] | 44.0[b] | 27.0[b] | N.A. | N.A. | N.A. |
| 1975 | 37.0[c] | 38.0[c] | 25.0[c] | N.A. | N.A. | N.A. |
| 1978 | 28.0[d] | 49.0[d] | 23.0[d] | 35.6[e] | 46.7[e] | 17.7[e] |

Note: Independent estimates refer to GNP in 1957 constant prices, while official statistics are national income calculated in 1970 prices. The 1970 prices involve an upward adjustment of agricultural prices from the 1957 constant prices, resulting in a larger share for agriculture than the independent estimates.
N.A. denotes "not available".

Sources: (a) From Table 13.2. (b) Ta-chung Liu and Kung-chia Yeh, "China and Other Asian Economies: A Quantitative Evaluation," American Economic Review 63:2 (May 1973), p. 218. (c) Robert F. Dernberger, "The Economic Consequence of Defense Expenditure Choice to China," in U.S. Congress, Joint Economic Committee, China: A Reassessment of the Economy (Washington, D.C.: Government Printing Office, 1975), pp. 460-499. (d) Projections made by Nai-Ruenn Chen, "Economic Modernization in Post-Mao China," in U.S. Congress, Joint Economic Committee, Chinese Economy Post-Mao (Washington, D.C.: Government Printing Office, 1978), pp. 202-203. (e) Derived from Yang Jianbai and Li Xuezeng, "China's Historical Experience in Handling the Relations Between Agriculture, Light Industry, and Heavy Industry," Zhongguo shehui kexue (Social sciences in China) No. 3 (May 1980), pp. 2-3. One recent Chinese official source gave personal service at only 13 percent of national income, significantly lower than the independent estimates. In 1949, there was an average of 5.66 service workers for every 100 residents in Beijing; in 1979, only 3.64 (Beijing Review 23:31 /August 4, 1980/, p. 15).

A comparison of the figures for 1975 and 1957 in Table 13.3 shows a very moderate decline of agriculture's share of the national product. Between 1957 and 1975, according to independent estimates, the agricultural share dropped a mere 2 percentage points compared to the decline of 9 percentage points during the slightly longer period between 1933 and 1952. The slight decline of the industrial share in the 1957–1975 period, according to the independent estimates, is the result of overestimating for the service sector. The official source indicates that the service sector actually declined during that period. The no-growth record of the industrial share between 1957 and 1975, however, would suggest that the pace of China's industrialization slowed considerably after 1957. The severe disruptions caused by the Great Leap Forward in 1958–1960 and the Cultural Revolution contributed to that slow progress.

Despite these setbacks, a comparison of China's sectoral distribution

Table 13.4
Relative Shares of Agriculture and Industry in the Combined Gross Output Values of Agriculture and Industry, 1949-1979 (in percent)

| Year | Agriculture | Industry |
|---|---|---|
| 1949 | 69.9 | 30.1 |
| 1952 | 58.5 | 41.5 |
| 1957 | 43.3 | 56.7 |
| 1960 | 20.1 | 79.9 |
| 1965 | 29.8 | 70.2 |
| 1977 | 25.0 | 75.0 |
| 1978 | 25.6 | 74.4 |
| 1979 | 25.7 | 74.3 |

Sources: Figures for 1949 and 1952 are from P.R.C. State Statistical Bureau, Ten Great Years (Beijing: Foreign Languages Press, 1960), p. 17. Figures for 1957, 1960, and 1965 are from Xue Muqiao, "Thirty Years of Strenuous Efforts," Hongqi (Red flag) No. 10 (October 1979), p. 45. Figures for 1977 are from Jingji yanjiu (Economic research) No. 4 (April 1979), p. 50; for 1978 are from Xinhua yuebao (New China monthly) No. 10 (October 1979), p. 126; and for 1979 are from P.R.C. State Statistical Bureau, "Communiqué on Fulfillment of China's 1979 National Economic Plan," Beijing Review 23:19 (May 12, 1980), p. 12.

with that of other countries during the post-World War II years (see Table 13.5) shows that the share of the modern sector in China's total product ranks among that of countries with a fairly high per capita product (in 1975, China's 38 percent was higher than the percentages for groups III and IV). But the large share of agriculture in the total product puts China in the group with a lower per capita income (China's 37 percent in 1975 was close to the 39 percent for groups V and VI). The share of the service sector in China's total product (25 percent) is smaller than the average of any other group.

Table 13.5
Comparison of Industrial Structure, China and Other Nations
(in percent)

| Share in Product | A Sector | M+ Sector | S Sector |
|---|---|---|---|
| China (1952-1957) | 43.5 | 33.5 | 23.1 |
| China (1975) | 37.0 | 38.0 | 25.0 |
| Groups I & II | 15.2 | 49.5 | 35.3 |
| Groups III & IV | 24.6 | 34.3 | 41.1 |
| Groups V & VI | 39.0 | 27.4 | 33.5 |
| Groups VI & VII | 48.0 | 19.6 | 32.4 |
| **Share in Labor Forces** | | | |
| China (1952-1957) | 72.9 | 16.1 | 11.1 |
| China (1978) | 74.0 | 16.5 | 9.5 |
| Groups I & II | 18.9 | 45.7 | 35.4 |
| Groups III & IV | 39.5 | 30.7 | 29.8 |
| Groups V & VI | 53.6 | 23.0 | 23.4 |
| Groups VI & VII | 59.3 | 18.8 | 21.9 |

Notes: Groups of nations are based on per capita income. Groups I and II are the highest income nations. Groups VI and VII are the lowest. Original figures do not add to 100.

Sources: The group figures for the early postwar years are from Simon Kuznets, Economic Trends in the Soviet Union: A Comparative Appraisal (Cambridge, Mass: Harvard University Press, 1963), Table VIII. The figures for China in 1952 and 1957 are from Ta-chung Liu, "Quantitative Trends in the Economy," in Alexander Eckstein, Walter Galenson, and Ta-chung Liu, eds., Economic Trends in Communist China (Chicago: Aldine, 1968), p. 127. The 1975 product shares are from Table 13.3. The 1978 labor shares are derived from three sources: (1) The total labor force in 1978 was reported as 400 million, of which 74 percent worked on farms (Xinhua yuebao /New China monthly/ No. 4 /April 1980/, p. 63). (2) Service and trade workers have dropped from 14.5 percent of the total labor force in 1957 to 9.5 percent in 1978 (Xinhua-Beijing, December 27, 1979). (3) The residual is counted as labor force for the M+ Sector.

A comparison of the distribution of labor force among the three sectors shows that China has a larger proportion of its labor force engaged in agriculture (A sector) and a smaller proportion working in the modern sector (M+ sector) than the averages of even the lowest per capita income group. The fact that the bulk of China's labor force remains in the agricultural sector is the most significant failure of China's industrialization effort during the past three decades.

## CHANGES IN PROPORTIONS OF CONSUMPTION AND INVESTMENT

A significant rise in the proportion of GNP devoted to capital formation is a prerequisite for modern economic development. Kuznets has identified three trends in the end-use of gross domestic product (GDP) as a result of modern economic growth. First, the private consumption share of GDP declines from its premodern economic growth level of 85–90 percent to less than 75 percent; second, government expenditures rise from 3–5 percent to 14 percent; and third, gross national capital formation rises from less than 10 percent to 12–20 percent.[8]

Some economists have characterized China's pre–World War II economy as a diminishing one in which capital formation was extremely low. The rate of investment for the period 1931–1936 was only 5 percent of GDP, based on 1933 prices, or 7.5 percent, based on 1952 prices. To promote rapid industrialization, the Communist government placed great stress on promoting capital accumulation at the expense of private consumption, thus producing a radical change in the end-use of the domestic product.

According to a study by Ta-chung Liu and Kung-chia Yeh (hereafter referred to as the Liu-Yeh study), private consumption (including communal services) accounted for 89 percent of GDP in 1933. It dropped to 73.9 percent in 1952 and declined further to 69 percent of GDP in 1957.[9] The share of government expenditures remained stable between 1952 and 1957. The proportion of gross investment in total expenditure registered substantial jumps from 7.5 percent in 1931–1936 to 19.1 percent in 1952 and 24 percent in 1957. Most of that change occurred during 1949–1952. If we assume that private consumption in 1949 accounted for a share not much less than 89 percent of GDP, like that in 1933, then the drop in the consumption share from 1949 to 1952 was drastic. In other countries, it took thirty to eighty years for private consumption's share of GDP to fall from 80 percent to 60–70 percent, as against a 15-percentage-point drop in only four years in China. During the first four years of Communist control, a series of measures reduced private consumption and promoted capital formation. These included the land reform program, which eliminated the country's wealthy landowner classes, and the large-scale confiscation of private property under the "three-anti" and "five-anti" campaigns (see Chapter 5).

The proportion of GDP devoted to consumption (private and public) further declined to only 60 percent during the turbulent years of the Great Leap Forward, when capital accumulation rose to an unprecedented level of 40 percent of GDP.[10] It rose to 72 percent in 1962 and dropped again to 67 percent during 1970–1978. In 1978, the share of consumption stood at only 64 percent, slightly higher than in 1959–1960 (see Table 13.6).

The high rate of capital formation estimated by the Liu-Yeh study for the 1960–1970 period and the capital accumulation reported by the Chinese government for 1970–1978 contrast sharply with those of other countries in the early post-World War II years. Table 13.7 compares the relative weights of various categories of expenditure in China during the 1952–1957 and 1970–1978 periods with those of

Table 13.6
Gross Domestic Product by End-Use, 1952–1978
(in percent)

| Year | (1) Personal Consumption | (2) Government Consumption | (3) Fixed Investment | (4) Changes in Inventory | (5) Export Surplus |
|---|---|---|---|---|---|
| 1952 | 73.9 | 7 | 19.1 | — | 1 |
| 1957 | 69.0 | 7 | 20.0 | 4 | 0 |
| 1961 | 63.0 | 8 | 19.0 | 10 | 1 |
| 1962 | 64.0 | 8 | 18.0 | 8 | 1 |
| 1963 | 63.0 | 8 | 20.0 | 7 | 1 |
| 1964 | 64.0 | 8 | 20.0 | 6 | 1 |
| 1965 | 64.0 | 8 | 23.0 | 5 | 1 |
| 1966 | 62.0 | 9 | 24.0 | 5 | 1 |
| 1967 | 65.0 | 9 | 21.0 | 4 | 1 |
| 1968 | 66.0 | 9 | 22.0 | 2 | 1 |
| 1969 | 66.0 | 10 | 22.0 | 2 | 1 |
| 1970 | 64.0 | 10 | 23.0 | 3 | 1 |
| 1970–1978 | 67 | | | 33 | |
| 1978 | 64 | | | 36 | |

Sources: The 1952 figures are from Ta-chung Liu, "Quantitative Trends in the Economy," in Alexander Eckstein, Walter Galenson, and Ta-chung Liu, eds., Economic Trends in Communist China (Chicago: Aldine, 1968), pp. 138–139. The 1957–1970 figures are from Ta-chung Liu and Kung-chia Yeh, "Chinese and Other Asian Economies: A Quantitative Evaluation," American Economic Review 63:2 (May 1973), p. 221. The 1970–1978 figures are from Renmin ribao (People's daily), October 20, 1979.

other non-Communist countries grouped by per capita product in the 1950s. The proportion of gross investment in China's total expenditure—23 percent in 1952–1957 and 33 percent in 1970–1978—ranks China among the countries with the highest per capita product (groups I and II). The proportion of gross investment devoted to consumption in the different country groups falls within a very narrow range. China's proportions of 67.6 percent (excluding communal services) in the 1952–1957 period and 57 percent (excluding government consumption) in 1970–1978 fall within the range of the low groups III–VII (see Table 13.7).

Under normal conditions, a high rate of capital formation would

Table 13.7
Shares of Various Uses of Gross Domestic Product,
China and Groups of Countries, 1952-1957, 1970-1978
(in percent)

| Countries | Private Consumption | Government Consumption | Gross Domestic Capital Formation |
|---|---|---|---|
| China | | | |
| 1952-1957 | 67.6 | 9.4 | 23.0 |
| 1970-1978 | 57.0 | 10.0 | 33.0 |
| Groups of Countries (Classified by per capita product) | | | |
| I | 64.9 | 13.0 | 21.2 |
| II | 61.8 | 13.6 | 24.5 |
| III | 69.8 | 12.8 | 17.4 |
| IV | 72.7 | 10.7 | 16.6 |
| V | 69.3 | 12.2 | 18.5 |
| VI | 73.0 | 11.2 | 15.9 |
| VII | 71.5 | 11.7 | 16.8 |

Note: Private consumption excludes communal services. Government consumption includes communal services (schools, hospital, etc.). Original figures for groups of countries do not add to 100.

Sources: Figures for China in 1952-1957 are from Ta-chung Liu, "Quantitative Trends in the Economy," in Alexander Eckstein, Walter Galenson, and Ta-chung Liu, eds., Economic Trends in Communist China (Chicago: Aldine, 1968), p. 141. Those for China 1970-1978 are from Renmin ribao (People's daily), October 20, 1979. The share of government consumption is assumed to be that of 1969-1970. Figures for groups of countries (1952-1957) are from Simon Kuznets, Economic Trends in the Soviet Union: A Comparative Appraisal (Cambridge, Mass.: Harvard University Press, 1963), Table VII.

lead to a high rate of growth in GDP. The Liu-Yeh study, however, found a low GDP growth of 2.8 percent a year between 1957 and 1970, compared to 8.9 percent for Taiwan, 10.5 percent for Japan, 8.1 percent for South Korea, and 3.4 percent for India. China's relatively low rate of growth in GDP resulted in a very high gross incremental fixed capital-output ratio (the increase of gross fixed capital divided by the increase of GDP). Based on the Liu-Yeh estimates, the ratio for China was 5.89, which was more than twice that of Japan (2.94) and three times that of India (1.96).[11]

Several economists have challenged the Liu-Yeh findings. Richard Eckaus has contended that the Chinese fixed capital-output ratio is equal to the highest average ratio estimated by Kuznets, which is for advanced countries. By comparison, the gross incremental capital-output ratios that Kuznets estimated for the less developed countries are 60 percent or less of the Liu-Yeh estimates for China. Eckaus suspects that the high capital-output ratio estimated by Liu-Yeh may reflect errors in either the numerator, the denominator, or both.[12]

Subramanian Swamy has argued that Chinese official investment statistics may embody two types of bias. The first is that of scope. The official Chinese definition is narrower than the customarily accepted UN definition, since the Chinese GDP excludes nonproductive services and the UN statistics include them. Second, the Chinese price system introduces an upward bias into the value of industrial items, including capital formation. To correct the price bias, Swamy converted the Chinese yuan investment figures into equivalent Indian rupee figures. With these conversions, the rate of Chinese investment (investment as a percentage of GDP) drops from 18.2 percent to 10.9 percent for 1952, and from 22.5 percent to only 12.9 percent for 1956. The new estimates yield an incremental capital-output ratio of 2.5, comparable to India's 2.3 in the same period.[13] Although Swamy's point about the upward bias in the Chinese price system is well founded, his "corrected estimates" are too low.

Recent official Chinese revelations tend to support the Liu-Yeh estimates. According to Chinese statements in 1979, the main reason for the high incremental capital-output ratio was inefficiency in carrying out investment projects. Since the Great Leap Forward, China's limited capital and technical resources have been spread too thinly among too many construction projects, each with an inadequate supply of construction materials and equipment. The result has been an unduly prolonged construction period.

> It took an average of only five to six years to complete a large or medium-sized heavy industrial construction project in the 1950s. Now it

> takes more than ten years. It took an average of only two to three years to complete a large or medium-sized light or textile industrial construction project in the past. Now it takes four to five years. . . . One year of these delays causes the country to increase wages alone by 5 billion yuan. This sum is equivalent to the total annual wages of 10 million low-wage workers.[14]

Inefficiency has also prevailed in the construction industry, one major component of the fixed capital investment. In the past twenty years, the level of mechanization in China's construction enterprises has been increased over twenty times. Yet, because of poor management and lack of worker enthusiasm, labor productivity has barely increased. In 1980, China's utilization rate of construction machines was only 50 percent, and the utilization rate was even lower for large machines. Official statistics reveal that the productivity of China's construction machines in 1980 was only one-eighth of that in the United States.[15] During the Fourth Five-Year Plan period (1971–1975), the investment required to build the capacity to produce one ton of steel was 80 percent higher than in the FFYP period, and the investment in facilities to produce one additional ton of coal was more than double that during the FFYP.[16] Moreover, because of poor planning and improper management, "many projects were often scrapped after construction started, wasting hundreds of millions of yuan."[17]

Official reports also explain why China has achieved a relatively rapid growth in industrial output while the living standards have remained extremely low. In the first place, the high rate of capital formation has directed most of China's resources into the capital goods industry, leaving very little for consumer goods. In the second place, the sluggishness of agriculture has limited the supply of raw materials for consumer goods. According to an official 1979 report, the per capita supply of staples declined between 1957 and 1978. Food grains dropped 3.2 percent, edible oils fell 33.3 percent, and cotton cloth slipped 2 percent.[18] These revelations confirm the Liu-Yeh estimate that per capita consumption in China during the 1957–1970 period grew less than 2 percent a year. The bulk of the population has failed to reap substantial material benefits during some thirty years of industrialization.

## CHANGES IN INDUSTRIAL STRUCTURE

Within China's industrial sector, there has been a significant change in the relative importance of producer goods and consumer goods in the total industrial output and in the roles of the steel, machine-building, and defense industries. Before 1949, consumer goods predominated in industrial production. Roughly 92 percent of industrial capital in the 1930s was invested in consumer goods industries,[19] and in 1933, 81 percent of the nation's gross value of industrial output and 76 percent of gross value added had been created by the consumer goods industries.[20] In 1936, textile and food processing alone accounted for 63 percent of the gross value and consumer goods as a whole accounted for 80.4 percent of the total gross value of China's industrial output (see Table 13.8).

The lopsided concentration on consumer goods industries resulted partly from foreign participation in the early stages of Chinese industrialization and partly from the Chinese entrepreneurs' inability to establish modern heavy-industry enterprises. Because the main goals of foreign capital were to process Chinese raw materials and to sell the finished products directly to Chinese consumers, consumer goods industries were a better investment than producer goods industries. This unbalanced development is not unique to China, however. Most

Table 13.8
Percentage Distribution of Total Gross Value of Industrial Output in China by Branch of Industry, 1936

| Branch of Industry | Percent |
|---|---|
| Electrical Power | 1.8 |
| Fuel Industries | 2.6 |
| Nonferrous Metals | 1.7 |
| Ferrous Metals | 0.9 |
| Metal processing | 8.8 |
| Machine-building | 1.5 |
| Chemicals | 2.3 |
| Textiles | 35.4 |
| Food processing | 27.6 |
| Others | 17.4 |
| Total | 100.0 |

Source: Zhao Yiwen, "Industry in Old China," in Tongji gongzuo tongxun (Statistical work bulletin) No. 16 (August 1956), p. 7.

developed countries have had the same experience during the early stages of industrialization.

When the new government embarked on its industrialization program in the 1950s, it was determined to change the pattern. Intent on establishing a comprehensive, independent industrial system, it earmarked the lion's share of industrial investment for the development of heavy industry. The proportion varied from a low of 76 percent in 1952 to a high of 87.7 percent in 1955, leaving only a minor share for textiles, food processing, and other consumer goods industries. There were several rationales for that decision. First, although China's industrial sector was extremely backward by modern standards, heavy industry was its weakest link. The Chinese economy could never be independent in the general sense if industry developed on the old pattern. Moreover, because there was a large proportion of untapped capacity in light industry, investment in light industry could be kept to a minimum. Furthermore, heavy industry is the foundation of modern defense. Although the policy of strengthening heavy industry was valid, it was carried to extremes. Between 1953 and 1979, an average of 90 percent of the industrial investment was allocated to heavy industry, resulting in a structural imbalance between producer goods and consumer goods supplies (see Table 13.9).

The differing rates of growth of light and heavy industry materially altered China's industrial structure. In 1949, consumer goods accounted for 73.4 percent of the total value of gross industrial output, and producer goods accounted for only 26.6 percent – a ratio of about 3 to 1. In 1957, the division was 51.6 percent for consumer goods and 48.4 percent for producer goods; by 1978, the share for consumer goods had dropped to 38.5 percent as compared to 61.5 percent for producer goods, almost reversing the early order of importance (see Table 13.10). According to W. G. Hoffmann's stages of industrialization, China had already reached the third stage in 1958 when producer goods exceeded consumer goods. Hoffmann's study did note, however, that it usually takes several decades for most industrial countries to progress from the first to the third stage.[21] China had traveled the whole road in only one decade.

The change in industrial structure is even more striking when the relative shares of the eleven major industries in various benchmark years are compared (see Table 13.11). The great loser has been the textile industry, which dominated Chinese industry for almost a century. In 1949, it accounted for 36.9 percent of the total gross industrial output value. Its share dropped to 19.1 percent in 1957, and by 1978, textiles accounted for a mere 11 percent of the total.[22] The rising group included the machine-building, chemical, petroleum, and steel industries.

The growth of the machine-building industry has been spectacular. In terms of gross output value, the industry grew from a minor position to become the leading area in the modern industrial sector. Its relative share advanced steadily from 2.7 percent in 1949 to 25.8 percent in 1972. Although this share is still below that in many advanced economies (34 percent in the United States and 31 percent in Japan), it is much higher than that in many underdeveloped countries. In 1979, China's machine-building industry embraced more than twenty branches, some of which—such as electronics and agricultural machinery—employed more than 1 million workers and employees.[23]

The steel industry was long identified as the "key link" of modern industry and received the lion's share of capital investment. Between

Table 13.9
Distribution of Investment Between
Light Industry and Heavy Industry
1952-1979
(in percent)

| Period | Light Industry | Heavy Industry |
|---|---|---|
| 1952 | 24.0 | 76.0 |
| 1953-1957 | 12.5 | 87.5 |
| 1958-1962 | 9.3 | 90.7 |
| 1963-1965 | 7.8 | 92.2 |
| 1966-1970 | 7.1 | 92.9 |
| 1971-1976 | 9.8 | 90.2 |
| 1977-1979 | 12.1 | 87.9 |

Notes: The terms "light industry" and "heavy industry" are not equivalent to "consumer goods" and "producer goods" industries. But in Chinese official statistics, they are always interchangeable.

Sources: Figures for 1952 are from P.R.C. State Statistical Bureau, Ten Great Years (Beijing: Foreign Languages Press, 1960), p. 61. Figures for 1953-1979 are from Hui Yangyiu, "Vigorously Develop Light Industry to Satisfy People's Needs," Jingji yanjiu (Economic research) No. 12 (December 1979), pp. 31-32.

Table 13.10
Percentage Distribution of Industrial Gross Output Value Between Producer Goods and Consumer Goods
1949-1980
(in percent)

| Years | Producer Goods | Consumer Goods |
|---|---|---|
| 1949 | 26.6 | 73.4 |
| 1950 | 29.6 | 70.4 |
| 1951 | 32.2 | 67.8 |
| 1952 | 35.6 | 64.4 |
| 1953 | 37.3 | 62.7 |
| 1954 | 38.5 | 61.5 |
| 1955 | 41.7 | 58.3 |
| 1956 | 45.5 | 54.5 |
| 1957 | 48.4 | 51.6 |
| 1958 | 57.3 | 42.7 |
| 1965 | 53.0 | 47.0 |
| 1970 | 55.6 | 44.4 |
| 1972 | 62.0 | 38.0 |
| 1973 | 62.0 | 38.0 |
| 1974 | 61.7 | 38.3 |
| 1978 | 61.5 | 38.5 |
| 1979 | 56.9 | 43.1 |
| 1980 | 53.3 | 46.7 |

Sources and Notes: 1949-1958 from P.R.C. State Statistical Bureau, Ten Great Years (Beijing: Foreign Languages Press, 1960), p. 90. 1965, 1970, 1972, 1973, and 1974 derived from output value estimated by Robert M. Field, "Civilian Industrial Production in the People's Republic of China, 1949-1974," in U.S. Congress, Joint Economic Committee, China: A Reassessment of the Economy (Washington, D.C.: Government Printing Office, 1975), p. 170. The 1978 figures are derived from the following procedures: (1) From Ten Great Years, p. 87; output value of producer goods in 1949 was listed as 3,730 million yuan and for consumer goods, 10,290 million yuan. (2) The 1978 output value for consumer goods was reported as increased 19.8-fold over 1949, and for producer goods, it rose 90.6-fold (Renmin ribao [People's daily], December 3, 1979). (3) The 1978 gross output value for consumer goods can be calculated as 214,032 million yuan, and for producer goods, 341,668 million yuan. (4) The share is 61.5 percent for producer goods and 38.5 percent for consumer goods. The 1979 figures are derived from output value of heavy and light industry in the P.R.C. State Statistical Bureau, "Communiqué on Fulfillment of China's 1979 National Economic Plan," Beijing Review 23:19 (May 12, 1980), p. 12. The 1980 figures are from Beijing Review 24:12 (March 23, 1981), p. 23.

1949 and 1979, total investment in the steel industry was 1.5 times that in textiles and other light industries. During the FFYP period, fixed investment allocated to iron, steel, and metal processing (machine-building is a component of metal processing) added up to 56.7 percent of the total investment. That figure compares with only 32.8 percent for Japan in 1956, 49.6 percent for the Soviet Union in 1928–1935, and 58.5 percent for the United States during World War II (see Table 13.12).

The share of metal processing in China's total industrial output shows signs of overexpansion. According to a study by Alfred Maizels, which grouped forty-eight countries according to per capita income of

Table 13.11
Percentage Contribution of Selected Industries to Total Gross Output Value of Industry, 1949–1972
(in percent)

| Gross Output Value of Industry | 1949 | 1952 | 1957 | 1965 | 1972 |
|---|---|---|---|---|---|
| Electric Power | 2.4 | 1.6 | 1.7 | 1.7 | 2.0 |
| Coal | 3.7 | 3.2 | 2.2 | 1.7 | 1.4 |
| Petroleum | 0.1 | 0.6 | 1.0 | 3.6 | 7.4 |
| Ferrous Metal | 1.8 | 5.1 | 8.0 | 6.3 | 6.6 |
| Machine-building | 2.7 | 5.2 | 9.5 | 18.4 | 25.8 |
| Chemical | 1.5 | 3.2 | 6.6 | 8.1 | 9.1 |
| Building material | 1.1 | 2.3 | 2.5 | 2.0 | 1.7 |
| Timber | 6.9 | 4.5 | 3.0 | 0.8 | 0.5 |
| Papermaking | 1.3 | 2.4 | 2.6 | 2.5 | 2.5 |
| Textiles | 36.9 | 29.7 | 19.1 | 13.0 | 11.0 |
| Food processing | 23.6 | 22.6 | 20.4 | 12.0 | 10.0 |

Sources: 1949, 1952, 1957--except petroleum from P.R.C. State Statistical Bureau, Ten Great Years (Beijing: Foreign Languages Press, 1960), p. 92. Petroleum from Chu-yuan Cheng, China's Petroleum Industry (New York: Praeger, 1976), p. 150. 1965 and 1972 except textiles and food processing from Chu-yuan Cheng, ibid, p. 151. Textiles share in 1978 was officially reported as 11 percent of total industrial output. Since the share of consumer goods industries in 1978 was almost identical with that of 1972 (Table 13.10), that figure is used for 1972. The ratio between textile and food processing was estimated by Field as 50.36 and 49.64 (see Robert M. Field, "Civilian Industrial Production in the P.R.C.," in U.S. Congress, Joint Economic Committee, China: A Reassessment of the Economy [Washington, D.C.: Government Printing Office, 1975], p. 162).

$100, $250, $500, and $1,000 in the early 1960s, the share of metal processing in total industrial output was 4 percent, 10 percent, 18 percent, and 29 percent, respectively.[24] In 1957, China still ranked with the country group with the lowest per capita income, but in terms of the relative share of its metal-processing industry (16 percent) in total industrial output, it ranked with the second and third country groups. By 1975, that share had exceeded 30 percent, putting China in the highest per capita income group. This fact suggests that the growth of Chinese metal processing has apparently exceeded the capacity of the national economy to absorb it.

Table 13.12
Ratios of Investment in Metals and Metal-Processing Industries to Investment in All Manufacturing: China, Japan, India, the Soviet Union, and the United States

| Country | Ratio |
|---|---|
| China | |
| (1953-1957) | 56.7 |
| Japan | |
| (1956) | 32.8 |
| U.S.S.R. | |
| (1928-1935) | 49.6 |
| (1928-1938) | 52.6 |
| (1928-1940) | 49.0 |
| U.S. | |
| (1904-1909) | 35.2 |
| (1909-1914) | 33.8 |
| (1914-1919) | 36.3 |
| (1940-1945) | 58.5 |
| (1947) | 34.8 |
| India | |
| (1956) | 47.9 |

Source: Chu-yuan Cheng, China's Allocation of Fixed Capital Investment in China (Ann Arbor: Center for Chinese Studies, University of Michigan, 1974), pp. 55-56.

## CHANGES IN GEOGRAPHIC DISTRIBUTION OF PRODUCTION FACILITIES

When the Communists came to power in 1949, the Chinese economy was a dualistic one, comprising a relatively modern sector along the coastal areas and a traditional sector in the vast interior region. The high concentration of modern industry and transportation in a few coastal areas had stemmed from the historical requirements of foreign trade and the existence of foreign interests, which were confined to the treaty ports. Most of the coastal cities were accessible to steam navigation and possessed adequate technical manpower.

The degree of geographic concentration changed little in the early years of Communist control. In 1952, industrial output in the seven coastal provinces (Liaoning, Hebei, Shandong, Jiangsu, Zhejiang, Fujian, and Guangdong) accounted for 68 percent of the national total (see Figure 13.1). The gross value of the industrial output of eight coastal cities (Beijing, Tianjin, Shanghai, Shenyang, Anshan, Luda, Fushun, and Benxi) in turn represented 55 percent of the coastal region total.[25] The spatial concentration of heavy industries and of the textile industry was particularly striking. Roughly 80 percent of the steel, 90 percent of the electric power, and 88 percent of the cotton cloth were produced in the coastal region. Even agricultural resources heavily favored this region. Although the seven coastal provinces take up only 11 percent of the total land area, they accounted for one-third of China's total cultivated area[26] and for the bulk of its modern transportation facilities. In 1949–1950, about 42 percent of the operating railway trunk lines were located in the coastal areas.[27]

The Chinese authorities regarded this high concentration as "irrational, both from the economic point of view and in respect to national defense."[28] It is expensive to ship minerals and raw cotton from their sources in North, Northwest, and Central China to the major metal-processing and textile centers in East China, and the coastal areas are also considered vulnerable to foreign attack.[29]

In view of these considerations, the FFYP called for locating most of the new industrial projects in Northwest, North, and Central China. Of the 694 major projects to be started during 1953–1957, more than two-thirds were to be placed in inland areas. The planned distribution of new large-scale enterprises under the control of the First Ministry of Machine-Building Industry and the Ministry of Electrical Equipment was 24 percent for the coastal areas and 76 percent for the interior areas. The major industrial centers to be developed included Lanzhou in Gansu Province, Taiyuan in Shanxi Province, Sian in

Figure 13.1
China: Changing Regional Shares of Industrial Output

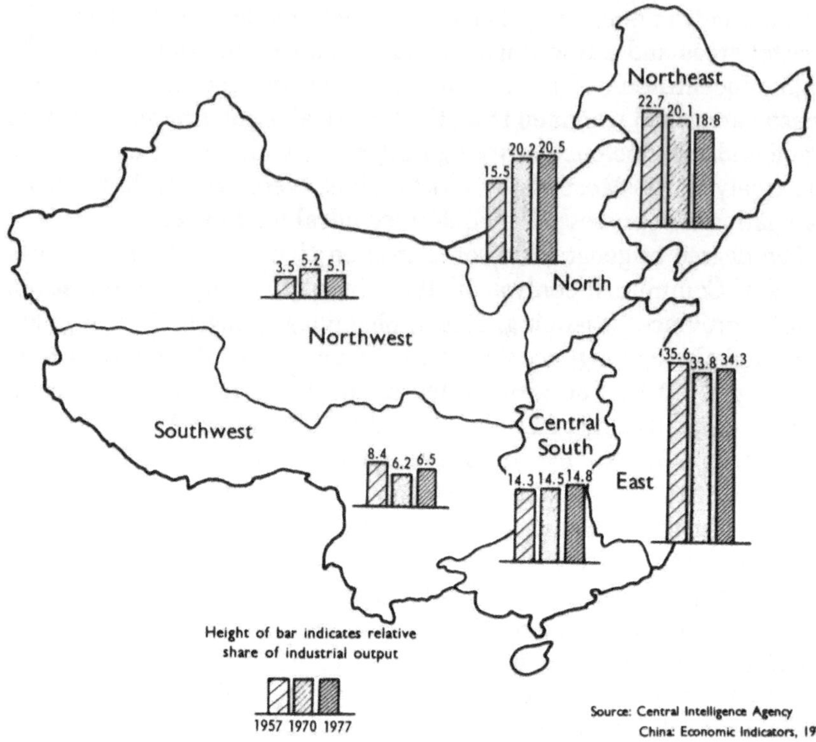


Shaanxi Province, Luoyang in Henan Province, and Wuhan in Hubei Province.

The policy of balancing industrial output between coastal and inland areas accelerated during the Great Leap Forward when millions of small plants were built all over the country. Had these small plants succeeded, they would have increased appreciably the share of industrial products coming from the interior areas.

The collapse of the Great Leap and the deterioration of Sino-Soviet relations caused a sharp turn in China's geographic distribution policy. The Sino-Soviet border stretching from Xinjiang to Heilongjiang was no longer a safe zone but a militarily vulnerable region. With the sharp decline in Sino-Soviet trade after 1960, China swiftly shifted the direction of its trade away from the Soviet bloc and toward

Japan and Western Europe. The old treaty ports along the coast resumed their pivotal position.

The shift of favor from inland to coastal areas was further reinforced during the adjustment period (1961–1965). Because of the need to make drastic cuts in capital investment, effective allocation of capital became the paramount concern of the planners, and preference went to the projects that could produce the highest profits. During 1961–1965, new emphasis was placed on the old industrial bases – such as Shanghai, Shenyang, Tianjin, and Guangzhou – where a small additional investment in existing plants could raise productivity substantially.

The year 1969 marked another turning point in the geographic distribution policy. Following repeated military clashes along the Sino-Soviet border in that year, China launched a new drive toward local self-sufficiency and preparedness in the event of a war with the Soviet Union. North China, Central China, and the Southwest received additional new investment. Two railways were constructed in the Southwest, and a dozen major industrial projects were built in Sichuan. The post-Mao leadership has reaffirmed these regional development policies by establishing six great regions, which are intended to function self-reliantly while working in close coordination with each other and to have a fairly harmonious development of agriculture and light and heavy industry.

Three decades of effort to balance the distribution of economic resources between the coastal and inland regions have produced mixed results. Statistics on the output of ten major industries show a marked shift of the relative shares. The shares of eight of the ten items produced in the coastal region (the exceptions are coal and sugar) declined continuously during 1952–1970, and the shares of crude oil, steel, chemical fertilizers, and cement registered a considerable decline (see Table 13.13). The gains of the inland areas were very conspicuous.

The decline portrayed in Table 13.13 has led some students of the Chinese economy to conclude that a fundamental change in the regional distribution of industry had taken place. Although that was true for a number of products, it was not true for industrial production as a whole. A study by R. M. Field, N. R. Lardy, and J. P. Emerson indicated that there was a slight increase in the inland share of total industrial production between 1952 and 1957.[30] But since 1957, there has been little change in the division between coastal and interior regions in terms of the total gross value of industrial output (see Table 13.14).

Table 13.13
The Share of Physical Output of Ten Major Industries in the Coastal Region, 1952-1970
(in percent)

| | 1952 | 1957 | 1965 | 1970 |
|---|---|---|---|---|
| Electric Power | 65.7 | 60.1 | 54.0 | 56.7 |
| Coal | 34.4 | 35.6 | 35.5 | 40.4 |
| Crude Oil | 75.0 | 40.0 | 16.2 | 13.3 |
| Steel | 84.6 | 83.3 | 63.6 | 55.5 |
| Chemical Fertilizer | 100.0 | 87.5 | 48.9 | 50.0 |
| Cement | 72.4 | 62.3 | 40.9 | 36.1 |
| Paper | 50.0 | 44.4 | 40.0 | 38.9 |
| Machine Tools | 90.0 | — | — | 79.6 |
| Cotton Cloth | 81.6 | 70.0 | 61.1 | 61.3 |
| Sugar | 40.0 | 33.3 | 46.7 | 47.1 |

Source: Charles Robert Roll, Jr., and Kung-chia Yeh, "Balance in Coastal and Inland Industrial Development," in U.S. Congress, Joint Economic Committee, China: A Reassessment of the Economy (Washington, D.C.: Government Printing Office, 1975), p. 89.

Table 13.14
Distribution of Gross Value of Industrial Output by Region, 1952-1973
(Percent of National Total)

| | Coastal Area | | | Inland Area |
|---|---|---|---|---|
| Year | Beijing, Tianjin and Shanghai | Other Coastal Areas | Total | |
| 1952 | 26.9 | 41.4 | 68.3 | 31.7 |
| 1957 | 25.2 | 39.2 | 64.4 | 35.6 |
| 1965 | 27.4 | 38.5 | 65.9 | 34.1 |
| 1970 | 28.1 | 37.6 | 65.7 | 34.3 |
| 1973 | 27.0 | 37.1 | 64.1 | 35.9 |

Source: Charles Robert Roll, Jr., and Kung-chia Yeh, "Balance in Coastal and Inland Industrial Development," in U.S. Congress, Joint Economic Committee, China: A Reassessment of the Economy (Washington, D.C.: Government Printing Office, 1975), p. 88.

The fact that the regional growth pattern of the gross value of industrial output shown in Table 13.14 is in conflict with the statistics in Table 13.13 indicates that the inland areas increased their relative share of industrial production only slightly. Table 13.14 is also not congruent with data showing unbalanced investment in favor of the inland region. Several factors have led to this result. First, although the physical output series (Table 13.13) included machine tools, it did not include the machine-building industry as a whole. During the 1957–1973 period, the leading sector within all industry was machine-building, which achieved an average annual growth of 20 percent. Machinery output alone accounted for about 42 percent of the increment in coastal industrial output.[31] Because machinery output was heavily concentrated in the coastal areas, adding machinery output to the data being considered offsets the movement in favor of the inland areas that the physical output series reveals. Moreover, during the 1950–1970 period, one major industry that was deconcentrated was the cotton textile industry, and such capacity in the inland areas increased from 10 to 20 percent of total industry capacity in about 1949 to 45 percent in the 1970s.[32] The textile industry depends on the cotton supply, and stagnation in the growth of cotton has constrained the rate of more growth of the inland textile industry.

Furthermore, the older industrial bases, such as Shanghai and Liaoning, possessed not only a technical labor force with long years of experience but also a wide range of modern industrial facilities offering various kinds of support. In Shanghai in 1970, 60 percent of the workers in the machine-building industry had more than seven years of experience, and they could produce a wide variety of products at various levels of quality. In contrast, despite the rapid growth in numbers of workers in Xian, Lanzhou, Taiyuan, and Luoyang, the bulk of the labor force in those new centers consisted of peasants, who lacked the skills required to operate complicated machinery and instruments. As a result, the rate of depreciation of fixed capital in those areas was extremely high, and productivity was generally lower than in the older industrial areas along the coast.[33]

The pattern of geographic distribution will become clearer if we replace the conventional division between "interior" and "coastal" areas with the concept of economic regions, which have a closer connection with Chinese economic plans. During the 1960s, the country was divided into seven economic coordination regions, many of which contained both coastal and inland areas. In 1977, the seven regions were merged into six (see Table 13.15).

During the FFYP period, the most rapidly developing areas were the

Table 13.15
Economic Coordination Regions, 1977

| Economic Regions | Coastal Areas | Inland Areas |
|---|---|---|
| 1. Northeast | Liaoning | Jilin, Heilongjiang |
| 2. North | Beijing, Tianjin, Hebei, Shandong | Henan, Nei Monggol, Shanxi |
| 3. East | Shanghai, Zhejiang, Jiangsu | Anhui |
| 4. Central-South | Fujian, Guangdong | Hunan, Hubei, Jiangxi, Guangxi |
| 5. Southwest | | Guizhou, Sichuan, Xizang, Yunan |
| 6. Northwest | | Gansu, Ningxia, Shaanxi, Xinjiang, Qinghai |

Source: U.S. Department of Agriculture, People's Republic of China, Agricultural Situation, Review of 1978 and Outlook for 1979 (Washington, D.C., June 1979), p. v.

less industrialized regions in Central and West China, which contributed less than 25 percent of the industrial output. Growth in the East was the lowest because of the decision not to let Shanghai continue to dominate industrial output. The East, however, remained the largest industrial region. North China was the fastest growing of the more developed regions, largely because the relatively backward provinces within the region (Shandong, Henan, and Shanxi) grew extremely rapidly.[34]

Between 1957 and 1977, in terms of growth rate, the Northwest ranked first, followed by the North, Central-South, East, Northeast, and Southwest. Even so, the Northwest made the smallest absolute contribution to the growth of industrial output, and the East made by far the largest. The long gestation period for investment in relatively underdeveloped regions was probably the chief cause of their smaller contributions. By 1977, the relative shares of industrial production of the six economic regions showed little change. In 1952, the two developed regions, East and Northeast, together had accounted for 54.9 percent of the country's total; in 1977, their combined share was 54.8 percent (see Table 13.16). The continuous reinforcement of Shanghai's position as the nation's chief industrial producer would suggest that the government's plan to shift industrial centers from

Table 13.16
Distribution of Chinese Industrial Production
by Economic Regions, 1952, 1957, 1965, 1970, 1975, and 1977

| Area | 1952 | 1957 | 1965 | 1970 | 1975 | 1977 |
|---|---|---|---|---|---|---|
| Total | 100.0 | 100.0 | 100.0 | 100.0 | 100.0 | 100.0 |
| North | 21.6 | 22.7 | 22.3 | 20.1 | 18.6 | 18.9 |
| Northeast | 22.9 | 15.5 | 18.0 | 20.2 | 21.5 | 20.5 |
| East | 32.0 | 35.6 | 34.1 | 33.8 | 33.7 | 34.3 |
| Central-South | 13.9 | 14.3 | 14.0 | 14.5 | 14.7 | 14.8 |
| Northwest | 2.6 | 3.5 | 4.6 | 5.2 | 5.0 | 5.1 |
| Southwest | 7.0 | 8.4 | 6.9 | 6.2 | 6.4 | 6.5 |

Note: Original percents do not add up to 100.

Sources: 1952, Robert M. Field, "Civilian Industrial Production in the People's Republic of China, 1949-1974," in U.S. Congress, Joint Economic Committee, China: A Reassessment of the Economy (Washington, D.C.: Government Printing Office, 1975), p. 171. Other years, Robert M. Field, Kathleen M. McGlynn, and William B. Abnett, "Political Conflict and Industrial Growth in China: 1965-1977," in U.S. Congress, Joint Economic Committee, Chinese Economy Post-Mao (Washington, D.C.: Government Printing Office, 1978), p. 246.

coastal areas to the interior did not materialize. By 1985, the investment in the Southwest, Northwest, and the North will have begun to pay off, but any significant change in the regional distribution of industrial output seems very unlikely.

## IMPACT OF STRUCTURAL CHANGES ON ECONOMIC GROWTH

The structural changes in China's economy since 1949 yield both positive and negative results in terms of industrialization, and modernization. Four of the positive results deserve mention. One, the component structure of GDP shows a steep rise for the share of industry and a concomitant decline for the share of agriculture. Two, within the manufacturing sector, there has been a significant rise in the metal products' share of total production and a decline in that of consumer goods. Three, a large proportion of the GDP has been constantly channeled into capital formation, despite an extremely low level of per capita income. And four, the distribution of industrial output, population, and transportation facilities between the coastal and inland regions has become somewhat more balanced over the years.

Several adverse trends also pose problems for China's modernization, however. The most notable disappointments have been the lack of a significant increase in per capita product since 1957, the failure to transfer the bulk of the country's labor force from agriculture to industry, the low labor productivity in agriculture and industry, and the absence of a tangible improvement in living standards.

*Lopsided Development*

The structural changes that brought about a rapid growth in the capital goods industry have hampered the growth of agriculture and of consumer goods industries and have placed strains on the Chinese economy. In particular, the lopsided expansion of the steel and machine-building industries has created a new structural imbalance in the economy and has become a major deterrent to Chinese industrialization.

First, the incessant expansion of the steel and machine-building industries has preempted the largest share of capital investment. Between 1952 and 1978, the steel industry, which employed some 3 million workers, absorbed capital investment 1.5 times that in light industry, which in 1978 possessed 60,000 enterprises and employed more than 10 million workers. The entire industrial sector took steel as the key link and had other industries serve steel production. The development of the steel industry required the expansion of the electricity, machine-building, and iron-ore mining, transportation, and fuel industries, which in turn needed increasing supplies of steel for basic construction. The whole process formed a vicious circle.[35]

Because light industry and the textile industry have been the prime sources of state revenue, the slow progress in those two industries has constrained capital investment. Between 1950 and 1977, the profits netted and taxes paid by the light and textile industries accounted for 29 percent of the total state revenue. That amount was equivalent to 70 percent of the state's investment for capital construction and thirteen times the investment in the light and textile industries. According to 1977 statistics, for each yuan spent on the light and textile industries, the state got back 52 fen (.52 yuan) in the form of profits and taxes as compared to only 6 fen (.06 yuan) received from heavy industry.[36]

Despite the vital role played by the light and textile industries in capital formation, those two industries received a diminishing share of investment. State investment in light industry accounted for only 2.5 percent of the total investment in 1953–1957, and its share dropped to 2.4 percent in 1958–1962, 1.8 percent in 1966–1970, and 1.9 percent in 1971–1978.[37] The share of investment in the textile industry was 10 percent in 1953–1957, 6.9 percent in 1958–1962, and 5.3 percent in 1966–1970, but it recovered to 7.9 percent in 1971–1975 and 10.2 percent in 1976–1978.[38] Lacking adequate investment, production facilities in those two industries rapidly degenerated, thereby impeding growth possibilities.

Second, the development of heavy industry was not linked effectively to that of agriculture and light industry. Heavy industry's development has become self-supporting. During the FFYP period, rolled steel allocated to light industry accounted for 21.3 percent of the total supply for industrial use. The ratio fell sharply to 13.7 percent in 1958–1962, 12.4 percent in 1966–1970, and to only 11.7 percent in 1978. Meanwhile, set equipment supplied by the machine-building industry to light industry amounted to only 6.1 percent of the total supply in 1972, and the ratio shrank year after year to a mere 2 percent in the 1975–1978 period. The failure to allocate adequate products of the capital goods industries to the consumer goods industries has also impeded the latter's growth.[39]

Third, the effort to expand the steel and machine-building industries has drained investment and materials from other basic industries (notably electricity, coal, and transportation), and the resulting sluggishness of those related industries has constituted a bottleneck for the entire economy. Official investigation reveals that the shortage of electricity in recent years has idled 20 to 30 percent of the industrial capacity.[40] In contrast, there is evidence of an excessive capacity in the steel and machine-building industries. By 1979, the Chinese steel industry was officially estimated as having the capacity to produce 55 million tons of steel. China turned out only 34 million tons in that year, however, because of shortages of coke, coal, and iron ore.[41] The same situation prevailed in the machine-building industry. In 1979 and early 1980, the slowdown of capital construction idled many machinery plants.[42]

Fourth, the lopsided expansion of the capital goods industry has also squeezed resources for housing construction. During the FFYP, investment in housing amounted to 9.1 percent of the total investment in capital construction. The rate declined sharply to only 4.1 percent in 1958–1962, rose to 6.9 percent in 1962–1965, dropped again to 4 percent in 1966–1970, and rose slightly to 5.7 percent in 1971–1975. During the twenty-six years between 1952 and 1978, China's investment in housing construction averaged only 5.8 percent of the total investment in capital construction, compared with 9.2 percent in the Soviet Union between 1928 and 1937 and 24.6 percent in the United States during 1920–1929. As a result, the average residential area per person has declined by 20 percent, from 4.5 square meters in 1952 to 3.6 square meters in 1978. Official statistics show that more than one-third of the households in urban areas faced severe housing shortages in 1980.[43] The housing shortage has affected workers' lives and lowered their enthusiasm and productivity.

*Excessive Rate of Capital Formation*

Although a high rate of capital formation is a necessary condition for rapid economic growth, China's rate has proved to be too high to sustain, given the low level of per capita income. Even among developed countries, few have been able to maintain an investment rate of more than 25 percent for a long period. The ratio of investment to GDP in China surged from 7.5 percent in the pre-World War II years to 24 percent in 1953–1957 and 40 percent in 1959–1960 before dropping back to 33 percent in 1970–1978. This rapid rate has not brought about a high rate of economic growth but has resulted in a steady decline of capital productivity for several reasons. First, because investment in capital construction outran the supply of construction materials and equipment, few projects could be completed on schedule, and construction costs jumped. Second, basic construction projects absorbed too large a share of the investment funds, leaving very little for renovation and maintenance of existing plants. Third, poor planning led to duplicate construction projects in almost every field, each competing for the limited supplies of materials, energy, and equipment.

The overall result is a high rate of capital formation but low capital productivity. During the FFYP period, for every 100 yuan invested, the country's newly added fixed assets were able to increase by 83.7 yuan, but in the 1966–1976 period, only 59.9 yuan were added, a 30 percent decline in capital efficiency.[44]

*Geographic Dispersion*

The geographic distribution policy represents a trade-off between optimum industrial location and maximum growth. The benefits of establishing new industrial centers in the interior (lower transport costs and reduced vulnerability to attack) had to be balanced against the concomitant need for a larger investment in social overhead capital and a lower rate of industrial growth in the short run. There is little doubt that the leadership was aware that the concentration of resources in the coastal areas and the postponement of inland industrialization would produce a higher rate of industrial growth. The rejection of that strategy reflects the leadership's determination to prevent the reemergence of a dualistic society. The decision, which appears to have been valid, has also affected economic growth in recent decades. Several points emerge from the analysis of China's geographic distribution policy.

1. The policy of regional self-sufficiency has caused great waste in capital investment and technical manpower. As an editorial in *Renmin ribao* noted in June 1980, "Thirty years of experience in construction have proved that, if every area builds on the same economic pattern, it will hinder the development of the superior conditions in each region and will even turn the superior conditions into inferior ones."[45] According to that Party organ, under the guideline of regional self-sufficiency, China put 40 percent of its coal-prospecting manpower and several billion yuan into searching for coal deposits in provinces south of the Chang Jiang in the past two decades, even though previous investigations had shown that there was little promise in those areas. Consequently, the state wasted immense amounts of capital and scored very few achievements.

2. Numerous reports indicate that production costs for identical industrial products have been much higher in the inland centers than in the old industrial centers because of a lack of supporting industries and the critical shortage of skilled labor.

3. The concentration of 75 percent of the new railway lines west of the Beijing-Guangzhou Railroad did little to relieve the burdens of the older railways in the coastal areas. Between 1950 and 1978, when the country's railway mileage increased 1.4 times, the volume of freight rose 9.7 times. Because 85 percent of the volume is still shipped on the old railways in the coastal areas, the capabilities of many major lines have reached their saturation point. The transport capabilities of many weak sections in the coastal areas can only meet 50 percent of the need. The concentration of new railways in the inland areas has thus created another bottleneck for the economy.[46]

In view of these problems, corrective measures were adopted in 1979 and 1980, and a "battle of readjustment" was launched to change the "irrational economic structure."[47] One major policy change was the sharp curtailment of the rate of capital accumulation. Chinese economists and central planners agreed that the 33 percent accumulation rate in the 1970–1978 period and particularly the 36.6 percent rate in 1978 were too high, crowding out private consumption and damaging incentives. The new guidelines want to reduce the rate of accumulation to 24 percent of GDP, similar to that in the FFYP period.[48]

Lowering the accumulation rate from 33 percent to 24 percent necessitated a 30 percent cut in overall capital construction,[49] and a major target for the cut was the metallurgical industry. In 1979, capital investment for the steel industry was slashed by 45 percent, compared with prior years. Construction of thirty-eight large and medium-sized projects was suspended, and more than 240 small iron-smelting plants and small mines were closed down.[50] The cut in capital construction was not confined to the steel industry, but extended to other heavy industries as well. Capital construction for the chemical industry in 1980 was trimmed by 30 percent.[51] However, the cut of capital investment in 1979–1980 failed to correct the imbalance, and the rate of accumulation in 1979 still accounted for 33.6 percent of national income. So, in 1981, further curtailment was undertaken. Total capital construction investment was to be reduced from the originally planned 55,000 million yuan ($36.3 billion) to only 30,000 million yuan ($19.8 billion), a slash of 45 percent. The construction of many well-publicized projects imported from abroad was halted or postponed.[52] The decision to curb capital construction on such a scale signaled a drastic change in policy.

In striking contrast, consumer goods industries, the long-neglected sector, received high priority in capital construction; government loans; the supply of raw materials, fuel, power, and transportation; and the introduction of new technology. In early 1980, the state extended a loan of 2 billion yuan to light and textile industries and provided $300 million (480 million yuan) in foreign exchange for the import of foreign technology and equipment.[53] For the first time in thirty years, the Chinese leadership was favoring light industry at the expense of the steel industry.

Another sector receiving priority in recent years has been housing construction. Capital investment allocated to housing projects rose from 6.9 percent in 1977 to 7.8 percent in 1978 and 14.8 percent in 1979. In 1978, 37.52 million square meters of housing areas were built in China's urban centers, up 33 percent over 1977. In 1979, 56.4 million square meters of housing areas were added, up another 50 percent over the preceding year. In 1980, the total floor space of housing projects went up 38 percent over 1979 and reached 78 million square meters, a record figure since the founding of the P.R.C.[54] The long-term goal set for the year 2000 is to attain an average residential area of 8 square meters per person, doubling that of 1978.[55]

As the consumer goods industries assumed primacy, the old textile and light industrial centers along the eastern coast regained prominence. At the 1979 National Conference of Light Industry Bureau Directors, Shanghai was designated to be a scientific and technological base for light industry throughout the country, an export base, and a modern production base in support of construction in the interior. Thus, China's geographic policy of development has come full circle. What began in the 1950s as a deliberate plan to locate industrial plants in the inland areas has been modified by the demands of the four modernizations and the new open door policy toward the West.

The adjustments outlined above represent a radical departure from the past and signal a new awareness on the part of the leadership that consumer welfare, labor productivity, and economic growth are interrelated. A high rate of capital accumulation cannot ensure a high rate of growth if workers lose their sense of initiative and enthusiasm. In a country like China, where the capacity of the agricultural sector to support industrialization is rather limited, there are competing claims on the scarce resources needed by agriculture, consumer goods, and capital goods industries. It is plausible to concentrate investment funds in one particular sector in order to speed up economic growth in the short run, but no unbalanced development strategy can be effective for long if it does not pay greater attention to the hitherto neglected sectors.

## NOTES

1. Simon Kuznets, *Toward a Theory of Economic Growth* (New York: Norton, 1968), pp. 96–97.
2. Ibid., p. 99.
3. W. G. Hoffmann, *The Growth of Industrial Economics* (Manchester, Engl.: Manchester University Press, 1958), chap. 2.
4. Simon Kuznets, *Modern Economic Growth, Rate, Structure, and Spread* (New Haven: Yale University Press, 1966), pp. 96–97 and 105–110.
5. Ta-chung Liu, "Quantitative Trends in the Economy," in Alexander Eckstein, Walter Galenson, and Ta-chung Liu, eds., *Economic Trends in Communist China,* p. 125.
6. Choh-ming Li, *Economic Development of Communist China,* p. 90.
7. *Jingji yanjiu* No. 4 (April 1979), p. 50.
8. Simon Kuznets, *Modern Economic Growth,* pp. 234–235.
9. Ta-chung Liu, "Quantitative Trends in the Economy," p. 138.
10. *Renmin ribao,* October 30, 1979.

11. Ta-chung Liu and Kung-chai Yeh, "Chinese and Other Asian Economies: A Quantitative Evaluation," *American Economic Review* 63:2 (May 1973), pp. 222–223.

12. See Eckaus's comment on the Liu-Yeh article in *American Economic Review* 63:2 (May 1973), pp. 232–234.

13. Subramanian Swamy, *Economic Growth in China and India, 1952–1970* (Chicago: University of Chicago Press, 1973), pp. 65–66.

14. Commentator, "Remove This Big Stumbling Block of Waste," *Renmin ribao,* July 10, 1979.

15. Zhou Shulian and Lin Senmu, "On the Question of Housing," *Renmin ribao,* August 5, 1980, p. 5.

16. *Jingji yanjiu* No. 2 (February 1979), pp. 12–13.

17. *Renmin ribao,* July 10, 1979.

18. *Jingji yanjiu* No. 12 (February 1979), p. 37.

19. Zhao Yiwen, *Xin zhongguo de gongye,* [Industry in new China], p. 15.

20. Ta-chung Liu and Kung-chia Yeh, *The Economy of the Chinese Mainland,* pp. 142–143.

21. W. G. Hoffmann, *Growth of Industrial Economics,* chap. 2.

22. *Hua-chiao jih-pao,* October 31, 1979.

23. Chu-yuan Cheng, *The Machine-Building Industry in Communist China,* pp. 225–226.

24. Alfred Maizels, *Industrial Growth and World Trade* (Cambridge, Engl.: Cambridge University Press, 1963), p. 54.

25. *Jihua jingji* No. 8 (August 1957), p. 13.

26. Kang Chao, *Agricultural Production in Communist China,* p. 295.

27. Yuan-li Wu, *The Spatial Economy of Communist China* (New York: Praeger, 1967), pp. 244–245.

28. P.R.C., State Planning Commission, *The First Five-Year Plan,* p. 40.

29. Wu Zhunyang, "The Problems of Geographical Distribution of Our Country's Industrial Construction Projects," *Xuexi* No. 10 (October 2, 1955).

30. Robert Michael Field, Nicholas Richard Lardy, and John Phillip Emerson, *A Reconstruction of the Gross Value of Industrial Output,* p. 16.

31. Charles R. Roll and K. C. Yeh, "Balance in Coastal and Inland Industrial Development," in U.S., Congress, Joint Economic Committee, *China: A Reassessment of the Economy,* pp. 88–92.

32. *Women zhengzai qianjin* [We are in the midst of advancing] (Beijing: Renmin Chubanshe, 1972), p. 75.

33. Chu-yuan Cheng, *The Machine-Building Industry in Communist China,* pp. 288–289.

34. Robert M. Field, "Civilian Industrial Production in the People's Republic of China 1949–1974," in U.S., Congress, Joint Economic Committee, *China: A Reassessment of the Economy,* pp. 155–156.

35. Wang Huide et al., "Is Priority for Increase of the Means of Production a Law Applicable to the Socialist Economy?" *Jingji yanjiu* No. 12 (December 1979), pp. 25–26.

36. *Renmin ribao,* May 30, 1979.

37. Hui yuanying, "Vigorously Develop Light Industry to Satisfy People's Needs," *Jingji yanjiu* No. 12 (December 1979), pp. 31–32.

38. Ibid.

39. *Gongren ribao,* November 7, 1979, p. 1.

40. *Renmin ribao,* May 29, 1979.

41. *Ta kung pao* (Hong Kong), March 27, 1979, p. 1.

42. Xinhua-Beijing, March 2, 1980.

43. Zhou Shulian and Lin Senmu, "On the Question of Housing," p. 5.

44. Editorial, *Renmin ribao,* March 24, 1979.

45. Editorial, "Fully Develop the Superior Conditions," *Renmin ribao,* June 30, 1980.

46. Commentator, "Transforming Old Railway Lines Is a Pressing Task in Railway Readjustment," *Renmin ribao,* July 4, 1979.

47. Commentator, "Make Concerned Efforts in Fighting Well the Hard Battle of Readjustment," *Renmin ribao,* November 23, 1979.

48. He Zhuo, "Readjustment of the Economy Is a Strategic Decision to Accelerate Modernization," *Jingji yanjiu* No. 5 (May 1979), pp. 9–10.

49. *Renmin ribao,* November 23, 1979.

50. Xinhua-Beijing, January 23, 1980.

51. Xinhua-Beijing, April 9, 1980.

52. Xue Muqiao, "Adjust the National Economy and Promote Overall Balance," *Jingji yanjiu* No. 2 (February 1981), pp. 25–31.

53. *Gongren ribao,* January 23, 1980.

54. *Beijing Review* 23:34 (August 25, 1980), p. 6, and 24:11 (March 16, 1981), p. 15.

55. Xinhua-Beijing, July 24, 1980.

# 14

# International Economic Relations

In the process of industrialization and modernization, foreign trade can play divergent roles. In some countries, it serves as a leading sector so that the expansion of exports stimulates technological change and opens up new markets, leading to rapid economic growth. In other countries, foreign trade becomes a balancing sector; imports serve as a means of breaking domestic supply bottlenecks, and the primary function of exports is to finance imports. China falls into the second category.

Until very recently, China pursued a policy of import substitution, purchasing plants that would produce commodities currently imported from abroad. Thus, imports of capital equipment were aimed more at reducing reliance on foreign economies than at improving China's competitive position in exporting to the world market. The import substitution policy, together with the large size of China's domestic market, explains the low level of China's foreign trade. Between 1949 and 1979, foreign trade accounted for only 5 to 8 percent of GNP.

Despite its relatively small role, foreign trade has constituted a vital channel for both equipment and new technology, which have become the driving forces in China's modernization. Imports of food grains since the early 1960s have helped to alleviate food shortages. It has been estimated that if China had completely cut itself off from imports between 1953 and 1957, the country's economic growth would have fallen from an average annual rate of about 6.5 percent to possibly 3 to 5 percent.[1]

In the modernization drive that began in 1978, China has unleashed a massive program to acquire Western equipment and technology in order to break development constraints and to accelerate the pace of industrialization. Foreign trade has been pushed to the forefront, assuming a much more important role than in earlier periods.

This chapter surveys the changes in China's foreign economic policies, the long-term trends (volume, composition, direction, and balance) of its foreign trade, its trade relations with the Western world in general and with the United States in particular, the role of foreign resources in China's modernization, and the prospects for China's foreign trade over the next decade.

## EVOLUTION OF FOREIGN ECONOMIC POLICIES

China's foreign economic relations reflect a complex interaction involving foreign policy and relations, internal political developments, and the dictates of economic necessity. Policies guiding international economic relations have evolved through alternating cycles of intensive acquisition of foreign technology and strong economic nationalism emphasizing self-reliance. The direction of Chinese foreign trade also shifted from the Communist bloc in the 1950s to the non-Communist world in the 1960s and 1970s.

### *The Lean-to-One-Side Policy, 1949–1960*

When the People's Republic of China was formally established in October 1949, the Soviet Union was the first country prepared to grant it diplomatic recognition. China's new leaders looked to Moscow as the most reliable source of support. In his famous speech, "On People's Democratic Dictatorship," delivered to the Sixth Session of the Seventh CCP Central Committee in June 1949, Party Chairman Mao Zedong ruled out the possibility of British or American aid and emphasized that "internationally, we belong to the side of the anti-imperialist front headed by the Soviet Union and so we turn only to this side for genuine and friendly help."[2]

Dependence on the Soviet Union in the 1950s produced one of the most remarkable technology transfers in modern history. Trade with the Soviet Union accounted for about one-half of China's total trade and provided the major impetus for China's industrialization efforts. From 1950 to 1959, the Soviets delivered $1.35 billion worth of equipment and helped China complete 130 projects, including factories for tractors, trucks, machine tools, and general equipment. In addition, the Soviets provided massive technical aid in the form of blueprints and technical data. More than 21,000 sets of scientific and technical documents were transferred to China. Thousands of Chinese specialists and workers were trained in the Soviet Union, and more than 10,000 Soviet experts were dispatched to China at various times.[3]

As a result of close cooperation, trade between China and the East European bloc registered a ninefold leap from only $350 million in 1950 to about $3 billion in 1959. Correspondingly, trade with the West fell sharply after 1952 and accounted for only 26 percent of China's total trade in 1955.

The period of Sino-Soviet cooperation did not last long, however. Ideological disputes and disagreements over economic development strategy in 1958 and 1959 culminated in an open break. In August 1960, during a severe agricultural crisis in China, Moscow suddenly called back all of its technicians and advisers and suspended the supply of equipment and essential materials. The abrupt action dealt China a profound blow and pushed its already weakened economy toward the brink of collapse. This bitter experience dramatized to the Chinese the high potential cost of dependence on any one country or any one source of supply.

### *The Self-Reliance Doctrine of the 1960s*

In the wake of the Sino-Soviet split, China's foreign economic policy took a sharp turn, and the doctrine of self-reliance became the new guideline. According to the official definition, self-reliance "means that a country should manufacture . . . all the products it needs whenever and wherever possible. . . . It also means that a country should carry on its general economic construction on the basis of its own human, material, and financial resources."[4]

Although self-reliance never meant autarky, it signified the deliberate pursuit of an import minimization policy. From 1960 to 1962, China's imports were cut back sharply. Trade with the Communist bloc plummeted from $3 billion in 1959 to only $1.1 billion in 1964. Trade with the Soviet Union, which accounted for 55 percent of China's total trade in 1959, dropped to less than 2 percent of the total in 1969.

In the mid-1960s, China began to plan a new expansion of foreign trade. From 1963 to 1966, China contracted with Japan and Western Europe for purchases of plants and technology worth more than $200 million. In addition, beginning in 1961, grain imports from Canada, Australia, and other Western suppliers became a major import item.

The campaign for self-reliance reached its height during the Cultural Revolution. In the active phase of the Cultural Revolution (1967–1968), trade relations with many countries were strained. The radicals in power generally supported strong economic nationalism, resistance to foreign influences, and reliance on domestic innovations for economic and technical development. Domestic turmoil in 1967 led to China's failing to fulfill export contracts and to attacks on embassies, and outbreaks of antiforeign hysteria damaged foreign economic relations.

*The Lean-to-the-West Policy, 1970–1976*

As normalcy gradually returned, Chinese policymakers began to weigh the cost of self-reliance against that of economic dependence on others. With the goal of accelerating development, a new policy line began to emerge and to modify the self-reliance doctrine. In late 1972, the Technical Import-Export Corporation, which had been abolished in the late 1960s, was reactivated, and China began to place orders to import large numbers of Japanese and Western plants. As part of a new diplomatic offensive, trade relations with the West improved dramatically, and the highlight of this period was the reopening of trade with the United States. China bought large quantities of steel, machinery, and equipment from Japan and Western Europe and increased its grain purchases from Canada and Australia. The aggregate value of turnkey contracts signed between late 1972 and late 1974 is estimated at $2.5 billion.[5] China's total trade soared from $4.4 billion in 1970 to $14.1 billion in 1974, with most of the growth coming in trade with non-Communist countries.

The massive acquisition of Western technology created unprecedented trade deficits, amounting to almost $1 billion for 1974 and 1975. The policy of trade expansion with the Western world soon triggered a fierce debate within China's leadership over the role of foreign trade and the orientation of foreign economic relations.

One group of pragmatist leaders, led by Zhou Enlai and Deng Xiaoping, consistently held that reliance on technical innovation from domestic sources would stretch out industrial modernization indefinitely and confine China to the ranks of second-class nations. Those leaders supported massive imports of Western equipment, large-scale plants, and technology to bring China up to the level of an efficient, modern industrial state as quickly as possible. In the document Some Problems in Accelerating Industrial Development (also known as the Twenty-Point Program), Deng prescribed a detailed program for the importation of critically needed advanced technology to be paid for by the export of China's coal, petroleum, and other natural resources.[6]

Deng's scheme proposed a strategy of development that other industrializing societies have commonly pursued. His premise was clear: China could save time and expense by acquiring certain portions of critically needed technology and equipment from the more advanced industrialized countries. The cost of those acquisitions could be partially offset by the products of the new plants.

In early 1976, however, the radicals rejected Deng's scheme and attacked him on the grounds that he had not only violated the inviolate precepts of independence and self-reliance, but he had also attempted to sell Chinese natural resources to foreign capitalists. Deng was removed from office in April 1976, and the acquisition of foreign plants dropped more than 20 percent from 1975. Trade turnovers in 1976 registered a 10 percent drop, despite an increase in Chinese exports.[7]

*The Great Leap Outward*

With the swift arrest of the Gang of Four in October 1976 and the subsequent purge of their followers, Deng's trade policy was quickly restored. Throughout 1977, Beijing's leadership showed considerable interests in industrially related technology and products from Western countries. The ambitious 1976–1985 plan announced in early 1978 proposed forms of economic interaction with Western companies that had once been regarded as unacceptable. In the dash for rapid progress, China embarked on a plan of massive acquisition of Western machinery and technology. An initial trickle of contracts in mid-1977 was followed by an upsurge in signing, which began in May 1978 and continued through December. Amounts contracted for total plant purchases reached $6.9 billion in 1978.[8]

To accelerate the inflow of Western technology, the new leaders reversed many long-standing policies toward foreign countries. The first major change was Beijing's willingness to borrow from the West to finance imports. In the past, China had adhered to the principle of balanced trade to avoid incurring foreign debts. In 1978, Beijing showed an increasing willingness to borrow, to sign barter agreements, to import materials to be reprocessed for export, and even to collaborate with foreign companies in joint ventures.

Formal commercial links were also expanded to promote trade. In February 1978, an eight-year trade agreement was signed with Japan calling for an exchange of $10 billion worth of Chinese oil and coal for an equal amount of Japanese plants and equipment. At mid-year, a trade agreement was signed with the European Economic Community setting up a framework for expanded trade. In December 1978, a Sino-French long-term trade agreement was also concluded in Beijing for a potential $13.6 billion of exchange through 1985.

Another novel move was the dispatch of thousands of China's top-flight students to attend Western academic institutions. That decision signified the leaders' determination to mine Western ideas and technology, and by the end of 1980, some 5,000 students were studying in Japan, the United States, and Western Europe. In 1977 and 1978, about 2,000 Chinese technicians and officials traveled to Western Europe, Japan, and the United States to investigate the Western state of the art in industrial processes and to negotiate for new equipment. Beijing also invited many Western experts and firms to China to conduct seminars on industrial topics. Although sales oriented, these seminars provided substantial information on new industrial methods. More than 250 such seminars were offered in the first six months of 1978.[9]

The new open door policy was begun at an opportune moment because the Western industrial countries had been hit hard by lagging growth rates at home and inadequate exports to the Middle East. Many Western industrialists eagerly sought the opportunity to enter what they regarded as a vast untapped market. A favorable climate was thus set for the rapid expansion of China's foreign trade.

The Great Leap Outward policy brought about an 82 percent increase in total trade during 1978 and 1979 (if calculated in constant prices, the growth was about 50 percent). It also produced a $3-billion trade deficit for those two years, the largest in P.R.C. history. Shortages of experienced engineers and the lack of infrastructure limited China's capacity to absorb the new technology. As bottlenecks and financial strains became evident, a slowdown of the acquisition spree seemed imperative.

Reacting to the rapid foreign exchange drawdown, as well as to a general rethinking of China's development policies, the Ministry of Finance in February 1979 suspended many late-1978 contracts that had been signed with Japan, France, and West Germany and ordered a moratorium on new major contracts. Major cancellations included a $14-billion Jidong steel project contracted for with West Germany and two nuclear power plants ordered from France. Several multimillion-dollar industrial projects undertaken by U.S. companies were also suspended in 1980, including an $800-million copper mine and concrete plant in Jiangxi Province that was to have been built by Fluor Mining and Metals Company and an iron-ore mine east of Beijing that was to have been built by Kaiser Engineers.[10]

The slowdown did not mean a return to self-reliance, however. At the June 1979 National People's Congress, the Chinese leadership strongly reaffirmed the decisions to liberalize and expand China's trade, and several new organizations were established to manage various aspects of foreign investment and trade. A Foreign Investment Control Commission was set up in July 1979 to supervise the approval of foreign investment. There was also an Import-Export Control Commission and a State General Administration of Exchange Control. As a major vehicle to attract private overseas capital, the Chinese International Trust and Investment Corporation (CITIC) was founded in Beijing and headed by veteran Shanghai industrialist Rong Yiren.

Various new measures were adopted to encourage foreign investment. On July 1, 1979, the NPC adopted a new Joint Ventures Law that permitted foreign participants to invest directly in Chinese industry. A dozen Western oil companies contracted to carry out seismic surveys in about eight concession areas spread across the Huang Hai and the Nan Hai. In December 1979, an agreement was signed with Japan for the joint exploitation of petroleum and natural gas in the Bohai Wan. A parallel agreement was also signed with two French companies, Elf Aquitine and CEP-Total, to undertake exploration and development in the northern Bohai.[11]

Strenuous efforts have also been made to bring in overseas Chinese and foreign private capital. Several special economic zones, similar to the export-processing zones in Taiwan, have been set up in Guangdong and Fujian provinces, where 80 percent of the overseas Chinese come from. Those special zones act as "islands" or "enclaves" for overseas investment, and plants set up in the zones enjoy preferential treatment.[12]

Compared with policies in the 1950s and 1960s, China's new policy has been characterized by flexibility and pragmatism. Its primary goal is to spur the inflow of Western technology within the limits of China's absorptive capacity and ability to pay. To attain this goal, the Chinese leadership is willing to reconcile its internal policies with international business and financial practices. The lifting of the bans on direct government-to-government loans, direct foreign investment, and China's participation in the International Monetary Fund and World Bank in early 1980 underscored Beijing intention to use foreign capital and Western technology to speed up the pace of modernization.

## LONG-TERM TRENDS IN FOREIGN TRADE

The evolution of China's foreign trade from 1949 to 1980 can be assessed in four major dimensions: the growth in the volume of trade, changes in commodity composition, the shift in the direction of trade, and variations in the balance of trade.

*Growth of Trade Volume*

The volume of China's foreign trade has fluctuated erratically since 1949. Between 1949 and 1959, the trade volume rose at an average annual rate of 18 percent. As a result of this increase, the growth rate of foreign trade outpaced the 10 percent annual increase in GNP. There were several reasons for this impressive performance. First, China's foreign trade had attained its peak level in 1928 and 1929, and those prewar records (in terms of constant prices) were not surpassed until 1954 on the import side and until 1955 or 1956 on the export side.[13] The rapid expansion of trade in the early 1950s was, therefore, in part due to the recovery from war and civil war. Second, the 1950s were a period of rapid, forced-draft industrialization when China's investment rose at an average annual rate of 24 percent. Of the total investment, approximately one-third was earmarked for the purchase of machinery and equipment, and one-half of the machinery and equipment needed were imported from abroad.[14] The high import component of capital investment entailed an upsurge of imports. Third, in the early 1950s, China benefited from a Russian loan of $1.3 billion, which enabled China to acquire large quantities of capital goods and military equipment under some form of deferred payment.

In the following decade, 1960–1969, the growth trends were reversed. Three successive crop failures in 1959–1961 produced an acute agricultural crisis, which spilled over into the rest of the economy. The contraction led to a drastic curtailment of investment, which in turn caused a sharp decline in imports. During this ten-year period, foreign trade not only failed to grow but actually declined in absolute terms. By 1969, the combined volume of imports and exports stood at 12 percent below the 1959 peak, although GNP had risen by approximately 40 percent in the same period. Thus, economic policy in this decade placed the emphasis on self-sufficiency and on the internal generation of growth.

The self-reliance doctrine, which was strongly emphasized in the 1960s, was substantially modified in the 1970s. After the disruption of the Cultural Revolution (1967–1969), the Chinese economy experienced a new surge of growth and expansion. Capital investment in industry during 1971–1972 increased dramatically. To facilitate the new expansion, China imported an increasing amount of machinery and equipment, including complete plants and technology. Trade turnover more than tripled between 1970 and 1975, the highest growth rate since 1949.

The rapid growth of trade volume in that period was mostly the result of price variations, because all trade statistics are expressed in current prices. A study by the CIA, which analyzed China's trade with non-Communist countries in current and constant prices between 1970 and 1975, showed that in terms of current dollars, China's trade turnover with non-Communist countries went up from $3,272 million in 1970 to $11,385 million in 1975, with an average annual growth rate of 28.2 percent. In terms of 1970 dollars, however, the 1975 trade volume was only $5,765 million, with an annual growth rate of only 12 percent.[15]

Although political turmoil in 1976 disrupted the trade expansion, growth resumed in 1977 and extended vigorously into the 1978–1979 period. Following the announcement of the Ten-Year Plan in early 1978, imports jumped by 58 percent and exports rose by 22 percent. The growth rate was scaled down somewhat in 1979 and 1980 under the new program of readjustment. Trade volume in the 1976–1980 period still registered a respectable 31 percent average growth rate, however. The growth of total trade volume, exports, imports, and trade balance from 1949 to 1980 is presented in Table 14.1.

*Commodity Composition*

China's exports comprise two major categories: traditional exports and energy exports. Four categories of products constitute the bulk of the imports: machinery and equipment, minerals and metals, chemicals, and agricultural commodities. Although the composition has remained unchanged since 1949, the relative share of each category has undergone profound changes.

In the early 1950s, China's exports basically consisted of food, food products, and nonferrous and alloy metals. Farm products, both foodstuffs and raw materials, accounted for roughly 70 percent of China's exports. After 1961, however, the export pattern altered drastically. After three years of crop failure in 1959–1961, the relative weight of farm products on the export list plummeted from a high of 70 percent in 1952 to a low of 20 percent in 1961. In compensation, exports of textile products (not including raw fibers) rose from less than 4 percent of the Chinese exports in 1953 to 16 percent in 1957 and 19 percent in 1958. The share increased sharply to 32.5 percent in 1960 and averaged 40 percent in 1961–1963.[16] With the improvement of the agricultural situation, foodstuffs regained the leading role in 1964. From 1966 to 1973, the export share of textiles and clothing stabilized at 21 to 25 percent, and in 1974–1978, at 19 to 24 percent (see Table 14.2).

In the 1970s, while foodstuffs and raw materials of agricultural and

Table 14.1
China's Foreign Trade, 1949-1980

| | China's Total Trade Turnover (Billion US $) | China's Exports f.o.b. (Billion US $) | China's Imports c.i.f. (Billion US $) | Trade Balance (Billion US $) |
|---|---|---|---|---|
| **Rehabilitation** | | | | |
| 1949 | 0.8 | 0.4 | 0.4 | Negl. |
| 1950 | 1.2 | 0.6 | 0.6 | Negl. |
| 1951 | 1.9 | 0.8 | 1.1 | -0.3 |
| 1952 | 1.9 | 0.9 | 1.0 | -0.1 |
| **First Five-Year Plan** | | | | |
| 1953 | 2.3 | 1.0 | 1.3 | -0.3 |
| 1954 | 2.4 | 1.1 | 1.3 | -0.2 |
| 1955 | 3.1 | 1.4 | 1.7 | -0.3 |
| 1956 | 3.1 | 1.6 | 1.5 | 0.1 |
| 1957 | 3.0 | 1.6 | 1.4 | 0.2 |
| **Great Leap Forward** | | | | |
| 1958 | 3.7 | 1.9 | 1.8 | 0.1 |
| 1959 | 4.3 | 2.2 | 2.1 | 0.1 |
| 1960 | 4.0 | 2.0 | 2.0 | -0.1 |
| **Readjustment and Recovery** | | | | |
| 1961 | 3.0 | 1.5 | 1.5 | Negl. |
| 1962 | 2.7 | 1.5 | 1.2 | 0.3 |
| 1963 | 2.8 | 1.6 | 1.2 | 0.4 |
| 1964 | 3.3 | 1.8 | 1.5 | 0.3 |
| 1965 | 3.8 | 2.0 | 1.8 | 0.2 |
| **Third Five-Year Plan** | | | | |
| 1966 | 4.2 | 2.2 | 2.0 | 0.2 |
| 1967 | 4.0 | 2.0 | 2.0 | Negl. |

| | | | | |
|---|---|---|---|---|
| 1968 | 3.8 | 2.0 | 1.8 | 0.2 |
| 1969 | 3.9 | 2.1 | 1.8 | 0.3 |
| 1970 | 4.4 | 2.2 | 2.2 | Negl. |
| Fourth Five-Year Plan | | | | |
| 1971 | 4.8 | 2.5 | 2.3 | 0.2 |
| 1972 | 6.0 | 3.2 | 2.8 | 0.4 |
| 1973 | 10.1 | 5.1 | 5.0 | 0.1 |
| 1974 | 14.1 | 6.7 | 7.4 | -0.7 |
| 1975 | 14.5 | 7.1 | 7.4 | -0.3 |
| Fifth Five-Year Plan | | | | |
| 1976 | 13.3 | 7.3 | 6.0 | 1.3 |
| 1977 | 15.2 | 8.1 | 7.1 | 1.0 |
| 1978 | 21.3 | 10.1 | 11.2 | -1.1 |
| 1979 | 29.4 | 13.8 | 15.6 | -1.8 |
| 1980 | 39.8 | 19.3 | 20.5 | -1.2 |

| | Average Annual Growth Rate of Total Trade Volume | Annual Growth Rate of GNP |
|---|---|---|
| 1949-59 | 18.3% | 10.3% |
| 1959-69 | -1.0% | 3.8% |
| 1969-79 | 21.7% | 7.6% |

Note: The trade turnover is expressed in current dollars. The CIA estimates are based on data gathered from China's trade partners. They are not dovetailed with Chinese official statistics. According to a Chinese official report, total trade for 1980 was $36.55 billion with a trade deficit of $570 million (Beijing Review 24:11 /March 16, 1981/, p. 15).

Sources: The 1949-1977 figures are from U.S. Central Intelligence Agency, China: Major Economic Indicators (Washington, D.C., February 1980). The 1978-1980 figures are from U.S. Central Intelligence Agency, China: International Trade, Third Quarter, 1980 (Washington, D.C., March 1981), p. 2.

Table 14.2
Commodity Composition of China's Exports, 1959–1978
(in percent)

| Commodity Category | 1959 | 1966 | 1968 | 1969 | 1970 | 1972 | 1973 | 1974 | 1975 | 1976 | 1977 | 1978 |
|---|---|---|---|---|---|---|---|---|---|---|---|---|
| <u>Foodstuffs</u> | 26 | 28 | 28 | 30 | 31 | 31 | 33 | 31 | 30 | 27 | 24 | 22 |
| Grains | | ( 7) | ( 7) | ( 6) | ( 5) | ( 5) | (11) | (11) | (10) | ( 6) | ( 5) | ( 4) |
| Meat and Fish | | (10) | ( 9) | (10) | (10) | (11) | (10) | ( 5) | ( 6) | ( 6) | ( 5) | ( 5) |
| <u>Crude Materials</u> | 26 | 22 | 21 | 22 | 21 | 19 | 18 | 22 | 27 | 25 | 26 | 26 |
| Coal | | | | | | | | ( 2) | ( 2) | ( 1) | ( 1) | ( 1) |
| Crude Oil | | | | | | | | ( 6) | (11) | (10) | (10) | (10) |
| Petroleum Products | | | | | | | | ( 2) | ( 2) | ( 2) | ( 3) | ( 2) |
| <u>Chemicals</u> | 3 | 4 | 4 | 4 | 5 | 5 | 5 | 6 | 4 | 5 | 5 | 5 |
| <u>Manufacturing</u> | 40 | 42 | 44 | 40 | 42 | 43 | 44 | 40 | 38 | 42 | 45 | 46 |
| Textile Yarn & Fabric | (19) | (14) | (14) | (15) | (17) | (15) | (16) | (14) | (15) | (17) | (15) | (17) |
| Clothing | | ( 8) | ( 9) | (10) | ( 8) | ( 6) | ( 6) | ( 5) | ( 5) | ( 6) | ( 7) | ( 7) |
| <u>Other</u> | 5 | 5 | 3 | 3 | 1 | 1 | 1 | 1 | 1 | 1 | * | * |
| Total | 100 | 100 | 100 | 100 | 100 | 100 | 100 | 100 | 100 | 100 | 100 | 100 |

Note: Totals may not add up to 100 because of rounding. Figures in parentheses are percents of particular commodity. * means Negl.

Sources: Figures for 1959 are from Alexander Eckstein, China's Economic Revolution (London: Cambridge University Press, 1977), pp. 250-252. The data have been arranged to be comparable with those of other years. 1966-1973 figures are from U.S. Congress, Joint Economic Committee, China: A Reassessment of the Economy (Washington, D.C.: Government Printing Office, 1975), pp. 646-647. The 1974-1978 figures are derived by the author from annual commodity composition data published by the U.S. government (see U.S. Central Intelligence Agency, China: International Trade, various years).

animal origin still represented about 35 percent of Chinese sales abroad, exports of energy products were of growing importance. In the mid-1950s, China had to import about a quarter of its crude oil and well over half of its gasoline, kerosene, and diesel oil. In the 1959–1961 period, China annually imported more than 3 million tons of crude oil from the Soviet Union and Eastern Europe. The operation of the Daqing oilfield in 1964 and the subsequent opening of the Shengli and Dagang oilfields in North China changed the picture completely. China achieved self-sufficiency in oil in 1965–1973 and has been a net exporter ever since, exporting about 2 million tons in 1973, 5.6 million tons in 1974, 10.5 million tons in 1975, 9.6 million tons in 1976, 9.1 million tons in 1977, 11.2 million tons in 1978, and 13.4 million tons in 1979. China's shift from a net importer to a net exporter of oil has been the most significant development in that country's trade composition.

Although China hopes that sales of oil will provide large amounts of foreign exchange, oil has accounted for only 10 percent of total exports in recent years. As the importance of agricultural products declined, intermediate and finished textile products assumed increasing roles. The share of textile products and clothing rose from about 10 percent in 1955 to 24 percent in 1978. In the 1979–1981 readjustment plan, the development of textiles and manufactured consumer goods received a high priority. As a result of increasing investment and material supplies, the consumer goods output in 1979 scored a 9.6 percent growth, surpassing the 7.7 percent growth of capital goods for the first time. In 1980, the output of consumer goods grew 17.4 percent, compared with 1.6 percent for capital goods.[17] Given the abundant supply of low-wage labor, China should be able to make further advances in exports of light manufacturing.

China's imports in the 1950s were dominated by machinery, equipment, and military goods, which together composed about half of the total imports. Next to machinery were chemicals, petroleum products, and textile fibers. In the 1960s, capital goods and military imports dropped to only one-third of total imports; at the same time, food grain imports rose tremendously. In the 1950s, China exported between 0.5 million to 1.6 million tons of rice annually and imported virtually no grain at all. Food imports jumped about tenfold in value in 1961, and during the 1961–1966 period, China imported 4.5 million to 6.5 million tons of grains annually, mostly wheat. Those imports then dwindled to a 3-million to 5-million-ton level until a poor 1972 harvest again pushed up grain purchases. They rose to a record of nearly 8 million tons in 1973 and 7 million tons in 1974. With better harvests, grain imports dropped to 3 million tons in 1975 and 1.9 million tons in 1976. A sharp upturn in wheat purchases took place in 1977-1979–6.9 million tons in 1977, 9.4 million tons in 1978, and 11 million tons in 1979. The increase in the amount of food grains imported stems mainly from the rapid growth of the urban population, from 50 million in 1949 to 110 million in 1978. Because the marketing rate of grain remains very low (almost 20 percent of output) and inland transport facilities are inadequate, some 40 percent of the grain supply for urban areas in the 1970s had to be imported from abroad.[18] Like its changing position in oil, China's shift from a net exporter to a net importer of food grains represents another significant change in trade composition (see Table 14.3).

Raw cotton was another major agricultural commodity purchased in increasing quantities, accounting for about 8 percent of China's import bill in the 1970s. Cotton imports reached a peak of 423,000 tons in 1973, and in the 1975-1976 period, they dropped to 150,000 tons. In 1979 and 1980 China stepped up cotton imports again as textile production increased 15.6 percent in 1979 and another 35 percent in 1980.[19]

Minerals and metals accounted for about 20 percent of all imports in the 1950s and for 30 percent in the 1970s. This category was dominated by finished steel, which made up more than two-thirds of the mineral and metal imports. Nonferrous metal imports were led by copper, nickel, aluminum, and lead. Improvements in Chinese steel quality and variety in 1979 and 1980 may lead to a diminishing share for this category of imports.

Chemical products averaged about 10 percent of China's total imports throughout the 1959-1978 period. Fertilizers have been the most important component of chemical imports, reaching 10 percent of total imports in 1970. As the foreign-built ammonia-urea modern complexes gradually come on stream, however, the relative importance of fertilizers in China's import list can be expected to decline gradually.

### *Direction of Foreign Trade*

China's foreign trade has not only been profoundly affected by its modernization program, but also by its foreign policy. Before 1949, China's trade was primarily oriented toward the United States, Japan, and Great Britain; trade with the Soviet Union and Eastern Europe was negligible. After 1949, the lean-to-one-side foreign policy made the Soviet Union China's major trading partner for a decade. By 1955, China's trade with the Communist bloc accounted for almost 75 percent of total turnover. During 1950-1952, when China's total trade

Table 14.3
Commodity Composition of China's Imports, 1959-1978
(in percent)

| Commodity Category | 1959 | 1966 | 1968 | 1969 | 1970 | 1972 | 1973 | 1974 | 1975 | 1976 | 1977 | 1978 |
|---|---|---|---|---|---|---|---|---|---|---|---|---|
| Foodstuffs | 1 | 25 | 23 | 19 | 16 | 16 | 20 | 20 | 12 | 9 | 15 | 13 |
| Grain | | (20) | (17) | (14) | (13) | (12) | (17) | (16) | ( 9) | ( 5) | (10) | ( 9) |
| Crude Materials | 20 | 17 | 16 | 17 | 17 | 19 | 20 | 19 | 14 | 15 | 21 | 17 |
| Textile Fibers | ( 6) | ( 7) | ( 5) | ( 5) | ( 5) | ( 7) | ( 8) | ( 8) | ( 5) | ( 5) | ( 9) | ( 8) |
| Chemical Materials | 8 | 12 | 17 | 17 | 15 | 13 | 9 | 8 | 11 | 10 | 13 | 11 |
| Fertilizers | ( 3) | ( 8) | (11) | (11) | (10) | ( 7) | ( 4) | ( 3) | ( 6) | ( 4) | ( 5) | ( 4) |
| Manufacturing | 60 | 45 | 43 | 46 | 52 | 51 | 50 | 52 | 62 | 65 | 51 | 59 |
| Iron & Steel | (15) | (11) | (15) | (15) | (18) | (18) | (19) | (16) | (21) | (24) | (22) | (28) |
| Machinery & Equipment | (40) | (22) | (15) | (13) | (18) | (18) | (17) | (22) | (29) | (30) | (17) | (18) |
| Other | 11 | 1 | 1 | 1 | * | 1 | 1 | 1 | 1 | 1 | * | * |
| Total | 100 | 100 | 100 | 100 | 100 | 100 | 100 | 100 | 100 | 100 | 100 | 100 |

Note: Totals do not always add up to 100 because of rounding. Figures in parentheses are percents for the particular commodity. * means Negl.

Sources: 1959 from Alexander Eckstein, _China's Economic Revolution_ (London: Cambridge University Press, 1977), pp. 250-252. 1966-1973 from U.S. Congress, Joint Economic Committee, _China: A Reassessment of the Economy_ (Washington, D.C.: Government Printing Office, 1975), pp. 646-647. 1974-1978 are derived by the author from annual commodity reports published by the U.S. government.

rose by 58 percent, its trade with non-Communist countries dropped sharply, by more than one-half.

The year 1956 marked a new turn in the direction of Chinese trade. Partly because of the dwindling of Soviet financial aid and partly because of the relaxation of Western restrictions on Chinese trade dating from the Korean War, trade with Japan, Hong Kong, and Southeast Asia increased. By 1957, China's trade with non-Communist countries had recovered to its 1950 level in absolute terms, although the relative share was still well below that of 1950.

In the wake of the Soviet suspension of all technical aid to China in 1960, trade with the U.S.S.R. dropped precipitously from a high of more than $2 billion in 1959 to a low of merely $45 million in 1970 (about 2 percent of the 1959 peak level), accounting for only 1 percent of China's total trade in that year. To fill the void, the Chinese leadership sought improved relations with the West (see Figure 14.1). By 1965, trade with the non-Communist world had recovered the 70 percent share attained in 1950. After 1970, the share continued to increase, reaching 88 percent in 1979, the highest level in thirty years (see Table 14.4).

*Japan.* The major beneficiary of the new orientation has been Japan. Before the 1937–1945 Sino-Japanese War, Japan was China's most important trading partner as geographical propinquity and historical cultural ties gave Japan an edge in competing with Western Europe and the United States for the Chinese market. Yet, before 1959, Japan's trade with China was negligible, accounting for less than 1 percent of the Chinese trade.

Sino-Japanese trade began to revive in the mid-1960s, and thereafter, Japan's share of China's foreign trade expanded steadily, reaching 20 percent during 1970–1973 and 26.7 percent in 1975. Over the same period, China became Japan's second most important export market, after the United States.

More than 80 percent of the products imported by China from Japan during the 1964–1979 period were in iron and steel, machinery and equipment, and chemicals (mainly fertilizers). The import share of steel rose from an average of 20 percent in 1964–1965 to 40–50 percent during 1968–1973. In the 1977–1979 period, China imported $4.45 billion worth of iron and steel from Japan, accounting for 51 percent of China's total imports from Japan.[20]

China's exports to Japan traditionally consisted of soybeans, raw silk, and mineral products. Beginning in 1974, crude oil emerged as China's leading export commodity to Japan, with shipments of 8.1

Figure 14.1
China: Trade Balance[a]

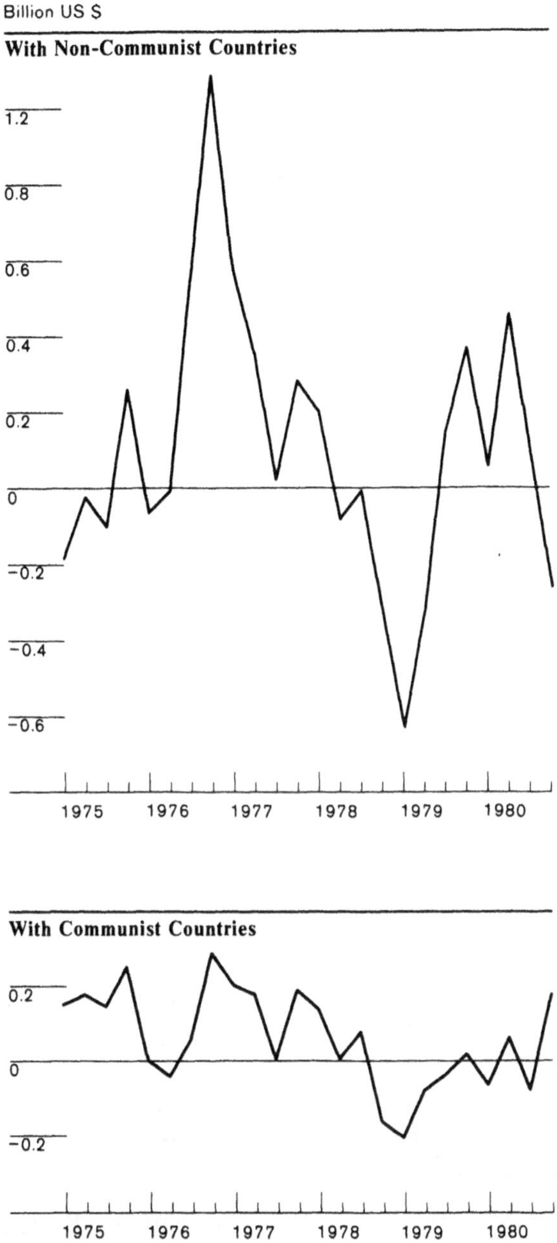


[a] f.o.b.

584280 5-81

Source: U.S. Central Intelligence Agency, *China: International Trade, Fourth Quarter, 1980* (Washington, D.C., May 1981), p. 1.

million tons in 1975 and 6.5 million tons in 1976. In February 1978, China signed a long-term trade agreement (1978–1985) with Japan, making oil and coal two major export items. Deliveries for the first five years were to total 47 million tons of oil and 9.2 million tons of coal. Quantities were to rise gradually to 1982 goals of 15 million tons of oil and 6.8 million tons of coal. Oil and coal exports over the life of the agreement were to total $10 billion. As China's crude oil output slowed down in 1979–1980, however, the Chinese found it very difficult to carry out the agreement. In 1979, China exported only 7.4

Table 14.4
Direction of China's Foreign Trade, 1950-1979
(in percent of total trade)

| Year | Trade with Non-Communist Countries[a] | Trade with Communist Countries | |
|---|---|---|---|
| | | Total[b] | U.S.S.R.[c] |
| 1950 | 71 | 29 | 26.4 |
| 1952 | 30 | 70 | 50.2 |
| 1955 | 26 | 74 | 51.0 |
| 1957 | 36 | 64 | 41.9 |
| 1959 | 31 | 69 | 47.9 |
| 1961 | 44 | 56 | 31.7 |
| 1963 | 55 | 45 | 22.3 |
| 1965 | 70 | 30 | 10.7 |
| 1967 | 79 | 21 | 2.9 |
| 1970 | 80 | 20 | 1.0 |
| 1972 | 79 | 21 | .9 |
| 1974 | 83 | 17 | 1.4 |
| 1975 | 84 | 16 | 1.9 |
| 1976 | 82 | 18 | 3.1 |
| 1977 | 84 | 16 | 2.2 |
| 1978 | 86 | 14 | 2.5 |
| 1979 | 88 | 12 | 1.3 |

a. U.S. Central Intelligence Agency, China: Major Economic Indicators (Washington, D.C., February 1980).

b. The 1950-1967 figures are derived from trade data in F. H. Mah, The Foreign Trade of Mainland China (Chicago: Aldine, 1971), p. 20.

c. The 1970-1979 figures are derived from annual trade reports published by the Central Intelligence Agency in various years.

million tons of crude oil to Japan, representing only 38 percent of the value of China's exports to that country. Although the quantity of crude oil exported remained almost unchanged in the first half of 1980, the price hike meant that its value was double that of 1979, so it accounted for 42.4 percent of the value of China's exports to Japan.[21]

Prospects for the Sino-Japanese trade have been enhanced by the long-term trade pact, which established an exchange of Japan's technology for China's natural resources. In 1978, when China signed many large-scale contracts for foreign technology, purchases from Japan accounted for 64 percent of the total orders, and in December 1979, Japan signed the agreement with China for joint exploitation of the offshore oil in Bohai Wan.[22] In early 1981, China unilaterally cancelled more than $1.5 billion of contracts for the purchase of plants and equipment from Japan signed in 1978, but Japan will still remain China's chief trade partner throughout the 1980s.

*Hong Kong.* Next to Japan, Hong Kong plays a unique role as China's second largest trading partner, its most important entry port, and its largest source of foreign exchange earnings. In the initial years of the People's Republic, China's leaders had to rely heavily on Hong Kong agents to conduct foreign trade, because of a lack of knowledge and experience and an inadequate foreign trade network.[23] Hong Kong also served as an intermediary through which China obtained strategic materials that the West had embargoed.

After 1952, as the Korean War wound down, China's imports from Hong Kong dropped sharply, but its exports to Hong Kong expanded tremendously. China supplied most of Hong Kong's grains, live animals, vegetables, and traditional medicine and maintained an export surplus that averaged about $350 million per annum in the late 1960s and increased substantially in the 1970s. Between 1960 and 1970, China had an accumulated trade surplus with Hong Kong of $3.58 billion, which became the prime source of China's foreign exchange.

In addition to the sale of merchandise, Hong Kong has also served as a conduit for overseas remittances; profits from P.R.C.-controlled banking and insurance companies, shipping agencies, retail outlets, and real estate holdings; as well as tourist receipts from the Chinese Travel Service. It has been estimated that China obtained more than $7 billion of foreign exchange from Hong Kong in 1980 alone.[24]

*Western Europe.* During the 1960s and 1970s, four of China's twelve leading trading partners were in Western Europe: West Germany, France, the United Kingdom, and Italy. During the 1975–1979 period, those four countries had a combined share of 13.3 percent of China's total trade. Of the four, West Germany ranked at the top in 1979, accounting for about 7 percent of China's total trade, followed by the United Kingdom, France, and Italy. Generally speaking, China exports foodstuffs, hides and skins, textiles, and light manufactures to Western Europe in exchange for machinery and equipment, chemicals, and finished steel products. In its modernization drive, China views Western Europe as an important alternative supplier to the United States and Japan for military equipment, steel mills, nonferrous metal plants, and nuclear power plants.[25]

*United States.* Prior to the founding of the P.R.C. in 1949, the United States was China's principal trade partner for many years. In 1936, for example, the United States accounted for 22 percent of China's exports and 20 percent of its imports. In 1946, the U.S. share reached 54 percent of China's imports and 48 percent of China's exports.[26] Even in 1950, U.S. trade still constituted 22.5 percent of China's total trade.[27]

The Korean War and the subsequent embargo caused a precipitous decline in Sino-American trade relations. In December 1950, under the authority of the Export Control Act of 1949, the U.S. government embargoed all U.S. exports to China. For more than two decades, trade relations between the two countries came to a virtual standstill. In 1969, as international relations changed, the U.S. government took several steps to relax tensions between Washington and Beijing and ended the embargo on June 10, 1971, by announcing a long list of nonstrategic U.S. commodities that might be shipped to China under general license. The historic visit of President Nixon to Beijing in February 1972 opened a new era in Sino-American relations. For the greater part of 1973 and 1974, continuous improvements in commercial relations were accompanied by rising trade and by an increasing number of visits by U.S. businessmen to China and Chinese technicians to U.S. plants.[28]

Starting from a negligible volume of $5 million in 1971, Sino-American trade spurted to nearly $1 billion in 1974. In 1973 and 1974, the United States emerged as China's number two trading partner, after Japan, and in 1974, China ranked second among the socialist states in trade with the United States, closely following the U.S.S.R.[29]

The rapid growth of Sino-American trade in 1973–1974 created rising expectations in the U.S. business community, which envisioned China as an untapped major market. Most of the U.S. trade with China in those two years was composed of farm exports, however, and the downturn in U.S. agricultural exports to China in 1975–1977 immediately lowered Sino-American trade to a very moderate level.

In 1975, the United States fell from fifth to sixth place among China's trading partners, and in 1976 and 1977, to eighth place. These percentages and rankings have varied primarily with the ups and downs of U.S. grain exports, indicating the unsettled nature of Sino-American trade.

In 1978, following the announcement of China's Ten-Year Plan (1976–1985), there was a new euphoria about the Chinese market, and many top U.S. bankers and corporation heads flocked to Beijing hoping to capture a share of that market. Two-way trade between the United States and the P.R.C. reached a new high of close to $1.2 billion in 1978, representing a threefold jump over the previous year. Trade volume surged to $2.3 billion in 1979, almost double that of 1978. Although the growth rates in those two years were phenomenal, they were the result of a Chinese resumption of large-scale purchases of U.S. agricultural products—a consequence of Chinese harvest cycles rather than the beginning of a trend of long-term growth.

During the eight years 1972–1979, Sino-American trade exhibited several peculiar features. In terms of trade turnover, unlike the U.S. trade with Taiwan and Japan, which grew steadily over the years, Sino-American trade was characterized by sharp fluctuations. As Table 14.5 and Table 14.6 show, Sino-American trade in 1974 was almost ten times that of 1972, but in the following three years, the trade volume dropped almost 60 percent. It then registered a threefold increase in 1978 and a 95 percent rise in 1979 (see Table 14.7). The

Table 14.5
U.S. Shares of P.R.C. Trade, 1972–1979
(in percent)

| Year | U.S. Share of P.R.C. Imports | U.S. Share of P.R.C. Exports | U.S. Share of P.R.C. Total Trade |
|---|---|---|---|
| 1972 | 2.3 | 1.0 | 1.6 |
| 1973 | 14.8 | 1.3 | 8.0 |
| 1974 | 11.0 | 1.7 | 6.7 |
| 1975 | 4.1 | 2.2 | 3.2 |
| 1976 | 2.2 | 2.7 | 2.6 |
| 1977 | 2.5 | 2.5 | 2.5 |
| 1978 | 8.4 | 3.2 | 5.6 |
| 1979 | 11.7 | 4.4 | 8.4 |

Source: Derived from data in Tables 14.1 and 14.7.

Table 14.6
Composition of U.S.-China Trade, 1972-1979
(in millions of current U.S. dollars)

| | 1972 | 1973 | 1974 | 1975 | 1976 | 1977 | 1978 | 1979 |
|---|---|---|---|---|---|---|---|---|
| U.S. Exports | 63 | 740 | 819 | 304 | 135 | 171 | 821 | 1,724 |
| Agricultural Commodities | 61 | 628 | 668 | 80 | 0 | 64 | 623 | 1,095 |
| Metals | 0 | 31 | 22 | 83 | 47 | 7 | 22 | 202 |
| Machinery & Equipment | 2 | 69 | 107 | 119 | 65 | 52 | 94 | 230 |
| Others | 0 | 12 | 22 | 22 | 23 | 48 | 82 | 197 |
| U.S. Imports | 32 | 64 | 115 | 158 | 201 | 203 | 324 | 591 |
| Food & Tobacco | 4 | 7 | 16 | 16 | 24 | 26 | 37 | 70 |
| Textiles & Apparel | 7 | 15 | 36 | 45 | 63 | 58 | 120 | 202 |
| Handicrafts | 8 | 15 | 20 | 22 | 42 | 49 | 45 | 34 |
| Bristles, Down & Feathers | 8 | 8 | 10 | 6 | 23 | 28 | 33 | 20 |
| Chemicals | 2 | 8 | 18 | 18 | 18 | 22 | 35 | 65 |
| Nonferrous Minerals & Metals | 2 | 8 | 11 | 40 | 21 | 12 | 37 | 137 |
| Others | 1 | 3 | 4 | 11 | 10 | 8 | 17 | 63 |

Source: Data are from the Department of Commerce and show exports f.a.s. and imports f.o.b.

Table 14.7
U.S.-P.R.C. Trade Volumes and Balances, 1971-1979
(in millions of U.S. dollars)

| Year | Total Trade | U.S. Exports | U.S. Imports | Balances | Ratio U.S. Exports to Imports |
|---|---|---|---|---|---|
| 1971 | 5.0 | --- | 5.0 | -5.0 | |
| 1972 | 95.9 | 63.5 | 32.4 | +31.1 | 2:1 |
| 1973 | 805.1 | 740.2 | 64.9 | +675.3 | 11.4:1 |
| 1974 | 933.8 | 819.1 | 114.7 | +704.4 | 7.1:1 |
| 1975 | 461.9 | 303.6 | 158.3 | +145.3 | 1.9:1 |
| 1976 | 337.3 | 135.4 | 201.9 | -66.5 | 0.7:1 |
| 1977 | 374.5 | 171.5 | 203.0 | -31.5 | 0.8:1 |
| 1978 | 1,188.2 | 864.6 | 323.6 | +541.0 | 2.7:1 |
| 1979 | 2,318.0 | 1,723.8 | 594.2 | +1,129.6 | 2.9:1 |

Sources: 1971-1977 from Martha Avery and William Clark, "The Sino-American Commercial Relationship," in U.S. Congress, Joint Economic Committee, Chinese Economy Post-Mao (Washington, D.C.: Government Printing Office, 1978), p. 752. 1978-1979 derived from data in National Foreign Assessment Center, China: International Trade Quarterly Review Fourth Quarter (1979), pp. 10-13.

sharp fluctuations corresponded to changes in the Chinese harvest, because food grains and cotton constitute the bulk of U.S. exports to China. If agricultural commodities are deducted from the U.S. exports, the track volume remains fairly stable.

As Table 14.8 shows, the four years of high trade turnover (1973–1974 and 1978–1979) were characterized by a high volume of U.S. agricultural exports to China (85 percent in 1973, 82 percent in 1974, 76 percent in 1978, and 64 percent in 1979). The years of low trade volume (1975, 1976, and 1977) were years in which U.S. agricultural exports were low or suspended (26 percent in 1975, zero in 1976, and 37 percent in 1977). Moreover, although some U.S. exports are perennial items, many are only one-time purchases, bought for a specific project or purpose. Examples are the $150-million Boeing jet sale and the $200-million M. W. Kellogg sale of eight fertilizer plants in 1973 and 1974.

U.S. imports from China, however, show a steady growth over the years and exhibit a predictable pattern. Between 1973 and 1979, imports of Chinese foodstuffs and tobacco constituted 10 to 14 percent of the imports from China; textiles and apparel from 23 to 38 percent; bristles, down, and feathers from 4 to 14 percent; and chemicals from 9 to 16 percent. In general, textiles and apparel have become China's principal export commodity to the United States, reaching 38 percent of the U.S. imports from China in 1978 (see Figure 14.2).

U.S. trade with the P.R.C. has run highly favorable balances most of the time, except for the two-year hiatus when China ceased to purchase U.S. agricultural products. In 1973–1974, U.S. exports to China amounted to seven to eleven times its imports. In 1978–1979, American exports still were three times its imports. This lopsided balance cannot be expected to continue for long.

In the 1980s, Japan, Hong Kong, Western Europe, and the United States will continue to be China's most important trade partners. As the data in Table 14.9 indicate, China has avoided overdependence on any one country since the early 1960s. In buying machinery and equipment in the 1965–1979 period, China placed orders with more than ten countries, preventing any one of them from dominating its trade in that area. In the 1980s, trade with Japan will continue to occupy the leading position, accounting for 20 to 25 percent of China's total trade, followed by 13–15 percent for Western European countries, 10–12 percent for Hong Kong, and 8–10 percent for the United States. These four major partners will account for approximately 60–65 percent of China's total trade, leaving the remaining 35 or so percent for more than 100 other countries.

Table 14.8
Composition of U.S.-China Trade, 1972-1979
(in percent)

| | 1972 | 1973 | 1974 | 1975 | 1976 | 1977 | 1978 | 1979 |
|---|---|---|---|---|---|---|---|---|
| U.S. Exports | 100 | 100 | 100 | 100 | 100 | 100 | 100 | 100 |
| Agricultural Commodities | 97 | 85 | 82 | 26 | 0 | 37 | 76 | 64 |
| Metals | 0 | .4 | 3 | 27 | 35 | 4 | 3 | 12 |
| Machinery & Equipment | 3 | 9 | 13 | 39 | 48 | 31 | 11 | 13 |
| Others | 0 | 2 | 2 | 8 | 17 | 28 | 10 | 11 |
| U.S. Imports | 100 | 100 | 100 | 100 | 100 | 100 | 100 | 100 |
| Food & Tobacco | 13 | 11 | 14 | 10 | 12 | 13 | 12 | 12 |
| Textiles & Apparel | 22 | 23 | 31 | 28 | 32 | 29 | 38 | 34 |
| Handicrafts | 25 | 23 | 17 | 14 | 21 | 23 | 15 | 6 |
| Bristles, Down & Feathers | 25 | 13 | 9 | 4 | 11 | 14 | 10 | 4 |
| Chemicals | 6 | 13 | 16 | 11 | 9 | 11 | 11 | 11 |
| Nonferrous Minerals & Metals | 6 | 13 | 10 | 26 | 10 | 6 | 12 | 23 |
| Others | 3 | 4 | 3 | 7 | 5 | 4 | 2 | 10 |

Source: Table 14.6

Figure 14.2
United States Trade with P.R.C.: Volumes and Composition

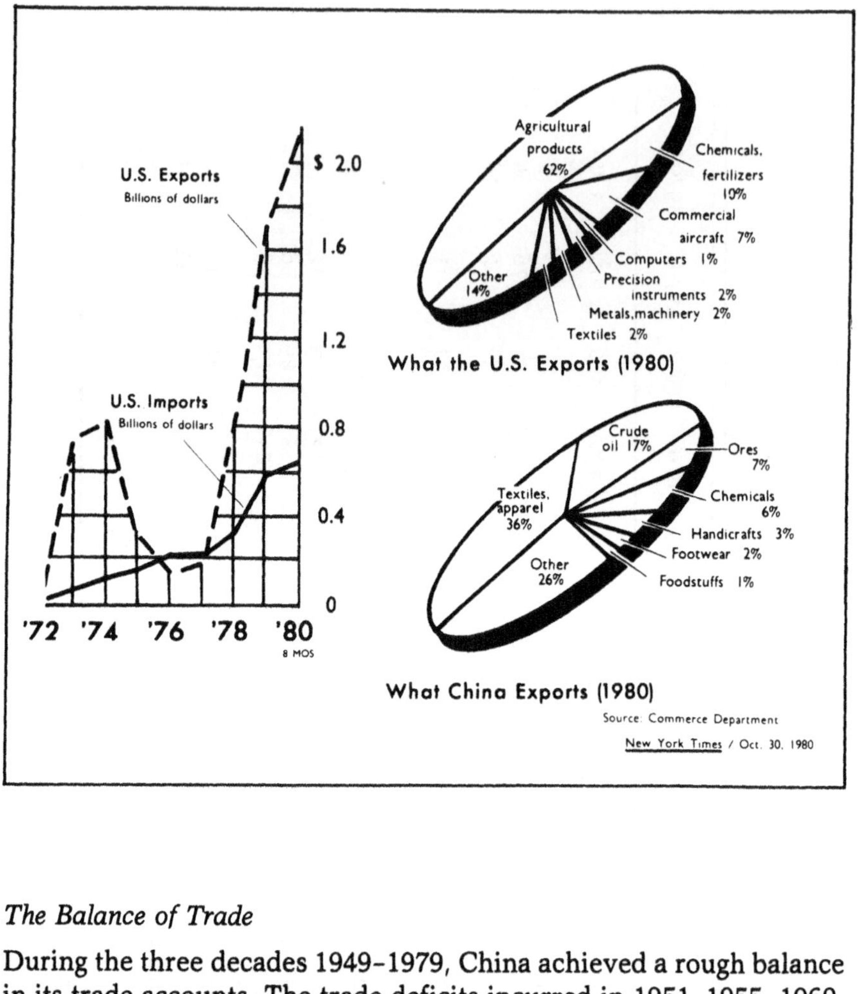


*The Balance of Trade*

During the three decades 1949–1979, China achieved a rough balance in its trade accounts. The trade deficits incurred in 1951–1955, 1960, 1974–1975, and 1978–1979 were offset by the surpluses of 1956–1973 and 1976–1977 (see Table 14.1).

In the 1951–1955 period, China consistently imported more from the Soviet Union than it exported to that country. During those five years, the cumulative import surplus was nearly $1 billion, which was mostly financed by Soviet loans to China. In the 1956–1965 period, as China began to pay off its debts to the Soviet Union, its trade balance with the Communist countries achieved a huge surplus totaling $2.24 billion. During that period, when China turned to Western Europe

Table 14.9
China's Trade with Twelve Major Partners:
Share and Rank in Selected Years, 1959-1979

| Country | 1959 | | 1961 | | 1966 | | 1970 | | 1975 | | 1978 | | 1979 | |
|---|---|---|---|---|---|---|---|---|---|---|---|---|---|---|
| | Share % | Rank | Share % | Rank | Share % | Rank | Share % | Rank | Share % | Rank | Share % | Rank | Share % | Rank |
| Japan | 0.5 | (10) | 1.5 | (10) | 14.9 | ( 1) | 19.9 | ( 1) | 26.7 | ( 1) | 24.8 | ( 1) | 22.9 | ( 1) |
| Hong Kong | 3.3 | ( 3) | 3.8 | ( 5) | 9.0 | ( 2) | 8.3 | ( 2) | 7.2 | ( 2) | 11.4 | ( 2) | 11.8 | ( 2) |
| West Germany | 4.5 | ( 2) | 2.7 | ( 6) | 5.1 | ( 4) | 6.3 | ( 3) | 5.6 | ( 3) | 6.5 | ( 3) | 6.9 | ( 4) |
| United States | — | — | — | — | — | — | — | — | 3.4 | ( 6) | 5.9 | ( 4) | 8.2 | ( 3) |
| U.S.S.R. | 47.9 | ( 1) | 30.3 | ( 1) | 7.5 | ( 3) | 1.0 | (11) | 1.9 | (12) | 2.5 | ( 9) | 1.3 | (12) |
| France | 1.3 | ( 7) | 1.8 | ( 8) | 3.7 | ( 7) | 3.6 | ( 8) | 4.1 | ( 4) | 2.0 | (10) | 2.2 | (10) |
| Malaysia/ Singapore | 2.1 | ( 5) | 2.1 | ( 7) | 3.4 | ( 8) | 4.4 | ( 5) | 3.9 | ( 5) | 3.5 | ( 5) | 3.3 | ( 6) |
| Canada | 0.2 | (11) | 5.1 | ( 3) | 5.1 | ( 5) | 4.1 | ( 6) | 3.4 | ( 7) | 2.6 | ( 8) | 2.3 | ( 9) |
| United Kingdom | 2.9 | ( 4) | 4.1 | ( 4) | 4.2 | ( 6) | 4.9 | ( 4) | 2.2 | (10) | 1.8 | (11) | 2.6 | ( 8) |
| Italy | 1.1 | ( 8) | 1.6 | ( 9) | 2.7 | (10) | 3.1 | ( 9) | 2.0 | (11) | 1.8 | (12) | 2.0 | (11) |
| Australia | 0.9 | ( 9) | 6.6 | ( 2) | 2.9 | ( 9) | 4.1 | ( 7) | 3.1 | ( 8) | 3.1 | ( 6) | 3.2 | ( 7) |
| Romania | 1.4 | ( 6) | 1.0 | (11) | 1.6 | (11) | 2.5 | (10) | 2.7 | ( 9) | 3.0 | ( 7) | 3.9 | ( 5) |
| Total of Above | 66.1 | | 60.6 | | 60.1 | | 62.2 | | 66.2 | | 68.9 | | 70.6 | |
| China's Trade Total | 100.0 | | 100.0 | | 100.0 | | 100.0 | | 100.0 | | 100.0 | | 100.0 | |

Source: Computed by the author from statistics from U.S. government publications of various years.

and Japan for complete plants and heavy machinery and to Australia and Canada for food grains, the result was huge trade deficits with those countries, which were partially compensated for by China's huge trade surpluses with Hong Kong and Singapore. The trade surplus with Hong Kong, plus overseas Chinese remittances, added up to roughly $600 million a year. This allowed China to pursue an unbalanced trade with Japan, West Germany, Canada, and Australia.

China suffered a record trade deficit in the 1974–1975 period, totaling about $1 billion. This deficit was the result of the depressed demand for Chinese exports caused by a worldwide recession and a sharp jump in the prices of China's commodity imports due to the energy crisis. When the Chinese authorities realized how seriously their trade balance was deteriorating, they cut back imports and achieved a $2.3-billion trade surplus in the following two years.

The large-scale acquisition of foreign technology and equipment in 1978 and 1979 again put China's trade balance in the red. The $3-billion deficit for those two years triggered the suspension of many whole plant equipment procurements contracted for with Japan and Western European countries. Chinese efforts in 1980 to correct the trade imbalance indicate that the leadership still adheres to its old international financial policies, historically among the world's most conservative.[30]

## MODERNIZATION AND FOREIGN RESOURCES

The four modernizations program greatly enhanced China's linkage with foreign resources and technology. The expansion of China's industrial capacity and the modernization of its defense system require the injection of foreign capital as well as a wide variety of advanced technology. In the 1978 plan, Chinese leaders estimated that the modernization drive would require capital investment totaling at least 1 trillion Renminbi ($600 billion) in the 1978–1985 period. As noted in Chapter 10, the 1978 and 1979 Chinese national income was officially reported as 317 billion yuan and 337 billion yuan, respectively. If the original investment plan is carried out, total capital investment for those two years alone would be around 250 billion yuan, or 38 percent of the total national income of 654 billion yuan for those two years. During the First Five-Year Plan period, the rate of investment to national income was only 24.2 percent, which many leading Chinese economists deemed appropriate for the country's economic level. Thus, the new investment rate seems highly excessive.

During the 1949–1959 period, China invested a total of 120 billion yuan (1957 prices), or $46.2 billion at the prevailing exchange rate. Approximately $10 billion of the investment fund came from the confiscation of private property; $1.3 billion came from Soviet loans and credits; and the remainder came from the agricultural sector through artificially low procurement prices for farm products and higher prices for industrial products sold to the rural areas. The price differentials, known in China as the "scissor gap," constituted the profit of the state-run enterprises. After 1960, as private property and Soviet aid ceased to be available, most new capital formation had to be generated through the profit of state enterprises, and those profits constituted as much as 70 to 80 percent of the annual state revenue. From 1952 to 1978, 97 percent of capital investment in industry came from the profits of the state's light and textile industries.[31] During the early and mid-1970s, the trauma of political storms and industrial unrest resulted in heavy losses for many state enterprises. In 1978, fully one-quarter of the state enterprises were operating at a loss. The average rate of profit for industry dropped precipitously from 24.3 percent in 1966 to only 16.4 percent in 1978.[32]

The drop in profits from the state enterprises has made it extremely difficult to finance the 1976–1985 plan announced in 1978. One major source of financing lies in the rapid expansion of exports, particularly crude oil and light manufacturing products. In the 1978 plan, the petroleum industry was expected to play a crucial role as a major foreign exchange earner to balance imports of increasing amounts of foreign machinery and equipment. But the performance of the petroleum industry in 1979 and 1980 was extremely disappointing. As the development of new oilfields lagged behind schedule, the growth rate of crude oil output fell sharply – 11 percent in 1978, 1.9 percent in 1979, and zero growth in 1980. Recent official reports indicate that the crude oil output in 1981–1982 can only maintain the 1978–1979 level. The 1979 and 1980 output showed a minuscule rise of 2.5 million tons, indicating that the petroleum industry had failed to play the crucial role assigned to it by the Chinese planners.

For all these reasons, a scaling down of capital investment and the acquisition of foreign capital became inevitable. In December 1978, the Eleventh CCP Central Committee decided at its Third Plenum to cut 30 to 40 percent of the investment scheduled in the original plan. Even after substantial revision of the investment plan, China still needed to import some $30 billion to $40 billion in plants, equipment, and technology (originally $60 billion to $70 billion). China's foreign reserves at the end of 1979 were estimated by JETRO (Japan External Trade Organization) at only $1.3 billion, and its holdings of gold were estimated at $2.23 billion. Total holdings of gold and foreign currency at the end of 1979 thus amounted to an estimated $3.5 billion, equivalent to approximately five and a half months' of imports from the non-Communist world in 1978.[33] Moreover, partly because of military overspending and partly because of the rise in procurement prices for agricultural products, China suffered a disastrous $11.3-billion budget deficit in 1979, the worst in its recent history.[34] The 1980 budget deficit was smaller, but it still reached $8 billion.

The critical shortage of foreign exchange and the huge fiscal deficit forced China to accept many arrangements that had been unacceptable in previous years, including direct government-to-government loans and joint ventures with foreign firms. Since the beginning of 1978, China has aggressively sought foreign bank loans. Japan has provided the largest single credit line, some $12 billion in 1979; France is the next largest source of credit, $7.6 billion. Export credits have also come from Italy, Canada, and several other countries. By the end of January 1980, China had obtained some $26 billion in government-guaranteed and commercial bank credits (see Table 14.10).

Efforts have also been made to bring in overseas private investment. In 1980, five special economic zones were established in Guangdong and Fujian provinces. In those special zones, the Chinese government promised to provide land and labor if the overseas investor would supply capital and technology. The local government would also provide preferential conditions and facilities so that foreign companies could establish enterprises in those areas. One major zone is located in Shenzhen, right across the border from Hong Kong. Beijing-controlled companies in Hong Kong are entering into joint ventures with Hong Kong companies to develop in Shenzhen not only light industry for export, but also large housing projects to be sold to Hong Kong residents. By the end of August 1980, Chinese factories had signed 3,200 contracts with foreign companies to process raw materials supplied by foreigners. There were also 170 compensation trade arrangements, according to which foreign companies provide high-technology equipment and are repaid in products made in China by using the equipment. China has also entered into offshore-oil-drilling contracts with more than ten foreign oil companies.[35]

In a larger sense, China intends to attract foreign capital through joint ventures in electric power, energy resources, the construction of ports and wharves, and raw and semiprocessed materials industries, precision machinery and electronics, and the exploitation of nonferrous metals.[36] The Joint Ventures Law promulgated on July 1, 1979, permits foreign investors to participate not only in the management but also in the ownership of an enterprise, which represents a radical departure from past practice. Two new organizations were set up at the same time to facilitate joint ventures and technology transfer: the Foreign Investment Control Commission and the China International Trust and Investment Corporation. In a joint venture, the law requires

Table 14.10
Export Credits to P.R.C., as of February 1, 1980

| Country | Date | Amount (million U.S. $) |
|---|---|---|
| Export-Import Bank Credits and Government Guaranteed Loans | | |
| U.K. | 12/78 | 1,200 |
| Australia | 4/79 | 56 |
| France | 5/79 | 7,140 |
| Italy | 5/79 | 1,000 |
| Japan | 5/79 | 3,625 |
| Sweden | 5/79 | 350 |
| Canada | 8/79 | 1,720 |
| West Germany | 10/79 | 1,100 |
| Belgium | 11/79 | 173 |
| | Subtotal | 16,364 |
| Commercial Bank Buyers' Credtis | | |
| U.K. | 3/79–4/79 | 675 |
| France | 4/79 | 500 |
| Canada | 4/79 | 100 |
| Luxemburg | 4/79 | 50 |
| Chile | 4/79 | 10 |
| U.S. | 6/79–10/79 | 28 |
| Japan | 8/79 | 8,004.6 |
| West Germany | 10/79 | 450 |
| | Subtotal | 9,817.6 |
| Total | | 26,181.6 |

Sources: U.S. Export-Import Bank, 1978 Annual Report (March 1979). China Business Review (July-August 1979), p. 50, also (September-October 1979), p. 21, and (January-February 1980), p. 57.

Note: The actual foreign loan owed by China will come to around $3.4 billion by the end of 1980 after the matured principal is deducted (Xinhua-Beijing, August 31, 1980).

a minimum foreign ownership of 25 percent, but no maximum foreign ownership is set.[37] Whatever the percentage of foreign holdings, the Chinese side appoints the chairman of the board of directors of a joint venture. To prevent any attempt at foreign unloading of outdated machinery and equipment, the law also stipulates that the technology or equipment provided by the foreign partners must be truly advanced and appropriate to China's needs. If this condition is not met, China may claim compensation; if it is met, tax breaks may be granted to foreign investors.

Foreign investors hailed the Joint Ventures Law as the first positive step toward establishing an apparatus for foreign investment on terms acceptable to China. The Chinese leadership aroused great expectations abroad for the new initiative but also cited four major advantages for China.

1. Joint ventures can attract advanced foreign technology and equipment.
2. China can expand its export markets through the new foreign connection.
3. Joint ventures can save China the cost of some capital investments, thereby freeing funds for other economic activities.
4. Joint ventures can help train technical administrators to run modern enterprises.[38]

Despite the government's high expectations, only a very limited amount of foreign capital had been commited one year after the adoption of the Joint Ventures Law. There are numerous reasons for this slow progress.

First, the law contains a number of references to specific laws that are still in the process of being drawn up. According to Peng Zhen, vice-chairman of the National People's Congress Standing Committee, some seventy decrees and regulations for economic work have either been prepared or are being drafted. By September 1980, China had only announced its income tax law. The income tax rate in joint ventures is 30 percent plus a local surtax, which brings the overall tax rate up to 33 percent. There are also provisions for tax holdings and tax reduction.[39] The adoption of the income tax law removed some uncertainty facing foreign businesses, but until other basic laws and regulations governing labor disputes, industrial patents, and foreign exchange control are promulgated, foreign businessmen will be reluctant to become involved in joint ventures in China.

A second group of deterrents lies in the low-wage system in China, together with a weak industrial safety program, the lack of labor discipline, and low labor productivity. As a consequence of the Cultural Revolution, quality control in many industries is lax, and delivery dates are not guaranteed. A third set of deterrents that is often cited includes the deficiency of supporting industries, the chronic shortage of electricity, and the antiquated transportation system, all of which make quick investment success very unlikely.

Moreover, since the function of a joint venture is to attract foreign capital, its ability to earn foreign exchange is likely to be a key determinant for Chinese approval. The Chinese authorities have made it clear that they will not provide foreign exchange for joint ventures. Thus, unless at least part of a joint venture's production is exported, the foreign participant will be unable to repatriate any profits.

Finally, as one Japanese economist has pointed out, foreign investors are concerned about the kinds of problems a private company founded on capitalistic principles may encounter in attempting to run a joint venture in a planned economic system that operates under a totally different set of rules. Numerous unknown factors of this sort create tremendous uncertainties.[40]

For all these reasons, the drive to attract foreign investment through joint ventures has achieved very modest results. Unless a legal system can be established quickly to set up laws and regulations regarding ownership, labor disputes, and means of repatriating profits, no large-scale inflow of foreign capital can be expected.

## FUTURE GROWTH OF FOREIGN TRADE

The modernization drive has markedly altered Chinese development policies. During the 1978–1980 period, not only foreign trade and commercial relations but the whole spectrum of P.R.C. attitudes toward the outside world became more open and liberal. As noted above, many previously prohibited policies and practices are now openly justified and welcome. These new policies, if continued, are bound to have a profound impact on Chinese economic relations with the rest of the world.

To accelerate the pace of modernization, capital investment must increase more rapidly than GNP, and a very sizable share of that investment has to be allocated to the expansion of factories, railways, and other modern facilities. Those facilities, in turn, require modern, technically advanced machinery and equipment and other installations that cannot be produced domestically and must be obtained abroad. Consequently, imports will have to increase rapidly. In 1978 and 1979, when national income rose by 10 and 7 percent, imports leaped by 40 and 35 percent, respectively, indicating a sharp rise in the marginal propensity to import. To sustain the pace of import expansion, exports will have to increase rapidly to provide the foreign exchange necessary to finance the imports. Some economists predict that China may enter an era in which foreign trade leads growth.[41]

Since all imports inevitably have to be paid for by exports, export potentials are the key to China's future imports. During the 1965–1980 period, China's exports increased from $2,035 million to $19,300 million, with an annual growth rate of 16.2 percent. In the same period, China's imports grew from $1,845 million to $20,500 million, with an annual growth rate of 17.4 percent. The disparity resulted in a sizable trade deficit for 1978–1980, which caused China to curb its imports in 1981.

Compared with other major countries, China's 1978 exports were rather small (see Table 14.11). They amounted to only 10 percent of Japanese exports and 7 percent of U.S. exports. China's exports were even smaller than those of the three tiny economic areas in

Table 14.11
China's Exports Compared with Those of Other Countries
1960–1978 (million U.S. dollars)

| Country | 1960 | 1970 | 1975 | 1977 | 1978 |
|---|---|---|---|---|---|
| United States | 19,651 | 42,659 | 107,130 | 121,150 | 143,570 |
| West Germany | 11,416 | 34,228 | 90,176 | 118,091 | 142,453 |
| Japan | 4,055 | 19,318 | 55,817 | 81,126 | 98,415 |
| France | 6,867 | 18,098 | 53,118 | 64,997 | 79,378 |
| South Korea | 33 | 835 | 5,081 | 10,047 | 12,711 |
| Taiwan | 164 | 1,428 | 5,301 | 9,349 | 12,682 |
| Brazil | 1,268 | 2,739 | 8,670 | 12,120 | 12,650 |
| Indonesia | 841 | 1,152 | 7,102 | 10,853 | 11,643 |
| Hong Kong | 689 | 2,514 | 6,019 | 9,704 | 11,208 |
| Singapore | 1,136 | 1,554 | 5,376 | 8,241 | 10,134 |
| China | 1,960 | 2,080 | 7,180 | 8,100 | 10,100 |
| India | 1,332 | 2,026 | 4,355 | 6,360 | 6,415 |

Note: All figures are f.o.b.
Sources: China's figures are from U.S. Central Intelligence Agency, China: International Trade 1976–77, (Washington D.C., November 1977), p.1, and China: International Trade 1977–78, (Washington D.C., December 1978), p.3. Other countries are from U.S. Central Intelligence Agency, Handbook of Economic Statistics 1979, (Washington D.C., 1979) pp. 77–78.

Asia – Taiwan, Hong Kong, and Singapore – and also smaller than those of South Korea, Brazil, and Indonesia. China's relatively small export volume reveals both the potential of and the constraints on China's future growth in foreign trade.

Three major barriers impede the rapid expansion of China's export trade. First, China's current exports are primarily composed of traditional items such as food, textiles, raw materials, and light manufactures. As shown in Table 14.2, during the 1969–1978 period, foodstuffs averaged 28.8 percent of China's total exports; crude materials, 22.9 percent; and textiles and clothing, 22.3 percent. Those three areas had a combined share of almost three-fourths of China's exports. In recent years, the share of textiles and clothing has been mounting steadily to become China's leading export area. Those goods, however, encounter the problems of an uncertain supply of raw materials, strong barriers from foreign protectionist actions, and keen competition from other developing countries. To support textile expansion, China imported from the United States alone $687 million worth of cotton and other raw materials during 1972–1979. In the 1980 crop year, China bought 2.2 million bales of U.S. cotton, worth nearly $700 million, and thus became the largest cotton customer of the United States, outstripping Japan and South Korea.[42] The cost of imported cotton in recent years has far exceeded the value of the textile products exported to the United States.[43]

Because exports of textiles are constrained by supplies of raw materials and the export market, the future of Chinese exports relies heavily on nontraditional products, particularly coal and crude oil. Between 1965 and 1975, the Chinese crude oil output grew at an annual rate of 20 percent, and in the early 1970s, it was expected that China would soon replace Saudi Arabia as the world's major oil supplier. The Chinese crude oil output peaked in 1978, however, and thereafter entered a period of stagnation, suffering zero growth for the 1980 and 1981 period.[44] Yet, in the same period, domestic consumption grew at 9.5 percent a year. Consequently, China was unable to fulfill its commitment to export 8.6 million tons of crude to Japan in 1980 and had to cut its crude oil commitment to Japan by 13 percent for 1981 and by 45 percent for 1982. Under the new arrangement, China is to export 8 million tons of crude oil to Japan annually in 1980, 1981, and 1982.[45] The slowdown in the crude oil growth rate suggests that China has run into difficulties in exploiting its existing fields. Although China harbors great hope for its offshore oil reserves, their size and quality are unknown, and exploration and development will be a long and expensive process. Until oil from the offshore fields begins to flow in the late 1980s, China's prospects for increasing its oil exports appear to be very dim.

The second major barrier to Chinese export expansion lies in its foreign trade system. Foreign trade in China is a state monopoly and is conducted principally through a group of foreign trade corporations (FTCs). There were eight of them in 1970, fourteen in 1974, and more than thirty in 1980. Until very recently, neither manufacturing units nor end-use entities in China concluded contracts with foreign firms. Instead, the FTCs acted as their agents in both import and export transactions. Since domestic producers have virtually no connection with foreign firms, they are ignorant about the nature and price of competitive products in the international market. As pure "order takers," their obligation is to fulfill the quotas set by their industrial ministry under the terms of its contract with the Ministry of Foreign Trade. The producers are not concerned about whether their goods can capture a foreign market. Under this system, there is a lack of communication between the production and the export organizations. Moreover, because all production plans are fixed by the central authorities, the individual firm has no way to revise them even if the international market has changed. Furthermore, a large percentage of manufacturing is done in small, scattered, and ill-equipped factories; they are inevitably slow to respond and adapt to the qualitative and quantitative changes sought by new foreign customers.[46]

The third major obstacle to export expansion stems from China's trade philosophy. Like the United States, China is not by tradition, or by need, a trading nation. In contrast to Taiwan, Japan, and South Korea, trade has occupied only a small fraction of China's gross national product. Aside from some limited trade undertaken to achieve foreign policy goals, the Chinese central planners have viewed exports merely as a means to obtain foreign exchange for needed agricultural and industrial imports. The lack of motivation for an export drive to conquer foreign markets makes any dynamic increase in nontraditional exports unlikely. China not only lacks the salesmanship to market its products aggressively, but it has not had to make broad adaptations for any foreign market.

For all these reasons, most economists think it unlikely that China can maintain the 1978–1979 20–30 percent growth rate of exports for the remainder (1981–1985) of the Ten-Year Plan. China's effort to increase exports rapidly during 1981–1985 faces a number of problems.

1. The demand for higher living standards is likely to curb the

growth of food exports, which have been China's major hard currency export earner.
2. The pressures of domestic demand and inadequate production capacity will limit the growth of light industrial manufacturing.
3. Rising protectionism, particularly at the behest of textile interests in Western countries, as exemplified by U.S. import quotas, will block any rapid expansion of Chinese textile exports.
4. The long lead time necessary to increase crude oil production, as well as a substantial rise in domestic demand, will inhibit the rapid growth of petroleum exports.

Taking these factors into account, real exports (exports calculated in 1978 prices) are likely to grow at an annual rate of 10 percent between 1981 and 1985, and real imports will grow at an annual rate of 15 percent in the same period. Table 14.12, based on these assumptions, estimates China's imports and exports, together with the debt incurred, for 1978–1985.

In the scenario presented in the table, imports from hard currency countries (non-Communist countries) would total almost $126 billion during 1978–1985, in terms of 1978 prices. Of this amount, China's capital goods import requirements could run on the order of $30 billion to $40 billion, or approximately 28 percent of the estimated total imports. The proportion is quite similar to that of 1974–1976, when capital goods accounted for 27 percent of imports, but is much lower than the proportion in the 1955–1960 period, when machinery and equipment represented 32 percent of China's total imports.[47] The trade deficit will result in a hard-currency debt of $21 billion by 1985, an amount that China could service with the bank credits pledged by foreign bankers.

To compensate for increasing imports and to repay the loans incurred, China has to step up its exports. In agricultural products, China will continue to export sizable amounts of meat, fish, fruits, and vegetables, primarily to Hong Kong, Japan, and Singapore. But the share of the agricultural sector in China's total exports is likely to decline from 24 percent in 1977 to less than 20 percent in 1985. Even if China is able to attain the ambitious targets set for agricultural output in the current plan, population increases and demands for improved living standards will hold down the growth of food exports.

In contrast to early optimistic projections that crude oil exports would sharply increase foreign exchange earnings, crude oil output, at an annual growth rate of 4 percent, can reach only 120 million tons in

1985. Most of China's crude oil will be needed for domestic consumption, and exports in 1985 are likely to be only 15 million tons a year. The projected 1985 crude oil exports amount to less than 5 percent of Saudi Arabian exports in 1979 and will contribute only modestly to China's foreign exchange earnings.

To increase its exports, China will have to rely on traditional products, particularly textiles, clothing, and footwear. During the 1977-1980 period, China boosted sales of those products and declared its intention of raising their share in total exports. Chinese trade delegations are touring the world seeking a better knowledge of foreign markets; trading corporations are increasing their efforts to produce goods to buyer specifications and to ensure prompt delivery; and textile plants specializing in export products have been set up. Given its abundant supply of low-wage labor, China should be able to

Table 14.12
China's Hard Currency Trade and Debt Estimates, 1978-1985
(in million 1978 dollars)

| | 1978 | 1981 | 1985 | 1978-1985 |
|---|---|---|---|---|
| Imports | 8,700 | 14,400 | 23,040 | 125,600 |
| Exports | 8,400 | 11,200 | 16,370 | 96,000 |
| Balance of Trade | -300 | -3,200 | -6,670 | |
| Year-end Debt | 1,000 | 4,300 | 21,000 | |
| Debt-Export Ratio | .12 | .38 | 1.3 | |

Assumptions:

1. Real exports between 1978 and 1985 assume an annual growth of 10 percent.
2. Real imports assume an annual growth of 20 percent for 1979-1980, 15 percent for 1981-1983, and 10 percent for 1984-1985.
3. Average annual real invisible growth is assumed to be a 10 percent increase in 1979-1980, 15 percent in 1981-1982, and 20 percent in 1983-1985.
4. The average interest rate on borrowing is assumed to be 7.5 percent.

Source: Business America (February 12, 1979), pp. 3-8.

make further advances in exports of light manufacturing products at the lower end of the technology scale. In the 1981–1985 period, Chinese textile exports may advance to win a 10 percent share of the world's textile exports, thus strongly competing with South Korea, Taiwan, Singapore, and Brazil in the international market.

Over the long term, China's huge population and untapped natural resources give that country great potential for foreign trade expansion. But, given the constraints mentioned above, its trade volume in the 1980s will remain rather small. Official reports reveal that the 1981 foreign trade volume would increase only 8 percent, compared to the 30 percent growth of 1979 and 1980.[48] That low growth would signify that unless China's crude oil industry achieves a new breakthrough, the country's trade volume in the 1980s may continue to lag behind those of Taiwan and Hong Kong.

## NOTES

1. Alexander Eckstein, *Communist China's Economic Growth and Foreign Trade,* p. 124.
2. Mao Zedong, "On the People's Democratic Dictatorship," in *Selected Works,* vol. 4, p. 417.
3. Chu-yuan Cheng, *Economic Relations Between Peking and Moscow, 1949–1963,* pp. 27–41.
4. Speech by Nan Han-chen, then chairman of the China Committee for the Promotion of International Trade, at the Asian Economic Seminar, Pyonguang, June 1964 (cited in Feng-hwa Mah, *The Foreign Trade of Mainland China,* p. 2).
5. Hans Heymann, Jr., "Acquisition and Diffusion of Technology," in U.S., Congress, Joint Economic Committee, *China: A Reassessment of the Economy,* p. 701.
6. *Xuexi yu pipan* (Shanghai) No. 4 (April 1976), pp. 20–28.
7. *Current Scene* 15:4–5 (April–May 1977), p. 23.
8. Central Intelligence Agency, *China: Post-Mao Search for Civilian Industrial Technology* (Washington, D.C., February 1979), p. 6.
9. Ibid., p. 3.
10. Linda Mathews, "China Runs Short of Cash, Suspends Big U.S. Projects," *Los Angeles Times,* August 25, 1980.
11. *Wall Street Journal,* December 10, 1979, and *China Business Review* 7:1 (January–February, 1980), pp. 23–28.
12. Xinhua-Beijing, January 15, 1980.
13. Alexander Eckstein, *China's Economic Revolution,* p. 245.
14. Chu-yuan Cheng, *The Machine-Building Industry in Communist China,* pp. 44 and 45.

15. U.S., Central Intelligence Agency, *China: Real Trends in Trade with Non-Communist Countries Since 1970* (Washington, D.C., October 1977), p. 10, Table 4.

16. Nai-Ruenn Chen, "China's Foreign Trade, 1950–1974," in U.S., Congress, Joint Economic Committee, *China: A Reassessment of the Economy,* p. 627.

17. Xinhua-Beijing, April 8, 1980, and July 11, 1980; *Beijing Review* 24:11 (March 16, 1981), p. 14.

18. David Bonavia, "China Turns to the Consumer," *Far Eastern Economic Review* 107:10 (March 7, 1980), p. 92.

19. The 1979 figure is from *China's Foreign Trade* No. 4 (July–August 1980), p. 6; the 1980 figure is from Xinhua-Beijing, July 11, 1980.

20. This figure is derived from trade data in U.S., Central Intelligence Agency, *China: International Trade Quarterly Review, 1979* (Washington, D.C., September, 1979).

21. JETRO (Japan External Trade Organization), *China Newsletter* (Tokyo) No. 27 (August 1980), p. 31.

22. *Wall Street Journal,* December 10, 1979.

23. Nai-Ruenn Chen, "China's Foreign Trade, 1950–1974," in U.S., Congress, Joint Economic Committee, *China: A Reassessment of the Economy,* p. 633.

24. *United Journal* (New York), May 30, 1981.

25. "China's Boom Is Europe's Boon," *New York Times,* November 25, 1978.

26. Chu-yuan Cheng, *The Chinese Market Under Communist Control* (Hong Kong: Union Research Institute, 1956), pp. 5–7.

27. William Clark and Martha Avery, "The Sino-American Commercial Relationship," in U.S., Congress, Joint Economic Committee, *China: A Reassessment of the Economy,* p. 505.

28. For details, see ibid.

29. In 1974, Sino-American trade of $934 million trailed only slightly behind the $958 million of Soviet-American trade.

30. According to official statistics, in 1980, China's imports went up 19.8 percent while exports went up 32 percent. The trade deficit dropped from $1,870 million in 1979 to $570 million in 1980 (*Beijing Review* 24:11 [March 16, 1981], p. 15).

31. *Jingji yanjiu* No. 2 (February 1980), p. 27.

32. Chi Hsin, "China Completed a Sharp Turn," *Chi-shih nien-tai* No. 2 (February 1979), p. 16.

33. JETRO, *China Newsletter* (Tokyo) No. 26 (June 1980), p. 20.

34. Wang Bingqian, minister of finance, report to the Third Session of the Fifth NPC, Xinhua-Beijing, September 1, 1980.

35. *Wall Street Journal,* September 10, 1980, p. 28.

36. *The New Trend of China's Foreign Trade* (Hong Kong: Economic Information Agency, October 1979), p. 15.

37. *Christian Science Monitor,* March 13, 1980.

38. South China Morning Post (Hong Kong), July 26, 1979.

39. *Wall Street Journal,* September 3, 1980.
40. Nobuo Maruyama, "China's System of Economic Management and Its Impact on Joint Ventures," JETRO *China Newsletter* No. 26 (June 1980), p. 3.
41. Alexander Eckstein, *China's Economic Revolution,* p. 274.
42. *Christian Science Monitor,* March 6, 1980.
43. *Hua-chiao jih-pao,* December 8, 1979.
44. Ibid., July 4, 1980, p. 1.
45. *Wall Street Journal,* September 12, 1980.
46. For details on this subject, see Eugene A. Theroux, "Legal and Practical Problems in the China Trade," in U.S., Congress, Economic Committee, *China: A Reassessment of the Economy,* pp. 536–599.
47. Alexander Eckstein, *Communist China's Economic Growth and Foreign Trade,* pp. 106–107.
48. Yao Yilin, vice-premier, report to the Third Session of the Fifth NPC (Xinhua-Beijing, August 30, 1980).

# Selected Bibliography

## ABBREVIATIONS

| | |
|---|---|
| *BR* | *Beijing Review* |
| *DGB* | *Da gong bao* [Impartial daily] |
| *GMRB* | *Guangming ribao* [Enlightenment daily] |
| *HQ* | *Hongqi* [Red flag] |
| *JHJJ* | *Jihua jingji* [Planned economy] |
| *JJYJ* | *Jingji yanjiu* [Economic research] |
| *PR* | *Peking Review* |
| *RMRB* | *Renmin ribao* [People's daily] |
| *TJGZ* | *Tongji gongzuo* [Statistical work] |
| *TJGZTX* | *Tongji gongzuo tongxun* [Bulletin of statistical work] |
| *TJYJ* | *Tongji yanjiu* [Statistical research] |
| *XHBYK* | *Xinhua banyuekan* [New China semimonthly] |

## I. PRIMARY SOURCES


Bo Yipo. "On the Correct Handling of the Relationship Between Accumulation and Consumption." In *Renmin shouce* [People's handbook], 1957, pp. 72–75.

Cai Yuanyuan. "Regional Specialized Production of China's Agriculture." *Jingji yanjiu* [Economic research] No. 11 (November 1979), pp. 30–35 (hereafter referred to as *JJYJ*).

Chen Boda. "Problems of Seizing Power." *Dong fang hong* [The East is red], a red guard newspaper published by the coordination office of red guards in the Beijing area, February 18, 1967, p. 1.

Chen Boyuan and Wang Min. "The Role of the Law of Value in Cotton Production." *Guangming ribao* [Enlightenment daily] (Beijing), December 9, 1978, p. 3 (hereafter referred to as *GMRB*).

Chen Muhua. "To Realize the Four Modernizations, Population Growth Must Be Controlled in a Planned Way." *Renmin ribao* [People's daily] (Beijing), August 11, 1979, p. 2 (hereafter referred to as *RMRB*).

Chen Xi, Huang Zhijie, and Xu Junzhang. "Effective Use of Energy Sources Is a Vital Issue in Developing the National Economy." *JJYJ* No. 5 (May 1979), pp. 20–24.

Cheng Shih. *A Glance at China's Economy*. Beijing: Foreign Languages Press, 1974.

Chi Ti. "Stable Prices and the Reasons." *Peking Review* 18:19 (May 9, 1975), pp. 17-20 (hereafter referred to as *PR*).

______. "General Task for the New Period: Industrial Modernization." *PR* 21:26 (June 30, 1978), pp. 7-9.

*China—A Geographical Sketch*. Beijing: Foreign Languages Press, 1974.

Chinese Communist Party (CCP). "Proposals for the Second Five-Year Plan for Development of the National Economy 1958-1962." *Xinhua banyuekan* [New China semimonthly] No. 20 (1956), pp. 164-170 (hereafter referred to as *XHBYK*).

CCP, Central Committee. "Resolution on Certain Problems of the People's Communes." *XHBYK* No. 24 (1958), p. 7.

______. "Resolution on the Establishment of People's Communes in the Rural Areas." NCNA-Beijing, September 9, 1958.

______. "Communiqué of the Tenth Plenary Session of the Eighth Central Committee of the Chinese Communist Party." NCNA-Beijing, September 28, 1962.

______. "The Twenty-Point Programme." *Issues and Studies* (Taipei) No. 8 (August 1977), pp. 77-99.

______. "The Decision on Some Questions Concerning the Acceleration of Agricultural Development." *Beijing Review* 23:12 (March 24, 1980), pp. 14-20 (hereafter referred to as *BR*).

CCP, Xushui Xian Committee. "Draft for Accelerating Socialist Construction to Enter Communism." In *Jihua jingji* [Planned economy] No. 10 (1958), pp. 15-17 (hereafter referred to as *JHJJ*).

Ching Hua. "How to Speed up China's Agricultural Development." *PR* 21:42 (October 20, 1978), pp. 8-11.

Chu Ching-ping. "The Basic Policy for Socialist Revolution and Construction." *PR* 20:12 (March 18, 1977), pp. 10-13.

Chung Chin. "China's Road to Industrialization." *PR* 20:14 (April 1, 1977), pp. 12-15.

"Constitution of the People's Republic of China" (adopted on March 5, 1978, by the Fifth NPC), *PR* 21:11 (March 17, 1978), pp. 10-11, and 22:20 (May 18, 1979), pp. 21-23.

Deng Liqun. *Shangpin jingji de guilü he jihua* [The law and planning of the commodity economy]. Beijing: Renmin Chubanshe, 1979.

Deng Xiaoping. "Speech at the Opening Ceremony of the National Science Conference." *PR* 21:12 (March 24, 1978), pp. 9-18.

______. "Speech at the National Educational Work Conference." *PR* 21:18 (May 5, 1978), pp. 6-12.

"The Development of State Capitalism in China's Industry." *Tongji gongzuo tongxun* [Bulletin of statistical work] (Beijing), No. 22 (October 1956), pp. 3-7 (hereafter referred to as *TJGZTX*).

Fan Maofa and Zhang Guofu. "Relations Between Planning and the Market in Socialist Economy." *JJYJ* No. 3 (March 1979), pp. 61-68.

Fan Ruoyi. "The Pricing Policy for Products of Heavy Industry." *JJYJ* No. 3 (March 1957), pp. 54–67.

Fang Yin. "China's Textile Industry." *China's Foreign Trade* No. 2 (February 1979), pp. 4–5.

Ge Zhida. *Guodushiqi de Zhongguo yusuan* [China's state budget during the transition period]. Beijing: Caizheng Chubanshe, 1957.

Guan Datong. "Characteristics and Superiorities of Urban People's Communes." *Xin jianshe* [New construction] (Beijing) No. 5 (May 1960), pp. 28–35.

*Guanyu youjihua anbili gaosudu fazhan guominjingji lunwenxuan* [Selected essays on the development of the national economy with proper proportion and high speed]. Beijing: Zhongguo Caizheng Jingji Chubanshe, 1979.

Gui Shiyong. "A System of Comprehensive Responsibility Must be Established in Industrial Production." *JJYJ* No. 6 (June 1978), pp. 17–22.

Guo Jiyan. "Proportions in Socialist Production and the Relationships Between Agriculture and Light and Heavy Industries." *JJYJ* No. 11 (November 1979), pp. 8–15.

Han Guang. "On the Development of Modern Industry." *BR* 22:12 (March 23, 1979), pp. 9–12.

He Jianzhang. "Problems in the Management of a Planned Economy Under the System of Ownership by the Whole People and the Orientation of Reform." *JJYJ* No. 5 (May 1979), pp. 35–45.

He Jianzhang, Kuang Ri'an, and Zhang Zhuoyuan. "The Problem of Profit Margin and Price of Production in a Socialist Economy." *JJYJ* No. 1 (January 1979), pp. 47–59.

He Jianzhang and Wu Kaitai. "A Few Questions About How to Accelerate the Development of Our Country's Agriculture." *JJYJ* No. 5 (May 1978), pp. 31–36.

He Liancheng. "On the Commodity System in Socialist Society." *JJYJ* No. 6 (June 1978), pp. 39–43.

Hu Changnan. "A Discussion of Price Scissors and the General Level of Prices." *JJYJ* No. 6 (June 1979), pp. 62–69.

Hu Qiaomu. "Act in Accordance with Economic Laws, Step Up the Four Modernizations." *RMRB,* October 6, 1978. English version, "Observe Economic Laws, Speed Up the Four Modernizations." *PR* 21:45 (November 10, 1978), pp. 7–11; 21:46 (November 17, 1978), pp. 15–23; and 21:47 (November 24, 1978), pp. 13–21.

Hua Guofeng. "Mobilize the Whole Party, Make Greater Efforts to Develop Agriculture, and Strive to Build Dazhai-Type Counties Throughout the Country." *RMRB,* October 21, 1975.

———. "Speech at the Second National Conference on Learning from Dazhai in Agriculture." *PR* 20:1 (January 1, 1977), pp. 31–44.

———. "Raise the Scientific and Cultural Level of the Entire Chinese Nation." Speech at the National Science Conference. PR 21:13 (March 31, 1978), pp. 6–13.

———. "Unite and Strive to Build a Modern, Powerful Socialist Country!"

Report to National People's Congress on February 26, 1978. *PR* 21:10 (March 10, 1978), pp. 7-40.

______. "Report on the Work of the Government to the Second Session of the Fifth National People's Congress on June 18, 1979." *BR* 22:27 (July 6, 1979), pp. 5-31.

______. "On Cultural Revolution, Chairman Mao, and Other Questions." BR 23:33 (August 18, 1980), pp. 12-18.

______. "Speech at the Third Session of the Fifth National People's Congress, September 7, 1980." *BR* 23:38 (September 22, 1980), pp. 22-29.

Huang Zhenqi, Xiang Qiyuan, and Zhang Chaozun. "A Review of the Discussion of the Basic Economic Laws Under a Socialist System by Economic Circles in Our Country Since the Founding of the People's Republic." *JJYJ* No. 10 (October 1979), pp. 27-32.

*Huihuang de shinian* [Ten glorious years]. Hong Kong: Sanlian Shudian, 1959.

"In the Communes–Ownership on Three Levels." *China Reconstructs* 22:1 (January 1974), pp. 35-38.

Ji Zhe. "China's National Capitalists: Past and Present." *BR* 23:17 (September 28, 1980), pp. 18-27.

Ji Zhengzhi. "A Few Problems in Setting Socialist Planned Prices." *JJYJ* No. 4 (April 1979), pp. 58-64.

Jiang Xueme. "On Coordinating Planned Readjustment with Market Regulation." *JJYJ* No. 8 (August 1979), pp. 52-57.

*Jianguo shinian* [Ten years of national reconstruction]. 2 vols. Hong Kong: Jiwen Chubanshe, 1959.

*Jiefang junbao* [Liberation army daily] Commentator. "A Fundamental Principle of Marxism." *PR* 21:28 (July 14, 1978), pp. 5-12, and 21:29 (July 21, 1978), pp. 9-15.

______. "Fundamental Change in China's Class Situation." *BR* 22:46 (Novem-16, 1979), pp. 9-13, and 22:47 (November 23, 1979), pp. 15-17.

Jin Guang and Xiong Yan. "A Correct Analysis Should Be Made of 'San-Zi-Yi-Bao.'" *RMRB,* May 12, 1980.

Jing Hua. "A Glimpse of Rural Life." *BR* 23:15 (April 14, 1980), pp. 17-27.

Li Debin. "Cotton Prices and Cotton Production During the Post-Liberation Period." *Beijing Daxue xuebao* [Journal of Beijing University] No. 2 (April 20, 1980), pp. 49-54.

Li Dehua. "Setting the Price According to Production Cost and Socialized Production." *JJYJ* No. 4 (April 1979), pp. 65-72.

Li Fuchun. *Report on the First Five-Year Plan for Development of the National Economy of the People's Republic of China in 1953-57.* Beijing: Foreign Languages Press, 1955.

Li Qiang. "Expanding China's Foreign Trade to Speed Up the Four Modernizations." *BR* 22:17 (April 27, 1979), pp. 15-16.

Li Qianheng and Zhang Yongtao. "Several Problems Relating to the Aim of Socialist Production." *Nanjing Daxue xuebao* [Journal of Nanking University] (Nanjing) No. 1 (1980), pp. 1-6.

Li Songlin. "Acceleration of Renovation for Fixed Assets Is the Basic Way to

Promote Labor Productivity in Existing Enterprises." *Nanjing Daxue xuebao* No. 1 (1980), pp. 36–42.

Li Xiannian. "Financial Work and Agricultural Co-operativization." *Da gong bao* [Impartial daily] (Beijing) November 8, 1955 (hereafter referred to as *DGB*.

Li Zhengrui, *Zhonghua renmin gongheguo nongyeshui shigao* [A draft on the history of agricultural taxes in the People's Republic of China]. Beijing: Caizheng Chubanshe, 1959.

Li Zhengrui and Zhang Zhuoyuan. "A Few Problems Concerning Rapid Socialist Modernization." *JJYJ* No. 2 (February 1979), pp. 2–11.

______. "Only Proportionate Development Can Insure High Speed." *BR* 22:19 (May 11, 1979), pp. 15–18.

Lin Yizhou. "The Peasant Problem in Democratic Revolution." *Hongqi* [Red flag] No. 5 (March 1961), pp. 27–29 (hereafter referred to as *HQ*).

Lin Zeli. "Initial Reform in Economic Structure." *BR* 23:22 (June 2, 1980), pp. 16–18.

Liu Chengrui, Hu Naiwu, and Yu Guanghua. "Link Planning with the Market: A Basic Approach to Reforming China's Economic Management." *JJYJ* No. 7 (July 20, 1979), pp. 37–46.

Liu Guoguang. "On Sustained High Rate of Growth." *JJYJ* No. 2 (February 1978), pp. 7–13.

Liu Guoguang and Zhao Renwei "On the Relationships Between Planning and the Market in a Socialist Economy." *JJYJ* No. 5 (May 1979), pp. 46–55.

Liu Rixin. "On the Relationship Between Agriculture and Heavy Industry." *DGB*, February 2, 1961.

______. "Agricultural Mechanization and Industrialization." *DGB*, July 15, 1963.

______. "On the Use of Foreign Trade." *BR* 23:34 (August 25, 1980), pp. 23–25.

Liu Shaoqi. *Political Report of the Central Committee of the Chinese Communist Party to the Eighth National Congress*. Beijing: Foreign Languages Press, 1956.

Liu Suinian and Zhou Ying. "Handling Correctly the Relationship Between Accumulation and Consumption in an Effort to Speed Up the Four Modernizations." *JJYJ* No. 4 (April 1979), pp. 8–15.

Liu Zheng. "Some Problems Concerning China's Population Growth." *JJYJ* No. 5 (May 1979), pp. 25–33.

Lu Luping. "Questions Concerning the Accelerated Development of Light Industry." *JJYJ* No. 2 (February 1980), pp. 26–33.

Lu Nan. "Pricing Manufactured Goods According to Production Costs Under Socialism." *JJYJ* No. 5 (May 1980), pp. 37–47.

Lu Nanru and Wen Min. "The Role of the Law of Value in a Socialist Economy and How the Law Relates to the Independence of an Enterprise." JJYJ No. 3 (March 1979), pp. 65–68.

Luo Gengmu. "The Three-Level Ownership System in Rural People's Communes." *Zhongguo qingnian* [China's youth] No. 1 (January 1, 1961), pp. 4–9.

Ma Yinchu. *Wode jingji lilun zhixue sixiang he zhengzhi lichang* [My economic

theory, philosophical ideas, and political standpoint]. Beijing: Caizheng Chubanshe, 1958.
_____ *Xin renkou lun* [A new treatise on population]. Beijing: Beijing Chubanshe, 1979.
Mao Zedong. *Mao Zedong xuanji* [Selected works of Mao Zedong]. 5 vols. Beijing: Renmin Chubanshe, 1951-1977. English edition, *Selected Works.* 5 vols. Beijing: Foreign Languages Press, 1965-1977.
_____. *Mao Zedong sixiang wansui* [Long live the thought of Mao Zedong]. 3 vols. Reprint. Taipei: Institute of International Relations, 1974.
_____. "On the Ten Major Relationships." *PR* 20:1 (January 1, 1977), pp. 10-25.
_____. "Note on Charter of the Anshan Iron and Steel Company." *RMRB,* March 22, 1977.
_____. "Talk At an Enlarged Working Conference Convened by the Central Committee of the Communist Party of China on January 30, 1962." *PR* 21:27 (July 7, 1978), pp. 6-22.
_____. "Uninterrupted Revolution." *BR* 22:1 (January 5, 1979), pp. 11-12.
Niu Zhonghuang. *Zhongguo shehuizhuyi gongyehua wenti* [Problems of China's socialist industrialization]. Beijing: Zhongguo Qingnian Chubanshe, 1956.
_____. *Woguo guomin shouru de jilei he xiaofei* [Accumulation and consumption in the national income of our country]. Beijing: Zhongguo Qingnian Chubanshe, 1959.
Peng Dehuai. "Letter to Chairman Mao." In Union Research Institute, *The Case of P'eng Teh-huai 1959-1968.* Hong Kong: Union Press, 1968.
Peng Kuang-hsi. *Why China Has No Inflation.* Beijing: Foreign Languages Press, 1976.
P.R.C., State Planning Commission. *Fazhan guominjingji Diyige Wunianjihua de mingci jinashi* [A concise explanation of terms used in the First Five-Year Plan for the development of the national economy]. Beijing: Renmin Chubanshe, 1955.
_____. *The First Five-Year Plan for the Development of the National Economy, 1953-1957.* Beijing: Foreign Languages Press, 1956.
P.R.C., State Statistical Bureau. "The Scale and Speed of Development in China's Basic Construction Investment." *TJGZTX* No. 18 (September 1956), pp. 4-6.
_____. "Basic Conditions in China's Construction Industry." *TJGZTX* No. 24 (December 1956), pp. 31-33.
_____. "Development of State Capitalism in China's Industry." *XHBYK* No. 2 (January 1957), pp. 66-70.
_____. "A General Survey of China's Socialist Industrialization." *XHBYK* No. 2 (January 1957), pp. 54-62.
_____. "A General Survey of National Industrial Capital." *Tongji gongzuo* [Statistical work] No. 1 (January 1957), pp. 31-33 (hereafter referred to as *TJGZ*).
_____. "Size, Structure, and Distribution of Total Employment in 1955." *XHBYK* No. 2 (January 1957), pp. 8-27.

______. "The Technological Level of Industrial Production in China." *TJGZ* No. 8 (April 1957), pp. 30–33.

______. "Several Major Problems Concerning the Methods of Measuring the Completed Investments in Basic Construction." *TJGZ* No. 10 (May 1957), pp. 4–8.

______. "A General Survey of the Distribution of Centrally Allocated Commodities in Past Years." *TJGZ* No. 13 (July 1957), pp. 29–31.

______. "Changes in the Price Ratios of China's Industrial and Agricultural Products Since Liberation." *TJGZ* No. 17 (September 1957), pp. 4–7.

______. "Great Achievements in China's Basic Construction in the Past Seven Years." *TJGZ* No. 17 (September 1957), pp. 1–3.

______. "Input-Output Coefficients of Major Products 1953–1956." *TJGZ* No. 18 (September 1957), pp. 18 and 33.

______. "Several Problems in the Compilation of 1957 Constant Prices of Industry." *TJGZ* No. 19 (October 1957), pp. 11–13.

______. *Woguo gangtie dianli meitan jixie fangzhi zaozhi gongye de jinxi* [The present and past of our country's iron and steel, electrical power, coal, machinery, textile, and paper industries]. Beijing: Tongji Chubanshe, 1958.

______. *Woguo guodu shiqi siying gongye diaocha tongji* [Survey and statistics of private industry in our country's transitional period]. Beijing: Tongji Chubanshe, 1958.

______. "A Preliminary Study of the Production and Distribution of Our National Income." *Tongji yanjiu* [Statistical research] No. 1 (January 1958), pp. 11–15 (hereafter referred to as *TJYJ*).

______. "Great Achievements in China's Economic Construction in the Past Nine Years." *TJYJ* No. 9 (September 1958), pp. 1–3.

______. "Rapid Development in China's Industrial Constructions." *TJYJ* No. 9 (September 1958), pp. 4–5.

______. "On the Fulfillment of the First Five-Year Plan." *RMRB,* April 14, 1959.

______. "On the Fulfillment of the 1958 State Economic Plan." *RMRB,* April 15, 1959.

______. *Ten Great Years.* Beijing: Foreign Languages Press, 1960.

______. "A Study of Gross and Net Output." *TJYJ* No. 2 (February 1958), pp. 27–30.

______. "Communiqué on Fulfillment of China's 1978 National Economic Plan." *BR* 22:27 (July 6, 1979), pp. 37–41.

______. "Communiqué on Fulfillment of China's 1979 National Economic Plan." *BR* 23:19 (May 12, 1980), pp. 12–15, and 23:20 (May 19, 1980), pp. 20–24.

Qian Jiaju and Feng Hefa. *Zhongguo shehui jingji zhidu* [China's social-economic system]. Beijing: Zhongguo Qingnian Chubanshe, 1955.

*Renmin Ribao.* Editorial, "More on the Historical Experience of the Dictatorship of the Proletariat." *XHBYK* No. 2 (1957), p. 6.

______. "Two Diametrically Opposed Lines in Building the Economy." *RMRB,* August 25, 1967.

______. Special Commentator, "Implementing the Socialist Principle to Each

According to His Work." *PR* 21:31 (August 4, 1978), pp. 6-15.
______. "How Marxists Look at Material Interests." *PR* 21:44 (October 13, 1978), pp. 5-10.
______. "The Truth About the Tian-An-Men Incident." *PR* 21:48 (December 1, 1978), pp. 6-17.
______. "Defend Truth, Oppose False Reports." *RMRB*, July 24, 1979, pp. 1-2.
______. "On the Aims of Socialist Revolution." *RMRB*, October 20, 1979.
______. "It is Imperative to Control Population Growth in a Planned Way." *RMRB*, February 11, 1980.
Rong Donggu. "Relations Between Energy Consumption and National Economic Development." *JJYJ* No. 6 (June 1980), pp. 49-55.
Shang Zheng. "It Is Imperative to Bring into Full Play the Positive Role of Rural Trade Fairs." *GMRB*, January 30, 1978, p. 3.
*Shijian shi jianyan zhenli de weiyi biaozhun lunwenji* [Collected essays on practice as the only criterion to examine the truth]. Hong Kong: Sanlian Shudian, 1979.
Su Xing. "The Two-Way Struggle Between Socialism and Capitalism in China's Rural Areas After the Land Reform." *JJYJ* No. 7 (July 1965), pp. 5-15.
______. *Woguo nongye de shehuizhuyi daolu* [The path of agricultural socialization in China]. Beijing: Renmin Chubanshe, 1976.
______. "Several Questions in Boosting Agricultural Labor Productivity." *JJYJ* No. 2 (February 1979), pp. 37-43.
Sun Jingzhi et al., eds. *Huadongdiqu jingjidili* [Economic geography of eastern China]. Beijing: Kexue Chubanshe, 1959.
______. *Huazhongdiqu jingjidili* [Economic geography of Central China]. Beijing: Kexue Chubanshe, 1959.
______. *Xinandiqu jingjidili* [Economic geography of southwestern China]. Beijing: Kexue Chubanshe, 1960.
Sun Liancheng. "On the Principle of Sole Responsibility for One's Own Profit or Losses." *JJYJ* No. 11 (November 1979), pp. 49-52.
Sun Shangqing. "Modernization: The Chinese Way." *BR* 22:45 (November 4, 1979), pp. 21-23.
Sun Shangqing, Chen Jiyuan, and Zhang Zhouyuan. "An Appraisal of the Discussion on Socialist Commodities and Prices by China's Economic Circles over the Last 30 Years." *JJYJ* No. 10 (October 1979), pp. 10-19.
Sun Shangqing and Zhang Er. "Some Theoretical Questions on Coordinating Planning with Marketing in a Socialist Economy." *JJYJ* No. 5 (May 1979), pp. 56-57.
Sun Yefang. "It Is Necessary Righteously and Confidently to Grasp Socialist Profit." *JJYJ* No. 9 (September 20, 1978), pp. 2-14.
______. *Shehuizhuyi de ruogan lilun wenti* [Certain theoretical problems of the socialist economy]. Beijing: Renmin Chubanshe, 1979.
______. "On Relations of Production—A Subject in Political Economy." *JJYJ* No. 8 (August 1979), pp. 3-13.
Sun Yefang, Liang Wensen, and Dian Jiangxi. "On Examination of Investment Result—With Respect to the Adoption of Capital Profit Rate as an Indicator." *JJYJ* No. 9 (September 20, 1978), pp. 26-31.

Tian Qi. "Several Problems in Revising the 1952 Constant Prices of Industrial Products." *TJGZ* No. 1 (January 1957), pp. 15-57.

Tong Dalin. *Agricultural Cooperatives in China*. Beijing: Foreign Languages Press, 1958).

______. "Transforming China's Agricultural Components." *BR* 23:4 (January 28, 1980), pp. 20-22.

Tong Dalin and Bao Tong. "Some Views on Agricultural Modernization." *RMRB*, December 8, 1978, p. 3.

Wang Dianwu. "A Suggestion That 'Net Output Value' Substitute for 'Gross Output Value' as the Major Economic Index." *JJYJ* No. 4 (April 1979), pp. 50-51.

Wang Huide et al. "Is Priority for Increase of the Means of Production a Law Applicable to the Socialist Economy?" *JJYJ* No. 12 (December 1979), pp. 25-26.

Wang Mengkui. "Proportions, Planning, and Speed." *JJYJ* No. 6 (June 1980), pp. 12-18.

Wang Xiangjia. "Bonus System in 100 Enterprises Under Experiment in Sichuan Province." *Jingji guanli* [Economic management] No. 1 (January 15, 19780), pp. 11-14.

*Women zhengzai qianjin* [We are in the midst of advancing]. Beijing: Renmin Chubanshe, 1972.

Wu Dange. *Guojia yusuan* [The state budget]. Shanghai: Xinzhishi Chubanshe, 1957.

Wu Jiang. "The Development of State Capitalism in the Initial Stage of the Transition Period." *JJYJ* No. 1 (February 1956), pp. 84-116.

______. "Transition from Capitalist Economy to State-Capitalist Economy." *JJYJ* No. 2 (April 1956), pp. 54-99.

Xiang Jiangquan. "On the Proportional Relationship Between Capital Construction, Accumulation and Consumption." *JJYJ* No. 4 (April 1980), pp. 40-48.

Xiao Zhuoji. "The Laws of Price Changes in China." *Zhongguo shehui kexue* [Social sciences in China] No. 3 (May 1980), pp. 41-52.

Xie Shirong. "Discussion on the Problems of Chinese-Style Modernization." *JJYJ* No. 1 (January 1980), pp. 38-45.

*Xinzhongguo ershiwunian* [Twenty-five years of the new China]. Hong Kong: Zhaoyang Chubanshe, 1975.

Xu Dixin. *Zhongguo guodushiqi guominjingji de fenxi* [An analysis of China's economy in the transitional period]. Beijing: Kexue Chubanshe, 1959.

Xu Qian et al., eds. *Jingji tongjixue jianghua* [Lecture on economic statistics]. Beijing: Tongji Chubanshe, 1957.

Xue Muqiao. "Struggle Between the Two Roads in the Economic Sphere During the Transition Period." *GMRB*, August 8, 1977. English version in *PR* 20:49 (December 2, 1977), pp. 21-28; 20:50 (December 9, 1977), pp. 12-15; 20:51 (December 16, 1977), pp. 9-11; and 20:52 (December 28, 1977), pp. 10-15.

______. *Shehuizhuyi jingjililun wenti* [Problems of socialist economic theory]. Beijing: Renmin Chubanshe, 1979.

______. *Zhongguo shehuizhuyi jingji wenti yanjiu* [Study of China's socialist economic problems]. Beijing: Renmin Chubanshe, 1979.

______. "Thirty Years of Strenuous Efforts." *HQ* No. 10 (October 1979), pp. 40–49.

______. "On Reforming the Economic Management System." *BR* 23:5 (February 4, 1980), pp. 16–21; 23:12 (March 24, 1980), pp. 21–24; and 23:14 (April 7, 1980), pp. 20–25.

Xue Muqiao, Su Xing, and Lin Zeli. *The Socialist Transformation of the National Economy in China.* Beijing: Foreign Languages Press, 1960.

Yang Bo. "The Relationship Between Accumulation and Consumption in the National Income of Our Country." *XHBYK* No. 22 (November 1958), pp. 63–64.

Yang Jianbai. "A Comparative Analysis of China's and the Soviet Union's First Five-Year Plan." *Xinhua yuebao* [New China monthly] No. 9 (September 1955), pp. 193–197.

______. *Zhonghua Renmin Gongheguo huifu he fazhan guominjingji de chengjiu* [The achievements of the People's Republic of China in rehabilitation and development of the national economy]. Beijing: Tongji Chubanshe, 1956.

______. *Jiefang yilai woguo guominjingji zhong jizhong zhongyao biliguanxi de bianhua* [Changes in several important ratios in our national economy since liberation]. Shanghai: Xinzhishi Chubanshe, 1957.

______. "The Problems of National Economic Equilibrium and Production Prices." *JJYJ* No. 12 (December 1957), pp. 40–56.

Yang Jianbai, He Jianzhang, and Jiang Lin. "On Prices of Production in the Socialist Economy." *JJYJ* No. 5 (May 1964), pp. 12–20.

Yang Jianbai and Li Xuezeng. "China's Historial Experience in Handling the Relations Between Agriculture, Light Industry, and Heavy Industry." *Zhongguo shehui kexue* No. 3 (May 1980), pp. 19–40.

Yang Yingjie. *Wuge nongyeshe he liubaige nonghu de diao cha baogao* [A report on a survey of five agriculture cooperatives and 600 peasant households]. Beijing: Caizheng Jingji Chubanshe, 1958.

______. "On Unified Planning and Decentralized Control." *JHJJ* No. 11 (November 1958), pp. 3–4.

______. "Several Problems in Current Planning Work." *Jihua yu tongji* [Planning and statistics] (Beijing) No. 14 (November 23, 1959), pp. 10–14.

Yao Jinguan. "Several Problems Relating to the 'Scissors' Difference Between the Prices of Industrial and Agricultural Products." *JJYJ* No. 12 (December 1978), pp. 32–36.

You Yunzhong. "Planning the Present Birthrate in Light of Supply and Demand of Labor Force in the Future." *JJYJ* No. 7 (July 1979), pp. 59–60.

Yu Guangyuan. *Lun shehuizhuyi shengchan zhong de jingji xiaoguo* [On economic effects of socialist production]. Beijing: Renmin Chubanshe, 1978.

______. "The Concept of Economic Effects in the Production of Material Values Under the Conditions of Socialism." *JJYJ* No. 2 (February 1978), pp. 43–52.

______. "Taking Agriculture as the Foundation Is the Basic Guideline in China's Socialist Modernization." *JJYJ* No. 3 (March 1979), pp. 2–14.

______. "A Discussion of the 'Theory of Socialist Economic Target.'" *JJYJ* No. 11 (November 1979), pp. 2–7.

Yu Guoyao. "Applying Economic Means to Readjusting the Irrational Structure of Agriculture." *GMRB*, January 17, 1980, p. 2.

Yu Qiuli. "Report at National Conference on Learning from Taching in Industry." *PR* 20:22 (May 27, 1977), pp. 5–23.

______. "Arrangement for the 1979 National Economic Plan." *BR* 22:29 (July 20, 1979), pp. 7–16.

Yuan Wenqi, Dai Lunzhang, and Wang Linsheng. "International Division of Labor and China's Economic Relations with Foreign Countries." *Social Sciences in China* 1:1 (March 1980), pp. 22–47.

Zeng Muye and Ding Jiashu. *Anlaofenpei yu sige xiandaihua* [To each according to work and the four modernizations]. Beijing: Zhongguo Caizheng Jingji Chubanshe, 1979.

Zhan Wu. "Implement in all All-round Way the Policy of 'Developing Simultaneously Farming, Forestry, Animal Husbandry, Fishery, and Sideline Production,' and Quicken the Pace of Modernizing Agriculture." *JJYJ* No. 2 (February 1979), pp. 30–36.

Zhang Chunqiao. "On Exercising All-Round Dictatorship over the Bourgeoisie." *PR* 18:14 (April 4, 1975), pp. 5–11.

Zhang Jingfu. "Report on the Final State Accounts for 1978 and the Draft State Budget for 1979." *BR* 22:29 (July 20, 1979), pp. 17–24.

Zhang Renfu. "Inquire Into the Reasonable Rate of Accumulation for Our Country from Historical Experience." *RMRB*, May 15, 1980.

Zhao Yiwen. "Industry in Old China." *TJGZTX* No. 16 (August 1956), pp. 7–10.

______. *Xin Zhongguo de gongye* [Industry in new China]. Beijing: Tongji Chubanshe, 1957.

Zhao Ziyang. "Study New Conditions and Implement the Principle of Readjustment in an All-Round Way." *HQ* No. 1 (January 1980), pp. 15-20.

Zhongguo shehui kexueyuan. *Zhongguo ziben zhuyi gongshangye de shehui zhuyi gaizao* [The socialist transformation of capitalist industry and commerce in China]. Beijing: Renmin Chubanshe, 1978.

*Zhonghua Renmin Gongheguo fagui huibian* [Compendium of laws and regulations of the People's Republic of China]. Beijing: Renmin Chubanshe, issued semi-annually since 1954.

*Zhongyang caijing zhengce faling huibian* [Compendium of laws and regulations on financial and economic policies of the central government]. Compiled by the Financial and Economic Committee, State Administrative Council. Beijing: Xinhua Shudian, Series 1–August 1950; Series 2–June 1951; Series 3–March 1952.

Zhou Cheng. "A Trial Exposition on the Question of Increasing Production and Income in the Rural People's Communes." *JJYJ* No. 6 (June 1978), pp. 23-26.

Zhou Enlai. "Report on Revision of the Major Targets in the 1959 Plan and on Stepping Up the Movement for Increasing Output and Economizing." *RMRB*, August 29, 1959.

Zhou Shulian, Tan Kewen, and Lin Senmu. "Why Does the Problem of Stretching the Battlefront of Capital Construction Remain Unresolved for a Long Period of Time?" *JJYJ* No. 2 (February 1979), pp. 12–18.

Zhou Shulian, Wu Jinglian, and Wang Haipo. *Lirun fanchou he shehuizhuyi de qiye guanli* [The scope of profit and socialist enterprise management]. Beijing: Renmin Chubanshe, 1979.

Zhou Zheng and Ji Zhe. "Class Status in the Countryside: Changes Over Three Decades." *BR* 23:3 (January 21, 1980), pp. 14–21.

Zhou Zhenhua. "On Some of the Features of Chinese-Style Modernization." *JJYJ* No. 8 (August 1980), pp. 36–41.

Zou Mu. "How Should We Analyze the Price Parities Between Industrial and Agricultural Products?" *JJYJ* No. 1 (January 1979), pp. 60–62.

Zuo Ping, Guo Dongle, and Mao Xincui. "On Country Fair Trade in the Present Stage of China." *JJYJ* No. 8 (August 1979), pp. 34–39.

## II. SECONDARY SOURCES

Ahn, Byung-joon. "The Political Economy of the People's Commune in China: Changes and Continuities." *Journal of Asian Studies* 34:3 (May 1975), pp. 631–658.

Aird, John Shields. *The Size, Composition, and Growth of the Population of Mainland China.* Washington, D.C.: Bureau of the Census, 1961.

American Rural Small-Scale Industry Delegation. *Rural Small-Scale Industry in the People's Republic of China.* Berkeley: University of California Press, 1977.

Andors, Stephen. *China's Industrial Revolution.* New York: Pantheon Books, 1977.

Axilrod, Eric. *The Political Economy of the Chinese Revolution.* Hong Kong: Union Research Institute, 1972.

Bardhan, Franab K. "Chinese and Indian Agriculture: A Broad Comparison of Recent Policy and Performance." *Journal of Asian Studies* 29:3 (May 1970), pp. 515–537.

Barnett, A. Doak. *Communist Economic Strategy: The Rise of Mainland China.* Washington, D.C.: National Planning Association, 1959.

______. *Uncertain Passage: China's Transition to the Post-Mao Era.* Washington, D.C., Brookings Institution, 1974.

Baum, Richard, ed. *China's Four Modernizations: The New Technological Revolution.* Boulder, Colo.: Westview, 1980.

Bergson, Abram. "Reliability and Usability of Soviet Statistics: A Summary Appraisal." *American Statistician* 7 (June–July 1953), pp. 13–16.

Brugger, William. *Democracy and Organization in the Chinese Industrial Enterprise 1948–1953.* New York: Cambridge University Press, 1976.

Buck, John Lossing. *The Chinese Farm Economy.* Nanking: University of Nanking, 1930.

______. *Land Utilization in China.* 3 vols. Nanking: University of Nanking, 1937. Reprint of Vol. 1. New York: Council on Economic and Cultural Affairs, 1956.

Buck, John Lossing, Owen L. Dawson, and Yuan-Li Wu. *Food and Agriculture in Communist China*. New York: Praeger, 1966.

Chang, John K. *Industrial Development in Pre-Communist China: A Quantitative Analysis*. Chicago: Aldine, 1969.

Chao, Kang. *The Rate and Pattern of Industrial Growth in Communist China*. Ann Arbor: University of Michigan Press, 1965.

______. *The Construction Industry in Communist China*. Chicago: Aldine, 1968.

______. *Agricultural Production in Communist China*. Madison: University of Wisconsin Press, 1970.

Chen, Nai-Ruenn. "The Theory of Price Formation in Communist China." *China Quarterly* No. 27 (July-September 1966), pp. 33–53.

______. *Chinese Economic Statistics*. Chicago: Aldine, 1967.

Chen, Nai-Ruenn and Walter Galenson. *The Chinese Economy Under Communism*. Chicago: Aldine, 1969.

Chen Ting-chung. "Planned Marketing by the State: Economic Fetters in Mainland China." *Issues and Studies* 14:1 (January 1978), pp. 28–39.

______. "The Pay Raise Program in Mainland China." *Issues and Studies* 14:2 (February 1978), pp. 1–11.

Cheng, Chu-yuan. *Monetary Affairs of Communist China*. Hong Kong: Union Research Institute, 1954.

______. *Income and Standard of Living in Mainland China*. 2 vols. Hong Kong: Union Research Institute, 1957–1958.

______. *The People's Communes*. Hong Kong: Union Research Institute, 1959.

______. *Communist China's Economy, 1949–1962, Structural Changes and Crisis*. South Orange, N.J.: Seton Hall University Press, 1963.

______. *Economic Relations Between Peking and Moscow, 1949–1963*. New York: Praeger, 1964.

______. *Scientific and Engineering Manpower in Communist China, 1949–1963*. Washington, D.C.: National Science Foundation, 1966.

______. "The Root of China's Cultural Revolution: The Feud Between Mao Tse-tung and Liu Shao-chi." *Orbis* 11:4 (Winter 1968), pp. 1160–1178.

______. "Growth and Structural Changes in the Chinese Machine-Building Industry, 1952–1966." *China Quarterly* No. 41 (January-March 1970), pp. 26–57.

______. *The Machine-Building Industry in Communist China*. Chicago: Aldine, 1971.

______. *China's Allocation of Fixed Capital Investment, 1952–1957*. Ann Arbor: Center for Chinese Studies, University of Michigan, 1974.

______. *China's Petroleum Industry: Output Growth and Export Potential*. New York, Praeger, 1976.

______. "Hua Kuo-feng, Really, Not an Enigma?" *New York Times*, February 28, 1976, Op-Editorial.

______. "China's Future as an Oil Exporter." *New York Times*, April 4, 1976.

______. "The Economic Thought of Mao Tse-tung." *Asian Thought and Society* 11:1 (April 1977), pp. 104–113.

______. "Leadership Changes and Economic Policies in China." *Journal of International Affairs* 32:2 (Fall/Winter 1978), pp. 255–273.

Cheng, Yu-kwei. *Foreign Trade and Industrial Development of China*. Washington, D.C.: University Press of Washington, 1956.

Chi Hsin. "The Left Deviation of Communization and the Great Leap Forward." *Chi-shih nien-tai* [The seventies] (Hong Kong) No. 10 (October 1978), pp. 30–37.

______. "China Completed a Sharp Turn." *Chi-shih nien-tai* (Hong Kong) No. 2 (February 1979), p. 16.

______. "De-Maoization Campaign in China." *Chi-shih nien-tai* (Hong Kong) No. 4 (April 1979), pp. 15–18.

*China's Foreign Trade and Its Management.* Hong Kong: Economic Information Agency, 1978.

Chou, Shun-hsin. *The Chinese Inflation 1937–1949.* New York: Columbia University Press, 1963.

Committee on Scholarly Communication with the P.R.C. *Report of the C.S.C.P.R.C. Economics Delegation to the People's Republic of China.* Washington, D.C.: National Academy of Science, 1980.

Cressey, George B. *China's Geographic Foundations.* New York: McGraw-Hill, 1934.

______. *Land of the 500 Million.* New York: McGraw-Hill, 1955.

Davin, Delia. *Woman-Work: Women and Party in Revolutionary China.* Oxford: Clarendon Press, 1976.

Dawson, Owen L. *Communist China's Agriculture: Its Development and Future Potential.* New York: Praeger, 1970.

Deleyne, Jan. *The Chinese Economy.* New York: Harper Torchbooks, 1973.

Dernberger, Robert F. "The Progress of Agricultural Transformation in Mainland China." *Issues and Studies* 14:10 (October 1978), pp. 59–97.

Domes, Jurgen. "The Doom of an Heir or the Failure of an Experiment?" In *Proceedings of the Third Sino-American Conference on Mainland China,* pp. 85–87. Taipei: Institute of International Relations, 1974.

Donnithorne, Audrey. *China's Economic System.* New York: Praeger, 1967.

______. "China's Cellular Economy: Some Economic Trends Since the Cultural Revolution." *China Quarterly* No. 52 (October–December 1972), pp. 605–612.

Ecklund, George N. *Financing the Chinese Government Budget, Mainland China 1950–1959.* Chicago: Aldine, 1966.

Eckstein, Alexander. *The National Income of Communist China.* New York: Free Press, 1961.

______. *Communist China's Economic Growth and Foreign Trade.* New York: McGraw-Hill, 1966.

______. *China's Economic Development.* Ann Arbor: University of Michigan Press, 1975.

______. *China's Economic Revolution.* London: Cambridge University Press, 1977.

Eckstein, Alexander, ed. *China Trade Prospects and U.S. Policy.* New York: Praeger, 1971.

Eckstein, Alexander, Walter Galenson, and Ta-chung Liu, eds., *Economic Trends in Communist China.* Chicago: Aldine, 1968.

Emerson, John Phillip. *Nonagricultural Employment in Mainland China, 1949–*

*1958.* Washington, D.C.: Bureau of the Census, 1965.

Field, Robert Michael, Nicholas Richard Lardy, and John Phillip Emerson. *A Reconstruction of the Gross Value of Industrial Output by Province in the People's Republic of China, 1949–1973.* Washington, D.C.: Foreign Demographic Analysis Division, Bureau of Economic Analysis, Department of Commerce, 1976.

Fountain, Kevin. "The Development of China's Offshore Oil." *China Business Review* 7:1 (January–February 1980), pp. 23–36.

Garth, Bryant G., ed. *China's Changing Role in the World Economy.* New York: Praeger, 1974.

Goodstadt, Leo. *China's Search for Plenty: The Economics of Mao Tse-tung.* New York: Weatherhill, 1972.

Gurley, John G. *China's Economy and the Maoist Strategy.* New York: Monthly Review Press, 1976.

Ho, Ping-ti and Tang Tsou, eds. *China in Crisis.* Vol. 1, *China's Heritage and the Communist Political System.* Chicago: University of Chicago Press, 1968.

Hoffman, Charles. *Work Incentive Practices and Policies in the People's Republic of China 1953–1965.* Albany: State University of New York Press, 1967.

______. *The Chinese Worker.* Albany: State University of New York Press, 1974.

Hou, Chi-ming. *Foreign Investment and Economic Development in China, 1840–1937.* Cambridge: Harvard University Press, 1965.

______. "Sources of Agricultural Growth in Communist China." *Journal of Asian Studies* 27:4 (August 1968), pp. 721–737.

Howe, Christopher. *China's Economy: A Basic Guide.* New York: Basic Books, 1978.

Hsia, Ronald. *Price Control in Communist China.* New York: Institute of Pacific Relations, 1953.

______. *Economic Planning in Communist China.* New York: Institute of Pacific Relations, 1955.

Hsiao, Katharine H. *Money and Monetary Policy in Communist China.* New York: Columbia University Press, 1971.

Ishikawa Shigeru. *Chugoku keizai hatten no tokei teki kenkyu* [Statistical studies of mainland China's economic development]. Tokyo: Ajia Keizai Kenkyujo, 1960.

______. *National Income and Capital Formation in Mainland China: An Examination of Official Statistics.* Tokyo: Institute of Asian Economic Affairs, 1965.

______. *Economic Development in Asian Perspectives.* Tokyo: Kinokuniya Bookstore, 1967.

Johnson, Chalmers. "The Failure of Socialism in China." *Issues and Studies* 15:7 (July 1979), pp. 22–23.

Kambara, Tatsu. "The Petroleum Industry in China." *China Quarterly* No. 60 (October–December 1974), pp. 699–719.

Klein, Sidney. "A Note on Statistical Techniques in Communist China." *American Statistician* 13:3 (June 1959), pp. 18–21.

Kuznets, Simon. "Capital Formation Proportions." *Economic Development and*

*Cultural Change* 8:4, Part 2 (July 1960), pp. 1-96.

______. "Quantitative Aspects of the Economic Growth of Nations, VI: Long-Term Trends in Capital Formations." *Economic Development and Cultural Change* 9:4, Part 2 (July 1961), p. 1-124.

______. *Modern Economic Growth, Rate, Structure, and Spread.* New Haven: Yale University Press, 1966.

______. *Toward a Theory of Economic Growth.* New York: Norton, 1968.

Lardy, Nicholas R. *Economic Growth and Distribution in China.* Cambridge: Cambridge University Press, 1978.

Li, Choh-ming. *Economic Development of Communist China: An Appraisal of the First Five Years of Industrialization.* Berkeley and Los Angeles: University of California Press, 1959.

______. *The Statistical System of Communist China.* Berkeley and Los Angeles: University of California Press, 1962.

Liu, Ta-chung. *China's National Income, 1931–1936: An Exploratory Study.* Washington, D.C.: Brookings Institution, 1946.

Liu, Ta-chung and Kung-chia Yeh. *The Economy of the Chinese Mainland: National Income and Economic Development, 1933–1959.* Princeton, N.J.: Princeton University Press, 1965.

______. "Chinese and Other Asian Economies: A Quantitative Evaluation." *American Economic Review* 63:2 (May 1973), pp. 215–223.

Liu, Jung-chao. "Fertilizer Applications in Communist China." *China Quarterly* No. 24 (October–December 1965), pp. 28–52.

______. "Fertilizer Supply and Grain Production in Communist China." *Journal of Farm Economics* 47:4 (November 1965), pp. 915–932.

MacDougall, Colina, ed. *Trading with China: A Practical Guide.* London: McGraw-Hill, 1980.

Mah, Feng-hwa. *The Foreign Trade of Mainland China.* Chicago: Aldine, 1971.

Maizels, Alfred. *Industrial Growth and World Trade.* Cambridge: Cambridge University Press, 1963.

Malenbaum, Wilfred. "India and China: Development and Contrasts." *Journal of Political Economy* 64:1 (1956), pp. 1–24.

Meyerhoff, A. A. "Development in Mainland China, 1949–1968." *American Association of Petroleum Geologists Bulletin* 54:8 (1970), pp. 1567–1580.

*The New Trend of China's Foreign Trade.* Hong Kong: Economic Information Agency, October 1979.

Nickum, James E. and David C. Schak. "Living Standards and Economic Development in Shanghai and Taiwan." *China Quarterly* No. 77 (March 1979), pp. 25–49.

Oksenberg, Michael, ed. *China's Developmental Experience.* New York: Academy of Political Science, 1973.

Orleans, Leo A. *China's Birth Rate, Death Rate, and Population Growth: Another Perspective.* Washington, D.C.: Government Printing Office, 1977.

Ou Pao-san. "Industrial Production and Employment in Pre-War China." *Economic Journal* 56 (September 1946), pp. 426–434.

______. "A New Estimate of China's National Income." *Journal of Political Economy* 54:6 (December 1946), pp. 547–554.

______. *1933 Chung-Kuo kuo-min suo-te* [China's national income, 1933]. 2 vols. Shanghai: Chung-hua Shu-chu, 1947.

Perkins, Dwight H. *Market Control and Planning in Communist China.* Cambridge: Harvard University Press, 1966.

______. *Agricultural Development in China, 1368-1968.* Chicago: Aldine, 1969.

______. "Plans and Their Implementation in the People's Republic of China." *American Economic Review* 63:2 (May 1973), pp. 234-240.

Perkins, Dwight H., ed. *China's Modern Economy in Historical Perspective.* Stanford: Stanford University Press, 1975.

*Provincial Agricultural Statistics for Communist China.* Compiled by the Committee on the Economy of China, Social Science Research Council and published by the same organization, New York, 1969.

Prybyla, Jan S. *The Chinese Economy.* Columbia, S.C.: University of South Carolina Press, 1978.

Rawski, Thomas. *Economic Growth and Employment in China.* New York: Oxford University Press, 1979.

Reynolds, Lloyd G. "China as a Less Developed Economy." *American Economic Review* 65:3 (June 1975), pp. 418-428.

Richman, Barry M. *Industrial Society in Communist China.* New York: Random House, 1969.

Robinson, Joan. *Economic Management in China.* London: Anglo-Chinese Educational Institute, 1975.

Rostow, W. W. et al. *The Prospects for Communist China.* New York: Wiley, 1954.

Schran, Peter. "The Structure of Income in Communist China." Ph.D. dissertation, University of California, Berkeley, 1961.

______. *The Development of Chinese Agriculture 1950-1959.* Urbana: University of Illinois Press, 1969.

______. "China's Price Stability: Its Meaning and Distributive Consequences." *Journal of Comparative Economics* 1:4 (December 1977), pp. 381-385.

Shabad, Theodore. *China's Changing Map.* Rev. ed. New York: Praeger, 1972.

Shen, T. H. *Agricultural Resources of China.* Ithaca: Cornell University Press, 1951.

Sigurdson, Jon. *Rural Industrialization in China.* Cambridge: Harvard University Press, 1977.

Skinner, G. William. "Marketing and Social Structure in Rural China: Part I." *Journal of Asian Studies* 24:1 (November 1964), pp. 3-43; Part II, 24:2 (February 1965), pp. 195-228; and Part III, 24:3 (May 1965), pp. 363-400.

Skinner, G. William and Edwin A. Winckler. "Compliance Succession in Rural Communist China: A Cyclical Theory." In Amitai Etzioni, ed., *A Sociological Reader on Complex Organizations,* pp. 410-430. New York: Holt, 1969.

Smil, Vaclav. *China's Energy, Achievements, Problems, Prospects.* New York: Praeger, 1976.

Swamy, Subramanian. *Economic Growth in China and India, 1952-1970.* Chicago: University of Chicago Press, 1973.

______. "The Economic Distance Between China and India, 1955-73." *China*

*Quarterly* No. 70 (June 1977), pp. 371-382.
Szuprowicz, B. O. and M. R. Szuprowicz. *Doing Business with the People's Republic of China.* New York: John Wiley & Sons, 1978.
Tang, Anthony M. and Bruce Stone. *Food Productions in the People's Republic of China.* Washington, D.C. International Food Policy Research Institute, 1980.
Terrill, Ross. "Peking: Waiting to be Westernized." *Atlantic Monthly,* 246:2 August 1980, pp. 8-11.
Traeger, Frank N. and William Henderson. *Communist China 1949-1969: A Twenty Year Appraisal.* New York: New York University Press, 1970.
Treadgold, D. W., ed. *Soviet and Chinese Communism: Similarities and Differences.* Seattle: University of Washington Press, 1967.
Tregear, Thomas R. *A Geography of China.* Chicago: Aldine, 1965.
______. *An Economic Geography of China.* London: Butterworth, 1970.
Tsou, Tang, ed. *China in Crisis: China's Policies in Asia and America's Alternatives.* Chicago: University of Chicago Press, 1968.
Uchida, Gengko. "Technology in China." *Scientific American* 215:5 (November 1966), pp. 37-45.
Ullerich, Curtis. *Rural Employment & Manpower Problems in China.* White Plains, N.Y.: M. E. Sharpe, 1979.
U.S., Central Intelligence Agency. *People's Republic of China: International Trade Handbook.* Washington, D.C., October 1976.
______. *China: Real Trends in Trade with Non-Communist Countries Since 1970.* Washington, D.C., October 1977.
______. *Handbook of Economic Statistics 1977, 1978, and 1979.* Washington, D.C., 1977, 1978, 1979.
______. *China: Economic Indicators.* Washington, D.C., December 1978.
______. *China: In Pursuit of Economics Modernization.* Washington, D.C., December 1978.
______. *China: Major Economic Indicators.* Washington, D.C., September 1979, and February 1980.
______. *China: Post-Mao Search for Civilian Industrial Technology.* Washington, D.C., February 1979.
______. *Chinese Coal Industry: Prospects over the Next Decade.* Washington, D.C., February 1979.
______. *China: The Steel Industry in the 1970s and 1980s.* Washington, D.C., May 1979.
______. *China: A Statistical Compendium.* Washington, D.C., July 1979.
______. *China: International Trade Quarterly Review 1979.* Washington, D.C., September 1979.
______. *China: A Preliminary Reconciliation of Official and CIA National Product Data.* Washington, D.C., December 1979.
______. *China: The Continuing Search for a Modernization Strategy.* Washington, D.C., April 1980.

______. *Electric Power for China's Modernization: The Hydroelectric Option.* Washington, D.C., May 1980.

U.S., Congress, Joint Economic Committee. *An Economic Profile of Mainland China.* 2 vols. Washington, D.C.: Government Printing Office, 1967.

______. *People's Republic of China: An Economic Assessment.* Washington, D.C.: Government Printing Office, 1972.

______. *China: A Reassessment of the Economy.* Washington, D.C.: Government Printing Office, 1975.

______. *Chinese Economy Post-Mao.* Washington, D.C.: Government Printing Office, 1978.

U.S., Department of Agriculture. *People's Republic of China, Agricultural Situation, Review of 1977 and Outlook for 1978.* Washington, D.C., May 1978.

______. *People's Republic of China, Agricultural Situation, Review of 1978 and Outlook for 1979.* Washington, D.C., June 1979.

______. *People's Republic of China, Agricultural Situation, Review of 1979 and Outlook for 1980.* Washington, D.C., June 1980.

Vladimirov, Iu. V. "The Question of Soviet-Chinese Economic Relations in 1950–1966." *Chinese Economic Studies* 3:1 (Fall 1969), pp. 3–32. Translated from *Problems of History* No. 6 (1969).

Walker, Kenneth R. *Planning in Chinese Agriculture, Socialization and the Private Sector, 1956–1962.* Chicago: Aldine, 1965.

______. "Collectivization in Retrospect: The Socialist High Tide of Autumn 1955–Spring 1956." *China Quarterly* No. 26 (April-June 1966), pp. 1–43.

Wang, K. P. *Mineral Resources and Basic Industries in the People's Republic of China.* Boulder, Colo.: Westview, 1977.

Wheelwright, E. L. and Bruce McFarlane. *The Chinese Road to Socialism.* New York: Monthly Review Press, 1970.

Whiting, Allen S. and Robert F. Dernberger. *China's Future Foreign Policy and Economic Development in the Post-Mao Era.* New York: McGraw-Hill, 1977.

Willmott, W. E., ed. *Economic Organization in Chinese Society.* Stanford: Stanford University Press, 1972.

Wu, Yuan-li. *An Economic Survey of Communist China.* New York: Bookman Associates, 1950.

______. *Economic Development and the Use of Energy Resources in Communist China.* New York: Praeger, 1963.

______. *The Economy of Communist China.* New York: Praeger, 1965.

Wu, Yuan-li, ed. *China, A Handbook.* New York: Praeger, 1973.

Yeh, K. C. "Soviet and Communist Chinese Industrialization Strategies." In D. W. Treadgold, ed., *Soviet and Chinese Communism: Similarities and Differences,* pp. 327–363. Seattle: University of Washington Press, 1967.

______. "Foreign Trade Under the Hua Regime: Policy, Performance, and Prospects." *Issues and Studies* 14:8 (August 1978), pp. 12–13.

# Index

For Product Safety Concerns and Information please contact our EU representative GPSR@taylorandfrancis.com Taylor & Francis Verlag GmbH, Kaufingerstraße 24, 80331 München, Germany

Batch number: 10726009

Printed by Printforce, the Netherlands